THE RIVER CHASERS

A History of American Whitewater Paddling

Sue Taft

To Carl & Beth Flynn,

Thanks for helping so many of us during our early years of boating!

Dan Demaree

Dan [illegible]

Susan L. Taft

Mimi (Hayman) Demaree

[illegible]

Printed in the United States of America

ISBN 0–9669795–1–6

Copublished by:
Flowing Water Press and Alpen Books Press
3616 South Road C-1
Mukilteo, Washington 98275

Distributed by:
Alpen Books
Mukilteo, Washington 98275
www.alpenbooks.com

Editor: Colleen Sayre
Cover and text designer: Eric Wargowsky

Special thanks to the following paddlers/photographers:

Ted Acton, Wolf Bauer, John Berry, Barbara Brown, Dan Demaree, Dave Guss, Robert Harrison, Bart Hauthaway, Al Holland, Tom Johnson, Julie Keller, Brandon Knapp, Justin Knapp, Rob Lesser, Kevin O'Brien, Jim Stuart, Carl Trost, American Whitewater, and Wilderness Systems.

Cover photo: Pillow Rock Rapid on the Gauley, Susan L. Taft
Back cover: Susan L. Taft

Dedication

This book is dedicated to all my paddling friends over the years, particularly among the Keel-Hauler Canoe Club, whose long-time friendships are a special embodiment of what the sport of whitewater brings to each of us.

Acknowledgments

This book would not have been possible without the support of family and friends, some paddlers, some not. But it would not have even happened had it not been for Marge, my oldest sister, who first took me canoeing when I was about eight; my father whom I was able to convince to buy a canoe for me when I was sixteen; and Dolf, my flatwater marathon partner who gave me my first taste of whitewater when I was twenty. I was hooked from that point on.

I want to acknowledge the help of everyone I interviewed, those who provided information, and those who fed me and opened up their homes to me while I conducted my research across the country. Whitewater paddlers are indeed one large extended family. There have been so many, but in particular I want to acknowledge Keith Backlund, John Berry, Stu Coffin, Dan Demaree, Bill Endicott, Bart Hauthaway, Davey and Jennifer Hearn, Ken Horwitz, Tom Johnson, Barb McKee, Pete Skinner, Jim Snyder, Jim Stuart, John Sweet, Carol Trost, Charlie Walbridge, Ron Watters, Jesse Whittemore, and Larry Zuk.

I also owe a special thanks to American Canoe Association for allowing me to rummage around their library and archives, American Whitewater and my friend Hank Annable for providing me access to a complete set of *American Whitewater* journals, and Judy Harrison for providing me access to *Canoe* magazine's archives. For the production of the book itself, I want to acknowledge with a special thanks to my friend and editor Colleen Sayre, who supported and encouraged me particularly in the final months of production; to my designer Eric Wargowsky, whose creativity in visual imaging and information brought the whole book together; to Lynne Gakavian, Marisabel Haddad, and Cindy Tolson for their support during final production; and to Rita Tessmann, my long-time paddling friend who provided the first editorial review of my work in progress.

Contents

"If you want to learn how much you can overlook or forget, just write a book."

Henry A. Pilsbry, 1949

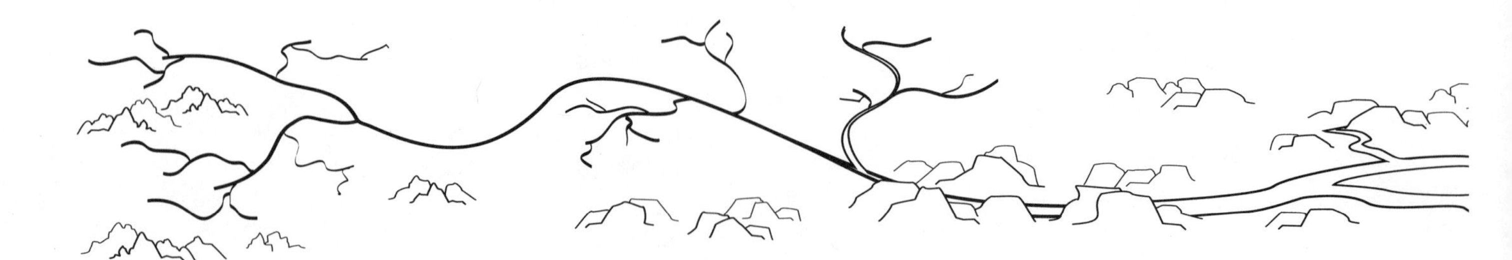

Introduction

Rain falls. Some evaporates. Some soaks into the ground, becoming groundwater, emerging later. And the rest accumulates, becoming surface water, gathering in larger and larger pools until it reaches a critical mass to overcome the resistance to flow. About one-third flows to defined channels; small channels merge to form larger ones, and so on. Rills become creeks, then runs, then streams, getting progressively larger to become a river, the grand accumulation becoming a watershed.

So it is with history. Events happen like falling rain. One event influences, accumulates with another and another, just as a rill becomes a creek, a run, a stream, and finally, a river of events that seems to carry the other smaller events along. Some events appear to stand alone and get lost only to emerge later, just as groundwater, to contribute and merge with other events. The river and its watershed—its history—are dependent upon all the creeks and streams. All contribute yet some influence more than others.

The history of whitewater paddling, its watershed, is the same. Seemingly disconnected events accumulate and merge, some as smaller streams, others as major tributaries but, the watershed is dependent on them all.

This history of whitewater in America is written to acknowledge and pay tribute to the people who have facilitated those significant events, the watershed events, which have brought about the evolution of the sport.

Preface

Five years ago, after sporadic whitewater paddling during the early '90s, I spent a summer traveling and paddling (backpacking, too) across the country. During that time, I realized how far the sport had come from when I began paddling in the mid-'70s. I also realized that many of the people I now paddle with have no idea how the sport evolved to this point: how slalom racing has contributed to much of our technique and designs; how the backgrounds and interests of the sport's pioneers in the '40s, '50s, and '60s shaped the sport; how materials (plastics) influenced and revolutionized the sport; how everything that came before has brought us to where we are and that without what seems to be trivial designs, techniques, and first descents, we would not be doing what we are today. Even paddlers who began in the '70s tend to trivialize what was done earlier, comparing first descents with those of today. But we forget that rivers commonly run by paddlers in 7-foot plastic kayaks were not trivial in 13-foot fiberglass kayaks. The routes were not always well known, the hazards well-scouted. The hydrodynamics of waterfalls were not well understood and those first run in the '70s were indeed pioneering runs although they were often less than 20 feet, not the multiples of that today. As one paddler told me of running the Gauley, "it would be significant if you didn't know where to go." And even then, knowing where to go, deaths continue to occur on the Gauley.

Much has changed in the sport in the last twenty-five years. In the mid-'70s, if you wanted to paddle whitewater you joined a club, bought a used boat or built a boat and much of your gear, learned to roll at winter pool sessions, and learned to paddle by getting on the rivers with other club members. Club trips provided camaraderie, shuttle arrangements, and someone who had paddled the river before, or at least was well-versed with what the guidebook said. Clubs are no longer necessary for the same reasons. Now you buy your boat and all your gear at a store, buy your instruction from a certified instructor or school, and check the internet to see what river is up and make arrangements to paddle with someone. Shuttle arrangements are easier, too. Now you can just show up at a put-in, and either buy your shuttle or hitch-hike because there are so many other paddlers around to give you a ride.

But some things have not changed. The lure of whitewater, its excitement and exhilaration and challenge, is integral to the sport and will not change. In talking with Jim Stuart while working on this book, he suggested that I use the title *The River Chasers*. The appropriateness of the title is twofold. First, the River Chaser was the first plastic whitewater kayak, for all practical purposes. It revolutionized the sport, not for the design itself, but for where plastic kayaks have brought the sport. And second, over the years regardless of the time, we have been and continue to be *river chasers*, seekers and chasers of the next whitewater experience.

View from the Bridge: 1945

Whitewater canoeing and kayaking—paddling–as a sport was in its infancy in America at the end of World War II. It was a sport based on the thrill of exploration and danger, and the development and mastery of newly found technique and skills. Its lure was the same as other young outdoor sports like climbing and skiing and often attracted the same participants. Like skiing, it was based on adaptations of long-used native equipment with a utilitarian purpose: transportation.

For both native canoes and kayak, the *materials* used for their construction, the *designs* of the craft themselves, and their respective paddling *techniques* were reflective of the environment (both physical and functional purpose) for which they were intended. Adaptations of native watercraft for whitewater during the sport's infancy were relatively few and were primarily associated with materials for construction. This was certainly the case for canoes since many of the native canoe designs adopted by European explorers, and later by modern craftsmen and manufacturers, already incorporated good river running design characteristics.

> ...The superior qualities of the bark canoes of North America are indicated by the white man's unqualified adoption of the craft. Almost as soon as he arrived in North America, the white man learned to use the canoe, without alteration, for wilderness travel... Indeed, the models and proportions used in many of these old bark canoes are retained in the canoes used today...[2]

A SPORT is defined as a physical activity engaged in for pleasure.[1]

The View from a Canoe

In 1945, whitewater was a new sport participated in by a scattered few across the country, although Americans had been engaged in whitewater canoeing for over fifty years, and more recently whitewater kayaking. Some of the earliest pioneers of whitewater used wood and canvas canoes (the first modern production canoes) that became available around 1880. Already known for the exploration of mountains in the Northeast by both climbing and skiing, Appalachian Mountain Club (AMC) members used canoes to explore rivers for the sport of it, for the purpose of running whitewater. (AMC was established in 1876 in Boston and expanded its chapters throughout the Northeast.)

During the early 1900's, members began running regular trips on increasingly difficult rivers in the Northeast. In the Spring, as flows permitted, trips included Miller's River, Deerfield, West, Souhegan, Contoocook,

[1] *Merriam-Webster Dictionary* (Home and Office Edition). Merriam-Webster Inc, 1995.

[2] Adney, Edwin Tappan and Howard I. Chapelle. *The Bark Canoes and Skin Boats of North America* Washington D.C.: Smithsonian Institution Press, 1983.

Pemigewasset, and Farmington rivers. Due to the lack of good roads suitable outside of urban areas for automobiles, canoes were often rented for the trips and transported by truck to the rivers. By the 1920's, the growing availability of automobiles and better roads allowed AMC's members to expand their whitewater river exploration beyond the normal reach of AMC's chapters in Boston, New York, and Connecticut.

One of the first published whitewater trip reports appeared in the June 1929 issue of AMC's journal, *Appalachia.* "Down the Piscataquog" by Elizabeth Knowlton was a report of the yearly Spring (April) run on the Piscataquog River. Another report published in the 1937 in *Appalachia* titled "Twenty Years of the Westfield River" by Alexander Forbes chronicled annual Spring trips on the Westfield River in Massachusetts beginning in 1914. The trips were two-day "over-nighter" trips from Cummington to Huntingdon through the West Chesterfield and Knightsville Gorges. (This predated the Knightsville Dam that inundated Knightsville Gorge. The section from Knightsville Dam to Huntington is rated Class II–III, III+ in high water, by today's standards.)

Thomas D. Cabot, his wife, and friends started running rivers in 1922 in the Boston area (perhaps the first to use canoe racks on their automobiles). Cabot wrote of these rivers in his article "Quick-Water Canoe Runs Near Boston" published in *Appalachia* in 1931. Another AMC member, John C. Phillips, also paddled and explored rivers in New England. Phillips teamed with Cabot to methodically explore rivers as far away as southern Maine over a three-year period in the early 1930's. The culmination of their efforts was perhaps the first American whitewater handbook and guidebook. Published in 1935, *Quick-Water and Smooth: A Canoeists Guide to New England Rivers* was the bible for paddlers in New England until the '60s.

Shuttle vehicle, 1943—courtesy of Ted Acton.

[3] Knowlton, Elizabeth. "Down the Piscataquog." *Appalachia* (June 1929): 221–223.

[4] Forbes, Alexander. "Twenty Years of the Westfield River." *Appalachia* (June 1937): 310–326.

AMC members helped put definition to the character of the developing young sport. John Worthington wrote:

> The ultimate object of technique in quick-water canoeing may be said to be–in serious travel, to arrive; pursued as a sport, the fun of it ...The canoeman is and must be his own master and his own teacher. He must learn the capabilities and the limitations of his canoe, the power and willingness of running water, and how best to use his own body to gain the Ultimate Object. He must observe, and he must use common-sense. As a good horseman and his mount act as a dynamic unit, so must the canoeman unite himself with his canoe. Like a horse, a canoe has individuality and temperament; it can shy, balk, buck, and roll. All this must be learned at first hand...
>
> While it would serve no useful purpose to formulate rules, some observations and suggestions may not be out of place... The first thing, then, is to know water — not a particular bit of water, but water generally, in all its manifold forms in a running stream, so that an unfamiliar complex of rocks, eddies, cross-currents, boils, and haystacks may be solved quickly. The tiniest brook, a gutter-stream running down Beacon Hill, is a river in miniature. A study, from a canoeman's viewpoint, of any stream is profitable. [5]

Through their pursuit of whitewater, AMC members also led in defining many different aspects of the young sport, particularly canoeing equipment, the development of paddling techniques, and the sport as a club activity. By the 1930's, many different designs and models of canoes were available from more than a half-dozen canoe manufacturers in the New England area alone. The "standard guide" model, an 18-foot canoe, was considered an all-around canoe that could be "run, dropped, poled, and portaged." [6] Canoe poling was a technique developed in the Northeast by loggers. Poles were used to "drop" down a rapid (perhaps the origin for the term drop for a rapid) and paddles were used to "run" a rapid. For short trips with no need for provisions for an over-night river stay,

> Any canoe will do ... , but it is best to have no keel, a fairly flat bottom, good sheer, high freeboard, alight [sic] tumble-home and strong canvas with plenty of "filler" [for impact and abrasion]. For double running with little baggage, a model 17 feet long 32 inches wide and 13 inches deep is about right. For one man, a 14-foot canoe is preferable. [7]

Whitewater paddling for canoeing first developed as "quick water" techniques that combined paddling and poling techniques. In 1934, AMC-Boston purchased a half-dozen used wood and canvas canoes from the estate of a wealthy sportsman to build a stable of canoes for member use. Members were now able to push the limits of river running and further define whitewater technique:

MANY OF THE BASICS of both canoeing technique and reading whitewater developed during the early years of the sport. In 1929, Worthington wrote:

> Some of us will recall a fine run on the Deerfield River just above Shelburne Falls, now, alas, obliterated by a dam... The problem was solved by running down to the first eddy, following the water into its lower end, and circling the eddy to its upper end, the canoe making a complete turn. This gave breath-catching time and a chance for a fresh start. The same maneuver was repeated in a lower-eddy. This brought one almost to the brink of the cascade, where its best channel could be seen close at hand and, from a standing start, the canoe could be carefully placed for the final descent. Note the value of reducing speed and the use of water power instead of muscle.
>
> ...The object, in downstream work, is not to drive the canoe; the water furnishes all the power needed for mere propulsion. Time is required, more time than the river is disposed to give. In heavy water especially, where swamping is a real danger, the pace should be reduced.
>
> ...One feature of quick water is that it may flow in any direction. The current does not always make for the best channel. At least that current which for the moment is carrying the canoe... So also, to avoid "haystacks", the big standing waves below a heavy run, sneak alongside between the Scylla of the haystacks and the Charybdis of the eddy. If the haystacks are to be run in midstream it is possible to

—continues on next page

[5] Worthington, John W. "Quick-Water Canoeing." *Appalachia* (June 1929): 268–277.

[6] Ibid.

[7] Cabot, Thomas D. "Quick-water Canoe Runs Near Boston." *Appalachia* (December 1931): 454–467.

avoid much wetting by swinging the canoe to a quartering position. This shortens the effective length of the canoe so that it may ride and not plunge.

...Use the cushion of backflowing water on the upstream side of a boulder; it will usually push you clear.

...With his knees well out in the bilges [i.e. kneeling low with knees spread as far as possible], the canoeman balances from his hips, keeping his body vertical. The canoe is allowed to rock freely and independently.

...The canoeman has, beside the usual paddle strokes and twists, many other strokes designed to turn the canoe or move it backward or from side to side. The drawing strokes are the more used and usually the more effective. They retard or, at least, do not accelerate. By a series of quick draws one may claw a canoe out of a bad position or keep it from being swept into one. One seems to take hold of a piece of water and pull himself toward it. The "cross draw," in which the position of the hands is the reverse of the normal one, uses the stronger back muscles more than the weaker arm muscles. To turn the canoe it is not paddled around but turned on a pivot, the bow or stern being held with the paddle and the river doing the turning... The side-pushing strokes are given greater force by using the gunwale as a fulcrum. In emergency anything goes, even paddling ahead, back paddling, or turning completely around voluntarily or involuntarily.[9]

WORTHINGTON'S "observations and suggestions" along with those of other AMC members eventually evolved into a progression of editions of AMC's *Whitewater Handbook.* The first edition was written by John Urban in 1965, the second by T. Walley Williams III in 1981, and the third edition by Bruce Lessels in 1994.

For ordinary light quick water one running single, or the stern man of a double may stand, the feet spread with one foot in advance. This may be practiced by standing in a subway car—a more severe test of balance... For heavier water, or where severe jolts may be anticipated, the canoeman should kneel, his knees well spread. In the kneeling position his weight is low, which makes for stability, and he can use to advantage the muscles of his back and arms. He grips with his thighs like the rider of a horse. Even in heavy water he must stand occasionally to pick out the course ahead. He should be prepared to change quickly his position from standing to kneeling or kneeling to standing, and his paddle, his extra paddle, and his pole should be ready to be picked up instantly.[8]

By the late 1930s, AMC's instructional methods for whitewater canoeing paralleled their other activities. Novices were trained using club equipment during club sponsored activities. In 1936, eleven trips on ten different rivers were part of the activities of AMC's General Outings Committee.

Although whitewater canoeing was limited to the availability of wood and canvas canoes, it was not limited to AMC members in the Northeast. Whitewater was found in pockets across the country although primarily in the Appalachians, often taking root from summer camp experiences. Camps from Canada to the southern Appalachians introduced canoeing in wood and canvas canoes to thousands of young paddlers. The American Red Cross started its water safety program in 1914 and began canoeing instruction at the National Aquatic Schools in New York and New England in the 1920s which gave further impetus to the growing sport of canoeing. National organizations such as the Boy Scouts and Young Men's Christian Association (YMCA) also promoted canoeing as an outdoor experience.

Whitewater canoeing in the Southeast had its roots in summer camps that offered canoeing with other outdoor activities in the 1910's. In 1914, a young camper, Frank Bell (Sr.), at French Broad Camp in North Carolina made his first canoe trip down the French Broad from Brevard to Asheville. For Bell, this was the beginning of a life of whitewater canoeing and exploration in the Southeast. As a young man, he founded Camp Mondamin for boys in 1922, and later Camp Green Cove for girls in 1945, in western North Carolina in which whitewater canoeing and exploration played a prominent role in the camp's activities. In 1923, Bell and fellow counselor George Blackburn took three campers on the first descent of the entire length of the French Broad starting at Hendersonville and ended at the Mississippi at Cairo, Illinois, a journey of almost 1,000 miles.

Bell continued exploration of southeastern rivers and in 1933, with Bill Childs, attempted the first descent of the Green River in North Carolina. Putting in below Lake Summit Powerhouse, they entered the Gorge (which drops up to 300 feet a mile) and destroyed their wood and canvas canoe within two miles. They walked and swam the remainder of the 16 miles to Lake Adger. Later in 1933, Bell led a Mondamin camp trip on the Green below the Gorge to the Atlantic.

[8] Worthington, John W. "Quick-Water Canoeing." *Appalachia* (June 1929): 268–277.

[9] Ibid.

Another camp in the Southeast, Camp Tate operated by Fritz Orr (Sr.), also encouraged canoeing and exposed many young campers to river exploration that ultimately led to their involvement in whitewater canoeing. One such camper was Hugh Caldwell who spent the summers of 1934 through 1937 at Camp Tate. In the early years, canoeing instruction at the camp was provided by a contingent of camp counselors from a YMCA school in Massachusetts. Caldwell's first multi-day excursion was a four-day canoe trip on the Chestatee River to the Chattahoochee in Atlanta, prior to dam construction that formed Lake Lanier.

But Bell, Caldwell, and Orr were not alone in their exploration of rivers in the Southeast. Ramone Eaton, another early pioneer, also began exploring in the 1920's and made many first descents of southern Appalachian rivers including the Nantahala on his own.

By 1945, although whitewater canoeing was already practiced in the Northeast and Southeast, differences in their practice were already evident based on the relative influences between a club-sponsored, organized activity versus an independent, less-defined activity. These differences were the source for changes that affected whitewater open canoeing over thirty years later during the 1970's.

Some of the first youth camps that provided canoeing as the central experience began in and around Algonquin Provincial Park in eastern Canada, the heart of native canoeing traditions. In 1902, Camp Keewaydin was established and within ten years began a tradition of wilderness river trips down the old fur trader rivers to James Bay such as the Abitibi, Missinabi, and Mattagami. In 1906, Northway Lodge, an all-girls camp, was established in Algonquin. Other camps, both American and Canadian, followed, including Camp Ahmek (later named Camp Temagami), Camps Tamakwa and Kandalore, and others sponsored by YMCA and Boy Scouts as well as private organizations.

Further Upstream

> The bark canoes of North American Indians, particularly those of birch bark, were among the most highly developed of manually propelled primitive watercraft. Built with Stone Age tools from materials available in the areas of their use, their design, size, and appearance were varied so as to create boats suitable to the many and different requirements of their users. The great skill exhibited in their design and construction shows that a long period of development must have taken place before they became known to white men.
>
> ... Bark canoes were designed for various conditions: some for use in rapid streams, some for quiet waters, some for the open waters of lakes, some for use along the coast.[10]

Native canoes of the eastern maritime region of New England and Canada (of the Micmac, Malecite, and Abenaki that included the Kennebec and Penobscot) were the first canoes seen by French and later by British explorers. The canoe designs reflected the waterways that were paddled, from small wooded streams, to large rivers, to coastal ocean waters.

Canoe length and width varied according to its purpose. For river use, canoes as short as 11 to 12 feet and 31 inches wide were designed for solo travel with light loads such as for hunting trips. Canoes as long as 21 to 22 feet and 33 inches wide were used for larger rivers with moderate loads.

[10] Adney, Edwin Tappan and Howard I. Chapelle. *The Bark Canoes and Skin Boats of North America* Washington D.C.: Smithsonian Institution Press, 1983.

The woods canoe of the Micmac used for smaller streams had a curved sheer with the lowest point of freeboard amidships with a generally flat-bottomed hull shape. Most had bow and stern rocker placed within the last few feet of the ends. Many also included a considerable amount of tumblehome.

Further inland, in the Great Lakes region and beyond to the north and west, native canoe builders such as the Algonkin, Cree, Ojibay, Sioux, Dakota, Teton, and Assiniboin had even more varied designs. The "crooked canoe"[11] design had a great deal of rocker from the middle to the ends, and was thought to be the evolutionary result of the whitewater requirements of the region's rivers.

Trappers and traders known as the Voyageurs in the watersheds of the Great Lakes and Hudson Bay in the late 1600's through the mid-1800's recognized the superiority of bark canoes over any water craft brought from Europe and quickly adopted them for exploration and the developing fur trade. Early on, canoes were purchased from native builders. By the early 1700's, a few French craftsmen began building canoes. As more and more and larger canoes were required for the Voyageurs and the fur trade, manufacturing centers, or canoe production yards, were established along the St. Lawrence from Montreal to Quebec City. However, as the fur trade diminished in the mid-1800's, along with demand for the large Voyageur canoes, demand for smaller birch bark canoes increased to satisfy the growing needs of affluent sportsmen. By this time, non-native materials such as nails and tacks, along with other modified construction techniques replaced traditional birch bark construction. In the mid-1850's, the first modern all-wood canoes were built in and around Peterborough, Ontario. Thomas Gordon of Lakefield and John Stevenson of Peterborough are often credited with simultaneous development of all-wood canoes around the summer of 1857. These all-wood canoes used plank and rib construction but the designs were based on traditional open river and lake designs of native builders, becoming known simply as "Peterboroughs." Although manufactured by many different craftsmen and companies, the all-wood canoes required precise workmanship and as a result, were only affordable to the growing affluent sportsmen population. Consequently, both their design and expense limited their use for whitewater.

Sometime around 1880, craftsmen in Maine made a change in both material and construction technique building wood and canvas or canvas covered canoes. In 1882, the B.N. Morris Canoe Company of Veazie, Maine, began production of less costly wood and canvas canoes. These were followed by Chestnut of New Brunswick in 1897, and E. M. White in 1889, and Old Town in 1898, both of Maine.

In addition to replacing bark with canvas, the building process was actually reversed. Bark canoes were traditionally constructed right side up, with the hull on the ground, starting with the bark outside material and adding the rest of the internal structure of ribs, gunwales, and thwarts. Wood and canvas canoes were constructed upside down, starting with the internal structure and finishing with the canvas outside material.

[11] Adney, Edwin Tappan and Howard I. Chapelle. *The Bark Canoes and Skin Boats of North America* Washington D.C.: Smithsonian Institution Press, 1983.

The less costly wood and canvas canoes allowed canoeing to become a leisure time pursuit for more than just the affluent. Liveries opened up on calm stretches of rivers and small lakes and ponds. Over the next thirty years, canoe clubs appeared in eastern and mid-western cities like New York, Philadelphia, Washington D.C., and Dayton. Many of the clubs had clubhouses on rivers or lakes where members stored their canoes.

The American Canoe Association (ACA) was founded in 1880 by twenty-three devotees of canoeing, all owners of finely crafted Peterboroughs. Although the ACA was established specifically as a canoeing organization, the organization and its members did not actively pursue river exploration. Instead, they concentrated on flatwater and canoe sailing competitions. Many of its members rejected the less expensive wood and canvas canoes that made river exploration feasible, calling them "rag" canoes.

NATIVE CANOE DESIGNS are the foundation for every open canoe made today, both flatwater and whitewater. We modern paddlers have not invented much. We have simply expanded upon the basics already established by native paddlers. Open whitewater canoes of the '70s and '80s with their flat bottoms, extreme rocker, and tumblehome are descendents of the "crooked canoes" of native canoe builders.

The View from a Kayak

Although native skin kayaks were also indigenous to North America, the first Europeans in America did not encounter them, nor even perceive them, the same way they did bark canoes. Skin kayaks were not the craft of choice for fur trapping or trading or even river exploration. As a result, the history of skin kayak adaptations for whitewater by Americans was very different than that of bark canoes.

Like wood and canvas canoes, until commercially made kayaks were available, only a few bold and affluent individuals used kayaks for whitewater. After running the Westfield in 1914, AMC member Alexander Forbes decided that a kayak was probably better suited for whitewater because of its inherent stability (because of sitting lower than kneeling in a canoe) and its ability to shed water (because of its covered deck). He designed a kayak similar to the "Alaskan Eskimo model, but with a flatter bottom for stability, with a fuller spoon bow for buoyancy in entering whitewater, and with a larger cockpit to expedite jumping out in case of capsizing or jamming a rock." [12] Forbes contracted its construction, similar to that of wood and canvas canoes. The kayak was built with wood ribs planked over and covered with canvas.

Forbes' kayak was first used in 1915 on the Westfield and proved suitable for whitewater. In 1920, he improved upon the design and contracted four kayaks built for use by fellow AMC members. As their skill and experience improved, they attempted and successfully ran rapids not previously run in open canoes. However, although a few kayaks were custom built by AMC members, canoes were clearly the craft of choice for whitewater for many of its members. Worthington, a proponent of canoes, wrote in 1929:

[12] Forbes, Alexander. "Twenty Years of the Westfield River." *Appalachia* (June 1937): 310–326.

> The kyack [kayak] has been used for sport in quick water, although it was obviously designed for use in the sea. It is exceedingly quick to turn and will live in water which would swamp an open canoe. But one cannot stand in it, or even kneel, or use a pole, or carry more than a trifle of dunnage. The use of the kyack in quick water is not recommended. [13]

Much of this preference may have been due to the native canoeing heritage of the Northeast and Canada and the presence of canoe manufacturers in this region that was also based on the native canoeing heritage of the region. However, as the availability of less expensive commercial European foldboat (folding kayak) imports became available in the 1930's, kayaks for whitewater began to gain acceptance, particularly as word spread regarding European wildwater touring in foldboats.

In 1932, Fred Launer and Dr. Charles Plummer of Salt Lake City kayaked the Green in Utah in a foldboat. The next year, Harold H. Leich of Washington, D.C., attempted to paddle the Grand Canyon. Although having previously paddled much of the Colorado starting at Grand Lake in Colorado, Leich destroyed his foldboat in Big Drop Rapid and ended up swimming to Hite where he walked out to Hanksville, Utah.

By the mid-1930's, even AMC canoeists began accepting foldboats for whitewater. Eugene Du Bois, a recognized leading sportsman and editor of the *New York Times,* extolled the benefits of whitewater paddling to fellow alpine skiers.

> Faltbootpaddeln [foldboat paddling] has sold itself readily to American skiers on the grounds that it is a proven European sport with a Teutonic origin, and that it requires much skill and gives back almost the same thrill as skiing. The boater with his collapsible kayak takes the same train he took as a skier; he wears a modified variety of the same clothes; and he uses the same water that previously served him in the form of snow. The skier concludes the obvious relationship between slalom and dodging rocks in river rapids; between cross-country and level paddling on still lakes; between ski jumping and taking a leap over a waterfall. [14]

In 1935, Joseph (Jack) Kissner, a German immigrant who began building foldboats in England in the early 1930's, established Folbot in New York. Now foldboats were manufactured domestically for the first time in North America. In 1939, Kissner along with DuBois and Roland Palmedo (both dedicated skiers) convinced the New Haven Railroad to emulate the train-foldboat trips that had gained popularity in Europe. On the first trip, about two hundred foldboaters departed by train from New York City for Falls Village, Connecticut, for a Sunday paddle down the Housatonic River to Flanders (a 20-mile Class II run). Other trips followed and received considerable attention in the *New York Times, Time, The Sun,* and other New York papers and Kissner specifically promoted his foldboats for use on whitewater rivers. (The Folbot

[13] Worthington, John W. "Quick-Water Canoeing." *Appalachia* (June 1929): 268–277.

[14] Folbot Catalog. 1935-1936.

catalog provided information beyond the standard information about the foldboats that he manufactured. The catalog also included instructionals, how-to's, and testimonials to encourage the public to take up the sport.)

As word spread about the rivers of the Colorado plateau with vast stretches of wilderness and whitewater, foldboaters from both the East and Europe traveled to run the Colorado River and its tributaries. Three French nationals from the Paris Museum of Natural History became the first to run the Colorado and Green Rivers in foldboats, and Genevieve de Colmont, the first woman. Antoine de Seynes, Bernard de Colmont, and Genevieve de Colmont brought their 15-foot foldboats to America to kayak unaided and without support down the Green and Colorado Rivers in Utah, in the summer of 1938. The trip started in southern Wyoming in September and reached Jensen, Utah, the first week of October. They ran all the drops with the exception of Big Drop in Cataract Canyon recording the trip on film as they went. They were eventually stopped by ice but reached Phantom Ranch in the Grand Canyon. All three were experienced kayakers having run rivers in Europe including a trip on the Nile. They were confident in their skills and wore helmets in the drops, unlike their American counterparts. The trip was Bernard's and Genevieve's honeymoon.

In 1938, W. Stewart "Stu" Gardiner, a young man from Salt Lake City, purchased a two-seater Folbot and began plans to run the Green River. Unable to convince any of his friends to join him, Gardiner made a solo run in October down the Green through Flaming Gorge to Split Mountain Canyon taking out at Jensen. The next year in September, Gardiner made a second run on the Green, but this time was joined by Alexander "Zee" Grant, Jr. of AMC. The following year, in 1940, Grant ran the Middle Fork of the Salmon along with two of his friends, Rodney Aller and Coleman T. Nimick, each paddling his own foldboat. Aller, an accomplished skier, already had a reputation as one of the most "expert river rats" in the East. Nimick, on the other hand, had virtually no previous river experience. Except for breaking paddles, and, for Nimick, a pin toward the end of the trip, their unaided mid-August trip was a success.

In 1941, Grant joined commercial river runner Norm Nevills and a small group for a trip down the Grand Canyon. Nevills had made the trip only twice before and agreed to allow Grant to participate "with the understanding that he and I would be separate parties, not responsible for each other, traveling together for mutual convenience." [15] Nevills insisted that the trip be made early in the season during high water so that his heavy boats would not crash into rocks. This meant a 30 knot current and 20 foot waves found only with a flow of at least 20,000 cubic feet per second (cfs). Grant designed a new foldboat hull based on this information along with recommendations of the manufacturer, Folbot, regarding the light craft's ability to endure such conditions. "The result, constructed from my sketches, was like nothing ever seen afloat before: a sixteen-and-a-half foot, folding, rubber-covered battleship" he named the Escalante after the explorer-priest who made the first crossing of the river. The folboat had "bulbous ends carved from balsa wood, and huge sausage-like sponsons along the sides, made from inner tubes of Fifth Avenue bus tires." The construction was much sturdier

Although David Thompson, Alexander MacKenzie, Simon Fraser, Meriwether Lewis, and William Clark explored rivers in the West a full 75 years before John Wesley Powell's epic exploration of the rivers of the Colorado plateau, it was Powell's discovery of the Colorado that sparked the interest in whitewater river exploration—river chasing—for many that followed. Powell's use of wooden boats that were rowed, not paddled, set the precedent for commercial river-running that followed, first in wooden boats and later in rubber rafts.

Thompson began a survey of western Canada in 1786 and was followed by Mackenzie's exploration of northern routes to the Beaufort Sea on the Arctic via the Peace, Slave, and Mackenzie rivers in 1789 and 1793 and Fraser's exploration of Canada to the Pacific via the Fraser River. Lewis and Clark began their exploration of America in 1804 following the Missouri and Columbia rivers and tributaries. Although their discoveries and accomplishments were noteworthy and affected the development and expansion of both the United States and Canada, none attracted the imagination for whitewater as Powell's exploration of the rivers of the Colorado plateau.

In 1869, and again in 1871–1872, Powell began a systematic and scientific survey of the Colorado River drainage starting on the Green in Green River, Wyoming. Powell's 1869 expedition was partially funded by the Illinois Natural History Society but the 1871 expedition was sponsored by the U.S. government. The precedent and tradition of rowing a boat on big water instead of paddling was established with Powell who designed the boats for the expeditions and they were designed to be rowed. His design was based on his experience of rivers of the Ohio and Mississippi Valleys with strong currents but with no rocks or obstacles obstructing the main flow. The design was round-bottomed with fairly deep draft and intended for two oarsmen to face upstream and row while a steersman steered from the stern. The idea was that the speed provided by the oarsmen would assist the sternman in steering. Only one boat was lost on the 1869 expedition that ended at

—continues on next page

[15] Grant, Alexander G. Jr. "Cockleshell on the Colorado- Through the Grand Canyon in a Foldboat." *American Whitewater* Vol. 4 No. 2 (Summer 1958): 6–13 (a reprint of an article originally published in *Appalachia*).

the mouth of the Virgin River, now under Lake Mead. The remaining boats survived the Colorado's treacherous and unexplored canyons and gorges. For the second trip in 1871, three new boats were built of the same design, but with a compartment amidships for buoyancy and cargo. Scholars questioned Powell's choice of men on the second trip because he already knew the nature of the river. They thought he should have included French-Canadian voyageurs who knew river running and had the skills to handle the rivers.

With the rowing tradition established, hunters, trappers, and prospectors like Nathaniel Galloway of Vernal, Utah, and Bert Loper of Hite, Utah, began rowing the rivers and canyons of the Colorado and its tributaries in the 1880's. Galloway designed and built lightweight cataract boats that revolutionized river running with oars. The boats were a lightweight skiff (about 400 pounds) 14 to 15 feet in length and 4 feet wide, flat-bottomed with a pronounced rocker (rake or curve fore and aft). Some were open but most had a cowling on the back (stern) of the boat to run backwards down drops. Galloway chose to row backward except in drops. He would spin the boat 180 degrees to run drops facing with the stern end (transom) forward. He used his oars to position himself for the drop and to maintain a speed slower than the current. By slowing the boat, he could maneuver down the drop avoiding rocks and holes without a steersman at all. The rockered flat-bottomed design allowed him to spin the boat on a dime and even surf or hold position in the current.

Galloway was the first to use the technique of rowing into the drops and the first to actually run many of the big drops. Prior to Galloway, many portaged the drops. Galloway's boat was greatly admired and in 1907, he was hired by Julius Stone to build four boats and serve as a guide on the rivers. This was the beginning of what would lead to the western tradition of commercial river running where boatmen rowed and catered to their guests. By the 1930's, the first commercial river trips were run on the Green, Yampa, and Colorado Rivers in Utah and the Salmon River in Idaho, among others.

[16] Grant, Alexander G. Jr. "Cockleshell on the Colorado—Through the Grand Canyon in a Foldboat." *American Whitewater* Vol. 4 No. 2 (Summer 1958): 6–13 (a reprint of an article originally published in *Appalachia*).

[17] Baldwin, Henry I. Correspondence to Stewart Coffin, 19 January 1986.

than standard foldboats and had considerably more sheer. Buoyancy was provided not only by the sponsons, but also by eight inner tubes and five beach balls inside the hull. [16]

Rapid River (ME), 1941 —courtesy of Ted Acton.

The trip began in mid-July following one of the wettest springs on record, with a gauge reading at Lee's Ferry of 25,900 cfs. Nevills was concerned about Grant's ability to run the large drops in the Canyon. Indeed, Grant fell out of his foldboat in Badger, the first major drop in the Canyon, and ended up climbing onto the back of the foldboat and paddling the remainder sitting backwards and on top. However, Grant, in his modified foldboat, ran most of the drops, portaging only Hermit and Lava Falls, as did Nevills and his group.

Word spread about Grant and his adventure through the Grand Canyon. Other paddlers, although not as famous Grant who was a nephew of President Franklin Delano Roosevelt, also paddled the Colorado. But Grant's adventures were well published. In 1938, Charles Mann of Pennsylvania paddled a foldboat on the Green through the Gates of Lodore all the way to Lee's Ferry on the Colorado. His adventure, though, was not widely publicized.

A club loosely called the "River Rats of America" arose from a small group of AMC paddlers including Zee Grant and accomplished what many considered "great feats out West." [17] Kissner further promoted this new sport with the publication of his book *Foldboat Holidays* published in 1940, a compilation of trip reports by pioneering foldboaters including Zee Grant, W. S. Gardiner, and Harold Frantz. In Europe, the movies of Seynes and Colmonts' trip down the Colorado were shown at club meetings that attracted other Europeans to explore rivers of the American West.

[*Author's Note:* The author of the article titled "Sun Valley and Yellowstone Park" in Foldboat Holidays is listed as W. T. Gardiner. Conversations with Stewart Gardiner's family indicate that the article was written by Stewart indicating a typographical error in the original publication of *Foldboat Holidays.* This error was repeated in subsequent editions titled *Folbot Holidays.*]

In 1940, the first official whitewater competition was held. It was sponsored by AMC, the only organized group involved in whitewater in North America at the time. Although a misnomer as a national race, the White Water Committee of AMC organized the first National White Water Championship (a wildwater race) on the Rapid River at Middle Dam in Maine. The race included classes for single and double foldboats, canoes, and Maine Guides. The race committee included Zee Grant as chairman along with others who later were involved in the early years of American Whitewater including Eugene DuBois, Stewart Gardiner, Lawrence I. Grinnell, and Roland Palmedo.

AMC trip, circa 1940s
—courtesy of Bart Hauthaway.

The race was held on July 6 and 7, 1940, and was sponsored by Royal Little, a committee member, head of Textron, and a leading figure in the financial world. The race ran from Richardson Lake to Umbagog Lake, a distance of 7 miles of Class III–IV water. Arrangements were made with the Brown Company, owner of the dam, for a release of 800 cfs. The channel of the river had been dynamited years before to make river driving of pulpwood easier, but which left sharp and jagged rocks. During a practice run, Roland Palmedo destroyed his folding kayak. Others damaged their kayaks and themselves on the jagged rocks. To finish the race required that the boater and boat cross the finish line together. Henry Baldwin recalled: "I barely qualified by holding on to the drifting sticks and cloth that had been my boat."[18] Zee Grant won the race in a folding kayak with the best time. Jack Kissner won the following year in 1941.

By 1945, whitewater kayaking in foldboats gained broader exposure across the country than did whitewater canoeing, partly due to the fact that folding kayaks were more easily transported. Because of their exposure, availability, and successful use on whitewater in the West, the practice of whitewater kayaking instead of whitewater canoeing took root in the early years of whitewater paddling in California, Colorado, and Washington.

Further Upstream

The origin of whitewater kayaks is not as straight forward as whitewater canoes. The first native kayak designs used for whitewater did not have specific design characteristics for whitewater like those of the crooked canoe. The designs, based on those of Inuit and other native kayak builders in the arctic regions of North America and Greenland, were for open water conditions, not rivers. Both open and decked kayaks were made of skin stretched on a frame of wood. The open kayak, the umiak, was designed for carrying loads, but it was also used for hunting whale and walrus and was often paddled by more than one hunter in pursuit of game. The decked kayak was designed for the solitary hunter.

[18] Baldwin, Henry I. Correspondence to Stewart Coffin, 19 January 1986.

Double-blade paddles were widely used by native kayakers, although single-blade paddles were also used. The blades of double and single-blade paddles were narrow, perhaps owing to the scarcity of both trees and large pieces of driftwood.

The major difference between bark canoes and skin kayaks is that the frame is entirely self-supporting for skin kayaks, in contrast to bark canoes where the bark "skin" is an integral structural part of the hull. The frame of a skin kayak does not need the skin for strength or support, whereas, without the bark "skin," the canoe falls apart. This skin-on-frame concept was adopted by the first modern builders of kayaks.

In 1859, a British paddler named John McGregor used a non-vulcanized rubber kayak 15 feet in length and 30 inches in width for river exploration. The design and construction was popularized throughout Europe and eastern North America with publicized accounts of his famous "Rob Roy" canoe trips. ("Canoe" was the term for a kayak in Europe for many years. "Canadian canoe" differentiated it from what was known in North American as a canoe.) MacGregor formed the Royal Canoe Club of England in 1866 and the popularity of the Rob Roy spread among English-speaking paddlers. In 1871, the New York Canoe Club was founded using imported Rob Roy canoes [kayaks]. Single-blade paddling of Canadian canoes was later adopted by club members in the early 1900's.

However, McGregor's Rob Roys were not readily adopted outside of Britain and North America, particularly among non-English language European countries for nationalistic reasons. Instead, Fridtjof Hansen, a Norwegian explorer, is credited with importing kayaking into Europe with his study and use of the native kayaks of Greenland. Just as with wood rib and plank canoes (Peterboroughs), modern European materials and construction techniques were adapted and allowed custom production on a limited basis for affluent European sportsmen. This changed in 1907 when Johann Klepper of Germany introduced the first commercially built folding kayak, called foldboats, based on the skin-on-frame concept but with modern materials. It was Klepper's commercially available foldboats that allowed kayaking to take root in Europe, particularly among Germanic language countries. Many European countries adopted folding kayaks and founded canoe [kayak] clubs and national organizations that were becoming the standard for sports in general. Foldboats, were specifically designed for travel by train, the most common form of European transportation.

Although Klepper is attributed with producing the first commercially available folding kayak, he is often mistakenly attributed as the inventor of the folding kayak concept. Perhaps the first folding kayaks were developed in 1863 by John Hagerman, a U.S. Army engineer, for use during fighting on the Tennessee River near Chattanooga. The idea died with the end of the Civil War.

During and after World War I, foldboaters, as users of folding kayaks were called, explored wildwater touring, attempting wilder sections of rivers in the Alps. As with AMC in New England, members of alpine climbing and skiing clubs adopted wildwater touring as a complimentary seasonal activity.

In the early 1920's, after a film was made that depicted wildwater paddling in Europe, Austrian paddlers began exploration of wilder and wilder rivers. In 1923, Austria reported eleven fatal accidents and the Austrian Canoe Association was described as "the direct kind of suicide club." Newspaper articles appeared with the title "Death rides along behind every kayak." [19]

THE DECKED KAYAK for the solitary hunter with a double-blade paddle became the basis for all modern kayaks, both flatwater and whitewater. However, the lineage to whitewater kayaks does not lie in their design characteristics since they were not designed for whitewater. Rather, it lies in the skin-on-frame and deck-with-cockpit concepts.

BY 1945, the young whitewater sport included canoeing and kayaking—canoeing, through native canoeing traditions, and kayaking, through its introduction by Europeans less than ten years before. But the young sport was largely dependent on individual pursuit with very limited organized participation and its development was further limited by the canoes and kayak. In particular, whitewater was limited more by the materials and construction of canoes and kayaks—materials not intended for whitewater but for general recreational use—than by their designs. Without materials that could handle the punishment of whitewater, the limitations of the designs and whitewater technique could not be explored. However, after 1945, post-war circumstances provided the impetus both for the organization of the sport and for the materials for canoes and kayaks to overcome and grow beyond earlier limitations. For whitewater, **materials** became the driving force behind the development of the sport, driving changes in **design** and **technique**. Whitewater now had an opportunity to develop fully as a sport.

In the few years before World War II, whitewater, the River, was born from the convergence of two streams: whitewater canoeing and whitewater kayaking. Both streams flowed from headwaters of native North American watercraft, but were still dependent on materials and construction not too far removed from that of the native watercraft. The River was small in volume and design and technique, and like crosscurrents roiling and interweaving, dependent on the individual flows from the two streams.

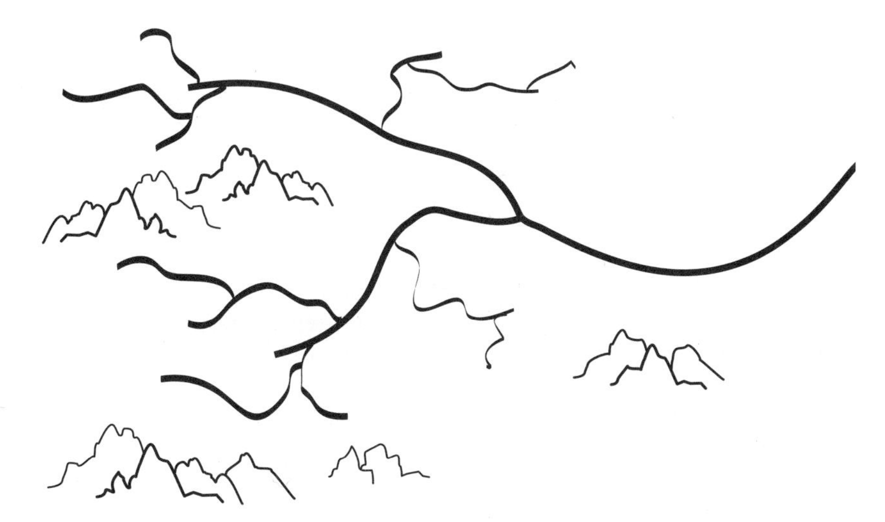

[19] Vesper, Hans Egon and John W. Dudderidge. *50 Years of the International Canoe Federation*, English Edition. Florence, Italy: International Canoe Federation, 1974.

The Infrastructure Building Years: Post World War II Through the '50s

THE FIRST OPPORTUNITY for whitewater as a sport to advance beyond limitations imposed by its adaptation of native watercraft came after 1945 with the application of new materials developed during World War II. The use of aluminum and fiberglass for canoes and kayaks provided the first materials that opened the boundaries of whitewater. Post-war circumstances, prosperity, and leisure time also provided increasing numbers of paddlers who organized clubs, both structured and not so structured, for the benefit of pursuing this young sport. The early clubs, our earliest facilitators, were scattered across the country from Appalachian Mountain Club and Buck Ridge Ski Club in the East to Washington Foldboat Club and River Touring Section of Sierra Club's San Francisco Bay Chapter in the West. Nestled in the middle of the country were a few scattered paddlers in Colorado who later became the founders of FibArk (First in Boating Arkansas River Club) and Colorado White Water Association.

Although by the early '50s we had new materials and new clubs, and had attempted to contact one another about our whitewater learnings, there seemed little urgent need to officially organize on a national basis. However, that changed in 1953 with an invitation to compete in slalom and wildwater competition in Europe. Not only did the invitation provide a purpose or a need for a national organization, but the purpose of the invitation itself, to compete in whitewater, demonstrated that we lagged behind our European counterparts. They appeared so far advanced in both their national organizations and technical skills that they were able to conduct international competition and had the technical skills to develop a new form of competition, slalom racing, something that only a few American paddlers had heard of. Competition, slalom, and wildwater, became the tie that bound our early facilitators together in a common pursuit, but just as importantly, competition became the means and motivation to advance skills and technique.

Our initial answer to the lack of national organization was the formation of American White Water Affiliation in 1954, an association of individuals and clubs scattered across the country, many of whom were already in contact with one another. It was a good start. However, our solution to the lack of technical skills and knowledge, particularly of slalom competition, was not as easy to resolve. Reading about it wasn't enough. We had to see it, and for this our European counterparts provided us with their assistance in the form of European competitors and paddlers drawn to the annual downriver race on

1945

Fiberglass materials available

Grumman aluminum canoes available

Fiberglass kayak built by Steve Bradley and Dave Stacey

Fiberglass canoe built by Tom Johnson

First Annual Royal Gorge Boat Race (Salida race)

First World Championships for slalom held in Geneva, Switzerland

1950

Invitation received by American paddlers to compete in '53 World Championships

First slalom demonstrations seen in America

Milo Duffek debutes new stroke at '53 World Championships

American White Water Affiliation (AWWA) organized

French team brings first closed canoe (C-2) to Salida race

1955

Americans compete in '57 World Championships in Augsburg, Germany

American C-2 built by Larry Monninger and Larry Zuk

American-built fiberglass kayak (paddled by Roger Paris) wins Salida race

First American C-1 built by Larry Zuk

1960

the Arkansas at Salida and the folklore of the wild rivers of Colorado. While some merely came to visit and paddle our rivers, others came and stayed. European champions like Walter Kirschbaum, Roger Paris, and Erich Seidel paddled and even taught among us in the '50s and '60s. Without their friendship and support and the universal sense of solidarity among paddlers, we would have remained far behind our European counterparts for many years.

In so many different ways, slalom and wildwater competition brought organization, advanced skills, and growth to the sport, all reasons to build the infrastructure necessary for a sport to grow. Competition also brought added impetus to explore and develop new materials, designs, and technique.

New Materials and Construction

Downstream of the convergence of whitewater canoeing and whitewater kayaking, the first major tributary entered the River. This tributary, fed by a cloudburst of new materials and construction processes, swelled from postwar events and developments, in particular, aluminum forming and fiberglass. (Technically, the terminology is fiber reinforced plastic, FRP. However, the term fiberglass is used throughout this book since it is the term most often used by paddlers to mean FRP.) Both developments represented significant leaps in technology with man-made materials for whitewater.

Aluminum forming, called stretch forming, permitted the production of even less costly and certainly more durable aircraft and watercraft than any previous materials and processes. Canoes became the beneficiaries of this technology. Fiberglass provided another less costly and more durable replacement material for the production of watercraft. Additionally, unlike aluminum forming, fiberglass construction permitted low-cost and relatively low-tech construction that allowed an individual to design and build his or her own boat, canoe, or kayak without the need to purchase it from a manufacturer. Of the two developments in technology, fiberglass was the more significant.

A third development, synthetic rubber (Neoprene and Duprene), provided man-made materials for survival and assault rafts, and pontoons for constructing replacement bridges during World War II. War surplus became an indirect contributor to whitewater canoeing and kayaking and its significance cannot be overlooked. These inflatables allowed the growing commercial river-running industry in the West to take more clients down rivers at one time. This resulted in less expensive trips thereby further increasing the growing client base and exposing increasing numbers of tourists to whitewater.

Bus Hatch of Vernal, Utah, and his cousin Frank Swain began exploring the Green and Colorado Rivers in the 1930s for pleasure. Like many of the small cadre of river-runners, Hatch dreamed of expanding his passion into a livelihood. He formed Hatch River Expeditions and used wooden boats to carry his passengers down river. After World War II, Bus and his son Don recognized that the availability of military surplus rafts and pontoons would allow them to expand their business making Hatch River Expeditions a viable business.

War surplus provided seven- and ten-man assault rafts. Large bridge pontoons in the mid-'50s replaced the smaller assault rafts as commercial outfitters tried to handle increasing numbers of guests on the Green and Colorado. At first, the rafts were powered by a single oarsman, the same as used in wooden boats and dories. As larger and larger rafts and different pontoon configurations came into use, a second oarsman was added. Experimentation continued for the best way to handle the pontoons and accommodate larger numbers of non-paddling guests including combinations with outboard motors mounted in various locations on a raft. By the '60s, rafts were predominant, replacing wooden boats on commercial trips on the Colorado or Green.

It was not until the early '60s that rafting for river-running significantly affected paddling in the East. However, its affect on whitewater was very unique and distinctive from that in the West.

Aluminum

As World War II drew to a close, the U.S. Government encouraged its wartime industrial suppliers to diversify and seek peacetime use of technology developed for the war effort. In that regard, Grumman Aircraft Engineering Company was no different than any other wartime supplier. Grumman Aircraft developed a great deal of expertise in stretch forming aluminum with their production of fighter planes and sought peacetime use of this technology. Stretch forming is ideally suited for production of aircraft since it can produce large curvatures by stretching or drawing the sheet over a form of the desired shape. Watercraft was one of the benefactors.

Aluminum refining uses a combination of smelting and a fused salt electrolysis to refine the metal from its oxide, primarily the mineral bauxite. Charles M. Hall in the United States independently developed the process in 1886 at the same time as Paul Heroult in France. The process became the foundation for the formation of what would become Aluminum Company of America (Alcoa). Since the process requires considerable amounts of electric power, aluminum refining is often located in areas with abundant hydroelectric power and near an ocean port for shipping in bauxite. In North America, one such area is Alma, Quebec, which is coincidentally in canoe country.

The idea of making a canoe from aluminum came about during a fishing trip in the Adirondack Mountains in 1944. William J. Hoffman, Vice President of Grumman Aircraft Engineering, wrote:

> We flew into Limekiln Lake from Fourth Lake and fished it for a day or two using a battered and water-logged 13' [foot] wood-and-canvas canoe. Then we decided to fish in Squaw Lake, which is several miles away. As there were not boats there, we had to carry our water-logged, paint-loaded canvas canoe that must have weighed at least 100 pounds. For a fellow who was not accustomed to carrying a canoe, this was too much. I decided then and there that someone had to do something about that problem. [1]

Hoffman determined that it would be a fairly simple stretch forming operation to form a canoe from two identical halves of aluminum, riveting the halves together at the keel. He also determined that a 13-foot canoe should weigh less than 50 pounds, far less than the waterlogged wood and canvas canoe that prompted the idea in the first place. He approached Grumman President Leroy Grumman and was given the go-ahead to build a prototype.

Since Hoffman's knowledge of canoe design was limited, he borrowed a 13-foot wood and canvas canoe from Macy's department store. After studying the canoe, he realized that the concavity in the bow and stern cheeks could not be formed since it was a reverse curve to the otherwise convex shapes. He and his assistants modified the shape to accommodate the stretch-forming process only keeping the most basic dimensions of the 13-foot canoe. The finished prototype of .032 skin weighed about 38 pounds, while the wood and canvas, although advertised at 50 pounds, weighed 64 pounds.

[1] Rockwell, Dwight Jr. Correspondence to Harry Roberts at Wilderness Canoe from Dwight Rockwell, Jr. of Rockwell and Newell, Inc. in New York (a marketing firm hired by Grumman), date unknown.

Materials and processes are specifically chosen for a product's required physical shape and properties. The specific choice and use of birch bark for canoes greatly affected the hydrodynamic aspects of canoe designs. Fortunately, it proved to be a remarkable material in that regard.

The use of stretch-formed aluminum for canoes also affected canoe design. Stretch forming, appropriate for convex shapes only, was not able to produce all the shapes and contours that even birch bark could since it could not produce compound shapes that required both convex and concave contours. Only one shape could be stretched or drawn at a time. For this reason, the fullness in a Grumman canoe's bow and stern was the result of the stretch forming process. It was not intentionally designed-in for hydrodynamic considerations for whitewater, but rather because concavity could not be formed into an otherwise convex canoe shape. The fullness of the bow was only later found to be an advantage for whitewater canoeing.

Grumman worked closely with Alcoa in selecting the appropriate alloys for the skin, extrusions for the gunwales, thwarts, and rivets. During this collaboration, Hoffman met Russell Bontecou of Alcoa who coincidentally came up with the idea of producing aluminum canoes about the same time. Bontecou had previously designed and produced a 17-foot canoe for Alcoa. However, without having Grumman's experience in stretch forming aluminum sheet, his canoe was made of eight pieces of sheet aluminum riveted together. The canoe was not only too costly to produce using Bontecou's process, but the canoe was unsightly as well.

Both Bontecou and Hoffman decided that a 17-foot canoe had more market potential than a 13-foot canoe. Taking Bontecou's canoe design, Hoffman made additional modifications to produce the shape. Thus was born the 17-foot Grumman canoe. Bontecou joined Grumman "with the understanding that he would handle canoe sales if Grumman went into production after the war."[2]

Under Hoffman's direction in manufacturing and Bontecou's efforts in sales, the first aluminum canoes were produced in 1945 in Grumman's facility in Bethpage on Long Island. The model line started with the 17-foot keeled canoe. It later expanded to include 13-foot, 15-foot, 17-foot, and 18-foot both keeled and shoe-keeled in standard and lightweight thicknesses. The canoes were made (and continue to be made the same way under the Marathon Boat Group name to this day) of 6061 aluminum alloy and heat-treated after forming to the T-6 temper. Although 6061 was weldable, Grumman chose to use rivets due to the brittleness remaining after welding. Production was later moved to Marathon, New York, as part of the Metal Boat Company of Grumman, although other Grumman facilities later produced or assembled canoes.

Thomas Cabot, of Cabot Corporation (and co-author of *Quick-Water and Smooth: A Canoeists Guide to New England Rivers)* claimed that Mr. Bontecou of Grumman approached him to design the ideal canoe. The result was the Grumman canoe that he specifically designed for "rapid water in mind with much fuller ends and somewhat less dead rise than the earlier birch bark and canvas models."[3] Dean Gray of the Gray family that owned Old Town Canoe was also said to be angry with Grumman because Grumman stole the design from one of Old Town's canoe designs.

[2] Rockwell, Dwight Jr. Correspondence to Harry Roberts at Wilderness Canoe from Dwight Rockwell, Jr. of Rockwell and Newell, Inc. in New York (a marketing firm hired by Grumman), date unknown.

[3] Cabot, Thomas. Correspondence to Stewart Coffin, 7 February 1985.

Aluminum canoes became commercially available primarily in the East through the small retail boat industry. No retailer could make a living selling only canoes so Grumman sold their canoes through retailers already selling other kinds of boats, including their own growing aluminum sport/fishing boats. However, then as now, shipping canoes was expensive and as a result, their use was concentrated near the manufacturer. For canoes, that meant in the East just as was the case for wood and canvas canoes. Due to their low cost and durability, aluminum canoes quickly replaced wood and canvas canoes for use in camps and rentals. Aluminum canoes also were quickly adopted for use in whitewater.

Fiberglass

In the mid-to-late '30s, a flurry of activity surrounded the development of fiber reinforced plastics. A variety of fibers, including linen, were used in resins that were also under development. The first fiberglass-reinforced composite was made in 1937, combining fiberglass wool (mineral wool or glass wool used as pipe insulation) with Bakelite™ (a phenolic resin) by researchers at Owens-Illinois. (Bakelite is a registered trademark of Union Carbide. Owens-Illinois later became known as Owens-Corning Fiberglass through a joint venture with Corning Glass.) With further advances in resin and fiberglass reinforcement developments, the potential of fiberglass reinforced composites for aircraft construction was realized and a task force was created in the early '40s at Wright Patterson Airforce Base in Dayton, Ohio, just down the road from Owens-Corning in Toledo. During the remaining years of the war, the Wright Air Development Center Structures Laboratory and Materials Laboratory generated mechanical and physical properties regarding glass fiber reinforced plastic composites. Their research later provided the emerging post-war fiberglass industry a platform to launch further investigations and research for practical applications of this new material. Airplanes, automobiles, and boats all soon benefitted from this new material.

In 1937, a researcher at DuPont invented the first polyester resin. It took two more years before the discovery of cross-linking polyester and a monomer (today predominantly styrene) which provided a usable commercial resin. Soon other chemical companies followed with their own polyester resin formulations, notably Union Carbide, American Cyanamid, Celanese, and Pittsburgh Plate Glass's (PPG) chemical division. Prior to the war, PPG introduced the first commercial resins. However, problems persisted with these resins until British Intelligence obtained secret information from Germany's research that overcame these problems. In 1942, American Cyanamid produced the first polyester resin, which was similar to today's resins. But the resins still had limitations for curing: they required heat to cure and would not cure in the presence of air. A relatively closed process or mold was required.

By the end of World War II, a catalyst, benzol peroxide, was available that provided for room temperature curing of polyester resins. Chopped and continuous strand mats for fiberglass reinforcement was also available from Owens-Corning, which provided all the necessary materials for post-war development for fiberglass construction.

Steve Bradley grew up on the water and in boats near Wood's Hole in Massachusetts where his father was a researcher. When he was 16 years old, Bradley built a foldboat from a kit purchased from Mead Glider in Chicago. In 1946, as an adult, he moved to Colorado to run Winter Park Ski resort. Two years later in 1948, his friend Dave Stacey, a Ph.D. physicist at the University of Colorado in Boulder, introduced him to a double folding kayak. [*Author's note:* The use of the term folding kayaks or foldboats and foldboating are differentiated from rigid kayaks as appropriate.] Bradley bought one himself from Folbot in New York and began paddling the Poudre outside of Boulder. Bradley, with his girl friend Ann (whom he later married), and Stacey, with his girl friend, scheduled a trip with Bus Hatch on the Yampa and Green. While practicing on the Poudre for the trip, Bradley and his girl friend wrapped the foldboat on a rock. The boat slowly shifted and sank out of sight. A few weeks later when the river level had dropped, Bradley retrieved pieces of the kayak and, incredibly, found the skin with only one small tear. He contacted Kissner at Folbot who sent a new frame in time for the trip with Hatch.

The Yampa and Green turned out to be a good introductory run and both Bradley and Stacey were hooked. Bradley realized that the sport was going to become expensive if he had to pay $250 for a new frame each time he hit a rock and wrapped a foldboat. Coincidentally, Bradley saw a feature article in *Life* magazine with Hawes of Pittsburgh Plate Glass (PPG) demonstrating how well an automobile fender made of fiberglass could handle the impact of hammer blows. Bradley contacted Hawes who provided him with all the necessary information to obtain the new material and build a kayak using it.

Bradley was not satisfied with the Folbot hull he used so he decided to design a better hull for whitewater. In order to design a new hull, Bradley took a correspondence course in basic naval architecture. He found "that hull design is as much an art, as much a matter of sense of proportion, of eye analysis, as it is an exact science."[4]

Bradley and Stacey designed and built a two man kayak (a double) mold that was a little shorter and beamier than their Folbot foldboats. Since Bradley first had to take the course, the double took almost six months to design. The mold was built as a male mold, which meant the kayak was layed-up on the outside. They managed to build two kayaks from the mold before it broke. This design was the first in a series of kayak designs, seven in total over approximately ten years.

Tom Johnson lived in southern California. Although he had not been in a canoe until he was 20 years old, he knew he wanted one. In 1938, not being able to afford a canoe, he decided to build a canoe for himself. He researched wood and canvas canoe construction and design before he designed his first canoe, an 11-footer. He lofted the design on butcher paper and then carved a scale model. Johnson built the canoe using green elm for the ribs, Philippine mahogany for the planking, and hickory dowels for the gunwales. A few years later, he designed and built a 13-foot canoe.

In 1948, while working for a hardware business, Johnson obtained optical rejects of Lucite™ sheets from Swedlow, a local company who thermoformed aircraft canopies, Johnson began experimenting with building a canoe made of Lucite. (Lucite is a registered trademark of an acrylic from E. I. Du Pont de Nemours and Co.) In order to thermoform the Lucite sheets, Johnson built an oven of concrete block using a natural gas burner and a heavy blanket for the lid. He also made a press to mold the heated sheets into the shape of a canoe. After much trial and error throughout the entire process, he built a canoe with a flange that became the keel and structural stiffener. The canoe gunwales were made by rolling over the shear to form its own lip. After the halves were molded, he glued the halves at the keel with a solvent. The finished canoe was 12 feet in length and weighed 92 pounds. Because the canoe was made entirely of Lucite, it was completely clear and appeared invisible in the water. When the canoe was in the water, it was not readily apparent what paddlers were sitting in. In fact, because the gunwales and keel were made of Lucite, the canoe disappeared when completely submerged. Unfortunately, the canoe was used only three times before it was dropped and cracked.

About this same time, the DuPont sales engineer who provided Johnson with assistance in working with Lucite also told him about fiberglass. Johnson built a male mold using the original plug used for the Lucite canoe. The completed fiberglass canoe had aluminum glassed into the keel for added rigidity

[4] Bradley, Steve. "Hull Design." *American Whitewater* Vol. 2 No. 3 (Fall 1956): 15–18.

and weighed only 22 pounds, 70 pounds lighter than the Lucite canoe. From this first experience building with fiberglass, Johnson continued building more canoes, even pulling molds from other canoes. In 1954, he designed a 15-foot canoe fashioned after a guide model.

Bradley and Stacey with their kayaks and Johnson with his canoes were the start of a revolution that propelled whitewater on its own course, a revolution possible only because of what fiberglass construction offered to the individual paddler. Fiberglass construction not only produced more durable canoes and kayaks, it provided paddlers with the opportunity to design and build their own boats with minimal expense, short-cutting the normal manufacturer-retailer cycle. But because fiberglass construction itself was new, learning about it required that paddlers learn much of it through their own experience. The use of fiberglass construction for canoes and kayaks was hindered by limited communication among groups and individual paddlers. Its use also required certain kinds of individuals who wanted to build and design their own craft and who were not intimidated by the whole experience. Bradley, Stacey, and Johnson were such individuals. Although they had very different backgrounds, they had a common interest and desire to experiment and explore, to tinker for the sake of their sport.

The Earliest Facilitators: the Cornerstone Clubs

Although aluminum and fiberglass had arrived, the evolving young sport needed more than just materials; it needed groups of paddlers to organize in some fashion for communication and exchange of ideas and experience. Clubs, whether well structured or loosely organized, were the medium to share and learn not only paddling techniques, but to provide a margin of safety in a sport with risk. The ramifications of new developments or advancements not only affected the organization of paddling activities and clubs, but the evolution or rate of progress of new developments was affected by the degree of organizational development. It was not surprising as clubs organized that their orientation was affected by various developments or circumstances associated in their geographic areas. With the availability of aluminum Grumman canoes, new clubs in the East continued to initially concentrate on whitewater canoeing, while other clubs across the country to the West concentrated on whitewater kayaking.

Before 1945, Appalachian Mountain Club (AMC) was the only club with organized whitewater paddling. AMC member Eliot DuBois felt that whitewater was a group sport, one that could be particularly associated with clubs oriented around the same geographic areas used for hiking, climbing, skiing, and paddling (mountainous areas). Dubois' prediction came true in the years immediately after World War II. Organizations of paddlers formed in the mid-Atlantic (Buck Ridge Ski Club), the Northwest (Washington Foldboat Club), California (River Touring Section of Sierra Club's San Francisco Bay Chapter), and Colorado (FibArk and Colorado White Water Association) that were often associated with other geographically related activities. These early clubs, the cornerstones of whitewater's infrastructure, were critical facilitators to the sport's development.

East Coast

After the war ended in Europe, three AMC chapters, Boston, Connecticut, and New York, restarted their pre-war activities, including whitewater paddling. The first notice came out in April 1945 from the New York chapter for a weekend to repair wood and canvas canoes in the club's stables. By the next year, AMC's whitewater canoeing program was back in full swing. AMC also purchased additional canoes, some of them the new aluminum canoes that had just become available from Grumman.

AMC trip on the Westfield (MA), circa early 1950s—courtesy of Ted Acton.

The use of foldboats also increased among club members as the exploits of Grant and Aller, two well-known AMC River Rats, on the Middle Fork of the Salmon and Grant's journey down the Grand Canyon were chronicled in AMC's own journal, *Appalachia.* Other members, including Eliot Dubois and his wife Barbara, members of AMC-Boston, and Roland Palmedo of AMC-New York, also espoused the use of foldboats over canoes for whitewater. (DuBois wrote a book, *Innocence on the Middle Fork,* from his experience solo foldboating the Middle Fork of the Salmon in 1942 before going to war.)

AMC trip on the Westfield (MA), circa early 1950s—courtesy of Ted Acton.

Interest in whitewater continued to grow and AMC's chapters organized White Water Committees to schedule and organize yearly trips. New rivers in the mid-Atlantic and Northeast were added each year to AMC's repertoire. In the early '50s, a small group of AMC canoeists, including Corning King, Louise Davis, and Ruth Walker, began a series of summer trips that explored whitewater all across the country. The series included trips on the Main Salmon, Hell's Canyon, Yampa, Green, and Glen Canyon with Hatch Expeditions providing support.

Canoeing in a Grumman canoe, circa late 1950—courtesy of Bart Hauthaway.

AMC's long history of paddling experience, almost forty years by this time, certainly contributed to their effectiveness in introducing new paddlers to the sport, as well as having equipment available for them for club trips. With its foundation in Worthington's "Quick-Water Canoeing" published in *Appalachia* in 1929, AMC's instructional programs continued to evolve for both canoes and foldboats and contributed to an increasing number of whitewater canoeists. Club trips were large enough, and odd enough, to attract attention. Hal Burton wrote an article about the attraction of whitewater and the kind of trips AMC members pursued for the *Saturday Evening Post* (April 25, 1953) titled "Wild Water? They Love It!" This kind of publicity further increased interest and club membership.

Shortly after World War II ended, a group of skiers banded together to facilitate ski trips, thus forming the Buck Ridge Ski Club in 1945. In the late-'40s, Buck Ridge expanded its activities to include whitewater canoeing, using Grumman canoes, and foldboating. Robert (Bob) McNair and his wife Edith (Edie) were two of the charter members that became involved in canoeing. Other early members included Jim Calkins, Don and Harry Rupp, Howard (Jeff) Wilhoyte, and Louise Walker. Paul Wick from Switzerland was one of the few foldboaters in the club. By the mid-'50s, the club had a Canoeing Committee with regularly scheduled canoeing activities. Members explored the rivers of the eastern mid-Atlantic and New England and developed their whitewater canoeing skills.

Instruction was also a part of Buck Ridge's activities under the leadership of Bob McNair. Although he corresponded with Eliot DuBois of AMC, McNair relied heavily upon the American Red Cross and their "Red Cross Basic Canoeing" course for information about canoeing. This became the basis for the club's whitewater canoeing technique. At the time, the Red Cross recognized that running rapids slower than the current prevented a canoe from burying into large waves (haystacks) and provided time to maneuver. However, maneuvering largely consisted of side slipping, often with back paddling strokes. The concept of ferrying was not well understood, nor even named or defined. Instead, canoes were kept in line with the current at all times, even when entering an eddy.

> Move into eddies broadside or from a downstream direction, keeping the canoe in line with the direction of the main current. When alongside the shore or bank, keep the upstream end of the canoe closer to the bank than the downstream so that the current will hold the canoe against the bank rather than catch it and pull it broadside out into the stream. [5]

McNair realized that there was much to learn about whitewater canoeing and being a mechanical engineer, read as much as possible in technical manuals about river hydraulics in an attempt to transfer the information into usable information for river running. The techniques he and others in the club developed were not only influenced by the American Red Cross course, but also by the state-of-the-art equipment: keeled Grummans with no flotation or thigh straps. In 1953, McNair circulated an article containing his observations of basic river hydrology and whitewater canoeing. The article contained a mix of American Red Cross basic canoeing and swift-river learnings with a slightly more advanced understanding of river hydrology. It illustrated that McNair was on the verge of grasping what the application of river hydrology would mean to whitewater canoeing technique. McNair had an understanding of what river features to avoid, but not yet a full understanding of what features to use, or how to use them, to work for the paddler.

Excerpts from an unpublished article "Hints on Reading Fast Water" dated June 1953 by Robert E. McNair read:

> The water velocity is not constant across the river. Friction along the bottom and shores slows the water. So it flows fastest on the surface in midstream and slowest near the bottom and along the shore. You must back ashore when landing or this current differential will turn your canoe around. And if you are compelled to swim in rapids you not only keep on your back with feet downstream but you also keep your feet at the surface so the current differential does not topple you end over end. There are also pockets of slow-moving water or still water in the eddies behind rocks. Your bowman must be careful not to put his end in them when the stern is still in fast water, but they can be welcome havens for those who are tired or in trouble.

[5] Hasenfus, Joseph L. *Canoeing.* Washington, D.C.: American National Red Cross, 1956: 359.

> You will want to spot those hidden rocks. In still water there will be no signs on the surface to mark a submerged rock, but in a current the rocks will be marked by waves. The faster the current and the closer the rock is to the surface, the bigger will be the wave… You will notice that the wave is right at the rock when the rock is at the surface but appears further downstream as the depth of the rock increases. You will also notice that there is a rock in the apex of a surface 'V' that points upstream, and that when there are two such obstacles the channel between them is marked by a surface 'V' pointed downstream. But note well that the 'V' pointing downstream is only the intersecting 'Vs' from the rocks on either side, and you must look for further signs to be sure that the channel between is indeed free of rocks.
>
> It is the standing waves or 'haystacks' that mark deep water and are the greatest delight of the canoeist. Like all river waves, these stand stationary while the water rushes through on its downstream course. They may be spotted by their characteristic shape and long length also by the fact that they appear in groups, a half dozen or more together at even downstream intervals… These waves therefore mark deepening water downstream of a clear path that lets the water through the rapid… So get in line with these waves to traverse the ledge or rock field. Continue through the waves if they are not so big as to swamp you, otherwise draw to one side when free of the obstacles and hit the waves where they are small. There is an interesting and useful corollary to this rule. When you are in rough and turbulent water and spot a nice quiet pool, avoid it like the plague. As you shoot past, sneak a look back and you will probably see that a hidden rock with water pouring over it protects this quiet spot.
>
> There are other lesser points that you will pick up later. In the meantime, use these rules with discretion… If you would be a keen observer of waterflow, if you would learn the special techniques of handling your canoe in swift water, and if you would practice the safety rules that have evolved from experience, then a new world of fabulous beauty can open before the bow of your canoe.[6]

WITH THE EXCEPTION of "swift water" articles published in AMC's *Appalachia* prior to World War II, very little was actually written about fast water canoeing. A few articles appeared in *Boy's Life* such as in the June 1954 issue "Reading White Water" by Ernest F. Schmidt. Excerpts appeared in the second issue of *American Whitewater* in August 1955.[7]

Although advanced in some areas, McNair's observations were not as advanced as others such as Worthington's 1929 "Quick-Water Canoeing" article. However, McNair's observations and learnings for whitewater canoeing expanded from the basics of this article to a new *River Canoeing Manual* in 1957 edited by David Mayer of the Southeastern Pennsylvania chapter of the American Red Cross and Buck Ridge Ski Club. McNair expanded on this later and wrote *Basic River Canoeing* which was published in 1968 by the American Camping Association. By this time, McNair was an acknowledged leader in whitewater canoeing technique that used back paddling and back ferrying to slow descent and maneuver in whitewater (passive techniques by today's standards).

[6] McNair, Robert E. "Hints on Reading Fast Water" unpublished. June 1953.

[7] Schmidt, Ernest F. "Reading White Water." Excerpt from *Boy's Life,* June 1954. *American Whitewater,* Vol. 1 No. 2 (August 1955): p22–23.

However, while Buck Ridge advanced toward the next level of whitewater canoeing skills, kayaking (foldboating) advanced in the West to the next level.

West Coast

Wolf Bauer, a German immigrant and member of the Mountaineers in Seattle, began foldboating with a group of fellow skiers and mountaineers in the mid-'40s. After a few years of foldboating and "getting into trouble,"[8] Bauer picked up a German book on using foldboats for river running and decided they needed to look at river running more "scientifically."[9] In 1948, Bauer with a small group of foldboaters from the Mountaineers, formed their own club, the Washington Foldboat Club, specifically for foldboating,

While canoeing technique evolved in the East, the Washington Foldboat Club developed their kayaking (foldboating) techniques, in the absence of outside information except for the German book on foldboating. Bauer and members of the club not only studied and paddled rivers, they also designed boats and evolved a technique and terminology from what they learned. This also influenced the design of their instructional programs. Bauer, being the engineer, skier, and climber that he was, also combined the art of paddling into this evolving technique.

Members used Klepper and Pioneer foldboats, both imported from Germany, as well as foldboats from Folbot in New York. Bauer used them all but preferred the Klepper T-6 model since the design was sufficiently maneuverable for river running. However, it was not totally adequate, at least for how Bauer wanted to paddle rivers. Coincidentally, Martin Geisler (a German toolmaker in Chicago) contacted Bauer with a new foldboat design, which he sent to Bauer for testing. Bauer did not like the design and requested two changes to complement the paddling techniques he was developing for river running: more rocker and a flattened stern, what Bauer called a skid stern. Unlike McNair's canoeing technique, Bauer's technique combined back paddling and back ferrying for maneuvering.

The skid stern worked. The foldboat could be slipped, or skidded, which allowed control in back paddling and back ferrying. The skid stern, with slight rocker along with buoyancy in the stern allowed Bauer's new technique to continue to evolve around advances in design. Technique evolved with design. In addition to the rocker and skid stern design, Whalecraft foldboats also initially had sponsons and a wavebreaking coaming that was fairly high above the deck, although the latter was eventually eliminated because of its tendency to stop the foldboat in a hydraulic. For over-night and extended trips, gear was packed in the middle towards the bow to keep the stern higher which also allowed the foldboat to spin easier.

The first foldboats of the new design were delivered around the 1946/1947 timeframe. Not only were the foldboats built to his design specifications, they had a thicker, three-ply black neoprene hull, custom colored canvas decks, and were half the price of the imports ($125–$150). Through most of the '50s, two-thirds of the foldboats in Washington Foldboat Club were from Whalecraft, the company formed by Geisler.

THE MOUNTAINEERS IN SEATTLE formed in 1906 and were pioneers in climbing as well as skiing in the Olympics and Cascades just as AMC was in the Appalachians of New England. A few members were immigrants from Europe and brought early climbing and skiing skills to the club. They also brought knowledge of European foldboating.

Harry Higman, a member of the Mountaineers, was a foldboater. Before World War II Higman retraced Vancouver's log. (George Vancouver, British explorer of the Pacific Northwest in 1792.) Later, Higman, as a scoutmaster, took his troop on a foldboating trip. One of his troop members, Wolf Bauer, knew of foldboating prior to his immigration to Seattle from Bavaria in 1925. As a boy, he was impressed by Higman's foldboat adventures. Bauer, one of three scouts selected as junior members of the Mountaineers, became a member of the Mountaineers in 1927.

[8] Bauer, Wolf. Interview by author, 26 June 1996.

[9] Ibid.

In order to grow its membership, the club offered courses through the Seattle YMCA and its Adult Hobby classes. Bauer felt that running rivers was more than just running whitewater and titled the course "River Touring" so as not to scare potential club members. In 1950, the first time the course was offered, fifteen people attended.

Washington Foldboat Club shuttle, 1956
—courtesy of Wolf Bauer.

By the mid-'50s, the Washington Foldboat Club had begun circulating "General Foldboating Terminology" within the club. It provided standard terminology for boats and gear, still water (fresh and salt), running water, technique and safety including standard signals, which the club thought was "prerequisite to the proper development of this paddle sport."[10] It was the culmination of Bauer's and other members' scientific study of river running in foldboats. Their running water terminology included very defined descriptions, almost fifty in total. Technique terminology included twenty different terms with descriptions. The level of detail clearly demonstrated the club's higher level of understanding of river hydrology linked to river running and river reading skills.

"General Foldboating Terminology" included seven river running descriptions and three technique descriptions involving eddies.

Eddy river running descriptions included:

Back Eddy The reverse reaction current, behind all objects in the path of flowing water. If center of back eddy, water wells up and flows toward object causing it. Back eddy has current on each side.

Eddy Line Defines the boundary between the eddy and the downstream flowing water on one or each side. It may be a sharp demarcation, or a series of small whirlpools. Water flows vertically down at this line.

Eddy Wall The raised portion and extension of the eddy line next to and behind the object under strong turbulent conditions. Taking the form of a wall of water falling continuously into the eddy along the eddy line.

Eddy Tail The downstream section of the eddy where it becomes narrow and begins to lose its upstream current direction.

[10] Washington Foldboat Club. "General Foldboating Terminology," date unknown (approx. 1955).

Side Eddy An eddy caused by an object or current-diverting obstruction, or by a central jet, past which water flows only on one side. Side eddy current is usually rotating in a horizontal plane.

Eddy Trap Narrow back-eddy in swift water preventing the turning of the boat between the opposite eddy lines, and having downstream exit blocked by another object or by difficult water.

Whirl Eddy A side eddy reinforced by direct current diversion causing full horizontal rotation of the mass of water, as by current splitting against a head wall.

Eddy technique descriptions:

Eddy Christy Swing or skid turn of boat moving over water surface at some speed in a turning arc. Boat is banked and steadied by means of flat-bladed paddle brace as it moves diagonally upstream out of an eddy into the main current or vice versa from current into an eddy. Also called telemark by the British. At slow speed the turn is a pivot while at high paddling and relative current-eddy speed the boat planes and skis as a ski in a Christiana turn. *(Note—some terminology was borrowed directly from skiing.)*

Eddy Anchor Momentary stop and positioning of boat in a back eddy, as behind a boulder in midstream. Boat may face upstream or downstream; it is not fastened by lines but only held by current and paddle control, or by hand against eddy-producing object.

Eddy Jumping Navigational procedure in graveyard type stretches in which paddler back-paddles from eddy anchor to pick his way slowly and to gain time for resting and scouting ahead.[11]

Although founded about the same time and for the same purpose, Buck Ridge Ski Club's level of development of river running and river reading skills lagged behind that of Washington Foldboat Club. This difference was due to many different factors. Bauer and Washington Foldboat Club concentrated on kayaking (foldboating) and had access to German how-to books with an emphasis on whitewater foldboating. McNair and Buck Ridge concentrated on canoeing using American Red Cross's canoeing manuals that had only minimal emphasis on river running, let alone whitewater canoeing. Although Bauer and McNair, leaders in their respective clubs, were engineers, Bauer's second major in geology further initially differentiated the development in river running and river reading skills between the clubs.

[11] Washington Foldboat Club. "General Foldboating Terminology," date unknown (approx. 1955).

While Washington Foldboat Club was well into the development of their instructional programs in the Seattle area, an informal group of whitewater paddlers, composed of foldboaters from the San Francisco Bay Area Sierra Club, organized in 1952 under the leadership of Bruce Grant. Grant, a canoeist and skier born in California, obtained his under graduate degree from Stanford in Mechanical Engineering and his masters from Columbia in New York. While in the East for his masters, he began paddling with AMC. Upon his return to California in 1952, he organized a group of Sierra Club skiers like himself into a paddling group. In seeking information about whitewater paddling, Grant corresponded with other paddlers around the country, including Bauer in Seattle, who influenced the name of the group to reflect river touring instead of whitewater. The group of Sierra Club paddlers became the River Touring Section (RTS) of the San Francisco Bay Chapter of the Sierra Club in 1953. River touring sections soon followed in other Sierra Club chapters and by the following year, Grant was the chairman of all river touring sections for all Sierra Club chapters. This provided Grant and Sierra Club's river touring sections a great deal of exposure (and influence) in whitewater paddling, not only in California, but also across the country.

Wolf Bauer in a folding kayak, 1956
—courtesy of Wolf Bauer.

The Inter-Mountains: Colorado and Utah

After World War II, foldboaters from the East, as well as the few living in Utah and Colorado, continued to explore whitewater on western rivers. Foldboats were considered ideal for extended touring by solo paddlers on remote stretches of wilderness rivers, like the desert canyons of the Colorado Plateau. Not only did foldboats have enough room to carry gear and supplies, but they could also be Eskimo rolled making recovery in heavy whitewater possible, something that canoes did not provide.

Increasing numbers of solo paddlers ran rivers both previously explored and unexplored (at least unexplored in a foldboat). Stewart Gardiner of Salt Lake City, Utah, continued his explorations after the war. In 1948, two foldboaters paddled the Royal Gorge run on the Arkansas for the first time. A few more women also began foldboating the rivers. In 1953, Nora Staley paddled the Canyon of Lodore in a foldboat, supported by Don Hatch.

In addition to solo paddlers, small pockets of loosely organized paddlers formed around Denver and Salt Lake City, the only two major population centers in the area. In the greater Denver area, a few small informal groups developed. One included Steve Bradley and Dave Stacey. Another small group comprised of Keith Anderson, Larry Jump, and Willie Schaeffler paddled their Klepper foldboats, purchased while in Europe on a business trip, on rivers throughout the area. In 1953, they may have been the first to run the Yampa River Canyon (also known as Bear Canyon) in foldboats.

Although the Salt Lake City area had a mountaineering club (the Wasatch Mountain Club formed in 1920), its club members primarily participated in mountaineering, hiking, and skiing. It was not until 1957 that members started running rivers, although in borrowed rafts instead of foldboats.

The presence of a war surplus center in Salt Lake City contributed to the use of inflatables instead of foldboats for river running in the area.

This surplus center also contributed to the use of inflatables by Boy Scout troops instead of canoes as in the East where the use of Grumman canoes was extremely popular in scouting. Instead of canoeing, rafting became a popular scout activity in the West, particularly in Utah, Arizona, New Mexico, and Idaho. Not only did the growing commercial river-running operations benefit from the availability of rafts and pontoons from the surplus center in Salt Lake City, the operations benefitted from the availability of young boatmen from scout troops throughout the area, ready and eager to become commercial boatmen.

In 1949, in a small, remote town in Colorado, the beginning of what at the time seemed an isolated event had far reaching effects on the young sport. The oldest (and continuous) whitewater (wildwater) race in the Western Hemisphere began on the Arkansas River in Salida, Colorado. The official story behind the origin of the race on the Arkansas is that it started over a cup of coffee in 1948. The unofficial story is that the race resulted when two drinking buddies challenged one another to a rowboat race from Salida to Canon City on the Arkansas in June to take advantage of peak snow melt and run off. They did not make it very far but publicity around the event prompted the local Chamber of Commerce to sponsor a race to gather locals and tourists into town to support local businesses. The race was called The First Annual Royal Gorge Boat Race and was held on June 17, 18, and 19, 1949 on a course from Salida to Canon City.

Word spread about the race; news of it made the United Press news wire. Coincidentally, two Swiss paddlers, Robert Ris and Max R. Romer, heard of the race while touring the United States and decided to enter. The race contestants used all kinds of watercraft, rowboats, foldboats, and canoes.

On the weekend of the race, the river was high and muddy and eliminated many of the would-be contestants merely at the sight of it. One paddler was Jack Kissner, who at the time was considered the reigning National White Water Champion with his previous win of the National White Water Championship (last sponsored by AMC in 1941). Although he participated in the race, he was not a registered contestant because registering for the race meant disqualification forever as an amateur in participating in any ACA sanctioned events due to the $1,000 purse for the winner. Near mile 23 of the 57-mile race, Kissner hit a log and capsized in his Folbot foldboat. He was pinned under the boat until nearby spectators rescued him. When asked if he would try to recover the expensive craft, he responded, "Oh no, I never ride in a boat I've tipped." [12] He said it was the 120th time he had to abandon a boat in his twenty years of experience.

Ris and Romer paddled a single foldboat and although they portaged frequently, they won the race and the purse. They were the only boat to finish the race out of the five that entered.

[12] "Swiss Boatmen, Ris and Romer, Win Salida-Canon City Ark River Boat Race; Only One Boat Finishes." Salida[Colorado] *Daily Mail Record* 20 June 1949.

Many of the competitors, including Ris, Romer, and Kissner, suggested that the racecourse was too long for a single day's race. Races thereafter were shortened and ended at Cotopaxi. Upon Ris and Romer's return to Europe, word spread about the race through their conversations with other paddlers. A European photographer and filmmaker by the name of Schwerla was also present at the race. His movies of the race were shown to foldboat clubs in Austria, Germany, France, and Switzerland. As a result of Ris and Romer's conversations, and Schwerla's movie, the first Europeans came to Salida to compete in the race in 1952.

The significance of the 1949 race was that it was the first time American paddlers, including local experts as well as the reigning National Champion, were actually pitted against European paddlers. The race clearly demonstrated the more advanced knowledge of whitewater techniques by Europeans. After all, Ris and Romer were not even top competitors in Europe and they handily won the Salida race.

The annual race became known as The Boat Race in the early years with handsome cash prizes under sponsorship of Salida's Chamber of Commerce. In 1950, Clyde Jones of Colorado won in a foldboat. Bob Ehrman of California was the winner in 1951 and 1952 prior to the influx of the European racers. Other American contestants included Larry Zuk, Willie Schaeffler, and Dick Stratton who later formed the Colorado White Water Association. Another well-known local contestant was Larry Compton, a Salida lumberman. However, like Ehrman, none of the other American paddlers could beat the European racers once they began entering the competition.

Two noteworthy events occurred at Salida at the races in 1952 and 1953. In 1952, the first Europeans since Ris and Romer entered the race. These included Andre Pean and Pierre D'Alencon from France who brought a canoe specifically designed for whitewater. No American had ever seen a canoe like this one. The open canoe was 15' 8" in length, 35 inches in width, 11 inches in depth amidships and 15 inches at the ends. The hull was flat-bottomed with 4 inches of rocker from the center to within a foot of the ends. This was considerably more rocker than any canoe currently built in America. The canoe was built of cedar strips and covered with fiberglass inside and out. It had a removable canvas deck with elastic that held the deck tight around the gunwales. A paddler knelt in large sacks that would fill with water while the rest of the canoe remained relatively dry. The canoe also had knee straps for better control, a simple idea yet one that had not occurred to American paddlers. The canoe was heavier than a Grumman at almost 80 pounds, largely due to the layers of fiberglass on the hull.

Neveu and Paris were second in the 1949 World Championships and were the World Champions in C-2 in 1951 and 1955. Roger Paris recounted they were surprised to learn how little the American paddlers knew about handling their boats in whitewater.

The following year in 1953, eighteen contestants entered including Erich Seidel of Germany and Roger Paris, Claude Neveu, Andre Pean, Raymond Zubiri (a Basque) and Pierre D'Alencon, all of France. Roger Paris came to the race with his C-2 partner, Claude Neveu. Erich Seidel, accompanied by Theo Bock, the owner of a chain of sporting goods stores in Germany, won the race.

The second noteworthy event occurred at the 1953 race when Seidel and Bock set up a slalom course on the river to demonstrate gate running. They staged a demo race and, of course, Seidel won and Bock took second, although

Although the canoe was a North American invention, the French adopted it and modified it specifically for whitewater years ahead of American paddlers. The roots of the French love affair with the open canoe can be traced to the early days of French trappers and traders, the Voyageurs, in the watersheds of the Great Lakes and Hudson Bay beginning in the late 1600's. Not only did the French readily adopt the birch bark canoe for exploration and trade in North America, but canoes were exported to France, the result of a love affair between the French and canoeing.

Joseph Cadet, a French Canadian familiar with birch bark construction, shipped birch bark canoe construction materials to France in 1766 to accompany him in his exile to France from New France in North America. Other French Canadians who returned to France also shared his love of the canoe and canoeing. Although this love affair may have been partially due to an appreciation for the practicality and craftsmanship of the craft itself, it may also have been due to the lasting memory of New France in North America, which was lost to the British. For whatever reason, canoeing became entrenched in the French paddlers' psyche, which later contributed to the French domination of whitewater canoeing in the early years of slalom racing.

he had not intended to compete, entering only at the last minute. This demonstration of a slalom race in a larger public forum was significant, especially considering the publicity that ensued.

While the former of the two events clearly demonstrated advanced canoeing as reflected in design and other innovations, the latter was the start of one of the most significant events to affect whitewater. The effects of slalom racing on the evolution of the sport in the early years were multifold and cannot be underestimated.

A New Facilitator: Competition

The first clubs learned much of what they knew about whitewater by trial and error and developed their own safety and education programs. Some intercommunication existed among clubs, particularly with the clubs in close proximity to one another. Buck Ridge and AMC chapters in the East and Washington Foldboat Club and Sierra Club Bay Chapter's RTS in the West communicated but their communication was limited and sporadic at best. No single organization represented or was aware of the activities of all paddlers across the country. Neither was there an industry that worked together to support paddlesports, let alone the sport of whitewater. This lack of national organization and infrastructure was painfully apparent when an Italian representative from the International Canoe Federation (ICF) sent an invitation to ACA to compete in a whitewater slalom race to be held in July 1953, in Merano, Italy. Although ACA purported to represent canoeing interests in America, their lack of involvement in whitewater activities was readily apparent. Spike Zywicki, ACA's Cruising Chairman, sent the invitation to Bob McNair of Buck Ridge. He in turn sent letters to Doug Brown of AMC-Connecticut and Eliot DuBois of AMC-Boston. They realized that not only could they not accept the invitation to compete since they had no way of notifying American paddlers, but they could also not decline in any official capacity since no one really represented whitewater paddlers. To further add to their frustration, they realized that Europeans were much further along in their technical skills. Competition of this nature, particularly associated with a new type of competition, slalom racing, clearly demonstrated advanced skills. *Competition, another tributary, entered the River, as did the third, European influence.*

Many of the Germanic language countries in Europe adopted folding kayaks and founded canoe [kayak] clubs and national organizations in the early 1900's. Until the early '20s, kayaking developed relatively independently within countries throughout Europe. That changed in 1923 when representatives from several national canoe associations were invited to convene at an international conference to arrange dates for future international regattas and establish uniform regulations for the construction of boats for competition.

Representatives from the national organizations of Austria, Britain, Canada, Czechoslovakia, Denmark, Germany, and Sweden attended the conference. Although ACA was invited, no representative was sent.

The organization that evolved from the conference became known as the Internationale Reprasentantschaft fur Kanusport (IRK). Its purpose was not only to "form a link between canoeing associations of various countries," but also to:

> Organize international competitions in paddling and sailing once a year and alternately in the various countries.
>
> Promote and foster foreign tourism through production of appropriate river guides.
>
> Introduce on maps, internationally recognized symbols for rivers in order to facilitate touring.
>
> Exchange canoeing information by mutually making available national publications on canoeing: through preparation of lectures and speakers, films, correspondence, etc... [13]

The organization and regulation of this sporting activity was firmly established in Europe. In order to organize international competition, dimensions were established for two current activities, flatwater canoe (kayak) and sailing canoe. Although Canadian canoes were popular in France owing to their import by French Voyageurs, Canadian canoe dimensions were deferred for input and exchange of ideas from ACA, the acknowledged authority on Canadian canoes.

However, attempts by IRK to forge closer links with ACA remained relatively unsuccessful. ACA ran independent regattas for sailing canoes and regattas almost exclusively for Canadian canoes including singles, pairs, and fours, perhaps fueled by their desire to remain elite as well as American. ACA did, however, report international races in their publication The Canoeist and sent representatives to a demonstration race at the Olympic Games in 1924.

For recognition by the International Olympic Committee (IOC) and qualification as an Olympic event, a sporting event required the support of a minimum of ten countries with national organizations supporting the event. Within ten years of the demonstration race, flatwater competition qualified and became an exhibition event for the '36 Olympics.

With the end of the war, changes occurred in the organization of IRK. In the spring of 1946, the still serving Swedish Vice President of IRK invited the national canoe associations to a Congress in Stockholm. At the congress, the use of the German name IRK was abolished and German was discontinued as the official language. The new organization became the International Canoe Federation (ICF) in English and La Federation Internationale de Canoe (FIC) in French, and French became the new official language. ACA soon became the officially recognized governing body for American canoeing and kayaking competition.

[13] Vesper, Hans Egon and John W. Dudderidge. *50 Years of the International Canoe Federation.* English Edition. Florence, Italy: International Canoe Federation, 1974: A7.

DuBois and McNair became the key people and driving force for the establishment of a national organization that represented whitewater interests. DuBois' job was to identify and contact other whitewater groups around the country including foldboaters, canoeists, and rafters. McNair's job was to learn as much as he could about slalom racing and attract ACA's interest since it was already recognized by ICF as the national governing body for flatwater competition. After much discussion and correspondence with scattered groups and individuals around the country, a memo on the "Formation of an Affiliation of White Water Groups" was sent to sixteen formal and informal groups on April 6, 1954.

Within a year, the American White Water Affiliation (AWWA) was seen as a medium for the exchange of ideas. The intention was to start on an informal basis with the intention that a formal organization would take shape as needed. Within the year, its purpose was further defined:

> To encourage exploration and enjoyment of wilderness waterways; to foster research, study and teaching of improved techniques and equipment designs for safely negotiating white water; to protect the wilderness character of our waterways for the growing number of those who are discovering the rewards awaiting the river tourist.

The Affiliation was described as:

> ... an affiliation of groups and clubs, professionals and amateur alike, who share a common interest in the AWWA purposes... Thus, the Affiliation is a channel for bringing together ideas, procedures and experiences. [14]

Although some parallels existed between the purpose established by AWWA and that of IRK (ICF's predecessor), the most notable difference was the absence of involvement in competition, even though the slalom racing invitation was the impetus for the formation of AWWA. Competition implied regulation and it seemed that the more free spirited souls involved in the establishment of AWWA did not seek to be regulated. Their purpose was to foster a sharing of information perhaps more befitting of the whitewater psyche. Their original purpose was to attract ACA's interest in the competition end of whitewater, fulfilling their role as the ICF recognized governing body.

The initial plan for AWWA was for representatives from each affiliated club to send packages of information to a Secretary who would in turn collect, collate, and re-mail the material to the other representatives, facilitating an exchange of ideas. This correspondence evolved into a magazine, the Journal of American White Water, or simply *American Whitewater.* (The actual name of AWWA's magazine was *American WHITE WATER.)* The first issue was published in May of 1955.

The importance of *American Whitewater* as the medium for an exchange of ideas could not be underestimated in the years to come. Neither could the importance of slalom competition and ACA's involvement as the recognized governing body for any canoeing and kayaking events, present or future.

[14] Grant, Bruce. "American White Water Affiliation." *American Whitewater* Vol. 1 No. 1 (May 1955): 32.

Although AWWA's purpose clearly steered clear of involvement in the regulation of competition, ACA apparently was not so sure. Perhaps the most telling statement about the relationship between the two organizations was written in a letter to AWWA by William (Dusty) Rhodes, Commodore of ACA, regarding his interest in the formation of AWWA and the impending publication of *American Whitewater.* His letter published in the first issue of *American Whitewater* for all AWWA affiliates to read said:

> Possibly because I think so much of the A.C.A., I am needlessly prejudiced (and/or nervous) when a possible rival appears on the scene. You and Bruce Grant have both relieved me by your friendly and cooperative letters. Though you will be a national affiliation, I am sure that for a while at least, most of your strength will be in the West. Possibly after a few months your magazine will catch on with A.C.A. people and you can take advantage of our organization... There is nothing whatever wrong with this and I can appreciate that you could be doing us a distinct service... [15]

At the time of AWWA's founding in 1954, ACA was already composed of nine divisions– eight in the United States and the ninth comprising all of Canada (although the Canadian Canoe Associations formed in 1902). ACA's organization included an executive head (the Commodore), National Officers, Board of Governors, Chairmen of National Committees (all elective offices), and an Editor of the *American Canoeist* magazine. Each division was headed by a vice commodore and had various committee members. Cruising, Sailing, and Racing (flatwater Olympic competition) were the three official activities.

Although perhaps more perceived by ACA than AWWA at the time, competition for whitewater interests developed between the two organizations. To support whitewater competition, ACA established the Whitewater Committee in 1955 as a standing committee and voted it in as a regular committee in 1956. The following year, ACA also established a Conservation Committee that seemed to compete directly with AWWA interests.

Some of AWWA's affiliates were caught in the middle of this competition. The Colorado White Water Association (CWWA) was formed in 1954 and for a time, was an extreme example of the split that could occur in clubs with AWWA and ACA associations. CWWA was an AWWA affiliate and many of its members fully supported it. Some of CWWA's key members were also responsible for *American Whitewater* in its early years, Joe Lacey and Dave Stacey as editors, Clyde Jones for circulation, and Roy Kerswill for the artwork. Other members regularly contributed articles. Another member, Larry Zuk, with a longtime family history in ACA in the East, promoted and supported CWWA's role as ACA's Rocky Mountain Division with full activity status in 1955. Over the next few years, the Rocky Mountain Division (alias CWWA) and ACA adopted many of the same initiatives as AWWA.

Another bone of contention developed between ACA and AWWA when AWWA accepted individual memberships as well as club affiliates. Again, then ACA commodore Rhodes wrote in an *American Whitewater* article in 1957 that ACA was an "organization of individuals," implying that AWWA's acceptance of individuals crossed-over a boundary between the two organizations.

[15] Grant, Bruce. "American White Water Affiliation." *American Whitewater* Vol. 1 No. 1 (May 1955): 32.

Rhodes went on to say, "The value of unity and order has been recognized by mankind since far back in the beginnings of history– so it is not strange that even such independent entities as canoeists should recognize the benefits of organization." [16]

Over the next few years, both organizations eventually settled into a state of co-existence, contributing significantly to whitewater in their own ways, AWWA through *American Whitewater* and ACA through competition, and both serving as mediums for the dissemination of information. AWWA allowed paddlers to read the how-to, and ACA, through their sponsorship of competition, allowed paddlers to see the how-to.

Slalom and Wildwater Competition

The letter from Italy inviting America to compete in slalom at the 1953 World Championships at Merano caught everyone by surprise. Only a few paddlers were even aware of slalom racing prior to this. The Washington Foldboat Club, one of the few who was aware, organized the first intra-club slalom race in America on May 29, 1953, on Nason Creek near Lake Wenatchee where gates were hung and competitors were timed with a stopwatch. About the same, time Erich Seidel and Theo Bock traveled from New York upon their arrival in America to Wilmington, Delaware, to meet McNair and other Buck Ridge members prior to traveling to Colorado for the Salida race in June 1953. (European racers and clubs knew McNair through his correspondence with them to learn more about slalom racing. Siedel competed in the 1951 World Championships for West Germany in slalom in F-1.) Seidel and Bock set up a demonstration slalom course for McNair and other Buck Ridge members before traveling to compete at Salida.

Later, during the fall of 1953, Buck Ridge, guided by McNair, organized a pilot slalom race held on Brandywine Creek at Rockport, Maryland. The next spring, Buck Ridge sponsored the first inter-club amateur competition on April 11, 1954 held on the Powder Mill Rapids of the Brandywine Creek near Wilmington, Delaware. The classes of competition were C-1, C-1W, C-2, C-2W, C-2M, F-1, and F-1W. The course had sixteen gates including two reverse gates.

DuBois of Boston-AMC set up slalom gates on the Black River in Vermont around the same time as Buck Ridge in 1954 also to demonstrate the sport to a few club members and to determine the suitability of the river for a race. AMC sponsored their first inter-club slalom race on the Black River in Vermont on April 30-May 1, 1955. Invitations were sent to New York-AMC, Buck Ridge, Ithaca Canoe Club, and Ledyard Canoe Club.

McNair became a major proponent for developing slalom racing in America which was seen as a means of improving technique for river-running, for cruising. It was not until 1955 that an unofficial English translation (from French) of the international rules for slalom racing was available to McNair who by this time was chairman of the National Slalom Committee of the ACA. Problems arose for American competitors with regard to the differences between metric boat dimensions in Europe and standard non-metric boat dimensions in America. In particular, the 15-foot Grumman was about a third of an inch too short for C-2 competition. Rigid kayaks were also barred from international competition.

IN THE EARLY '20S, wildwater races were held in Europe on rivers such as the Isar and Traun using foldboats. By the end of the '20s, articles on wildwater techniques appeared in many different countries and the first standard dimensions were established for wildwater competition. The short single was 4.2 to 4.35 meters in length and 65 to 72 centimeters in width (approximately 14 feet by 27 inches). The Eskimo kayak was 4.9 to 5.2 meters in length and 46 centimeters in width (approximately 16 feet 6 inches by 18 inches).

Though wildwater racing preceded slalom racing, it was slalom racing that became the first internationally recognized competition for whitewater. Since many of the European whitewater paddlers were also skiers, the idea of negotiating rocks just as negotiating slalom poles in skiing evolved into developing slalom on water instead of snow. In the fall of 1932, the Swiss organized the first slalom on a lake. The following fall, the first slalom on wildwater was held on the Aar. Slalom races spread to other countries and rules and regulations were established. Max Vogt of Switzerland founded the Comitee International du Slalom in 1936 as the representative committee for IRK for the control of slalom. In 1937, the International Kayak Slalom Committee prepared the new rules for slalom competition.

—continues on next page

[16] Rhodes, W. J. "The American Canoe Association." *American Whitewater* Vol. 3 No. 1 (Spring 1957):19–20.

In 1955, ACA became embroiled in the amateur status controversy when they published the provisions for governing the amateur standing of boatmen racing in whitewater and slalom events in the United States. The provisions and definition of an amateur were provided to accommodate ACA's interpretations of regulations from ICF, the United States Olympic Committee (USOC), and the International Olympic Committee (IOC). The rules provided that an amateur:

> May receive fair and reasonable compensation for traveling expenses.
>
> May not accept any money for traveling expenses to be paid to a trainer, masseuse, friend or relative.
>
> May not compete as a representative of a corporation or business or club or organization.
>
> May not exploit fame for money, salary, gifts, or by presenting himself in the sponsored time of any radio station.
>
> May not bet or risk money on a canoeing event.
>
> May not enter or compete under a name other than his own.
>
> May not knowingly compete with professionals.

A professional was considered anyone who teaches, trains, prepares, participates, or agrees to participate in any canoeing activity, or any closely associated activity, for money or reward of any nature. In addition, anyone declared a professional in any one branch of canoeing (paddling, sailing, slalom, or cruising) is considered a professional for all. And, once declared a professional, that person could not regain amateur status. These very rigid rules immediately caused controversy for anyone having competed in the Salida races or any competitor who had worked for any outfitter at any time.

In 1958, a British paddler wrote of the differences in amateur status between the American and European whitewater sport. "In Europe a man is a professional only if he competes in a canoeing contest for money. Engaging in the canoeing trade or writing about it does not affect his amateur status. You are making things difficult for yourselves, particularly when you have to pick representatives for international events." [17]

In 1956, ACA was recognized by ICF as the governing body for slalom racing, and three years later for wildwater racing. Slalom races began springing up across the U.S. and Canada. Over the next few years, races were held in the East sponsored by AMC and Buck Ridge; in Colorado sponsored by CWWA; in Washington by the Washington Foldboat Club; and in Canada by the Ontario Voyageurs and British Columbia Canoe Club.

The U.S. Championships (later called the National Championships) in slalom began in 1956 and in wildwater in 1959. The first two U.S. Championship races in 1956 and 1957 were held in Colorado at the Salida race. The slalom champions those first two years were Colorado boaters Carol Kane in

The 1948 ICF Congress ratified slalom rules and decided to hold World Championships every other odd year. The first was held on the Rhone in Geneva in 1949. By the early '50s, hull shapes and dimensions of whitewater canoes and kayaks were pretty much standardized. Klepper was the major manufacturer in Europe and contributed significantly to the development of whitewater competition and the standardization of canoe and kayak dimensions. ICF rules established classes for three boats: foldboats (F-1), single canoes (C-1), and double canoes (C-2). Rigid kayaks (R-1) were added in 1958.

Participation in the World Championships for slalom increased throughout the '50s. Races were held throughout Europe on the Steyr River in Steyr, Austria, in 1951; the Passiro River in Merano, Italy, in 1953; the Sava River in Tacen, Yugoslavia, in 1955; the Eiscanal (Ice Canal) in Augsburg, Germany in 1957; and back on the Rhone in Geneva in 1959. For many years, the Austrians dominated in the foldboat classes while the French initially led in the Canadian canoes, later followed by the Czechs.

In 1958, the ICF Congress met in Prague and finally adopted rules for wildwater racing, based on rules adopted the year before by ICF's Wild Water section. ICF rules established classes for four types of boats: foldboats (F-1), rigid kayaks (K-1), single canoes (C-1), and double canoes (C-2) for every wild race with the exception of the World Championships where no rigid kayaks were allowed. Wild Water Racing Championships were also established on a biennial basis the same year as the Slalom World Championships and in the same region, though not necessarily in the same country.

[17] Blanford, P.W. "Letters from Readers." *American Whitewater* Vol. 4 No. 1 (Spring 1958): 5.

F-1, Larry Zuk and Dick Stratton in F-1, Roy Kerswill and Larry Zuk in C-2, and Larry and Paula Zuk in C-2M. However, European competitors easily won the classes in which they were allowed to compete.

The First Eastern Slalom Championships were held in April 1956, on the Salmon River near Middletown, Connecticut. It was co-sponsored by AMC-Boston, Connecticut, and New York Chapters, and Buck Ridge. The Eastern Championships continued thereafter and coincided with the National Championships in the years the nationals were held in the East.

HANS KLEPPER was instrumental in supporting the development of whitewater kayaking from its very beginnings. Not only was this demonstrated by his hospitality for visiting athletes and sponsorship of world champion competitors, his early involvement helped to establish standard kayak dimensions that supported both flatwater and whitewater competition, a sound business decision.

Three Colorado boaters, Eric Frazee, Carol Kane, and Dick Stratton went to Germany in 1957 to compete in the World Championships in Augsburg, Germany, the first U.S. Team ever to go to Europe. Stratton and Kane were considered the top kayak (foldboat) racers because they had won their respective races at Salida that year. Frazee, only 17 years old, placed second at the race. All three competitors were guests of Hans Klepper for part of the time they were in Germany and purchased new foldboats from Klepper. Kane and Frazee chose slalom models but Stratton chose the T-65, a combination slalom and downriver design 14' 6" in length.

Frazee, Kane, and Stratton initially thought that a man-made canal such as the Eiscanal at Augsburg would be a piece of cake after having trained on the Arkansas. However, the Eiscanal was known for its narrowness and unpredictable water fluctuations by European competitors. During their pre-race training runs, the American racers learned of the skill level required for the Eiscanal, as well of the skill of the other competitors.

IN AN ARTICLE in the 1998 FibArk White water Festival Program, Carol Kane was credited with having won many International Women's Kayak titles from 1955 to 1962 and placing 5th at the 1957 World Championships in Augsburg, Germany. However, her only entry in World Championship competition was in 1957 (as listed in *The River Masters*[18]) where she placed 16th out of 17. It is assumed that the International titles were the result of competition in the International races at Salida.

Both the European canoe and foldboat competitors, including the C-2 teams, regularly rolled during the practice runs. In fact, the course was designed specifically to test the rolling skills of the competitors. This was the downfall of the American competitors. Neither Frazee nor Stratton was able to finish either of their two runs, finishing DNF in F-1 slalom. Kane, with less than two years of foldboating experience, only completed her second run and finished 16th out of 17. The American competitors were clearly years behind the Europeans. Competition was taken so seriously in Europe that at that time grandstands were built along the courses for spectators who showed up rain or shine to watch the races. Safety was also taken very seriously at the races. Trained swimmers were placed strategically along the course for rescue.

In 1958, the National Championships were held in the East on the West River in Jamaica, Vermont, with no western boaters in attendance. The clubs that participated were all from the East: AMC-Boston, AMC-Connecticut, AMC-New York, Buck Ridge, Canoe Cruisers Association of Washington, D.C., Ontario Voyageurs Kayak Club of Toronto, and Norwich University Outing Club of Northfield, Vermont. All the competitors were in the forefront of canoeing and foldboating skills. The National Champions based on this race were Eliot DuBois in F-1, Sauer and Wescott in C-2, Edie and Bob McNair in C-2M, and Bob Harrigan in C-1. The May 12, 1958 issue of *Sports Illustrated* covered the National Slalom Championships.

The following year in 1959, the National White Water Slalom Championships were again held in Colorado (where the Roaring Fork joins the Colorado) with two additions: wildwater races and competitors from the East. Both Erich Seidel and Walter Kirschbaum of Colorado, having established their U.S. residency, won their kayak specialties, slalom for Seidel and wildwater (downriver) for Kirschbaum. But this time, paddlers from the East

[18] Endicott, William T. *The River Masters: A History of the World Championships of Whitewater Canoeing.* Washington, D.C.: William T. Endicott, 1979.

dominated all canoe events. John Berry and Bob Harrigan of the Canoe Cruisers Association won in both C-2 wildwater and slalom. The domination of canoeing by paddlers from the East and kayaking by paddlers from the West began.

Competition's Other Facilitators

With competition came other facilitators, events, and people that accelerated the evolution of whitewater in America. The annual race at Salida was one such event. It became the mecca for European and American racers alike throughout the'50s. These pilgrimages brought an inter-mingling of European and American paddlers learning and sharing from one another. Mostly Americans were learning from the Europeans, but it became a two-way street for innovation.

European influence was integral to the sport's evolution in America. Some came for the Salida race and to explore western rivers before returning to Europe. Others visited a few times before being drawn permanently to stay and become American citizens and to pass on their knowledge to American paddlers. Three such Europeans were Erich Seidel, Walter Kirschbaum, and Roger Paris.

Salida

For the 1954 race, French racers returned in greater numbers including Andre Pean, Pierre D'Alencon, (Miss) Raymonde Paris, (Mrs.) Jeanette Pean, Serge Michel, and Raymond Zubiri. Roger Paris also returned and won the downriver event in kayak (F-1), having switched from C-2. The C-2 team of Pean and D'Alencon and C-2W team of Paris and Pean easily won their races in canoes similar to the French canoe first brought in 1952. (D'Alencon was the World Champion in C-1 in 1949 and Pean placed second in C-2 with his partner Musson in 1951.) Both French canoes were purchased by Colorado paddlers and used the following year by two American teams in 1955, Roy Kerswill and Bud Parks and Paula and Larry Zuk.

In anticipation of ICF's recognition of ACA's governing body status for whitewater competition, in 1954 ACA began to establish their influence in whitewater competition, and in particular, the Salida races. The Salida Chamber of Commerce, who sponsored the race for business purposes, wanted to attract more American talent and at the same time guarantee the race's amateur status by ensuring the race was ACA sanctioned. But ACA sanctioning also meant new rules. ACA could not sponsor a professional race due to their tie with ICF and IOC through flatwater competition and a separate amateur class was added to avoid any conflict. Unfortunately, this meant that previous American winners, including two-time winner Bob Ehrman of California, were no longer considered amateurs having won prize money in previous years and could not participate unless they competed in classes that pitted them against superior European paddlers. This allowed new American competitors to enter the amateur division. Laurence Compton, a Salida lumber dealer, became the first American to win the amateur division that year, which included the Klepper trophy, sponsor of the amateur class.

Raymonde Paris, Roger's younger sister, and Jeanette Pean competed in the slalom and downriver races becoming the first women contestants to paddle the entire length of the downriver race. Outfitted in bikinis and necklaces with no lifejackets, they paddled their canvas decked whitewater strip canoe. (No one wore life jackets or helmets for the slalom race. However, life jackets were worn for the downriver race.) Although they were not eligible to compete for any of the prizes (they were women competing in men's classes), many local competitors raised objections for even allowing them to enter the races.

After the race Paris, Pean, D'Alencon, Michel, and Zubiri remained to explore the local rivers, and with Larry Compton and Volney Perry ran Royal Gorge of the Arkansas. The more difficult drops and sections were portaged. However, Zubiri, who went to races in Europe demonstrating the roll and was known as the "Eskimo Roll Champion of the World," failed to roll in the Gorge. His foldboat was badly damaged; the frame was broken into pieces. Compton also swam, but his boat was not damaged as severely.

In an article written by Roger Paris for the November 8, 1954 issue of *Point de Vue-Images du Monde,* the more difficult stretches were described by Paris as Class V and even Class VI.[19] In 1955, racers came from France, Germany, Austria, Switzerland, and Yugoslavia (by way of Switzerland) and included returning racers Pierre D'Alencon, Roger Paris, Claude Neveu, Andre Pean, Jeanette Pean, Raymonde Paris, all of France, Henry Kadrnka of Yugoslavia, Charles Dussuet and Jean Paul Roessinger of Switzerland, Walter Kirschbaum of Germany, and Rudi Pillwein of Austria, winner of the downriver race that year. Aside from the attendance by a large number of champion European racers, a watershed event occurred at the race that year: the appearance of an all-fiberglass decked canoe paddled by the Swiss team of Roessinger and Dussuet. The canoe was not just fiberglass over wood as was the 1952 canoe, but an all-fiberglass canoe with one long middle cockpit specifically designed with an integral deck; it was a closed canoe. The deck was not an afterthought.

The canoe was described as "an oval shaped tube pinched together at the ends, about 15 ½ feet long, with a relatively small cockpit for two, beginning about 4 feet from the stern and ending about 3 feet from the bow, and with a beam of about 34 inches."[20] The canoe also had very little upsweep at the sheer from the midsection to the bow and stern. The presence of this canoe at Salida had lasting effects on materials, design, and technique for whitewater canoes and provided impetus for American innovation.

Tom Telefson of California was also at the race in 1955. He raced in a fiberglass kayak, designed by Robert C Lyon, which was really more like a decked touring canoe. Although Telefson did not win, it was the first time a fiberglass kayak was entered in the race. However, the canoe paddled by Roessinger and Dussuet overshadowed its presence.

[19] Paris, Roger translated by John Sibley. "White Hell." *American Whitewater* Vol. 1 No. 3 (November 1955): 19–22.

[20] Kerswill, Roy and Larry Monninger. "Revolutionary Fiberglass Canoe." *American Whitewater* Vol. 1 No. 3 (November 1955): 6.

The following year in 1955, the race was billed as America's International Race. ACA's involvement prompted further changes with regard to sponsorship. Eleanore Frye wrote of these changes:

> Since the ACA took a dim view of the Salida Chamber of Commerce sponsoring the race, holding that it was a publicity stunt rather than a sporting event, a group of Salida sportsmen organized FibArk, and this organization now is the sponsor of the race. FibArk is the abbreviated form of First in Boating Arkansas River Club.
>
> ... The establishment of a Rocky Mountain division of the ACA enabled the race to have close ACA scrutiny, insuring strict adherence to Association rules. Since the race is the roughest of America's downriver races and a pioneer in that type of racing, the ACA is watching it closely to formulate future rules. [21]

FibArk, nevertheless, continued to regard the race as a business instead of merely as a sporting competition. Very few of its members were even paddlers. FibArk sent invitations each year to canoe federations in European countries, inviting them to send a team, offering $300 plus room and board to each competitor on the team. This did not violate European amateur rules for competition, only ACA's rules.

The 1956 race was the first official American National Slalom Championship and International Slalom event. Seidel and Wuerfmannsdobler, recent immigrants living in the Salida area, took first and second slalom.

In the International Slalom event, Seidel won beating Roger Paris. However, Paris won the downriver event. In the women's International slalom event, Fritzi Schwingl of Austria, winner of more than one hundred races, finished first in her class with a time far ahead of most male competitors. (Swingl was second in F-1W at the '49 and '51 World Championships. She became the World Champion in 1953.)

In 1958, Paris again won the downriver race but this time his win was embroiled in controversy. Paris was at Salida to race a Klepper kayak. (After beating Klepper's sponsored racer in 1956, Paris was sponsored by Klepper.) However, because the downriver race allowed any boat to be used, experimental boats were also entered in the race. Tom Telefson showed up again with another fiberglass kayak, one modeled after a 17-foot Swedish wood Olympic flatwater sprint kayak. Prior to the race, Telefson had taken the wood Olympic kayak to Tom Johnson and the two of them made a mold to build the design in fiberglass. However, Telefson was not a serious racer and there was doubt that he could handle the flatwater design on the river. During practices on the downriver course in the preceding couple of days before the race, Paris and Telefson exchanged kayaks. Telefson could handle the more forgiving design of Paris' Klepper and at the same time, Paris realized the flatwater design in the right hands could win the race. Paris raced and indeed won in Telefson's kayak. Belgian Marcel Beaujean, who placed second behind Paris, protested the use of the fiberglass kayak but he lost his protest.

[21] Frye, Eleanore. "America's International Race." *American Whitewater* Vol. 1 No. 1 (May 1955): 27.

CURIOUSLY, although the seeds of controversy were planted, in 1959 AWA's Racing Editor, George Siposs, concluded from the Nationals held in Glenwood Springs that although folding and rigid kayaks competed against one another, the rigid kayak had no particular advantage over the folding kayak. However, his observation was based solely on the relative skill of the paddlers, particularly since the fiberglass kayaks were essentially the same design as the folding kayaks, and were often paddled by less experienced American paddlers.

Paris and Telefson after kayak exchange on the Arkansas at the Salida (CO) races, 1958. Paris is wearing a leather bicycle helmet in Telefson's fiberglass kayak—courtesy of Carl Trost.

Paris and Beaujean arguing about Paris' use of Telefson's fiberglass kayak at the Salida (CO) races, 1958—courtesy of Carl Trost.

This protest became the seed of controversy that followed the racers back to Europe, the use of foldboats versus the new fiberglass material in competition. The controversy ultimately resulted in the establishment of two separate kayak classes, F-1 for foldboats and K-1 for fiberglass kayaks for the 1961 World Championships. These two classes existed separately for only four years until the superiority of fiberglass was firmly established as the material for competition. By the 1965 World Championships, only the K-1 class remained.

European Immigrants

Not only did Europeans visit to race, a few stayed and taught. Erich Seidel from the Klub Munchen Kayak Fahren (the touring kayak club of Munich) came to Salida for the first time in 1953. Seidel worked for Klepper who sponsored him in races. In 1954, he and his wife emigrated and settled in Salida. The next year, Xaver Wuerfmannsdobler from the same club in Munich came for the Salida race and lived with Siedel for a time. Local newspaperman George Oyler gave him a job and even sponsored him for citizenship. Seidel and Wuerfmannsdobler explored rivers together, with Wuerfmannsdobler often working safety from shore on many of Seidel's first descents. They also taught kayaking to local junior and senior high school kids. One of their students was Eric Frazee who competed in Europe at the 1957 World Championships.

Seidel's influence was felt through his teaching and exploration. He explored the rivers of Colorado, Utah, and California, and was responsible for many first descents in a foldboat. Seidel was a small man, about 5' 6" and 130 lbs. He had an I-can-run-this attitude and did the first descent of Brown's Canyon in full flood during the spring of 1952. He dropped into a huge, almost river-wide hole that still bears the name Seidel's Suck Hole. While he escaped in one piece, the sticks and fabric of his foldboat washed out.

Although at that time Seidel was considered one of the greatest hydraulic technicians with a dependable roll, the Upper Merced in California provided him with a memorable experience. As he came down the river, he saw a funnel shaped sinkhole that spanned the width of the river, the bottom of which was about 8 feet below the river level. He literally shit when he saw what he was headed for.

Seidel never really found a work niche in America. His work was always secondary to his paddling and in the early 1970s, he moved east to New York. Seidel eventually moved back to Munich.

Although Erich Seidel was considered one of the greatest hydraulic technicians of the time, the irony is that it took him about twenty years to learn to roll. He grew up in Saxony and read a German translation of a book written by an author from the Canadian northwest. The book described how native paddlers could roll without a paddle using only a "stone." To Seidel the whole idea of using a stone implied throwing his weight to help with the roll. However, he was never able to accomplish this. He eventually figured out that there was an error in the translation. The "stone" should have read slate which he realized after a visit to British Columbia where he saw slate along the rivers he paddled. He then understood that native paddlers used a piece of slate, a flat stone, for surface area to roll their kayaks, the same flat surface area that a paddle blade provided.

Another German, Walter Kirschbaum, came to the Salida race in 1955. Kirschbaum was the World Champion in F-1 slalom. However, unlike Seidel, he did not immediately immigrate, instead visiting and exploring the rivers of Colorado and Utah returning to Germany each year. While paddling in Colorado prior to emigrating, he also made many first descents, particularly on more difficult sections of the upper Arkansas than Seidel attempted. Kirschbaum made a solo run of Pine Creek Rapids in his folding kayak in 1957.

In 1959 after competing in the World Championships, he came back to America. This time, he stayed for good. Kirschbaum became the first to paddle Cataract Canyon without portaging any of the drops. He encountered considerable problems in getting on the river in the first place, which required that he enlist the aid of an attorney to obtain permission from the Park Service to run the Canyon. His successful run on the Cataract Canyon proved his ability to attempt the Grand Canyon. In 1960, Kirschbaum left Lee's Ferry in June in one of his own designs, a 16-foot kayak with a canvas deck on a fiberglass hull. He became the first kayaker to run the Grand Canyon without portaging. The level was about 40,000 cfs. Kirschbaum was accompanied by Ted Hatch of Hatch River Expeditions who ran a motorized pontoon with six selected passengers including Tyson Dines, the attorney who helped Kirschbaum get permission to run on Cataract Canyon. Kirschbaum's only swim was in Hance Rapid where he flipped and lost his paddle. He climbed back on, grabbed his spare paddle, and finished the run.

Aside from his many first descents, Kirschbaum also introduced many American kayakers to the Duffek stroke. Kirschbaum also influenced non-kayakers. John Berry attributes Kirschbaum with having shown him how to play a river. Like Seidel, Kirschbaum taught anyone who was interested in learning whitewater.

Walter Kirschbaum won the World Championships in F-1 in 1953 in Merano, Italy. But he isn't famous for his win. Instead, Miroslav (Milo) Duffek, a former Czech canoe champion, is more famous, although he took second to Kirschbaum's first. On the first day of the World Cup slalom races, Duffek won with a new technique that became known as the Duffek stroke. Kirschbaum finished second, but noticed Duffek's stroke. He practiced it and used it the next day to win the race. Later, there was much controversy regarding Duffek's second place. The story regarding Duffek's loss and Kirschbaum's win is that Duffek threw the race in order to defect from communist Czechoslovakia. Had Duffek not purposely allowed his bow to hit a pole at gate 14, which gave him a 100-second penalty, his score of 310 would easily have beaten Kirschbaum's score of 330.5. Because he took second, Duffek was able to quietly defect. Had he taken first with the use of his new stroke, he would have been unable to slip away because of the publicity that would have followed him—literally.

WALTER KIRSCHBAUM was a kayaker in the late '30s in Bavaria in one of Hitler's youth programs. He was drafted into the army at the age of 16 and was sent to the Russian front where he was captured and held as a POW. When he was finally repatriated in 1948, his health was poor from the imprisonment and he became an alcoholic.

Kirschbaum was never able to overcome his wartime psychological experience. As long as he was paddling on a river, he controlled his alcoholism and his memories. He lived for long wilderness trips. "I live to paddle my boat—the only time I am free."[22] Although he had a premonition about dying by drowning, he never stopped paddling. In 1972, while living in New Mexico he drowned in his bathtub when he fell and hit his head.

Walter Kirschbaum July 1969
—courtesy of Al Holland.

In an early article in *American Whitewater,* Bruce Grant speculated on the future of whitewater paddling and how its growth might occur. He likened it to the growth of skiing in America and noted that three things, with similarities to skiing, could bring about growth in the sport.

> At least three primary ingredients seem indicated—the teacher, the river, and the supporting organization. The right combination of these elements could easily have a spectacular impact on the whitewater sport and point the way for future development... The teacher must be a master of modern technique with either the double or single paddle. He will probably be a Swiss, French, or Austrian since the art is most highly developed in those countries. He will have been successful in European wildwater and slalom competitions and will have been a top performer in the Arkansas River event. He will believe that the highest use of white water skill is to broaden the range of wilderness rivers one can tour in safety. His teaching skill and promotional instinct will be his outstanding abilities. No doubt he will also be handsome.[23]

The description seemed to be meant for Roger Paris. In a newspaper article, he was described as a "handsome 29-year-old daredevil who teaches skiing in northern California."[24] Like Kirschbaum, Paris did not immediately emigrate. After his first visit in 1953, he came back in 1954 at the invitation of Bob Herman, a racer who lived in California. Paris stayed with Herman near Cloverdale, California, where they paddled and trained together. Paris taught Herman how to roll his kayak and Herman took Paris paddling on the Russian, Eel, Trinity, and Klamath Rivers. They saw very few people in kayaks and often those they saw were paddlers from Sierra Club's river touring sections.

Paris returned year after year before immigrating to Colorado in the early '60s. During those intervening years, he paddled on rivers throughout the West and worked for Hatch Expeditions exposing countless paddlers to his paddling abilities and advanced technique.

THREE TRANSFORMATIONS occurred in the late '50s that were the result of competition. The first was the beginning of the transference of European paddling skills to American paddlers. The second was the domination of competition of canoeing events by paddlers from the East and kayaking by paddlers from the West. And finally, the beginning of the "passing of the torch" from older (greater than 30 years of age) to younger paddlers (less than 30), which foretold of significant changes yet to come in the '60s.

In the West, the Salida races in 1957 saw 17 year old Eric Frazee, trained by Seidel, place second beating older paddlers with many more years of experience. In the East, the Third Annual Eastern White Water Slalom Championships race on the West River in Vermont in 1959 and its accompanying downriver race marked the beginning of the torch pass with college-age members of Penn State Outing Club participating and doing well. The younger Bill Bickham took first place beating favorite Bob Harrigan in C-1 slalom by 36 seconds.

[22] Anderson, Fletcher. Interview by author, 23 November 1998.

[23] Grant, Bruce. "Things to Come." *American Whitewater* Vol. 2 No. 1 (Spring 1956): 27–28.

[24] "Frenchman Wins Third Title in Arkansas River Boat Races." AP Wire Service, Salida Colorado, June 16, 1958.

AWWA: Cornerstone for Whitewater

Although competition was a facilitator for the developing sport, in itself it could not provide the supporting knowledge and information such as river ratings, instructional books, and guidebooks needed to both supplement and complement competition. Both ACA and AWWA contributed to this knowledge and information. But neither organization was large and ACA had its hands full with the organization of competition. AWWA by its mere purpose statement was perhaps better able to provide and support the knowledge and information necessary for the developing sport. AWWA became the cornerstone for whitewater.

Coincidental to the formation of AWWA, the Western River Guides Association was formed in February of 1954. The purpose of the organization was multifold including preserving the natural resources and providing an exchange of ideas on technique, equipment, and safety. However, its primary purpose was as a trade organization that promoted commercial river running. The first president was Don Hatch of Hatch River Expeditions.

AWWA's founder is often considered to be Eliot DuBois of AMC-Boston, also the first Secretary in 1954. However, there were many early members of a truly national cross-section who were integral to AWWA's development in the early years. Those members who were either on the first executive committee or part of the original correspondence that established AWWA included Eliot DuBois (AMC-Boston), Bruce Grant (founder of the RTS in California), Laurence Grinnell (Cornell in New York), Wolf Bauer (founder of the Washington Foldboat Club), Clyde Jones (Colorado White Water Association), Steve Bradley (Colorado White Water Association), Oscar (Oz) Hawksley (Central Missouri State in Missouri), Walter F. Burmeister (AMC-Boston), W. S. "Stu" Gardiner (Salt Lake City), Don Rupp (Buck Ridge Ski Club), Bob McNair (founder of Buck Ridge Ski Club), Harold Kiehm (Prairie Club in Illinois), Marvin McLarty, and Wolfgang Lert. All were active participants in whitewater paddling activities.

WALTER BURMEISTER, Laurence Grinnell, Oz Hawksley, and Bob McNair later wrote some of the earliest guide and how-to books. Burmeister wrote a series of guidebooks including *Appalachia White Water.* Grinnell wrote *Canoeable Waterways of New York State.* Hawksley wrote *Missouri Ozark Waterways,* and McNair wrote *Basic River Canoeing.*

True to the original intent of AWWA was the distribution of information among affiliates. In a letter dated June 8, 1956, AWWA Secretary Bob McNair wrote to Affiliates and Prospective Affiliates:

> This is our first mailing of interclub exchange material in 1956. We would like to send much more so please give us thirty copies of all trip schedules, instruction outlines, et cetera, that you prepare for your own members. Then write a few memorandums just for us. This is the opportunity to try out new ideas before presenting them to the entire membership in AWWA... At first the AWWA was just a link between clubs. So much valuable information came to light in the information exchange that the magazine was created to make it available to individuals. But the original AWWA service, the exchanger of information between clubs, still goes on... Be sure to circulate your notebook of exchange material among your members.[25]

[25] McNair, Robert E. Correspondence from American White Water Affiliation Secretary Robert E. McNair to Affiliates and Prospective Affiliates, 8 June 1956.

As the affiliation grew, new members and affiliates replaced the original founders. Additionally, the structure of the affiliation evolved as intended by its original founders. In the early years, committees were established as needed to address a variety of concerns such as membership, safety, and conservation, all a part of the organizational infrastructure needed to grow the sport.

By the end of 1956, the individual membership was 440 with ten affiliated clubs or groups that were in contact with thirty more. Before year's end, an executive board was in place followed by the completion of a constitution and by-laws. At the heart of the Affiliation was a General Committee made up of representatives of affiliated clubs. The service committees of Safety, Conservation, Membership, and Editorial were formed. Bruce Grant was the Executive Secretary with Bauer, DuBois, Grinnell, Hawksley, Clyde Jones, Harold Kiehm, McNair, and Don Rupp as board members. Four committees were established: Membership, Guidebook, Safety, and Conservation. Colorado White Water Association provided considerable support to AWWA's journal, *American Whitewater,* from its membership, with Dave Stacey and Joe Lacy as editors and Roy Kerswill, and Clyde Jones for art and circulation assistance.

Five years after its founding, AWWA members recognized the need for more structure if it was to survive with its current rate of growth. It was not by accident that the Affiliation existed the first five years without a formal organization. "The people who started AWA [AWWA] avoided picking a ready-made constitution, and chose instead to let organizational structure evolve slowly." [26] A preliminary study for an organization plan was launched and it was soon realized "that people who like the outing sports usually have an aversion to 'stuffy' organization" and that "the plan should be simple and flexible, yet set forth some guiding principles of operation for the Affiliation." [27] This resulted in the formulation of a Constitution and By-laws.

The Constitution and By-laws provided for a General Committee comprised of representatives from the affiliated clubs. Other members of the General Committee were the chairmen of the Service Committees, and members of Advisory Committee. At the time, the Service Committees included Safety, Conservation, Membership, Editorial, and Guidebook Committees.

The Constitution and By-laws also established the name of the organization as the *American Whitewater* Affiliation with the initials AWA, a change from AWWA, with its incorporation in 1959. By 1959, aside from the original affiliates that included AMC, Buck Ridge, Colorado White Water Association, Foldboat Club of Southern California, Ithaca Canoe Club, Prairie Club, Sierra Club, and the Washington Foldboat Club, new affiliates were added including the Canoe Cruisers Association, American Youth Hostel in Columbus (Ohio), Ozark Wilderness Waterways Club, Penn State Outing Club, Outing Club of the Wisconsin Hoofers, and Kayak and Canoe Club of New York.

Affiliates and members were actively involved in slalom racing since competition was a large part of many paddlers' lives, even for those wishing only to develop their river-running skills. To accommodate this interest in competition, a racing editor was added to *American Whitewater* in 1959 (although ACA controlled whitewater competition in slalom and down river racing as the national governing body for ICF). George Siposs of the Ontario Voyageurs

[26] Editor. "Proposed Constitution and By-laws of the AWA." *American Whitewater* Vol. 4 No. 4 (Winter 1959): 27.

[27] Hawksley, Oz. "How Not to Become Extinct." *American Whitewater* Vol. 4 No. 3 (Fall 1958): 34.

was the first racing editor and "Racing News" became a regular department in the magazine along with "Letters from Readers," "From Your Editor," "Conservation Comment," "Safety," and "Book Reviews."

In the early years, key elements of AWWA's long-lasting stewardship for Whitewater were established as caretaker of the river-rating system, safety code, river conservation, and as a medium for the exchange of ideas and information, offshoots of its original purpose statement.

To encourage exploration ... of wilderness waterways...

The Guide Committee was established in the spring of 1955. Its purpose was multifold and included trying,

> to reach an agreement in principle and in as much detail as possible amongst cruising groups on the use of a standard method for rating the difficulty of cruising streams; to clarify understanding of river problems by seeking uniformity in methods used to describe portages, scenery, river flow rates, distance tables, mapping symbols and riverside signs, etc... ; to compile an accurate listing of guide information now available; and to disseminate this information for the use of future authors.[28]

The committee sought to gain consensus, not ramrod or impose any rules and regulations on its affiliates, an important aspect instilled by the founding members that embodied the spirit of the organization.

The Guide Committee members included a representative group of paddlers: Bruce Grant of California, Wolf Bauer of Washington, Oscar (Oz) Hawksley of Missouri, Sydney Jackson of Wisconsin, Lawrence Grinnell and Arthur Bodin of New York, Walter Burmeister of New Jersey, and Howard (Jeff) Wilhoyte of Pennsylvania. This group also brought representation of a variety of whitewater rivers and conditions from across the country.

Coincidental to the formation of AWWA's Guide Committee in 1955, Larry Zuk and other CWWA club members began writing trip and scouting reports. Zuk's reports were quite detailed and included directions for the put-ins and take-outs along with U.S. Geological Survey (USGS) river level information. His maps included mile markers and descriptions of how to run the rapid and what to expect. In 1955, trip reports and maps were completed for the South Platte around Deckers, Cache La Poudre near Fort Collins Water Works, Arkansas river below Salida, Blue River near Dillon, Eagle River near Wolcott, Gunnison River below Gunnison, and Colorado and Roaring Fork Rivers near Glenwood. The information was passed on to ACA for their effort (similar to AWWA's) to classify rivers for cruising. ACA used an official log so that the member could receive a cruising certificate and have the trip officially recorded in the ACA log under the auspices of the National Cruising Chairman. The final use of the information was different for the two organizations: AWWA used it for guidebooks and ACA used it for certification.

In order for IRK to "promote and foster foreign tourism through production of appropriate river guides" and "introduce on maps, internationally recognized symbols for rivers in order to facilitate touring,"[29] IRK also recognized the need for a river classification system or rating system. In 1924, IRK proposed a river classification system based on seven grades: Grades I–II were for quiet water and Grades III–VII for wild water. Soon after, the first combination how-to and guidebook came out in Germany (1925) *Wildwasserfahrten in Kayak und Falboot* by Alfred Heurich. Others guidebooks followed. In 1932, the IRK Congress accepted the Austrian proposal that established wildwater classification using Grades WW I through VI, with WW VI being the limit of the possible. The six-grade international classification system was thus born. However, the scale was neither adequately described nor officially adopted by the International Canoe Federation until 1954.

[28] Wilhoyte, Jeff. 'Guide Committee Report.' *American Whitewater* Vol. 1 No. 4 (Winter 1956): 6–7, 9.

[29] Vesper, Hans Egon and John W. Dudderidge. *50 Years of the International Canoe Federation*, English Edition. Florence, Italy: International Canoe Federation, 1974: A7.

AWWA's Guide Committee immediately recognized that one of the biggest challenges for paddlers was the lack of a single rating system for rivers. Eight different rating systems, or scales, were in use, including three from Europe. Three that they knew of that were in regular use in the country included those used by FibArk, the Washington Foldboat Club, and a scale predominantly used by commercial river runners, sometimes called the Deseret Scale. Their survey of the different systems showed that the rating increments in use were similar and covered nearly the same range of difficulty except for some of the most difficult rapids. While the FibArk and Deseret scales were too simplistic with insufficient descriptive notations, Washington Foldboat Club's river classification chart was the opposite with very detailed descriptive notations based on the kind of water (their local rivers) and type of craft (foldboats).

The FibArk Scale predated the arrival of the International Scale in Colorado and was based on a scale of seven gradations. It was based solely on the section of the Arkansas River used for their annual race and normal runoff for the June race time. The scale was very simple: 1 (placid), 2 (slow), 3 (average), 4 (fast), 5 (navigable), 6 (dangerous), and 7 (very dangerous. The "eighth" designate, greater than 7, was defined as barely navigable.

The Deseret Scale was used primarily by commercial rafters of the Colorado River Plateau, hence the term Deseret Scale. (The Deseret Empire is associated with followers of the Church of the Latter Day Saints in Utah and adjacent areas of Arizona, Idaho and Wyoming, approximately encompassing the Colorado River plateau.) It was based on a scale of one to ten and took into account the big volume rivers, the Colorado and its tributaries, seen nowhere else in the country. Compared to the six-point International Scale, eight corresponded to roughly Class VI when taking into account the differences in craft, such as a raft versus a kayak.

The name for the Deseret Scale may have its roots with Les Jones, a kayaker and commercial boatman for his cousin, Don Hatch (Hatch Expeditions). In 1953, Jones first began to use his ten-grade river classification scale. He later combined his scale with his own river profiles that became detailed scroll maps for use by river runners on many rivers in Colorado and Utah.

Washington Foldboat Club's River Classification Chart[30]

Class	River Speed Compared to Back-Paddle Speed of 3 MPH	Obstacle Channel Recognition	Passage around Bends, Stationary Objects	Passage thru or by Jumps, Fences, Stacks, Eddies	Passage thru or by Rapids, Chutes, Drops, Riffles	Suitable and Safe Limit for:
A	Less	Easy	Easy	Hardly Noticeable	None Present	Beginner green
B	Some or more	Easy	Easy thru	Easy thru	Easy thru	Beginner instructed
I	Variable	Readily in time	With attention	Thru with attention. Readily by	Thru with attention. Readily by	Beginner practiced
II	More	Usually in time	With alertness	Thru with care. Small hydraulics	Thru with analysis while paddling	One-season practiced paddler or average
III	Often fast	Sometimes difficult from boat	With care backpaddle, or inspect	Thru only with skill. Not always by easily	Inspection may be required. Usually by	Experienced good foldboater
IV	Usually fast and turbulent white water	Difficult. Frequent inspection required	With great care and skill	Thru with experience and spray cover. Not by easily	Inspection required. Some team support indicated.	Expert with available support
V	Very great velocity	Seldom possible from boat	Detailed inspection analysis required. Restricted passages	Large dimension hydraulics. Special techniques	Steep gradients. Extremely turbulent. Inspection. Long and continuous	Team of experts only

Speed Scale (still water)

3 MPH: Easy Touring Paddling Stoke, Average Person in Single
3.5 MPH: Easy Touring Paddling Stoke, Average Couple in Double
6 MPH: Short Stretch High Sprint Speed for Single
7 MPH: Short Stretch High Sprint Speed for Double
2.5–3.5 MPH: Hard Reverse Back-Paddling Speed

Note

River stretches are classified according to navigational skill and experience required to travel within safe limits with good foldboating gear by experts.

Washington Foldboat Club's River Classification Chart (consisting of Class A, B and I through V) made its rounds of AWWA affiliated clubs. Dave Stacey of CWWA reviewed it and proposed a system based on how hard it was to run the rapid. Being familiar with the FibArk scale, he expanded on its range, from 0 to 10 in even numbers, and descriptions.

0 Surface is almost smooth but may be fast moving.
2 Water is not calm, but causes no one trouble.
4 Average men have no trouble, beginners may.
6 Very good men get through almost always, average men may have trouble.
8 The best boatmen in the world have a 50–50 chance of getting through without a spill (in a kayak).
10 Impossible, never been run.[31]

[30] Washington Foldboat Club River Classification Chart circa mid-1950s'.

[31] Zuk, Larry. Cruise Committee Report No. I, 1955.

Based on an initial survey, the committee agreed that a six-point system seemed to cover the range of whitewater paddled but also felt that higher numbers might be required for very difficult rapids and stunt type situations. Flatwater was given a separate three-point rating system. Their initial survey included Ratings A, B, and C for flatwater that were primarily based on current speed. The ratings for 1 through 6 (not Roman numerals at the time) were left to be defined but the experience of a paddler was anticipated with 1 being a practiced beginner, 2 an intermediate, 3 an experienced, 4 as highly skilled, and 5 and 6 depicted as a team of experts.

By the winter of 1957, the committee completed their survey of the various rating systems used in America and worked in cooperation with the ACA's Cruising Committee to study the grading systems used in various European countries. Their final recommendation supported the use of the International Scale first promulgated by the Nautical Section of France's Alliance de Tourism and officially adopted by ICF in 1954. The International Scale was first published in the Winter issue of *American Whitewater* in 1957.

The International Scale[32]

Smooth Water

Rating	River or Individual Rapids Characteristics	Approx. Minimum Experience Required
A	Pools, Lakes, Rivers with velocity under 2 miles per hour	Beginner
B	Rivers, velocity 2-4 mph	Beginner with River Instuctions
C	Rivers, velocity above 4 mph (max. back-paddling speed) may have some sharp bends and/or obstructions	Instructed and Practiced Beginner

White Water

Rating	River or Individual Rapids Characteristics	Approx. Minimum Experience Required
I	Easy—Sand-banks, bends without difficulty, occasional small rapids with waves regular and low. Correct course easy to find but care is needed with minor obstacles like pebble banks, fallen trees, etc., especially on narrow rivers. River speed less than hard back paddling speed.	Practiced Beginner
II	Medium—Fairly frequent but unobstructed rapids, usually with regular waves, easy eddies, and easy bends. Course generally easy to recognize. River speeds occasionally exceeding hard back paddling speed.	Intermediate
III	Difficult—Maneuvering in rapids necessary. Small falls, large regular waves covering boat, numerous rapids. Main current may swing under bushes, branches or overhangs. Course not always easily recognizable. Current speed usually less than fast forward paddling speed.	Experienced
IV	Very Difficult—Long extended stretches of rapids, high irregular waves with boulders directly in current. Difficult broken water, eddies, and abrupt bends. Course often difficult to recognize and inspection form the bank frequently necessary. Swift current. Rough water experience indispensable.	Highly Skilled (several years experience with organized group)
V	Exceeding Difficult—Long rocky rapids with difficult and completely irregular broken water which must be run head on. Very fast eddies, abrupt bends and vigorous cross currents. Difficult landings increase hazard. Frequent inspections necessary. Extensive experience necessary.	Team of Experts
VI	Limit of Navigability—All previously-mentioned difficulties increased to the limit. Only negotiable at favorable water levels. Cannot be attempted without risk of life.	Team of Experts (taking every precaution)

[32] Wilhoyte, Jeff. 'Guide Committee Report.' *American Whitewater* Vol. 2 No. 4 (Winter 1957): 28–31.

The International Scale[32]

In expanding on the International Scale, the committee attached a point range for each rating based on a variety of factors. The points were based on factors related primarily to success in negotiating rapids, affecting both success and safety, and factors related to a safe rescue. The ratings were written without regard for boat type or special equipment such as spray covers since covers were considered a necessity for rapids with ratings from III to VI.

While the committee was able to successfully promote the use of the International Scale, particularly with regard to rating rapids and rivers for paddlers (canoeing and kayaking) as a common reference, other common references for guidebooks were not as straightforward. Aside from establishing a common rating reference, another important aspect of rating a river for a guidebook was in establishing a reference point for river level or volume. Across the country, various federal organizations tracked river flow using gauges, particularly USGS and Army Corps of Engineers who provided flow information for some watersheds, especially for those associated with river levels for hydropower, irrigation, and barge traffic control. However, relating the information to river levels for paddling was not always done.

As early as 1950, Wolf Bauer began to use Army Corps gauges to evaluate river levels in the Seattle area for paddling. However, in the absence of USGS or Corps gauges, paddlers established their own relative gauges. Some gauges were based on relatively random assignment of marks on bridge abutments, but others were developed specifically to provide paddlers with useful information relative to other rivers in the same and adjacent watersheds. Randy Carter of Virginia developed a river marking system (the Randy Carter System) with just that in mind, "to give the canoeist the height of the river in terms of what the canoeist needs."[34] The basis of his system established zero as the lowest water height that "an expert canoeist" could run the river. Zero meant scraping over shallows and ledges which also corresponded to about 3 inches of water over the shallows. But if bottoming stopped the canoe, the river was less than zero. Once zero was established, a road or bridge abutment, readily visible from highway or phone location, was then marked in 1-foot increments, often to the highest level of 5 feet.

Randy Carter was an open canoeist who explored the rivers of Virginia, Eastern West Virginia, and the Smoky Mountain area of North Carolina. His method was later adopted by and maintained by canoe clubs in the mid-Atlantic including the CCA, Coastal Canoeists, Blue Ridge Voyageurs, and the North Carolina Canoe Club as well as H. Roger Corbett, an author who carried on Carter's guidebook traditions.

Along with river classification and reference level information, guidebooks also needed common descriptions and codes for maps. Again, in their absence, individuals developed their own codes and systems. Although a code for river maps was in use in Europe, none of the American authors (Walter Burmeister, Lawrence Grinnell, Bruce Grant, Eliot DuBois, and Randy Carter) compiling information at the time used it. In 1959, Randy Carter's guidebook, *Canoeing White Water in Northern Virginia and Northeastern West Virginia,* became the standard by which others were measured. Carter went to great extent to establish, record, and document river levels to paddleable levels using his river marking system. (Later review of the information collected by Randy Carter for small streams showed a rough correlation that RC zero corresponded to approximately 2 feet on USGS gauges.) With the help and cooperation of

IN THE EARLY DAYS of the Washington Foldboat Club and before Wolf Bauer was aware of the International Scale, Bauer realized that rivers needed to be classified or rated for their difficulty. He decided to rate rivers from 1 through 5 with 5 being unrunnable. His rating was based on the ability of the best kayaker (foldboater) in the group and only a few could handle the rivers rated at 4. A class 3 or 4 rapid was impossible for a beginner to successfully run.

It was not until Erich Seidel visited Bauer (around 1956) that Bauer became aware of the International Scale. Seidel was surprised at the difficulty of rivers paddled by the club, who took him through a rock garden rated 3-4 by their standards. Bauer reported that Seidel was not only surprised by the difficulty but also by the fact that Bauer and the others played in the jets.

Yet in 1958, a British paddler wrote of obvious differences between the American and European whitewater sport. One of the differences was,

> the optimistic way you appear to grade rivers. Some of your contributors talk of tackling grade V and VI rivers as a matter of course. In Europe "grade VI" means what it says—the absolute limit of difficulty-which is usually interpreted as impossible. Grade V is almost as bad and usually avoided by even the most expert canoeist [European canoeist means kayaker] ... if it is at all possible to canoe [kayak] a river, by European interpretation it is not grade VI.[33]

WOLF BAUER, in addition to using Army Corps gauges for level reference, also developed his own map system codes. He made a map that contained rivers only and which also contained instructions for where to find the appropriate roads for the put-ins and take-outs. The map was continually updated and in 1965, was in its fourteenth printing.

[33] Blanford, P.W. "Letters from Readers." *American Whitewater* Vol. 4 No. 1 (Spring 1958): 5.

[34] Carter, Randy. *Canoeing White Water River Guide.* Oakton, Virginia: Appalachian Books, 1967: 28.

CCA members, all of the rivers covered in the book were marked with gauges viewable from highways, which greatly added to the usefulness of his guidebook.

Walter Burmeister began paddling and compiling his guidebook materials in the early '40s. However, the real difficulty for him was really in finding a publisher (although the paddling and research was difficult enough as it was). There were no publishers who felt there was enough of a market for such a book. It was not until Buck Ridge extracted West Virginia and Pennsylvania river descriptions from sections of his manuscripts for mimeographed publication (200 copies in 1957) that his dream of a published guidebook became a reality.

By the late '50s, there were more 16 mm movies available (both German and American) than guidebooks and instructional books. The movies ranged from movies of trips, to races, to instructional movies on technique.

Although Burmeister's books significantly affected paddling in the East, his first two volumes had no references to river levels. Much of his research was done before he was aware of the International Scale, and he rated many rivers after-the-fact. This, combined with the fact that he ran rivers in a foldboat, never a rigid fiberglass kayak, meant that his river ratings were questionable in the first place, even at the time of their publication. Regardless, Burmeister paddled and catalogued many first descents in his foldboat, often years before any others attempted the same runs.

To foster research ... for safely negotiating whitewater...

The Safety Committee began soliciting input for a safety code in 1956, much of which elicited strong opinions. The suggestion of being a good swimmer as a requirement was met with considerable criticism, many pointing out that swimming after an upset was absurd. The suggestion that life jackets be worn at all times also solicited strong opinions. There was also considerable discussion regarding loose ropes or painters and the safety aspect with snagging either paddler or river objects. The use of riverside throw lines was also seriously questioned for their practicality due the concern of loose ropes in the water. One of the few suggestions that elicited little criticism was the hazard associated with cold water. The use of spray skirts was also encouraged, but so, too, was the issue of making sure the skirt could be released.

The Safety Committee finally submitted a draft of the Safety Code for comments in 1957. The Code included provisions for wearing life jackets, dressing for the air and water temperature, and carrying essential equipment in waterproof bags. It specifically addressed required equipment such as a spare paddle, bow and stern safety lines, repair kit, sponge or bailing container, a spray deck, and in Class IV and V rivers, a pith-type crash helmet should be considered. The Code further addressed the use of lead and rear-guard boats and the responsibilities of other boaters to stay in that order. By 1959, final changes were made and the Safety Code was accepted.

The Code contained eight sections: Personal Preparedness and Responsibility, Boat Preparedness and Equipment, Group Equipment, Leader's Responsibility, On the River, On Lake or Ocean, If You Spill, and If Others Spill. Key provisions of Personal Preparedness were: never boat alone, be a competent swimmer, wear your life jacket, and support your leader. Within

Leader's Responsibility, the leader was to have full knowledge of the river and the participants in his group as to their abilities. A key provision of If You Spill was to stay with the boat and stay upstream of the boat.

In 1957, Donn Charnley (Washington Foldboat Club member), Chairman of the Safety Committee, began the practice of publishing accident reports. He passed along seven accident reports that totaled ten deaths in the spring of that year. Deaths occurred due to hypothermia and drowning, including three boy scouts and their scout master on French Creek in Pennsylvania during a high water run.

To protect the wilderness character of our waterways...

River conservation was an integral part of AWWA from its early beginnings. The first issue of *American WHITE WATER* in May of 1955 included an article titled "Echo Park Dam: Is it Needed Now?" by Steve Bradley about the controversial Echo Park Dam and the need to preserve versus satisfy future water needs for growth of the region.

The Conservation Committee was formed in August of 1956, comprised of committee members with conservation positions in other outing organizations. It was always the intention of AWWA to coordinate efforts with other like-minded organizations. In November of the same year, ACA voted to elevate its Conservation Committee from a fact-finding committee to full-standing committee status.

The newly formed Conservation Committee, under the leadership of chairmen Oz Hawksley and Dan Bradley, struggled with where AWWA should stand on different issues. Consensus was difficult to obtain. However, one thing they did agree on was that the most important national issue was the Wilderness Preservation Act.

In 1956, a wilderness bill was introduced for the first time in Congress. In the ensuing years, the reality of the impact of political forces on conservation issues was an early lesson learned by the Conservation Committee. The year 1957 saw a spectrum of conservation issues and exposed their weaknesses. The Wilderness Act that looked so promising did not pass. The Committee was further disillusioned by further encroachments into river conservation with a proposed dam on the Clearwater in Idaho and the change of Dinosaur National Monument to national park status that still did not guarantee protection from preventing the damming of the Green within the park's boundaries. The Committee learned that nothing in the Act precluded the Secretary of the Interior from investigating the suitability of reservoir and canal sites.

The 85th Congress in 1958 still could not pass the Act, but it did pass appropriations for detailed engineering plans for the Bruces Eddy Dam on the North Fork of the Clearwater in Idaho. To gather support in fighting the Bruces Eddy Dam, AWWA introduced its first wilderness outing as a joint venture in 1959 with the Sierra Club, led by Lou Elliott and Oz Hawksley. Designed as a base camp trip located near runs on the Selway, Lochsa, Middle Fork, and North Fork of the Clearwater, the wilderness outing's purpose was to expose a greater number of their members to the potential loss should dam construction gain approval.

IN 1920, the Federal Water Power Act was enacted and the Federal Power Commission was created. The Commission was given authority to issue hydroelectric power licenses to any project deemed to be in the public interest. Less than a year later in 1921, a joint venture made up of Southern California Edison, Utah Power and Light, and the U. S. Geological Survey launched a series of map-making/surveying expeditions to identify potential dam sites for the entire Colorado river basin. The expeditions were lead by Colonel Claude H. Birdseye and in 1921, they ran the San Juan and upper Colorado basin; in 1922, the Green; and finally, in 1923, they were ready to survey the Colorado through the Grand Canyon. The greatest impact of these surveys was the identification of twenty-two potential dam sites. The first dam proposed was Boulder Dam, the largest man-made structure on the earth in 1935.

Immediately after the war in 1946, the Bureau of Reclamation put before Congress the Colorado River Storage Project. This project outlined the construction of five main storage and hydroelectric dams on the Colorado and its tributaries that would spread across six states and include a dozen lesser projects. The centerpiece for the project was Echo Park Dam on the Green and included Glen Canyon Dam on the Colorado, Navajo Dam on the San Juan, and Flaming Gorge on the Green. Echo Park Dam would have affected Dinosaur National Park. Congress heard the nationwide uproar and although funding for the Colorado River Storage Project was passed in 1955, funding for the Echo Park Dam was deferred. Conservationists and other groups managed to kill the dam. However, when the Echo Park Dam in Dinosaur National Monument was killed, planning for the Glen Canyon dam was speeded up. In October 1956, President Eisenhower pushed a button from his desk in the White House that began the first explosions marking the beginning of Glen Canyon dam construction.

With all the controversy around the Echo Park Dam, the other dam on the Green, Flaming Gorge Dam, also went largely unnoticed. It, too, was begun in 1956.

OSCAR (OZ) HAWKSLEY was a champion for conservation and active in the Ozarks. He was a professor at Central Missouri State College in Warrensburg.

Almost forty people participated in what was considered the pioneering runs on three branches of the Clearwater. Roughly half of the number were AWWA members and the other half were Sierra Club river tourists. Bay Chapter's RTS provided ten-man rafts with boatmen for the non-paddlers on the river trips. The outing included two days paddling the Lochsa and three days on the North Fork. The river trips began with about a dozen kayaks and canoes but finished with less than half. One foldboat and one fiberglass kayak were totally destroyed.

One of the purposes of the trip was to demonstrate to Federal authorities that there was legitimate interest in keeping the Clearwater dam free. However, the threat of roads into wilderness areas and their impact on the rivers also became apparent to both AWWA and Sierra Club organizations. The bulldozing of materials into the rivers for road construction made some stretches of the rivers particularly hazardous with sharp and unstable rock piles both submerged in and along the riverbanks.

Due to the difficulty of the rivers encountered, the experience level of paddlers, and the difficulties of a combined raft and boat flotilla, AWWA decided that future trips would be for kayak and canoe paddlers rated skilled and expert and with enough rafts to support them with supplies and to transport their families.

By 1959, because of the growing paddling population and increasing use of old and new rivers and areas alike, AWWA was becoming aware of,

> encroachments on our favorite rivers—dams, highways, and other "improvements" both public and private. Many of them are not necessary, but their construction brings great material benefit to everybody from local contractors to steel mills, and so they draw hoops of support form local chambers of commerce and business clubs. Who is it that keeps demanding these improvements?... It is the Army Engineers, the Bureau of Reclamation, the National Park Service, and other empire-building government agencies, and the chambers of commerce and business organizations, and their representatives in State and National governments.[35]

For bringing together ideas, procedures and experiences.

AWWA, through *American Whitewater,* was the medium for the exchange of ideas and information that was critical to the development of the sport. Although many different ideas, procedures, and experiences were shared, perhaps the most important information concerned skills on technique and river running, and on fiberglass construction of canoes and kayaks.

Technique

Paddling techniques evolved somewhat independently in pockets (clubs) across the country. The exchange of ideas through *American Whitewater* provided a more rapid, and to some extent, more uniform evolution of technique

[35] Bradley, Don. "Conservation Comment." *American Whitewater* Vol. 5 No. 1 (Spring 1959): 29–31.

and skills. This rate of evolution was also greatly influenced by advanced skills brought by European competitors and the dissemination of information regarding those advanced skills as well as by slalom competition itself.

Toward the late '50s, more paddlers were exposed to the Eskimo roll, which was the subject of many articles. In 1957, one inventive paddler, Carlos Yerby of Bay Chapter's RTS, designed the "Eskimo Roll Trainer." It consisted of two ten-gallon barrels attached together with three boards. The midsection contained a seat but because there was no cockpit or solid hull, the trainer would not fill with water. Using the trainer, the paddler could learn the rolling sequence using the long method or extended roll, proceeding to the pawlata or sculling method, and finally the short or screw method. [*Author's note:* The screw roll was the same as we know it today although some people gained greater leverage with their paddle by going to the extended roll.] Once it was learned in the trainer, the paddler could switch to his own boat to practice the technique. CWWA members also developed similar aids to assist with learning the roll. Their idea used inner tubes on the bow and stern of the kayak during pool sessions.

In addition to exposure to the Eskimo roll, American paddlers also studied the basic paddling techniques of the Europeans. They recognized that holding their paddles in the air while going through a series of waves was a mark of inexperience. It was noted that an expert, while reading the river, always had one blade (meant for kayakers) in the water. It was determined that there were two important reasons for "not holding the paddle high in the air. First, to minimize loss of time in applying the stroke or brace; and second, to keep the center of gravity low. Holding the paddle high in the air decreases stability."[36] It was also learned that the expert leaned forward at the waist, not back against the seat rest and that control was established by bracing the knees firmly inside the boat and with regard to leans, "the vertical axis of the kayak should lean with him."[37]

However, of all the techniques learned from the Europeans, the most important was the Duffek stroke. In 1953, the new stroke hit the slalom world. Milo Duffek adapted his namesake stroke from his canoeing experience using a bow draw with a brace. He used his adapted kayak stroke as a pivot or momentum changer where he planted the blade forward and pulled or drew the blade as a rudder.

Until the introduction of the Duffek stroke, only forward strokes and backstrokes were used to maneuver a kayak. If the kayak was to be moved sideways, the paddler reached out to the side and pulled over, while leaning to increase effectiveness. For turning the kayak around, the backstroke was used. However, in turning around a 360-degree slalom pole, the stern was usually caught by the current and carried down stream. The Duffek stroke offered a more successful alternative. It allowed a single stroke to accomplish what before required a series of strokes. (A 360-degree slalom pole was a solitary pole around which a paddler had to do a complete 360-degree turn.)

Although upstream maneuvering and use of river current was essential in river poling, many paddlers did not tie in the use of upstream maneuvering to paddling. (Because canoe poling was predominantly found in the East, many paddlers elsewhere were not familiar with it.) With the introduction of the Duffek stroke and slalom racing to American paddlers, it became obvious that

On July 30, 1927, Hans Eduard Pawlata (also known as Edi Hans) of the Vienna Kayak Club performed the first Eskimo roll and wrote of the technique in his book *Kipp Kipp Hurra im Reinrassigen Kayak* in 1928. Leo Fruhwirth, an Austrian, later demonstrated a series of rolls in a borrowed folding kayak at an IRK meeting in 1928. The same year, Franz Schulhof, another Austrian, provided instructions with illustrations in an article in the magazine of the German Canoe Association. In 1932, he produced a film demonstrating the technique.

[36] Grant, Bruce. "White Water Form." *American Whitewater* Vol. 1 No. 4 (February 1956): 8.

[37] Ibid.

using river currents and differentials was also a major component of technique. The Duffek stroke and its use of currents were enlightening to many. Peter Whitney recognized this and shared his observations in an article in 1959.

> One objective is always to let the river do as much of the work as possible, and hence to present the boat to the current in such a way that it cannot be broadsided unless you want it to turn. That means planning every move from swifter into slower water and vice versa. I have seen Paul Bruhin, the Swiss kayak star, run a rapid on the Housatonic that the rest of us thought problematic if not difficult; then turn and paddle up it again, cross it repeatedly, and draw the teeth of each of its separate problems. Paul gets five rapids' worth where the rest of us used to get but one. The Duffek technique relies heavily on the paddle as a pivot, and on the boat's having a certain relative velocity in the water. Thus current differentials are more critical than in the old-fashioned forward and back-stroking methods.[38]

However, in addition to providing a more uniform evolution of technique and skills, the exchange of ideas also illustrated the differences between East and West. In 1957, DuBois wrote:

> It is a well documented fact that New England canoeists are predominantly backpaddlers, whereas Colorado canoeists and foldboatists paddle forward to achieve control of their boats. This has been attributed to many causes: New Englanders are conservative; Coloradoans are more dashing, and the Salida race provides a strong stimulus for forward paddling. If you paddle forward on a New England river you may easily be moving over the bottom three times as fast as you would if you were backpaddling. If a portion if the bottom sticks up and whallops you, as often happens, the whallop will be nine times greater. On Colorado rivers there are souseholes, and forward paddling ploughs through them.[39]

Wolf Bauer and the Washington Foldboat Club were perhaps the first to accumulate knowledge of river currents and technique specifically for kayaking. A series of articles by Bauer in *American Whitewater* through the late '50s disseminated much of what they learned including terminology that reflected parallels to skiing where appropriate. The terminology included terms such as eddy turn, eddy christy, eddy jumping, figure 8-turn or figure S-turn, stack or roller surfing, and ferry surfing.[40]

[38] Whitney, Peter. "Let's Go Upstream." *American Whitewater* Vol. V No. 2 (August 1959): 15–18.

[39] DuBois, Eliot. "Slide Rule and Paddle." *American Whitewater* Vol. 3 No. 2 (Summer 1957): 23–24.

[40] Bauer, Wolf, "Playing the River." *American Whitewater* Vol. 2 No. 1 (Spring 1956): 5–8.

The eddy turn used "a modified paddle brace" and "the boat and paddler may bank as much as 60 to 80 degrees to balance the opposing current force." The eddy christy was also a banked turn,

> except that it is accomplished in faster opposing eddies such as jets... The eddy line is crossed more toward the opposing current at about 50 to 70 degrees. The paddler uses maximum paddling speed up to an instant of entering the opposing current, after which the bow and boat are raised into planing position, requiring a slight downstream lean or bank, as well as light skidding paddle brace... If there is no eddy wall to climb over, you may plane halfway across the jet in a smooth skidding turn. Weight is shifted aft as you cross the eddy line, then forward after the full hull is planing.[41]

A considerable part of Washington Foldboat Club's instructional program was playing on rivers and was described in Bauer's 1956 article, "Playing the River." Playing follow-the-leader under controlled conditions with eddies was an important part of the instructional program. The figure S-turn or figure 8-turn is:

> a double alternately banked turn crossing two eddy lines. It requires strong side eddies on each side of a rather narrow jet or main central current. Additional skill will allow the paddler to perform the S-turn without paddle skid-brace simply by shifting his weight to counterbalance the current.
>
> [*Author's note:* Bauer's use of the term paddler, instead of the terms kayakist, canoeist, and foldboater, was not a commonly used term elsewhere at the time.]

Surfing was also an integral part of developing boat control and technique. "Stack or roller surfing or planing, as well as ferry-surfing, is a fun maneuver we have developed to practice balance and forward lean." Mastery of ferry surfing was considered important,

> ...as there are occasions for upferrying in swift currents in places where minimum loss in downstream boat position is allowable during a crossing... If the play spot happens to have a stack or series of stacks reaching across a small river between two side eddies, then the scene is set for real fun. The eddies are your ski-tows and the center jet or current with standing waves provide high-speed thrills across its surface in graceful christies, undulating banked turns, and swift upstream ferry surfing back and forth.[42]

[41] Bauer, Wolf. "Let's Understand the Eddy." *American Whitewater* Vol. 3 No. 3 (Fall 1957): 25–30.

[42] Bauer, Wolf. "Playing the River: Some Ideas from an Expert." *American Whitewater* Vol. 2 No. 1 (Spring 1956): 5–8.

In Bauer's exploration of technique and current, he pushed the known paddling limits. "In determining the upper limits (of surfing), I have been able to hover ahead of smooth green stacks in a deep channel and by extreme forward lean [to] cause the boat finally to dive and turn completely over in an upstream somersault."[43]

Not only did Bauer's series of articles explain terminology and technique, but they also explained river hydrodynamics for paddlers. In his first article related to this topic in 1957, Bauer covered the complexities of eddies. Bauer felt that:

> understanding and recognition (of hydrodynamics) is at least half the battle, training and exercise to reflect the other... If we can understand the components of the pure forms (of eddies) and basic types, then we can at least partly conject about the mechanics of these many interfering and confused hydraulics. This understanding will allow the paddler to react to their forces with the appropriate boat tilt, brace, forward or back-stroke, body lean or shift, respect or disregard. He may then use their action as a navigational aid (for controlling the boat), or as a means for engaging in the many play-maneuvers that his kayak is capable of performing.[44]

Bauer identified three basic types of eddies: the back-eddy, the side-eddy, and the whirl-eddy. Bauer defined the back-eddy as "the center reverse current flowing upstream on the surface toward the object causing it." The eddy line "defines the boundary between it and the down-stream current on each side, this line having various characteristics in relation to stream velocity and depth, as well as shape and size of object causing the eddy." The eddy walls "may be likened to ... the bow-wave of a boat—the faster and more blunt the boat and bow, the steeper and higher the bow wave. Thus eddy walls may vary in height from inches to several feet in height." The eddy tail "is the turbulent area extending downstream from the end of the eddy where the split current more or less rejoins and dissipates its energy in small whirls and cross currents." A souse-hole or souse-eddy is an "extreme form of the back-eddy (and sometimes side-eddy) requiring high current velocity against sharp-edged objects to form high eddy walls."[45]

In trying to address river-running safety and rescue (as he did with the Mountaineers with mountain safety and rescue), Bauer decided to study eddies "up close and personal." He did this at first by diving in rivers with scuba tanks but soon gave this up due to the danger of the weight of the tanks. He then tried snorkeling, which was not only less dangerous, but proved more successful. By snorkeling on rivers, Bauer determined that in the green eddy stage, where water was not yet flowing over the rock, the eddy had a tail downstream of the rock. He also determined that the shape of the rock determined the size of the eddy and whether the rock was streamlined upstream or downstream. The white eddy stage was where the water poured over the rock. The eddy formed was always lower than the rest of the water so that the water pouring over the rock created an air pump and aerated the water in the eddy. Bauer correlated all of this to new and evolving hull designs and paddling techniques in addition to its use for rescue.

[43] Bauer, Wolf. "Playing the River: Some Ideas from an Expert." *American Whitewater* Vol. 2 No. 1 (Spring 1956): 5–8.

[44] Bauer, Wolf. "Let's Understand the Eddy." *American Whitewater* Vol. 3 No. 3 (Fall 1957): 25–30.

[45] Ibid.

Side eddies were differentiated from back-eddies and were characterized as having stronger rotational currents "on the surface due to the nature of the underwater condition and depth of the river bed and bank on one side... From the well-developed side eddy to the whirl eddy is only a short step and matter of degree, although the causes are not quite the same."[46] The whirl eddy was really a side eddy with stronger upstream currents, hence whirl, that would take the paddler back up towards the obstruction causing the eddy. Because the white eddy was aerated, it was difficult to get out of, forming a trap, hence the term white eddy trap.

Terminology has changed since the '50s. Some terms were retained but many others were lost. ACA's *Canoeing and Kayaking Instruction Manual* published in 1987 includes only the eddy turn. Gone is the eddy christy. There are only three descriptions for eddies: black eddies, white eddies, and boiling eddies. Side eddies, back eddies, whirl eddies, and jets are also gone. Eddy walls are simply eddy lines and stack, roller, and ferry surfing are simply surfing. White-eddy traps were appropriately described for the skill at the time. Today, the white eddy trap is known as a play hole of today. Souseholes and suckholes are referred to as holes, hydraulics, or reversals and large holes with very strong upstream currents are called keepers, for their ability to keep a boat.

Fiberglass Construction

The first article involving fiberglass construction was published in *American Whitewater's* third issue, November 1955, and was written by Roy Kerswill and Larry Monninger. "Revolutionary Fiberglass Canoe"[47] described the process they used to build a male canoe mold modeled after Roessinger and Dussuet's canoe first seen at the Salida races the same year. Their mold was of plywood and spaced wood strips covered and faired with plaster (keeping in mind that the mold would have to be torn out after the canoe was laid up). They relied on the advice of Fiber-Resin Corporation in California, a fiberglass materials supplier, in the use of the materials as well as a suggested lay-up. The resulting 16-foot canoe weighed about 50 pounds.

Although Kerswill and Monninger's article was the first to appear in *American Whitewater,* Dave Stacey wrote an article titled "The Fiberglass Kayak" that was first published in CWWA's newsletter *The Spray* about a year before.[48] The article shared some of the experiences that he and Steve Bradley accumulated in the previous five years of building fiberglass kayaks. The article was published again in *American Whitewater's* Winter 1957 issue for greater distribution to paddlers.[49]

In the article, Stacey guided the novice through the high level steps from designing the boat to the more detailed steps of building the mold. He included information about the materials, resin and cloth, and suppliers. The article provided insights into the importance of design and how Bradley read books on marine engineering, spending several hundred hours working on the first model, a double. Bradley's next design was a single, the Colorado. He suggested that the first time builder swipe a boat design using a folding kayak as the mold. Since they were building with male molds, swiping was as simple as covering the hull with plaster (it could be easily removed when finished because it was water soluble and did not damage the foldboat skin) to obtain a rigid surface against which to lay-up the fiberglass and resin.

[46] Bauer, Wolf. "Respectfully Yours—the Eddies." *American Whitewater* Vol. 3 No. 4 (Winter 1958): 9–12.

[47] Kerswill, Roy and Larry Monninger. "Revolutionary Fiberglass Canoe." *American Whitewater* Vol. 1 No. 3 (November 1955): 6–8.

[48] Stacey, Dave. "The Fiberglass Kayak." *The Spray* 1954/55.

[49] Stacey, Dave. "Building a Fiberglass Kayak." *American Whitewater* Vol. 2 No. 4 (Winter 1957): 12–14.

For someone wishing to design his or her own mold, Stacey described how he and Bradley built a mold starting from drawings, using bulkheads or forms (the same as building with one-off strip construction techniques). He explained "it's an awful lot of work; but the mold can be used many times"[50] in contrast to using a foldboat as the mold.

Stacey provided quite a bit of detail regarding working with the materials and some of the lessons they learned. Because of the relative infancy of the fiberglass industry, they became aware of how little the suppliers knew about their own materials and how to use them. Stacey suggested that anyone wishing to build a fiberglass kayak should write letters to the suppliers asking for information and advice. However, Stacey also provided suggestions about what worked best for them including release agents, bubble removal techniques (using a rolling pin or squeegee), and time of cure. He recommended applying the resin to all the layers at one time with two or three people helping with the operation.

In addition to his input on Stacey's article on building fiberglass kayaks, Bradley also wrote two articles on hull design, the second of which was published in the same issue as Stacey's article.[51] In the articles, Bradley provided, in layman's terms, what he had learned about design. The articles discussed the three basic attributes of hull design: profile or sideviews and the effects of rocker; plan or topviews, and symmetry; fishform, and anti-fishform (swedeform); and cross section and the effects of flat, U, V, and combination bottoms as well as sidewall flare (concave), flam (convex), and tumblehome. All attributes were discussed in their relation to the performance or handling of a canoe or kayak in whitewater.

AWWA, THROUGH ITS FOUNDERS, AFFILIATES, AND MEMBERS, embodied the psyche of whitewater paddlers, those people drawn to the thrill of exploration, danger, and the mastery of skills. Whitewater paddlers, then as now, were free-spirited, yet they acknowledged that some degree of organization or structure was required that was associated with the preservation of the sport through conservation and safety and without hindering the inherent nature and draw of whitewater. AWWA was the cornerstone on which whitewater as a sport was built, and through its stewardship, continues to carry-on the spirit and embrace changes as necessary to ensure its future.

Building on the Cornerstones: the Growing Infrastructure

In the latter half of the '50s, the popularity of whitewater slowly grew, and with it came growth to the cornerstone clubs along with the formation of new whitewater clubs across the country. These new clubs were reinforcements, adding to and building up, the growing infrastructure of the young sport. Larger metropolitan areas, particularly in the mid-Atlantic region, often supported more than one club. But the formation of structured clubs was not the only source of growth. Non-structured whitewater activity also grew, particularly in less populated areas with fewer paddlers to support a structured club.

[50] Stacey, Dave. "Building a Fiberglass Kayak." *American Whitewater* Vol. 2, No. 4 (Winter 1957): 12–14.

[51] Bradley, Steve. "Hull Design." *American Whitewater* Vol. 2 No. 3 (Fall 1956): 15–18 and "Hull Design—Part II" Vol. 2 No 4 (Winter 1957): 6–9.

Economic conditions in the United States affected whitewater activity. By 1955, the American economy was strong which was attributed to the "Eisenhower prosperity."

During the first ten years after World War II, a blossoming in turnpike (toll) construction occurred, predominantly in the East. In 1956, the Interstate Highway Act passed providing for federally funded highway development across the country, the effects of which were felt by paddlers not only as they explored rivers further from the local paddling areas, but across the country as well. The influence of the Act cannot be downplayed, particularly into the 1960's.

Many women paddling in the '50s were spouses of paddlers: Barbara DuBois (wife of Eliot) and May Jane Sawyer (wife of Fred) of AMC, Edie McNair (wife of Bob) of Buck Ridge, and Paula Zuk (wife of Larry) of CWWA. However, single women, or women with non-paddling spouses, were also involved in whitewater. AMC had Marjorie Hurd (an early open canoeist), Helen Fair, Ruth Walker, and Louise Davis among others. Carol Kane of Colorado was a racer, downriver and slalom, one of the few in the country at the time. Sierra Club's Elsa Bailey participated in many trips, and even had a rapids named after her– Bailey Falls on the Stanislaus.

New England

AMC was *the* club in New England primarily due to chapters that expanded and developed throughout the region. Their activities influenced many paddlers through technique and safety instruction and club-sponsored competition and trips. AMC's influence was also felt nationally through the involvement of its members in AWWA committees and activities. In 1958, the Inter-Chapter White Water Committee formed to share information, establish a uniform rating system for rivers and canoeists, sponsor races, and communicate with other organizations, particularly AWWA. Eliot DuBois, one of AWWA's founders and a proponent for slalom racing, continued his support and involvement in AMC's slalom racing efforts, working closely with Bob McNair of Buck Ridge. The first Eastern White Water Slalom Championships were held on the West River at Salmon Hole in 1958, co-sponsored by AMC and Buck Ridge.

In the latter '50s, AMC expanded its club-sponsored trips beyond its rivers in New England. In 1955, AMC sponsored a month-long series of trips in the West that included the Yampa through Yampa Canyon, the Green through Lodore, Echo Park, Whirlpool Canyon, Split Mountain Canyon, and the Salmon River in Idaho. Hatch River Expeditions provided the support for these trips.

By this time, approximately 400 of AMC's 6,000 total membership were active in whitewater canoeing. Trip schedules for the combined chapters totaled more than sixty using fleets of 17-foot shoe-keeled Grumman canoes for whitewater canoeing. AMC also developed what was considered an excellent safety program based on teamwork, and a rating system for paddlers based on skill and experience. Paddlers were rated as novice, intermediate, expert or instructor, ratings that also matched the river ratings from novice to expert. Leaders and co-leaders took registration for trips. Because leaders were not always familiar with all of the new paddlers, the chairman in charge of canoeing activities kept a file of all canoeists in contact with AMC (members and non-members alike). The file actually contained a record of a canoeist's qualifications as rated against AMC standards. "This is actually a simple and workable system that has developed with the recognition that whitewater canoeing must be a 'controlled' group sport." [52]

In 1959, the death of a novice member during a training session greatly affected AMC and challenged their safety record. The tragedy occurred on the Charles River in late March during a training session sponsored by the White Water Canoeing Committee. While practicing strokes on a flatwater pond above the dam in Waterton, a husband and wife team, wearing no life jackets, was swept over the dam. The husband was trapped in the hydraulic while the wife was swept downstream. Icy water and the lack of a life jacket were contributors to his death. The death shocked AMC members and resulted in a great deal of internal assessment of AMC's training and safety practices. It also helped to stir additional debate regarding the rating of paddlers.

Mid-Atlantic

Considerable growth in whitewater paddling occurred in the mid-Atlantic region in the latter '50s with the formation of four new clubs involved in whitewater. Buck Ridge Ski Club was the only club until a group of paddlers formed the Canoe Cruisers Association (CCA), specifically as a whitewater club, followed by two other clubs, which, like Buck Ridge, did not initially form solely for whitewater activities. These later clubs were the Penn State Outing Club (PSOC) and Explorer Post 32. A fourth, the Kayak and Canoe Club of New York (KCCNY) organized specifically for whitewater at the end of the '50s, becoming one of the first clubs in the East to emphasize kayaking as much as canoeing.

Since Buck Ridge members viewed slalom competition as a valuable skill-building activity, the club's involvement in slalom competition and instruction dominated activities throughout the'50s. It included support of slalom racing through its annual Brandywine Slalom and co-sponsorship of other races with neighboring AMC chapters.

Just two years after their first introduction to slalom in 1953, the effect of slalom racing and correspondence with other AWWA affiliates was evident in Buck Ridge's whitewater canoeing skills, which were disseminated through instruction and river trips. Under the leadership of Bob McNair, Buck Ridge in conjunction with the Southeastern Chapter of the American Red Cross began conducting basic canoeing courses in 1955, which became known as the "Red Ridge College of Canoeing Knowledge." (The name "Red Ridge" was formed from the combination of Red Cross and Buck Ridge.) The course lasted three days and was held at a YWCA camp with access to rivers with novice to intermediate whitewater for instruction. [*Author's note:* Red Ridge was emulated by groups in the East for canoe instruction into the '70s, often using McNair's Basic River Canoeing as the manual.] As with Washington Foldboat Club's course, the Red Ridge course provided lectures on "fluid flow and water reading." [53] The course was held every other year and drew paddlers from up and down the East Coast and the Midwest.

[52] Sawyer, Fred. "White Water Canoeing with the AMC." *American Whitewater* Vol. 3 No. 3 (Fall 1957): 4–6.

[53] Wilhoyte, Jeff. "The Red Ridge College of River Canoeing Knowledge." *American Whitewater* Vol. I No. 2 (August 1955): 17.

In addition to slalom competition sponsorship and instruction, Buck Ridge was also actively involved in river trips. By 1958, the club schedule included seven weekends for skilled and expert paddlers including the Cheat River, and seventeen relatively easy moving water weekends for less experienced members. Because members participated in races wherever possible, they often took advantage of paddling other nearby rivers. During race trips in Colorado, members paddled many different rivers.

In May of 1956, the Montgomery Sycamore Island Club on the Potomac near D.C. (founded in 1885 for fishing, paddling and swimming) sponsored the first Potomac River Whitewater Race. The race was actually the idea of Andrew J. (Andy) Thomas, a flatwater racer associated with the Washington Canoe Club in D.C., to get publicity for whitewater in the hopes of getting ACA to recognize whitewater as a viable sport. The race ran from the base of Great Falls to Sycamore Island. The race committee was comprised of a small group of paddlers with Andy Thomas as chairman and included Bob Harrigan. The Montgomery Sycamore Island Club's only real involvement was that it was the finish line for the race. The committee required that all racers be good swimmers and "at home in whitewater," as approved by the race committee. Among the racers that first year were O.K. Goodwin in a foldboat, Bob Harrigan and Phil Scott in a tandem canoe, and John Berry and Ramone Eaton in solo canoes.

The committee was pleased with the turnout for the race and decided to organize as a club for whitewater activities. The Canoe Cruisers Association was founded during the fall with Andy Thomas (considered the founding father), Bob Harrigan, Roger Arnold, Jim Johnson, and Osgood Smith as founding members. Their intention was to sponsor regular paddling schedules as well as periodic training courses such as the White Water Training Program that was first held in September of 1956, just before the club's actual formation. Others including Dick Bridge and John Berry, who later became two of the clubs prominent members, joined soon after the club was formed.

In the first few years, CCA established three activities: organized trips, yearly instruction (for members and non-members), and an annual Potomac River Whitewater Race. The early trips were primarily family-oriented, but as members' skills developed, they explored rivers beyond the local Potomac area.

Exposure to Buck Ridge and the Brandywine Slalom drew some paddlers toward racing. Soon, two contingents developed racers led by Berry and Harrigan, and cruisers led by Andy Thomas. However, some racers, like Berry and Harrigan, also continued their cruising in earnest, using their whitewater slalom skills to explore more complex rivers.

Exploration for Berry and Harrigan opened up when Burmeister's book became available in 1957. Burmeister rated Confluence to Ohiopyle, the Middle section on the Youghiogheny (Yough) in southwestern Pennsylvania as Class IV. They paddled it and found it relatively easy for them, so they ran the Loop section. Later the same year, along with CCA members Osgood Smith and Jim Johnson, they paddled the Lower Yough.

John Berry began canoeing as a boy near Winchester, Virginia, during the mid-'30s. He bought his first canoe, a Thompson, in the late '30s and started paddling on the Potomac. After receiving his business degree from Wharton, he lived in the D.C. area paddling mostly alone on area rivers. On one of his trips on the Shenandoah, he ran into Randy Carter and Ray Eaton and from them, found out about CCA, a club that was forming in the D.C. area. (Berry was one of the few early influential white-water paddlers who was not an engineer.)

Dick Bridge attended the White Water Training Program in September 1956 after noticing an ad in a Washington paper about a canoeing class. He became one of the first members after CCA's founding. He was also the father of (now) three generations of cruisers and racers with his sons, Charles and John, and grandson, Andy.

John Berry on the Yough (PA) in a 16-foot Old Town guide model, 1958—courtesy of John Berry.

Also that same year, Berry and Harrigan ran sections of the upper Cheat in West Virginia. In the spring of 1957, they ran the Cheat Gorge for the first time, which included an unexpected over night stay at High Falls with Dick Bridge, Todd Miles, and Earl Mosburg. Over Labor Day weekend, Berry and Harrigan led a group on the New in West Virginia, putting in above Thurmond and taking out at Fayette Station three days later. Soon the Yough, Cheat, and New became regular club trips for advanced paddlers. (Because of the absence of interstates, these trips often occurred over long weekends.)

In the fall of 1957, Berry and Harrigan marked the bridge support at Albright for the Cheat canyon using Randy Carter's system. They estimated that their trip the previous spring was probably at 1½ feet and made arrangements with Pete Morgan, the gas station owner at the bridge, to send them daily postcards with the recorded water level from the bridge. During the winter of 1958, five CCA members began planning a whitewater film of the Cheat Canyon from Albright to Jenkinsburg. The group led by Harrigan, included Berry, Bridge, Miles, and Mosburg, the original group that ran the Canyon the first time. The river's wild beauty and remote grandeur impressed all of them. Their plans included renting two Bolex H-16 three-lens cameras and using 16 mm Kodachrome single perforation film to permit the addition of a sound track. From their trip on the Cheat the previous spring, they determined that the ideal level was probably around 2½ to 3 feet. They also knew that it would probably take two or three trips to film all of the footage they envisioned.

After a very wet April and May, the level did not drop below 3 feet until May 22nd soon after which the filming began. The actual filming took three 3-day trips. Harrigan, Miles, and Berry paddled 15-foot solo canoes while Bridge and Mosburg paddled an 18-foot tandem Grumman. As with any movie making, it required much scouting, set-up, and rehearsal. However, the outcome was included in a 25-minute movie narrated by Bob Belton (a Navy doctor) titled *Give Us a River.* It was probably the first movie in the East to document the sport of whitewater.

The CCA was primarily a canoeing club throughout much of the '50s. It was not until Dan Sullivan ran into Berry, Harrigan, and Bridge who told him of a newly formed club, that a foldboater joined the canoeists. Sullivan began paddling with them and while they introduced him to rivers in the East, he introduced them to rivers in the West. In 1959, Harrigan, Berry, and Bridge joined Sullivan on the Yampa. Like members of AMC and Buck Ridge, CCA members, predominantly canoeists, traveled West to explore and expand their paddling skills.

Dan Sullivan canoed as a teenager but his dream during undergraduate and law school was to paddle a kayak on rivers around the country. After completing his law degree in 1953, he purchased a Klepper T6 and paddled on rivers in the mid-Atlantic. The next two years, 1954 and 1955, he traveled to Colorado and paddled the Colorado near Grand Junction, the Roaring Fork, and the Crystal, running into and paddling with western boaters on some of the rivers. On his first trip to Colorado, a colleague of Ron Bohlender showed Sullivan how to roll. When he returned home, he practiced his roll eventually replacing his paddle with a cedar shingle, making it smaller and smaller until he could hand roll a foldboat. Every summer for the next several years, Sullivan returned to the west, paddling the Yampa and Green Rivers along with Cataract Canyon, and Glen Canyon of the Colorado.

Although cruising was Sullivan's real interest, he also competed in slalom and wildwater races and traveled to Colorado for the Salida race a few times during the '50s. The first time he went to the Salida race he flew to Denver and borrowed a boat from Ron Bohlender to race in. He shipped back two of Bohlender's kayaks that were fiberglass hulls with decks of Herculite, the first to arrive in the East.

In central Pennsylvania, whitewater activities developed in two different organizations that were involved in outdoor activities in the latter '50s: the Penn State Outing Club (PSOC) and Explorer Post 32, a Boy Scout explorer post. Under the leadership of Tom Smythe, a faculty advisor associated with Penn State University, PSOC's outdoor activities grew to include whitewater canoeing. By 1959, PSOC with about 950 members was considered the largest among university outing clubs and had a separate canoeing division. With Bill Bickham as the Canoe Division chairman, they sponsored nineteen trips on rivers up through Class III. A few members also had the skills to handle open canoes on more advanced rivers, scouting and running Black Moshannon Creek, sixteen miles of a remote river with 870 feet of vertical drop.

Boy Scout troops and Explorer Posts became involved in whitewater to different extents across the country in the '50s. In the East, whitewater canoeing dominated. However, in the West rafts were considered the whitewater craft of choice. The location of a large military surplus facility in the Salt Lake City area facilitated the use of rafts among troops and posts in the region. Three Boy Scout organizations from South Cottonwood Ward (Salt Lake Council, Utah), Twin Falls (Idaho), and Los Alamos (New Mexico) Explorer Post became the source of river boatmen for commercial outfitters throughout the West.

The Salt Lake City Council of the Boy Scouts of America started an outdoor adventure program for their Explorer Scouts. Scout leader John Cross (Senior) from Orem, Utah, bought surplus life and assault rafts and led the first trip of Explorers through Glen Canyon in 1947. After a few years, the Explorer program was discontinued, although a few other Scout leaders, including John Cross, Al Quist, and Malcolm "Moki-Mac" Ellington, continued with trips and exposed a whole generation of scouts to river running. The Snake River Council in Twin Falls, Idaho, also sponsored rafting, beginning with their first Middle Fork of the Salmon trip in 1959. The Snake River Councils still maintains an institutional/commercial permit on the Middle Fork.

However, Los Alamos Explorer Post 20 was responsible for starting many young men in their careers as boatmen. Earl Perry, author and boatman wrote: "For years the Post was a mother of boatmen—the alumni populated river outfits all over the west."[54] In 1956, James H. (Stretch) Fretwell and Robert C. Emigh unsuccessfully tried to form a post around a core of outdoor activities in Los Alamos. Rafting, however, worked. Stretch and his wife Patricia were the main advisors. In 1957, they hired Ken Sleight to take the Post on the San Juan. Within a year, the Post began running rivers with their own surplus military rafts and equipment. The Post ran one- and two-day trips on rivers like the Rio Grande, Conejos, and Rio Chama, and one- or two-week trips on the Salmon, Cataract Canyon, Lodore, and Desolation Canyon. In 1960, the Post made a final run of Glen Canyon before its inundation.

The Post used small five-man life rafts and developed many specialized techniques for their use in river running. The rafts were considered the smallest practical size for running heavy rapids and held two Explorers, an oarsman and a passenger with their gear. The Post developed their own rowing practices that proved effective on rivers less than 16,000 cfs. For heavy whitewater, they followed the practice established earlier by Galloway of turning the stern downstream, bow upstream, so that the oarsman could face the rapids.

[*Author's note:* The Post is over 40 years old and shows no sign of dying. It includes both young men and women. Some alumni including Dave Carlson and Russell Sullivan established their own river-running operations. Many more became professional boatmen.]

On May 30, 1959, three PSOC members, Bill Bickham, Dave Kurtz, and Tom Smyth, drove to Ohiopyle with three Grumman canoes and ran the Lower Yough scouting, running, and lining their way down to Indian Creek. The next day they ran the Upper Yough from Sang Run to Friendsville, perhaps a first descent. They lost a canoe to the river. Bickham, in a 15-foot Grumman, thought he could run a slot, but he did not make it. He hiked out after unsuccessful attempts to unwedge the canoe.

Concurrently in the latter '50s, Kurtz, a graduate student at Penn State and member of PSOC, established Explorer Post 32. Although the post focused on a variety of outdoor activities in its early years, by 1957, canoeing had become one of their main activities. Through Kurtz's association with PSOC, he developed skills that he passed onto his Explorers. Through AWWA, he also became aware of slalom racing. Following directions in articles in *American Whitewater,* Kurtz made slalom poles and set up a slalom course to introduce the Explorers to slalom racing using Grummans.

The fourth group to organize for whitewater activities in the mid-Atlantic was the Kayak and Canoe Club of New York (KCCNY), which officially formed in January, 1959 with Peter Whitney as the first chairman. Situated

[54] Perry, Earl. Correspondence to author 22 December 1998.

between AMC and Buck Ridge, they learned from both organizations. But, like AWWA, KCCNY chose a more loosely structured organization. Unlike AMC and Buck Ridge, the group was comprised of both open canoeists in Grummans and double (tandem) foldboaters. With importers of European foldboats in the New York City area, a variety of foldboats were available to club members including Klepper, Pioneer, Sioux-Hart, and Cheaveaux. The emphasis on kayaking was certainly integral to its membership since the word kayak was in the club's name and KCCNY was essentially the first club in the East to emphasize kayaking as much as canoeing.

In addition to the availability of European foldboats, the New York City area also offered the benefits of European foldboaters who contributed to the advancement of American paddlers in the club, as had occurred in Colorado, but on a smaller scale. Paul Bruhin, a Swiss watchmaker, came to New York City in 1959 and stayed for two years. During that time, he exposed numerous paddlers, both within and outside the club, to the Duffek stroke. Bruhin is credited with the spread of the stroke's use in the East.

Southeast

Although whitewater clubs did not appear in the Southeast until the late '60s, the camps of the southern Appalachians, with their strong whitewater paddling programs, continued to grow and exposed many young campers to whitewater canoeing. As soon as Grumman canoes were available, many of the camps turned to them for instructional use, which further advanced their efforts in whitewater canoeing instruction. Key camp instructors and facilitators for whitewater in the Southeast included Frank Bell (Senior), Hugh Caldwell, John Delabar, Ramone Eaton, and Fritz Orr (Senior).

Under Frank Bell's leadership, Camp Mondamin for boys and Camp Green Cove for girls continued to introduce young men and women to whitewater canoeing. Bell's friend Ramone Eaton, Vice President of the American Red Cross, introduced Bell to canoeing the Nanatahala and Chattooga Rivers during the late '40s and early '50s. Through their friendship, Eaton's experience with the Red Cross's canoe instruction influenced many different camps in the Southeast, though the instruction was modified based on Eaton's own whitewater canoeing experience.

John Delabar, a teacher in the D.C. area, was also an active instructor and proponent of whitewater instruction at Camp Mondamin, spending almost twenty-five years teaching canoeing at the camp. Although aluminum canoes were not as easily damaged, he taught his campers to be just as careful with them on the river as they would be in wood and canvas canoes. He felt that because aluminum had a tendency to stick to rocks, it was even more critical to develop the skills to avoid rocks rather than to run over or into them.

Camp Tate, owned by Fritz Orr, also had an emphasis on whitewater canoeing. Before its closure in 1938, it exposed a young camper, Hugh Caldwell, to whitewater canoeing which became a life-long interest. As an adult Caldwell, a professor of philosophy at the University of the South in Sewanee, Tennessee, spent his summers working at camps. In 1952, he made a solo descent of Section III of the Chattooga in an 18-foot Grumman, unaware of the run's difficulty prior to the start. That same year, Caldwell was introduced to the Nantahala by Ramone Eaton, also an instructor at the camp. His friendship with Eaton contributed to Caldwell's development as a whitewater facilitator and pioneer in the Southeast, including his role as director of Camp Merrie-Woode's canoeing and tripping program.

Camp Merrie-Woode, one of the oldest camps for girls in the Southeast, was purchased by Fritz Orr who expanded the camp's canoeing program. With the help of Ramone Eaton and Hugh Caldwell, the camp became known for the instruction of young women in whitewater canoeing, just as Camp Mondamin had for young men.

Midwest

Although often a good distance from whitewater rivers, clubs organized in the Midwest from western Pennsylvania to Wisconsin, Arkansas, and Missouri. Canoeing groups with strong whitewater programs developed in both Pittsburgh and Columbus through American Youth Hostel (AYH) clubs exploring rivers throughout Pennsylvania and northern West Virginia including some of the first pioneering runs on the Yough. (CCA members on the Yough for the first time in 1956 saw the remains of a wooden canoe with AYH on the bow, presumably from Pittsburgh AYH.)

In Chicago, the Prairie Club, headed by Harold Kiehm, was already established when AWWA formed. (Harold Kiehm was one of the founders of AWWA.) The Hoofers, associated with the University of Wisconsin in Madison, developed their own whitewater group exploring the rivers of Wisconsin and Minnesota. (Cal Giddings, of Utah, started his whitewater canoeing in Grummans with the Hoofers while doing post-doc work at the University of Wisconsin.) The Ozark Wilderness Waterways Club started in the fall of 1956 under the guidance of Oz Hawksley. (Oz Hawksley was one of AWWA's founders.) Their most direct inter-club contact was with CWWA during the '50s that started as an exchange of information between Hawksley and Larry Zuk of CWWA and developed into inter-club river trips. Both clubs participated in joint trips on the San Juan and Colorado rivers in the late '50s.

Inter-Mountains

The races at Salida provided an opportunity for many Colorado paddlers to get together once a year not only to compete against one another, but to swap stories and information. From this evolved other occasional gatherings, story swapping, and movie sessions. Many paddlers took movies (8mm and 16mm movies) of their river trips and showed their films at club gatherings. Larry Zuk moved to Colorado in the early '50s and became involved in canoe instruction for the Denver Red Cross where he met other paddlers and heard about the growing interest in whitewater paddling. Interested in expanding on the occasional gatherings, Zuk sent a letter in April, 1954 to twenty-one "canoe[i]sts and whitewater enthusiasts"[55] including Keith Anderson, Steve Bradley, Tyson Dines, Clyde Jones, Larry Jump, Roy Kerswill, Lt. Joe Lacy, Willie Schaeffler, Dave Stacey, and Dick Stratton. In the letter, he called for a meeting to "establish a friendly type of local organization for the exchange of river information and to discuss the possibilities of developing more slalom

[55] Zuk, Larry. Correspondence address listing, 13 April 1954.

races, canoe courses in techniques and safety and to schedule more group cruises for this summer."[56] The result was the formation of the Colorado White Water Association (CWWA) in 1955.

Both cruising (river running) and racing were club activities from the start. A Cruise Committee was formed in 1955 and provided a trip schedule starting at the end of May and going through Labor Day weekend. Their first year's schedule included trips on the South Platte, Cache La Poudre, Arkansas, Blue, Eagle, Gunnison, and Colorado Rivers. The Salida race and Clear Creek Race, a slalom race sponsored by the club, were also on their first schedule.

In 1956, paddlers from Buck Ridge joined a group of paddlers from Colorado and ran the Yampa and the Green. The group, composed of four kayaks and two canoes, included Erich Seidel, Roger Paris and two others in kayak, and the McNairs and Zuks in the two canoes (open canoes with spray covers). Hatch Expeditions, with regular rafting customers, provided support for the paddlers. Roger Paris played in Moonshine in Split Mountain Canyon on the Green, which was considered a daredevil stunt at the time.

By the late '50s, CWWA trips regularly included runs on the Yampa, Colorado, Gunnison, Arkansas, Roaring Fork, Poudre, North and South Platte, Blue Taylor, Clear Creek, Eagle, and Rio Grande Rivers. The club had a membership of more than 100 in the combined Denver, Boulder, and Greeley areas.

Although CWWA was like other clubs with their support of cruising and race schedules, CWWA members had two other interests that the other clubs had not yet developed: building with fiberglass and designing new boats. CWWA's newsletter, *The Spray,* became one of the vehicles used to disseminate information on how to build with fiberglass and where to buy materials for boat building. Articles by Steve Bradley and Dave Stacey, Larry Monninger, Roy Kerswill, Larry Zuk, and others often first appeared in *The Spray* even before *American Whitewater.* The other vehicle was in learning-by-doing, sharing boat-building information by working with other experienced builders.

Many CWWA members became innovators in designing and building boats. One of Bradley's and Stacey's earliest kayak designs, the Salmon, was produced by many paddlers in the region. A scout troop in New Mexico re-produced about twenty-five kayaks for their troop. Larry Zuk built his first kayak in 1955, the Falcon, from a mold he built based on a Klepper slalom kayak design. In the late '50s, Ron Bohlender designed and built fiberglass kayak hulls with Herculite decks. New canoe designs were also popular, modeled after the fiberglass canoe of Roessinger and Dussuet at Salida. Zuk teamed with Larry Monninger in 1957 to build their version of the decked canoe that was one of the first versions of a truly closed canoe, or C-2. Art Kidder changed the Roessinger and Dussuet design, incorporating bow and stern cockpits along with a center cockpit for carrying gear, which was also classified a C-2. (Kidder's C-2 predated the Old Town "Berrigan" designed by John Berry and Bob Harrigan in the '60s.) In 1959, Zuk designed and built a closed solo canoe (a C-1), the Merlin, with an elongated centered cockpit. All in all, during the late '50s, CWWA members built the first fiberglass kayaks, C-2s, and C-1s, many of which were the first American designs.

By 1957, CWWA members were well known to Don Hatch who solicited their business offering trips down the Grand Canyon and Middle Fork of the Salmon. He particularly pushed the Middle Fork and Main Salmon trips as appealing to the "small boat enthusiast."[57]

[56] Zuk, Larry. Correspondence to "Fellow River Rat(s)." 14 April 1954.

[57] Hatch, Don. Correspondence to "Fellow River Rats." 23 January 1957.

CWWA members in their fiberglass kayaks made many first descents in Colorado in the '50s. These kayaks allowed them to explore smaller volume rivers than previously permitted because of the limitations imposed by raft size, or suitability of open canoes, or the durability of foldboats.

Another innovator was Leslie (Les) Jones, a civil engineer from Heber City, Utah. His river-running experience began by helping his cousin Don Hatch (son of Bus Hatch) run float trips for the Sierra Club. In the early '50s, Jones designed and modified his own boats for river running using an oar-rigged decked aluminum canoe for his solo runs. Jones also designed and built an aluminum kayak. To record his solo runs, he mounted a camera on a football helmet with an inverted paint can over it for protection. In 1954 and 1955, he ran Cataract Canyon by himself before Lake Powell covered up the worst drops. In 1957, he rowed the Grand Canyon, also solo. Later that year he also rowed, again a solo run, from the Gates of Lodore to the mouth of Split Mountain Canyon in less than ten hours. The next year, Jones made a solo run through Glen Canyon at high water in record time. His 300-mile run from Lee's Ferry to Temple Bar on Lake Mead took only six days. When the gates of Glen Canyon Dam were closed in 1963, Jones and Ulrich Martin (a champion German kayaker) ran the Colorado at record low water in kayaks. Jones used his custom-built aluminum kayak that was only 19 inches in width.

California

Although a few small clubs, like the White Water Klub of Sacramento, developed whitewater activities, whitewater paddling in California primarily developed from Sierra Club's Bay Chapter RTS. Under the leadership of Bruce Grant, all of Sierra Club's River Touring Sections continued a strong alliance with AWWA. Bay Chapter's RTS organized both instructional and cruising activities. However, because it was a section of a Sierra Club chapter, both paddlers and non-paddlers participated in whitewater trips with rafts provided for the non-paddlers. With conservation as the cornerstone of the Sierra Club, conservation-oriented paddling activities included both cruising and what were called obituary trips on rivers destined for inundation.

Many of Bay Chapter's paddlers were avid foldboaters including Elsa Bailey, Frank (Red) Cockerline, Maynard Munger, Fen Salter, Carl Trost, and Bryce Whitmore who made many first descents on rivers in California and Oregon. Standard foldboating runs in the late '50s included the American at Fair Oaks (the Yough of the West), the Molekumne below Powerhouse (a standard beginners run), the Merced, and the Feather before the Oroville dam was built that inundated the upper gorge. The American in particular provided a full range of whitewater conditions, and along with its proximity to San Francisco and Sacramento, became a popular destination and proving ground for whitewater paddlers.

Under the leadership of Bryce Whitmore, the year 1958 was one of the most ambitious in the '50s for sponsored outings starting with training programs and included pool sessions to teach bracing and rolling. The year's trip schedule included the Yampa and Green Rivers through Dinosaur National Monument, the Green through Lodore Canyon, Glen Canyon with Georgie White (an obituary trip to see the canyon before the dam construction was complete), and the Main Salmon with Hatch Expeditions. Paddlers from the

East joined in on the Salmon trip, including the Rupp brothers from Buck Ridge who paddled tandem open canoe. Roger Paris was also on the trip working as a boatman for Hatch.

Over the years, many Sierra Club members ran into Roger Paris on different river trips throughout the West, often when Paris worked for Hatch Expeditions but sometimes when he paddled on his own. On some occasions, Paris joined them on rivers, and although many members wore big kapock life jackets, he never wore one. After all, he had a dependable roll. His example sparked some members to stop wearing life jackets. However, on one trip, when Paris joined Sierra Club paddlers on the Feather, he dumped in a Class III drop and swam; he did not roll his kayak. That reversed the trend he had started earlier. Many figured if Paris could swim in a Class III drop then they most certainly could also and started wearing their life jackets again.

In the mid-'50s, members began experimenting with fiberglass construction. One of the first members was Bryce Whitmore, a chemist, who obtained samples of polyester resin. His first kayak was a fiberglass version of a Klepper foldboat. He used silicone as a mold release and layed up fiberglass directly on the foldboat. His second design, the Peanut, was less than 10 feet in length. Instead of laying up fiberglass on an existing kayak, he built a mold using cross-sections of wood at 1-foot intervals and lithograph plates (thin aluminum plates) to span between the cross-sections. The plates left abrupt joints at the transitions in the hull making a very crude mold. Subsequent molds for longer kayak designs were made the same way and were used by many club members to build their own kayaks.

RTS later progressed to plaster and then finally fiberglass molds in the '60s. The club made a new mold every year and rented out the molds for $10 making up to $1,000 per year on mold rental alone.

DURING THE '50s, Tom Johnson continued with his own innovations, although they were not completely paddling oriented. He made some of the first fiberglass helmets for Lockheed for fighter pilots. The helmets were a customized hand lay-up with a crushable urethane foam liner. This work brought him in contact with an attorney who handled a patent dispute between Lockheed and DuPont over use of the urethane foam. The patent attorney later asked Johnson if he could make fiberglass gun stocks filled with rigid urethane foam, which he did. The process he developed used by Armalite to make military survival guns. One of the men he worked with at Armalite eventually became Vice President of Hollowform, a custom rotational molder in southern California.

Pacific Northwest

Washington Foldboat Club continued their instructional, cruising, and slalom racing activities throughout the '50s. Their instructional program, like Buck Ridge's Red Ridge College, was an important part of the clubs' activities. The club continued to offer their "River Touring" course through Seattle's downtown YMCA. The course supported the club's membership growth with about twenty new members each year. Course materials evolved with Wolf Bauer as the principle instructor supported by his ongoing research into whitewater paddling technique and river hydrology.

The "River Touring" course offered by Washing Foldboat Club included topics that covered equipment, technique, party management, and navigation. Equipment included the care and treatment of foldboats, and students were taught to assemble and disassemble foldboats properly.

Technique covered all the strokes necessary for handling the kayak on moving water. Back paddling and back ferrying and the strokes necessary to accomplish back ferrying were the predominant aspects of the technique. The paddle brace was basic to the course. (The paddle was long and the kayaker could therefore shift hands to further extend the brace.) Back paddling was also a key ingredient to back ferrying.

In his research of river hydrology and characteristics of the local rivers, Bauer determined there were ten classic problems encountered by kayakers and taught these in the course. The classic problems were narrow, tight, and cluttered bends; headwall bends with or without whirl-eddy, fences, or surges; S-turns with bouncing current; side-slip riffles; split two-level channels; flood channels; deep vertical-surge eddy channels; graveyard sections at green and white eddy stage; full roller-eddy rapids; and single or multi-stage drops.[58]

Party management covered both safety and rescue. Safety incorporated the use of a scout or lead boat along with a sweep boat and river signals, developed by the club used on each trip. Lines and painters with flotation were installed on each kayak so that whenever the paddler flipped, the kayak could be pulled into a nearby eddy. Throw lines, first aid kits, and repair materials were all a part of managing the party. The repair materials consisted of tool glue, clamps, twine and electrical tape.

The term river touring was appropriate for many of the club's activities. River trips included overnights similar to multiple-day wilderness trips. Their foldboats were designed to carry gear for overnight camping, but not for small tight and technical rivers of the rivers higher in elevation in the coastal mountains. As a result, their trips were focused around larger rivers in the area, or sections of rivers at lower elevations with more water and less elevation gradients. This did not change until club members began building and using fiberglass kayaks in the mid-'60s, one of the last cornerstone clubs to do so.

Canada

Two whitewater clubs also organized in Canada in the '50s were influenced by their proximity to American clubs and their own European immigrants. In the West, the British Columbia Kayak and Canoe Club (BCKCC) organized in Vancouver, British Columbia in the mid-'50s became the first Canadian AWWA affiliate. With its close proximity to Seattle, the club participated in inter-club activities with Washington Foldboat Club.

The Vancouver area, like Seattle, Toronto, and New York City, had a number of immigrants with paddling experience or connections in Europe. Vernon Rupp, a well-known Vancouver paddler, had a connection through relatives to one of the most influential clubs in Europe, the Kayak Klub of Rosenheim (KKR), whose membership included Hans Klepper, and later Toni Prijon.

In the East, Ontario Voyageurs organized to include paddlers around metropolitan Toronto. Like other large metropolitan area such as New York City, the club had a number of European immigrants among its members. With its proximity to New England and the Mid-Atlantic, Ontario Voyageurs participated in inter-club activities with AMC and Buck Ridge including slalom races. Many of the club's members were also very actively involved with AWWA, including George Siposs who was the Racing Editor for *American Whitewater.*

[58] Bauer, Wolf. "Introduction to River Navigation." *American Whitewater* Vol. V No. 3 (November 1959): 17–20.

Whitewater's Industry

Whitewater and paddlesports in general lacked a real industry from which to buy products. Wood and canvas canoe manufacturers like Old Town and Chestnut, and aluminum canoe manufacturers, primarily Grumman, were the industry, often supplying the few accessories, such as paddles, that were available. With the exception of Folbot in New York and Whalecraft in Chicago, all other foldboat manufacturers were European. Many other accessories were either homemade or borrowed from other sporting activities. Army surplus was a good source of waterproof bags and wool clothing for whitewater paddling. There were still few how-to books and very few guidebooks. Each club, or group of paddlers, explored unknown territory with regard to the sport of whitewater. However, in spite of the many obstacles, the sport continued to grow throughout the '50s.

An indication of growth is the recognition that there is a market for goods or services. By the mid-'50s, the popularity of whitewater paddling gained the attention of the boating industry, in particular, the aluminum boat industry. Grumman (called the Metal Boat Company in Marathon, New York) was joined in the market for aluminum canoes by Aluma Craft Boat Company in Minneapolis, Arkansas Traveler Boats in Little Rock, Star Metal Boat Company in Goshen, Indiana, and Freeland Sons Company in Sturgis, Michigan.

Competition for the foldboat market increased with the importation of most of the major European foldboats including Hammer Foldboats by Banton Corporation in San Francisco (retailed by Ski-Hut in Berkeley), Hart-Sioux (French) by Foldcraft in Pennsylvania, Klepper in New York, and Pioneer Foldboats by Sportsman's Equipment Company in Pennsylvania. By the late '50s, Klepper had six models of foldboats: the slalom, the T-65 (combination design for slalom and touring), the T-66 (for the racer who wants more room and stability), the T-6 (single touring), T-8 (double touring), and the Aerius (a large unsinkable touring kayak with built in sponsons).

By the late '50s, fiberglass was no longer an experimental material and fiberglass boats, both kayaks and canoes, competed with all the other materials. In 1957, Colorado Kayaks of Greeley, Colorado, began advertising in *American Whitewater.* The ad read:

> All New—Fiberglass Kayaks; very light weight, permanent color, practically indestructible, no upkeep. Just the boat you're looking for! No more worries about rocks and snags. This boat designed specifically for use in whitewater by members of the Colorado White Water Association.[59]

The following year, Waterways Unlimited of Denver also began advertising in *American Whitewater.* Their ad was for "the only true whitewater canoe, designed especially for river running." The canoe was described as "a revolutionary sleek design made of tough, resilient fiberglass" and very lightweight at 80 pounds with the cover. It was 17 feet long, 36 inches wide, 14 inches deep with 5 inch rocker, no external keel, and with under-gunwale flotation and steel ends. The watertight cover had kneeling bags to "allow canoe to be righted and reentered right in the middle of the rapid!"[60] Waterways Unlimited, owned by Larry Monninger and Marion Schultz borrowed

[59] Colorado Kayaks. Advertisement. *American Whitewater* Vol. 3 No. 3 (Fall 1957): 20.

[60] Waterways Unlimited. Advertisement. *American Whitewater* Vol. 4 No. 1 (Spring 1958): 26.

heavily from the first fiberglass canoe brought by the French teams for the races at Salida in 1952. Both the Rupp brothers and McNairs of Buck Ridge purchased canoes from Waterways Unlimited for whitewater canoeing.

In 1957, Pierre Marquette Fiberglass Boat Company of Scottville, Michigan, introduced a 16-foot fiberglass canoe. The canoe was the first commercially available fiberglass canoe to compete directly with Grumman. (Even Grumman entered the fiberglass canoe market for a short time in the early '60s.) The canoe was approved for use by the Boy Scouts after testing by the Boy Scout National Supply and was made available to scout and other camps across the country. The testing found that that it withstood "shocks and rough handling much better than conventional materials."[61]

By the end of the '50s, fiberglass canoes and kayaks along with aluminum canoes, began to make in-roads into the foldboat and traditional wood and canvas canoe markets. A few of the foldboat manufacturers, particularly Chauveau, espoused the ability of their foldboats to compete with the rigidity of a fiberglass kayak in competition while still being easily transportable (folding). Of the many wood and canvas canoe manufacturers, Old Town probably felt the most competition for their whitewater canoes by aluminum canoe manufacturers and backyard fiberglass builders. After all, their canoes had been used by AMC for whitewater in New England for years. In an ad in the Spring 1959 issue of *American Whitewater,* Old Town touted the use of their wood and canvas canoes, using a photo and endorsement from John Berry in his 16-foot Old Town canoe in the Cheat Canyon.

However, the same issue of *American Whitewater* contained a report for the first time on the availability of a new material for canoes. Thompson Royal-Craft of Cortland, New York, introduced their 16-foot Royal-Camper canoe made of Expanded Royalite. This material consisted of five layers, two outside skin layers for strength and durability with a center core layer of the same material but "blown" into a foam layer. Thompson Royal-Craft touted that the core layer therefore provided buoyancy that eliminated the need for built-in end tanks or styrofoam blocks. The color was impregnated into the outside layers that meant that no refinishing was required. AWWA reported, "The Thompson people had a sample of Royalite which they subjected to an impact test together with a 1/16 inch sheet of 61ST6 aluminum and a 1/8 inch fiberglass sheet. The Royalite showed up very favorably."[62] It took another thirteen years before this new material would leave its mark on whitewater canoeing.

[61] Editor. "New Products." *American Whitewater* Vol. 2 No. 4 (Winter 1957): 25.

[62] Editor. "Product Information." *American Whitewater* Vol. 5 No. 1 (Spring 1959): 38.

View from the Bridge

THE SPORT OF WHITEWATER IN AMERICA took shape in the '50s. Prosperity and modern materials, both the result of the end of World War II, helped to form that shape. Both also provided the impetus that grew the sport, contributing to the establishment of a foundation—its infrastructure—on which the sport could continue to build.

It was also a time of discovery. There was much excitement. The sport was young. It was new in so many different ways. There was so much to learn, to see, to try, so much to share. Paddlers in the '50s were like kids in a candy shop with all the new rivers to run and to explore using boats of the new materials with new techniques.

Events of the '50s also set in motion changes that revolutionized whitewater paddling as it had previously existed. The sport was not at its pinnacle as had been previously thought. The convergence of fiberglass construction and the Duffek stroke, both watershed events in their own right, contributed to a paradigm shift in thinking for whitewater. The interactions of new materials, design, and technique were well on their way to surpassing the previous pinnacle, onward toward the next.

Three small tributaries associated with new materials, the European influence of America, and whitewater competition entered the River. Draining their own unique watersheds, each tributary was fed by events, like cloudbursts, that added to their flow. As the River grew, fed by its tributaries, its current was also affected. Design and technique, the current, was not only influenced by the flow primarily from materials, but also by the other two tributaries. As the growing River surged, it entered a new region that helped to confine its flow within a streambed, which shaped and molded its flow and further defined the River, just as the growing infrastructure helped to define the new sport.

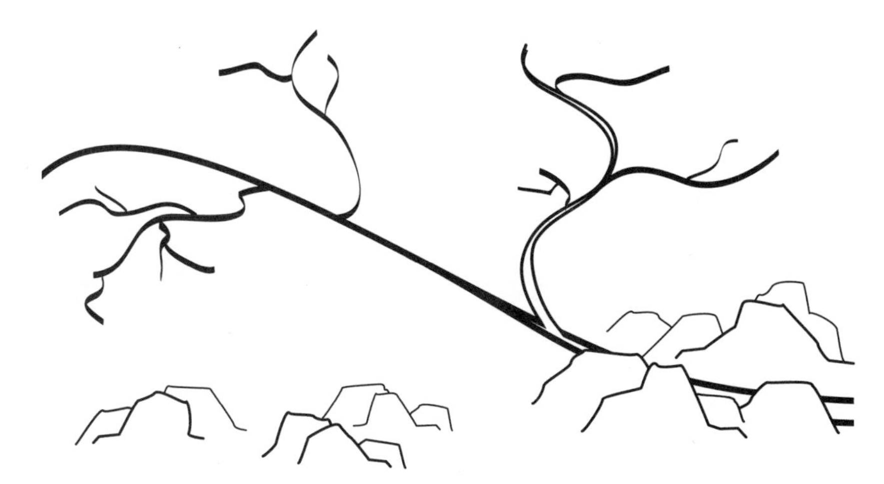

Toward the Diverging River: the '60s

DURING THE '50S, the fundamental elements of the sport were set; the cornerstones on which the infrastructure was built were laid. The '60s reinforced it all through growth; the addition of new clubs and paddlers, the influence of Europeans, and the growing market. Competition spread, contributing to the sport's growth in many different ways including ACA's role as the owner and facilitator of whitewater competition. AWA, too, continued its role as the steward of the sport and provided a medium for the exchange of ideas and information.

But the '60s were also a time for transition, from old thinking to new, and from old paddlers to young. Transitions also occurred from old materials to new (fabric and wood to fiberglass), from old designs to new (folding downriver kayaks and open canoes to slalom kayaks and closed canoes), and from old techniques to new (a series of individual strokes to a single Duffek). Fiberglass and competition cemented these transitions.

The '60s were also the beginning of the transition from the older, first generation of modern whitewater paddlers to young Baby Boomer paddlers, who were influenced by everything associated with the '60s in America. Older recreational weekend racers gave way to more serious, often younger racers who devoted considerable time and effort to winning, to competing with and against the Europeans with the ultimate goal of competing in the Olympics. All of this contributed to a divergence in the sport, between cruisers—river runners—and racers in the late '60s, that set the stage for the rapid changes that occurred in the '70s.

1960

First descent of Upper Gauley in rafts by Sayre Rodman and group

Natan Bernot helps young Explorers build European C-1s and C-2s

Stu Coffin and Bart Hauthaway, the first real manufacturers of whitewater canoes, kayaks, and paddles, began operations in New England

Last World Championships with F-1 and R-1 classes for kayaks

First commercial outfitters in Ohiopyle, Pennsylvania begin operations

1965

American back-yard builders and designers in full-swing copying and modifying European whitewater designs

American racer break into top ten at '67 World Championships, (Barb Wright in K-1W) in Lipno, Czechoslovakia

First descent of Gauley in kayaks and C-1s led by John Sweet

ICF announces inclusion of slalom in '72 Olympics in Germany

1970

Competition

Competition's role as a facilitator for the developing sport grew into the '60s. It not only provided advancements in technique and designs used for competition, it also benefitted cruising. With their sport's infrastructure established during the '50s, American paddlers now had an opportunity to catch up, to narrow the skill gap between European and American paddlers. In the '60s, slalom and wildwater competition came to the forefront and were the force that narrowed the gap. However, the influence of European paddlers continued to remain a key facilitator, through instruction of technique and through design.

European Influence

American paddlers, including the first of the Baby Boomer generation, were influenced by three European paddler-instructors: Walter Kirschbaum, Roger Paris, and Milo Duffek, all three world-class kayakers. During the '50s, Paris' and Kirschbaum's influence was felt through their participation in competition and river running and many paddlers witnessed their skills and technique. But it was their time instructing paddling associated with the Colorado Rocky Mountain School where they left a lasting impression on a younger generation of paddlers. Although Milo Duffek left his mark on American paddlers in the late '50s through his namesake stroke, in the early '60s he also left a lasting impression on American paddlers who were taught by him and witnessed his skill and technique.

Walter Kirschbaum and Roger Paris

In 1959, Walter Kirschbaum came to America to race at Salida and to run rivers. While in Colorado, he paddled with Roger Paris who suggested he contact Colorado Rocky Mountain School (CRMS), a prep school in Carbondale, Colorado, for a teaching position in order to remain in America. Kirschbaum settled in the Denver area teaching French and German at Colorado Academy and taught during the summer at CRMS.

Roger Paris (known by many simply as Rog-ét) ran Sierra Club's ski school for eight winters and lived in their Claire Tappan lodge beginning in the late '50s. He continued going back to France and Europe during the summers to race and mountain guide. Paris immigrated to the United States permanently in the early '60s. Paris also taught kayaking at CRMS in the summers. In 1964, he and his wife Jackie (a well-known American K-1W racer), were invited to stay at the school. Throughout the '60s, the Parises held a summer kayak program on the Crystal River near the school. In 1970, when CRMS discontinued its summer kayak program, the Parises continued kayak instruction with their own summer program.

IN THE EARLY '60s, Czech paddler Jan Sulc railed against the use of the term "Duffek stroke." He maintained Duffek had "merely exported it" since the stroke was used by other Czech paddlers who had also borrowed it from their paddling of Canadian canoes.[1]

EUROPEAN PADDLER Paul Bruhin (a Swiss watchmaker) influenced a number of American paddlers. During 1959 and 1960, he lived in New York City and was associated with KCCNY. During this time, Bruhin paddled and raced throughout the East influencing many, including Dave and Jan Binger, Bill Prime, and Bill Heinzerling of KCCNY, as well as others outside the club. Bruhin used the Duffek stroke and taught it to many paddlers in the East. Upon Bruhin's return to Switzerland in 1961, he became a student of Duffek.

Observing noted paddler Bob McNair of Buck Ridge paddling an open canoe, Bruhin asked why he didn't use knee straps in his canoe. When McNair responded with what Bruhin considered a less than satisfactory answer, Bruhin then asked why he (McNair) used an eyeglass strap when he paddled. McNair responded "Why... so I don't lose them. I can't paddle without them."[2] Bruhin made his point and McNair began using knee straps. (McNair later credited Roger Paris and Paul Bruhin with suggesting the use of knee straps.)[3]

[1] Editor. "Letters from Readers." *American Whitewater* Vol. VII No. 1 (May 1961): 3.

[2] Southworth, Tom. Interview by author 2 January 1998.

[3] McNair, Bob. "Making Knee-Straps for a Canoe." *American Whitewater* Vol. VII No. 1 (May 1961): 16–17.

With its two world famous kayak instructors, CRMS's summer kayaking program developed a reputation that drew paddlers from across the country. Being a program associated with CRMS as a prep school, CRMS also attracted younger generation paddlers to the prep school curriculum, paddlers like Fletcher Anderson (Colorado) who attended the prep school in the early '60s, and Dave Nutt (Maine) and John Holland (California) in the later '60s. Paris considered Nutt and Holland two of his best students. Eric Evans (New Hampshire) also came to CRMS not as a student, but to train with Paris.

FLETCHER ANDERSON, a well-known and accomplished kayaker and racer in the '70s, wrote of Kirschbaum's influence: "I learned three things from this man: how to paddle backwards, how to do a draw stroke, and how to do an eddy turn." [4]

KIRSCHBAUM'S AND PARIS' influence spread across the country through their students. It also spread through paddlers who witnessed Kirschbaum and Paris as guides and boatmen for Hatch Expeditions on rivers throughout the West.

Milo Duffek

During a visit to Europe in 1962, George Topol of the Ontario Voyageurs learned that Milo Duffek planned a visit to the United States in the summer of 1964. (After the '53 World Championships in Italy where he "lost" to Walter Kirschbaum, Duffek defected from Czechoslovakia and moved to Switzerland.) Upon his return, Topol contacted AWA to suggest they arrange with Duffek to provide instructional sessions during his visit. In the summer of 1964, Milo and his wife Irmgard, also a kayaker of renown, provided instruction during a tour of seven AWA affiliates in British Columbia, California, Colorado, Maine, Ontario, Washington, D.C., and Washington state. Their visit also included recreational paddling (cruising) with their hosts as they traveled the country.

KCCNY sponsored a week of instruction on the Rapid River in Maine with twenty participants from KCCNY, Buck Ridge, AMC, and Mohawk Rod and Gun Club (Ontario). In Toronto, the Duffeks were sponsored by the Ontario Voyageurs Kayak Club. The session was held on the Madawaska River at Barry's Bay, Ontario (near the future site of Madawaska Kanu Centre) with many American paddlers in attendance including Bart Hauthaway and Barb Wright (KCCB), Nancy Abrams (CCA), and Jane Showacre (formerly CCA, living in Denver).

Duffek's championship style was apparent to those who attended the sessions. Dave Binger (of KCCNY) wrote: "His strokes are lovely combinations, each one leading to the next in a seemingly effortless and highly effective pattern." Teaching a proper backstroke,

> Duffek combined the backstroke with a leaning draw stoke on the other side (reverse, of course), followed by a back thrust on that side, draw on the other, back stroke, draw, and so on, resulting in a smooth and highly controlled backward progress through the water. Similarly, a forward turn, to the right, let us say, would begin with the same strong back thrust, which then by a subtle turn of the wrist and change in blade angle would become a hanging draw, also on the right. The effectiveness of these combinations must be seen to be appreciated. [5]

[4] Written in September 1976 on a photograph of Walter Kirschbaum, taken by Alfred E. Holland, Jr. July 1969.

[5] Binger, Dave. "Milo in America." *American Whitewater* Vol. X No. 3 (Winter 1964–65): 7–9.

Martin Vanderveen of Denver wrote of a technique rarely seen prior to Duffek's demonstration.

> To make a gradual turn in either direction Duffek showed the students how to lean the boat 30 degrees **away** from the direction of the turn while keeping the torso upright and continuing to paddle on both sides. This offers an obvious advantage in competition in that it allows the paddler to turn without losing headway or even slowing down.[6]

Duffek also demonstrated leaning a boat fully on its edge until his shoulders were submerged and then recovering, a bracing technique rarely seen among American paddlers. By the session's end, many of the novice paddlers in attendance mastered the technique, a testimonial to Duffeks' teaching skills.

Milo Duffek from Winter 1964/65 issue of *American Whitewater.*

Duffek demonstrated the application of his skills and technique on what was considered "formidable stretches of water"[7] including the upper stretch of the North Fork of the Feather. Duffek paddled this stretch with three other California boaters, Walter Harvest, Don Golden and Noel DeBord, while others filmed them from the road. He also demonstrated no-hands and one-hand rolls as well as rolling in a strong current, again techniques rarely seen by American paddlers. Movies and photographs, which later became valuable teaching aids, were taken using an underwater window at CRMS's pool where Duffek demonstrated his one-hand roll. Barb Wright of KCCB wrote "Esquimautage Sans Paddle" for *American Whitewater* using photographs she had taken of Duffek.[8] (The Winter 1964/65 issue of *American Whitewater* has excellent photos of Duffek in action. All photos show him without a helmet or a life jacket, the norm at the time, especially among European racers.)

Sierra Club Bay Chapter's RTS held their "Duffek session" on the North Fork of the Feather (since de-watered by Pacific Gas & Electric). Peter Whitney, author of *White-Water Sport*, was one of the participants and came away from the experience with two main conclusions. One was a strong feeling of having heard a lot of it before, having paddled with Bruhin at KCCNY, and the other was the importance of constant practice. However, Whitney was very much impressed by what he had learned from Duffek in person.

Beyond the on-the-water demonstration of technique, off-the-water discussions with Duffek also provided paddlers with a considerable amount of information, in particular the latest thoughts on boat design. This was a particular interest to CWWA members since many were designing and building kayaks. Al Bennet shared a summary of what he learned during off-the-water discussions in the "Milo in America" article in *American Whitewater* that chronicled Duffeks' visit.

Bennet learned that there were three common hull shapes in kayaks: flat bottom hulls illustrated by the Baschin (European) slalom hull, sloped-sided hulls with pronounced curves as in the Klepper R-7 design, and crescent-shaped

[6] Vanderveen, Martin. "Milo in America." *American Whitewater* Vol. X No. 3 (Winter 1964–65): 9–11.

[7] Whitney, Peter D. "Milo in America." *American Whitewater* Vol. X No. 3 (Winter 1964–65): 12–13.

[8] Wright, Barbara. "Esquimautage Sans Paddle." *American Whitewater* Vol. X No. 3 (Winter 1964–65): 14–15.

hulls as in the Bohlender or Boston designs. Boat widths of 24 inches were considered optimum since anything wider could interfere with the use of newer hanging strokes. The bow of many of the more successful designs had a high breakwater extending all the way to the front (usually in the form of a high center ridge on the front deck). Flat or shallow decks with pronounced gunwale lines were considered difficult to control (were edgy) because they tended to catch waves and upset the boat in heavy water. It was also felt that flat or shallow decks "[made] turning more difficult particularly when a strong lean is used."[9] (This was a characteristic that was capitalized on in designs of the '70s.) The importance of being tight-in-the-boat, including having a proper seat and use of knee or thigh braces, was also garnered from the discussions. (This is obvious now but was not at that time, even in C-1s and C-2s.)

New Cornerstones

Regardless of the development of any national organization for competition, grass root efforts to support competition at the local level for setting up races, either slalom or downriver, required a great deal of effort by a number of people. The clubs of the '50s, AMC chapters, Buck Ridge, Colorado White Water Association (ACA's Rocky Mountain Division), and Sierra Club's Bay Chapter RTS, remained the facilitators of competition into the '60s. Other more recently formed clubs such as CCA, PSOC, and KCCNY also became involved in promoting and sponsoring competition.

By the end of the '50s, the first of the Baby Boomers began competing and winning. For much of the '60s, the competitors were of mixed generations. Four groups, Explorer Post 32, CCA, Ledyard Canoe Club (an outing club associated with Dartmouth College) and Kayak and Canoe Club of Boston (KCCB) left lasting legacies (albeit forgotten in later years).

Author's note: In the "Milo in America" article in *American Whitewater's* Winter 1964–65 issue, there are several contributing authors, split into separate sections by author. Each author is noted in the text and endnotes as appropriate.

Explorer Post 32

The two State College groups, PSOC and Explorer Post 32 with PSOC member Dave Kurtz as its advisor, had a synergistic effect on one another. The paddlers of PSOC were primarily undergrads, grads, and professors associated with the university. The paddlers of Post 32 were teenagers. However, as unlikely as it would seem, it was the Explorers who had the greater influence on the sport initially.

Soon after the Post's interest turned to whitewater in 1957, Dave Kurtz and his Explorers bought used Grummans from a canoe livery. At this time, Kurtz was as much a student of whitewater as his Explorers. A serendipitous meeting four years later with Natan Bernot, a Yugoslavian slalom racer taking graduate engineering courses at Penn State University accelerated the Post's whitewater activity, particularly in competition.

In 1961, Kurtz organized a trip on the Susquehanna for his Explorers where he also planned to set up a slalom course to practice technique in their Grumman canoes. While Kurtz and his Explorers were getting ready for the trip, Natan Bernot walked by and noticed slalom poles in Kurtz's car. Kurtz, having heard of Bernot's reputation as a paddler, "barreling down rapids with a wild technique,"[10] was reluctant to pursue any prolonged conversation with him in the presence of his Explorers. But the Explorers were instantly fascinated with Bernot and convinced Kurtz to allow him to join them on their trip.

[9] Bennet, Al. "Milo in America." *American Whitewater* Vol. X No. 3 (Winter 1964–65): 11–12.

[10] Kurtz, David. Interview by author 4 March 1997.

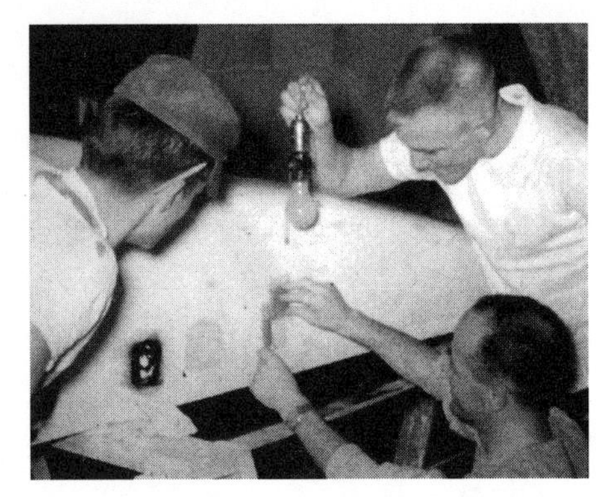
Guss, Bernot, and Southworth (left to right) pulling a Yugo I mold —courtesy of Dave Guss.

BEING A CHEMIST HIMSELF, Kurtz took this limited exposure to fiberglass construction and design and ran with it. Kurtz later became a supplier of materials for many boat builders in the State College area as well as a designer of his own series of slalom kayaks, the DK (for Dave Kurtz).

On the Susquehanna trip, Bernot paddled with each of the Explorers in their Grummans, sharing his knowledge and excitement of slalom racing. Although he provided little actual instruction, he was an instant inspiration to them. After all, he had competed in World Championship competition and told them that *"if they had a good boat and would train, they too, could compete in the World Championships."* [11] The Explorers took what he said to heart. The trip, along with subsequent experiences with Bernot, turned out to be one of the major influences in not only Kurtz's life, but also the lives of his young Explorers, particularly Tom Southworth and Dave Guss.

When Bernot returned from the trip, he designed (on paper using "the family of curves") a C-1, later called the Yugo I, for the Explorers. ("C-" implies a closed canoe, either a C-1 or C-2, not just a decked canoe.) The C-1 had a long cockpit with a sprayskirt that was attached to the boat. The design was completely symmetrical: midsection to bow and to stern, symmetrical in all four quarters. Following Bernot's instructions Guss, Kurtz, and Southworth made the plug for the mold. The plug was made using wood-strips which were then sanded, filled in with putty, painted with layer upon layer using different colors to judge fairness, and then wet sanded to the final finish. Again following Bernot's instructions, they made a female fiberglass mold from the plug split along the centerline.

The Explorers made four boats during the winter of 1961–62. The first boat from the mold was lopsided in weight, one half weighing quite a bit more than the other, with an overall weight of close to 80 pounds. Kurtz, Southworth, Guss and another Explorer, Hank Yeagley, paddled the boats at the Brandywine Race that spring competing against the top racers (in Grummans) of Buck Ridge, KCCNY and PSOC. The "kids" blew them away with their new C-1s as well as with their *youth.* The "little club of kids" did it. They took first, second, and third (Guss, Southworth, and Kurtz) beating PSOC's perennial winner, Bill Bickham. Their success at Brandywine further fueled their enthusiasm.

Although the Explorers dethroned perennial favorite Bill Bickham at Brandywine, Bickham turned around and beat the Explorers by a second in his Grumman at the Nationals later that year. However, he too, knew that *real* closed canoes were the future in racing and asked the Explorers to build a C-1 for him, which they did, forging a friendship between Bickham and the young Explorers.

Dave Guss in a Yugo I on the Lower Yough (PA) —courtesy of Dave Guss.

[11] Kurtz, David. Interview by author 4 March 1997.

Bernot also provided the Explorers with a C-2 design, a true end-holer with cockpits at bow and stern. The design was called Poliester 1, also symmetrical in all four quarters as was the Yugo C-1, and was paddled by Yeagley and Les Bechdel, a newer member of the Post. During the Winter of 1962, after Bernot returned to Yugoslavia, Kurtz along with Yeagley, Southworth, Bechdel and Guss, attempted to learn to roll their boats. After five straight days of pool sessions, they were still unsuccessful. Kurtz finally contacted John Berry of CCA who was able to provide a detailed enough explanation that Kurtz was successful the next day. The rest soon followed although it took Southworth almost five weeks to learn. At the '63 World Championships at Spittal, Southworth provided the audience with excitement by rolling three times in one of his runs, although ultimately finishing 21st out of 22.

Les Bechdel at Esopus Race (NY) circa 1965 —courtesy of Bart Hauthaway.

For the 1963 World Championships, Bernot designed a second C-1, the Yugo II, which he also provided to Kurtz. Three of the Explorers attended the team trials in the West and wrapped up the C-1 class.

Less than two years after Bernot told them they "could," four Explorers, Southworth and Guss paddling C-1 and Bechdel (only 15 years old) and Yeagley paddling C-2, were accompanied by Kurtz and Bickham (racing C-2M with Barb Wright) to the '63 World Championships in Spittal, Austria. Although finishing either last or within a few places of last in both slalom and wildwater, the young Explorers finished their races at the World Championships. Kurtz in C-1 finished only a few places ahead of his Explorers and Bickham and Wright in C-2M finished last.

At the next World Championships in 1965, Southworth and Kurtz again went to the World Championships, again held on the Leiser in Spittal. This time in slalom, Southworth finished 11th out of 29, two places ahead of Kurtz.

The Post became a magnet for young paddlers interested in whitewater and attracted young men including Steve Draper who later became a National Champion and Rich Brown who founded Norse Paddle Company while still an Explorer in the '60s. Ex-Explorers, with Kurtz, continued to paddle and formed the Wildwater Boating Club of Bellefonte in the mid-'60s, which provided a place to build and store boats. Bechdel and others racers were members of the Bellefonte club.

BECHDEL, having switched to K-1, placed third at the Eastern Kayak Championships and did not make the '65 team since only two K-1s were allowed from the East. Instead Bechdel traveled West with Bickham, to cruise and explore rivers.

When Explorer Posts were allowed to become coed in the late '60s, Post 32 did too, and became Post 111. Gay Gruss paddled C-1 with the Post and later raced C-2M with Mark Fawcett of Buck Ridge whom she later married.

Ex-Explorers from the Post became national champions in the '60s and '70s. Tom Southworth was National C-1 Slalom Champion in 1964, 1966, and 1967, C-2 Slalom Champion with fellow Explorer Dave Guss in 1964, and C-2M Slalom Champion with Mariner Nancy Abrams in 1966, 1967, and 1970. Les Bechdel was National K-1 Slalom Champion in 1967 and C-2 Slalom Champion with Dave Kurtz in 1966, 1967, and 1968. Gay Gruss became National Wildwater C-2M Champion with Mark Fawcett in 1966, 1967, and 1968 and National Slalom C-2M Champion with Fawcett in 1969. Steve Draper became National C-2 Slalom Champion in 1971 with Frank Schultz.

Two other Explorer Posts in the mid-Atlantic also developed young whitewater paddlers in the '60s and into the '70s, using the rivers of West Virginia, western Maryland, and southwestern Pennsylvania as their playground. One Post was located north of Baltimore in Bel Air, Maryland, with Carl Flynn as an advisor. Flynn exposed many young paddlers to whitewater including boat building. (Flynn moved around the country for his job, each time setting up and teaching boat building, and whitewater paddling, to anyone who wanted to learn.) The Post's alumni included well-known racers and paddlers of the '70s including Dan and Dave Demaree, National K-1 Slalom Champion Dan Isbister, John (Johnny Wonder) Regan, and John Connelly, who started his own rafting company, Eastern Expeditions, in Maine.

Another Post, also in Maryland, was located south of Baltimore in Howard County. Explorer Post 757 with advisor Doug Woodward, built many boats including kayaks and Czech C-2s. In Post 757, many young paddlers began in C-2 before moving on to kayaks. Also among its members were well-known racers and paddlers including C-2 Wildwater Champion Brad Hager (Hager was National Wildwater C-2 Champion in 1969 with Norm Holcombe and in 1970 with Bill Endicott), Eric Nielson, who started Cheat River Outfitters in West Virginia, and Jesse Whittemore, one of the first squirt masters.

In the late '60s, with other Explorer Posts going coed, Post 757 merged with a Girl Scout troop in the area and two young women became involved in whitewater as a result of the merger, Mimi Hayman (C-1) and Nancy Rayburn. Hayman paddled the Grand Canyon in a C-1, perhaps the first woman to do so, and as she says, "the first woman to swim out of a C-1 at Crystal and Lava."[12] Woodward moved to Atlanta in 1970 and started Explorer Post 49 with the assistance of Georgia Canoeing Associations (GCA) members.

CCA

CCA was different. It was comprised of older (relatively speaking) paddlers compared to Post 32 and PSOC. However, these older paddlers, often with sons and daughters of their own, left a legacy for young men and women by taking active roles in Mariners, Explorer Posts of young women, and later their own youth program called the C-CATS (CCA Training Squad). This active role resulted in Olympians and World Champions of the '70s and '80s.

[12] Demaree, Mimi. Interview by author 15 February 1997.

From CCA's inception, competition played a major role in the activities of the club, though balanced with club sponsored trips. John Berry and Bob Harrigan were proponents of slalom racing while continuing to cruise and explore. Berry and Harrigan often competed against one another in C-1 and raced together in C-2 (until 1968 when Harrigan dropped out due to an injured shoulder).

In 1963, Ray Eaton and Randy Carter came up with the idea of having a race in lower Smoke Hole canyon on the South Branch of the Potomac to bring attention to its possible inundation. They approached CCA to organize the race. (The actual racecourse was changed, at Berry's suggestion, to the North Fork of the South Branch near Petersburg, Virginia.) Berry and Harrigan organized the first race with the help of Alma Cowherd, owner of the hotel in Petersburg, along with other local sponsors, fashioning the race more like the Salida race by getting the whole town involved. Racers contributed to the local economy by staying in town and buying gas and food.

In the Spring of 1964, John Berry promoted the formation of a new Slalom Division within CCA. Its purpose was to promote "advancing white-water skills through slalom practice and the use of specialized craft and equipment, by means of selected, small-group trips on both difficult and seldom-explored streams." [13] The cost for its membership was an extra $5 to buy slalom poles.

The formation of CCA's Slalom Division, along with interest and support of members, provided a wellspring for young racers. Three families in particular, the Hearns (with Mary Alice and Carter), the Bridges (with Dick and Rosemary), and the McEwans (with Bob and May "Skipper"), participated in and promoted both slalom and downriver competition.

Another youth program, this one for young women, was also supported by CCA. The Mariners, under the leadership of Annavieve Abrams, Mary Ollry, and Betty Riedel were exposed to "everything about water" [14] by CCA members such as Dick Bridge, Ed Gertler, Jim Stuart, and "Uncle" Dan Sullivan. The Mariners tried rowing at the Washington Canoe Club (D.C.), sailing on the Potomac and Chesapeake, and whitewater canoeing. Another Mariner troop, Troop 214 with May McEwan as an advisor, also participated in whitewater activities, often blending both groups into one.

The young women who participated in the Mariners included Carrie (Lyn) Ashton, Terry Franz, Chris Stevens, Peggy Elliot, Barb Snyder, Panilee Ikaree, Karen Modine, and Nancy Tighe. They all cruised and raced together although only a few took racing seriously. Nancy Abrams was one young woman who did. In 1967, Annaviev Abrams took a small group of young Mariners to the World Championships in Czechoslovakia to watch her daughter compete. A new member, Carrie Ashton, joined them. After watching Nancy compete, it became Ashton's goal to compete in Europe. Ashton not only competed in World Championship competition, she also competed in the '72 Olympics.

By 1967, the group's membership was less than the minimum needed for Girl Scout regulations and was dissolved. However, in its years of existence, the Mariners provided an opportunity for some of the first young women to become involved in whitewater. This was before Title IX of the Civil Rights Act of 1972 required schools to equalize women's sports programs with men's

EVENTUALLY, Petersburg residents took over the organization of the race. The downriver and slalom races drew racers and non-racers alike across the East and exposed countless numbers of people to the sport in general into the '70s.

Author's note: The effects of the Petersburg races were far-reaching. A friend of mine, Hank Annable, one of the founders of the Keel-Hauler Canoe Club, witnessed his first competition at Petersburg around 1968. It was also the first time he had seen a closed C-1. That started the club's foray into whitewater. Annable even joined CCA to participate in their trips to the Yough and Cheat and other rivers in southeast Pennsylvania and West Virginia, bringing knowledge of the rivers back to the club.

[13] Vanderveen, Martin (Retiring AWA Secretary). "The Secretary's Soap Box." *American Whitewater* Vol. IX No. 4 (Spring, 1964): 15.

[14] Brown (Synder), Barbara. Interview by author 6 February 1997.

programs. Granted, whitewater did not directly benefit, but the fact that women were encouraged to participate in physical sports brought some women to whitewater.

Ex- Mariners Nancy (Abrahms) Southworth and Carrie Ashton became National Slalom Champions over multiple years. Abrams became the National C-2 M Champion in 1966, 1967, and 1970 with Tom Southworth (Ex-Explorer) and 1969 Champion with John Bridge, son of CCA member Dick Bridge. Carrie Ashton became National Slalom Champion in K-1 and C-2M. In 1972, she became National K-1 Slalom Champion, and in 1973 she became National C-2M Slalom Champion with Russ Nichols. In addition to Nancy Abrams and Carrie Ashton, in the late '60s and into the '70s, many of the top female racers were ex-Mariners. Terry Franz was on the U.S. team for the '67 World Championships.

KCCB and LCC

With the introduction of slalom racing to AMC members by Eliot DuBois in 1954, some members became immersed in slalom practically to the exclusion of anything else. The group favoring competition argued that the growth of the sport with regard to equipment and technique could be attributed to slalom competition. Those supporting slalom did not want trips scheduled on slalom race weekends that would interfere with their slalom racing. The other side of the argument did not care about slalom at all and did not want their weekend trips to be scheduled around races. The much smaller competition-oriented group was much more vocal and split from AMC around 1961 to form the Kayak and Canoe Club of Boston (KCCB). This group included John Urban, who had headed up AMC's Whitewater Committee, Sumner Bennett, Bart Hauthaway, and one of the most recent members to AMC, Barb Wright, formerly of Washington D.C. and CCA. The members of KCCB, though small in number, concentrated their efforts on racing.

In reality, KCCB was a club in name only. Only Bart Hauthaway and Barb Wright were regular members. However, their contributions went beyond merely being a couple of competitors. Hauthaway and Wright helped push innovations in competition, and interacting with Jay Evans, coach of Dartmouth's Ledyard Canoe Club, they established new standards for kayaks in competition. They also pushed toward innovations in boats and paddles. Wright prompted both Stu Coffin and Hauthaway to design kayaks and paddles for her use. She was determined to be the top U.S. K-1W paddler and compete in Europe and sought every innovation to achieve this: from training techniques (English gate), to training with Milo Duffek on his 1964 visit, to bringing back boats and paddles from Europe to be improved upon.

Wright was a Ph.D. biochemist. She practiced English gates in a pool in her backyard and encouraged others to do so. Wright was also very gracious in helping young paddlers. She assisted Les Bechdel, supporting his efforts to change from C-1/C-2 to K-1, by helping him bring back a kayak from Europe after the '63 World Championships and providing kayaking instruction to him. The Cohasset Invitational Slalom on the tidal basin rapids at Mill Rapids to provide an almost year-round slalom course was her idea. She encouraged very young slalom racers to participate.

Wright, however, also cruised and was considered a hotshot, a "heavy-water woman" by conservative AMC standards.[15] With her friend Stu Coffin of AMC, she paddled the Rapid, Dead, and Kennebec Rivers of Maine. She also paddled rivers in Colorado with Bill Bickham, Dick Bridge, Dan Sullivan, Peter Reilly, and Phil Hugill. In 1967, the year she retired, Wright was the top ranked female paddler.

While KCCB members were still of an older generation, members of the Ledyard Canoe Club at Dartmouth in New Hampshire were Baby Boomers. But both clubs had an impact on one another and their legacies to the sport were very different.

The Ledyard Canoe Club (LCC) was founded in 1920 with two objectives: "encouraging and stimulating of interest in canoeing and other aquatic sports among the resident students of Dartmouth College" and, "providing of the proper facilities for such activity on the Connecticut River."[16] In the '60s, these two objectives provided the foundation for LCC that established a force-to-be-reckoned-with in slalom competition and propelled American competition to new levels.

Dartmouth alumnus Robert J. (Jay) Evans was first introduced to whitewater canoeing during his tenure as a headmaster at a country day school in western Virginia in 1956. On a rainy day in February, he and his 6 year-old son Eric ran Goose Creek with Ramone Eaton and Randy Carter. Though a miserable day and trip, his interest in whitewater was piqued. Evans' interest was further heightened in 1959 while a coach at a country day school in Massachusetts when he watched slalom races on the West River with his son. Due to a lack of gate judges, Evans was corralled into gate judging and witnessed Barb Wright capsize in her kayak in a gate he was judging. The next year, Evans returned and was commandeered into paddling in the bow of an F-2 with Ron Bohlender from Colorado. Evans' interest now shifted from canoeing to kayaking, slalom racing in particular. The next year, in 1961, he ordered a fiberglass kayak from Klepper, one of the first Klepper fiberglass kayaks in the country [although it took almost a year to arrive].

In 1962, Evans returned to his alma mater as an admissions officer bringing his interest in slalom racing. Evans soon became involved with LCC and hung gates at Dartmouth's indoor pool for winter practice. Evans spent a considerable amount of time during the summer and fall of 1962 trying to learn to roll his kayak. It wasn't until the next spring that he was successful, with assistance from Barb Wright (KCCB). Soon, two members of LCC, Chris Knight and Brad Dewey, joined him in his practice and were followed by others. The next Spring, in March of 1963, LCC sponsored the first in-door slalom taking advantage of Dartmouth's new pool. The course had ten gates and required a roll during the race. Jay Evans won, defeating ten other competitors. LCC also sponsored the first Mascoma Slalom on the Mascoma River near Dartmouth that same spring. The following summer, Chris Knight placed third in K-1 at the Eastern Slalom Championships on the West River near Jamaica, Vermont.

[15] Wright, Barbara. Interview by author, 6 July 1997.

[16] Evans, Jay. Correspondence to author 10 January 1996.

THE TERM "ENGLISH GATE" was coined by members of the Ontario Voyageurs in honor of its inventors. In England, it was called the "Wiggle" test [17] and timed competitions were a part of both indoor and outdoor training. Wright showed Evans the English gate test and they incorporated the idea of a roll in the traditional wiggle test.

By 1963, Evans' influence on LCC was beginning to be noticed. That year, an 18 year-old Dartmouth student, Jonathon (Jo) Knight, narrowly missed first place in the hotly contested Eastern Slalom Championships. It was his first season of competition and only his second major slalom competition. Evans himself had seriously taken up racing and was promoting European style training with weight training and running, including English gate as a critical part of training during the winter.

By the mid-'60s, LCC's paddling program was in full swing. Indoor training included English gates as well as pool slaloms with other competitors from KCCNY and KCCB. Along with sponsoring local slalom races, including the spring race on the Mascoma, Evans also began a training camp on summer weekends on the Rapid River.

Eric Evans at Tariffville Gorge (CT) circa 1965 —courtesy of Bart Hauthaway.

With its success, LCC attracted more young athletes. Many of the top racers developed from its membership in the '60s including Wick Walker, John Burton, David Nutt, and Eric Evans (Jay's son). These racers were some of the first young men to devote their paddling efforts almost exclusively to racing. They were joined by young women including Peggy (Nutt) Mitchell and Carol Fisher.

By "providing... the proper facilities for such activity on the Connecticut River," [18] LCC provided a site (albeit flatwater with a current) to hang permanent gates, a place to store equipment, and a place to build boats. As many as one hundred sixty boats were built during one three-year period in the second half of the '60s, much to the chagrin of early designers and builders, Bart Hauthaway, Stu Coffin, and later Sam Galpin with High Performance Products, who were trying to make money in New England.

LCC also sponsored European racers to train during the summer, an arrangement that turned out to be a two-way benefit. In 1968, LCC (through Wick Walker) invited Lida Sirotkova, the '65 World Slalom Champion in C-2M and K-1W member on the '67 Czech team, to join them for a series of races and training camps. She provided considerable assistance to the team and was invited back the following year. Other paddlers were later brought over to train including two British paddlers, Dave Mitchell and John MacLeod.

EVANS competed and enjoyed the Hudson River Derby Giant Slalom. He won the race in 1965, 1968, and 1969. In 1967, at 42 years old, he won the senior class. In 1969, he ended his personal competition to become the U.S. Team coach.

LCC members and alumni became National Champions from the '60s through the '90s. Eric Evans was nine-time National K-1 Slalom Champion from 1969 through 1978, with the exception of 1970, and in 1972 held National titles for both slalom and wildwater. Fellow LCC member David Nutt held the National titles for slalom and wildwater in 1970 and became the K-1 Wildwater Champion in 1968 and 1974. In the same year as David's dual championship, his sister Peggy also held dual National titles in K-1W Slalom and Wildwater and became the K-1W Wildwater Champion in 1971.

Carol Fisher followed Peggy and became the National K-1W Wildwater Champion from 1972 through 1976 and again, from 1981 through 1984. Later in the '90s, another Dartmouth and LCC alumnus, Dana Chladek, became three time National K-1W Slalom Champion beginning in 1987, World Champion in the 1988 World Cup, and two time Olympian winning bronze in the '92 Olympics and silver in the '96 Olympics.

[17] Siposs, George. "Test Your Slalom Skill in Still Water." *American Whitewater* Vol. VIII No. 2 (Autumn 1962): 18–19.

[18] Falcon, Thomas. *The Ledyard Canoe Club of Dartmouth: A History.* Hanover, New Hampshire: Dartmouth, 1967.

Although LCC paddlers were primarily kayakers, two members left their mark in C-paddling. Wick Walker became the National C-1 Slalom Champion in 1968 and John Burton, in 1971. In 1970, John Burton also became the National C-2 Slalom Champion with Tim Schell. Burton and Walker were also coaches for various U.S. Teams throughout the '70s.

Wick Walker at Tariffville Gorge (CT) circa 1965 —courtesy of Bart Hauthaway.

The Racers and the Races

The 1960 National Whitewater Slalom Championships (coincident with the Eastern Whitewater Slalom Championships) were held in the East on the West River. Unlike the first Nationals held in the East in 1958, clubs from both the East (CCA, PSOC, KCCNY, AMC, and BRSC) and West (FibArk and CWWA) were represented. The East's domination of canoeing and the West's domination of kayaking were clearly demonstrated by the race results.

With the Nationals held in the East, races at Salida were billed as the International and Western American Slalom and the International and U.S. Championship Downriver races. (The Salida race was always termed a downriver race. Changes to that term were slow to come in the U.S. even though terminology in the World Championships was wildwater.) Paul Bruhin (Swiss) of KCCNY won the International Slalom competition in F-1 beating Erich Siedel (second) and Eric Frazee (third) of CWWA. In R-1, the only class in the Western American Slalom, Bryce Whitmore of Bay Chapter's RTS won followed by Ted Young (second) and Ron Bohlender (third), both of CWWA.

The 1961 National Championships were split between two races held in Colorado: the National Slalom Championships sponsored by FibArk at Salida and the National Downriver Race on the Roaring Fork sponsored by CWWA. However, team selection was made by ACA for the World Championships in Dresden prior to either race in order to allow enough time to travel and train in Europe for the three classes: K-1, K-1W, and C-2. The team members for the other classes were announced later. ACA, Klepper, and Old Town contributed to travel expenses; however, the individual team members paid most of their own way.

The team of paddlers who represented the U.S. at the '61 World Championships included only kayakers from the West. However, the C-2 teams were from both the East and the West. Of the paddlers selected, only Berry and Harrigan (CCA), Bob Worrell and Conrad Swenson (CWWA), Ted Young (CWWA), and Richard Schraner (CWWA) went to Europe. Since no other American women entered the F-1 wildwater class, Brigitte Schraner asked and received permission to enter, although in the end, she did not compete.

Berry and Harrigan ordered a boat from a West German manufacturer in Stuttgart: a "banana boat" (a descriptive name for its appearance). It was an end-hole closed C-2 unlike anything they had ever seen before: its hull was very rounded and only 30 inches in width. Berry and Harrigan found out it did not meet ICF's minimum width requirements, being almost an inch narrower than allowed. They were without a boat to race until they learned that Worrell and Swenson who made arrangements to borrow a boat from the East Germans, only planned to compete in the slalom race. That provided Berry and Harrigan the opportunity to use it in the wildwater race.

John Berry and Bob Harrington at the 1962 Brandywine Race (DE) —courtesy of John Berry.

The '61 World Championships were only the second time American champions competed against Europeans on their home turf. Previously, Harrigan expressed his doubts about the superiority of European slalom skills to Paul Bruhin. Bruhin responded, "You will see." [19] And see they did at Dresden. The dam controlled Rote Weisseritz was the fastest water Harrigan had encountered, save for a few flooded West Virginia mountain streams. The river had no real eddies and was more like a river in Colorado, fast with few obstructions and eddies. Both Berry and Harrigan admitted it was a challenge just to run it safely, let alone negotiate any obstacles such as gates.

Worrell and Swenson managed to survive their first slalom run where they had dumped in earlier practice runs, but their second run was DNF (Did Not Finish). The reverse was true for Ted Young in F-1. He was DNF on his first run but "survived" his second. The final American tally was Worrell and Swenson 21st in C-2 slalom; Young was 36th in F-1 slalom and 35th in F-1 downriver; Dick Schraner finished 37th in F-1 downriver. Berry and Harrigan did not even place. However, they learned much from what they saw, including boat design ideas and technique. They also noted that European paddlers used fast but short choppy strokes in their canoes in comparison to Berry and Harrigan's longer, slower strokes.

The list of races across the United States and Canada continued to grow. In 1962, races included the Hudson River Whitewater Derby and Giant Slalom, Brandywine Slalom, Potomac River Race, Third Western Canadian Slalom and Downriver Races on the Chilliwack River in British Columbia, Clear Creek Slalom in Colorado, and the First Annual Root River Race in Sault Saint Marie, Ontario. Bay Chapter's RTS sponsored their first race on the North Fork of the Feather in the Sierras. Roger Paris proclaimed the race the "hardest slalom ever set in the United States." [20]

In 1962, the National Championships for slalom and wildwater were held on the North Fork of the Feather (in the West for the first time outside of the traditional Colorado race sites.) ACA awarded Bay Chapter's RTS the Nationals for kayak but decided to keep the canoe Nationals in the East due to lack of western competitors. By this time, many races combined R-1 and F-1 into one class, K-1, and the Nationals in 1962 on the North Fork of the Feather followed this practice.

At the National Kayak Slalom Championships, seventeen-year-old Claud Burk from Salida beat Eric Frazee, also of Salida, and Bill Prime of KCCNY who was trained by Paul Bruhin. This stunned many paddlers at the race. The K-1W Champion was Elizabeth Wheelwright of Seattle, the only woman who finished. Kay Harvest and Candace McDonald were both DNF. Roger Paris did not attend although he had set the course. Instead, he worked with his wife Jackie, grooming her for the next World Championships in 1963.

Another bit of controversy arose at the race, again involving amateur status and taking on a new height that indirectly involved AWA. The competition was sponsored by Bay Chapter's RTS, an AWA affiliate, and held in compliance with ACA requirements. The morning of the race, visiting ACA Commodore Ted Jacobs approached Bryce Whitmore and warned him

[19] Harrigan, Bob. "The U.S. Team in East Germany." *American Whitewater* Vol. VII No. 3 (November 1961): 4–13.

[20] Siposs, George. "Racing Report." *American Whitewater* Vol. VIII No. 2 (August 1961): 20.

that he would probably be ruled a professional and that his participation as a contestant might "contaminate" the other contestants. Because of the ACA regulations that stated that a man may not make money from activities "closely associated" with canoeing, Jacobs determined Whitmore was a professional because of his summer job as a raft guide. When other AWA members urged Whitmore to enter in protest, he was warned that the precedence had already been set with the disqualification of Utah boatman Les Jones who often worked for Hatch Expeditions. Whitmore decided not to enter and later received a written apology from Jacobs stating that ACA decided to extend river guides the same exemption given to summer camp counselors who teach canoeing.

The following year, 1963, was a World Championship year with the championships held on the Lieser in Spittal, Austria. This was the last World Championship competition that included separate kayak classes in F-1 and R-1. ACA's selection for the U.S. team was based on past Slalom Chairman Bob Harrigan's point system with modifications based on the 1962 National results to eliminate discrimination against western paddlers. Domination of all canoe classes by the East continued as well as domination by the West in K-1 wildwater.

Because the selection was based on 1961 results, it eliminated many of the up and coming younger paddlers from competing at Spittal, particularly C-paddlers such as Dave Guss, Tom Southworth, Hank Yeagley, Mark Fawcett, and Dick Shipley. Based on the National Kayak Slalom Championships at Salida, the selection was supported with the exception of the exclusion of Walt Harvest in R-1 downriver. However, adjustments to the team were made since individuals still were responsible for paying their own way. This allowed some of the younger team members who did not make the team, but were able to pay their own way, to compete.

The '63 World Championships were an eye-opening experience for the eleven American paddlers who went to Spittal: Dave Kurtz, Tom Southworth, Barbara Wright, Barb Krebs, Bill Prime, Dave Guss, Hank Yeagley, Les Bechdel, Ted Makris, Dan Makris, and Bill Bickham. (Ted and Dan Markis were the only paddlers from the West.)

Natan Bernot invited the team to train with the Yugoslavian team in Ljubljana, Slovenia, but only Guss and Southworth accepted. Bernot and fellow coach Vaclav Nic also hosted and provided training advice to other Post and PSOC competitors from State College who came later for the race. Bernot was head of canoeing in Yugoslavia and was probably single-handedly responsible for the presence of U.S. canoeists in Europe. Nic was considered the master of the sport and trained all the youth in Yugoslavia.

ACA'S ROLE in supporting and developing competition cannot be understated in spite of controversies surrounding amateurism and team selection. Aside from ACA's role as the official governing body with ICF, ACA's internal infrastructure throughout the '60s through its divisions supported the expanding development of slalom and wildwater races across the country. However, ACA's other activities outside of whitewater benefitted from growth associated with whitewater competition and the people it brought into the organization. Until 1967, California, Arizona, New Mexico, Washington, Oregon, and Idaho were all included in the Pacific Division. In that year, the Northwest Division was established, splitting off Washington, Oregon, and Idaho, which was partly attributed to growth associated with whitewater competition. One of the key proponents for whitewater was Tom Johnson who was the Pacific Division Vice Commodore from 1962 to 1967.

Nic taught the technique of using short, vertical paddle strokes held close to the boat for C-paddling. Tom Southworth wrote of the experience:

> At first their [the Yugoslavian team] training schedule was restricted to flat water. "Training" consisted of paddling 10 [,] 100 meter sprints; practice also included paddling through stillwater gates in every conceivable manner. It was immediately apparent that they paddled much more rapidly using short, quick strokes with short, narrow (6.5 to 7 inches wide) paddles. We also learned that it was not at all easy to imitate their style; thus it became increasingly apparent that their paddling skills were not the result of week-end excursions but of long hours of hard practice and many competitions."[21]

Barb Wright wrote of her training experiences and observations with the Yugoslavian team:

> [training consisted of] ... practice in a series of gates negotiated in special sequences and directed by the coach who held a stop-watch on each run. Trainees made run after run until gradually the techniques required for this series were learned and seconds shaved from the initial running time. Practice was so intense that even their superbly conditioned paddlers lay inert and exhausted, heads resting on boat decks between runs... The laminated, lightweight slalom paddles used by the Europeans are short (about up to the mouth), rigid, and have a relatively small, flat blade area. This flatness permits feathered blade, in-water recoveries, and in fact, any underwater paddle motion, with a minimum chance of twisting, and with least water resistance. The small blade area allows for greater rapidity in actual strokes per minute. It would seem, in fact, that the Europeans take about three paddle strokes to just one of ours during gate negotiation and probably twice as many between gates. Such endurance, of course, demands practice and conditioning. Their mastery of and complete reliance upon the pry-away at each boat end, plus their combination power/direction strokes, is highly evolved as contrasted with American slalom paddlers... Forward momentum is attained and maintained with these short, choppy stokes which end at the body. There is practically no follow-through... There is never any careful deliberation in "lining-up" for the next gate. The approach is consistently on a direct-line basis, and with confident disregard for the angle of difficulty involved... European canoeists use continuous combination strokes even when centered in a gate. By keeping the paddle in constant motion, slight corrections are more quickly and surely accomplished.[22]

[21] Kurtz, Dave aided by Tom Southworth, Barbara Wright, and Bill Prime. "World Championships, 1963." *American Whitewater* Vol. IX No. 3 (Winter 1963/64): 7–22.

[22] Wright, Barbara. "World Championships, 1963." *American Whitewater* Vol. IX No. 3 (Winter 1963/64): 12–13.

It was evident that the techniques used by American C-paddlers were very different from those of their European counterparts. Except for the brief time that Bernot paddled with Post 32 and PSOC members in State College, very few American canoe paddlers had ever witnessed European canoe paddlers. Most of the previous European racers and immigrants to America paddled kayaks. Although the Americans felt their paddling technique was inferior, they proved they were better at rolling their canoes.

A month before the World Championships, Southworth and Guss saw the course for the International Slalom (held) on the Tacen in Yugoslavia (site of the '55 Worlds) without water. Later, they were horrified to see the course with water. Although the river was dam controlled, there was little water for the race due to less rainfall than normal. During pre-race runs, almost half of the seventy Yugoslavian racers upset and half of those were scraped up pretty badly on the course. The course was much more difficult than any encountered previously by American paddlers, but the American C-1s were the only ones who did not upset at the pre-race runs.

Aside from a few of the State College area paddlers, only Prime arrived early. Prime met Bruhin and Bruhin's mentor and coach, Duffek, to paddle and train with them and the rest of the Swiss team a few days before the race. The rest of the American team arrived shortly before the race providing very little warm-up training or preparation for the course.

The American C-1s, as were a few other European boats, were too short (by a centimeter) and fiberglass and resin were added to meet the minimum length requirement. Although many competed in slalom and wildwater, they used their slalom boats for wildwater competition. Of the American paddlers, Prime had the best finishes: 40th out of 48 in F-1 slalom and 19th out of 26 in F-1 wildwater. The remainder of the team finished last or within a few places of last.

Wildwater racing took a back seat to slalom racing, particularly among paddlers in the East. Not only did many not specialize between slalom and wildwater racing, they often did not own a boat designed for wildwater, only slalom. Wildwater (downriver) racing remained an event found primarily in the West, attributed to the long running history of the Salida Races. This changed in 1964 with the addition of a second wildwater race in the East (to the established Potomac Whitewater Race, the Petersburg race) on the Loyalsock in Pennsylvania. Finally the East had its own wildwater championships.

Slalom racing continued its domination with an ever-increasing number of events, particularly in the East. In 1964, the National Canoe Championships, along with K-1W National Championships, remained in the East on the West River. The Men's National Kayak Championships and Women's Slalom was held on the Arkansas at Buena Vista. And for the fourth year, the Pacific Invitational Slalom was held on North Fork of the Feather.

West River Race (VT) 1967 —courtesy of Jim Stuart.

The 1964 race schedule had almost twenty races, with fourteen slalom races including two giant slaloms in the East. Races were held on the Salmon River in Connecticut, Black Moshannon and Loyalsock in Pennsylvania, Potomac in Virginia, Mascoma in New Hampshire, Brandywine in Delaware, Hudson and Esopus in New York, West in Vermont, and Cheat in West Virginia. Races in the West included the National Kayak Championships on the Arkansas in Colorado, the Salida Race and South Platte in Colorado, and the North Fork of the Feather in California.

The first year that a C-2W Champion was crowned was 1964. Many women became involved in competition through C-2M. C-2W teams often formed at the last minute to compete, from a pair of C-2M teams. However, due to a lack of competitors, C-2W classes were often not held in every race, the same as C-2M for the same reason. C-2W was also not a recognized class in World Championship competition.

During the early '60s, there was often more than one "national champion" in a given year because of the rivalry between the East and West and the lack of nation-wide race organization. Racers in the West would not acknowledge the "national" races held in the East and visa versa. Many competitors did not consider it fair that a single national race held in the East or West should determine national championship status since it was difficult for all to attend in either location. Additionally, because of the long-standing running of the Salida race, many of its regular racers felt it was truly the "national" race and that anyone who won it was the "national" champion.

K-1W racers from the East, notably Barb Wright, and the racers from the West, Jackie Paris and Kay Harvest, rarely race against one another. Although all of them at one time claimed to be "the best," it was not until the World Championships in 1965 that they actually competed. Barb Wright decisively beat both Jackie Paris and Kay Harvest.

The schism between East and West domination of K-1 began to reach a climax in 1965. Roger Paris was elected Team Captain for the '65 World Championships. The system for selecting the team had not yet been agreed upon by all involved and was considered one of the duties of the ACA National Slalom Chairman. The '61 and '63 teams were selected by the Harrigan system (Harrigan was the '62 National Slalom Chairman and from the East), which used a point system based on two races in the East and two in the West. However, Ron Bohlender (from the West), the '63 National Slalom Chairman, did not agree that the system placed the racers in "perfect order."[23] Kurtz, the '65 National Slalom Chairman, with the assistance of racers and other advisors, attempted to develop different systems that could be agreed upon. His report totaled ten pages but in the end, none of his systems were accepted. The final decision was that each Divisional Slalom Chairman would make his own list that was tallied with the other chairmen for the final team selection for all canoe classes and K-1W. The exception was for the hotly contested (between East and West) K-1 spots that were determined by the team captain, in this case, Roger Paris. Ten kayakists were invited to compete for positions on the team at a training camp held at the CRMS. At least that was the plan. However, team selection was made by a vote at a small meeting of the Eastern Slalom Chairmen that was not

[23] Kurtz, Dave and Tom Southworth. "Racing Report: Selection of the U.S. Team." *American Whitewater* Vol. X No. 4 (Spring 1965): 15, 18–20.

announced to other Divisional Slalom Chairmen of ACA. Naturally, this created quite a bit of tension in East-West relations. Of the team selection process *American Whitewater's* editor Whitney wrote:

> Except for Roger Paris, those chosen were Easterners. The Pacific and Mountain Divisions were allocated one team place in addition to that of Roger Paris, team captain and one alternate. No Eastern kayakists turned up at the Colorado training session or the National K-1 Championships at the Feather... No Easterner, to the best of your Editor's recollection has ever held the U.S. K-1 championship since the title became a worthwhile prize to compete for—five years, more or less.[24]

1965 East and West Race results for slalom K-1, and K-1W

East K-1 Charles Bridge, William Prime, Al Zob (Canadian), Heinz Poenn (Canadian), and Les Bechdel. U.S. entries only included Jo Knight, and Eric Evans.

West K-1 Walt Harvest, Ted Young, Noel DeBord, Marin Etter, and Dave Morrissey

East K-1W Barb Wright, Terry Franz, and Jan Binger

West K-1W Elsa Bailey, and Kay Harvest

In 1965, the National Canoe Slalom Championships and Eastern Kayak Championships were held in May on the West River in Vermont. The National Wild Water Canoe Championships and Eastern Wild Water Kayak Championships were held on the Potomac in Virginia. The Men's National Kayak Singles Championship (Slalom) and Pacific Invitational Slalom and Wildwater Races were held on the North Fork of the Feather in the Sierras.

From the race on the Feather, Walt Harvest was declared the K-1 National Slalom Champion. In spite of the controversy, the final team selection was fairly representative of both eastern and western interests. On the team for K-1 slalom were two paddlers from the East, Charlie Bridge and Jo Knight, and two from the West, Walt Harvest and Roger Paris. K-1 wildwater members were from the West; Noel DeBord, Roger Paris, and Mike Stanley. The rest of the team competed in slalom and wildwater and included Kay Harvest, Jackie Paris, and Barb Wright for K-1W; Dave Kurtz, Tom Southworth, and Wick Walker for C-1; and Mark Fawcett and Dick Shipley, Bill Heinzerling and Rowan Osborne, and John Connet and Jim Raleigh in C-2.

KAYAKIST, which paralleled the term canoeist, was the term often used in the '50s and '60s for paddlers in kayaks.

The 1965 U.S. Team did not do well in Spittal. The European course was much harder than they anticipated, particularly for wildwater. In contrast to Spittal in 1963, the 1965 river conditions were fast and high due to an abundance of rain. (Mark Fawcett, a C-2 racer, wore two life jackets for the race.) However, the team improved in their standings. Joe Knight finished 29th out of 47 in K-1 slalom. (Paris finished 36th and Duffek finished 42nd.) Barb Wright finished 12th of 19 in K-1 slalom and Tom Southworth was 11th of 29 in C-1 slalom and 15th of 25 in C-1 wildwater.

IN 1958, Walt Harvest and his father built their own fiberglass kayaks, a symmetrical touring design of their own, that was four meters in length and 70 cm (28 inches) in width. During the summer of 1959, father and son spent a week on the Klamath running Class III water. While driving in their MG TD with their two glass kayaks on top, Walt made a comment to his father: "What would be the likelihood of passing another sports car on the road with two kayaks on top?"[25] When a Porsche with two kayaks passed in the other direction, both sports cars immediately made a u-turn. It was Roger and Jackie Paris. From that point on, Walt became a protégé of Roger who helped to develop his paddling skills.

One of the lessons learned from Spittal in 1965 was that the U.S. paddlers had the same level of equipment and basic skills but needed more polish. However, another major lesson was that there was a big difference in pursuing competition as a hobby versus a sport; conditioning and training made the critical difference.

The first Canadian team went to the '65 World Championships in Spittal. The team was made up of Roger Parsons and Ross Durfey in C-1, Heinz Poenn, Manfred Baur, and Eckhart Rapin in K-1. As Harrigan and Berry had done in 1961, the Canadian team ordered boats from a European manufacturer for delivery for the races. However, it turned out that the workmanship was bad and the boats were very heavy. After having destroyed his wildwater canoe earlier on the day of the opening ceremonies and parade,

24 Whitney, Peter D. "A Correction." *American Whitewater* Vol. XI No. 5 (Summer 1965): 14.

25 Harvest, Walter. Interview by author 14 June 1997.

CZECH AND SLOVAK paddlers were particularly tolerant and helpful of American paddlers. The relationship between paddlers from Czechoslovakia and America first began in 1963 when Kurtz and his Explorers went to the World Championships. Czech and Slovak C-paddlers took the young Americans under their wing. Perhaps their assistance stemmed from an acknowledgement that North America was the home of canoeing and saw the potential of the young paddlers. In 1961 Czech paddler Jan Sulc wrote to AWA and said, "Our nation, just as you, is first of all a canoe, not kayak nation, like Germany."[27]

Author's note: Anti-Germanic sentimentality is perhaps one reason why canoeing caught on in Czechoslovakia instead of kayaking and contributed to Czechoslovakia's dominance in C-1 and C-2 for many years in the World Championships.

In 1964 Karel and Vretka Novak, '61 C-2M Slalom World Champions, came to the United States and paddled in Colorado with American paddlers. Karel, as president of the Slovak Racing Club, later assisted American paddlers in Europe. Tom Southworth lived in Slovakia and trained with the Slovak Racing Club for the '67 and '69 World Championship. Milan Horyna, another C-2 expert, also befriended Americans training in Europe. Karel Knapp, the Czech coach in 1965, was also very helpful although his friendliness was suspect by Czech authorities. Knapp defected to West Germany in 1967. The relationship expanded in 1967 when the Czech team played host to the American team, primarily through the efforts of team manager Bill Reilly (1967 to 1971) who spoke fluent Czech.

Because of close ties established between Czech and American paddlers, a few Czech paddlers contacted their American counterparts to sponsor them after they defected. When Josef Sedavic and his wife Jirina (Czech C-2M Champions) defected after the '67 World Championships, they contacted Mark and Gay Fawcett of Buck Ridge. The Sedavics later competed as Americans in the '71 World Championships. Stanislaus Chladek and his wife Erna (C-2M) also defected and came to America.

Roger Parsons wrote of the exhilaration and comfort when the Canadian team marched in the parade and heard applause and shouts of "Bravada Kanada." Canadian C-1 paddlers finished 25th and 28th out of a field of 28 while their K-1 paddlers finished slightly better at 34th and 35th out of 38.

The controversy regarding American rankings and team selection was finally resolved in time for the next World Championships. In 1966, ACA's National Slalom Committee approved a Rotation Plan for National Championship White-Water Slalom and Wildwater races. For K-1 and K-1W slalom and wildwater, the nationals rotated among three ACA divisions: the Rocky Mountain Division, Pacific Coast Division, and all the divisions of the East. As soon as enough competitors existed outside of the East, it was intended that canoeing would also rotate. Additionally, a Team Selection Method was finally accepted. The top three from each class in both slalom and wildwater in the East and the West were selected by the National Chairman based on rankings within each group and named to the National Team for the World Championships. This went into affect for the '67 World Championships.

By this time, the major difference between the East and West rankings was the difference in the ages of the racers. Racers from the East were often younger (predominantly late teens to late twenties) than those from the West. With the exception of Fletcher Anderson of Colorado, many of the ranked racers from the West were older than those from the East. Whitewater activity in the East clearly developed and encouraged younger racers. This was particularly true for young women who came into the sport through Mariners and later, coed Explorer Posts.

The Nationals on the Wenatchee in 1967 was the first time many at the race had seen racers from the East. Eric Evans and Peggy Nutt (now Mitchell), both considered the top K-1 paddlers in the East, competed at the race. For many of the West Coast racers in attendance, Nutt was the first woman they had seen that "paddled like a man."[26] She trained with Jay Evans.

In 1967, there were twenty-four slalom races in the East but less than ten in the West split between California and Colorado. With the availability of more races to prepare for, the National Team selected for the World Championships in Lipno, Czechoslovakia, was by far the strongest to date. The team was also comprised of the youngest members, many in their late teens and early twenties, including Sandy Campbell, Eric Evans, and Dave Nutt (all associated with LCC) in K-1; Terry Franz and Nancy Abrams (Mariners) in K-1W; and, Tom Burton (LCC), Tom Southworth (PSOC), and Wick Walker (LCC) in C-1. Jo Knight, a favorite, did not make the team due to injuries sustained in an automobile accident. However, in addition to being the youngest team to attend a world championship, they were also the most successful with the most team members finishing well in the middle of the pack for K-1 slalom, C-1 slalom, and C-1 wildwater. ACA's goal for 1967 had been to place someone in the top ten in world competition. Barb Wright placed 9th out of 17 in K-1W slalom. The U.S. had finally broken into the top ten.

Barb Wright was 41 years old in 1967 and was often the oldest competitor at races, both nationally and internationally. At the World Championships in 1967, as was her custom, she had a couple of shots of whiskey before the race to calm down.

[26] Liebman, Paul. Interview by author 7 February 1999.

[27] Sulc, Jan. "Letters from Readers." *American Whitewater* Vol. VII No. 1 (May 1961): 3.

After the '67 World Championships, the Swiss magazine *Touring* released the official ICF statistical survey assessing present international standards in whitewater kayak and canoe. On the basis of results of the '67 World Championships, the U.S. team was ranked fifth behind East Germany, Czechoslovakia, West Germany, and Switzerland boosting the U.S. in front of Austria and France for the first time. For wildwater, the U.S. team was ranked ninth.

With Wright's success, sights were set for additional placings in the top ten at the next World Championships in 1969 at Bourg St. Maurice in France on the Isere River. ACA created National Slalom Training Centers with eight training camps established in 1968: Northern New England under Jay Evans, Southern New England under Guy Newhall, California under Tom Johnson, Midwest under Eric Olsen in Wisconsin, Northwest under Al Zob, Mid-Atlantic under Dan Sullivan, and Rocky Mountains under Dave Morrissey.

Per the 1966 Rotation Plan, in 1969 the National Kayak Slalom Champions were held in the West on the Arkansas at Buena Vista, Colorado, and the National Canoe Slalom Championships remained in the East. As was the case in previous years, K-1 and K-1W national champions were from the West.

The National Slalom and Wildwater Committee recognized the need for designated coaches, trainers, and team managers if the team was to be successful in the next World Championships. In anticipation of the '69 World Championships, Jay Evans was appointed Trainer and Coach, and Bill Riley Manager. Assistant coaches, both appointed and volunteer, also assisted during the championships in France and included some older racers including John Connet, Bart Hauthaway, Tom Johnson, and Ted Young.

For the first time, the team had slalom and wildwater specialists, five each, and the balance of the team competed in both. The team was composed mostly of paddlers under the age of 25: Lucile (Barb) McKee, Tom Southworth, Paul Liebman, Louise Wright, Mark Fawcett, Dave Kurtz, Ben Parks, Jon Evans, Al Chase, Brad Hager, Norm Holcombe, Dave Nutt, Peggy Nutt, Les Bechdel, Eric Evans, John Burton, John Bryson, Don Joffray, Gay Fawcett, Dick Church, Ed Bliss, John Holland, and Art Vitarelli.

Although none on the team broke into the top ten at Bourg St. Maurice, overall individual improvement continued in all classes. However, the C-2M team took bronze medals in slalom and wildwater, placing third out of four in slalom and third out of five in wildwater.

After the '69 World Championships, ICF announced that slalom (not wildwater) was chosen as a demonstration sport for the '72 Olympics in Munich, Germany. That announcement forever changed the sport.

THREE distinct pockets of competition evolved for a time in the '60s: in the East, Colorado, and California. The East dominated canoeing, first open (decked) and then closed canoes (C-1 and C-2). Colorado and California rivalry dominated kayaking early in the '60s, partly influenced by European immigrants like Walter Kirscbaum and Roger Paris at CRMS. But this rivalry eventually gave way to the East for kayaking as well, much of it due to Jay Evans' influence and his "Dartmouth boys." Throughout the '60s, the East also contributed to a younger group of racers, perhaps more dedicated than before, encouraging young men and women through programs under the guidance of Jay Evans at Dartmouth (LCC), Dave Kurtz with his Explorers, and CCA members with support of young women in Mariners. All of this helped to narrow the gap between American and European racers in international competition, setting the stage for what many considered the ultimate venue in international competition, the Olympics.

Competition's Other Benefactors: Design, Technique, and Boat Building

Competition drove almost everything in the sport. Because of that, the sport changed forever when the F-1 class was dropped from competition, which signaled the acceptance of the superiority of fiberglass construction and rigid kayaks. This acceptance propelled the development of modern kayak and canoe hull shapes for slalom and downriver competition. The last vestiges of the influence of pre-World War II materials on design could be eliminated. Kayak shapes evolved away from the traditional "touring" hull of a folding kayak. Canoes became permanently decked, or closed, emulating kayaks. Modern materials finally allowed preconceived notions about design to change. Changes in technique in turn affected design. Both complimented one another and spawned additional advancements. Added to this was the ability for each paddler to design and build his own boat, which resulted in increased numbers of new designs.

In the early to mid-'50s, fiber reinforced plastic (FRP) construction primarily meant the use of fiberglass cloth, mat, and roving as the fiber reinforcement. However, by the late '50s and early '60s, other reinforcement materials came into use to improve the properties of the lay-ups, particularly for increased resistance to impact and therefore, durability, complimented by newer and better resins. True "composites" had arrived.

The Wild Water Commission promoted the inclusion of rigid and folding kayaks in the same event at the 1962 Congress of the ICF. However, the Chairman of the Commission also promoted retaining "the traditional shape of the kayak and the canadian [sic] canoe. For the sake of socalled [so-called] progress we see far too many 'monsters' on our rivers..."[28]

[28] Thelen, H. (Editor). "Congress Topics." *ICF Bulletin* International Canoe Federation No. 3 1962 (July 1962).

Design

In competition, as well as cruising, American paddlers in the mid-to-late '60s continued to look to Europeans as the experts in many different areas of paddling, including design. With few exceptions, new designs were purposed for competition, either slalom or wildwater. However, they were also used for cruising. As soon as a new European boat was available in an area, builders quickly adopted and pirated it. That was the beauty of fiberglass construction. A mold could be made practically overnight. European designs provided a kick-start for American paddlers and certainly influenced many early American designs, many of which were often no more than minor changes to pirated European designs.

American paddlers thought European designers were superior without realizing that the early to mid-'60s was also a transition time for them; they didn't really have a "lock" on the materials or designs themselves. Not only was fiberglass construction new, but designing for a truly rigid material like fiberglass was also new. Klepper and others recognized that the "water flow technology" (terminology used by Dieter Stiller)[29] was different for fiberglass. Gone was the hull concavity due to water pressure between cross-sectional members as well as the chines (whether intentionally or unintentionally the result of concavity between longitudinal structural members). The hull was truly rigid, even under water pressure, and they realized they had much to learn. Hull hydrodynamics were much different for a rigid hull. However, American paddlers didn't know that the Europeans didn't know it all.

The transition time for European designers and manufacturers was relatively long in acknowledging the effects of fiberglass construction on design. For manufacturers such as Klepper, they were not quick to introduce an unproven design or concept that might hurt their reputation. Their approach to design and manufacturing was very methodical and therefore, slow. When a mold was created, it was not "quick-n-dirty." The mold was built to produce consistent results for 200 to 300 boats. This further increased the time required to produce and introduce a new design.

Kayak Evolution

In the early '60s, with the exception of imported Klepper fiberglass kayaks, very few other European kayaks were available except those brought back from Europe by racers and other paddlers. (Racers even cut boats into three pieces to bring them back on a plane.) For kayak designs, Klepper was the acknowledged leader.

In 1961, Klepper came out with two fiberglass models, the SL-61 (slalom) and Quirl (downriver). The SL-61 was advertised as a 13' 9" x 24" kayak comparable to the folding SL-59 hull weighing in at 42 pounds. In 1962, a few fiberglass kayaks manufactured by Herbert Baschin in Stuttgart, West Germany, were bought back by American racers and paddlers. Two characteristics differentiated Baschin kayaks from Klepper. One was the two deck bulges, "crocodile eyes," that served as knee-braces, or knee bumps. The other was the centerline seam down the hull, the kayak mold was split side to side, not deck to hull. In 1963, Baschin ceased production and was later purchased by Klepper. However, Klepper discontinued the knee bump design and the concept was lost for a time by European designers.

[29] Stiller, Dieter. Interview by the author 26 June 2000.

Beginning in 1951, Klepper introduced new slalom folding kayaks each year for the World Championships. Each new design had its own designation, "SL" followed by the year. The last folding kayak designed for world championship competition was the SL-59. The SL-61, a fiberglass kayak, was the exception but thereafter, the year numbering was shortened to just the last digit, hence the SL-5 was the fiberglass kayak designed for the '65 World Championships.

In 1965, Klepper introduced the SL-5, one of the first kayaks in the evolution toward lower volume designs. Although the stern was low enough to sneak gates and sneaking gates was not a common practice, the SL-5 was later recognized for that ability. In 1967, Klepper introduced the SL-7 and the following year, the SL-8 (Slalom 8), continuing the slow methodical evolution with somewhat lower volume designs and lower decks. The SL-8 was teamed with another model, the Trabant, that Klepper referred to as their "standard" slalom model. A wildwater racing/downriver boat, the Fighter, and the Minor, a junior K-1 for 7-13 year olds, were also produced providing a more complete line of kayaks.

Klepper's Minor was the first commercially produced kayak for children. It was about 8 feet in length, 20 inches in width, and about half the weight of an adult kayak. The cockpit size was the standard adult. Other Europeans manufacturers followed suit with junior slalom designs in the 10-foot range. KCCNY, WKC (Washington Kayak Club, formerly the Washington Foldboat Club), AMC and other clubs supported kids in paddling and regional designers also designed and built kayaks for kids at about the same time. This included Vern Rupp in Seattle, Walt Harvest in California, and Bart Hauthaway in Boston whose design was eventually manufactured by Old Town. Kids were encouraged to participate in slalom competitions and junior slalom courses were designed and set up for them.

Duffek's own kayak design became available in the mid-'60s, not as a manufactured hull as the Klepper, but as a home-built hull that was molded again and again across the country. The Duffek hull brought two characteristics to slalom: a softened bow V and hard chines. As the boat was eddied, the softened V in the bow (a U shaped V) tracked and caught the current which allowed the boat to accelerate. Its hard chines allowed the paddler to carve during surfing while maintaining position and control by using the chine like a rail or keel using leans and weight shifts. (This did not become common in racing designs until the late '70s.)

A few Mendesta kayaks from Belgium also showed up in the mid-'60s, and in 1967, Tom Johnson in Kernville, California, became a distributor for them in the West.

Another European design from Czechoslovakia called the Vertex was developed for the '67 World Championships. It was a good design but it was not available to American paddlers until after the Championships.

In the mid-'60s, American designers and builders began producing designs similar to their European counterparts. The early designs of Bart Hauthaway, John Urban, and Stu Coffin in the East were influenced by European designs, following Klepper's lead with high volume and moderate rocker.

By the late '60s, the most sought after European design was the Special Slalom, developed by the newly emerging designer Tony Prijon for the '69 World Championships. The only model available to American paddlers was the British modification, the Isere, which proved to be slightly better. Kurtz brought back an Isere and the design was soon pirated. The boat was in great demand. Ledyard made their own mold and Jim Stuart with Tim Fahey of the Wisconsin Hoofers built at least fifty Iseres, renamed WHOC Slalom Kayaks, to meet the demand for them.

The difference between the Special Slalom and the British Isere versions was that the Isere's seat position was one and a half-inch farther forward than the Special Slalom. In 1970, after discussions with Jim Stuart, Prijon changed the Special Slalom's seat position to match the Isere's.

There was a difference between the European designers of C-1s and C-2s and kayak designers regarding the sharing of designs. C-1 (and C-2) designers Bernot, Benes, Hahn and others were not as concerned about their designs being pirated and often gave their designs away. However, kayak designers such as Klepper, Prijon, and Lettmann were very concerned and felt that many of their designs were stolen from them through pirating. In reality, the designs actually were stolen since no royalties were generated for the designs from the multitude of pirated molds. The difference in view point regarding the pirating of designs between C-1 and K-1 designers was the result of the difference in market potential between C-1s and K-1s. Kayaking was always much more popular than C-paddling, particularly in Europe for cruising, and therefore had more potential for generating revenue.

Concurrent to the trend toward lower volume kayaks by European designers, Mel Schneller, a designer and builder in Marysville, California (apparently unaware of the SL-5/SL-7 lower volume decks), designed what was considered a radically low volume K-1 for slalom racing. Schneller organized a small group of paddlers to form the Feather River Kayak Club in Marysville where the Yuba River joins the Feather. They practiced slalom on the Yuba and perfected shallow-water slalom techniques for low-water levels which were available to them much of the time. Schneller's kayak design was based on these shallow-water techniques and was a low volume kayak with high rocker, particularly noticeable compared to other kayaks at the time. Unfortunately, the group spent so much time perfecting their technique with the design that they were unable to handle bigger water. At the '70 National Kayak Slalom Championships on the Wenatchee in Washington, paddlers from the group had considerable difficulty on the big water of the Wenatchee, 6,000 to 8,000 cfs, which was almost ten times the volume they were used to practicing on. Paul Liebman, a C-2 racer from Philadelphia, recalled that Gate 1 was a straight shot but with the big water, even that gate was difficult for the Marysville group to run cleanly. Unfortunately, the paddlers and Schneller's design were dismissed as inadequate and the low volume design's concepts were lost. Schneller was ahead of his time but he was isolated and neither his design nor his technique caught on. When he died of a heart attack toward the end of the Burnt Ranch Gorge run on the Trinity on Labor Day in 1971, the spirit of the Marysville group died with him. So, too, did his innovations in design.

Schneller K-2 on the Rogue River (OR) 1971
—courtesy of Carl Trost.

In the East another designer, James Stuart (CCA) also designed a low volume kayak, the Tri-S or SSS (Super Sonic Sneak), and introduced it the Summer of 1967. The design was a little like a wildwater boat with a narrower hull in the bow with a bow V (more than Hauthaway's Czech kayak version) and the stern was a little wider but with less rocker. Acknowledging that the Duffek and Hauthaway Czech kayaks were slow, the bow V of Stuart's design was an attempt to "snag water on entrances to eddies as well as on exits, to hook the boat into the current." [30] The bow was designed to facilitate fast entry and exits on upstream gates. The overall asymmetry with its wildwater-like design was for speed over the whole course. However, the critical change in the boat was its low deck, particularly in the stern, designed intentionally to sneak gates (hence its name). "The stern deck centerline and seam line in profile actually dipped downward from the cockpit, and then up again to the tip of the stern. There were alligator eye knee-braces [borrowed from the earlier Baschin model] to compensate for the lowered deck." [31]

The first model in 1967, although well thought out from the design standpoint, was not properly faired and in 1968, a second iteration was made that eliminated the imperfections. For a short time, Stuart went into commercial production of the Tri-S with another CCA member.

Like Schneller's design, the Tri-S was ahead of its time. Both designs, as was the trend toward lower volume hulls, were short-lived for partially the same reason: low volume boats were not thought to be able to perform well on large volume rivers. The announcement that slalom would be included in the '72 Olympics and that the course would be at Augsburg, Germany, meant the artificial course would have big, pushy water. As a result, design strategy completely shifted away from low volume hulls with low decks to high volume with high decks.

Closed Canoe Evolution

Just as with the design transition from the limitations of folding kayak to fiberglass construction in kayaks, so, too, did canoes undergo a design transition. Prior to fiberglass, canoes retained some of their heritage shapes, particularly when it came to a deck. Decks were added to keep water out in whitewater but were not an integral part of the design, nor were they necessary for structural purposes. Whitewater canoes, prior to fiberglass, were merely decked canoes. However, fiberglass construction allowed decks to become a permanent structural part of the design. With the use of fiberglass, C-1s and C-2s permanently split from traditional canoe designs to become permanently decked canoes, or closed canoes for whitewater.

However, unlike with kayak designs, no C-1 or C-2 designs were available from Europe in the late '50s or early '60s until Bernot's designs appeared. As a result, evolution of C-1 design in America took a somewhat different turn. American designers were pretty much on their own for a few years. In 1959, Larry Zuk designed and built the first truly closed C-1, the Merlin, and paddled it at the Nationals held on the Roaring Fork in Colorado in 1959. Since the Merlin was the only boat of its kind, not fitting into any canoe class and looking more like a kayak, Zuk was forced to compete in the kayak class.

At the race that year were three paddlers from the East, John Berry, Bill Bickham, and Bob Harrigan, all competing in decked canoes. Berry recognized the potential of Zuk's closed design and upon his return home, Berry

[30] Stuart, James. Email correspondence to author dated 31 May 2000.

[31] Ibid.

designed and built a closed C-1. It was tippy and narrow with low ends and premiered at Brandywine in 1960. Neither Harrigan nor Bickham were impressed with it. In fact, Harrigan would not even paddle it and Bickham called it the "Monitor." Only Paul Bruhin paddling with KCCNY was impressed. "*That* is a C-1. Now learn to paddle it!"[32] Later the same year at the Nationals held on the West River, Berry's C-1 was the only one of its kind and easily beat the other decked canoe competitors including Harrigan and Bickham. This was two years before the Bernot design was paddled by the Explorers of Penn State.

John Berry in his first C-1, the Monitor, West River Race (VT) 1962 — courtesy of John Berry.

Bernot's 1961 design, the Yugo I, provided the first European C-1 design that met ICF requirements for competition (4 meters by 90 centimeters with bow and stern higher than amidships). His second design, the Yugo II, was much lower in volume and had a rounded deck with low edges emulating kayak designs of the time. It was ahead of its time. Other C-1 designs retained the higher volume seen in earlier designs.

In the mid-'60s, Stu Coffin obtained and modified a German C-1 and John Berry and Jim Raleigh cut down a Czech C-2 to make a C-1. Kurtz also picked up another Czech C-1 design from Ludek Benes of Bratislava at the '65 World Championship. It also was a high volume design extremely popular for competition and cruising. Many used the design until it became obsolete with the changes in C-1 dimensional requirements for the '71 World Championships.

After Stuart's low volume Tri-S kayak debuted the previous summer, Tom Southworth modified the Benes C-1 design during the winter of '67–68, lowering the deck (and volume) and taking about 2-inches out of the rocker. The design, the Lumas, was actually a faster design and able to sneak gates, similar to the Slipper C-1 design in 1976. The Lumas was named after the prep school Southworth attended when he designed the boat. Don Joffray made the '69 team using a Lumas design.

The most notable change in designs at the '69 World Championships did not come from slalom competition, but rather from wildwater competition. Alain Feuillette, a French designer and paddler, introduced a radical wildwater C-2 design called "La Tub" which revolutionized wildwater designs with three significant changes. The first was that the cockpits were moved toward the center of boat, away from the ends. The cockpits were also offset to allow the paddlers to be closer to the boat's side along with providing a clearer view for each paddler. The second change included a more bulbous bow to prevent the bow from burying into waves. The third change, again to keep the boat riding higher in the water, was the addition of the delta wing stern, particularly useful in keeping the stern from bottoming over ledges.

La Tub signaled the radical change that occurred in the '70s between boats that could be used by cruisers from those used exclusively by racers because of their complete specialization for racing. This specialization was also an indication of the divergence between racers and cruisers.

Since open canoes were not used in competition except in smaller local races, there was nothing driving any changes in their design. For whitewater in general, Grummans dominated, particularly the 15-foot and 17-foot shoe-keel models.

THE MONITOR was the Union counterpart to the Confederate Merrimack, both ironclad warships. They were both preposterous looking at the time but the Monitor even more so since the deck was extremely low and it had a raised turret amidships, very much like a raised cockpit of a C-1.

IN AN INTERVIEW by John Sweet, John Berry recalled:

> How does a guy pushing 40, who flies a desk all week, and has a wife and four kids... beat someone like Bickham? In a better boat, much better.[33]

[32] Sweet, John R. "Going for Gold: The Evolution of C-1 Slalom in the United States." *Whitewater'79* The United States International Slalom Canoe Association: ACA National Slalom Committee: (1979): 13–20.

[33] Ibid.

Technique

With more sophisticated designs, the limits of paddling technique for canoeing and kayaking were pushed. Aside from competition, new designs and new composite materials allowed paddlers to run more demanding whitewater, pushing the limits of boating abilities all around.

In the '50s, with some exceptions where European paddlers and instructors were available, almost everyone was self-taught. By the '60s, a growing group of paddlers began to understand the finer points of technique, using the big muscle groups, the Duffek, leans, and draws. Stylistically, the techniques were still in development, but fundamentally, the basic technique was already there.

Many of the improvements in cruising technique were a carryover from slalom that evolved at the same time. Slalom's popularity increased all over the country. Some cruisers realized that slalom skills greatly added to their cruising abilities with techniques such as ferrying, eddy turns, peel-outs, stroke efficiency, and the use of river currents to their advantage. As technique and river running skills advanced and improved, the level of difficulty of the rivers that were run increased.

Kayaking

In the early '60s, a coalescing of technique and design began to take shape. Peter D. Whitney in his book *White-Water Sport* referred to it as the "'crystallization of style." [34] Much of this crystallization evolved around the Duffek stroke and leans (which in turn affected designs).

[*Author's note:* The following quotes are from Whitney's *White-Water Sport.* [35]] Whitney wrote,

> All [kayaks] have V profiles at bow and stern, some flattening amidships, and rounded arcs at the sides. The typical modern slalom boat, with rocker in its keel, may have a V carried from bow to stern, but widening out to an all-but-flat midsection. Its bottom may curve into the upward slope of the sides, or it may have sharp chines (the angles between bottom and sides) for some part of the hull. The reason for the latest outbreak of design rethinking has been the emphasis on leaning in the more modern kayak technique. A kayak is leaned nowadays for the sake of turning it more easily; that means that designers are tempted to make a boat that is easier to lean and has yet more pronounced rocker when leaned than it does at the actual keel.
>
> Above water, the foredeck section of a kayak is customarily somewhat higher than the poop, the extra elevation being used to steepen the roof angle of the canvas deck [of a folding kayak]. The purpose of this is to throw off heavy waves the more quickly… As for cross-section above the water line, there has been a recent tendency to abolish the sharp distinction between bottom and deck—to round the gunwale so that the bottom curve continues around under the canvas, and indeed,

White-Water Sport was written by Peter Dwight Whitney in the late '50s and published in 1960. Whitney was a member of AMC and KCCNY in the East before moving to California where he became a member of Bay Chapter's RTS. He was active in AWA, served as editor of *American Whitewater,* and was exposed to paddling across the country, particularly during the time of advancements and changes in the sport in the late '50s and early '60s.

In the preface for his book, Whitney acknowledged AMC, KCCNY, and Sierra Club, as well as Paul Bruhin, Ernest Svaton, and Lawrence Zuk and the contributions of Oscar Hawksley, Lawrence Monninger, Arthur Kidder, Frank Cockerline, and Bryce Whitmore, paddlers from the East and West.

[34] Whitney, Peter Dwight. *White-Water Sport: Running Rapids in Kayak and Canoe.* New York: The Ronald Press Company, 1960.

[35] Ibid.

> to the very cockpit edge... For the new ways of paddling, it permits the kayakist to lean extraordinarily far, yet to right himself smoothly with paddle brace or esquimautage.

The French term esquimautage (eskimo-tahj) included "the idea of rolling over [on] one side and coming back[up] on the same side, as well as the complete 'eskimo-roll' in which the paddler goes over one side and comes back the other."

The Duffek was recognized as an important stroke because it was often combined with a strong lean and a powerful forward stroke. "Until Duffek, nobody had ever dared to lean onto his paddle quite so hard and to hang from it." It was recognized that the stroke maintained forward energy capitalizing on centrifugal force around the pivot using the current.

A powerful and proper forward stroke was also recognized as important.

> Exerting the blade as far forward as is comfortable and—for a straight punch—fairly close to the hull, push your upper fist out in something very similar to a boxer's straight punch delivered at eye level. Your lower hand, used as a fulcrum, is drawn back with appropriate wrist-twisting to achieve the proper blade angle. The paddler's body is erect, though with a little lean forward. The torso swings around a firm spine; power will be wasted if there is too much body movement.

As were leans.

> The paddler should study from the beginning the effects of leaning the kayak... by swiveling his hips, a paddler can make a moving kayak turn without so much as touching his paddle to water. The turn is somewhat "against nature" inasmuch as the paddler must lean to the outside, the opposite of what he does in bicycling and ice skating... [Lean in on] high-speed turns with heavy use of the paddle blade as a pivot.

Braces, both forward (now called a high brace) and backward (a low brace), were combined with forward strokes and back strokes and were done both forward and aft of the cockpit. For a brace in the mid-section,

> ...perpendicularly abeam of the paddler, we have come to the threshold of the Duffek or hanging turns. This brace is done with the upstream, concave paddle face, and a high upper arm. This brace can be turned into a drawstroke to move the boat sideways by bringing the slightly bent upper arm directly above the head (so that water from the upper blade drops on the hair). The blade is pulled toward the boat while lean is maintained as long as possible. The firmness of this brace and drawstroke have to be experienced to be believed. But be sure to maintain that 90-degree angle of paddle from [the] boat, or much of the stabilizing effect is lost.

Whitney recognized that technique was a combination of strokes, braces, and leans but it was also recognized that changes of blade angle with the current were equally important. "More important for his development as a subtle paddler, though, he changes the outline of his paddle stroke [for forward or back strokes] and varies his blade angle."

Understanding the effects of leans and blade angle in current, paddlers experimented with new combinations. In 1959, a few Colorado boaters "invented" and practiced a new kayak stroke they called the Colorado Hook. It was actually a cross draw and took advantage of what was learned from the Duffek.

> The stroke is executed at speed when entering or leaving fast moving water. The greater the velocity differential, the greater the effectiveness of the Hook. The blade from the side of the kayak that will be on the outside of the turn is crossed over to the inside and inserted into the water toward the bow in such a way that it digs in or hooks. Simultaneously the body is leaning toward the outside of the turn. Balance is then maintained by feathering or turning the blade to control the amount of hook.
>
> The hook as done in a kayak is entirely different from the crossover in a canoe because of the difference in length and rocker of the boats and because of the entirely different balance and lean of each. There are several fringe benefits of the Colorado Hook. One is that in reaching out ahead of the body the paddler can take advantage of a current before he himself enters it and sooner than he would if he were reaching to the side only. He can reach through a gate or up into a current when smack-dab alongside underbrush or a wall. The Hook will naturally work better with certain shapes of kayaks, and it will work only under particular circumstances. The inside lean on a turn should be forgotten, and the last forward stroke should be made on the side which will be inside at the turn. It is not easy to get aquainted with, but this thrilling spine-twister will give you a new sensation in kayaking, and will enable you to execute a snappier turn than you ever though possible.[36]

In a letter to the editor dated March 17, 1961 (published in May 1961 AWA), Czech paddler Jan Sulc claimed that the Colorado Hook was not a powerful new stroke but one that was tried and dismissed, and if used in Europe, would bring "smiles to the faces of the spectators."[37]

Although there was much agreement on the Duffek and leans, there was much controversy about whether to feather paddle blades or not, especially among racers trying to determine the greatest advantage of equipment and technique. Articles appeared in *American Whitewater* in the early to mid-'60s justifying both positions and later included discussions about the best size of the blade (blade area) and "spooning" of a blade's profile. Eventually, feathered paddles and spoon blades won out. The profile of the blade and power face continued to evolve into the '70s (and continues to do today).

[36] Lake, Leo C. "The Colorado Hook." *American Whitewater* Vol. VI No. 1 (May 1960): 6–7.

[37] "Letters from Readers." *American Whitewater* Vol. VII No. 1 (May 1961): 3.

Canoeing

At the same time changes in kayak technique were recognized as a result of Duffek's influence, others including McNair recognized the evolution in canoeing from the '50s into the early '60s also directly related to some of these changes. McNair wrote:

> Until about 1950 our Buck Ridge "style" was limited to picking the right filament of water and dodging the last minute rocks. We knew that flat water techniques (and paddlers) were inadequate and that our sideways skidding was effective on many rivers. This technique was not quite adequate for the Lehigh Gorge and each year Buck Ridge approached this trip with some trepidation. Then the Appalachian Mountain Club taught us about back paddling and setting. We built the back paddling reflex into our canoeists and put great emphasis on discretion. The cross draw made hand shifting unnecessary in the bow, but sternmen were encouraged to shift sides in setting so the powerful reverse quarter sweep (pried off the canoe) could get the stern over in initiating the setting maneuver.
>
> Now the eastern clubs face a new revolution in canoeing technique. We have always been on the lookout for new ideas and for two years our spies have brought back hints of a new technique. The rumors have become a roar that can no longer be ignored by those who would maintain their "expert" status. The first clue came when we studied movies of ourselves in action, and saw how much time was wasted shifting the paddles from side to side. In Colorado we found that the splash covered canoe had to be driven **forward** to get through monstrous waves or souse holes. From the Northwest we learned to "play the river." From Roger Paris of France we learned of the paddle braces and the related techniques developed in European slalom. All these things added up to a new technique, a new chapter of fun in the evolution of canoeing.
>
> Perhaps the characteristic of the new technique is the rapport between a paddler and his canoe. The old school said you kneel to lower the center of gravity. We said the purpose was to get the point of contact with the canoe down to the waterline. Now the purpose is to hold the canoe with the knees so you can force it to bank in some maneuvers. It appears that knee sockets or straps will be needed to do this with most canoes. With a firm hold on the canoe our whole body can swing into action.
>
> Another characteristic of the new style is driving the canoe forward in many maneuvers. Actually the ability to shift back and forth from forward technique to backward technqiue is essential, the ability to do an eddy turn, then a set in quick succession.

> The new maneuvers depend on some new paddle strokes. A new hand-hold increases our backing power for setting; the paddle brace (borrowed from folding kayaking) adds stability to our eddy turns; the pryaway replaces the cross draw in heavy water and slalom;[note this] the sculling strokes come into whitewater because they keep the paddle in the water when sudden corrective action or bracing may be needed. Most important is a ban on shifting hands on the paddle. It has become taboo. They realized this because they needed both sides to have braces in heavy water.
>
> Those who aspire to such rivers as the Cheat, the Hudson, or the Arkansas will need these new techniques... Of course the real reason for the new technique is that it is more fun. "Playing the river" is an inseparable part of the new technique. By playing in the rapids we develop the skill for tougher rivers and we also have more fun with the same rapids than ever before.[38]

Author's note: I noted that there is no real mention of hydraulics in *White-Water Sport,* and little discussion of playing in a river except for ferrying and wave surfing. Whitney discussed navigating in whitewater by using "sliding" or ferrying to avoid obstacles. He suggested that a canoeist should not try to steer through rock gardens but use sideways strokes and ferry glides using eddies. He acknowledged that with the advent of the Duffek in kayaking that allowed forward turning, that the trend for canoeing was changing from hanging back (back paddling) to paddling forward through a rapid. But Whitney also admitted for canoeists that the practice of ferrying (or setting) was "more firmly entrenched" implying it would take longer for advances in technique to come to canoeing. However, it should be noted that Whitney's observations were also based on open canoeing since his book was written before closed canoes were commonly used.

Just as it was recognized in kayaking that being firmly positioned or tight in the boat was required for better boat control, particularly with the increasing use of leans, so, too, was it recognized for both open and closed canoes. The use of knee straps finally became a common practice in the mid-Atlantic and Northeast although it was slower to be adopted in the Southeast.

As Whitney wrote, canoeing technique had similar parallels to kayaking:

> More modern canoe technique, however, increasingly parallels the kayak methods in preferring a brace on the upstream face [of the paddle] wherever possible.
>
> In standard technique, as practiced in many clubs in this country, the bow position is for the less well-trained paddler or for the woman, or at least the lighter and less strong member of the team. This corresponds to the realities of still-water canoeing in the straight-keeled canoe, where a stern-heavy canoe is desired and steering is largely in the hands of the stern paddler. In this case, it is usually the bow man who adapts to the preferences of his stern man, and more often than not he has to paddle on the left side [note don't change sides]... In most canoe clubs using standard technique, a well-trained paddler who is content to stay in the bow is a pearl beyond price... This differs, as will be seen, from the situation in the European canoe, where the positions are much more equal and where the bow position may even be the place for the more powerful paddler. The two schools of paddling differ in how much they allow the bow paddler to cross over. All agree that crossing is a special situation and that the normal position is to have one paddle on each side. But the standard American technique allows so many exceptions to the bow man in whitewater that the rule seems to be honored more in the breach than in strict observance. The bow paddler is continually reaching over

[38] McNair, Bob. "The Evolution of Canoeing Style." *American Whitewater* Vol. VI No. 1 (May 1960): 16–17.

> his "off" side for the cross-bow draw. He does not change his hands, however, for fear of losing the paddle. The reason for cross-bow work is that the drawstroke is stronger and safer than the pushing and prying strokes the paddler must otherwise use to turn his off-side.
>
> The J-stroke is supplanted in whitewater by a harder curve, swinging the paddle blade under the boat, which is sometimes called the C-stroke. In hard slalom turns, the last half of this stroke may be a vicious pry against the gunwale. These prystrokes (ecart in French) are far more common in European than American canoeing.[39]

American Red Cross's instruction was primarily geared toward flatwater although their manual *Canoeing,* published in 1956, included a chapter on canoeing swift rivers. With its foundations in flatwater and using wood and canvas canoes, only the pushaway stroke was taught. The pry or pryaway was not used since it used the gunwale and was therefore not aesthetically pleasing for use in a wood and canvas canoe. The practice of tandem paddlers (particularly in Grummans) switching sides to take advantage of their strong sides including the use of both bow and stern draw strokes, over crossdraws and prys, was hard to give up. It wasn't until Bernot actually demonstrated it was better to stay on one side that many paddlers were convinced of the needed change.

In 1966, Whitney, as retiring *American Whitewater* editor, wrote of the changes in technique and also skills across the country since the early '60s.

> The Eskimo roll was known to only a few, mostly in the Rockies and the Far West; many easterners thought it a stunt without value in either competition or cruising... The screw roll, in turn, was known by still fewer kayakists; most of them still relied on the long paddle methods. The Duffek technique was just something to talk about.[40]

About canoeists he wrote, "many used the sitting position by preference" and in regard to river-running advances, "the Neversink Gorge was then considered an all-but-unrunnable horror."[41] (Today KCCNY schedules training runs on the Neversink.)

Boat Building

Fiberglass and its offspring, composites, allowed the individual to not only build any design, but also provided a boat that was easily repairable. This was significant. It took the realm of making boats away from established manufacturers like Old Town and Grumman for canoes, and Klepper and Folbot for kayaks, and put it into the hands of anyone. As did the designs, fiberglass and composite construction also evolved in pursuit of stronger and lighter materials, particularly for competition.

Colorado builders were at least five years ahead of the rest of the country in the early '60s and got a further boost when Tom and Jane Cooper became involved with CWWA around 1960. The Coopers, Tom, a chemical engineer

[39] Whitney, Peter Dwight. *White-Water Sport: Running Rapids in Kayak and Canoe.* New York: The Ronald Press Company, 1960.

[40] Whitney, Peter D. "From Your Editor." *American Whitewater* Vol. XII No. 1 (Summer 1966): 38.

[41] Ibid.

and Jane, a lab technician, owned Plasticrafts, a plastic forming company for architectural plastics and injection molding in Denver, Colorado. They began building kayaks and canoes with other CWWA members and, through their business, supplied fiberglass cloth, mat, roving, and resin in quantity to other builders. It eventually turned into a side business. They rented a small building next to Plasticrafts where they made kits and rented molds. Cooper developed his own resin mix for boat building made of two-thirds standard surfacing resin and one-third flexible resin.

Builders across the country obtained information on how to build and what materials to use through a variety of sources, including Astrolite Industrial Plastics in Oakland, California, and Plasticrafts, who both advertised in *American Whitewater*. In the early to mid-'60s, although most builders used cloth and mat with iso-polyester and epoxy resins, Dynel and nylon cloths were also used by American builders to enhance impact properties of their lay-ups, which were the first true composites. This was occurring at the same time Klepper and other manufacturers in Europe were methodically perfecting their proprietary lay-ups using strictly fiberglass cloth and mat with polyester resins.

In the East, Kurtz, Coffin, and Berry experimented with materials. In the early '60s, Berry relied on materials and resins from Herters in Minnesota and later Defender Industries in New York. However, the resins were not modified with flex agents (as was Cooper's) which meant that experimentation with materials other than fiberglass, such as nylon and polypropylene, resulted in delamination.

The State College area with Dave Kurtz and John Sweet, both chemists, was also a center for much experimentation with resins and lay-ups. They experimented with different polyester resins, and later epoxies and vinylesters as they became available. Both Sweet and Kurtz also supplied materials to other builders, as did Cooper in Colorado.

ETHAFOAM is a registered trademark of the Dow Chemical Company.

Jim Raleigh was another racer and boat builder in the East who furthered advances in the use of materials at the same time. He experimented with the addition of polypropylene and nylon to fiberglass lay-ups as well as the use of epoxies. Raleigh also experimented with selective reinforcement using different fabrics. In order to build lighter race boats, he began the practice of using Ethafoam™ (polyethylene foam) for walls. By 1968, many boats built in the East followed the practice.

The use of walls in boats was not a common practice in the West and did not really catch on. Many boaters in the West bought Harvest's air bags during the '60s that were not available in a split design for use with walls. Instead, boats built in the West relied on extra reinforcements in the lay-ups to obtain structural rigidity without walls.

With all of the experimentation in the East, which was attributed to the desire for lighter and stronger boats for competition, boatbuilding and materials knowledge soon caught up to and surpassed that in the West. However, one person in particular in the late '60s and early '70s was a key facilitator and equalizer for advancements in both the East and the West. That person was Bill Clark.

Clark worked for IBM in Poughkeepsie, New York, and became involved in paddling in the mid-'60s. He bought a flatwater trainer and, although it was very light, he realized it wouldn't take any abuse. Clark decided he wanted to build boats that didn't fall apart so he read about advanced composites used in the growing aerospace industry. Through his work at IBM, he had access to literature and obtained the most recent information from the Society of Plastics International (SPI) and even obtained a copy of a handbook for epoxy resins. Because many of the epoxy resins available required heat to cure properly, he built a curing oven large enough for a kayak. Clark also realized that vacuum bagging (a relatively new technique developed for aerospace) provided better resin-to-fiber ratios and therefore, more durability with lighter weight. His first vacuum bagged, oven cured epoxy kayak was built around 1967.

The first boat built in this manner was an Urban kayak from a mold Clark and another IBM engineer built. Because the mold was required to withstand the same temperatures as the boats during curing, the molds were made with similar materials. Clark incorporated heaters in the mold by weaving copper wire into a layer of heavy fiberglass roving. He also used electric blankets to heat the molds. This provided him with good temperature control as well as the resin viscosity needed for proper fiber impregnation during the curing process.

Clark and his cohorts formulated and tested coupons to develop their lay-up and oven conditions and even post-cured the epoxy resins to increase impact properties. Combined with vacuum bagging, they were able to build a much lighter and more durable boat than ever before.

Both racing and cruising benefited from this technology and Clark exposed many builders in the East including Dave and Bill Nutt, (racers) and Jackson Wright to this process. In 1970, Clark moved to Colorado to work at IBM's Boulder facility. Two years later in 1972, he began building his lightweight, vacuum-bagged boats in Colorado. He paddled with local CWWA members and introduced many builders to his advanced techniques including Tom Derrer who founded Eddy Line in Boulder in 1971.

IN THE LATE '60S, American builders advanced light years ahead of their European counterparts in boatbuilding and were well prepared for further advances available in the '70s.

Cruising

In the West it was called boating; in the East it was called paddling. But one thing that western boaters and eastern paddlers had in common was an interest in cruising or river-running.

Shuttle vehicle circa 1963 —courtesy of Dave Guss.

The numbers of both organized clubs and loosely knit paddling groups grew throughout the '60s. While competition was very dependent upon organized clubs, cruising was not. And because there was a limited number of paddlers around the country, the circle was small. As a paddler, you often knew almost everyone else in your area, or on your home rivers.

Clubs provided instruction. Many clubs started winter pool sessions to practice rolls, a technique that increased in use by cruisers as it became obvious it was more than just a neat trick. Clubs also provided instruction and assistance in building boats since there were few boats available for purchase. Back yard builders in the early years usually served a single region, particularly due to shipping difficulties. The boundaries of clubs often blurred as paddlers of advanced skills often found one another.

However, not all cruisers actually participated in any kind of club or organization. This was particularly true in less populated areas of the West. Paddlers in Utah and Colorado (the two paddling areas during the '60s outside of California and Washington) often paddled alone or in very small groups. They had so far to go to get to water. Their season, when spring runoff was considered safe, was very short. Rivers with water later in the summer often required permits. It often took a paddler longer to develop his skills because there just were not the rivers and time available as in the East.

Cal Giddings was a paddler in Utah who encountered these problems. A native of Utah, Giddings started paddling with the Hoofers while at the University of Wisconsin pursuing his post-doc in chemistry. His first whitewater experience was the Flambeau River in 1955, and later the Wolf, Namekagon, and Upper Flambeau rivers. When he returned to Utah the following year, he rafted the Yampa and Split Mountain section on the Green with the Wasatch Mountain Club, on the club's first whitewater trip using borrowed rafts from an area Boy Scout troop. (Giddings had climbed with the Club while a grad student at the University of Utah.) With his exposure to whitewater canoeing from Wisconsin, Giddings decided that kayaking was preferable to rafting. Since no kayaks were available in the area, he and Bob Green designed and built (with the help of Giddings' wife, an artist majoring in sculpture) a mold to produce a fiberglass kayak approximately 13 feet in length and 32 inches in width. Giddings was unaware of CWWA's boat building activities.

In the mid-'60s, Giddings obtained a Duffek kayak from paddlers in Colorado that was narrower than his previous design. He made a mold and produced many kayaks for use by Wasatch Mountain Club paddlers. Throughout the '60s, Giddings and other Wasatch Mountain Club paddlers explored rivers already routinely rafted, but they also explored rivers too small for rafts higher in the mountains.

Middle Fork of the Salmon (ID), 1969
—courtesy of Carl Trost.

Because there were so few paddlers in kayaks in the area, much of what Giddings did was new and much of what he learned about technique was self-taught. Giddings taught himself to roll using a book and then he taught others. However, one of his challenges was always finding others to paddle with him. The Wasatch Mountain Club drew many of its members from the university. Unfortunately, Giddings discovered that one of the challenges of paddlers associated with a university, or attracting young from a university, was that they often moved on. Giddings related this in an interview:

> I kept trying to get people involved in kayaking around here [Salt Lake City area]. In fact, there were many times I wanted to go, even for a short one like down on the Provo River, and I couldn't find anyone who could or would go. I mean, there was practically a zero population of kayakers in this area… I was rather isolated attempting to built up a group of people… if I could get two or three people, I felt pretty lucky to go anywhere, and to the extent that I could do that, I used to go out and try these various things that were around here.[42]

In the latter half of the '60s, in the East the use of closed boats (both canoes and kayaks over strictly open canoes) increased from the mid-Atlantic north into New England and in the Midwest. However, there were also regions in the East where open canoes dominated and very few closed boats were seen, either canoe or kayak, such as in the Southeast. In the West, with few exceptions, paddlers used kayaks.

[42] Whitney, Peter D. "From Your Editor." *American Whitewater* Vol. XII No. 1 (Summer 1966): 38.

In the early '60s, women were not always welcomed on river trips. Longtime KCCNY member Ed Alexander recalled trips in the early'60s led by Walter Burmeister, early explorer and guidebook author:

> Those were the days of marathon-type outings under the leadership of Walter Burmeister. Walter had navigated most every river imaginable and was an expert on river classification. He would not begin a cruise unless he was assured of no less than a 25- to 30- mile paddle to the next takeout... Walter was stunned by the appearance of three women on one of his cruises! He instinctively suggested that the day would be far too rough a grind for them to possibly accompany us. Marianne Goldstein, Miriam Alexander and Rosemarie Peter insisted that they could do it, and were determined to prove the tripleader wrong—even if it took them every last ounce of their individual and collective strength.[43]

By the mid- to late '60s the number of women grew with the participation of younger paddlers, both men and women.

In the '60s, whitewater cruising exploded in three different regions of the country: West Virginia, a region of its own, the Southeast, and the Sierras in California. Each region had their own distinct circumstances for the development of whitewater cruising.

West Virginia, the Mountain State, and surrounding rivers in southwestern Pennsylvania (Yough), and western Maryland (Upper Yough) became *the* destination of many paddlers, particularly with the advent of fiberglass boats. It also became the wellspring for the growing commercial rafting industry and the phenomenon called *the Gauley.*

Paddlers in the Southeast paddled exclusively in open Grummans (15-foot for solo and 17-foot for tandem). Without the benefit of AMC and Buck Ridge, they developed a different style of whitewater canoeing: aggressive with massive flotation. This area eventually developed to become the new home of whitewater open canoeing, Royalex canoes, the movie *Deliverance*, and Nantahala Outdoor Center (NOC).

Like West Virginia, the Sierras opened up with the advent of fiberglass boats. Its steep and technical creeks demanded even better materials. It became the proving ground for plastic kayaks and the wellspring for the revolution of plastic in whitewater.

IN WEST VIRGINIA many of the Army Corps dams are for flood and pollution control combined with providing sufficient water downstream for barge traffic. Dams upstream from the Kanawha valley on the New and Gauley are for that purpose. In the Southeast many of the TVA (Tennessee Valley Authority) dams are for electric as well as flood and barge traffic control.

West Virginia

West Virginia, although a destination for CCA, PSOC, and AYH trips, was still largely unexplored. There were many Class IV and V rivers waiting for first descents with minimal portaging in fiberglass boats.

Perhaps because of the domination of canoeing in the East, C-1s, not just decked canoes, were paddled by many racers and cruisers of expert caliber on many of the Class IV and V rivers in West Virginia. These C-1 paddlers included Bob Burrell, Paul Davidson, Norm and Jim Holcombe, John Sweet, and Charlie Walbridge. They were later joined by other Midwest C-1 paddlers

[43] Giddings, Calvin. Interview by Roy D. Webb, 3 July 1984.

including Hank Hayes, Doug Miller, Dean Tomko, and "Fearless" Fred Young, all paddling their big volume Hahns and modified Hahn C-1s as the boats of choice for drop-pool rivers typified in West Virginia.

It wasn't until the early to mid-'60s that West Virginia spawned its own home paddlers. In 1965, Bob Balhatchet and Charlie Mallory of the Kanawha Valley near Charleston independently entered the Petersburg race in open canoes. Both met at the race. They realized that many more out-of-state paddlers were at the race than paddlers from West Virginia and that the race was sponsored by an out-of-state club (CCA). They also realized that West Virginia needed a club of its own. Instead of forming a club in a single city area, they formed the West Virginia Wildwater Association (WVWA) to encompass the entire state, just as Colorado White Water Association had done almost ten years before. Many of the early members were in the Charleston area and many were associated with Union Carbide in Charleston. Idair Smookler, a Union Carbide librarian, was the first woman member and was also the glue behind the organization for many years.

Another early member from the northern part of the state was Bob Burrell who moved to Morgantown in 1961. He bought a canoe and paddled the South Branch of the Potomac. Over the next few years, he paddled other West Virginia rivers in decked open canoes. Burrell and another paddler from Morgantown, Paul "Doc" Davidson, became serious about whitewater. Burrell, as did Balhatchet and Mallory, also attended the Petersburg race in 1965 which exposed him to C-1s and better paddling skills. Soon he and Davidson became members of WVWA.

Burrell and Davidson paddled many of the rivers throughout West Virginia and with the help of other WVWA members scattered across the state, compiled a detailed guidebook modeled after Carter's guidebook classic about Virginia whitewater. In the late '60s, they printed *A Canoeist's Guide to the Whitewater Rivers of West Virginia.* In 1972, McClain Printing of Parsons, West Virginia, took over the next two editions and the title was changed to *Wild Water West Virginia.*

Burrell removed his name as author after the second edition when he felt it attracted too many paddlers to West Virginia. Burrell was right. A lot of paddlers were attracted to West Virginia and the guidebook was the reason out-of-state paddlers came to paddle its rivers. [*Author's note:* I was one of those paddlers.] Their guidebook did indeed open up West Virginia's whitewater to the rest of the whitewater world. West Virginia became a mecca for paddlers. The rivers ranged from small streams tumbling off mountainsides with flows less than 1,000 cfs to larger volume valley rivers with flows greater than 5,000 cfs. It had many un-dammed rivers, particularly in the Cheat watershed, that paddlers could catch in the spring or after heavy rains the rest of the year. It also had a few dammed rivers like the New with regular releases for downstream pollution and barge traffic control throughout the summer and fall. West Virginia had everything a whitewater paddler could want. And it also had *the Gauley.*

The Gauley

In whitewater, there are some rivers that develop a following and become beloved by the people who paddle them. Sometimes it is because of the challenge the river offers. But when the experience level of the paddlers increases, it often loses its following as the paddlers move on to more challenging rivers. But some rivers retain their mystique and their following and continue to inspire paddlers. The Gauley is such a river. It has been the object of affection and protection which has shaped its role in American whitewater history.

Sayre Rodman and Jean Winne were young rock climbers who met at a Pittsburgh Explorers Club meeting in the early 1950's. Although their interest was rock climbing, they found themselves hooked on river running with a group of climbers from the D.C. area who rafted rivers during the winter when it was too cold to climb. Ray Moore from Alexandria, Virginia, in particular had a keen interest in river exploration. He took the Rodmans on their first river trip in late Fall of 1955 on the North Branch of the Potomac from Gorman to Kitzmiller. They returned to Pittsburgh, purchased a 6-foot by 12-foot surplus military raft and ran Crooked Creek, a local stream. The Rodmans adopted the same technique they had been shown by the D.C. climbers: the rafts were rowed forward using the technique of western river runners, ferrying and slowing the raft's descent. After their first run, they purchased a second raft so that each could row solo.

The Rodmans used the flexible oarlocks that were glued onto the military rafts instead of rigid rowing rigs used in the West. Repairs were often required after a couple of trips, including re-gluing the oarlocks and the repair of rips and tears. The Rodmans used a lot of rubber cement and duct tape.

As they progressed in their river explorations, their rowing technique and river-running skills improved. As their skills evolved, they ran more difficult rivers with less portaging. Because they did not use a rigid rowing frame, they were able to maneuver using the raft's own flexibility combined with its relatively small size. Their technique often involved ferrying sideways but they also used rocks to maneuver, bouncing off a rock to change direction, turning, spinning, and even pinballing into another rock. They could also tip the rafts on edge to squeeze through a narrow slot.

Since many of the Rodmans' runs were either first descents or at least descents that were unknown to them, they scouted many drops and portaged those they felt were unrunnable for their skill. Sayre developed a knack for "listening" to an upcoming drop to decide whether to run or scout. If the drop emitted a deep base sound, they would stop and scout. If the sound was more of a wooshing sound, they would run it without scouting.[44]

In the early summer of 1956, the Rodmans went to Ohiopyle and ran the lower Yough through to Connellsville. They explored the headwaters of the Potomac and then moved on to the Cheat. By this time, the Rodmans had encountered Berry and Harrigan many times on rivers and had become friends. Before running the Cheat, the Rodmans received a trip update from Berry and Harrigan on what to expect.

Ray Moore, who had originally introduced the Rodmans to rafting, continued to pore over topographical maps in search of harder and harder rivers with more remote access in the mountains of West Virginia. He rarely ran any river section twice. For him, the thrill was partly the first descent, of which he and his other climbing/rafting friends made many, unbeknownst to any other boaters at the time.

[44] Rodman, Sayre. Interview by author 5 November 1998.

As the Rodmans' skills developed they joined Moore on these explorations. Moore first noticed the Gauley in 1959, before the dam at Summersville was erected, and assembled a trip that included the Rodmans. They put in above Summersville and took out at the dam site, running the section that is now inundated by the dam. It was a high water run (about 5,000 cfs) and they flushed down the river.

In the Spring of 1961, the Rodmans put together their own two-day trip putting in above Summersville and running to Swiss. The group of six rafters from Pittsburgh included the Rodmans, Ralph and Kay Krischbaum, and two others. Rodman had not been on the section from Summersville to Swiss and was not prepared for what was to become known as Iron Ring. (The best guess for water level was someplace between 1,000 to 2,000 cfs.)

At Iron Ring, a raft rowed by one of the women stalled and was pulled under, squirting the raft out a distance down stream. Rodman recalled, "There were no waves to mark the spot. It just took the raft down and spit it out."[45]

> ...[Iron Ring,] the one where one of us nearly got it. The river swings out of a big pool, past a huge partly submerged slab about 30 feet long as I remember it, then goes over a pair of moderate waterfalls fairly close together.
>
> A couple of people ran it happily. Then a girl got too close to the upstream end of the slab, and the river took her and the 6-by-12-foot raft like a trout taking a fly. Lots of water goes under the slab, as we were too dumb to see at first. The suck-under wasn't against the slab, but about 10 feet out in the current.
>
> Anyway, she yo-yoed around under the slab for awhile and then was spit our under Waterfall No. 1, quite OK but with regretable but understandable lifelong reservations about serious whitewater fun.
>
> The boat with 6-foot oars in the oarlocks still popped out a bit later. Those who'd not yet run it still haven't—they carried... The strangest thing is that the suck-under didn't create any waves... It certainly didn't look like anything special. It was non-violent-looking water.[46]

The experience cooled the Rodmans' interest in first descents and extreme river runs. In the mid-'60s, their interest turned to western rivers and they began a series of trips on the Middle Fork of the Salmon, the Yampa, and Green Rivers.

Although run only that one time in 1961, word circulated among paddlers about the Gauley. John Sweet, too, pored over maps looking for new rivers to explore. He heard about the Gauley. In 1965, on one of his three-day weekend trips to the New, he decided he wanted to make the run. But it wasn't until 1968, two years after the Summersville Dam was completed, that he had the opportunity.

On Labor Day in 1968, Sweet and his party put in at Summersville dam for a run to Swiss. The water level was about 1,200 cfs. Sweet was accompanied by three other C-1 paddlers, Jim Holcombe, Norm Holcombe, and Miha Tomczic from Slovenia, and Jim Stuart and Jack Wright, both in kayaks. The

[45] Rodman, Sayre. Interview by author 5 November 1998.

[46] Downing, Bob. Whale Rock: *The New and the Gauley.* Akron, Ohio: Bob Downing, 1983: 98–99.

run to Swiss turned into a very long day. Only an orange and a candy bar remained after lunch, which they all later fought over. They ran much of the river without scouting. They did scout what later became known as Pillow, Iron Ring, and Sweet's Falls. (However, no drops were named that day.)

Jim Stuart remembers that at Pillow Rock, "Jimmy [Holcombe] was the only right-handed C-1 and could not draw away from the Room of Doom. He pounded into the wall, smashed his glasses, and ripped his knee straps out. He had to jury rig a fix, but was loose in the boat for the rest of the trip."[47] The paddlers on that first closed boat descent knew it was going to be a "river of reckoning."

At the end of the day, buying food at a local store, they learned of a new dam planned by the Army Corp of Engineers that would inundate the river they just paddled. This prompted Stuart to become active in fighting the dam. In order to assist in its defense, the river and rapids needed an appropriate description including naming of the rapids. Stuart organized a CCA trip in October of 1969 with the intention of documenting the trip and naming the rapids. The trip became known as the infamous Lost Paddle Trip and included Peter Brown, Barb Snyder, Kent Taylor, Bill Funk, Ed Richmond, Gorman Young, and Al Jenkins guided by Jim Stuart. All paddled kayak except for Kent Taylor.

Bill Funk at Pillow Rock Rapid, Gauley (WV) 1969 — courtesy of Barb Brown.

Some of the original names remain from that trip: Initiation, Iron Ring, Sweet's Falls, Pillow, Junkyard, and Canyon Doors. Many of the rapids on the lower section were renamed after the Stuart trip. Peter Brown was nervous about coming to Pillow Rock and although still upstream from it, kept asking what was coming up at the next drop. Stuart replied, "I don't know, something insignificant." But at that level, 2,200 cfs, the next drop was anything but. At the bottom, Brown angrily yelled back "Insignificant huh?" Stuart wrote it down, as he did that day with the other names of rapids as they paddled the river.

[47] Stuart, James. Email correspondence to John Sweet, 4 May 1998.

Snyder lost her paddle in the rapids below where the Meadow enters. Not having a spare, they spent considerable time trying to find it. About the experience, Stuart later wrote:

> Like idiots, Bill Funk, Kent Taylor, and myself went swimming along the undercut edges of lower Lost Paddle looking for her paddle. This was probably Bill's or my idea. For almost an hour we clung along the rocks on both sides at water level, reaching into the undercuts with our hands trying to locate it. We looked for such a long time, because not to find it meant we had to hike out, which ultimately we did. We were young, ignorant, and crazy not aware or afraid of swimming at 2,200 cfs amidst all those siphons. Actually, it was kind of interesting[48]

The rapid was named Lost Paddle. Seven years later Snyder's paddle, with her name inked into the blade, was found by paddlers of the Gauley. It was returned to her, worn in places from abrading against rocks, but still useable.

The Southeast

Whitewater paddling in the Southeast developed first on the eastern drainages of the Appalachians in camps and later on the western drainages through the scientists and engineers from Oak Ridge and Eastman Kodak in Tennessee. The camps, Mondamin, Merrie-Woode, Green Cove and other Boy Scout camps, had a long-standing tradition of teaching open canoeing. This tradition continued with whitewater paddling that carried over throughout the Southeast.

As with West Virginia, there were no whitewater clubs or paddling organizations until the mid-'60s. There was no also racing. Cruising was done by loosely knit groups of ex-campers and counselors on the eastern drainages and scientists and engineers on the western drainages. There was also little cross-cultural exchange between paddlers of the North and South, particularly in the western drainage. The exceptions were Ramone Eaton, Randy Carter, and Louis Matacia, all open boaters from Virginia and Maryland who traveled to the eastern drainages to paddle. In 1962, AWA's John Bombay paddled with canoeists in Tennessee and discovered none had even heard of closed canoes.

In the '50s and '60s, camp counselors and ex-campers including Fritz Orr Jr., Hugh Caldwell, and Bunny Johns (all of Camp Merrie-Woode), John Delabar (Camp Mondamin), Payson Kennedy and Bob Benner were often joined by Randy Carter and Ramone Eaton in exploring and making first descents of the rivers of the Southeast. (Payson Kennedy learned canoeing at a scout camp in northern Georgia in the early '40s. Bob Benner was a counselor at the same camp.) As they explored, they developed a different style of open canoeing. Instead of relying on backferrying techniques used by AMC and Buck Ridge, the southeastern boaters were aggressive. This was not a conscious difference, but was more related to not knowing what could or should be done. They paddled rivers that otherwise might not have been run in open canoes in other areas of the country. In 1964, Section IV of the Chattooga was first

48 Stuart, James. Email correspondence to author, 29 January 2000.

STYROFOAM is a registered trademark of the Dow Chemical Company.

run solo by Fritz Orr, Jr. and Hugh Caldwell in 15-foot shoe-keel Grummans, and Al Barret and Bunny paddling tandem in a 17-foot shoe-keel Grumman. Fritz's canoe was lost at Soc-Em-Dog. It never came up and was never found.

Many first descents were made in 15-foot (solo) and 17-foot (tandem) shoe-keel Grummans with no decks. The paddlers knelt but were not strapped in and there was no flotation added to the canoe. Eventually, after the loss or damage of too many canoes, flotation was added in the form of an inner tube and later progressed to large Styrofoam™ blocks. The use of Styrofoam was finally stopped when paddlers realized that the tiny beads that broke off the blocks polluted the rivers.

In 1966, two alumni of Camp Mondamin with young families, Horace Holden and Billy Crawford, decided the best way to continue their interest in canoeing, and at the same time encourage participation in the sport, was to form a club that became the Georgia Canoeing Association (GCA). The officers in the first year (1967) were Billy Crawford (President), Payson Kennedy (Vice President), and Horace Holden (Secretary, Treasurer and newsletter editor). Of the early years of GCA, longtime member Payson Kennedy recalled:

> Several impressions come to mind in thinking about those years. Perhaps the most obvious is the extent to which paddling skills and knowledge have improved since then — at least, in part, I think as a product of the training programs, mutual encouragement and shared experiences provided by the GCA. In 1968 the preferred boat was the Grumman shoe keel and no one had thought of adding extra flotation. We had seen a few folding kayaks but no rigid kayaks. One of our members, Ben Falmlen, did paddle an early version of the Royalex ABS boat. Many of our members had learned to paddle in wood and canvas boats [from the southeastern camp experiences] and subsequently had a dread of hitting rocks that is unknown today. The newsletter warned prospective trip participants that the Nantahala and section 2 of the Chattooga were for advanced paddlers and that if the water level on the Chattooga was above 1.25 feet the trip would be cancelled. The Nantahala was listed as Class 4-5. Some of us, though, were already running section 4 of the Chattooga on unofficial trips with just the most experienced of our paddlers. It is interesting that although we regularly portaged Bull Sluice and Corkscrew and ran the sneak at Seven-Foot, we often ran Woodall Shoals, Jawbone and Crack-in-the Rock, and some even attempted Soc-em-Dog on our first section 4 trip... One other impression is the extent to which the GCA was truly a family club. On most trips many entire families participated. Often there were non-paddling activities for family members... On easy trips we often took even the younger children along in the canoes... On more difficult trips a few adults often stayed around camp to take care of the younger children.[49]

[49] Kennedy, Payson. Correspondence to Anna Belle Close, 29 May 1984. Published in *The Eddy Line* Vol. 30 No. 5 (May 1995): 13–14.

In the late '60s, GCA expanded their interest in whitewater paddling beyond open canoeing. In 1968, Holden, Kennedy, and Crawford attended the Petersburg race and found that many racers expressed interest in attending a race in the South. On July 4th of the following year, GCA sponsored the first Nantahala Whitewater Race with the assistance of members of CCA including John Sweet. As with the Petersburg race, GCA had assistance from local businesses Bryson City Jaycees and the owners of the Hemlock Inn.

The Petersburg race exposed Kennedy to closed boats and he, too, soon started building C-boats with John Berry's help and advice. In 1970, a paddler and Explorer Post advisor from the Baltimore area, Doug Woodward, moved to Atlanta. He not only brought kayaks with him and showed them what could be run, but he also brought his boat-building skills.

The Sierras

Bay Chapter's RTS members explored the rivers of the western slopes of the Sierras, particularly in the central and northern areas in their folding kayaks in the '50s and into the early '60s. As in West Virginia, the advent of fiberglass boats expanded the exploration of more difficult river sections that were higher in elevation up in the Sierras.

The size of the river drainages of the Sierras is limited by their combined geography and climate. The mountain corridor is bounded by California's vast central valley to the west and desert conditions to the east and south. Winter snows melt relatively quickly leaving a very narrow paddling season after which there may be no rain to speak of until the next winter. California depends almost completely on snowmelt for water for the entire state. Water is a precious commodity, perhaps more so than in any other state. The rivers are gauged and dammed for flood control, irrigation, and electric and may not always be available for whitewater boating.

Carl Trost, initially a folding kayaker, adopted fiberglass kayaks for his scientific approach to river exploration. Trost was an electrical engineer. He was always asking, "What's upstream and why doesn't anyone run it?" [50] Trost set a precedent for paddlers of the Sierras to follow in their quest of new rivers; he had a method to his river exploration. Trost obtained plan and profile maps of water flows from USGS and Army Corps of Engineers for rivers and then compared flow data and profiles with actual conditions while scouting a river before even putting on to run. When no other information was available, he used a standard topographical map. Trost limited the rivers he explored to what he perceived to be his own paddling abilities and that of fiberglass kayaks. His upper limits were gradients of 50 feet/mile and flows of 1,000 cfs. Trost called himself a "3-digit boater" which meant that he normally ran no more than 999 cfs, which were often levels on the wane of snow melt.

In his explorations, Trost discovered many rivers. He came up with Carl's Law: "Rivers look nice at the bridge." [51] Trost knew that Native Americans and early settlers established river crossings where it was easy to cross and that many of those remain. The implied second part to Carl's Law: "A quarter mile downstream, it always starts—all hell breaks loose." [52] John Sweet had a similar saying, "All streams that run along roads must have drops at the bend that you can't see," [53] implying that it always looks nice from the road.

[50] Trost, Carl. Interview by author 17 June 1997.

[51] Ibid.

[52] Ibid.

[53] Sweet, John. Interview by author 19 December 1996.

Elsa Bailey on the Owyhee (OR), 1960
—courtesy of Carl Trost.

A second wave of paddlers associated with Bay Chapter's RTS began exploring and cruising. Other paddlers formed their own clubs or loosely knit groups. Paddlers in the second wave made many of the first descents in the '60s and into the early '70s in higher elevations of the Sierras, as their fiberglass kayaks allowed. Trost gladly shared the wealth of information he collected on rivers. The first unofficial guidebook for California came out in November 1969. It was actually a report for the state's water protection plan and was based largely on Trost's information that had been used for trip reports for the Bay Chapter's RTS newsletter. The compiled information became an instant guidebook. Charles Martin, who moved to California in 1966 and was one of the second wave of explorers, used Trost's information and expanded on it with his own to create *Sierra Whitewater,* a loose-leaf guidebook in 1971. (In 1974 it became a regular guidebook.)

Dick Schwind of Oregon worked on his own guidebook in the late '60s and early '70s. Schwind and Martin agreed to cover different rivers with some overlapping information. Martin's *Sierra Whitewater* covered the rivers of northern California rivers that fed from the Sierras into the Sacramento and south to the Kern River in the southern Sierras. Schwind's *West Coast Touring: the Rogue River Canyon and South* covered the non-Sierra draining rivers from the Rogue south to San Francisco and was published in 1974.

The Sierras now had their own guidebook. Just as Trost had asked over ten years before, "What's upstream and why doesn't anyone run it?" the next wave of boaters was ready to ask the same question and to push even farther. All that was needed was a boat that could take it.

Whitewater's Cornerstone: AWA

AWA was "a channel for bringing together ideas, procedures, and experiences" particularly for activities associated with cruising. However, the division between racers and cruisers affected the organization and its affiliates. Much discussion focused on the benefits of competition and how it could elevate the standard of boating. But at that time, many cruisers were reluctant to accept that they needed to be elevated, an opinion they did not commonly share with racers. AWA continued to support cruising as well as other aspects of whitewater which made it the cornerstone for the sport.

In 1961, AWA Secretary Dave Morrissey acknowledged that there seemed to be a universal controversy involving competition. While attending Bay Chapter RTS's first sponsored race on the North Fork of the Feather, he observed a common thread: many of the boaters considered themselves cruisers and were not particularly interested in racing, or were even hostile towards it. Perhaps some of their hostility was towards all of the attention that competition was receiving, that is, that it was the end-all or quintessence of the sport as some believed. His observations concluded "that these same boaters have not progressed very far in accepting and executing some of the high strokes, despite Peter Whitney's fine book." He acknowledged that "this same lack of technique is very evident in Colorado,"[54] the secretary's home state. After discussions with Peter Whitney and Roger Paris, it was decided that the best approach for elevating the standard of boating was to sponsor a national boating week where all affiliate members could gather and train under the top competitors. The national boating week should also conclude with a North American Championship so as not to exclude Canadian affiliates.

Continuing with the cruiser versus racer skills debate, Morrissey further heightened the debate by contending that FibArk, a new affiliate in 1962 (though its members were not new to whitewater) was primarily made up of racers and their cruising ability suffered for that. Erich Seidel, a long time FibArk and CWWA member, was quoted saying, "We are not interested in developing average boaters, only in developing winners." Morrissey, in his last "Secretary's Soap Box," continued the discussions:

> FibArk's leading U.S. trained boaters have developed their skill in this race [Salida downriver and slalom] to a high degree. At the same time their lack of skill in handling rapids is exceedingly unusual in view of their success in wildwater racing and their accessbility to fine white-water conditions. One must conclude that over-specialization in this one race has contributed markedly to their lack of development of the refined techniques of our sport. This certainly has hindered their development as boaters and would greatly reduce their chances of success in a difficult wildwater race in which course conditions were not familiar... [their] technique consists of paddling like hell through rapids. The current slalom races and most wildwater races emphasize power rather than technique. This also has allowed them to retain a high degree of success with outmoded back-paddling techniques in slalom racing. Their success is due to poor competition rather than their own improvement.[55]

Morrissey is referring to the poor race finishes of kayakers from FibArk to represent the U.S. team in World Championship competition in the early '60s. Morrissey went on to indicate the other extreme that the attitude of some that

[54] Morrissey, Dave (AWA Secretary). "The Secretary's Soap Box." *American Whitewater* Vol. VII No. 2 (August 1961): 31–32.

[55] Morrissey, Dave (Retiring AWA Secretary). "The Secretary's Soap Box." *American Whitewater* Vol. VII No. 4 (Spring, February 1962): 27.

IN THE EARLY '60S, the front and back cover photos of *American Whitewater* were split equally between cruising (including rafting) and slalom racing but little wildwater racing.

"we are just a cruising club and we don't want to be bothered by racing" has its drawbacks. "Competition brings out such [new] techniques and allows the average boater to become familiar with such strokes."[56]

The same year George Topol suggested that AWA sponsor Milo Duffek during his 1964 visit to North America. AWA did and the Duffek sessions were primarily attended by paddlers interested in slalom competition.

A few years later Bob Simmonds, AWA's Secretary wrote:

> Probably the most important choice facing the affiliation in 1966 is that between continuing our recent movement toward the slalom-oriented European point of view and a return to our earlier primary concern with river cruising, whether wilderness or not. It has become cliché in our sport to say that there is no conflict between racing and cruising; that slalom merely sharpens the skills needed for river touring. To a great extent this is no longer true. Slaloms are no longer won, indeed are rarely even entered, in traditional cruising canoes. The modern slalom canoe is most emphatically not a touring model. It has little cargo space, all of it sealed by sprayskirts which are mandatory even on flat water because of the low freeboard, and the inflexible paddling position requires frequent breaks to restore circulation to the limbs. By contrast, the Grumman or Old Town is a magnificent cruising vehicle, permitting changes of position while paddleing from kneeling to sitting, to standing; capable of transporting vast volumes of gear... Even the attitudes of cruisers and racers have diverged. Our most successful International slalomist, queried about the fabled beauties of Pennsylvania's Pine Creek, dismissed it as "the kind of water where you can watch birds," and in this very journal, another racer suggested that we find good slalom sites and encourage the Corps of Engineers to build dams there. Once we accept the fact that the dichotomy exists, we are faced with our choice. Shall we concentrate on slalom, with cruising considered worthwhile only on the toughest rivers, thus restricting ourselves to a relatively small but hightly dedicated group, or shall we serve the tens of thousands of paddlers on the small placid streams; the ones who fish, picnic, and photograph birds and flowers, but who are not really interested in organization, competition, Milo Duffek, or Selecting the American Team... Let us hear from the membership on this topic.[57]

Three years later in 1969, the announcement of the inclusion of slalom in the 1972 Olympics signaled the divergence between cruisers and racers. The announcement also signaled divergence in many other aspects of the sport.

In 1963, AWA reached 1,000 paid members with growth of approximately 25 percent in that year alone. In 1964, ten years after its founding, AWA had more than 55 affiliates. This included clubs in New Mexico, Missouri, Tennessee, Alaska, Michigan, Kansas, Wisconsin, and Illinois as well as the early clubs and affiliates of the Sierra Club in California, AMC in New England, AYH in

[56] Morrissey, Dave. (Retiring AWA Secretary). "The Secretary's Soap Box." *American Whitewater* Vol. VII No. 4 (Spring, February 1962): 27.

[57] Simmonds, Bob (AWA Secretary). "The Secretary's Soap Box." *American Whitewater* Vol. XI No. 4 (Spring 1966): 26–27.

the Midwest, and college outing clubs. Canadian affiliates were also located in Quebec, Ontario, Alberta, and British Columbia. The Boy Scouts of America was an affiliate with Explorer Posts in Sanselmo, California (Post 15), State College, Pennsylvania (Post 32), and Los Alamos, New Mexico (Post 20).

By 1969, AWA had more than 1,600 members and approximately 100 affiliates including international affiliates such as the Canoe Club of Milano, Italy, and the Indooroopilly Canoe Club of Australia.

The debate surrounding competition versus cruising also brought debates surrounding the merger of AWA and ACA. Discussions began in 1961 regarding merging AWA, a cruising group, and ACA, a racing group, to bring the full force of both organizations into the sport. Some members acknowledged that AWA's emergence prompted ACA to take notice of whitewater paddling, which was one of the AWA's original intentions. Other members objected to any discussions saying the competition between the two organizations was healthy and that if there was to be any merging, let ACA become an affiliate.

Eliot DuBois, one of AWA's founders, expressed his objections to any merger based on ACA's organizational structure (a slam at ACA). He wrote, "The period of time during which an organization can effectively serve its membership is inversely proportional to the length of its by-laws".[58] The controversy surrounding amateur status at the 1962 National Kayak Slalom on the North Fork of the Feather further fueled the debate, but also the animosity between the two organizations. Martin Vanderveen, AWA Secretary in 1963 wrote:

> The ACA has as its undisputed province the government of racing, the rules of amateurism, and the representation of the United States in international competition. We recognize this jurisdiction and do not challenge it. If, on occasion, we disagree with specific actions or rulings we will try to express our disagreement in a constructive manner. The ACA has other functions which are equally legitimate... The AWA is interested in all phases of white-water sport. Racing is a part of the sport—and without infringing on ACA prerogatives, we will encourage it, we will publish race schedules and results in our journal, and we will give our members and affiliates advice and encouragement... Among other things, the AWA has devoted considerable effort to encouraging the compilation of river guides. ACA has published some river guides; to this we say, "Bavo!" The more work done along these lines by any and all sources, the more the entire sport will benefit. There are many such fields in which both organizations have a sincere and legitimate interest; and all work done by both organizations furthers the sport... AWA and ACA are both dedicated to the development and betterment of the sport. While we may approach this goal through different channels, in the last analysis our interests are the same and there is no reason for any but a friendly feeling between the two organizations.[59]

[58] "Letters from Readers." *American Whitewater* Vol. VII No. 4 (Spring, February 1962): 3.

[59] Vanderveen, Martin. "The Secretary's Soap Box." *American Whitewater* Vol. IX No. 3 (Winter, 1963/64): 28.

ACA and AWA remained separate organizations and AWA continued its evolution just as its founders had intended. In the fall of 1967, AWA leadership proposed a new constitution and by-laws to conform to incorporation regulations provided for under "General Not for Profit." The organization was incorporated in 1961, and supported the growth from twenty-one affiliates in 1958 to nearly 100 in 1967. However, the first few Articles of the Constitution, including the Purpose, remained unchanged. The most significant changes provided for a nine-member Board of Directors and Executive Committee to replace the Executive Director.

Strong opinions were voiced regarding the changes. Some voted against the adoption because of the institution of a Nominating Committee for the Board that was felt could lead to a "self-perpetuating oligarchy in which the grassroots majority would have no power to unseat an undesirable establishment."[60] Another criticism concerned successive terms. However, the final tally was 335 in favor and only ten opposed. The provisions of the new constitution provided for at least one, but not more than two candidates from each of the six regions of U.S. One Canadian was selected at-large.

AWA provided a medium for discussions through its magazine, *American Whitewater,* which was the only national magazine to focus exclusively on whitewater activities. The actual name of AWA's magazine changed during the '60s from *American WHITE WATER* with white water as two words to *American WHITEWATER* with whitewater as one word. This reflected the same change that occurred with the name of the organization in 1959 from AWWA (American White Water Affiliation) to AWA (American Whitewater Affiliation). With the exception of a brief time mid-year in 1966 during an editorial department transition, the magazine continued relatively uninterrupted as the medium for communication. Throughout the '60s, articles focused on wilderness runs and cruises in trip reports. The "Racing News" section continued to report race results. Much of the information related to paddling technique was associated with slalom racing and training. AWA also reported its continuing efforts in conservation and safety through reports from the conservation and safety chairmen published in *American Whitewater.*

Conservation

The primary focus of AWA's conservation efforts throughout the '60s was to provide information to its members. AWA as an organization did not often take an active role in conservation except through the individual efforts of its members.

Prior to and into the early '60s, the main thrust behind river conservation was to battle against a few dams that threatened the most extraordinary rivers. Many of these fights focused on dam sites on the rivers of the Colorado basin. However, in the later '60s, much of the attention shifted to California that was in the throes of dam building. Because these dams directly affected rivers paddled by AWA members, much was written in *American Whitewater* about them, in particular, the New Melones Dam on the Stanislaus and the Auburn affecting the North and Middle Forks of the American. The New Melones Dam was an Army Corps of Engineer project while the Auburn Dam was a

[60] Houk, Ted. "Letters from Readers." *American Whitewater* Vol. XIII No. 3 (Winter 1967/1968): 2.

Bureau of Land Reclamation project. Congressional authorization for the New Melones dam for irrigation storage was given in 1962 before the popularity of the river for its recreational value was realized and developed. The dam created a reservoir from the town of Melones up to Camp Nine and flooded the "Upper Stanislaus" and "Lower Stanislaus" runs. Both were very popular and heavily used by commercial rafters and outfitters. Gerald Meral, a Bay Chapter RTS member, was key in the fight to save the Stanislaus.

In 1964, an article in the Spring *American Whitewater* issue titled "Death of a River System" brought attention to the California Water Plan with its effects on the Eel, Trinity, Feather, Mad, and Klamath rivers. Later the same year, heavy rains in northern California caused a thousand-year-flood on the Eel. Many articles were published in ensuing issues regarding logging policies that contributed to the devastation. It was a time of an awakening awareness among paddlers and others throughout the country and AWA was active in spreading the news to its members.

In 1965, the Wild Rivers Bill was introduced by Senator Frank Church (ID) and Representative John Race (WI) to establish a National Wild Rivers System similar to the pattern established by the National Wilderness System. One key definition of the bill was that the rivers shall be "free-flowing." Rivers proposed for protection included the Salmon from North Fork to Riggins, the entire Middle Fork, Clearwater from Kooskia to Powell on the Lochsa and to Thompson Flat on the Selway, the Rogue from Grants Pass to the Pacific, Eleven Pointe from Greer Springs to Highway 142, and part of the upper Rio Grande. Other possible rivers included the Cacapon, upper Hudson, Skagit, Susquehanna, and Wolf.

In the Spring of 1967, CCA member Bob Harrigan contacted Bill Prime of KCCNY to assist in taking a party of twenty-four down the Hudson Gorge on May 6. The party consisted of Senator (Dem. N.Y.) and Mrs. Robert Kennedy, Secretary of the Interior and Mrs. Stewart Udall, Peter Lawford, James Whittaker (conqueror of Mt. Everest), three CBS photographers, a *New York Times* correspondent, and ten children including Caroline Kennedy, Dennis Udall, and Stephen Smith, Jr. The trip was used to dramatize river sports, water pollution control, and the pending Wild Rivers Bill that was hung up in Congress. The Hudson was chosen because it was a wild, clean river within 200 miles of New York City that became severely polluted as it passed through major metropolitan areas. As little as ten years prior, the Gorge's whitewater was considered unrunnable. AWA members were tasked with arranging safety for the entire trip. Harrigan was the organizer and Bill Bickham, the trip leader, took charge of a group of seven canoes. Bill Prime was in charge of five kayaks including one for Senator Kennedy, and a group of professional rafters from Pennsylvania (including Sayre Rodman) took the rest of the party down in rafts. Other KCCNY members assisted bringing the total to approximately sixty people on the river that day.

As befitting other political battles of the time, river-conservation activity also engaged in battles for legislation to gain protection prior to dam-building planning or after proposed dams were defeated for other reasons. This amounted to legislation to protect wild and scenic rivers. The Scenic Rivers Bill passed the House and was signed into law (Public Law 90-542) with the passage of the Wild and Scenic Rivers Act on October 2, 1967. A year later, the National Wild and Scenic Rivers System was established and included the Middle Fork of the Salmon and Clearwater including the Lochsa and Selway in Idaho, Rio Grande in New Mexico, Rogue in Oregon, Wolf in Wisconsin, and St. Croix in Wisconsin and Minnesota. States also independently passed their own legislation to protect other rivers within their boundaries and not covered by the national legislation.

Unfortunately for California, only the Middle Fork of the Feather was included in the national legislation. California's own Wild and Scenic Rivers Act of 1972 proved inadequate to provide complete protection from the state and federal agencies with jurisdiction, and funding, to build dams.

Safety

In 1963, AWA's Safety Code, first adopted in 1959, was revised for the first time to reflect advancements in the sport. One of the more significant revisions was the addition of a ninth section containing the International River Classification, otherwise known as the International Scale. The adoption of the International Scale, although supported by many, also spawned discussions regarding the interpretation of the River and Rapids Rating System brought about by its inclusion in the Safety Code. One member wrote of the two current thoughts: "Take the system literally and agree with less than 5 per cent of our boaters are experts; this means that a III rapid is the ultimate for most of us." Or, "The other school wants to upgrade our boaters so that everyone can do a III and IV rapid (that means everyone is an expert). Most of those desiring the strict literal interpretation are in Colorado, and those wanting a more liberal interpretation are on either coast."[61]

Under Section I (Personal Preparedness and Responsibility) only one revision was made: the addition of "Know and Respect River Classification," in reference to the new ninth section. Under Section II (Boat Preparedness and Equipment), specific recommendations were added regarding installing flotation devices in the boat along with changes in bow and stern safety line (painters) recommendations.

Under Section VI (On Lake or Ocean), an added item included the mastering of the Eskimo roll by a "kayakist on tidal or large lake waters" and the "canoeist should learn to right, empty of water, and board a swamped canoe." In Section VII (If You Spill), more specific instructions were added regarding what to do in holding onto your boat, but also importantly, when to leave your boat for safety's sake. The old rule of never leaving your boat was amended. The old Code used to say that the boat should be left only under special circumstances. The revised section included those circumstances "if rescue is not imminent and water is numbing cold or worse rapids follow, then strike for the nearest shore." In Section VII (If Others Spill), a change was made to include "... rescue his boat only if this can be done safely."

By the mid-'60s, discussions also began surrounding the disregard of AWA's safety boating regulations and the hypocrisy of publishing articles and photos that went against the Safety Code:

> We are frequently prodded by not-so-good boaters as to why we do not raise a voice of disapproval about the fact that some of these experts do not rigidly adhere to our safety code in respect to lifejackets and the "don't boat alone" rule.

[61] Jones, Clyde (Retiring AWA Secretary). "The Secretary's Soap Box." *American Whitewater* Vol. VI No. 4 (February 1961): 43.

These requests for our opinion arise every time the word goes around that one of our crack boaters negotiated a 80-foot-per-mile-drop river wihout his guardian angel buddies and without a jacket. It also is brought up when participants in a class III-plus slalom do not wear lifejackets but only a helmet and wetsuit (sometimes). Before making any quick and harsh statements on this subject, we must look at these new approaches to our safety rules with consideration, because there may be good reasons that make these people deviate from our safety code... First, these people are experts, class IV (and up) boaters... Second, they can eskimo-recover under nearly any condition in rapids that most of us would not even consider running right-side up! Their need for a lifejacket is not as great as for the average boater- in fact, the jacket may interfere with their esquimautage [roll]. Thirdly, the type of water these people frequent contains vicious currents, souse-holes, and whirlpools where a lifejacket can be disadvantageous, since it does not allow the swimmer to dive down and swim out. Fourthly, in a slalom, where the ultimate performance of strokes is required, a bulky lifejacket can obstruct a boater's movements... Of course, rescue crews should be stationed along he course. Fifth and last, our safety code is written for the benefit of the average of all boaters, beginners and experts... But our code is not law... To our average boater we have to say, "Put on that lifejacket and go out only in groups." To our expert we have to say, "Remember your mishap will put a blot on our sport; please wear that jacket where possible, and find some buddies for your next Class IV trip.[62]

DUFFEK didn't wear a helmet or lifejacket in 1964 during the AWA sponsored "Duffek sessions" held across the country. During the '60s, there were very few photos in *American Whitewater* that showed Europeans wearing any type of safety equipment, although some American paddlers shown did.

While the Safety Code and discussions surrounding it remained a focus for the Safety Committee, other safety related discussions were encouraged among the affiliates. One discussion and controversy that first began in 1958 was in regard to Roland Palmedo's proposition of AWA's sponsorship of a national patrol similar to the National Ski Patrol. To the consternation of Palmedo, discussions continued into the '60s with individual clubs taking the lead instead of AWA. AWA's role under the leadership of Safety Chairman Red Fancher proceeded with outlining standards and recommendations for clinics, sponsored by clubs, and assumed that as the sport developed, the system would become as sophisticated as needed. CWWA was one such club that began a process of setting up a rescue unit. Ontario Voyageurs and Buck Ridge also investigated the use of river patrols or rescue units in their areas.

Kayaker with no PFD on the Tuolumne River (CA), 1969 — courtesy of Carl Trost.

AWA pursued a similar approach regarding promoting safety as a part of whitewater instruction (and standardizing instruction without dictating it). In 1962, AWA offered suggestions through *American Whitewater* for a series of instructional programs to prepare students for Class 2 whitewater. The series consisted of four sessions followed by a trip on moving water. The first, a classroom session, included a lecture on simple paddle bracing and strokes using Whitney's *White-Water Sport* and discussions of reading Class 2 water. The second session, in a heated pool, was used to demonstrate and practice strokes. The third session, back in a classroom, included discussions of boat

[62] Bombay, John. (AWA Safety Chairman). "Safety as We See It." *American Whitewater* Vol. XI No. 3 (Winter, 1965/66): 22–23.

types, advanced strokes and advanced river reading (Class 3). The last session included discussions concerning safety and safety equipment in preparation for the final session on water.

Another discussion in the early '60s regarding the debate of rating paddlers for their own safety grew. AMC-Boston had classified members according to their skill level, based on a five-grade system ranging from Beginner to Leader. Other clubs considered similar member classification systems. AMC-NY and Ontario Voyageurs leaned toward adopting a four-grade system equating it to the International six-grade classification of rivers leaving Class V and VI to the super-experts who were considered beyond classification. However, by the Winter of 1962–1963, Ontario Voyageurs, under pressure by its members, abandoned efforts to rate boaters. With the exception of AMC-Boston, many other clubs eventually abandoned forced rating of their members as well. Instead, many clubs adopted a self-rating system to provide guidance to club paddlers.

The Growing Industry

As the number of whitewater boaters grew, so, too, did the market for products and services. Commercially available books, boats, and gear developed throughout the '60s.

Books

THE AVAILABILITY OF BOOKS displaced some of AWA's early functions as a medium to disseminate information. However, since American Whitewater was the only national publication devoted to whitewater, it continued to facilitate the dissemination of information with reprints of articles. Advertising in the magazine also supported the growing commercialization of the sport.

In the early '60s, both Burmeister's and Carter's guidebooks were expanded upon for publication beyond mimeographed copies. John Berry of CCA led the charge to have Burmeister's books published in their entirety and in the spring of 1963, Volumes 1 and 2 were published by CCA. In 1962, Carter's guidebook, *Canoeing Whitewater River Guide,* was expanded to cover rivers in northern Virginia, northeastern West Virginia, and the Great Smokey Mountain Area of North Carolina.

Burmeister was difficult to work with because he would not allow anyone to edit his work. His works included gradient information derived from topographical maps but had no river level information. As paddlers started using his books, they realized that he may not have run many of the more difficult river sections he described, writing his descriptions instead from viewing topographic maps and walking some of the sections. Burmeister either swam or walked most of the Gauley and Meadow. However, the value and effort of his guidebooks could not be underestimated. Over the course of his research, he purchased more than 4,000 topographic quadrangles and logged over 100,000 driving miles. He used seven double and three single folding kayaks over the years, losing several while attempting to run more difficult rapids.

Although Burmeister and Carter covered many of the same rivers, Carter wrote primarily for canoeists while Burmeister wrote for folding kayakers. Additionally, many paddlers knew that Carter had indeed paddled every river he wrote about due to the accuracy of the descriptions.

By the mid-'60s, other guidebooks were available and covered many rivers in the East. Pittsburgh AYH published their own guidebook, *Canoeing Guide to Western Pennsylvania and Northern West Virginia.* Volume I of *Blue Ridge Voyages* by H. Roger Corbett, Jr., and Louis J, Matacia, Jr. was published in 1965. Volume II was published the following year. AMC published their *AMC New England Canoeing Guide* under the guidance of Ken Henderson and Stewart Coffin in 1965. However, publication of guidebooks for rivers in the West lagged behind. With the exception of *Missouri Ozark Waterways* by Oz Hawksley, guidebooks for western rivers were late in coming.

By the time many of the later guidebooks were published, the International Scale was known across the country. However, there was still little standardization among boating groups. The International Scale gained wider use in the East and may have been more consistent regarding ratings. However, because of the popularity of rafting and the use of rafts and of independent scales associated with rafting, a much broader, and different, interpretation of the International Scale was found in the West. This lack of standardization, along with the "rafting scale" based on 1 through 10, resulted in a greater disparity in rating rivers in the West. Some clubs designated their best boaters as Class IV boaters and then rated rivers accordingly. The lack of guidebooks further exacerbated the situation.

In the early '60s, Les Jones provided a series of maps of western rivers based on the Deseret Scale. His maps were available as 7-inch wide continuous scroll maps and were available for Green, Cataract Canyon, Grand Canyon, Westwater Canyon, and Dolores of the Colorado River watershed; Middle Fork of the Salmon, Main Salmon, Hell's Canyon of the Snake, Selway, Lochsa, and Clearwater Rivers of Idaho; Columbia Big Bend and Fraser from Tete Jeune Cache to Yale in Canada; Rogue in Oregon; and Grijalva in Mexico.

In the '70s, Dick Schwind's *West Coast River Touring* adapted the International Scale by dividing each class in two (1, 1½, 2, 2½, etc. through Class 4½) and eliminated Classes IV and V as unrunnable. Schwind also attempted to provide more detailed flow information beyond just high/low or optimum designations. He designated an optimum flow as a flow "with plenty of water to cover all but the widest shallow regions and eliminate most of the picky rock dodging that occurs when the river flow is too low. The water should not be so high as to cover all the rocks or wash out many eddies since they provide the rock dodging that makes the sport exciting."[63] He also went beyond this simple flow description using stream gauge information available through various state and federal agencies for California and Oregon rivers.

The first instructional book for whitewater canoeing and kayaking, *White-Water Sport,* was written by Peter Whitney and published in 1960. Like Carter's guidebooks which set the precedent for guidebooks that followed, Whitney's *White-Water Sport* set the precedent for instructional books that followed. Whitney included information on river hydrology (why there are rapids, types of rapids, how water behaves), how to run rapids, kayak and canoe design, equipment and gear, how to paddle kayak and canoe (tandem), safety, slalom and downriver racing, and how to organize trips.

[63] Schwind, Dick. *West Coast River Touring: Rogue River Canyon and South.* Beaverton, Oregon: The Touchstone Press, 1974.

[*Author's note:* I found one particular area of interest in Whitney's *White-Water Sport,* one that I heartily agree with and that has not changed in the last forty years.

> The paddle is the most neglected element in the triad of man, kayak, paddle. That is odd, since the paddle defines the sport—we are "paddlers"... Boaters who spare no expense on their kayaks may make it a virtue to compromize on paddles, buying the cheapest models with plywood blades ... as if they were disposable items, like paper cups... The paddle should be understood from the first as a vital element in the kayakists stability and safety and should be chosen with the same care as a tennis racquet or a golf club.[64]]

Whitney only briefly mentioned solo canoeing, concentrating instead on tandem canoeing.

> The special single canoe for competition is a much shorter boat, hardly longer than a kayak and some 30 inches wide. The paddler sits very near the middle, in a cockpit hardly larger than that of the kayakist. He makes times in competition that are well behind kayaks and double canoes, but the discipline of his craft is widely recognized as the most difficult of all on the river.[65]

The techniques that AMC used for their instructional programs were incorporated by John Urban into the their first instructional book, *A White-water Handbook for Canoe and Kayak,* published in 1965. A review of the book indicated that unlike *White-Water Sport* that was aimed toward the general reader as well as whitewater paddler, Urban's book was more detailed as a "no-nonsense training manual for whitewater cruising."[66] The book itself, like Whitney's *White-Water Sport,* was written during a period of transition in the sport when equipment and descriptions of technique were soon out of date.

By the time *Basic River Canoeing* by Buck Ridge Ski Club (with Bob McNair as the principle author) came out in the Spring of 1968, advancements in open canoeing technique were at a plateau so that the technique described in the book was fairly advanced and current. The book was a compilation of everything the club had learned from their involvement in the Red Ridge College of Canoeing beginning in 1955 and was updated with the most recent innovations and knowledge of open canoeing.

While *White-Water Sport, A Whitewater Handbook for Canoe and Kayak,* and *Basic River Canoeing* emphasized basic cruising techniques with some reference to racing techniques as applied to cruising, Jay Evans' *Fundamentals of Kayaking,* first published in 1964, concentrated specifically on whitewater racing. Serving as LCC's slalom coach, and as a racer himself, Evans kept detailed notes and perfected the instructional technique that proved to be so successful for LCC's young racers.

[64] Whitney, Peter Dwight. *White-Water Sport: Running Rapids in Kayak and Canoe.* New York: The Ronald Press Company, 1960.

[65] Ibid.

[66] Peekna, Andres. "Book Review." *American Whitewater* Vol. XII No. 4 (Spring 1967): 11.

Another publication geared specifically for racing also came out in 1964. George Siposs, of Ontario Voyageurs and later of Haystackers Club of southern California, published a pamphlet titled *From Start to Finish* that included the psychology of racing along with training information including physical and mental preparation.

Boats and Gear

Paddlers across the country experienced similar difficulties in finding the proper boats and gear as well as the materials to make their own. Often, each club in an area had one person who bought bulk building materials and resold them to other club members. Molds were often owned and rented out by a club. Pirating was common. Clubs often became their own mini-factories for boats and a few backyard builders developed as an outgrowth. Some backyard builders even found a market among paddlers who didn't build their own boats.

The first whitewater boat manufacturers, backyard builders who advertised, developed in areas with the longest or most active whitewater activity, although none lived solely off their business or enterprise. Most built boats mainly on demand and either advertised in ads in club newsletters and *American Whitewater* or relied on word-of-mouth.

Waterways Unlimited of Colorado continued building their version of the French canoe used at the Salida races in 1952, although the market in the West was limited. Ron Bohlender and Walter Kirschbaum, also of Colorado, sold their fiberglass kayak hulls (with canvas or other non-fiberglass synthetic materials for the deck) to paddlers primarily in the West. Although Kirshbaum supplied a limited number of hulls in the Colorado area, the Bohlender hull (as it was called) was shipped East and was one of the few commercial hulls available.

In the early '60s, other short-lived boat manufacturers sprang up in the West and later the East. In 1960, Husky Kayaks manufactured by Cooper Fiberglass Products in North Surrey, British Columbia, advertised a European designed kayak, Model S2S, in *American Whitewater.* In 1962, in California, Walt Harvest and his father Ove came out with a fiberglass kayak that was advertised as a 25 pound, 13' by 28" kayak. In 1963, Hasbrouck Plastics in Hamburg, New York, advertised fiberglass kayaks.

Aside from boats, other paddling gear and accessories were often homemade and therefore not in as great a commercial demand. *American Whitewater* was the source of plans along with where to buy the materials, particularly for wetsuits and spray skirts of neoprene. Some paddling clubs became local informal retailers. Entrepreneurial club members who supplied boat-building materials to club members often expanded to include lifejackets, helmets, paddles, and other paddling gear. Some of these informal retailers eventually expanded into full-time retail outlets. As was popular in the late '60s, the Dartmouth Co-Op was formed and sold Co-Op made waterproof nylon paddling jackets, adjustable hockey helmets, and Flotherchok life vests.

In 1965, Tom Johnson's wife Virginia made what was probably the first neoprene spray cover for his C-1. Virginia used scrap wet suit material and an inner tube for the cockpit seal.

ALTHOUGH MOVIES were not commercially available in the '60s, some clubs, as well as AWA, produced movies for instructional purposes. AWA felt that an integral part of safety was the mastery of skills in maneuvering boats. To assist instructors, AWA produced *"Canoe Training"* in 1965, and later produced a movie on kayaking.

Bay Chapter's RTS also produced movies in the '60s for instruction: *"Beginners Whitewater"* and *"Advanced White-Water Kayaking"* in 1962, and *"Gung-Ho with Duffek"* in 1964 after Duffek's AWA sponsored tour.

Flotation for kayaks was an exception in homemade gear. Walt Harvest resolved this by inventing vinyl flotation (air) bags. In 1964, he started Harvest Enterprises and sold 20 mil vinyl float bags that were made for him by a pool liner company.

It was the exploding racing scene in the East in the early '60s associated with AMC and KCCB that was the most fertile for the first real manufacturing of boats and equipment. The first manufacturers, Stu Coffin (AMC) and Bart Hauthaway (KCCB), were rivals and sometimes collaborators. Both were encouraged by Barb Wright in their manufacturing endeavors.

Stu Coffin

THE C-1 AND C-2 BANANA MODELS later became known as the Boston models. In total, Coffin built about 100 kayaks, 50 each of his C-1 and C-2 models, 2,000 canoe paddles, and 1,000 kayak paddles. The Boston Kayak later became known by paddlers as the Coffin kayak.

Stewart (Stu) T. Coffin was an engineer who worked in the electronics industry in the Boston area. He was also an avid paddler and AMC member. Coffin compiled AMC's first *New England Canoeing Guide* in 1965. He met Barb Wright for the first time soon after she moved to the Boston area from D.C. in 1960. Wright returned from Europe with a fiberglass kayak paddle with a broken blade and asked Coffin to make her a feathered kayak paddle. Coffin had been making wooden canoe paddles for a couple of years by this time. With no previous knowledge of fiberglass, Coffin dove into the project. He made a paddle using aluminum tubing for the shaft and sold his first fiberglass paddle to Wright in 1962. During the same time, Wright was using Bohlender hulls with a fabric deck and so encouraged Coffin to add a fiberglass deck. This led Coffin to design the Boston Kayak and in 1963, he sold the first one. Soon after, Wright encouraged Coffin to design and build a C-1, similar to the Bernot design she had seen at slalom races. Coffin sold a Banana C-1 in 1963 to Bill Heinzerling of KCCNY. When Wright and her C-2 partner Bill Bickham returned from Europe in 1963, they brought back a Yugo C-2 and in the same fashion, Coffin built the Banana C-2 and sold it Bickham. With three whitewater boat molds and canoe and kayak paddle molds, Coffin was in business. All three boats sold for under $200. Kayak paddles were $15 and canoe paddles were $9.

Coffin's knowledge of working with fiberglass grew with experimentation. He used milled fibers with resin to strengthen its use as an adhesive and experimented with various lay-ups for his boats and paddles. Coffin also developed many different innovations in the fiberglass construction of boats. He developed the use of sealed through-holes for bow and stern grab loops and used an overlapped seam on all decked boats instead of a butt joint seam. He also developed a technique to make lighter boats by eliminating the use of a gelcoat. (Hauthaway borrowed this technique, too.)

Coffin's greatest innovations were developed for his paddles. In 1963, he introduced a standard design with pressure molded glass/epoxy blades with metal tips on an aluminum shaft also covered with glass/epoxy. The blades were flat, oval shaped, and measured 8½ inches by 20 inches.

In the '60s, canoe paddle length depended on where the paddle was used in the canoe, open or closed boat, bow or stern, and not particularly on the paddler's physical dimensions (height, arm length, body length). The paddle used in the stern of an OC-2 was typically 69 to 72 inches. Bow lengths were typically in the 66-inch range. The most common lengths overall were between 60 to 69 inches. For C-1s and C-2s, the lengths were usually 57, 60, or 63 inches for competition and slightly longer 60, 63, and 66 inches for cruising. T grips were preferred 30 to 1 by paddlers for whitewater.

The average length of kayak paddles was 81 inches (206 cm) for slalomists with the extremes being 74 (188 cm) to 84 inches (213 cm). The average length for cruising was 84 inches (213 cm) with extremes of 81 inches (206 cm) to 87 inches (221 cm).

Coffin noted in 1968 that kayak paddle length seemed less to do with a paddler's height but corresponded to kayak length. He also observed that the trend was toward spooned blades away from flat blades and wondered if that was going to be the next innovation in canoe blades. Blade angle was pretty much considered to be slightly less than 90 degrees.

However, Coffin felt that his innovations for paddles were also his downfall. During the mid-'60s, he switched from composite blades to ABS (Acrylonitrile-Butadiene-Styrene), a thermoplastic, to increase production. Although a thermoplastic can be heated and formed into a shape or thermoformed, Coffin experienced a lot of problems thermoforming ABS with an aluminum shaft. He then attempted to mold and adhere two sheets of ABS with adhesive onto a shaft. Nothing proved to be successful. In 1969, Coffin sold all of his fiberglass paddle-making equipment and molds to Sumner Bennet. John Field soon took over the operation, naming it Illiad.

Coffin's biggest problem as a manufacturer was shipping his products. Boats were either picked up at his place or he delivered them at races. Shipping kayaks either by common carrier (freight) or air was not practical due to the damage that frequently occurred. Paddles were not much easier. Because of their length, paddles could not be shipped by parcel post (U.S. mail). Although Coffin did ship paddles by common carrier, it was a terrible experience for him so he often preferred a pick-up or race delivery, the same as with boats.

Bart Hauthaway

Bartlett (Bart) M. Hauthaway started paddling with AMC using one of the Grumman canoes in their fleet in the late '50s. On one trip, he saw Eliot DuBois paddling a solo folding kayak. Hauthaway ordered one the next day and never got into a Grumman again.

When Barb Wright moved to the Boston area, she advertised in a Boston paper to find people to paddle with. Hauthaway attended an English gate demo Wright arranged at a pool at MIT and was impressed by the potential abilities of a kayak. He thought he was a competent paddler. However, after seeing the English gate demo, he realized he had much to learn. Hauthaway attended the next Brandywine slalom and saw Dan Sullivan (CCA) roll his kayak during the race. Hauthaway was now really hooked.

Hauthaway, influenced by Wright, obtained a Bohlender hull. He was not entirely satisfied with its performance and decided to design and build his own fiberglass kayak. As did Coffin, Hauthaway learned about building with fiberglass and became involved in manufacturing paddles as well as boats. In 1963, Hauthaway introduced his first kayak paddle: 82½ inches in length and 3 pounds in weight. The blade was pear-shaped (Wright's idea) and the area was oversized (and advertised as such). Wright was always looking for a competitive edge and at the time, large blade areas were considered

Bart Hauthaway —courtesy of Bart Hauthaway.

an advantage. There were both similarities and differences between the Hauthaway and Coffin paddles. Hauthaway pressure molded with iso-phthalic polyester; Coffin used epoxy. Hauthaway used a wood shaft; Coffin used epoxy covered aluminum.

Unlike Coffin, Hauthaway was a slalom competitor and actively participated in many of the slalom races in the East including indoor slaloms at Dartmouth. It was said that Hauthaway was fascinating to watch doing English gates, that watching Hauthaway was like watching a water ballet. He competed in Europe in 1965 and was a coach in 1969 for the U.S. team.

Hauthaway was influenced by what he saw in skills and designs in both America and Europe. As did Coffin and others, he both borrowed designs from Europe (the Hauthaway Czech C-1 had no real modifications in the design from the original Czech C-1), and designed his own. By 1968, his boats and designs were well known in the East. With the exception of his junior-sized slalom kayak, much of what he designed and built was for himself.

Hauthaway was approached by Old Town in 1968 and in 1969, that company began manufacturing his whitewater kayaks: the junior model, a slalom model, and two wildwater models. Old Town also offered his feathered adult kayak paddles (spooned model) and his pear-shaped flat blade. For the '69 World Championships, Old Town loaned six slalom kayaks and two wildwater kayaks to the team. Both were Hauthaway designs.

The arrangement with Old Town provided that Hauthaway design for Old Town but he could also continue to build and sell kayaks on his own. This arrangement soon led to disagreements. Many paddlers continued to buy directly from Hauthaway, partly due to better craftsmanship. However, the larger problem was the difference in motivation between Hauthaway and Old Town. For Old Town, building whitewater kayaks was a business opportunity directly related to the growing whitewater market and the potential generated by the '72 Olympics. For Hauthaway, financial concerns were only a small part of why he designed and built boats.

[*Author's note:* Hauthaway was known for his meticulous craftsmanship in fiberglass but he never really experimented or built beyond traditional fiberglass/polyester lay-ups. Although now in his 80s, Hauthaway continues to build small fiberglass craft and I scheduled my visit with him for an interview around his boat-building activities. Upon arriving at his residence, the smell of styrene practically floored me. (I build almost exclusively with epoxies for that reason, and with a mask). A tour of his work shop revealed an extremely clean area, well-built, meticulously clean molds, and superb hand lay-up craftsmanship in the hull he had just completed (a Wee-Lassie-type canoe).]

The Divergence: The Real Impact of the Olympic Announcement

The divergence between cruising and racing and between cruisers and racers began almost from the beginning of whitewater. In the early to mid-'60s, this split became more evident and often centered around age, youth, and the transition between the first whitewater paddlers and the first Baby Boomers. For a brief time in the mid-'60s, racers over 30 years of age, represented by KCCB, and racers under 30, Dartmouth's LCC, competed together. However, youth ultimately won out as advanced skills developed. This was also the beginning of real athleticism with paddlers solely dedicated to racing, personified in Dave Nutt's contribution of speed and Eric Evan's technically-correct runs. The course of divergence was finally set with the announcement of the inclusion of whitewater competition in the Olympics, the ultimate venue of athleticism and youth.

The divergence also helped to set the course of ACA and AWA and the young industry. Although discussions began again within AWA as to whether it would be time to merge AWA with ACA to support this effort, the debate regarding the merger subsided at the end of the '60s as the roles of both organizations became more clearly defined. ACA had its "brass ring," Olympic competition. AWA had everything else for a time.

For the young industry, the divergence meant more than just a split between cruisers and racers. It also meant that everything associated directly with cruisers and racers such as boats and gear, designs and technique, had the potential to diverge.

THE 1969 ANNOUNCEMENT set in motion changes that were more far-reaching than readily apparent at the time. Like a building weather front, the first rains of the Olympic "event" began. The announcement ultimately affected the future course of the River. The divergence set in motion events that were bolstered in the '70s by still others. It firmly established the basis for the growing paddlesport industry and even two new forms of competition, first squirt and later rodeo. But before these changes could occur, the early affects of two additional building cloudbursts which started in the late '60s, needed to build. These early rains from building cloudbursts were commercial rafting in the East and Walt Blackadar.

Commercial Rafting in the East

The founders of commercial rafting in the East started their businesses as extensions of a weekend lifestyle of paddling rivers. It began in 1963 in Ohiopyle, Pennsylvania, on the Youghiogheny, the Lower Yough. Ohiopyle and the river had long been a destination for tourists, brought first by railroad from D.C., Baltimore, and Pittsburgh for its natural beauty, waterfalls, and mountains. In the late '50s and early '60s, the area also attracted a growing population of whitewater paddlers from throughout the East and Midwest.

Commercial rafting in the East actually started on the "Grand Canyon of the East." Ed McCarthy (not to be confused with Ralph McCarty) began leading raft trips on Pine Creek in Pennsylvania eight years earlier in 1955.

Lance Martin of Pittsburgh and his friend Karl Kruger began guiding rafts down the Yough in 1963. In 1964, they decided to call themselves Wilderness Voyageurs. Martin and Kruger were briefly joined by a third partner, Ed Coleman, who spent much of his summer guiding canoe trips in Algonquin Provincial Park in Ontario. As with Ed McCarthy on Pine Creek, their passengers paddled the rafts with canoe paddles and were led by experienced guides. This practice clearly differentiated commercial rafting in the East from the West and became the standard throughout the East.

Author's note: I began my whitewater paddling with members of the Mad Hatters (east of Cleveland) and Keel-Haulers (west of Cleveland) in 1976. I built my first kayak, a Bronco, in the garage of the Lewis family, members of the Mad Hatters.

In the meantime, Ralph McCarty of Mentor, Ohio, along with other paddlers that eventually formed the Mad Hatter Canoe Club, began paddling the whitewater rivers of western Pennsylvania and New York in canoes. In 1966, McCarty and his family rafted the Yough. Within a few years, he started Mountain Streams and Trails (MS&T) with duckies (small solo rubber kayaks) on the Connoquenessing in western Pennsylvania but soon moved MS&T to the Yough.

Coleman, after his brief partnership with Martin and Kruger, began his own rafting company, Laurel Highland River Tours. The Lower Yough was now rafted by three companies which were soon joined by a fourth, Whitewater Adventurers founded by Wendell Holt and Bob Marietta (locals to Ohiopyle) in 1967.

These early rafting entrepreneurs held "real jobs" early on. McCarty was a machinist/inventor who managed a shop that used his invention for metal machining. Coleman was a high school chemistry teacher. Martin was an Olivetti equipment salesman and Kruger worked for the American Red Cross.

In the East during the '60s, there were no regulations controlling commercialized rafting on rivers and the businesses grew as fast as the market allowed. There were no quotas or limitations to the number of rafting companies or rafters on any given stretch of river. The only limitation was crowding and perhaps the loss of adventure because of it.

Partially because of crowding and partially to seek additional business opportunities, commercial rafting spread out from the Yough into West Virginia on the Cheat, New and Gauley, and southeast to western Maryland on the Upper Yough and beyond.

The roots of almost all of the rafting companies in the East can be traced one way or another to the four Ohiopyle companies. Coleman himself left Ohiopyle and started Wilderness Tours on the Ottawa. Some companies were started by Ohiopyle guides who struck off on their own. Jon Dragan started Wildwater Expeditions Unlimited on the New after leaving Wilderness Voyageurs in 1967. Imre ("Attilla") Szilagi was an Ohiopyle guide who founded Appalachian Wildwater on the Cheat. John Connelly was a guide for Wilderness Voyageurs and started Eastern Expeditions on the Kennebec and Penobscot in Maine.

Other rafting companies hired guides with Ohiopyle-related experience to start their companies. For NOC (Nantahala Outdoor Center), Payson Kennedy hired Jim Holcombe who was a guide for Wilderness Voyageurs.

Some sought advice directly from one of the Ohiopyle companies before starting their own operations. Jim Greiner started Wildwater Limited on the Chattooga after talking with Martin and Dragan.

Blackadar

Walter (Walt) Lloyd Blackadar, a young surgeon from the East, settled in Salmon City, Idaho, in 1949. Instead of just reading about the wilderness life that attracted him in his youth in New Jersey, he now had the opportunity to live it. In Idaho, that also meant running whitewater. Having started running rafts in the Idaho tradition with oars and sweeps, he became interested in kayaking in 1965 when he met Nelson Riley, a kayaker from New York.

In 1966, Riley drove to Idaho to paddle whitewater. The following year, he returned with his two sons and six other paddlers to join Blackadar on a Middle Fork trip, guided and supported by Blackadar. The cost to them for the trip was a kayak for Blackadar and one for his friend, Joe Kinsella.

With those two kayaks, Blackadar and Kinsella tackled the local rivers. However, their attempt to run the Main Salmon below Deadwater with limited kayaking skills and with no roll, resulted in the loss of both kayaks. Blackadar needed a teacher. He read an article in *American Whitewater* written by Barb Wright about rolling without a paddle[67] and contacted Wright directly in Boston. At this time in 1967, the 41-year-old Wright had reached the peak of her competitive paddling career. She was the K1-W National Champion and the first American paddler to place in the top ten (9th) in World Championship competition.

The following summer, in 1968, Wright went to Idaho to give Blackadar lessons in kayaking and rolling in exchange for a trip on the Middle Fork. Blackadar invited many of the top ranked paddlers in the United States and Canada on the trip. The party included Ron Bohlender of Colorado; Barb Wright of KCCB; Jan and Dave Binger of KCCNY; six paddlers from Ontario Voyageurs including Herman and Christa Kerckhoff and four Idaho paddlers. The 1968 Middle Fork trip began Blackadar's association with paddlers from the East and his lifelong friendship with Wright. It was the first of many trips organized by Blackadar on rivers in Idaho and other western Rivers, including the Grand Canyon.

Although Wright realized that Blackadar would probably always revert to muscling his roll instead of using his hips and perhaps never develop the finesse of a slalom paddler, she had a great deal of respect for his ability to read water and his relative ease of handling big water. After all, he had spent quite a bit of time learning to read water while maneuvering rafts down Idaho rivers. Blackadar often told Wright, "put a log in the river, it will get down"[68] referring to watching how the currents carried the log downriver. Blackadar had a flair and bravado for life which found its realization in whitewater kayaking, and that caught the attention of others.

[67] Wright, Barbara. "Esquimautage Sans Paddle." *American Whitewater* Vol. X No. 3 (Winter 1964–1965): 14–15.

[68] Wright, Barbara. Interview by author 6 July 1997.

View from the Bridge

COMPETITION was the driving force for whitewater throughout the '60s. It was the underlying force that shaped the sport. It drove the need for lighter, more durable boats and ushered in the transition from old materials to fiberglass to advanced composites. It drove the transition away from designs dependent upon the structural requirements of the old materials and techniques based on the old designs. Kayaks evolved toward shapes that took advantage of technique that used the "new" hanging strokes, away from the folding kayak touring hull to one with more parabolic shapes between deck and hull. Closed canoes, C-1s and C-2s, evolved in shape parallel with kayaks. Competition was the underlying force that helped Americans develop the basics for the new techniques by the middle of the '60s and before the decade was done, placed a women in K-1W in the top ten in World Championship competition.

Competition also benefitted cruising from construction to designs and to technique used for river running. The publicity of competition certainly exposed increasing numbers to the sport. This in turn fed existing clubs and contributed to the formation of new clubs. The young industry certainly benefited from the growing number of paddlers and the increasing demand for goods and services, not just for competition, but for cruising.

Competition also drove the changes that led to the Divergence between cruisers and racers, between cruising and racing. The Olympic announcement forever changed the sport and once and for all, finalized the split. But the Divergence also meant more than just a split between cruising and racing. Going into the '70s, it affected the roles ACA and AWA played in the future representing whitewater interests. The Divergence also affected the market place and the future of the industry.

The River now diverged with two parallel channels, cruising and racing. For a time, neither one was more dominant than the other, although surface crosscurrents, design and technique, flowed from racing toward cruising. The River's flow began to feel the effects of the first rains of the three building cloudbursts: the Olympics, commercial rafting, and Blackadar.

The Golden Age of Paddling: the '70s

THE '70S WERE A PIVOTAL TIME for building the character of the sport we know today. Everything prior set the stage from our whitewater origins to building the supporting infrastructure to the divergence in paddling in the '60s between racing and cruising, now called river-running in the '70s. The '70s solidified it all and the industry, as we know it today, emerged.

The '70s are often called the Golden Age of Paddling because of the freedoms we enjoyed: pushing the limits of the sport (Walt Blackadar), receiving recognition beyond our own sport's boundaries *(Deliverance* and ABC's *American Sportsman),* attaining a level of skill and stature in whitewater in our own right (C-1 Bronze Medal at Munich in '72 and C-1 sweep at Jonquierre in '79), developing the confidence to invent new aspects of the sport (Gemini C-2s, Max C-1s, rodeo and squirt), to be finally free of our dependence on measuring up to European standards.

We paddled many rivers when we wanted (water levels permitting) and how we wanted, free of over-crowding and other restrictions. As individual paddlers, we designed and built our own boats and made our own gear. We were independent, with the kind of independence that comes from doing it all for ourselves. But with all of this came circumstances that moved the sport away from its previous facilitators, the individual paddlers and their clubs, towards the adolescent industry that supplied the goods and services to the growing number of whitewater paddlers. But also with that, in some way, came the loss of our independence. We lost the skills and ability to build and even repair boats and gear because of the materials they were made from (thermoformed and rotationally molded plastics). However, boaters who previously would not have become involved because of the need to build their own boats and gear, came into the sport and brought diversity to our core community. Our numbers increased to the point that restrictions were imposed on us by various governmental agencies. Our access to rivers was threatened for the first time, as were the rivers themselves for various dam-building projects. We also had some of our first real river deaths, of paddlers that were part of our core community. These were not just accidental deaths brought by inexperience or other circumstances.

All of these things are part of the character of the sport today. Those of us who were part of the '70s often reminisce about the times and mourn its loss, but we must also acknowledge that it, too, was an integral part of the continuing evolution of the sport, and not something that should be bemoaned. Rather it should be celebrated for what the sport is today. We must recognize that we were there at the beginning.

1970

Walt Blackadar's article about his first descent of Turnback Canyon on the Alsek appears in a summer issue of Illustrated

Deliverance debutes in theaters across the country

Jamie McEwan wins bronze in C-1 at '72 Olympics in Munich, Germany

First plastic (rotationally molded) kayak produced for whitewater, the River Chaser, by Hollowform

First thermoformed plastic canoe produced for whitewater by Blue Hole

Canoe, first commercial paddlesport magazine, published

Guidebooks available for most areas of the country

1975

First American designed kayak, the Slipper, raced in '75 World Championships in Skopje, Yugoslavia

First stern squirt, by Bob Robison, in Max II C-1

American designed C-1s (Max II and Slipper) and C-2 (Gemini) raced at '77 World Championships in Spittal, Austria

First rodeo in Stanley, Idaho

Perception enters plastic kayak market with the Quest

Last of large composite manufacturers, Hyperform (formerly HIPP), out of business

Mad River begins production of ME, OC-1

American C-1 slalom racers sweep medals at '79 World Championships at Jonquierre, Quebec

1980

The Rains of the Summer of '72

In the early '70s, three independent events fed the River: the Olympics, the movie *Deliverance,* and Blackadar's adventures. Just as a cloudburst and accompanying torrential rain can change a river's flow and channels, these three events changed paddling in subtle ways.

The Olympics of August of 1972 in Munich were the first to include whitewater slalom racing. The Olympics epitomized youth and was the ultimate venue of competition. The inclusion of slalom racing drove home that slalom racing was a sport for youth. It swelled competition's tributary and channel, though its effects were not solely limited to racing and racers.

The second event, the release of the movie *Deliverance,* also came during the summer of '72. It debuted in July in theaters in Los Angeles and New York and by the Fall, had been seen across the country.

The third event, a compilation of the adventures of Walt Blackadar, epitomized the opposite of the other two. Blackadar was not young, nor did his skills necessarily model the sport. He was also a person in fact, not fiction. But a *Sports Illustrated* article about his solo run down the Alsek, published in the Summer of '72, attracted recognition of his accomplishment. Though preceded by other pioneering extreme paddlers in the '30s, '40s, and '50s like Stewart Gardiner, Zee Grant, Erich Seidel, and Walter Kirschbaum, the news of their exploits rarely reached beyond the paddling community. Blackadar, on the other hand, gained national recognition. *Deliverance* and Blackadar fed the river-running channel.

The First Olympics

ACA spent much of the latter half of the '60s organizing and gathering support for World Championship competition with the thought of possible inclusion of whitewater in Olympic competition. Finally in 1969, ACA sanctioned the first formal U.S. team for the World Championships in Bourg St. Maurice, France, just in time for the Olympic announcement.

In 1971, the International Olympic Committee (IOC) made their final decision regarding whitewater at the Munich games. Their decision was that whitewater would be a full-scale event, not just a demonstration sport, and that it would include only slalom, not wildwater. The event would have only four classes: K-1, K-1W, C-1, and C-2. Both C-2M and team classes were not included in Olympic competition.

The decision to exclude wildwater and C-2M forever affected competition and the sport itself. Wildwater competition was relegated to second-class status which over time resulted in the loss of support, and even funding, by official racing organizations.

Dropping C-2M meant that now only one event was open to women, K-1W. Women who paddled C-2M had often paddled C-1 to help develop their skills. With the loss of the C-2M the number of women closed C-boaters dropped (although there was never a large number of them in the first place).

C-2M was excluded because men and women cannot compete against each another according to Olympic rules. It was not excluded, as was commonly thought, to eliminate the defection rate of eastern-block athletes.

Concurrent to IOC's decision, International Canoe Federation (ICF) came out with new slalom rules in 1971. The most important change reduced the minimum width for C-1s to 70 centimeters (cm) for slalom although it was not immediately adopted by all designers and racers. In the first year, only Hahn and Gaybo Limited in Europe built 70 cm C-1s.

The 1971 race schedule in the U.S. and Canada grew to include over fifty races running from March until October providing racers with ample opportunity to compete. It was also the last year that U.S. Whitewater Team members for the World Championships were selected from East and West races, the practice established in the '60s. The K-1 team had East and West racers but K-1W, C-1, and C-2 teams were entirely made up of racers from the East with the exception of the C-2M team of Josef and Jirina Sedivec, former Czech Champions living in California. Roger Paris was selected as the team coach. The '71 U.S. team in World Championship competition improved their standing in 11 out of the 18 events and held their ground on three more. At the conclusion of the '71 World Championships, the U.S. was ranked the sixth best nation in slalom in the world.

For Olympic competition, IOC required head-to-head competition, or qualifying trials, for Olympic team selection. The U.S. Olympic Team Selection Method was changed in 1972 to accommodate this requirement. In July, the first Olympic Trials were held for slalom on the Savage in Maryland. July 27 was the official day of training on the course. July 28 and 29 were reserved for the two preliminary runs and July 30 was set for the final runs. Qualification for entry into the final trials was determined by competition in one of the five ACA divisional regions: Pacific, Northwest, Rocky Mountain, Western, and Eastern Region comprising the Middle States, Atlantic, Central, Eastern, and Dixie divisions.

Although ACA had spent much of the latter half of the '60s preparing for World Championship competition and the dream of the Olympics, there was still much to do to organize and prepare to send a team to the Olympics. ACA began supporting training camps in the East and West in 1970. Training camps were held on the Wenatchee in Washington and the Yough in Pennsylvania. In 1971, they were held again on the Yough and Tariffville in Connecticut. However, aside from the training camps, individual racers were still on their own regarding training and preparation. Racers qualifying for the national team were provided structured support and coaching.

Because 1970 was an off year, having no World Championship competition, some American racers went to Europe on their own after the U.S. Nationals to compete against prospective European Olympic racers. Eric Evans and Dave Nutt competed well against the young European K-1 racers. Bill Endicott and Brad Hager, and John Burton and Bill Funk competed in C-2. Peggy Nutt competed in K-1W and John Sweet and Jamie McEwan competed in C-1.

But aside from using races to train, racers also needed a place, or center, at which to train. For the '72 Olympics, three centers provided extended training opportunities: LCC at Dartmouth, Philadelphia Canoe Club (PCC), and Peanut Butter Park in California.

The most unusual short-term training center during the Winter of 1972 was held on the Kern in Kernville, California, facilitated by ACA Commodore Tom Johnson. Providing an opportunity for paddlers to train year round, without taking time off over the winter, the training camp ran from February 1 through April 22 and concluded with the annual races on the Kern.

The racers camped in the local park in town. The term Peanut Butter Park became synonymous with the training camp, a term used by Angus (Sandy) Morrison because of the preponderance of peanut butter sandwiches eaten by the racers. They trained all winter on the Kern and in the spring hit the race circuit. Five Olympians attended the first Peanut Butter Park training camp: Jamie McEwan, Angus (Sandy) Morrison, John Holland, Carrie Ashton, and Cindi Goodwin.

Prior to the trials, Jay Evans was selected as coach for the Olympic team. He in turn selected an A squad made up of the athletes likely to make the Olympic team. Although being on the A squad did not guarantee making the team, it did provide some preferential treatment including an invitation to a training camp Evans held at Augsburg, the site of the Olympic slalom races held during the spring before the team trials. Many of the A squad attended Evans' training camp at Augsburg. The A squad included Dave Nutt, Dwight (Sandy) Campbell, and Eric Evans in K-1; Linda Hibbard, Louise Holcombe, and Peggy Nutt in K-1W; Sandy Morrison, John Sweet, and Jamie McEwan in C-1; and Steve Draper and Walter (Butch) Rogachenko, Bill Endicott and Brad Hager, and John Burton and Tom Southworth in C-2. All were paddlers from the East.

Trials on the Savage were held in July. They were organized by a small group of local paddlers headed up by Ted Allender and Joe Monahan of Appalachian River Runners Federation (AARF), long time Maryland and West Virginia paddlers, along with ACA National Slalom Committee members Mark Fawcett, Tom Cooper, and former champions Bill Bickham and John Berry.

The Trials provided a few surprises and individual disappointments. In C-1, John Sweet was unable to compete due to a shoulder injury (Shoulder Snapper on the Tygart in West Virginia is named for it). In K-1, western paddler John Holland beat out eastern favorite Dave Nutt (Evans' favorite). In K-1W, Peggy Mitchell (Nutt), considered the top female racer at the time (coached by Evans), flipped and missed her roll at Ledyard Rock during the trials. She did not make the team either.

The other disappointment came when the C-2 team of Bill Endicott and Brad Hager, though placing third in the trials, could not compete because only two C-2 teams were allowed according to Olympic regulations. Evans invited Endicott to the Olympics as an unofficial assistant coach, a position he undertook at his own expense.

The final Olympic team included Jamie McEwan, Sandy Morrison, and Wick Walker in C-1; Eric Evans, John Holland, and Sandy Campbell in K-1; Carrie Ashton, Cindi Goodwin, and Louise Holcombe in K-1W; and Tom Southworth and John Burton, and Russ Nichols and John Evans in C-2.

In preparation for the Olympics, Jay Evans consulted Al Merrill, Dartmouth's cross-country skiing coach, who had the experience of taking a team to an Olympics. One piece of advice Evans followed was the suggestion to copy the best in the sport and improve on it. Evans instituted racing sweats as uniforms to encourage team spirit. The racers became known as the "little green men" because of Evans' choice of Dartmouth green. Evans also shot Super 8 movies and recorded commentary for each racer's run which proved to be valuable in improving performance.

Another piece of advice that Evans followed (which was unpopular) was the two-week break from training after the Savage team trials. The parents of the racers wanted them to train continuously before leaving for Europe. Evans stuck with the advice and was proved right when the British team burned out from over-training and did not do as well as expected.

Evans also kept the racers out of the Olympic village until necessary, another unpopular decision. Merrill maintained that the excitement of the Olympic village environment was a heady experience, one that could prove detrimental. Evans kept the racers near the slalom course site in Augsburg as long as possible prior to the start of the Games.

The old Eiscanal (Ice-Canal) in Augsburg was modified for the Olympics. Although often used for slalom competition, it had not been used for the World Championships since 1957. The new Eiscanal had facilities for 30,000 spectators with 10,000 grandstand seats of which 4,000 were under cover. The course was 600 yards in length and the depth of the water varied from 18 inches to 4½ feet with a speed of 17 feet per second.

Many racers trained at the new Eiscanal which was available for training almost a full year prior to the Olympics. The new Eiscanal course was notorious for its ferocity and fluctuations. Precise but slow moves (relatively speaking) were thought to be the winning combination and large volume designs were considered the way to achieve that. Both Klaus Lettmann and Toni Prijon came out with high volume K-1 designs for the new course: the Mark IV from Lettmann and Olympia 400 from Prijon. Prijon designs swept the medals in K-1.

Since C-1s were already large volume designs, the only major change anticipated for the Olympics was the reduction in width to 70 cm. Many C-1 racers used the latest 70-cm design from Hahn for the Olympics.

As anticipated, Europeans dominated slalom racing. All of the gold medals for slalom were won by the German Democratic Republic (East Germany). However, American Jamie McEwan shocked everyone. As was the custom, the higher ranked paddlers were given early numbers down the course. Because of his low ranking, McEwan was the 32nd racer toward the end of the C-1 class. By the time McEwan made his second run, the presumed bronze medal winner was already being interviewed. While the interview was taking place, the event announcer's play-by-play of McEwan's run could be heard in the background. As McEwan's run down the course continued, the growing excitement in the announcer's voice became evident. The interviewer and presumed bronze medal winner began to notice the crowds' response. As everyone's attention turned to McEwan's run, the incredulous and disappointed look on the interviewee's face told the story as Jamie finished the course winning the bronze.

McEwan's win was a shock because he had not become a serious racer until after the Olympic announcement in 1969. For the '71 World Championships, McEwan paddled an 80 cm C-1, not having made the change to a narrower 70 cm C-1. McEwans best and only finish in World Championship competition prior to the Olympics was a 17th place finish in 1971. While in Europe during the Summer of 1971, McEwan ran the new course at Augsburg. At

Zoom Flume, the current threw him into the concrete wall and he bloodied his hand. On his second run, he broke his boat. He did not attempt a third. Upon his return home to America, he almost gave up on competing in the Olympics. However, his good friend Wick Walker convinced him otherwise and McEwan made up his mind to go for it. He drove to Pennsylvania, bought epoxy from Norse, and made a boat from John Sweet's 70 cm Hahn mold. Although McEwan was determined to make the team, the knowledge that he had not successfully run the new Eiscanal course at Augsburg remained on his mind the entire year.

Olympic team coach Jay Evans used the same questionnaire used by professional football teams to develop psychological profiles of the racers on the team. Based on McEwan's psychological profile, Evans asked McEwan what place he thought he'd finish in the Olympics. When McEwan responded that he'd place 6th, Evans asked him who he couldn't beat. McEwan named only two. McEwan then added a few other names but changed his mind and said he could beat them, too. Evans told McEwan that what he was really saying was that he could win the bronze.

ALTHOUGH MCEWANS' FINISH was considered by some to be a fluke, the gradual ascendance of Americans in slalom racing through the '60s was not a fluke. With the assistance of European immigrants like Erich Seidel, Roger Paris, and Walter Kirschbaum, Americans were instructed in and exposed to advanced European experience on American soil. Others like Natan Bernot (Yugoslavian), Paul Bruhin (Swiss), and Miloslav and Irmagard Duffek (Czechs living in Switzerland) assisted American paddlers whenever they were in Europe for training and competition.

Deliverance

The movie *Bride of the Colorado* was made in 1927 taking advantage of recent publicity generated by the Bureau of Reclamation's decision to build a dam on the Colorado below the Grand Canyon. The movie fit the genre of the silent movies of the '20s. It was shot using Colorado boatmen as doubles in Cataract and Glen Canyons on the Colorado. Instead of a rescue scene from an oncoming train, the movie's climactic rescue scene was shot at Hermit Rapid. After all the trials and tribulations of shooting the movie in December, the movie's partners fell into dispute over who owned the rights and the movie was never released. However, unlike *Bride of the Colorado,* another movie based on the impending inundation of a fictional wild river, *Deliverance,* made it to the theaters during the Summer of 1972.

Based on a novel by James Dickey, *Deliverance* portrayed what could go wrong (and then some) for four Atlanta businessmen on a weekend of canoeing and hunting down an isolated stretch of a river about to be inundated by a dam. Practically overnight, *Deliverance* popularized whitewater canoeing, particularly open canoeing of the Southeast. The movie dramatized the exhilaration of whitewater and brought many new paddlers to the sport. The movie also led to what became known as the Deliverance Syndrome. With rumors that the Chattooga was the site for the filming of the movie, many

AS DOUG WOODWARD recalled, *Deliverance* "belonged as much to the GCA [Georgia Canoeing Association] as it does to Warner Brothers."[1] Not only was the movie filmed on the Chattooga and Tallulah Rivers, but three GCA members acted as stuntmen and technical advisors. They were brought in after the film crew lost equipment trying to shoot at Rock Jumble and Deliverance Rock (so named during the filming) on Section IV of the Chattooga. Payson Kennedy (founder of NOC) and Doug Woodward (co-founder of Southeastern Expeditions) doubled for Ned Beatty, and Claude Terry (Southeastern Expeditions' other founder) doubled for Jon Voight.

Both NOC and Southeastern Expeditions were founded in 1972, coincidental with the release of *Deliverance.*

[1] Woodward, Doug. "Deliverance." *The Eddy Line* Vol. 32 No. 1 (January 1997): 14–17.

novice paddlers attempted the river. In 1973, the river claimed the lives of eight people who tried to emulate Burt Reynolds. Eleven more died during the following three years.

The Deliverance Syndrome was not relegated to the Chattooga alone. Deaths occurred all over the country in the ensuing years, many attributed to novice paddlers attempting whitewater runs. Eight lives were lost in Ohio in 1973 due to paddlers running rivers with low-head dams. California had twenty-eight river-running fatalities, most involving inflatables. Many of the deaths were attributed to the lack of life jackets, although only three of the fatalities involved canoes and kayaks, two from canoeing and one from kayaking. The three-fold increase over the previous two years was attributed to the growing popularity of the sport due to *Deliverance.*

FOR YEARS "DUELING BANJOS" was the unofficial theme song of paddlers across the country and was often heard from car stereos wherever paddlers congregated.

IN 1974, THE CHATTOOGA, known as the Deliverance river, was the first river in the East to receive Wild and Scenic designation. It is also the only Wild and Scenic river that offers commercial whitewater trips.

Blackadar

Although an easterner, Walt Blackadar began to evolve into the role of a western cowboy almost from the moment he moved to Idaho. During the summer of 1968 with his assembled who's who of paddling for his Middle Fork trip, the legend of Blackadar began. Blackadar did everything in grand style. He put on an incredible show. Blackadar played the responsible leader not only ensuring that all were safe on the trip, but that all had fun. Blackadar was the real thing.

In the Spring of 1970, Blackadar tasted the thrill and excitement of big water in high water spring runs on the North Fork of the Payette, the Jarbridge, and the Middle Fork of the Salmon. For the summer, he organized another grand trip, this time down the Colorado through the Grand Canyon with its world renown as big whitewater. Altogether, twenty-seven paddlers, including some that were on his '68 Middle Fork trip, joined him.

SEVEN CANADIANS were among the American paddlers that accompanied Blackadar on his 1970 Grand Canyon trip. The returnees included Barb Wright and Canadians Herman and Christa Kerckhoff along with four others. The new paddlers consisted of both river runners and racers, including Al Chase from Oregon, Gunter Hemmersbach from California, Roger Parsons from Toronto, and Linda Hibbard, Sumner Bennet, and Jack Wright from the Northeast. All were kayakers except for Chase in his C-1.

The trip provided Blackadar an opportunity to find his niche in paddling circles. At 49 years old, he was often older than many others he paddled with. Although he lacked the technical skills of many of the paddlers on the trip, Blackadar proved he had developed a style that worked for big water, "his own brash western style of boating."[2]

American Whitewater published an article written by Blackadar in the Winter 1971 issue. The article was titled *"I Dig Hair—Big, Not Long"* that described his big water technique. In the article, Blackadar's motto was, "When in Hair relax and keep your paddle high and dry." He compared his technique with the current techniques of canoeing and kayaking which promoted paddling slower than the current (backpaddling) for canoeing and faster for kayaking. Paddling slower than the current "let the boat climb the waves," but paddling faster than the current, faster than the oncoming wave, offered no chance for the boat "to rise and ride over the challenge but rather the boat cuts through and becomes unstable." The third choice of "floating at the speed of the wave is very stable until it reaches the brink and then tends to get flipped back from the crest." Using this knowledge he developed his big water technique.

[2] Watters, Ron. *Never Turn Back.* Pocatello, Idaho: Great Rift Press, 1994.

> ...a boater can relax, almost go to sleep, even in huge hair until his boat reaches the summit of each wave. At that instant a brief but definite downstream feint or if necessary stroke/brace combination prevents the expected upstream flip and lets one again relax for a couple of seconds until the next crest is reached. This feint is actually a fluff rather than a stroke, and usually never hits the water; however it does shift the body weight, and if the wave has been read properly, nothing more is required, even for a big wave. If the feint proves insufficient, it is then continued on into a stroke or brace to which one then commits himself as much as necessary..." [3]

Blackadar also defended his perceived showmanship as demonstrated by his nonchalant attitude of entering waves sideways or even backwards. He explained that he chose backwards for entering waves so that he could shift his weight back over the rear deck, even reaching toward the stern in a high brace using the stern as a sea anchor allowing the bow to climb the wave. Sideways approaches allowed him to brace over the waves but also allowed him to drive forward or backwards to avoid danger. His instructions were to "forget the angulation of one's boat, relax until reaching the crest of a wave, and look for danger... Read water at a glance, react only if needed." [4] Blackadar also emphasized the need for an infallible roll. Only a screw roll would do. A put across or layout roll had no place in big water.

Blackadar used a somewhat extended screw roll by sliding his inactive hand toward the inactive blade thereby extending the reach and leverage of his roll. Blackadar was a powerful paddler, compact with big strong shoulders and a low center of gravity. His big chest and lungs allowed him to hold his breath until the time was right to roll.

Blackadar recommended specific paddling gear for big water. He recommended life vests with 33 pounds of flotation found in the Grand Canyon type vest, not the commonly used life vests with only 10–15 pounds of flotation. He recommended the use of unspooned paddles for big water and promoted paddles from Iliad. He also recommended the addition of a rescue handle in the form of a T-grip affixed to the rear deck of a kayak about a third of the way toward the stern. Blackadar and Jim Henry designed the rescue handle in 1970 on one of Blackadar's Idaho trips. The Henrys, founders of Mad River Canoe, often paddled with Blackadar during summers in the early '70s.

The 1970 Grand Canyon trip also fed Blackadar's need for recognition. Some said he was crazy, but many paddlers on the trip came back to join him on trips in the following years. Word spread of his reputation. The time was right, and ripe, for Blackadar to do something adventurous, to really gain the recognition he sought. When he saw an article about Turnback Canyon on the Alsek in Alaska, Blackadar thought this could satisfy him.

Blackadar was told by many experienced paddlers that there was no way to paddle Turnback Canyon, a five-mile stretch of dangerous water in a narrow gorge. The sheer volume of water was awesome and barely above freezing with chunks of iceberg floating in it. Blackadar was unsuccessful in his attempt to organize a small group of the most highly skilled kayakers for a trip during the summer of 1971. Even Blackadar's good friend Barb Wright told him it

[3] Blackadar, Walt. "I Dig Hair—Big, Not Long." *American Whitewater* Vol. XVI No. 4 (Winter 1971): 132–134.

[4] Ibid.

was too harebrained. Others told him the same thing and to put it on the backburner. Instead, Blackadar ran it alone. This time, recognition of his feat went beyond the paddling community.

Blackadar kept a daily diary of the experience and upon his return, wrote to a few major magazines to publish an article based on his writings. *Sports Illustrated* recognized what he had done and Blackadar's story, "Caught Up in A Hell of White Water" was published in the August 14, 1972 issue. When the article came out, coincidental to the Olympics, word spread in the whitewater community beyond the United States. Blackadar was in the national limelight along with the youthful Olympians.

Immediately after paddling Turnback Canyon and even before the *Sports Illustrated* article came out in 1972, Blackadar looked for his next challenge, his next bit of recognition. During the Summer of 1972, Blackadar and two of his Idaho paddling friends, Roger Hazelwood and Kay Swanson, attempted another Alaskan river, the Susitna through Devils Canyon. Devils Canyon proved to be far worse than even Blackadar expected. After harrowing and grueling paddles, portages, and swims, they barely made it out of the canyon alive. Hazelwood and Swanson climbed out of the gorge at Devil's Horn, although neither knew the fate of the other. Nor did they know the fate of Blackadar. Swanson eventually caught up with Blackadar downstream of Devil's Horn, surprised to see him in one piece. Hazelwood's fate was unknown until he was spotted on a ledge in the gorge by the expedition's pilot a day later. Hazelwood was eventually rescued by a helicopter from Air Force Rescue in Anchorage. Their expedition was not the success that Blackadar had hoped for. It did not garner the same recognition for Blackadar as Turnback Canyon had.

While Blackadar was on the Susitna trip, he was approached by Bob Duncan, a producer for American Broadcasting Company (ABC) *American Sportsman* series. Duncan wanted Blackadar to assist with a kayaking piece that was to be aired during the summer as a precursor to the Olympics. Instead of accepting the invitation himself, Blackadar recommended Barb Wright for the piece. Titled "Challenge," the piece showed Wright instructing William Shatner (of the popular *Star Trek* series) in whitewater kayaking. It was filmed on the Salmon in Idaho from Pine Creek Rapids to Panther Creek.

With the TV publicity associated with the "Challenge," *Deliverance,* and Olympic slalom coverage, Blackadar approached Duncan about filming another piece for *American Sportsman,* one that Blackadar felt would really wow the audience with big water paddling. Two years later, in 1974, Duncan was ready to shoot Blackadar's idea, a kayaking run through the Grand Canyon. Blackadar handpicked the paddlers and included Linda Hibbard who had been on his 1970 Grand Canyon trip, Carrie Ashton and Jamie McEwan, both '72 Olympians, and his friend Kay Swanson. John Dondero, a young paddler from Idaho who owned Natural Progression kayaks, supplied Lettmann Mark IV kayaks for the trip. Dondero also accompanied them in his own kayak as crew support which included filming the others with a camera attached to his helmet.

Just before the Grand Canyon shoot, an unfortunate accident occurred that deeply affected Blackadar. During the years after Turnback Canyon in 1971, Blackadar expanded his paddling beyond Idaho. Often while in the East for medical conferences, he paddled on the more well known Class IV–V eastern rivers. In 1973, he paddled the Chattooga with Payson Kennedy, Claude Terry, Les Bechdel, Doug Woodward, and others. At that time, he met Julie Wilson, a young paddler from Georgia, and invited her to paddle with him in Idaho. The next winter, she left her job for an extended adventure of skiing and paddling, joining Blackadar in Idaho in late April. On the first paddling trip, Blackadar led Wilson and three other paddlers on a trip on the West Fork of the Bruneau. Wilson drowned on the Bruneau. Her death shook Blackadar and although it haunted him, Blackadar went forward with the Grand Canyon shooting.

EMORY CLIFFORD KOLB AND HIS BROTHER ELLSWORTH made the first movie of a run down through the Grand Canyon in 1911–12. It was shown for years and set the precedent for garnering public interest in river running exploits.

On the river, Blackadar provided the ABC crew with everything they needed for a good show. His performance in Lava Falls was spectacular. He kept everyone spellbound. Blackadar ran the drop on the river right, which was not the normal route. He disappeared entirely, no boat, no Blackadar, for what seemed an eternity. Even McEwan exclaimed "God Bless!" when he finally appeared upright at the bottom. Blackadar said in front of the camera that although the current pulled him out of the boat, he managed to crawl back in to roll up. It was made for TV.

Soon after Blackadar's Grand Canyon appearance on *American Sportsman,* he was contacted by Roger Brown, a film producer from Summit Films in Colorado. Instead of just shooting a documentary of high-adventure sports that included kayaking with skiing, hang gliding, and rock and ice climbing, Brown wanted to make a movie with a story line that included them all. The script centered around two characters who sought help from well-known climbers and kayakers. The climbers chosen for *The Edge* were Yvon Chouinard and Mike Covington. John Deahl and Tom Hamilton were chosen for hang gliding. The kayakers chosen were Walt Blackadar and the much younger Fletcher Anderson, men who were exact opposites in many ways except for their egos. The kayaking scenes were shot in the Grand Canyon and included another spectacular made-for-the-movies run by Blackadar in Lava Falls. Although *The Edge* showed promise in early showings in Idaho and Colorado in 1976, it failed to attract audiences removed from the paddling scene.

After *The Edge* was finished, Blackadar made a proposition to Brown: to film Blackadar's second attempt at Devils Canyon on the Susitna. Brown liked the idea and successfully sold it to ABC. In the Spring of 1976, a team of five paddlers was chosen for the July trip. Brown chose Cully Erdman and Billy Ward, both from Colorado. Blackadar chose John Dondero, who supplied kayaks for the trip, and Roger Hazelwood, who was with Blackadar on his first attempt in 1972. At the last minute, a young but persistent Alaskan paddler named Barney Griffith blackmailed his way onto the team by attempting to upstage Brown and Blackadar with his own solo descent to be made just days before filming began.

Devil Creek Rapids, which was portaged by Blackadar, Hazelwood, and Swanson on the 1972 trip, was successfully run by Erdman and Ward. Even the 18-year old Griffith ran it successfully. However, Blackadar, was unsuccessful, swimming at the bottom of the drop after two attempts, evidence of his age at 53. The rest of the trip also turned out to be a personal disappointment for Blackadar. Even the final film edited by *American Sportsman* left everyone disappointed when it aired in February of 1977. Although it showed the awesome forces of big water, it also focused on Blackadar, his physical and mental struggles, and left little impression of the successful runs by the other kayakers.

Walt Blackadar on the Susitna (AK), 1977—courtesy of Rob Lesser.

By the mid-'70s, others outside of Blackadar's inner circle were following in his footsteps, organizing and attempting runs on difficult and inaccessible Alaskan rivers by small groups of paddlers. Rob Lesser, a paddler and climber from Idaho who had lived in Alaska, organized his own trip on the Susitna in 1977 with Al Lowande and Ron Frye, a C-1 paddler. Blackadar wanted to try it again. Having a difficult time arranging a group of his own, he contacted Lesser and joined his trip. Blackadar, Frye, Lesser, and Lowande entered Devils Canyon. Upon reaching Devil Creek Rapids, Frye chose not to paddle the rest of the canyon. Frye was also concerned about his wife who had not returned from a hike in bear-inhabited tundra after flying in to High Camp to watch the group paddle through the Canyon. Blackadar, Lesser, and Lowande continued without Frye. Devil Creek Rapids, and specifically the section previously named by Blackadar as the Nozzle, was again Blackadar's nemesis. Blackadar was forced to climb out of the canyon after losing his boat, as did Lowande. Lesser portaged around the last part of the Nozzle, successfully running the rest of the canyon by himself.

In 1978, Blackadar was once again asked to participate in another *American Sportsman* piece, this time on Cross Mountain Canyon on the Yampa with Eric Evans, nine time National K-1 Slalom Champion in the '70s. Instead of showing big water adventures, *American Sportsman's* intention for the piece was to draw attention to the potential inundation of Cross Mountain Canyon for a hydroelectric dam. To demonstrate contrasts between low water and high water runs, the piece required two separate shootings. Footage for the low water run was shot in the early spring of 1978 before snowmelt raised the water levels. The high water run was expected two months later. In the meantime, after the first run through Cross Mountain Canyon, Blackadar traveled East and paddled the Gauley at 7,500 cfs with Richard Furman and Al Parker who later died in a plane crash scouting a kayaking run. Blackadar also paddled the New gorge at 50,000 cfs with Furman and Lee Miller.

Before the high level run was made, Blackadar returned to Idaho and made a run on the South Fork of the Payette. On May 14, 1978, while on the South Fork, Blackadar drifted into a log that was obscured by a wave. His boat pinned, trapping him inside and Blackadar drowned. He was 55 years old.

Author's note: I recommend Ron Watter's biography of Blackadar, *Never Turn Back*, for additional insight into Blackadar's life as a "whitewater pioneer."

Paddlers across the country were shocked by Blackadar's death, regardless of their personal feelings about him. He was not always well liked in the paddling community. His bigger than life image and ego sometimes clashed with other paddlers. This was particularly true outside western boating circles. His lack of technical finesse on rivers in the East sometimes contributed to disdain among eastern boaters, particularly those who did not appreciate the differences between eastern and western style paddling, between eastern and western rivers. But Blackadar had a charismatic character that lent itself not only to the TV audience, but was the stuff of legends. He loved to meet and paddle with people from all over the country. Granted, it provided him a stage to talk about himself and his exploits, but it also provided others in the paddling community an opportunity to enjoy him as a person. Blackadar always went out of his way for people. He invited many people to visit and stay with him in Idaho to paddle. He knew how to tell a good story. He knew how to reinvent reality. His life and death contributed to the history and the future of the sport.

In 1978, a 6,000-foot mountain peak in the St. Elias range overlooking Alsek's Turnback Canyon was named Mount Blackadar by the Canadian Permanent Committee on Geographic Names.

Shelby Canyon of Turnback Canyon on the Alsek —courtesy of Rob Lesser.

After the Summer of '72, the sport did indeed grow, although not directly the result of the Olympics as anticipated. Instead, the making of *Deliverance* and the emergence of Blackadar were the major watershed events that contributed to the growth in river running and the future of the sport, not the Olympics. Perhaps this was in part because of the obvious differences between *Deliverance* and Blackadar, and the Olympics. Slalom racing was a sport for the young, for athletes. Watching the slalom runs during the '72 Olympics on a man-made course was probably the first time many people, including some paddlers, had seen a slalom race. Many people probably found it interesting and perhaps fascinating, but the race bore little resemblance to river running. It is doubtful that many people, save for some youth, seriously considered getting into whitewater because of it. The connection between slalom racing and river running, then as now, is rarely made because many televised slalom races occur on man-made rivers or rivers altered for racing. But anyone who saw *Deliverance* or read about or watched Blackadar on ABC's *American Sportsman,* or Barb Wright teaching Captain Kirk about whitewater, could fantasize and even seriously consider the possibility of whitewater for themselves.

The **fictional** *Deliverance* followed by the **factual** Blackadar was a powerful one-two punch. The continued televised appearances of Blackadar on American Sportsmen on Sunday afternoons throughout the mid-'70s further expanded the audience exposed to whitewater and river-running. At the same time, there was no continued televised coverage of slalom racing. Slalom racing was not included in the next Olympics in 1976. Neither was there any

American televised coverage of World Championships from Europe throughout the '70s. Instead, river running began to take the place of competition in driving the future of the sport.

A Subsequent Deluge

It was often said after the Olympic announcement in 1969 that 1972 would be the year that the sport of whitewater would come into its own, the result of inclusion in the Olympics. It was anticipated that as with skiing in the '60s, the televised slalom races at the Olympics would attract many new participants in the sport and usher in a new era of growth. Many people thought whitewater paddling would be the *next* big sport.

In anticipation of coming into its own, many people in the sport prepared for the growth that was expected as a result of Olympic competition, particularly the young and eager whitewater component of the paddlesport industry. In 1969, Old Town loaned boats to the U.S. Team for the '69 World Championships. In 1971, High Performance Products (HIPP), a new and eager manufacturer, supplied boats for the '71 World Championships. The next year, HIPP obtained a license from Klaus Lettmann to build his designs and supplied the '72 Olympic U.S. Team with Lettmann boats.

HIPP SUPPLIED THE U.S. TEAM with the Olymp Mark IV K-1, Mistral Mark II C-1, and Team Mark II C-2, all specifically designed for the Augsburg course. However, not all members of the team used Lettmann designs for the Olympics. Jamie McEwan used a Hahn C-1.

ACA was also eager to support the anticipated growth in whitewater. ACA felt it was important to protect designers and manufacturers from the pirating of designs and because they felt that competition was the source of the anticipated growth, protection of designs used in competition was particularly important. John Wilson, the public relations official for the '71 U.S. Whitewater Team, wrote about "the Big Debate," to copy or not to copy, that began in earnest at the '71 Whitewater Championships in Merano, Italy. His article appeared in *American Whitewater* in the Winter 1971 issue. It was an appeal in support of American manufacturers of whitewater boats, which at the time only involved Old Town and HIPP.

> Original and successful new boat designs often involve 500 to 1,000 hours of work. Many evolve only after years of experimentation. The professional boat designer must amortize this in the purchase price of his boat. He can protect his design with a copyright. However, the designer, not the government, must enforce the copyright through the courts. This might take two or three years and in the meantime the boat in question has probably become obsolete... England and some other European countries are strict about not allowing copied boats to compete in major races. There the officials of the sport enforce the copyright rules instead of the courts. In other countries, such as West Germany, paddlers themselves enforce no copying by vigilante techniques, such as breaking a copied boat in the dark of the night. Not a very happy situation.[5]

[5] Wilson, John. "The Big Debate." *American Whitewater* Vol. XVI No. 4 (Winter 1971): 115–116.

Wilson's assertion that a copyright was sufficient to protect a design was a common misconception. A copyright only protects the design on paper. Once the design is made into an object, only a patent can provide protection. However, Wilson's assertion that the owner of the copyright is responsible for enforcement through the courts is correct. The same also applies to a patent. Its protection is only guaranteed through enforcement by the assignee of the patent.

Wilson did not propose the use of extreme measures taken by other countries in protecting manufacturers and designers. Instead, he proposed that although copying was deemed acceptable in the '60s because of the unavailability of large numbers of commercial boats, the situation had changed in the '70s. Old Town and HIPP, the current manufacturers, were able to produce sufficient numbers relatively inexpensively and, therefore, copying of designs by small builders was deemed unacceptable. Wilson also argued that because HIPP supplied boats at no cost to the '71 U.S. Team (a total of fifty-three boats for the thirty-four team members), American paddlers should support the current legitimate manufacturers like HIPP.

ACA's Slalom Committee tentatively agreed with Wilson's proposition because they felt support of manufacturers was integral if whitewater was to grow. Although the committee acknowledged that enforcement was a problem, they also felt that failure to support the manufacturers was detrimental to growth since the manufacturers might not find it economically feasible to continue to develop new boats for competition.

However, neither Wilson's nor ACA's view on the matter was widely accepted, particularly among non-racers. Michael Harman, President of the Washington Kayak Club, responded to Wilson with a rebuttal in a follow-up letter published in "Letter from Readers" in the Summer 1972 issue of *American Whitewater.* In his letter, Harman pointed out the reasons why boats were copied in the Seattle area. Not only were the well-known brands, Old Town and HIPP, unavailable, but if they were available, their cost would be much higher than acceptable due to the cost of freight from the East. It was, therefore, cheaper for a paddler to build a copy of a boat than to buy one. Harman also pointed out that many considered boat building a part of the sport itself. Harman reasoned that if pirating of boats was to be eliminated, then boats must be available locally and cheaply. His proposed solution was for designers to either license local builders to build their designs or work directly with major clubs to build molds with royalty arrangements for personal use only by club members, not for resale.

The discussions surrounding pirating demonstrated the divergence between the interests of racers and river runners. The interests of a very visible and vocal few, racers and their supporters, were superimposed on the largely invisible and quiet majority who continued doing their thing, running rivers for the pleasure of it. However, after 1972, paddlesports, both flatwater and whitewater, experienced an increase in the number of participants. For whitewater, this increase was for river running and pleasure, not for competition. Many factors contributed to this increase, including the energy crisis of 1974 and a general increase in interest in outdoor sports. Paddlesports provided recreation without gasoline consumption as opposed to other recreational boating activities. For Grumman, canoe demand peaked in 1974 and was attributed to both the movie *Deliverance* (a Grumman was used in the movie) and the energy crisis. In that single year alone, Grumman produced 33,000 canoes. Many new canoe and kayak manufacturers began production during this time to satisfy the increasing demand. Within a few years of the discussions around "the Big Debate" and protecting the future of the sport by protecting the manufacturers from pirating, river running began to drive whitewater. The pirating and protection discussions were ultimately made moot.

With increased participation in paddlesports, the next event—the introduction of plastics—was poised to affect the sport, particularly whitewater. The future of the sport would not be in competition or composites.

Fortunately for the whitewater market, two non-paddlesport companies, Uniroyal and Hollowform, adapted their experience in plastics to produce canoes and kayaks. Uniroyal chose Royalex™ (Royalex is a registered trademark of U.S. Rubber Company, Uniroyal's predecessor) and its accompanying process of thermoforming to make canoes. Hollowform chose rotational molding, and the use of the polyethylene, to make kayaks. This paralleled what occurred after World War II with Grumman and aluminum forming technology in producing aluminum canoes. Had it not been for these non-paddlesport companies, the history and timing of the introduction of new materials into paddlesports may have been different. None of the existing paddlesport manufacturers had the technology nor the financial support (except for Old Town) to experiment with plastics. The paddlesport market on its own was not large enough to warrant it. Had it not been for Uniroyal and Hollowform identifying a potential market in paddlesports, the entry of plastics undoubtedly would not have occurred as soon as it did in the '70s. Uniroyal and Hollowform essentially kick-started plastics in paddlesports.

THE DEMAND FOR NEW MATERIALS is not always driven by the need for better materials. For whitewater, that could be lighter, more durable, or stronger materials, but also by market and economic considerations, typically the need to produce more products faster or cheaper. For competition, lighter, not necessarily stronger and more durable materials, were needed. Plastics were neither lighter than composites nor did the size of the market for competition justify the costs associated with plastics and their processes. However, for the rest of the paddlesport market, including river running, plastics were not only suitable for durability and strength, the growing market could justify the costs.

In 1959, U.S. Rubber Company obtained a copyright for the name Royalex for a multi-layer laminate with an inner core of foam. The same year, Thompson Royal-Craft introduced a canoe of Expanded Royalite material, the same material as U.S. Rubber's Royalex. Although not specifically intended for whitewater, a few of the canoes from Thompson Royal-Craft were purchased and used by whitewater paddlers including John Berry. Unfortunately, the canoes were heavy and paddlers did not accept them for whitewater, or any other kind of paddling.

In the early '60s, Uniroyal, the successor to U.S. Rubber, began to promote Royalex as a light and rigid material for use by the automotive industry. It was initially used for motor covers for large trucks. Over approximately the next five years, Uniroyal explored other uses for Royalex including auto bodies, large truck cabs and fenders, and boats. In 1968, they approached White Canoe in Maine with the idea of using it for making canoes. White Canoe, a longtime producer of high quality wood and canvas canoes, scoffed at the idea saying no one would buy a plastic canoe. Undeterred, Uniroyal decided that canoes thermoformed of Royalex was a good idea and proceeded on their own. They copied a canoe (thought to be a 16-foot Old Town with fuller ends chosen for easier thermoforming), built a mold, and peddled canoes to rental outfitters. The canoe became known as the Warsaw Rocket, named after the original manufacturing site of Royalex in Warsaw, Indiana.

Uniroyal hired a company to assist in marketing the Warsaw Rocket and showed the canoes at boat shows. Paul Rivers, then owner of Rivers and Gilman in Maine who purchased White Canoe (the company that only a few years earlier dismissed the notion of plastic canoes), saw one at a show. In the early '70s, Rivers and Gilman requested and received a canoe for testing and began ordering unfinished hulls, choosing to complete the boats themselves.

Uniroyal was willing to sell unfinished hulls to anyone who would place a minimum order of twenty. Others soon followed Rivers and Gilman's practice, including Blue Hole, Mad River, Seda, Shenandoah, and Perception, and began producing their own versions of the Warsaw Rocket. Except for different thwart and seat placements that affected hull width with accompanying subtle hull changes, they all manufactured essentially the same canoe. Though the design coincidentally worked well for whitewater because of its fuller ends, just as the original 17-foot Grumman had worked, neither the design nor the marketing by Uniroyal targeted whitewater paddlers specifically. This changed when Blue Hole not only outfitted and marketed their version of the Warsaw Rocket for whitewater, but also decided to thermoform their own design specifically for use on whitewater.

Tom Johnson first met Don Carmichael while developing fiberglass gun stocks filled with rigid urethane foam for Armalite. At the time, Carmichael told Johnson of his dream of producing plastic parts such as a canoe or kayak in a single mold by simply pouring plastic into the mold. Carmichael later became VP of Hollowform, a company that could do just that.

Hollowform was a proprietary molder of rotationally molded products in southern California. In 1973, Don Carmichael, the new VP of the Marine Division of Hollowform, contacted Tom Johnson about canoe and kayak designs to produce them in polyethylene by rotational molding. Based on his 1970 Bronco kayak design, Johnson made a plug for a mold for rotational molding. In 1973, Hollowform produced the first rotomolded kayak of Johnson's new design, the River Chaser.

The kayak was 13 feet in length and molded to produce a double layer of cross-linked polyethylene. The inner layer was foamed to increase rigidity while reducing overall weight (because a foamed layer is less dense than a nonfoamed layer). The seat and walls were made of Ethafoam and the footbraces were an aluminum bar, the type that was often called a suicide footbrace.

The first Hollowform ad appeared in *American Whitewater's* Winter 1973 issue. New River Chasers sold for $129.95 plus tax and shipping. Shipping from California to New York was $27. Thousands of River Chasers were sold across the country over the next five years. In 1978, the River Chaser II model retailed for $299. Comparable composite kayak designs retailed from $300 to $375.

The plastic in the early River Chasers was not always properly cross-linked. This sometimes led to permanent hull deformation in the heat, particularly when the kayak was tied down too tight on racks on a hot sunny day. Improper cross-linking also often resulted in cracks on impact with rocks and even normal handling abuse. Johnson took a trailer load of kayaks to Ohiopyle for the guides to test in their day-to-day activities. Dan Demaree recalled that the first ones were easily broken but that the second trailer load held up well. [6]

In 1973, the same year the River Chaser was introduced, LPA Plastics of Quebec, a sailboard manufacturer, introduced their own plastic kayak design, the River Runner. The River Runner was an entry-level kayak for general recreation, not a whitewater kayak, and was sold as a package with a paddle. However, the concept behind its production and distribution was unique. The River Runner was molded in a factory-on-wheels, a semi with a trailer, described as the "smallest [rotational molding] machine in the world." [7] LPA's manufacturing and distribution concept was to produce kayaks, one per hour, on site at a warehouse, and then move on to the next site. For two years, Pierre Arcouette, owner of LPA Plastics, trailered his factory-on-wheels across the country producing kayaks for outfitters and retailers. Rutabaga in Madison, Wisconsin, owned by Gordy Sussman, was one retailer where Arcouette molded kayaks. Unfortunately, Rutabaga was in a retail/commercial zone, not a manufacturing zone, and the operation was shut down by the city. In 1975,

[6] Demaree, Dan. Interview by author 31 August 2000.

[7] Arcouette, Pierre. Interview by author 5 September 2000.

Arcouette produced kayaks at the National Sporting Goods Association (NSGA) show in Chicago.

A few other rotational molders also produced plastic kayaks like Hollowform, although their entry into the market was often short-lived. One exception was White Brothers of Ontario, part of Algonquin Distributors associated with Kayko Industries in Ontario. White Brothers produced their own version of Arcouette's River Runner for many years throughout the '70s and '80s.

Tom Johnson and his River Chaser — courtesy of Tom Johnson.

Tom Johnson provided Hollowform with two other designs, a second kayak designed more for river touring and a 15-foot canoe copied from a Willet canoe design (a Washington builder of wood and canvas canoes).

Hollowform, like Uniroyal, was not solely involved in the production of kayaks or canoes. It was merely part of their business, and not a large part at that. During the later '70s, Hollowform's management changed often, eventually resulting in the sale of the company to another plastic molding company that decided to get out of the plastic kayak business. However, by this time, Perception, like Blue Hole who was dedicated to producing and marketing to whitewater paddlers, had begun production of rotationally molded kayaks.

With Holloform's demise, Johnson ended up with the canoe mold for his design and Bill Masters, founder of Perception, purchased the kayak molds to Johnson's designs, both the River Chaser and the un-named touring kayak mold. Perception never produced the River Chaser. However, the touring kayak was later produced under the Aquaterra name.

THE KAYAKERS OF CALIFORNIA were the first to benefit from Hollowform's location in southern California. The Sierras provided the testing that showed the suitability and superiority of plastic kayaks for whitewater. With their rotationally molded kayaks, California paddlers pushed the limits of the sport. They were able to run what was previously considered unrunnable because they were no longer limited by the durability of their boats.

The open canoeists of the Southeast were the first to benefit with Uniroyal's Warsaw Rocket that Blue Hole, located in eastern Tennessee, specifically outfitted and promoted for whitewater. Like the kayakers of California, the open canoeists of the Southeast pushed the limits of the sport. The Southeast also soon followed as the new center for rotationally molded kayaks with Hollowform's successor, Perception, who set the course for the market and industry in the '80s.

The New Face of the Industry

Plastics cemented the dominance of river running over competition. But plastics also established the industry's position as the provider of goods and services in the future of the sport. The industry, in particular the boat manufacturers, were poised to share, and even take over, the role of facilitator of the sport from individuals and their clubs. With the transition away from composites that the individual paddler could build with in his or her own garage, to plastics that required expensive equipment beyond the paddler's capabilities, the face of the industry changed and so did the sport.

Blue Hole and Perception, unlike Uniroyal and Hollowform, were founded as paddlesport companies by paddlers specifically for the whitewater market. They took the technology and combined it with an understanding and knowledge of whitewater, and the specific needs of the whitewater paddler. These two companies shaped the future of the sport.

Blue Hole

In the late '60s and early '70s, paddlers on the western side of the Appalachians in the Southeast from the Tennessee Scenic River Association (TSRA), the East Tennessee White Water Club (ETWWC), the Tennessee Valley Canoe Club (TVCC), and other small groups, paddled their open Grummans on whitewater in Tennessee. However, as they developed their paddling skills and ventured onto more difficult rivers, standard Grummans were not the boats of choice. Instead, a beefed up shoe-keeled Grumman was needed. Don Bodley and Don Hixon of Chattanooga ordered and sold special Grummans, built of a heavier gauge sheet and with seven ribs instead of five. Bodley's and Hixon's business name was Canoeist Headquarters. Looking for something better, they eventually ran across a 16-foot keel-less canoe built by Pierre Marquette of Michigan that proved to be suitable for whitewater. Because the canoe was made of cloth instead of chop, it proved to be a more durable canoe than other fiberglass canoes they tried. Bodley and Hixon began to sell the Pierre Marquette canoe. Using duct tape for repairs and truck inner tubes for flotation, paddlers were able to run more and more difficult rivers of the Cumberland plateau. Although the Pierre Marquette canoes were better suited in some ways, Bodley and Hixon also recognized that its design had a tendency to submarine while a Grumman did not due to its fuller bows. Not wanting to get into building their own fiberglass canoes, Bodley contacted Darrell Leidigh of Mohawk in Florida to build a whitewater canoe to their specifications: fullness in the bow and stern, rounded bilge, and with cloth instead of chop.

THERE WAS LITTLE MINGLING between the paddlers of the Tennessee valley (ETWC, TSRA, and TVCC) on the west side of the mountains and the paddlers of the eastern side of the mountains (GCA and Carolina Canoe Club, CCC). While the paddlers on the east side developed their own style of paddling with pioneers including Bob Benner, Hugh Caldwell, Ramone Eaton, Horace Holden, Payson Kennedy, and Fritz Orr, Jr., the paddlers on the western side followed McNair's *Basic River Canoeing.*

Bob Lantz, who happened to work in the aerospace industry in Nashville, Tennessee, as a structural engineer, was also a paddler. In the late '60s, he received a letter from Uniroyal about a material, Royalex, with potential aerospace applications. Lantz paid little attention to it when he first received it. It wasn't until he was on a one-year assignment for NASA in Langley, Virginia, that he ran across the letter in his files. This time, the letter caught his attention and he contacted another paddling engineer, Bill Griswold, about it. Based on Royalex's structural information contained in the letter, Griswold and Lantz realized that Royalex had three characteristics beneficial for whitewater: it would slide over rocks better than aluminum or fiberglass; it had good impact resistance (although it could tear); and it had its own built-in internal flotation.

Griswold contacted Uniroyal and found that they had previously investigated marine applications and built a powerboat and a canoe. Griswold also learned that a canoe made of Royalex was already available through Rivers and Gilman of Maine. He also learned that he could buy hulls directly from Uniroyal. Coincidentally, around the same time, one of Rivers and Gilman's canoes made it into the South. Although it was outfitted as a touring canoe rather than a whitewater canoe, word spread about its whitewater potential. Hearing this, in 1971, Lantz and Grizwold, and two other friends, decided to purchase hulls from Uniroyal.

In order to protect the Royalex hulls from tearing, Lantz and Griswold designed the outfitting to include structural gunwales and large flattened thwarts. Although they only had four hulls to outfit, Lantz and Griswold designed and bought a die for the extrusion of aluminum gunwales to their design and specifications. They designed gunwales of a lower temper aluminum, T42, to allow bending and attached the gunwales with rivets and washers in a one inch rivet pattern to prevent tearing and rivet pull-through. The gunwale cross section itself used a wider outwale to shed water. A narrower inwale was used for ease of dumping a water-filled canoe. This was not a standard approach to gunwale design at the time since many builders used a wider inwale for seat attachment. The gunwales also had ridges that ran lengthwise along the inside surface against the Royalex surface to further prevent slipping that might result in a tear.

Unlike the gunwales, the thwarts and seats were a higher temper and therefore stiffer to prevent bending. Seat height was designed to allow sufficient room underneath for kneeling for whitewater (unlike the Rivers and Gilman hull). The deckplates were also designed as a structural part of the gunwale system but included a solid handle and perforations to allow water to drain. Every bolt used was stainless steel and had a locknut for vibration while being transported on top of a car.

The first four canoes had no seats because the canoes were intended exclusively for their own whitewater use. But before Lantz and Griswold completed the first four hulls, they realized that not only did the hull shape itself appear to be good for whitewater (full ends and rounded bilge), other paddlers might also want one. Lantz decided to brand them with a company name. He chose the name Blue Hole (after the deep, blue fishing and swimming holes on many of the rivers in the area) and designed a logo for decals. The logo was affixed to the first four canoes before the company existed as a business.

Lantz and Griswold paddled and tested the canoes. They found that the canoes performed as expected; everything they designed for the canoes worked. Until this time, a broached canoe was not easily repairable. Now they found that all they had to do was pull the canoe off the rock, stamp it out, and use a limb to bend the gunwales back into shape. The Royalex did not tear.

In 1973, Lantz and Griswold purchased fifty hulls from Uniroyal and in October delivered their first canoes, the first ten going to Don Bodley in Chattanooga. The first ads for Blue Hole also appeared in *American Whitewater*. Lantz recognized very early that the market for the canoes was large enough for more than a backyard operation. In 1974, Lantz partnered with two other paddlers, Bill Peeton, a chemistry professor at Vanderbilt, and Roy Guinn, an air conditioning controls technician for Robert Shaw. All three worked at outfitting canoes in their spare time. Lantz was the first to leave his full-time job. In early 1974, Blue Hole moved from Nashville to new facilities in Sunbright, Tennessee. Blue Hole continued to purchase and outfit Uniroyal's Royalex hulls. More than 150 hulls were manufactured in this manner. Peeton eventually left Blue Hole for a position in Germany leaving Lantz and Guinn as the owners of the business.

Although Uniroyal's Warsaw Rocket hull was a fairly decent hull for whitewater, from the very beginning, Lantz wanted to design and manufacture a hull specifically for whitewater. It took about a year to design and build an oven. After producing about 175 canoes from the Warsaw Rocket hull since Blue Hole's founding in 1975, they introduced their own thermoformed canoe design. The design was nominally 16 feet (15' 9") and incorporated fullness into the ends with more freeboard than the Warsaw Rocket. It was called the OCA design, O for open, C for canoe, and A for the model.

The OCA was a tandem design but thwart and seat placement allowed for solo paddling, either by paddling it forward or backward depending on the paddler's thwart placement preference. In 1976, Blue Hole's second model was introduced, the OCA-17A. It was essentially the same hull as the OCA except that 18 inches was added to the middle extending the hull to a little more than 17 feet in length. Two other designs followed: the 16-foot Challenger and 17-foot Wanderer.

Although there were other manufacturers of Royalex whitewater canoes using the Warsaw Rocket hull, Blue Hole was the only manufacturer located in the Southeast, which was recognized as the prime whitewater open canoeing region in the country. Blue Hole's OCA proved ideal for the rivers of the Southeast.

Although Blue Hole wasn't into manufacturing kayaks, toward the end of the '70s, Lantz recognized that rotational molding was the future of the sport.

Perception

In 1971, while at Clemson, Bill Masters was introduced to whitewater canoeing using a Grumman on the Chattooga. Masters was a junior engineer at a manufacturer of polyester fiber. He became interested in whitewater kayaking and began building kayaks using a borrowed mold and overruns from the mill. His word-of-mouth business grew and he moved production to Liberty,

South Carolina. Masters met Don Hamilton one day when Hamilton stopped by to inquire about kayaks on his way to paddle Section III of Chattooga in his Grumman. They soon began paddling kayaks together.

In 1972, Masters started Marbaglas, a business that rebuilt molds for the synthetic marble industry, all the while continuing to build kayaks on the side. In 1974, after graduating from college with a degree in electrical engineering, Masters worked as an electrical design engineer for about a year, but he continued to build. During this time Masters decided to expand into paddle making. In 1975, he became a partner in New World Paddles with Keith Backlund, Don Hamilton, and Steve Scarborough.

Keith Backlund began carving wood canoe and kayak paddles in the late '60s. In 1971, Backlund and fellow Olympic hopeful Drew Hunter hit the East coast racing circuit together. In 1972, Hunter won the Yough Slalom with a paddle made by Backlund. At the time, all the top racers used European wood paddles from Prijon and Kober. Backlund's wood paddles became popular and Backlund and Hunter formed Dagger Paddles in 1972. In 1974, Dagger Paddles was put on hold due to Hunter's move to Colorado and Backlund started Wood-Lyte Paddles, which folded within a year. A year later in 1975, Backlund, then living in the Southeast, started New World Paddles with Hamilton, Masters, and Scarborough as partners.

The name New World was given to distinguish their technology from the old world paddles of Kober and Prijon. Kober used veneer and Prijon used hardwood edges in the blades. The difference between Backlund's Wood-Lyte and New World paddles and Europe's Prijon and Kober paddles was that Backlund shaved away wood for the fiberglass reinforcements. He didn't just add glass reinforcement on top of the wood. Backlund's paddles combined the properties of glass with wood to achieve a better and lighter paddle made of wood, glass, and epoxy. This was the beginning of selective reinforcement with different synthetic fibers, and at the same time, the selective use of different woods and grain combinations to achieve the desired blade properties. It was, however, a labor-intensive process to build New World Paddles. In 1976, they began to mass-produce a Kober-type paddle replacing the veneer with glass. These new mass production paddles became the Dagger brand. The hand crafted, custom paddles remained the New World brand. During the same time, Hamilton went into production of all fiberglass paddles under the name Harmony Paddles.

While New World was making paddles, Masters continued production of fiberglass kayaks on the side, initially under the name Fiberglass Technology. In 1976, he changed his business name from Fiberglass Technology to Perception. He added two canoes to his product line with the purchase of Warsaw Rocket hulls from Uniroyal. Both canoes were made from the same Warsaw Rocket hull, but were outfitted differently: the Nantahala with wood gunwales and the Chattooga with aluminum gunwales. Masters practically duplicated Blue Hole's extruded gunwale for his Chattooga model. This created considerable tension between Blue Hole and Perception, particularly since both were located in the Southeast, although on opposite sides of the Appalachians, and both vied for the same market. In 1977, Masters introduced a third canoe, the HD1, short for Hahn Design 1 (later called the Hot Dog 1). The HD1 was a Hahn C-1 hull with sides extended up for use as a solo open canoe (13 feet in length) and was initially introduced in fiberglass.

During the '70s, the link between the innovations for boats and paddles was not merely coincidental. Both benefitted from the development of the other, their development often intertwined due to the influence of the men involved. The link between Backlund and Masters was not an artificial one as they each worked to pursue and perfect their respective crafts.

ONE OF HOLLOWFORM'S biggest detractors, and safety hazards, was the use of foam walls and seat to support the flexible plastic hull. Masters' use of rotationally molded vertical walls integrated with a molded seat (which he patented) in the Quest overcame many of the early safety concerns associated with plastic kayaks from Hollowform.

STANCIL WAS INCREDIBLY ARTISTIC and contributed that creativity to the team of Masters and Stancil. The early trademark indented tape lines on all Perception hulls was his idea. The indented tape lines symbolized flowing water and gave a strong statement to Perception kayaks that all paddlers would come to recognize. Stancil was also the designer of the famous Perception logo which contains William Masters initials. The connected and blended W placed above M appears as a canoe in the center with a kayak on either side.

WOODEN PADDLES, affectionately called "sticks" by their hard core users, is a phenomenon primarily associated with the East. In 1972, about the same time as Backlund began producing wood paddlers, Mitchell Paddles in New Hampshire was started by British paddler Dave Mitchell who apprenticed under Toni Prijon. Mitchell initially produced wood paddles patterned after Prijon's paddles but he later adopted many of the same reinforcements using wood, glass, and epoxy.

In 1980, Homer King started Silver Creek in North Carolina patterning paddles after the trend set by Wood-Lyte, New World, and Backlund Paddles with glass reinforcements and edgings. Other paddle makers followed including Gonzo, Rainbowave, and Sidewinder.

About this same time, Masters and his brother-in-law Allen Stancil saw their first Hollowform kayak while paddling their fiberglass kayaks on the Chattooga. From that moment, they decided rotational molding was the way to manufacture kayaks. Soon after in 1977, Masters and Backlund built the woodstrip prototype of the Quest. (In 1973, Backlund worked for David Hazen, a noted woodstrip canoe builder in Oregon. Backlund passed on the technique of using woodstrip construction for building canoe and kayak prototypes.) In 1978, Perception introduced the Quest.

The same year, the New World partnership terminated. Backlund bought out Hamilton and Masters and retained the New World name. Backlund moved back to West Virginia and a year later, started Backlund Paddles. Backlund continued his paddle-making craft that influenced others including Jim Snyder, Jesse Whittemore, Phil Coleman, and John Regan who helped to carry on the mystique of wood paddles generated by Appalachian small shop craftsmen. The name Dagger remained with Scarborough and Brandy Lesan, Scarborough's college roommate, who was brought in to help make paddles.

In 1979, Masters thermoformed the HD1 in Royalex as a challenge to Blue Hole and the other thermoforming canoe companies. It was the first short plastic canoe on the market. The HD1 was ahead of its time for open canoeing techniques. It required a higher skill level of many OC-1 paddlers who were used to paddling rather forgiving 15-foot and 16-foot canoes, not short 13-foot hulls designed for slalom racing. However, Masters had no real intention to pursue the canoe market. He already knew he was going after the rotationally molded kayak market.

Masters' attempt at contracting kayak manufacturing to a custom rotational molder was a disaster. The molder he hired was unable to produce his kayaks alone. Masters had to work closely with the molder, fixing the machine and learning what worked and what didn't work. At this point, he decided to mold his own kayaks. He designed and built his own machine and oven from scratch, a rock-n-roller that used a forced air oven. Masters and Stancil molded kayaks during the week and delivered them on weekends. The second kayak that Perception introduced to the market was the Mirage that was influenced by Lettmann's Mark IV and Mark V hulls. In 1979, Perception introduced the Sage, the first rotationally molded C-1. Perception now had two kayaks and a C-1 in their line of rotationally molded products.

Masters pushed the market for plastic kayaks with Perception and gained the acceptance of consumers, not only for the durability of the plastic, but for his designs and warranty. The warranty issue was particularly important to consumers since manufacturers of fiberglass kayaks provided no real warranty. Masters also produced kayaks with adjustable seats and thigh braces that were not available from any other kayak manufacturer.

Aside from Perception's rotationally molded products, Masters used his entrepreneurial spirit to take the industry to a new level, particularly with the marketing of paddlesport products. He established a dealer network across the country and because his production was not as labor intensive as fiberglass or composite construction, he could provide a low cost product without the wait. In the late '70s, Masters attended and exhibited at the National Sporting

Goods Association (NSGA) tradeshows. During one show, he shared a booth with Aquaterra of Roanoke, Virginia, who initially made skirts and bags for Perception. Masters expanded his own business holdings with the purchase of Aquaterra to bring accessory production under his control.

Masters read business information voraciously and attended every business seminar given by the Small Business Administration (SBA). He absorbed business information whenever possible. He sold stock in his company to raise capital. He also patented many different ideas and trademarked many different names associated with the sport. Some of Masters' patents and trademarks were disputed by others in paddlesports. They felt their ideas, and ideas that were considered common knowledge in paddlesports, had been borrowed upon too heavily for his patents and trademarks.

Masters was a paddler and entrepreneur who became a rotomolder for the paddlesport market. In essence, Masters did what Hollowform was not able to do.

MANY EVENTS, both within and outside of paddlesports, came together in the '70s, providing the impetus for the evolution of whitewater paddlesports. Uniroyal and Hollowform helped to kickstart the beginning of the plastic industry within paddlesports. Blue Hole and Perception used the momentum, not only of that provided by Uniroyal and Hollowform, but other events including the making of *Deliverance* and the emergence of Blackadar that contributed to the growth of the sport and increasing numbers of whitewater paddlers. Not only were Blue Hole and Perception at the right time, they were in the right place, in the Southeast which was an area that became a destination for many paddlers with its long paddling season and many good whitewater rivers.

A Competing Composite Manufacturer: HIPP

Plastics could not compete with composite construction for racing. Its weight and the cost of its molds were restrictive to the needs of the small whitewater racing market. However, the market was also insufficient to support large manufacturing companies. Two companies with high hopes of success building composite boats, High Performance Products (later called Hyperform) and Phoenix, were successful for a short time. Even before Perception's inception in the late '70s, High Performance Products was the first company to bring real business practices to the young industry. However, neither High Performance Products nor Phoenix could compete with plastics and the changes they brought.

Composites remained the realm for competition. In the late '60s and into the '70s, American domination of the aerospace industry benefitted composites in paddlesports. In 1973, Kevlar™ became available and revolutionized composite construction for canoes and kayaks. (Kevlar is a registered trademark of DuPont de Nemours.) Although Kevlar was the first high-strength, lightweight material that significantly improved whitewater composite construction, its impact on whitewater paddlesports in general was overshadowed by plastics. Composite construction in general was more costly than plastic and since Kevlar added significantly to the cost, it was relegated to use primarily for racing canoes and kayaks.

High Performance Products (HIPP) was originally the idea of Tom Wilson, a member of the '67 National Wildwater Team while with the MIT whitewater club. With the financial assistance of Sam Galpin in 1969, HIPP was officially incorporated and initially produced two of Wilson's designs, the Vector K-1 and C-1 slalom boats. In 1970, with the anticipation of business growth from the aftereffects of the Olympics, HIPP moved production to a larger facility in Hingham, Massachusetts. Over the next year, Galpin traveled to Europe and obtained exclusive manufacturing rights for both Prijon and Lettmann designs. By the 1971 season, HIPP's line included four slalom K-1s, three wildwater K-1s, four touring K-1s, one surfing K-1, one junior K-1, two slalom C-2s, two slalom C-1s, one wildwater C-1, two wildwater C-2s, and 2 semi-open C-2s. HIPP supplied all the boats for the U.S. Team for the '71 World Championships. Unfortunately, the resin used in the team boats was sensitive to UV light. Exposure to sunlight degraded the properties of the composite so the boats had to be kept out of the sun as much as possible.

In contrast, in 1971 while HIPP had the latest Prijon and Lettmann designs, Old Town retained those designs by Hauthaway that were used for the '69 World Championships. Old Town had only kayaks for wildwater, slalom, touring, and a junior model. In just two short years, Old Town was not competitive with HIPP.

E-GLASS STANDS FOR electrical fiberglass. S-glass stands for structural fiberglass.

HIPP marketed their own composite construction calling it Mithril, elve's armor. Mithril was a laminate with E-glass that actually varied from time to time depending on whatever synthetic fibers (cloths) were available. Diolen, made in Europe, was the preferred cloth though was not always available. Mithril was developed to maintain cost as much as possible but it was also more durable than a straight fiberglass layup. The resin used in Mithril was a modified iso-phthalic polyester for use with E-glass and synthetic layups. At times Mithril contained strips of carbon and S-glass for stiffening.

In 1971, HIPP also hired Les Bechdel as a sales rep. Bechdel developed a strategy to market to the many new specialty stores who sold hiking, backpacking, and cross-country ski equipment to like-minded consumers, instead of the traditional marine stores who sold everything from canoes to johnboats. He rep'd, paddled, and even gave lessons as he traveled across the country promoting the product and the sport. Bechdel was successful and by 1972, HIPP had a nationwide dealer network shipping railcar loads to Whitewater Sports in Colorado who handled distribution in the West. HIPP also established a nationwide sales rep network to service the new specialty stores. HIPP also advertised in *American Whitewater* and the newly formed magazine, *Canoe.*

By 1973, Galpin and Wilson began to disagree on various business decisions. In 1974, they parted ways and Wilson established his own company, Phoenix, in Kentucky. Bechdel also left HIPP to join Wilson and his other partners Linda Hibbard, a racer, and Peter Rice, the owner of a chain of stores called Blue Ridge in the mid-Atlantic.

Phoenix opened its doors with Wilson as the general manager, Bechdel in charge of production, Rice in charge of marketing, and Hibbard in charge of product development which included accessories like spray skirts and air bags. Realizing that river runners were using outdated slalom boats, Bechdel traveled to Europe to buy the rights to build boats designed specifically for river running. He negotiated with Mendesta for the Match, a hot racing boat, along with other river running and touring designs.

Everyone at Phoenix was convinced that whitewater was at the threshold of a new level of activity. They recognized how both the Olympics and *Deliverance* contributed to it. They also knew that it was more than just building boats, that it involved gear and accessories that were being developed just for whitewater. However, almost as soon as its doors opened, Phoenix felt the effect of plastics and Hollowform, just as HIPP was feeling it. Bechdel recognized the impact and potential of plastics and told the others that the technology would make Phoenix obsolete. Bechdel left in 1975, a year after Phoenix was founded. Unlike HIPP, Phoenix survived by diversifying its composite production and benefitting from economic subsidies for its location in Kentucky which was an economically depressed area. However, Phoenix never achieved the dreams that were envisioned for it.

In addition to the upstart Phoenix, with management who knew everything about his operations, Galpin also faced other coincidental events over the next few years that seriously threatened his business. Prior to the energy crisis in 1973–74, the list price for a kayak was $299 (wholesale was 40 percent of list) and shipping was free to retailers with orders of 75 or more. When price controls were lifted in 1974, Mithril's material costs increased 40 percent in the first 60 days. Polyester resin increased from $0.29 to over $1.00 per pound. By the end of 1974, the cost of a boat doubled yet the paddling consumer was not willing, nor able to pay for the increase. Although Kevlar became available in limited amounts in 1973 and 1974, it was too expensive to incorporate into the Mithril layup. Neither was it compatible with the polyester resin used to make Mithril. The price of a boat that the market would bear was controlled by the cost of the homebuilder and shipping cost. Shipping alone was formidable at $40. The energy crisis also contributed to the unavailability of some of the materials used in Mithril. As Galpin recalled, "In 1974, the entire economics of business unglued, all hell broke loose." [8]

In 1975, IOC announced that slalom racing would not be included in the '76 Olympics. About the same time, the popularity of Hollowform's plastic River Chaser began to affect HIPP sales. Arcouette's rolling factory of River Runners also hurt HIPP's sales. The combination of the loss of slalom racing in the Olympics and the impact of plastics was lethal.

Galpin did many things to help his business survive. He substituted less expensive mat and woven roving for cloth. He experimented with new layups including wet pre-pregs. However, orders went unfilled and the boats that were sold experienced quality problems. Galpin even changed HIPP's name to Hyperform in an attempt to transform the company's image.

Galpin also made the decision to pursue rotational molding using urethane resins. Instead of using polyethylene which required heat to cure and therefore the use of an oven, Galpin planned to rotationally mold kayaks without an oven using ambient cure thermosetting urethanes. Rotational molding would distribute an even layer of urethane within a mold. Because no heat was needed, inexpensive composite molds would work replacing the expensive metal molds needed for polyethylene. Although his process was hyped in the November 1979 issue of *Modern Plastics,* his rotomolded urethane whitewater kayak never made it to the market. Galpin was never able to "get the chemistry right." [9] A prototype melted when it was left on top of a sales rep's car on a hot August day in Houston.

During the mid-'70s HIPP held almost 40 percent, on the order of 2,000 to 3,000 boats a year, of all composite boats produced. This was considerable considering that an estimated half of all boats were produced by backyard and home builders. The top producers in the world were HIPP, Phoenix, and Seda in America and Prijon and Lettmann in Europe.

[8] Galpin, Sam. Interview by author 18 January 1997.

[9] Ibid.

Galpin officially closed Hyperform in March of 1978, about one year after he stopped production of composite boats. Early the following year, he sold Hyperform to Old Town, molds and all. Along with the molds, Old Town obtained licenses for Prijon and Lettmann designs.

The Rest of the Industry

The rest of the industry evolved to encompass all those things that individuals and clubs previously provided, slowly replacing the individuals and clubs as facilitators of the sport. Like innovations in materials for boats, there were innovations in new equipment, particularly innovations by paddlers for paddlers.

One innovation often taken for granted was readily adjustable footbraces. Prior to the introduction of Yakima footbraces in 1975, footbraces were fairly crude. One type was called the suicide footbrace which consisted of a bar, either spring-loaded or with holes and cotter pins, that slipped into slots or holes on either side of the interior walls for leg length adjustment. It was called a suicide footbrace because a paddlers foot or leg could slip past the bar potentially trapping the paddler in a pin situation. Another type of footbrace was the predecessor of the Yakima consisting of two different sizes of aluminum tubing with holes for cotter pins to allow for leg length adjustment. Interestingly, Yakima footbraces were not designed by a paddler. They were designed by Otto Lagervall, a machinist, who began his business, Yakima Industries, making music stands in Yakima, Washington.

The need and desire grew to buy specialized equipment and gear designed for paddling such as clothing, helmets, and life jackets. With the growth came the potential for a small but growing cadre of entrepreneurial paddlers to eke a living out of what they enjoyed doing most, making an avocation into a vocation, meager though it was.

Other Kayak Manufacturers

In the '70s, kayaks became the domain of whitewater, particularly with the advent of plastic kayaks. Although plastic kayaks caught on quickly in some areas, composite kayaks (and closed canoes over open canoes) still dominated in many areas. Many more were built for river running than racing during this time. Some paddlers continued building their own boats but because of the growing market for kayaks, many new paddlers instead began to purchase kayaks providing a market for an increasing number of local backyard and garage builders.

Shipping costs and logistics were the greatest barriers for cross-country sales, particularly for the smaller builders. As a result, small builders often remained local builders catering to local paddlers, selling both direct and through local retailers. Sometimes local meant an entire geographic area like the Southeast or Northwest. The small builders often built pirated and outdated designs, with minor modifications, from European designers, particularly Lettmann and Prijon. A few builders like Peter Kauput of Easy Rider, Tom Derrer of Eddyline, Lee Moyer of Pacific Watersports, and Dick Held of Whitewater Boats obtained permission to build copies from the designers. Other builders, like Dan Ruuska of Natural Designs, built only their own designs.

Builders learned their boatbuilding skills on their own, through participation in clubs, or while working for other small builders. Tom Derrer learned much from Colorado builders Bill Clark and Tom and Jane Cooper, owners of Plasticraft, when Derrer first started Eddyline Kayak Center in Boulder, Colorado, in 1971. Others learned a great deal from Charles Walbridge's *Boatbuilder's Manual,* a compilation of information and dinner conversations with Jack Wright, John Birdsong, and others. His first printing of 500 copies in 1973 was soon replaced with a second, revised edition. Subsequent editions throughout the '70s included the latest information in advanced composites. The fourth edition, printed in 1979, included information from Steve Rock on vacuum bagging and epoxy resins, Gary Myers on health and safety, and Chip Queitzsch on laminate design. Many manufacturers in the industry also used Walbridge's manual.

In the East and Midwest while HIPP (Hyperform) and Phoenix dominated the composite market, many other small builders also contributed to the market including Millbrook Boats, Rapid Design, Hurka Industries, Sports Equipment, and Apple Line. In its early years, Noah, owned by Czech immigrant Vladia Vahna, also imported and manufactured kayaks in the Northeast before relocating to the Southeast.

Dan Ruuska seaming an Outrage, 1977—courtesy of Rob Lesser.

Rapid Design, Hurka, and Apple Line were a string of kayak companies with a common thread. Rapid Design originally contracted Joseph Hurka, a materials specialist with his own R & D company who developed foam cored skis, to develop a synthetic paddle using Kevlar. After the paddle was developed (made of Kevlar and urethane foam weighing less than 3 pounds), Rapid Design was unable to pay Hurka due to financial problems and Hurka ended up with the paddle design and their remaining inventory. Although Galpin of Hyperform tried to buy the paddle design, Hurka instead manufactured the paddles and two of the designs in the inventory and started the company bearing his name. The original designer of Rapid Design kayaks, Stan Zdunek, later approached Hurka to use a mold to build a few for his personal use. This was the beginning of Apple Line that eventually carried a complete line of kayaks and both closed and open canoes before going bankrupt. Apple Line was also known as Amsterdam Boat Works, Kellogg & Miller Boatworks, and a few other business names.

Small builders also sprung up in the inter-mountain West outside of Colorado as a result of the increasing number of paddlers. Natural Progression Kayaks in Idaho was owned by John Dondero who often paddled with Blackadar. Dondero built large volume modified Lettmann Mark I and IV kayaks for the local rivers. He built many of the kayaks used by Blackadar and others for their big water expeditions. Another builder was Dick Held who owned Whitewater Boats by Dick Held in Utah. Held built some of Tom Johnson's designs. The TJ1 was Johnson's Bronco and the TJ2 was Johnson's Hoback. Held also built Johnson's Snake.

Many of the small builders came and went throughout the '70s and into the '80s. However, three manufacturers in the West who began even before the events of 1972 continued to grow and expand. Seda was established in 1969 in southern California, followed by Easy Rider in 1970 in the Northwest, and Eddyline in 1971 in Colorado. Seda and Easy Rider were more than just boat manufacturers; they also imported (or eventually manufactured in the case of Seda) paddles and other accessories. All three eventually adapted their product lines beyond whitewater when plastics began to dominate the whitewater market in the mid-to-late '70s.

Perhaps enduring longer than anywhere else in the country, slalom was really a recreational aspect of whitewater in the Northwest throughout much of the '70s. The Washington Kayak Club promoted whitewater and specifically slalom racing for many years. This provided a strong client base for both Easy Rider and Eddyline, who relocated to the Seattle area from Colorado. (Seakayaking, for which Easy Rider and Eddyline are now noted, was not really in the picture in the Northwest until the affects of the Divergence finally took hold in the Northwest in the later '70s.)

Peter Kauput, a German born aerospace engineer, and his wife Barbara started Easy Rider to cater to local Seattle slalom racers. Easy Rider built many of the latest designs including the Augsburg K-1, Munich C-1, Winner C-1, and Swing C-2. Kaupat also imported Kober paddles and other accessories. Working with Hahn, he provided some of the first commercially available C-1 designs for slalom racers.

Tom Derrer, originally of the Seattle area, returned there with his company Eddyline after graduating from college in Boulder, Colorado. While in Colorado, he built two designs, a Bonet kayak called the Combie which was a combination slalom and touring design, and a big volume kayak design from John Urban in Boston. In Washington, he established a working relationship with Werner Furrer, one of area's local designers. Using what he learned while in Colorado under Bill Clark's tutelage, Derrer built Werner's designs as vacuum bagged epoxy/S-glass layups using an oven to heat cure the epoxies. Eddyline became one of the first manufacturers to vacuum bag boats.

In the late '60s, Werner Furrer's son, Werner Furrer, Jr., began slalom racing. Because he was smaller than the average racer, Furrer, Sr. began designing kayaks specifically for him. Around 1973, when the East German designs began to evolve to lower volume designs for sneaking gates, Furrer Sr. realized he needed to learn more about designing kayaks. In 1974 he bought a computer and wrote his own software, a fairing program for designing boats. His designs expanded to both slalom and touring kayak designs.

Furrer, like Natan Bernot, designed as an engineer or naval architect, lofting plans from drawings instead of using the shave and foam or cut and paste technique used by many other American and European designers.

Although Furrer's program was for fairing only with no hydrostatic calculations, it was a precursor to present day boat design CAD programs, perhaps one of the first used by any whitewater designer in America. Tom Derrer learned much from Furrer. Derrer followed Furrer's lead when he began designing his own kayaks.

The first kayak design of Furrer's built by Eddyline was the WSL-6, a high volume slalom kayak followed by the WSL-7, WSL-9, and WSL-10 in 1976. Furrer gave his designs designations, not names, in the order of their design. However, with the availability and acceptance of the River Chaser, the demand for composite kayaks quickly evaporated. The following year in 1977, Eddyline produced its first seakayak and began to move away from the whitewater market.

Two other builders also began building kayaks in the Northwest in the early-to- mid '70s. Natural Designs and Pacific Water Sports were both started by laid-off Boeing engineers. Natural Designs was started by Dan Ruuska who designed and built only his own kayak designs. Ruuska's Outrage series were specifically for river-running.

Pacific Water Sports, started by Lee and Judy Moyer, was a little different than the other builders in that it was started more as a retail business ordering Iliad paddles, wetsuits, and other paddling accessories for the local Seattle paddlers. Realizing that boats were also needed, and not wanting to rip-off molds from designers, the Moyers contacted designers to ask for the rights to build their designs. Neither Sam Galpin at HIPP nor Tom Wilson at Phoenix Kayaks gave then the rights to build their American designs. Instead Moyer, through the efforts of a friend, obtained rights to build the Scarab, a British boat designed for the '72 British Olympic team. Eventually, like Eddyline, the Moyers' boat building business moved away from whitewater toward seakayaking.

Throughout the '70s, the controversy raged regarding pirated designs. It was a particular sore point for HIPP and Phoenix who obtained licenses for the designs they built. Perhaps the most copied boat was Lettmann's Mark IV which was also modified. Neither HIPP nor Lettmann benefitted. Perhaps one person, more than any other, was inadvertently responsible for this: Keith Backlund. While building boats for PSOC at Penn State, Backlund was asked to make a mold from a new Lettmann Mark IV which had just been brought into the country. As payment, Backlund was given one of the boats from the new mold. From that boat, Backlund made another mold which he in turn sold to KCCNY. Almost immediately after building the molds, Backlund traveled west to California, running rivers and racing as he went. Many quick-and-dirty overnight molds were made at rivers and races along the way and more kayaks were made from those molds. Some of these molds became the source for modified Mark IV designs. Bill Clark's Mistle design was a modified Mark IV. Backlund eventually sold his kayak to Riley Carsey in southern California. Carsey later sold a Mark IV kayak from the mold he built to Don Banducci who owned Yakima. The proliferation of Mark IV's and modified Mark IV's continued across the country. This all occurred while HIPP attempted to sell its licensed Mark IV kayaks.

Other Canoe Manufacturers

Like Blue Hole's entry into plastic canoes, other small local manufacturers like Tanana in Arkansas and Shenandoah in Virginia purchased and outfitted Warsaw Rocket hulls. In 1973, Mad River, a composite canoe manufacturer, also bought and outfitted a Warsaw Rocket and soon wrapped up the New England market. The next year, Mad River owner Jim Henry designed the Explorer, a V-hulled river running canoe, for Royalex construction and Mad River began production of their own thermoformed canoe designs. Old Town also came out with their own thermoformed hulls about a year after Blue Hole introduced the OCA, although Old Town did not specifically market their canoes for the whitewater market like Mad River or Blue Hole did.

Jim and Kay Henry began building boats while paddling with KCCNY in the late '60s. In 1971, they started Mad River and in 1972, Tubbs of Vermont (snowshoes) approached them to build canoes to counter their seasonal business. The relationship lasted less than a year after which Mad River began to purchase Warsaw Rocket hulls from Uniroyal. Initially, Mad River contracted the production of their thermoformed canoes. In early 1977, the Henrys moved all of Mad River's thermoforming operations in-house.

With the exception of the Northeast and Southeast, interest in whitewater open canoeing slowly began to diminish in many areas of the country. Not only did the growing interest in whitewater kayaking affect open canoeing, but the replacement of open canoes by closed canoes (C-1s and C-2s) in whitewater competition also contributed to diminishing interest. Sales for whitewater open canoes did not grow like that of kayaks.

Open boaters also had fewer choices of models unlike kayaking where new designs were introduced at least every other year by European designers for World Championship competition. Both open canoe design and technique stagnated for a time during the mid-'70s. The plastic whitewater open canoe market was dominated by Blue Hole with its 16-foot OCA model, Mad River with its 16-foot Explorer, and Old Town with its 17-foot Tripper. All three models were used for tandem and solo paddling. Grumman canoes, both the 15-foot and 17-foot shoe keel models, also continued to be popular for whitewater. This did not begin to change until interest in open canoe slalom began to increase, which in turn provided new designs for river running.

With no differentiation between open canoes and closed canoes in slalom racing during the '60s, open canoes were not competitive with closed canoes and their use in slalom races pretty much discontinued. With that, interest in open whitewater canoeing began to wane. Fortunately, the New England area never lost its love of open canoes and in 1970, the Penobscot Paddle and Chowder Society sponsored the First Annual Whitewater Weekend, largely through the efforts of two of its members, William and Fern Stearns. The weekend included the National Wildwater Open Canoe Race, co-sponsored by ACA and USCA, on 22 miles of the Dead River in Maine. From this developed a renewed interest in whitewater slalom open canoeing competition which helped to spark renewed interest in open whitewater canoeing in the Northeast.

John Sweet raced in the '74 Open Canoe Nationals held on the Dead in Maine. Although other short experimental canoes (11 feet in length with very little freeboard) were used in the race, Sweet won the race using a 13-foot open canoe he built by adding freeboard to a Hahn C-1 hull, minus the deck. Around the same time, John Berry, now living in upstate New York, noticed many of the open canoes used in New England were Old Towns and Grummans. Berry noted that many of the paddlers were "pulling their arms from their sockets" [10] in trying to turn the canoes. They needed an open canoe with rocker designed for slalom. In 1975, Berry took the largest volume slalom C-1 hull that he had, a Czech 80 cm C-1, and raised the sides to add freeboard to make a 13-foot OC-1. He called it the Flasher. The name Flasher came from John Berry's wishful fantasy to have a logo made which showed an old man in

[10] Berry, John. Interview by author 15–16 January 1997.

an overcoat exposing himself. Fortunately, his fantasy, and logo, never came to fruition. Berry's next OC-1 design, the Flashback, was again based on an old slalom C-1 hull. The name Flashback was a reference to the past using a C-1 hull as the source of the design. However, the market for these new designs was small. Berry was able to provide them through his one-man boat building business, Millbrook Boats.

In 1978, Berry did the same with the Hartung C-2 hull, one of the hottest hulls of its time, to make an OC-2, which he named the ME. (This was the same design of Horst Hartung C-2 that was borrowed by Austrian racers at the '71 World Championships.) The ME was an abbreviation for "Maximum Exposure" referring back to the Flasher idea. Berry built a few ME's and took them to the Nationals at the Yough that year. On the spot, Carrie Ashton and Bunny Johns bought one, raced it, and won the OC-2W class only 5 seconds behind the OC-2M team of McKee and Sweet.

Coincidentally, Barb McKee and John Sweet showed up at the '78 Open Canoe Nationals with their own OC-2 built from the Hartung C-2 hull. Sweet and McKee, too, had taken the hull and built up the sides to make it into an OC-2. However, their Hartung had tumblehome instead of flare that Berry incorporated in his ME design. McKee and Sweet won their class, OC-2M. Both their time and Ashton and Johns' time in OC-2W beat the OC-2 class by more than 50 seconds.

Kay and Jim Henry of Mad River were also at the race. They approached Berry about obtaining rights to the design (as did a rep for Perception). In 1979, Mad River began building the ME, first in composite construction and then in a Royalex version. Although in 1977 Mad River had introduced their own design, the 15-foot Courier which was a shortened Explorer, it was the ME that became one of the most popular whitewater canoes, even more popular as an OC-1 than an OC-2 for which it was originally designed.

John Berry is often considered the father of modern whitewater canoeing and of C-1 paddling. His influence was felt through his racing, his designs, his boat building, and his teaching. In 1970, Berry bought a ski-lodge in Waitsfield, Vermont, with long-time paddler and fellow CCA member Henri DeMarne. Henri DeMarne obtained his formal instruction in canoeing while a young man in France. While living in the D.C. area in the '60s, he became involved with CCA's instructional programs, teaching others what he had been taught about canoeing. Berry spent much of his off-season, non-skiing time building and designing boats. After moving to Riparius, New York, he expanded his paddling activities to include instructional clinics for canoeing. Although he continued building boats for his one-man operation, Millbrook Boats, he also spent a great deal of time teaching in clinics that were often attended by members of AMC-Boston.

Berry turned his attention back to open canoeing and many of his new designs were open canoes. Throughout the years, Berry built more than 1,000 boats which included over 30 of his own designs, some used only once. He built about 300 Sweet-Hahns, 300 Berrigans, 200 modified Czech C-1s, 60 Flashbacks, and about 40 Flashers.

[*Author's note:* During my interview with John Berry, I found that he doesn't consider himself a real designer. He figured that almost anything he did at the current state of design was an improvement. Taking existing designs, some not his own, he used the cut-and-paste or chop-and-bondo school of

JOHN BERRY SOLD MILLBROOK BOATS to John (Kaz) Kazimiercsyk in 1988. Kaz continues Berry's tradition of designing and building composite open and closed canoes, and competing, too.

design to come up with a new design. Although he said he learned by trial and error, he undoubtedly had a great deal of intuition about design that proved successful.]

While Blue Hole and Mad River dominated the Royalex whitewater canoe market in the '70s, Old Town initially had the opportunity to do what Perception and Blue Hole did in the whitewater market. Had Old Town pursued the whitewater market, both Blue Hole and Perception might have been displaced or supplanted.

Old Town, too, saw the benefits of Royalex for canoes. They hired Lew Gilman away from Rivers and Gilman to develop their own thermoforming process. Old Town initially entered the plastic canoe market using standard Royalex sheets from Uniroyal. However, they soon began to specify the placement of ABS and foam layers in the laminate. In order to show a distinction between their product and others, Old Town marketed their laminate as Oltonar.

In 1974, the Gray family, long-time owners of Old Town, sold Old Town to Johnson Worldwide Associates. For many different reasons, the new owners decided against continuing to specifically pursue the whitewater market in kayaks and canoes. Instead, Old Town developed its own use for rotational molding and continued to market to the larger (and also growing) recreational market that was considered more dependable than the whitewater market.

Gilman recognized what rotational molding could do for the non-whitewater market. He also recognized two limitations in using Royalex (Oltonar) for canoes. One limitation was that defects in Oltonar sheets supplied by Uniroyal were not found until thermoforming had begun, which was too late in the process. This was not the case for rotational molding. Rotational molding resins (powders) could be tested prior to molding. The second limitation was that Uniroyal owned the patents for Royalex and was the only supplier.

In order to overcome these limitations, Gilman wanted to produce a multi-layer laminate similar to Royalex using rotational molding. He visited Hollowform in California to familiarize himself with rotational molding. Old Town then hired Pierre Arcouette who had developed the first skin-foam-skin process twelve years earlier for rotational molding. (Hollowform used a form core to stiffen their canoe and kayak hulls with limited success.) With Old Town's success with Royalex hulls, Gilman was given the go ahead to pursue the process.

Gilman designed the rotational molding machine, oven and all, and the canoe itself that was molded with the new process. (Gilman opted to design a rock-n-roller, the same as Perception.) However, it took considerably more time than expected to produce the multi-layer laminate, which first required perfecting the multi-layer drop process. Finally in 1983, Gilman and Old Town succeeded and introduced their patented multi-layer laminate: a polyethylene foam layer sandwiched between two other non-foamed polyethylene layers. The laminate was used in their new Discovery line of canoes. With the exception of weight, it was superior to Royalex in many ways.

The Discovery line of canoes was initially marketed to the rental market, not the whitewater market. Old Town demonstrated its durability with the now-famous ads showing a canoe being thrown from their factory roof.

THE RELATIONSHIP between Uniroyal and paddlesport manufacturers was unusual. Uniroyal not only supplied Warsaw Rocket hulls but early-on, also outfitted hulls themselves and supplied Royalex sheets for thermoforming. As more manufacturers began thermoforming their own canoes, they followed Old Town's lead by specifying the placement of ABS and foam layers in the laminate. For whitewater, manufacturers specified more foam in the hull for a thicker finished laminate to eliminate oil canning and in the ends for impact resistance. Others areas of the laminate were thinned to reduce overall weight. However, with the exception of Old Town who called their specified material Oltonar, the material was mostly referred to as Royalex regardless of the lamination variations from manufacturer to manufacturer.

Retailers

In the '70s, many of the boat, paddle, and accessory manufacturers did not have established dealer networks or sales reps. Manufacturers often sold to anyone who bought their product in quantity. Many sold to retailers and individual paddlers alike and local stores often carried locally manufactured products. Outdoor stores were not exclusive to whitewater and sold all kinds of outdoor equipment in addition to paddlesport equipment. As the sport grew, specialty outdoor stores began to appear and were often associated with specific destinations for an outdoor activity. Many of the paddlesport destination stores were located on rivers, often associated with raft outfitters in the East such as on the Yough or the Nantahala and in the West on the South Fork of the American. Credit cards were not in wide use, particularly in paddlesport stores. Paddlers took cash to the rivers to buy gear.

While shipping costs and logistics were a barrier for cross-country sales of boats and paddles, the same was not true for the rest of the accessories. At first, a few companies imported and distributed many of the paddling accessories. However, some like Seda and Extrasport expanded into manufacturing the accessories themselves.

In the fall of 1968, Joe Sedivec and his wife Jirina, former C-2M Wildwater World Champions, emigrated from Czechoslovakia to southern California. A year later they formed Seda and began manufacturing boats and accessories. In 1973, Seda introduced one of the first multi-chambered personal flotation devices (PFDs) that met the newly approved U.S. Coast Guard's use of polyethylene foam. (With their new regulations, the Coast Guard began the use of the term PFD, to replace life jacket.) Seda's new PFD was one of the first comfortable PFDs replacing the imported Harishok for whitewater.

In 1976, Danny Broadhurst and Alex Khanimirian started Extrasport as an importer of boats and accessories. Like Seda, Extrasport later began manufacturing their own accessories, one of which was a front zippered PFD.

Like boats, paddles were often manufactured by a local paddle builder who often had a local following. Many manufacturers preferred to sell direct because the logistics of shipping paddles was almost as difficult as shipping a boat. The U.S. Postal Service (USPS) had strict weight and dimension restrictions that were unsatisfactory for shipping kayak paddles. United Parcel Service (UPS) requirements were not stable and often changed. At times, paddles longer than 86 inches were considered oversized and were not accepted for shipment. Some paddle manufacturers tried shipping by Greyhound. One manufacturer, Hurka, even tried shipping the paddles in halves and letting the dealers assemble them. Unfortunately, too many paddles were assembled incorrectly. As a result, many of the smaller manufacturers relied on a system of pickups and dropoffs at races.

Since many of the paddling destination stores were seasonal, catalog sales provided year round service to paddlers. Two of the more prominent catalog businesses for whitewater were Northwest River Supplies (NRS) in the West and Wildwater Designs in the East.

In 1972, Bill Parks, a kayaker turned rafter, started NRS in Idaho. While Wildwater Designs provided accessories for whitewater canoeing and kayaking, NRS provided equipment to private boaters, particularly whitewater rafting in the West. Initially begun as a re-distributor of equipment, NRS evolved into a manufacturer of rafting and other whitewater equipment serving both the private boater and commercial outfitter.

In 1973, Charles Walbridge (author of *Boatbuilder's Manual)* started Wildwater Designs. His experience in running the Gauley prompted him to design a PFD with more flotation like a Mae West, but with more comfort. Walbridge borrowed on the Harishok design and made PFD kits with thicker foam in the panels. He also added foam over the shoulder for additional buoyancy which gave the PFD its name, the HiFloat. Wildwater Designs eventually expanded its products to include spray skirts, wetsuits, paddling jackets, gloves, and booties.

Other Services

As the market grew in the '70s for goods, boats, and other gear, it also grew for other services. Not only did the growth lead to more guidebooks for areas and rivers not previously covered but more instructional books were also written. In addition, the size of the paddling public finally reached critical mass to support magazines associated exclusively with paddlesports.

Rogue River (OR) —courtesy of Carl Trost.

By the mid-'70s, guidebooks for rivers in the East were already being revised. In 1975, the second edition of Burrell and Davidson's *Wildwater West Virginia came* out as did other new guidebooks for New England including Ray Gabler's *New England White Water River Guide.* During the same time, the first guidebooks were just coming out for rivers in the West including the first for Washington, Oregon, and California. In 1971, Werner Furrer, Sr. published *Water Trails of Washington* with later editions in 1973 and 1979. In 1974, Dick Schwind's *West Coast River Touring: Rogue River Canyon and South* for Oregon and northern California came out as a supplement to Charles Martin's earlier book for California.

In 1974, Scott and Margaret Arighi wrote a combination how-to and guidebook titled *Wildwater Touring* for rivers in Oregon and Idaho. Similar, more generic how-to books were published such as *Whitewater* by Norman Strung, Sam Curtis, and Earl Perry that condensed in less than 200 pages the basics of whitewater rafting, canoeing, kayaking, and boat building into one book. By the mid-to-late '70s, a growing number of how-to type books became available including *The All-Purpose Guide to Paddling* edited by Dean Norman in 1976, *You, Too, Can Canoe* by John Foshee in 1977, *The Complete Guide to Kayaking* by Raymond Bridge in 1978, and *Wildwater: The Sierra Club Guide to Kayaking and Whitewater Boating* by Lito Tejada-Flores, also in 1978.

Other very specific how-to books were also published including Thomas S. Foster's *Recreational White Water Canoeing* in 1978 (which received a less than flattering review by *American Whitewater's* reviewer David Smallwood who noted it was "far outdistanced" by others previously published including books by McNair and Urban).[11] Walbridge's *Boatbuilder's Manual* in 1973 was the first complete how-to for building composite boats for whitewater. Revisions

[11] "Book Reviews." *American Whitewater* Vol. XXIII No. 3 (May/June 1978): 114–115.

throughout the '70s provided the latest composite information. (Unlike many books published in the '70s that are now outdated, Walbridge's *Boatbuilder's Manual* is still sought today even though the last revision is out of print.)

Until the early '70s, only journals of organizations, AWA's *American Whitewater* and AMC's *Appalachia,* provided information to paddlers. (The name of AWA's journal changed from *American **White Water*** to *American **Whitewater**,* whitewater as one word, with the Spring 1971 issue.) However, they were available only to members. The same was true of ACA's newsletter, *American Canoeist,* which carried paddling articles for the general paddling population with some information about whitewater, particularly associated with slalom and wildwater competition.

The early to mid-'70s was a time that many small, specialized outdoor-type magazines came and went. With the growth in backpacking, *BACKPACKER* was launched in 1973. Harry Robert's *Wilderness Camping* was the precursor to *Canoe Journal,* a specialized paddlesport magazine specifically for canoeing.

In April 1973, the first issue of *Canoe* was published, on the heels of the Olympics, Blackadar, and *Deliverance. Canoe* was published by Peter A. Sonderegger through much of '70s. Spencer Stone was the publisher during the last years of the '70s. Though not exclusively dedicated to whitewater, the magazine provided coverage of the excitement that whitewater drew. Other magazines followed with *Down River* in 1974 and its short-lived, follow-on *River World* until 1979. Both were published by World Publications. With the demise of *River World* in 1979, *Canoe* remained the only commercial magazine dealing with whitewater. *(Canoe* is the only non-organization-supported paddlesport magazine that has endured to the present. In the '80s *Canoe* was published by John Viehman, currently the publisher of *Backpacker,* and James S. Povec before Judy C. Harrison took over in 1985 and continued until retirement in 1998.)

Unlike an organization's journal that is supported by its members, a magazine is supported by it advertisers and readers. A magazine's editorial content is, therefore, influenced by its advertisers and readers. By the late '70s, *Canoe* was the "Official magazine of the American Canoe Association" and suffered from the "inevitable conflict of flat-and whitewater paddlers."[12] *Down River,* long regarded as a quality magazine, suffered from the loss of its long-time editor, Eric Evans, who provided sustained support for whitewater. *American Whitewater* was still the only magazine dedicated to whitewater.

Other services that developed in the '70s were associated with paddling instruction. Before the '70s, there were few professional, paid instructors for whitewater. Roger Paris and his school in Colorado on the Crystal River was the most well-known. However, the growing number of new paddlers was large enough to support a growing market for paid instruction. Paddlers were willing to pay for instruction instead of just reading the how-to's or get instruction through a club. And not all paddlers sought instruction solely for competition. Many new paddlers sought the basic skills of river running.

The demand was still not sufficient to make a living from instruction alone. Most instructors worked part time, supplementing their incomes with other paddling activities such as boat building or raft guiding. Other paddlers-turned-instructors found employment through a new phenomenon, Outward Bound-style adult camps that provided outdoor experiences related to instruction in an activity. In the Outward Bound-style camps or centers, adults were

DURING THE LATE '70S AND EARLY '80S, AWA's membership did not continue to grow as was expected from the number of whitewater paddlers participating in the sport. Many advertisers chose to advertise in other magazines that were read by the larger paddling population than AWA's membership. Unfortunately, since the content of *American Whitewater* depended on member input, its content suffered with minimal articles and information. This in turn further discouraged advertisers from using *American Whitewater.*

[12] Editor. "Message from the AWA Directors." *American Whitewater* Vol. XXIII No. 1 (January/February 1978): 4.

Camps incorporating whitewater paddling specifically for kids also gained momentum during the '70s. Camp Mondamin in the Southeast continued its long history of developing whitewater paddlers. But while Camp Mondamin directed its instruction toward canoes, Valley Mill Camp in Maryland was one of the first camps directed at kayaking for kids. Valley Mill was established in 1956 by May and Bob McEwan as a summer camp. In the early '70s, under the direction of their son Tom, the camp took a more serious turn toward whitewater instruction for river running. Racing was encouraged as a way of developing better river-running skills.

Valley Mill's whitewater camps ran nine weeks during the summer. In the early '70s, a "tenth week" trip was added into the program. The trip destination varied from year to year. In the '90s, trips included Seven Sisters on the Rouge in Quebec and the Green Narrows in North Carolina.

Graduates of Valley Mill Camp included ten-time National C-1 Wildwater Champion Andy Bridge, '88 Olympic K-2 Gold Medalist Norm Bellingham (flatwater sprint), and three-time National K-1 Wildwater Champion Dan Schnurrenberger.

Other commercial rafting businesses in the '60s and early '70s hired college students as guides, typically young men. Young women were not often hired as guides. The process to become a guide typically followed four steps: start as a raft passenger in year one; work as a raft guide in year two, become a kayak support guide in year three; become a racer or river-runner.

[13] Demaree, Dave. Interview by author 15 February 1997.

not catered to as was the practice with earlier so-called dude ranches in the West. Instead, adults actively participated in activities. In the East, whitewater rafting was one such activity where customers paddled the rafts instead of merely being passengers. Whitewater paddling became the basis for two businesses with paddling schools for adults: Madawaska Kanu Camp (MKC) in Ontario and Nantahala Outdoor Center (NOC) in North Carolina. MKC later changed their name from Camp to Centre.

MKC was begun specifically for paddling instruction with an emphasis on slalom racing. Hermann and Christa Kerckhoff, '69-'71 Canadian C-2M National Champions, started MKC in August of 1972. With the assistance of Austrian K-1 World Champion Kurt Presslmayr, MKC was modeled after European ski schools with a five-day course providing top instructors, good food, and lots of atmosphere. In their first year, the Kerckhoff's brought in Austrian K-1 Olympic Silver Medalist Norbert Sattler as an instructor. Over the next few years, additional World Champions were brought in as instructors including Austrian Gerhard Peinhaupt, '77 K-1 Wildwater World Champion, West German Bernd Heinemann, '73 C-1 Wildwater World Champion, and Gisela Grothaus, the K-1W Wildwater World Champion from 1973 through 1978. Throughout the '70s and '80s, many American racers attended MKC at some point in their paddling careers, drawn by the excellent program and European instructors. Some top Americans racers later returned to MKC as instructors including Kent Ford, Linda Harrison, and Davey and Cathy Hearn.

NOC was started the same year as MKC by Horace Holden and Payson Kennedy. In addition to paddling instruction, NOC provided instruction for many other outdoor activities including backpacking and rock-climbing. In its early years, NOC provided paddling and rock-climbing instruction for Carolina Outward Bound. Holden and Kennedy also opted to provide commercial rafting on the Nantahala following the advice and the lead of Jon Dragan. (Jon Dragan started his own commercial rafting operation, Wildwater Unlimited, on the New in West Virginia about the same time.) Commercial rafting became the moneymaker (and still is) for NOC.

Holden and Kennedy's motivation to start NOC was to provide for their own lifestyle: they wanted to paddle. NOC's commercial rafting and instruction provided that opportunity. Over the years as NOC grew, it also provided employment for many other paddlers. Because NOC hired paddlers to become raft guides, including women, it became the place for racers to work and train at the same time.

In 1973, Louise Holcombe and Carrie Ashton, members of the '72 Olympic team, were hired to teach courses incorporating slalom racing techniques. NOC's instructional program continued to grow and in 1975, Kennedy hired Les Bechdel to teach kayaking. Later in the '70s, Gale Coward from ACA taught an ACA instructor clinic for NOC instructors. This was the beginning of a relationship between NOC and ACA that led to NOC's influence on ACA's whitewater instructional programs beginning in the '80s.

By the end of the '70s, instructional programs providing paddling and instructional vacations were found across the country. Multiple-day clinics were held by Sierra Rivers Paddle School and Whitewater King Canoe and Kayak School, both in California, Sundance Kayak School in Oregon, Snake

River Kayak School in Wyoming, Wolf River Lodge in Wisconsin, Saco Bound in New Hampshire, Slick Rock Kayaks in Utah (owned by Cully Erdman), and White Water Sports in Seattle. Some, like Sundance and Slick Rock, combined instruction with raft supported multi-day river-running trips.

College outing clubs began incorporating whitewater paddling in the '50s and '60s, often providing instruction to their members. In the '70s in the Southeast, instruction in whitewater expanded beyond outing clubs to instructional programs offered by community colleges. In 1970, Bob Benner, author of *Carolina Whitewater,* began a paddling program in Morganton, North Carolina, at Western Piedmont Community College. The following year, Benner started the Southeast Intercollegiate Canoe Races among community colleges in the Southeast. Unlike college outing clubs which often attracted younger college-aged students, the community college courses were often attended by older students which was more typical of local community colleges.

The Effects of Growth on the Rest of the Sport

The growth of the '70s, associated with the onslaught of young Baby Boomers taking up the sport, was felt across the country. Paddling activities expanded everywhere and whitewater clubs formed in practically every state. Local paddling populations even grew in areas like Idaho and Alaska with small overall populations.

In 1970, it was estimated that over fifty thousand canoes were sold annually and that four million people went canoeing. Yet in 1970, the combined total membership of the three national paddling organizations, ACA, AWA, and USCA (U.S. Cruisers Association), was only about two thousand members. New paddlers to the sport, young Baby Boomers, were not typical of the previous generation. Many Baby Boomer paddlers were influenced by the anti-establishment and flower child sentiment of the '60s. Membership in an organization was not a necessity.

Although whitewater clubs formed across the country, whitewater paddlers in particular did not generally join any national organization. For many paddlers, a club was merely a convenience to have a group to paddle with. Throughout the '70s, AWA never had more than a thousand members and ACA's whitewater membership numbers, with the exception of racers, did not change dramatically. Whitewater paddlers were acknowledged as loners. In 1971, Bob Burrell, co-author of *Wildwater West Virginia,* wrote:

BY THE END OF THE DECADE IN 1979, there were five organizations vying for the support of paddlers: ACA, AWA, USCA, ARA (American Rafting Association for private rafters), and NORS (National Organization for River Sports). However, their combined membership was still a small percentage of those participating in paddlesports.

> The sport's main appeal is that it is something he can do that few other people can. It gets him into areas where few other people are capable of entering. He sees things most people never lay eyes upon. His equipment is often homemade thus lending an additional do-it-yourself charm to the activity. The various oddball (to the public) qualities of the sport are probably what attracted him to it in the first place. Paddlers are remarkably resourceful and independent. They enjoy doing their thing, but alone and in their own way. [14]

River Running

During the early '70s, the interstate highway system neared completion in many areas providing better roads and access to rivers. Their awareness increased by the availability of guidebooks and magazines. River runners, not just racers, traveled cross-country to paddle new rivers. Many paddlers continued to travel for paddling weekends and vacations in spite of gas shortages and prices.

Carl Trost in Chamberlin Falls on the North Fork of the American (CA), 1970—courtesy of Carl Trost.

Paddlers in the East headed West to paddle the high volume and wilderness rivers they read about: the Arkansas, Colorado, Snake, Main and Middle Fork of the Salmon, Rogue, and Kern. Paddlers in the West headed East to paddle the Kennebec, New, Gauley, Upper Yough, and Chattooga. As they traveled, paddlers learned about the differences between rivers of the East and the West: low volume technical drop-pool versus high volume continu-

[14] Burrell, Bob. "On Staying Small—A Minority View." *American Whitewater* Vol. XVI No. 3 (Fall 1971): 74–77.

ous whitewater and gradient/boulder induced holes versus volume induced holes. They discovered why their respective techniques and instincts for running whitewater were different. Beyond the East versus West differences, paddlers in the West learned that the rivers of the Sierras, though smaller in volume, were every bit as difficult because of their tightness and steepness as other typical western-style big volume rivers. Paddlers in the Northeast discovered that the rivers of the Southeast were different: ledges and undercuts versus boulder strewn.

Until the '70s, river runners, with the exception of racers/river runners, tended to paddle their local home rivers and, therefore, developed techniques and styles customized for their experiences. As paddlers traveled beyond their local rivers, the regional and geographic differences and opinions were evident. Many discussions, over dinner and in magazine articles, revolved around these differences, often not about how the differences evolved and were appropriate for their specific circumstances, but which one was better and why. Discussions about rolls, the sweeping western roll versus the screw roll, were prevalent.

Admittedly, when eastern paddlers traveled west they were often intimidated by the high volume and huge holes that could be paddled through instead of avoided. Western paddles who traveled east were also often out of their element on small, tight, technical rivers with "frowny face" holes that needed to be avoided.

The three regions that exploded with whitewater activity in the '60s, West Virginia, the Southeast, and the Sierras, came into their own in the '70s. Each developed under distinct circumstances with distinct personalities.

Hole-riding on the Lochsa (ID), 1977 —courtesy of Rob Lesser.

West Virginia

West Virginia developed its own genre of paddlers associated with the commercial rafting industry. Commercial rafting provided the means, income, and housing for many young paddlers, typically college-aged males, to do what they wanted to do most—paddle. Some worked as raft guides to train for racing. Others worked as raft guides so that they could spend their free time running rivers or building boats and paddles and tinkering with new designs. Some attended college at the University of West Virginia in Morgantown just to be able to paddle the rivers year round.

The genre developed with the flavor of the small mountain river towns that the paddlers inhabited: Ohiopyle in Pennsylvania, Albright in West Virginia, and Friendsville in Maryland, which were the places to be. These paddlers were the antithesis of paddlers coming in for the weekend from D.C. "Grunge" was the trademark of these dedicated paddlers: barefoot, always with a great stick (wooden paddle), and a boat in any condition. The rest of the gear didn't matter. The stick was one thing they shared in common with the racers of D.C. But unlike the racers of D.C. who used European-made paddles, they used paddles from their own, Keith Backlund, or one of his many protégés including Jim Snyder.

Paddlers like Jim and Jeff Snyder, Phil Coleman, Mike Fentress (a transplanted Californian), Don Morin, Jesse Whittemore, Roger Zbel, and others were not bounded by anything. They ran rivers, like the Big Sandy, Cheat, and Upper Yough so often that they knew them like the back of their hands. They also experimented with boat design and technique, which ultimately led to an entirely new aspect of the sport in the realm of the third dimension, below the surface, which became squirtboating, a sub-sport of its own in the '80s.

Even the Burned-Out Canoe Club developed as the opposite of the West Virginia Wildwater Association. The club's first rule was no meetings. Its second rule was that members had to paddle the New River Gorge, meaning that only a certain level of paddler could be a member. This typified the rebellion against the establishment that was part of the times.

Southeast

During the '70s, the Southeast became firmly entrenched as the new home of open canoeing, called open boating, with its own new technique and style. What began in the Southeast in the '50s and '60s was furthered with the use of the Southeast's own Royalex Blue Hole canoes. Payson Kennedy became well-known for canoeing the Chattooga, particularly Section IV, as well as other rivers in the Southeast. He helped to further the new, more aggressive style of open boat paddling by incorporating styrofoam blocks in the mid-section of Blue Hole canoes. Not only did the blocks provide flotation, they could also be carved to provide thigh braces.

However, paddlers began to really push the limits of open boating with the availability of more nimble canoes like Mad River's Explorer. Robert Harrison initially began open boating and developing his skills on the Chattooga in an Old Town Tripper but purchased an Explorer when they became available. In 1977, using a Mad River Explorer stuffed with inner tubes, Harrison made the first descent of all the drops of the Upper Gauley in an open boat. He continued pushing the limits with runs on the Upper Yough, Russell Fork, Ripogenus Gorge, and Overflow Creek.

Perception's 13-foot HD-1, the first short plastic canoe, also became available about the same time as the Explorer. Bob Miller from North Carolina was noted for making high water runs on the New and steep creek descents in the Southeast in his HD1. Equipped with front and rear airbags he "was one of the first canoeists to regularly and consistently roll in heavy water." [15]

Interest in pushing the limits of open boating grew across the Southeast. Although the first short canoes came out of a more traditional purpose, slalom competition, pushing the limits also meant pushing the limits of design. This ultimately led to the concept of short canoes as whitewater playboats designed specifically for river running and playing on tighter, more technical rivers. For that, the Southeast would lead the way in the '80s.

[15] Harrison, Robert. "Evolution: Open Canoes for Whitewater." *River Runner* Vol. 7 No. 4 (June 1987): 42–43, 47.

Ramone Eaton is often credited with the expansion of whitewater open canoeing in the Southeast which had far-reaching effects beyond the Southeast. Eaton was described as a southern gentleman who influenced many paddlers with his grace and style. NOC carries on his name in their tradition of open canoeing. Benner dedicated his book, *Carolina Whitewater: A Canoeists Guide to the Western Carolinas,* to Eaton: "A man who canoes as he lived—with grace and charm laid his paddle to rest on April 25, 1980. It will be awhile before another like him will paddle with us." [16]

Sierras

What began in the late '60s with exploration in higher elevations in the Sierras jumped by leaps and bounds with the use of plastic Hollowform kayaks in the '70s. Steep descents known as steep creeking began with California Baby Boomers in their plastic kayaks including Lars Holbek, Richard Montgomery, and Chuck Stanley.

In the late '60s and early '70s, Montgomery and Stanley boated with Dick Sunderlund, who was considered a little crazy and beyond his time in what he attempted. Montgomery and Stanley became role models for Holbek who joined them in the latter '70s in their exploration and exploits in plastic kayaks.

The trio of Holbek, Montgomery, and Stanley began a series of first descents in the mid-'70s in the high Sierras. They were probably the first to do steep-creeking, California style. The trio looked at the current guidebooks for river sections considered unrunnable and ran them. For them, almost anything was possible in their plastic kayaks.

Unlike other areas of the country, in California there was little resistance to the use of Hollowform kayaks. Their acceptance as a replacement to fiberglass kayaks was almost immediate. Not only were Hollowform kayaks more indestructible, but plastic kayaks were able to keep up with rafts because they could slide over gravel bars like rafts (instead of hanging-up or getting damaged like fiberglass kayaks). California paddlers were also not as caught up in tradition and in the past as other areas. Paddlers in California had experimented with designs and tinkered with fiberglass and composites, always looking for improvements for river running and for kayaks that could withstand abuse. Holbek recalled that it was logical that California paddlers would readily accept the change.

Safety and Conservation

The '70s were also a time of increased regulation by federal and state governments. Safety, with Ralph Nadar and other consumer protection groups behind it, became part of that regulation. The U.S. Coast Guard became more involved in watersport activities for small, non-powered craft. It was also a time of heightened environmental and conservation awareness which brought increased regulation. For whitewater in the '70s, this increased regulation meant both governmental support and interference, particularly where safety, conservation, and river access were concerned.

[16] Benner, Bob. *Carolina Whitewater: A Canoeist's Guide to the Western Carolinas* (Fourth Edition). Hillsborough, North Carolina: Menasha Ridge Press, 1981.

(Fearless) Fred Young on Baby Falls on the Tellico (TN), 1979—courtesy of Rob Lesser.

Safety

Safety was a growing concern among older paddlers even before the growth of whitewater in the '70s. AWA's Safety Code was in the process of being revised in light of the fact that rivers deemed unrunnable ten years earlier were being run routinely. Frances Cutter, Chairman of Sierra Club's Bay Chapter River Touring Section, wrote of his concerns for the safety of the sport in the Autumn 1970 issue of *American Whitewater*. Cutter felt that the excellent safety record in the West was partially due to luck, but also to better safety precautions including the wearing of PFD's and helmets, even on easy water, and the use of flotation. However, Cutter was concerned about the paddlers who were extremely skilled and trying "truly fantastic things… Unless we start a new drive for river safety, someone won't make it, one of these days." [17] He felt that the point had been reached where,

> safety in terms of equipment and know-how ends and safety in terms of psychology takes over… [It is] something other than love of fresh air and exercise [that] drives those who defy reason by most boating standards; those who find floodstage and class V rivers the only worthwhile water, attempt daring and dangerous stunts, whether for attention or fun, run alone or even take inexperienced boaters into situations where they will be obviously dumped. [18]

By this time, many of the first and older generation of paddlers were replaced as active river runners by younger and bolder Baby Boomers, a generation that didn't want to be bounded. But it was the older generation, not the younger, that held offices in clubs and organizations and often wrote articles and letters to AWA. Because the younger paddlers were pushing the limits of paddling with their fiberglass and plastic boats, even as the older paddlers had done in their time, discussions occurred regarding taking risks and regulating the people who take them. Some clubs even attempted to regulate the risk its members were allowed to take by implementing rating systems.

Like AMC in the '60s, Sierra Club's Bay Chapter implemented a rating system for its members. Class I was considered a Novice Boater, Class II an Intermediate Boater, and Class III an Advanced Boater. For Class III, a boater needed to have the ability to roll consistently on both sides in white water using the screw roll and at least one other roll. Any RTS officer, training leader, or trip leader could certify paddlers for Class I and II. However, Class III certification required approval of a member of the executive committee. Rating systems like this were probably one of the main reasons why many of the experts running dangerous water in California and New England were not members of either club.

[17] Cutter, Francis. "Letters from Readers." *American Whitewater* Vol. XV No. 3 (Autumn 1970): 2.

[18] Ibid.

Tremendous controversy erupted with the publication of the Summer 1973 issue of *American Whitewater* with a photo of Martin Begun running Potter's Falls in a C-1 on its cover. Begun ran the 15-foot fall on the Crooked Fork Creek in Tennessee the previous January. He wrote of his run: "Much to our surprise there was nothing to it, and now everybody is doing it. It's even a lot of fun backwards." [19]

Martin Begun committed suicide on March 26, 1974. No one knows why. He was an accomplished and skilled C-1 boater.

The controversy centered around two issues. One was the fact that AWA would include such photos in *American Whitewater* since this was deemed contrary to their safety standards. After all, it might encourage others to do the same (which it did). The other issue was the preconceived notion and suspected dangers of running falls. In spite of all the controversy, *American Whitewater* included additional photos submitted by Begun in the May/June 1974 issue where he gave tribute to Mark Hall who was actually the first to run the falls. Begun wrote: "Potter's Falls *is not* a 'daredevil' stunt if one is an expert in a decked boat. The only daredevil was the guy who tried it first. The numerous safe runs since then have proven this. It is largely the unique structure of this particular falls that makes it such." [20] Now finally, someone had formally printed the idea that not all falls are the same and that some can be run successfully and safely.

By 1979, many waterfalls were run for the first time. Rob Lesser ran Ohiopyle Falls (18 vertical feet) on the Lower Yough in 1974 much to the chagrin of local guides who had made plans to do it themselves with an aborted attempt the year before. In 1975, Great Falls on the Potomac, with a total drop of 65 feet in 200 yards (the Spout is 22 vertical feet) was run for the first time by Tom McEwan, Dan Schnurrenberger, and Wick Walker. Its first descent was kept a secret for many years. In 1979, *Canoe* published an article written by Wick Walker titled "Waterfalls: Forbidden Fruit or Calculated Risk?" The issue included as its cover photo a shot of Whit Deschner's run of Pilchuk Creek Falls (15 feet) in Washington. Photos of (Fearless) Fred Young's C-1 run of Ilgen Falls (31 feet) on the Baptism River in Minnesota, and Rob Lesser's run of Ohiopyle Falls were included in the article. With *Canoe* being the "Official magazine of the American Canoe Association," an editor's note accompanied the article.

> The following article is bound to be viewed as controversial at best and irresponsible or reckless at worst. But our interest in the subject of waterfalls is one of reportage—that truly expert paddlers have and will continue to run waterfalls, pushing their skills to the limit of human endurance, until such time as 1) the water stops, or 2) they stop. Thus, the following discussion recognizes the activity only as an extreme deviation from sound boating practices... [21]

[19] Begun, Martin. "What's Going on Here?" *American Whitewater* Vol. XVIII No. 2 (Summer 1973): 57.

[20] Begun, Martin. "Daredevils." *American Whitewater* Vol. XIX No. 3 (May/June 1974): 92–93.

[21] Walker, Wick. "Waterfalls: Forbidden Fruit or Calculated Risk." *Canoe* Vol. 7 No. 1 (February 1979): 56–59, 68.

Sue Taft on Wonder Falls of the Big Sandy (WV), 1978.

[*Author's note:* By the late '70s, falls running was becoming fairly common, particularly of falls that had proven to be relatively safe. Over Memorial Day weekend in 1978, a small group of paddlers from Keel-Hauler Canoe Club, including myself, ran Wonder Falls (18 feet) on the Big Sandy in West Virginia. Because of low levels (less than 6 inches) on the Cheat, we hiked to Wonder Falls with a couple of kayaks for some falls running and a picnic. The oldest member of the group to run it was Jim Waters, aged 54. By this time, falls running had become blasé.]

During 1973, a number of fatalities from river running accidents were reported in the news. Disturbed by it, Carl Trost provided the first thorough evaluation of fatalities and accidents in California which was published in the September/October 1974 issue of *American Whitewater.* In 1973, twenty eight people died as a result of river running accidents, eighteen involved inflatables. Two deaths occurred while canoeing and one while kayaking. This total number was more than three times seen in the previous two years: eight in 1971 and seven in 1972. Many of the fatalities were attributed to the lack of PFDs worn by the victims. The rise in fatalities was also attributed to the growing popularity of the sport and the Deliverance Syndrome (regardless of what type of craft was used, canoe or inflatable.)

Spurred by Trost's analysis, AWA included an accident report form in *American Whitewater* journals to report accidents with anonymity ensured. Information requested included type of boat, water conditions, and type of PFD. A survey of fifty-one reports received covering 1970 to 1975 by Bev and Fred Hartline of Washington Kayak Club indicated that experienced paddlers were far less likely to be involved in accidents. Based on preliminary findings, they concluded that experienced paddlers took precautions such as wearing appropriate attire for hypothermia, wearing PFDs, and were perhaps paddling within their abilities.

The U.S. Coast Guard was also concerned about the increase in fatalities and accidents. In 1975, they directly requested input through letters sent to the canoe industry and the paddling community including members of ACA, AWA, and USCA. Requested input included the need for leveling flotation regulations for canoes, similar to what was done for powerboats. Their rationale was that self-righting canoes would reduce fatalities. The Coast Guard initially anticipated that the first draft of standards would be available within a year, although no time limit was given for any decision.

The canoe industry in the early '70s was represented by a subchapter of the National Marine Manufacturers Association (NMMA). The subchapter was dominated by the three big manufacturers, Old Town, Chestnut, and Grumman. By the mid-'70s, other canoe manufacturers entered the picture, though not strictly whitewater manufacturers, including Lincoln, Mad River and Wenonah. The canoe manufacturers were leery of the two new kayak manufacturers, HIPP and Phoenix, who made kayaks exclusively (and primarily for whitewater). However, when the Coast Guard floated the idea of requiring leveling flotation, the canoe and kayak manufacturers along with Sonderegger, the publisher of *Canoe,* formed the Canoe and Kayak Industry Council to fight off the perceived threat to the industry.

To obtain input from the paddling community, a copy of the Coast Guard letter was reprinted in the September/October 1975 issue of *American Whitewater.* The issue also included copies of member responses already sent to the Coast Guard and solicited further input from AWA members. The letter was also copied and re-printed in other journals, magazines, and club newsletters. The result was an avalanche of mail not only to the Coast Guard, but to congressmen and senators opposing any regulations regarding leveling flotation for canoes.

Right on the heels of the Coast Guard's inquiry, Jay Evans presented his viewpoint regarding the recent spate of deaths and the use of open canoes in whitewater. In a letter to the Editor published in the September/October 1975 issue of *American Whitewater,* Evans emphatically stated "**Never use an open canoe beyond a Class II rapid!**" He further wrote,

> Perhaps someday there will be legislation against the misuse of the open canoe in rapids. But until that time all we can do is to urge people to leave their open canoes to the lakes and gently flowing rivers for which they are so ideally suited. For whitewater? Learn to use the nimble kayak, or the maneuverable and deck covered C-1 or C-2.[22]

Member responses were overwhelmingly against Evans' viewpoint, although AWA acknowledged they could only publish a sampling of the letters they had received. But Evans didn't stop there. He wrote another letter that was published in *Down River.* This letter was the basis for a reponse from Ramone Eaton, Retired Senior Vice President of the American Red Cross, published in the January/February 1976 issue of *American Whitewater.* In his letter, Eaton expressed his concern that Evans was the coach for the '72 U.S. Olympic team and therefore, might be perceived as knowing what he was talking about, espe-

[22] Evans, Jay. "Letters from Readers." *American Whitewater* Vol. XX No. 5 (September/October 1975): 156.

cially by the Coast Guard who might take his opinions seriously. This was a particularly valid concern in light of other attempts to regulate and legislate canoeing and kayaking activities for the purpose of safety.

Over the next couple of years, the Coast Guard continued their pursuit of leveling flotation for canoes. ACA Commodore Chuck Tummonds, a boat manufacturer, was very concerned that any resultant regulations would prohibit private building and drive up the price of canoes. He was also concerned that it could eventually lead to the regulation of kayaks, too. In 1977, Tummonds facilitated the formation of a task force to deal directly with the Coast Guard in a unified effort. The result was the River Safety Task Force (initially called the Kayak and Canoe Safety Task Force) comprised of a group of paddlers from ACA, AWA, and USCA including Dick Bridge (long-time ACA and CCA member), Frank Despit (longtime ACA member and Safety Chairman for ACA's Middle States Division), O.K. (Ollie King) Goodwin (AWA Safety Chairman), Mike Reynolds (USCA), and Charlie Walbridge (ACA Safety Chairman, appointed by Tummonds in 1976).

ACA's role in the River Safety Task Force was partially sparked by Chuck Tummonds' interest in slalom racing and the death of a slalom racer at the Icebreaker Slalom in Unadilla, New York, in October 1975. Gene Bernardin drowned due to foot entrapment after capsizing during his C-2M run. It was the first fatality documented due to foot entrapment. Bernardin's death, in front of numerous other racers, stunned the racing community and demonstrated how even a Class I–II river with a swift current can be deadly.

The Coast Guard's efforts were further supported by two technical reports prepared by independent research firms in early 1978, although deficiencies in the Coast Guard's accident report data were noted in both reports. In September of 1978, Bob Lantz of Blue Hole, as a member of the Canoe and Kayak Industry Council, presented a written statement to the Canoe Subcommittee of the National Boating Safety Advisory Council at a public meeting held in Chicago. In the statement, Lantz and the Council critiqued the findings of the two research reports that supported leveling flotation.

From the 1977 accident data, the two highest and overwhelming accident causes were "apparent operation error" and "bad judgment." The two greatest contributing factors were "lack of swimming ability" and "PFD not worn or used."[23]

Thinking that interpretation of accident data by non-paddlers might have contributed to erroneous conclusions, the River Safety Task Force, representing the paddling community, volunteered to review the accident reports. In November, the Coast Guard finally invited representatives of ACA, AWA, and USCA to review the data for the 1977 canoeing fatalities. Their findings did not support the reduction of accident fatalities through implementation of leveling flotation. Instead, their findings supported basic canoe instruction as given by the American Red Cross, and PFD usage. Within a few months, in early 1979, the Coast Guard set aside their efforts to institute leveling flotation regulations and instead concentrated their efforts on public education. The efforts to block flotation regulations had succeeded. The Coast Guard conceded they were impressed that a group of paddlers would volunteer to spend long hours reviewing accident reports.

In early 1979, with the Coast Guard's decision to set aside flotation regulation, the industry's sole reason to remain united was gone and the Canoe and Kayak Industry Council was disbanded. The paddlesport manufacturers saw only a single need for an organization, to ward off any perceived threats of regulation that might threaten their livelihood, instead of deriving any other

[23] Walbridge, Charlie. *River Safety Task Force Newsletter* Vol. 3 No. 1 (1979).

benefits for marketing purposes. However, the River Safety Task Force saw an opportunity to continue to support the paddlesport community. Although the leveling flotation threat was one of the seeds behind its formation, the Task Force's main objective was to collect accident information involving non-powered watercraft and evaluate the causes to propose solutions to reduce accidents in the long-term. With this information, the Task Force could then work with other groups and government agencies in "educating the public to the need for instruction before setting out on the river, [and the] development of equipment standards and tests and evaluation of rescue techniques. The goal is to do all of this through education and the establishment of voluntary standards, rather than through a push for more government regulation."[24] Their motto became "Education, Not Regulation."

The River Safety Task Force under the leadership of ACA's Safety Chairman Charlie Walbridge became an important contributor and driver regarding river safety and accident awareness. ACA took the lead and published newsletters for the Task Force that compiled and evaluated accident reports. The newsletter also provided a medium to distribute safety information to a growing group of interested individuals and organizations, both private and governmental, regarding river safety. The first *Best of The River Safety Task Force Newsletter* was published by ACA in 1982 for the years 1976 through 1982 and has continued periodically since then.

CHUCK TUMMONDS, along with O.K. Goodwin (AWA's Safety Chairman), helped Walbridge adopt the philosophy of "Education, Not Regulation" which by the mid-80's was widely supported by governmental agencies across the country.

The Coast Guard, with their heightened awareness of the causes of canoeing and kayaking accidents, provided a grant to the American Red Cross that was used to make an educational movie for the general public. In 1977, the movie *The Uncalculated Risk* was released and was used to educate the public across the country. (*The Uncalculated Risk* was made by Russ Nichols Productions. Nichols was a racer and whitewater paddler with two previous movies, *Whitewater Self-Defense: The Eskimo Roll,* and *Fast and Clean.*)

AWA continued their efforts regarding river safety and in 1978, AWA's River Signals Committee came out with hand and paddle signals that became a common means of communication on rivers. The major signals were Help, Emergency; Stop; All Clear; Run Right/Run Left; Attention and like AWA's Safety Code, became the standard for whitewater paddlers across the country. However, except for the growing use of carrying stuff-bag throw bags by paddlers, very little other preparation was made by whitewater paddlers for rescue. Paddlers in pockets around the country developed some novel approaches to rescue, however this was limited. River guides of whitewater outfitters were the exception. Many outfitters developed methods of rescuing "swimmers" and freeing pinned rafts. However, this often did not include rescuing paddlers in canoes or kayaks.

With the increase in the availability of manufactured boats and gear (and perhaps partially due to early problems associated with Hollowform's plastic kayaks), AWA decided to develop an equipment approval program in 1978. Their idea was to have one person manage a group of testers across the country and develop performance criteria with the assistance of manufacturers and paddlers. The manufacturers could then be made aware of defects or problems associated with their products and make appropriate changes. If the changes were made, then the product could receive the AWA seal of approval. If the manufacturer declined to make the changes, the tester's findings along with a

24 Walbridge, Charlie. *River Safety Task Force Newsletter* Vol. 1 No. 1 (1977).

reply from the manufacturer was published for the public's consideration. The equipment approval program did not gain a great deal of support and was very short-lived.

Conservation and Access

Coming into the '70s, dam building was already perceived as the biggest threat to whitewater. The '70s not only brought increased regulation and legislation, but with the energy crisis and droughts, they also brought more reasons to threaten more rivers with even more dams. Growth of the sport and increased numbers of participants were thought to be one weapon in defense of dam building efforts. Frances Cutter, Chairman of Bay Chapter's River Touring Section wrote in the Autumn 1970 issue of *American Whitewater:* "We would like to see more people on our rivers—how can we sell river conservation to the reservoir recreationist? Unfortunately, we expect a drop-out rate of over three fourths in our beginner programs, and it is these people who are the conservationists most valuable allies." [25]

California was one of the states most embroiled in dam building controversies. During the '70s, it was discovered that the National Wild and Scenic River System established by congressional act in 1968 did not really protect rivers. Any river designated as Wild and Scenic was never completely protected. The Act did not specifically safeguard the water quality either. Individual state laws sometimes further exacerbated the situation. Unfortunately for California, that was the case. Only the Middle Fork of the Feather was included in the national legislation and the California Wild and Scenic Rivers Act of 1972 was inadequate to provide complete protection from the different state and federal agencies with jurisdiction and funding to build dams. In 1976, the Tuolumne battle exploded when three dams were proposed with complete disregard for the Wild River Study classification given to a Class IV to VI stretch given by Congress the previous year.

The battle to "Save the Stanislaus" from the New Melones Dam was hard fought. Because of the popularity of the river among whitewater paddlers, the Army Corps of Engineers attempted to leverage the excitement of the Olympics and its man-made course in their favor. The Corps started touting the use of dams for artificial courses, specifically in support of the New Melones Dam. For ACA, the ICF recognized governing body for paddlesport competition, this was of particular interest. In the July/August 1972 issue of *American Canoeist,* ACA reported that there was a new spirit of cooperation with the Corps regarding the use of dams to support slalom racing. However, the actuality of it happening became embroiled in discussion and the Corps may have merely dangled a carrot to gain support among paddlers. Carl Trost of California wrote: "If a destroyed river can justify a slalom course, then a slalom course can justify more destroyed rivers." He warned: "It is possible that in our eagerness we may be grasping for a two-edged sword and grasping for the wrong end." [26] Despite its heavy private and commercial use, the Stanislaus was lost.

However, after the '72 Olympics, enthusiastic paddlers contacted their Congressmen and the Corps for the development of man-made slalom courses. Ray McLain of ACA and other AWA paddlers pulled together a Manmade Slalom Course Committee to study manmade courses. One course was proposed for the Cincinnati (Ohio) area on Bear Creek on old abandoned

[25] Cutter, Francis. "Letters from Readers." *American Whitewater* Vol. XV No. 3 (Autumn 1970): 2.

[26] Trost, Carl. "Build a Slalom Course, Destroy a Dozen Rivers." *American Whitewater* Vol. XVIII No. 1 (Spring 1973): 16–18.

farmland. Although there was little opposition (even the Nature Conservancy didn't care about the piece of land), there was also insufficient support for the project. Other projects like the eighteen-gate manmade slalom course on Denver's South Platte gained considerable support. The Platte River Greenway Foundation and CWWA supported and funded the development of the course. Its dedication was held on Memorial Day of 1978.

However, another dam proposed for a manmade course was planned for the Mulberry River in Arkansas and this one stirred up much controversy. The Mulberry was one of the best wilderness whitewater rivers in a five-state area encompassing Arkansas, Oklahoma, Louisiana, Tennesee and Mississippi. ACA supported it while other groups did not and the controversy pitted paddler against paddler. The manmade course on the Mulberry was never built

Until this time, conservation efforts were mostly focused on blocking the construction of dams. But with the growing numbers of paddlers, access to rivers in the form of allocations and use restrictions also became an issue. At first, allocation issues primarily revolved around rivers in the West in an attempt to preserve wilderness settings. Beginning in 1972, the Grand Canyon management plan severely restricted use of the Colorado River by private boaters from 1972 to 1980. Over 97 percent of the people who ran the canyon were on commercial trips. Less than 3 percent were on non-commercial trips. Over 90 percent of non-commercial applicants were turned away. In 1974, approximately 70 percent of the private applications for the Grand Canyon were refused with the adoption of the 92 percent to 8 percent commercial to private allocations.

In 1974, representatives from ACA and AWA participated in Interagency Whitewater Committee meetings with the National Park Service (NPS), Bureau of Land Management (BLM), and the U.S. Forest Service (USFS) regarding access and usage allocations for private boaters, particularly for canoe and kayak paddlers. The following year, ACA established their own River Rights Action Committee to support river runners' rights and access. As the popularity of whitewater increased into the late '70s, allocation restrictions were placed on more rivers for private boater trips including the Rogue in Oregon and the Middle Fork of the Salmon and Selway rivers in Idaho.

Allocation restrictions also hit the Lower Yough in Ohiopyle, the birthplace of eastern commercial rafting. By the mid-'70s, an estimated 75,000 floaters used the river. This included private raft trips, commercial trips by the four outfitters on the river, and private hardboaters, a term given to paddlers of canoes and kayaks. In 1975, Pennsylvania's Bureau of Parks commissioned a study that affected commercial and private allocation. A final decision by the Bureau of Parks boiled down to a daily allocation of permits for 192 hardboaters and 768 rafters, commercial, not private. Park officials acknowledged the lopsidedness of the figures against hardboaters even though they acknowledged that hardboaters were the safety factor on the river—it was hardboaters who were often the ones saving rafters.

Actual execution was a nightmare for the state park. In 1978 when as many as 95,000 people converged on the Yough to either raft or paddle, the first-come-first-served basis for hardboater permits resulted in long waits and irate tempers among hardboaters. Even greater numbers continued in the following years: 105,000 in 1979, 115,000 in 1980, and 138,000 in 1981. The state park instituted new management plans that included a new put-in and take-out (with buses to haul boats and gear to a larger private boater parking area and the purchase of a "token") and half-hour launch windows from 8:00 am to 1:30 pm. Paddlers caught sneaking on the river without a permit were fined $50.

The popularity of the Lower Yough continued for two main reasons: it is a Class III/IV river at normal levels and therefore provides a good training ground for new paddlers; it is dam controlled and always has water when many other rivers do not. [*Author's note:* Some of us would argue that a "6 inch" release is an adequate summer release.]

Use restrictions also surfaced in California in the early '70s regarding access and navigability issues. Claims of non-navigability by landowners on the Russian River, with its many popular Class I to III runs, led to a fight to preserve access and use. In the East in 1974, a favorite long time Class II–III run on the Lehigh River in eastern Pennsylvania was closed to paddling when a local rod and gun club forbid access to an old railroad bed that provided take-out access.

In 1977, Upper Yough (Maryland) access issues exploded regarding the put-in at Sang Run. Local landowners, riled up over the implementation of Maryland's Wild and Scenic Regulations, thought they would lose control over the use of their land. Unfortunately, whitewater paddlers were the unwitting victims of their ire. Since the Upper Yough was (and still is) considered one of the top Class V runs in the East, its access issue gained AWA's attention. (Perhaps this was partially due to the fact that AWA, considered by many as an "eastern" organization, had a number of members who regularly paddled the river, including it directors.)

In October 1978, Tom McEwan, brother of Jamie McEwan, was arrested for trespassing at the Sang Run put-in. A non-profit fund was set up by CCA and supported by AWA to help defray his legal costs. The trial, without a jury, was scheduled for the day before election day in November which illustrated how highly politicized the issue was at the time in the local area. McEwan was found guilty and fined $1.00. The verdict was appealed and was declared Non Pros (non prosequitor) for failure on the part of the plaintiff to respond to the court for the appeal. In essence, the verdict was dismissed.

AWA cut its teeth on access issues with the Upper Yough and began efforts to become actively involved in river access and conservation issues. Gone were the days of merely reporting issues to members to rely on their letter-writing efforts. The following year in 1978, AWA started working with American Rivers Conservation Council (ARCC). ARCC was founded in the mid-1970's by a group of river runners and AWA members including Oz Hawksley of Missouri, Gerald Meral of California, and Calvin Giddings of Utah. In 1979, under the guidance of AWA President Pete Skinner, AWA began to take the lead of the five national paddling organizations in conservation efforts. Skinner brought new energy, dedication, and ideas to the defense of rivers. AWA began discussions (again) with ACA to find areas for mutual cooperation of common interests, even beyond conservation. The same year, the Corps of Engineers completed their *Preliminary Inventory of Hydropower Resources,* a six-volume tome listing over 11,000 existing and new power sites under investigation. It was apparent that dam building for flood control was no longer the Corps' weapon. The new weapon was energy. AWA had its crusade, and challenge, ahead for the '80s.

The Gauley

Although safety and conservation concerns came to the forefront in the '70s concerning many different rivers, the Gauley in particular, had its own story. In 1970, Jim Stuart and Jon Dragan, owner of Wildwater Expeditions Unlimited located on the Newriver, ran an exploratory raft expedition on the Gauley to determine its use for commercial rafting. With the first annual fall release from the Summersville Dam by the Corps the weekend of September 22–23, 1973 (2,500cfs), word spread about the Gauley. The Gauley became one of the premier Class V rivers in the East. Paddlers from across the country began to flock to run it during the annual fall releases.

As the Gauley's popularity grew, increasing numbers of paddlers, clubs, and organizations joined the battle to preserve the river and its near-wilderness setting. The Gauley River Downriver Race was used as a tool to publicize and stop the project. The battle waged for much of the '70s. However, in the end, the dam was doomed by the Corps itself. The Corps used out-of-date and inaccurate topographic maps from surveys prior to World War I to design the dam and reservoir. When the Corps received newly surveyed maps from the U.S. Geological Survey (USGS), they discovered the dam they designed was 200 feet higher than the rim of the gorge itself. The entire project was scrapped when the cost of re-designing the project exceeded the cost-to-benefit ratio. By 1978, the project was declared dead.

With the increasing numbers of paddlers running the river, it was inevitable that there would be a serious mishap, or death, among its paddlers. However, the first paddler's death was not one of an inexperienced or first time Gauley paddler. The first death was that of an experienced expert paddler, Bob Taylor, on August 27, 1997, on a river he knew so well.

Taylor was 35 years old and had more than ten years of experience on big and small rivers throughout the East. A native West Virginian, he paddled with KCCNY while living in New Jersey, later returning to live and paddle in his home state. Taylor, well known for his surfing ability, came out of his boat after pausing to surf the holes in the second drop of Lost Paddle. "Despite rescue efforts by other members of his party (a total of five) he was swept downstream into a boulder sieve where he was forced underwater and trapped. It took rescuers several days to recover the body. [27]

Much was written about Taylor's death. It shook the eastern whitewater community. The accident was thoroughly studied, perhaps moreso than any other because Taylor was considered an expert paddler and knew the river so well. And perhaps it was thoroughly studied because the death occurred on the Gauley, a river that was capable of such accidents but none of which had occurred until Taylor's death.

[27] Walbridge, Charles. "Fatal Accident on the Gauley River." *American Whitewater* Vol. XXII No. 6 (November/December 1997): 193–198.

Ward Eister, another one of West Virginia's own expert paddlers and co-author of the 1985 revision of *Wildwater West Virginia,* wrote "A Eulogy and Warning."

> It was one of those things that never should have happened. It never happens to us or anyone close to us does it? Except this time.
>
> We must try to learn from this tragedy. To me, the most important lesson is that it was not a freak accident. It was inevitable. Not inevitable for Bob, but for someone. I realized 3 or 4 years ago that I was paddling increasingly more dangerous waters routinely to find challenge. When we were learning, we took all precautions on Class 3 water because it was difficult for us then. Now, some paddle Class 5 water nonchalantly and yet the danger is significantly greater. Yes, it was inevitable. Yes, it will happen again. The vast number of paddlers now guarantee that it will. Let us be more aware of our surroundings to make sure that we are not the one. [28]

Idaho Big Water Paddler, Selway (ID), 1976
—courtesy of Rob Lesser.

Blackadar's Legacy

Although Blackadar was not the first to run big remote water (Powell may be considered one of the first), his exploits occurred at the right time and in the right media to inspire others. Blackadar's particular legacy was that of extreme adventure paddling, particularly running extreme big water and paddling in remote areas in small self-contained parties, or sometimes even alone. His legacy captivated fellow Idaho paddlers including Rob Lesser who paddled with Blackadar on occasion. After Blackadar's death, Lesser carried on his legacy, particularly on rivers of the North American extreme northwest in Alaska (Turnback Canyon on the Alsek and Devil's Canyon on the Susitna) and British Columbia (Grand Canyon of the Stikine). In 1977, Lesser made a solo run on the Susitna. Lesser established his own name as a big water paddler expanding beyond North America. Later, Montana paddler Doug Ammons followed in Blackadar's footsteps by running big remote whitewater, as did Alaskan Andrew Embrick.

Still others explored remote water beyond North America in South America, Central America, and in the Himalayas in Asia. In 1975, AWA President Cal Giddings, AWA Executive Director Jim Sindelar, along with Dee Couch, Gerry Plummer, and Chuck Carpenter, traveled to Peru and made the first descent of the Apurimac, the longest tributary of the Amazon. The descent was a 300-mile trip with a total elevation drop of about 10,000 feet and included a 60-mile canyon whose rim rose up to 15,000 above the river.

[28] Eister, Ward. "A Eulogy and Warning." *American Whitewater* Vol. XXII No. 6 (November/December 1997): 190.

About the same time Giddings thought about exploring South America, Wick Walker sought to explore whitewater in the Himalayas and settled on a self-contained expedition down the Wong Chu River in Bhutan starting at 15,000 feet of elevation. Efforts to gain permission began in 1975. The initial trip length was reduced from 30 to 10 days with six team members instead of nine before permission was finally granted in 1981. The final team consisting of Wick Walker (trip leader), Les Bechdel, Eric Evans, Ed Hixson (expedition doctor), Jamie McEwan, and Tom McEwan, successfully completed the first American descent of a river in Asia and the first descents ever of the Thimpu, Paro, Fo, and Amo rivers. Hixson, a part-time paddler, wisely opted out of the more difficult sections of the river.

Aside from the effort taken to obtain permission in the first place, a considerable amount of effort was taken to ensure the trip was successful, and safe. As Evans wrote:

> In the month prior to the trip, everyone but Ed Hixson (who was in China) spent a week on the Gauley and Russel Fork rivers in West Virginia and Virginia, respectively, shaking down gear, rescue techniques, and communication methods on the water... But even more important than our safety gear and preparations was our attitude. We wanted to err on the side of conservatism, and we pledged to support any team member who wanted to portage a rapid.[29]

American Sportsman also continued their involvement in filming big water runs and first descents. In 1979, ABC was granted permission to film the first kayak descent of the Arun River in Nepal and chose Cully Erdman, Phil Freedman, and Tom Ruwitch to make the run. In 1979, *American Sportsman* also wanted to film a high water run of Cross Mountain Canyon and arranged for Eric Evans, Norbert Sattler (Austrian K-1 World Champion), and Cully Erdman to run it. After looking at the first drop with a large keeper, normally portaged at high water, Sattler declined to run. Evans ran it, although he was held underwater for a very long time. Erdman also ran it but he was seriously injured and nearly drowned which required helicopter transport to a nearby hospital. This also provided for excellent TV and became a topic of discussion across the country. Evans later confided to fellow racers that he felt an obligation to run it because of the money he was paid. However, he also said that he would not let money influence his decision again.

In 1981, ABC's *American Sportsman* was granted permission to film a legal run of the Niagara Gorge of a team of four kayakers lead by Chris Spelius, who had previously made three other successful but illegal runs. On October 15, 1981, Spelius with "partners in crime" Ken Lageren and Don Weedon, were joined by Carrie Ashton for the first legal run of the Gorge.

The previous illegal Niagara Gorge runs by Spelius, though not inspired by Blackadar's paddling in remote areas, were inspired by Blackadar's big water exploits. In the mid-'70s, Chris Spelius, a raft guide and slalom racer, left Utah to work at NOC. Before moving East, he heard about attempts to set-up a commercial raft company on the Niagara Gorge, attempts that resulted in deaths in 1973 and again in 1975. On August 19, 1975, three rafters drowned on an experimental run down the Niagara Gorge. Toronto based Niagara

In October of 1980, Spelius and Lageren ran the Niagra Gorge. The following August, Spelius ran it with Don Weedeon, a protégé of Cal Giddings. However, this time the run ended with a Keystone Cops-type chase with helicopters. They were pursued by both U.S. and Canadian law enforcement officers who strictly enforce the laws against such illegal activities. Spelius escaped capture but Weedon was caught. In the media, Spelius was referred to as "Charles, the guy who got away."

Soon after *American Sportsman's* filming of the Niagara Gorge descent, the focus of publicity began to shift from the adventure and bravado of first descents to that of river preservation and conservation. In 1982, *American Sportsman* filmed the first descent of the Grand Canyon of the Stikine in British Columbia, run by Don Banducci, Rick Fernald, Lars Holbek, Rob Lesser, and John Wasson. However, unlike many of their previous shows, the focus of the first descent and filming was to bring conservation attention to the river to preserve the river and protect it from environmental damage.

[29] Evans, Eric. "In the Land of Thunder Dragon." *Canoe* Vol. 10 No. 3 (June 1982): 34–43, 58–59.

River Gorge Tours ran an experimental raft, a 37-foot rubber raft with a forty horse motor designed by engineers from Cornell for the Gorge. The raft held thirty people, two crewmembers and twenty-eight volunteers and flipped on a monstrous wave above the Whirlpool.

Enchanted by its sheer volume (a 55-foot drop with a release of 100,000 cfs on summer days for hydropower generation), Spelius and longtime paddling friend Ken Lageren of Idaho decided to risk arrest and attempt the Gorge. They successfully ran the Gorge on October 30, 1977 at 110,000 cfs although both were caught, arrested, fined $100, and had their kayaks seized.

Women

Women paddlers often encountered two extremes in the '70s. One was the friendly, almost nurturing (actually more along the line of fatherly) environments exhibited by family oriented clubs that participated in paddling activities outside of whitewater. The other was the fairly hostile male locker room mentality environment more typical of groups (often not clubs) associated exclusively with whitewater. Walbridge recalled that he was often surprised and appalled to see how far this mentality went, that some of the guys would act like a bunch of Neanderthals. The latter was particularly true in the early to mid-'70s, even in clubs where the core of the whitewater paddlers consisted of young men. Women were still considered the weaker sex. Whitewater was a macho thing. However, the environment slowly changed through the '70s. This was, in part, attributed to the overall effects of Title IX of the Civil Rights Act of 1972 that required schools to equalize women's sports programs with men's programs. Over time, Title IX changed thinking regarding women in sports.

Donna Berglund, Lochsa (ID), 1972 —courtesy of Barbara Brown.

In addition to a hostile environment, women were also subject to hostile equipment that was always too big because it was designed by men for men. Women were also not afforded the same opportunities for employment in whitewater. Many raft outfitters would not hire women. NOC in North Carolina and Whitewater Adventurers owned by Imra Szilagi in West Virginia were two exceptions.

But in spite of it all, women in small numbers paddled in the early '70s. Some paddled pretty much exclusively for competition like Peggy (Nutt) Mitchell and Cathy Hearn while others were both racers and river runners like Carrie Ashton, Donna Berglund, Louise Holcombe, Barb McKee, and Nancy Wiley. Still others, like Mimi (Hayman) Demaree and Julia Schmidt, were river runners almost exclusively. Both Demaree and Schmidt were unique in that they paddled C-1 and were guides for Whitewater Adventurers in West Virginia.

Nancy Wiley was often the only woman paddling heavy whitewater on trips in a multi-state area around her home in Colorado. In the East, there was actually an opportunity for all-women trips with greater numbers of women paddling. Around 1972–73, Barb McKee recalled being part of a high level run on the New Gorge in West Virginia that was an all-woman trip and included Donna Berglund, Kathy Felton, and Julia Schmidt.

By the latter '70s, the changes that occurred in the sport for women were significant. Just as Blackadar's media attention highlighted whitewater paddling, so, too, did publicity of women in the sport in both competition and river running. In competition, Linda Harrison's win at the '78 Pre-Worlds in Jonquierre (a full 22 seconds ahead of the next competitor) and her four-time National K-1W Slalom Champion status in the late '70s brought much needed media attention. Harrison's aggressive style inspired comments that compared her paddling style to that of a man. Cathy Hearn's performance at the '79 World Championships in Jonquierre, where she medaled in every K-1W event, including an individual gold in slalom, and was sometimes over-shadowed by the American C-1 medal sweep, also brought attention to women. Cathy Hearn's medals included individual and team classes.

Although some women might take offense at a statement that compares women to men, for Linda Harrison, it was indeed a compliment for her style, concentration, and skill.

More women entered both competition and river running as these changes occurred. In general, the trend toward lower volume boats, including slalom, although not intentionally designed for women, often benefitted them. The number of women grew to the point that women became a new niche within the market. Paddles were made in shorter lengths and with smaller shaft sizes. Other gear was also made in smaller sizes to better fit women. Paddling clinics also developed at schools like NOC that were taught by women for women.

The Road to Jonquierre (Competition's Hidden Legacies)

One aspect of the divergence between racers and river runners was that it drew a smaller group of youthful paddlers solely dedicated to competition. After the '72 Olympics, many older European competitors that had hung in there to compete in an Olympics retired from competition. However, with the discontinuation of slalom for the '76 Olympics in Montreal and later for the '80 Olympics in Moscow (the United States boycotted the Moscow Olympics anyway), many thought interest in competition by young paddlers would decline. After all, only the World Championships remained. For some, the draw of competing in the Olympics (Five Ring Fever) affected their decision to switch from whitewater slalom to flatwater sprint.

California racers Candi Clark, Carl Toeppner, and Chuck Lyda were joined by Jamie McEwan and Angus Morrison after the '75 World Championships to train under Andy Toro in California for flatwater for the '76 Olympics. Wildwater racers Carol Fisher and Leslie Klein also trained and competed in flatwater for the '76 Olympics. In the late '70s, Chris Spelius, a rodeo and slalom paddler, also made the switch, albeit temporarily. One of the benefits of their flatwater training was that they brought back to whitewater improvements in training and stroke technique. Morrison was a dual National Champion in C-1 Slalom and Wildwater in 1978. McEwan, however, tried to come back to slalom in 1977 but, admittedly, was too late. He was left behind by the new era of designs and younger paddlers.

For other racers, the World Championships were enough. Although having come a long way since their first World Championships as a team in 1961, the best finish for American racers was a bronze in Wildwater team C-1 at the '71 World Championships in Merano. McEwan's bronze at the '72 Olympics proved that the young American paddlers were within grasp of a World Championship win. For American paddlers in particular, there was still much to be gained. However, training for competition was only one part of winning. The other part was having the best kayak and canoe designs to train and compete in and American paddlers were still very dependent on designs from Europe.

The trend that started before the Olympics toward lower volume boats to sneak gates, particularly kayaks, was only temporarily halted by the larger volume designs that came out specifically for the Olympic Augsburg course. After the Olympics, the low volume trend resumed, incorporating flatter decks and pointed ends. Lettmann and Prijon pursued their own courses in low volume kayaks, both producing successful designs. For Prijon, it was his Treska and Sanna kayaks. For Lettmann, it was his Mark V and VI.

During the same time frame as the development of low volume kayak designs for World Championship competition, European designers also grappled with what the next generation of slalom canoe (C-1 and C-2) designs would be. The changes that first started in 1971 for C-1s, with width reduction to 70 cm, continued in 1973 with the elimination of bow and stern height requirements for both C-1 and C-2. (The 1973 changes also allowed concave hull shapes for wildwater boats. This change was a break from hull criteria brought to wildwater from flatwater designs.) These changes were significant enough that there was no single school of thought that guided the next generation of canoe design. The trend toward lower volume and gate sneaking opened the doors to new ideas in designs. New technique and many new designs were introduced, although no single design stood out signifying the beginning of the next step in canoe evolution.

Canoe design again had the opportunity to emulate kayak design as it had in the early '60s with the introduction of fiberglass construction. However, that was not to be. C-1 and C-2 design, and accompanying technique changes, took advantage of the inherent differences between kayaks and canoes. The combination of width reduction for C-1 and elimination of bow and stern height requirements for C-1 and C-2 set the stage for advances in C-paddling like none previously seen. Although there was international resistance to big change, everyone expected that if a country hit it right on, with boat design and accompanying technique change, they would blow everyone else away. However, no one, not even the Europeans, had a crystal ball for the canoe designs of the future.

Following McEwan's Olympic bronze win, a spirit of can-do and experimentation followed for American paddlers and designers. In the mid-70s, dependence on European designs was challenged by new, young American paddlers.

America's Kayak Design: the Slipper

In the late '60s and early '70s, there were a few American kayak designers like Werner Furrer, Dave Kurtz, and Jim Stuart, but their designs fell short of their European counterparts. None were used in World Championship competition as American World Championship team members continued to use the latest European designs.

Werner Furrer, Sr. had his WSL series of kayaks designed for his son, Werner, Jr. Dave Kurtz had his DK series, the most popular being the DK-5 based on Prijon's Slalom Special. Jim Stuart's series that started with the Nimble and progressed to the Shadow and the Whisper were designed with the help of naval architect Jim Miller of Annapolis using measurements from a variety of the best European boats available.

In 1974, racing proponent Chuck Tummonds, who owned Sports Equipment Inc. in Ohio, was irked that American racers were dependent upon European designs. This meant that they were often unable to train for competition using the latest European design. At a spring slalom race, Dan Demaree overheard Tummonds tell Dave Kurtz that he was willing to pay for or sponsor an American who could design a winning slalom kayak. Demarree, a young slalom racer and raft guide, volunteered to design the kayak but was politely rebuffed by Tummonds.

During the summer, Demarree traveled to Europe and competed in the Europa Cup slalom races. While in Europe, he ordered the latest Lettmann design, the Mark V. Demaree spent time with Klaus Lettmann who showed him how he designed and built boats using foam to make a plug. Demaree also spent a great deal of time with Austrian Norbert Sattler, the '73 K-1 Slalom World Champion, learning about European training methods. Sattler, a designer who began designing with Prijon in 1973, also taught Demaree about the theories behind Lettmann and Prijon designs. After Demaree's Mark V kayak was run over by a van at a race, Sattler suggested Demaree replace it with a Treska kayak, a kayak Sattler had co-designed with Prijon. Demaree traveled to Prijon's factory and bought a kayak. Demaree also spent time with Prijon learning about kayak design as he had done with Lettmann.

WHILE THE REST OF THE COUNTRIES trained and raced in large volume boats designed for the Augsburg course for the '72 Olympics, the East German kayak team trained and raced in Hartung designed low volume cut-down boats. The boats were so cut down that knobs had to be added to the bow and stern ends to remain legal. However, East German K-1 slalom racer Siegbert Horn switched his Hartung design for one of Prijon's at the last minute to win the gold.

Chuck Tummonds and Dan Demaree (left to right) working on the Slipper kayak mold, 1974 —courtesy of Dan Demaree.

In the early '70s, the major difference in design theory between Lettmann and Prijon was the notion of features that worked like a keel. Lettmann's designs were essentially keel-less; the bottom surface of the hull contained no feature that acted like a keel and the chines remained soft to slip in the current. Prijon on the other hand, incorporated a slight V in the hull that acted like a keel and harder chines to lock into the current.

Upon his return from Europe, Demarree approached Tummonds about designing a new kayak. This time, Demaree, armed with what he had learned from Lettmann, Prijon, and Sattler, convinced Tummonds that he knew what he was talking about. During the fall, Demaree lived at Tummonds' house while they designed and built five prototype designs. Demarree contributed the designs and Tummonds the fiberglass and molding technology to the project. Over the winter months that followed, Demaree, along with fellow racer and guide Dan Isbister, narrowed down the five prototypes to one using timed runs on a flatwater slalom course with current. The design chosen was named the Slipper. The following summer, Chuck Stanley and Dan Isbister paddled Slipper kayaks at the '75 World Championships. Although their finishes were disappointing, Isbister was 43rd and Stanley was 46th out of 63, Tummonds' goal was fulfilled. Americans paddled an American designed kayak at the World Championships.

Dan Isbister in a Slipper kayak at Unadilla (NY) slalom, 1975 —courtesy of Dan Demaree.

Unfortunately, the American K-1 finishes at the '75 World Championships did not reflect the ability of the Slipper design. European racers recognized that it was clearly fast. Two European companies pirated the design and produced their own version with modifications in the deck. After the Championships, Demaree and Tummonds licensed the design to Phoenix who sold a couple thousand in the U.S. alone. The Slipper kayak went from the hottest race boat, "a specialized slalom design … radical low volume kayak … not recommended for most recreational paddlers" in the mid-'70s to "a whitewater play-boat … a favorite of those who love enders and pop-ups … for regional recreational fun or kayak racing"[30] in the late '70s.

[30] Phoenix Products, Inc. Advertisement brochures, not dated.

America's C-2 Innovation: the Gemini

At the '75 World Championships, the American C-2 team of John (Johnnie) Evans and Carl Toeppner of California showed up with a new C-2 design from Evans that incorporated offset-center cockpits. Although the concept was not entirely new, the bow and stern height requirements eliminated in 1973 provided the opportunity for the concept to work for slalom. (The concept had been incorporated in a wildwater C-2 design by Alain Feuillette, called La Tub, for the '69 World Championships.)

Evans had recognized that slalom courses were being designed around the use of low volume kayaks and the trend for gate sneaking. The courses were tighter; the gates were closer together. End-hole C-2s were not able to keep up with the trend. To Evans, the logical solution was positioning the paddlers closer together to get through gates. His offset-center design was based on the 1971 Hartung hull, a hull designed as an end-hole C-2 with fairly deep or high volume ends. This hull, combined with the close placement of the center cockpits (around 12 inches), resulted in a boat that was not as maneuverable as it could have been. It was not even as maneuverable as the current end-hole designs. John Holland nicknamed it the Monitor because it sat so low in the water it couldn't be hit, in the case of the C-2, by slalom poles, not by cannon fire.

THE HARTUNG DESIGN used by Evans was the same design that was pirated from the Polish team by two Austrian racers at the '71 World Championships. The racers borrowed two C-2s from the Pole's boat building, swam them across the Drau River, pulled a deck mold from one and a hull mold from the other, and then returned them, all during the same night. However, in their haste they forgot to note which end was which and inadvertently seamed the deck and hull on backwards. Their mistake was discovered a few weeks later at an international slalom race where they became the subject of much laughter and embarrassment.

Although Evans and Toeppner made the team by winning the Nationals with the Monitor, they finished 23rd out of 26 at the World Championships. However, the idea provided the impetus for another American, Steve Chamberlin, to design his own C-2.

The next year, in 1976, Chamberlin introduced the Gemini Mark II (the Mark I version didn't have enough rocker) which was the first successful offset-center C-2 design. Chamberlin was a dual National Champion that year, with his wife Sue in C-2M and Joe Stahl in C-2, easily beating all other competitors.

Chamberlin recognized that the volume in the ends of Evans' C-2 was the barrier to the success of the concept based on a previous discussion he had with West German Bernd Heinemann at MKC. Heinemann told Chamberlin that the key to success in handling the bow (in end-hole C-2s) was to get the bow paddlers' weight as far back toward the middle as possible. This was not an easy proposition for Chamberlin who, in his 30's, outweighed his younger teenaged partner Joe Stahl in the stern. Chamberlin recognized that offset-center cockpits were the solution. He designed the Gemini from scratch taking the volume out of the ends.

Chamberlin used a Feuillette mold, filled it with foam, and whittled away much of the foam toward the ends to reduce the volume while keeping the middle section fairly intact. This became the Gemini Mark I version that was then modified to become the Mark II used at the '76 Nationals. The '76 Nationals were held on the Kern and was a year that turned out to be a low water year. The course was a Class II/III course at best. Since the trend had always been toward large volume boats for large volume rivers, the question was whether the concept would work on large volume rivers. It was proven the next year at the '77 World Championships in Spittal and subsequent races on other large volume European rivers.

Chamberlin refined the design and used a third iteration (the Mark III version) for the 1977 season. At the '77 World Championships in Spittal, all three American C-2 teams paddled Geminis while the European competitors paddled end-hole C-2s. Although none of the Americans placed at the Championships, the concept was clearly recognized by all as superior. By the '79 World Championships in Jonquierre, not a single end-hole C-2 was used by any competitor. All competitors used offset-center C-2 designs.

As with other radical design changes, technique also had to develop and evolve. Unlike some other changes, this one proved to be more forgiving. Stability actually increased over end-hole C-2 designs because the weight centers shifted in and down giving a lower center of gravity. Previously for end-hole C-2s, courses had a bias based on gate positions that required difficult moves for either bow right or left. With offset-center designs, there was no longer a good or bad side related to the bow paddler's position for any given slalom course.

[*Author's note:* In the mid-'80s, I switched from paddling a Seda end-hole C-2, a mid-'70s design, for river running to a modified Paramax, the 1982 design. (The original Paramax was designed for the '81 World Championships by Hearn, Lugbill, and the Garvis twins.) After a few initial surprises and adjustments, learning the differences between paddling a high volume end-hole C-2 and a low-volume offset-center C-2 with edges, the latter's superiority was clear.]

America's C-1 Design and Technique Innovations

While Americans in their new kayak and C-2 designs did not place at the '75 World Championships, the presence of Americans paddling American-designed boats was an inspiration to other young racers, particularly for a group of young paddlers in CCA's youth program, the C-CATS. For them, the Summer of 1975 was the start of a series of smaller, random events with long term effects. The young C-2 team of Jon and Ron Lugbill, both under 16 years of age, made the U.S. team and competed at the '75 World Championships. After watching European C-1 paddlers, the Lugbills were convinced that the Europeans could be beat and Jon and Ron split up to concentrate on C-1. They also recruited another neighbor, Bob (Bumbo Blitzkreig) Robison to join them in training.

Cathy and Davey Hearn, two other young C-CATS members, attended three weeks of slalom classes at MKC during the summer. While there, Davey used a new low volume European C-1, the Roock-Schmidt, which had a fairly high volume bow but a low volume stern.

At the end of that summer, an invigorated group of C-CATSs including the Hearns, Lugbills, Kent Ford, and Bob Robison, got back together to train. And train they did. With coach Jack Brosius, they worked throughout the winter in the David Taylor Model Basin. The Model Basin was where the Navy tested models of new boat and ship designs. It was essentially a 500-meter long indoor swimming pool that provided an opportunity for the young paddlers to train year round.

The trend the following year in 1976 for all C-1s from Europe continued to evolve toward the gate-sneaking characteristics of kayaks. Hearn, Robison, and the Lugbills decided to try their own hand at making a new C-1 design.

THE SANNA, named after the Saane River in Europe, was a design collaboration between Toni Prijon and Norbert Sattler. [*Author's note:* I found that the design's name was sometimes spelled Sanna, and other times as Sahne by various American authors.]

Using a plug from a Sanna kayak, the latest design from Prijon, they modified the plug to design their first C-1, the Max II. (There was no Max I.) Although the new design was crude (it was not even symmetrical side to side) and not properly faired, they trained in the design during the winter of '76–'77. They were joined by Kent Ford who also trained in a new design from Tummonds, the Slipper C-1. Coincidentally, for the '76 paddling season, Tummonds, with input from Kent Ford, decided to use the Slipper as the basis for a C-1 version of the kayak.

There was nothing very scientific about the modifications made to the Sanna for the Max II design, nor for many of its descendents. Few changes were made to the basic kayak designs except for modifications required for the wider minimum width requirements for C-1s, about four inches. The kayak decks and hulls were cut lengthwise with the exception of the ends (to keep the plug together). Aside from the different starting points, that is the different kayaks used, the only other difference between the Max II and the Slipper C-1 design was that the gap additions for the Slipper C-1 was properly faired. The gap for the Max II was filled in with straight surfaces resulting in straight sides and a flat bottom with hard transitions in the bottom surface. The Max II had roughly the same amount of rocker as the Slipper C-1 but had flat surfaces in the hull with transitions fore and aft of the cockpit like a jacked up hot-rod. These unfaired transitions and hard edges proved to be serendipitous. The Max II also had its widest point after the cockpit, behind the paddler, instead of at the cockpit center.

Jamie McEwan at the '77 Nationals on the West (VT), 1977—courtesy of Dan Demaree.

In the winter of '76–'77 during training at the David Taylor Model Basin, the beginnings of a new C-1 technique began to take shape with the low volume C-1s, particularly with the Max II. At the Model Basin, the slalom poles were hung from a catwalk that was about 60 feet above the water. Because of the excessive length of the ropes holding the slalom poles, the bottom of the poles were placed in the water, often inadvertently at different depths, to dampen their swing when hit. After practice, the game was to see who could drive the bow of their boat under the pole that was deepest in the water without moving the pole. Because it was difficult to determine whether the water or the boat moved the pole, the game was changed to see how far up the pole the bow could reach requiring that the boat's bow swing high out of the water. This required a stern pivot or a stern squirt. Robison did it first by leaning the wrong way. He also did it in his Max II, the C-1 with *the flat hull surfaces and transition aft of the cockpit.* The Max II hull shape, as unfair and strange looking as it was, played an important role in Robison's successful stern pivot. After seeing Robison's performance, the others followed. They all practiced this new move and incorporated wrong-way leans and stern pivot moves into their slalom technique.

At the '77 World Championships in Spittal, the young American C-paddlers in C-1 and C-2 showed promise, although they finished out of the medals. However, the superiority of the Gemini offset-center C-2 design was clearly established. The young and inexperienced Garvis twins, Mike and Steve (nicknamed the Garvi), were not expected to do well but posted the fastest time in their class. Unfortunately, with penalties they finished out of the medals in fourth place. Three of the four C-1 paddlers on the team were young C-CATSs. Robison, in a Max II, had the best finish in 4th place followed by Ron Lugbill in 6th, and Ford in 7th, both paddling Slippers. An older Jamie McEwan, the fourth C-1 on the team, finished 15th.

Two other young C-CATSs, Davey Hearn and Jon Lugbill, attended the Championships as members of the wildwater team. This proved fortuitous because it provided them the opportunity to watch the slalom competition. It would also be the last races they would merely watch for many years to come. As Endicott recalled, for Hearn and Lugbill, merely watching the race as spectators "probably fueled 15 years of payback."[31] For the young C-CATS C-paddlers, Robison's finish confirmed that they were on the right track with their Max II design and new technique. The '77 World Championships proved to be the end of one era and the beginning of another for C-1 competition.

While American C-paddlers showed promise, American K-1 hopes were dashed. Eric Evans finished a disappointing 13th in his last World Championships. However, in K-1W, Linda Harrison medaled with a bronze. Harrison picked up the trend established by Wright in the '60s of American women outperforming men in their respective kayak classes in the World Championships.

In 1978, the first Pre-Worlds were held at Jonquierre, Quebec, the site of the '79 World Championships, the first-ever scheduled in North America. At the Pre-Worlds, American finishes in slalom C-1 and C-2 clearly established the beginnings of American reign and superiority in these classes. In C-1 slalom competition, the American paddlers dominated, winning gold, silver, and bronze medals as well as 5th, 6th, and 8th using their latest design, the Super Max (a streamlined version of the Max II). While three entries for each class were allowed for each country in World Championship competition, six entries were allowed in the Pre-Worlds. Hearn won gold, followed by Ron Lugbill with silver and Ford with bronze. Robison finished out of the medals in 5th and Jon Lugbill 8th. In C-2 slalom competition, two American teams medaled with gold and silver finishes. Ron Lugbill and Hearn won gold followed by the team of Jon Lugbill and Robison with silver.

At the '79 World Championships at Jonquierre, American C-1 paddlers swept the medals and won the team event. An iteration of the Super Max, the Ultra Max, was made for the race and was used by Jon Lugbill and Robison.

THE K-1 CLASS was always considered the "King" of all slalom classes with its quality of competition and intense competitiveness. A country's stature in slalom racing was measured by its number of K-1 World Champions. Both the C-1 and C-2 classes, though often very competitive, played second fiddle to K-1. The other two classes, K-1W and C-2M (unfortunately, the only classes involving women) varied in their levels of competition over the years. Until the '70s, the quality of international competition in K-1W was considered low. The reverse was true for C-2M which had always been very competitive in international competition. Its exclusion from Olympic competition contributed to a reversal in its competitiveness.

With East Germany and Czechoslovakia no longer supporting C-2M teams, only three countries entered C-2M slalom competition at the '73 World Championships: United States, France, and the Netherlands. The American team of Carol and David Knight finished 1st followed by Paul Liebman and Leena Mela in 2nd.

At the '75 World Championships, there were five C-2M slalom entries. All three American entries placed, sweeping the medals in the class. The American team of Marietta Gilman and Chuck Lyda took gold followed by Rasa D' Entremont and George Lhota with silver and Michele Piras and Steve Draper with bronze. (In wildwater C-1, Al Button won bronze, the first individual medal finish in wildwater World Championship competition.)

By the late '70s, the roles of K-1W and C-2M reversed with a lower quality of competition for C-2M. The '81 World Championships were the last for the slalom C-2M class.

[31] Endicott, William. Interview by author 27 January 1997.

Hearn competed in his Super Max. Although the changes in the Ultra Max were not considered substantial, the ends were narrowed reducing bow and stern volume and the deck was flattened (ridges were added for strength). The Ultra Max had more rocker and could spin faster. The Super Max and Ultra Max and the associated technique incorporating aggressive cross-paddling and stern pivot turns were clearly superior. Previous slalom racers, including John Evans and Wick Walker, pioneered cross paddling but Ford, Hearn, the Lugbills, and Robison perfected it. Combined with the new designs and stern pivot moves, the C-CATSs shaped the future of slalom competition.

Jon Lugbill at the '79 World Championship at Jonquierre (Quebec), 1979 —courtesy of Jim Stuart.

Although the American team, particularly in C-1 and C-2, was expected to do well at the '79 World Championships, no one predicted how well. In addition to five gold medals, two silver, and two bronze, the American team won the ICF trophies in both slalom and wildwater for the most team points overall. In C-1, Jon Lugbill won gold, Davey Hearn, silver, and Bob Robison, bronze. In team competition, the C-1 team won gold finishing an incredible 74 seconds ahead of the British team. The C-1 wildwater team of Chuck Lyda, Kent Ford, and John Evans won silver.

Even the U.S. team members paddling kayak did well. Cathy Hearn medaled in every K-1W event, slalom and wildwater, individual and team. She won an individual slalom gold. The slalom K-1W team of Cathy Hearn, Linda Harrison, and Becky Judd took gold, along with the wildwater K1-W team of Carol Fisher, Leslie Klein, and Cathy Hearn. Although the American men's K-1 team improved with the best finish ever for K-1 with Chris McCormick's 5th place finish, K-1 medals in World Championship competition still remained an elusive goal.

However, another event occurred at Jonquierre aside from the spectacular American sweep in C-1. While warming up for the race, Jon Lugbill performed a bow pivot. After the race the C-CATS experimented and found the best use for this new technique. Bow pivots were more effective in slower current than faster current. This had different implications and uses than the stern pivot

IN THE MID-70'S, although a few racers came out of California, clubs from the East, in particular CCA and PCC, provided many of the core racers on the U. S. teams.

CCA's access to the Dickerson canal and David Taylor Model Basin clearly drew competitors to CCA for year-round training. In addition to Ford, Hearn, the Lugbills, and Robison, the Garvis twins and Joe Jacobi were all C-1 benefactors of CCA training. K-1 and K-1W paddlers also trained with CCA including Chris McCormack, Cathy Hearn, and Yuri Kasuda.

PCC's core racers included Paul Liebmann, Steve and Sue Chamberlin and John Burton. In 1975, one third of the U.S. team in 1975 was from PCC.

and set the course for more than just slalom competition. The group of young C-paddlers were well on their way to changing the future of the sport in many different ways.

THE REMARKABLE CONVERGENCE of opportunities (people, places, and events) culminated in the ascension to power of American C-1 paddlers on home turf in Jonquierre, the heart of canoe country in North America. While materials (plastics) revolutionized river running, C-1 design and the accompanying advances in technique revolutionized competition. The edges and the wrong-way or offside leans associated with those edges resulted in bow and stern pivot turns that affected the sport outside of slalom competition and supported advances in river-running technique. It also contributed to the birth of a new sport: squirtboating.

Competition's Legacies: Two New Sports

By the mid-to-late '70s, river running was more than just getting down the river. Playboating became a significant part of the experience, playing in holes and surfing waves. Hot-dog maneuvers developed with names like pop-ups, end-overs or enders, and pirouettes. Paddlers became addicted to surfing and spent hours at one wave. The result was the birth of two new sub sports, squirt and rodeo.

Squirtboating developed from the low volume designs and associated techniques that developed for slalom racing in the '70s, particularly associated with C-1. Rodeo, on the other hand, was an indirect result of the divergence between competition and river running. With the divergence and the specialization that evolved around slalom and wildwater competition, showing off was removed from the realm of river runners. But the need to demonstrate paddling abilities did not disappear. While offside leans and pivot turns became entrenched in slalom racing technique, competition of a different sort developed in Idaho. Rodeo, the public performance and demonstration of skill (hot-dogging) met a need for river runners.

Squirt

Offside leans using an edge were not entirely new with the new low volume C-1 designs of the late '70s. Offside leans in kayaks came into use with some of the first lower volume slalom kayaks developed in the late '60's and early '70s. Jim Snyder recalled seeing Eric Evans intentionally "drop his outer rail into the current"[32] to turn the stern of his kayak at the National Slalom Championship in 1970 on the West River. Evans' move was more than just tail sliding the stern of his kayak and it caught Snyder's attention. Offside leans using an edge had been done before, but the full effect of it needed an appropriate time and place for it to take its place in the sport, just like the Duffek stroke in the '50s.

[32] Snyder, James. Interview by author 15 February 1997.

While Hearn, the Lugbills, and Robison developed their new slalom technique with what they learned from their stern pivot moves, Phil Coleman, a racer turned raftguide turned steep creekboater in West Virginia, developed the same moves for kayak. Coleman had his eyes open to the benefits of low volume race boats for river running. Using a Sanna mold that he owned (the same design used to derive the Max II), Coleman made kayaks of heavy lay ups specifically for river running. Sometime around 1979, Coleman described the move he made out of an eddy above Tear Drop in the Cheat Canyon by saying he was "squirted" out of the eddy. The term squirt stuck.

Rodeo

In June of 1977, Joe Leonard, a small raft outfitter in Stanley, initiated the idea of a rodeo for Idaho's paddlers. His idea was simple: a hole-riding contest where a paddler proved he was macho by dropping into a big hole while at the same time being creative and artistic, much like bronco riding. Here was an opportunity to demonstrate river-running skills. The result was the first Stanley Rodeo.

The idea caught on and in the next year, Salmon River Days was added. Word spread and attendance at the rodeos became more than just a reason to show off paddling skills. The rodeos grew, drawing paddlers not only from other western states, but from the East as well. The rodeos became opportunities for paddlers to network and exchange ideas, the same as the early nineteenth century fur trapper rendezvous.

Paddlers from the East, often with an invitation from Blackadar, began to travel to Idaho to paddle in the early '70s. In 1976, Rob Lesser recalled running into only a handful of paddlers from the East including Fearless Fred Young from Illinois and Pete Skinner from New York. Two years later, Lesser counted 26 paddlers from California, Colorado, Kentucky, Illinois, New York, and Wisconsin who attended Idaho's rodeos and paddled Idaho's rivers.

As with cowboy rodeos, the equipment used was the same used in river running. Rodeos became the "Signature of the '70s" for playboating and were an expression of the different styles of paddling.

View From the Bridge

MUCH HAPPENED DURING THE DECADE OF THE '70s, the Golden Age of whitewater. The sport grew considerably and took on many new characteristics. It even took on a younger look.

The growth was fueled by many events, both directly and indirectly associated with the sport itself. The Olympics, *Deliverance*, and Blackadar and the publicity associated with all three certainly contributed. Its excitement and thrills lured a younger, brasher generation, a product of the '60s. The political and sociological changes brought on by the times included environmental and conservation awareness that also contributed to the growth.

The Divergence, begun in the '60s, was finalized in the '70s. Racers and river runners would never to be one again. Racing designs, both slalom and wildwater, became so specialized that only ex-racers used them for river running. Materials, advanced composites and plastics, further reinforced the split. With that split and specialization came new designs specifically for river running and the emergence of a new character, playboating, facilitated by the indestructability of plastics.

This new character became a combination of river-running and playboating. Paddlers, who were formerly called canoeists and kayakists (and later kayakers) in the '60s, finally became known as boaters, even beyond the West where the term originated. Canoes and kayaks became more widely known simply as boats. The industry classified them as whitewater playboats. Boaters affectionately nicknamed plastic boats "Tupperware" boats, after the Tupperware Party fad of the '70s.

The introduction of plastics coincident with the sport's growth and the new character playboating provided the momentum that began to shape the industry and change the facilitators of the sport. No longer were individuals and clubs the only key facilitators. The industry began to take over those roles. However, individual facilitators still left their marks in developing squirt and rodeo. It would be these newest facilitators, those associated with the industry, that would drive the sport during the '80s.

The River was now braided. What had been two channels, simply racing and river running, was now more complex, taking on different characteristics. Racing was more than just slalom and wildwater. It began to expand to competition in general, fed by rodeo, competition for river runners, and playboaters. But the river running channel, too, took on a different character. River running was more than just running a river. It now had a new aspect to it: playboating.

The materials tributary fed both channels. Plastics fed river running and advanced composites fed racing. The currents, the designs and techniques, associated with each channel grew stronger with the increased flow in volume from the new materials.

However, while the currents of the river running channel did not feed into racing, the reverse was sometimes true. This cross-current fed two new sports emerging within river running—squirt and rodeo—and helped to change the character of river running through playboating. The two channels were now much broader encompassing racing-competition and river running-playboating.

Plastics and Playboating: the '80s

BEGINNING IN THE SUMMER OF '72, the Golden Age of the '70s was filled with events that forever affected the course of whitewater. The events brought unprecedented growth and ushered in the beginning of the sport as we recognize it today. The events of the '80s centered around the new subsports from the '70s—squirt and rodeo—offspring of playboating.

We lost our innocence in many different ways. Experts and friends could die on rivers. Laws designed to protect rivers could be ignored. River freedoms could be taken away with quotas. But in the '70s, we also began to learn about how to work within the system rather than **fight it**. In the '80s, we used these lessons to help preserve the essence of our sport: our rivers.

The greater contribution of the '70s, plastics, further shaped the future during the '80s: playboating was a sport driven by plastics. Because of plastics, we gradually lost our homemade inclinations. We could use plastic to buy plastic. We could attempt things we might not have attempted in fiberglass, and we gained free time between paddling weekends because we were free of repairing boats and gear. Our skills developed and playboating grew.

Plastic changed how we paddled. We didn't need to belong to a club in order to build a boat or get instruction. In the '80s, we gravitated away from the regimented club outings and towards small groups of paddlers, which became especially true as whitewater's popularity continued to increase. Dam controlled rivers during the height of paddling season became crowded. Paddlers looking to get away from the crowds found themselves paddling on smaller and smaller rivers and creeks more suitable for smaller groups. Creekboating emerged.

Whitewater was always a chosen lifestyle. But plastics changed the demographics trend of who became a paddler. Two types of paddlers emerged: those that made a living paddling and those that lived for paddling. The sport grew enough to support more than just a few who made a living paddling, paddlers who worked as summer raft guides and winter ski instructors, racers turned instructors, whitewater specialty store owners, manufacturer reps, custom boat builders and designers, and even the eastern (Appalachian) custom wood stick makers.

The excesses of the '80s, with the growing trend toward extreme sports, helped to develop a new paddler demographic that lived for paddling. These new paddlers were often well-educated professionals, yuppies, living in urban settings. They didn't need to make their boats and equipment. Plastic boats and plastic cards took care of that. Living to paddle as an obsession was not new. It was always the hallmark of a whitewater paddler, but now with plastic and paddling schools it was easier for more would-be paddlers to become real paddlers. By the mid-to-late '80s, the first paddlers of the next

1980

Whittemore designs the Millennium Falcon squirtboat

Snyder designs the Baby Arc squirtboat

Perception introduces the Dancer

Hydra introduces the Mustang to compete against Perception

Blue Hole introduces the Sunburst

1985

Snyder designs the Jet, the most popular squirtboat ever

Blue Hole ceases operations

Dagger founded

USCKT formed; ACA loses Olympic canoeing and kayaking sponsorship

NOWR founded

1990

generation—Generation-X—were also lured toward whitewater. Though small in number, their growing numbers would begin to reflect subtle changes in the sport, precursors of major changes to come.

Gary Carlson wrote in 1988 in *American Whitewater* of the young professional's plight who lived for paddling.

> The fact that you spend your weekends dropping over waterfalls, that you wear the same pair of river shorts for 48 straight hours, or that you exercise the discretion of a street person as to where you sleep would not necessarily reinforce your business image. [1]

However, plastic and the industry also took away our individuality. Our boats and gear looked like everyone else's. We became part of the masses of plastic boaters. Squirt was one answer to maintaining our individuality with its mystery moves and graphic boats and helmets that set squirtboaters apart from the rest. Individuality was furthered with the trend of the '80s towards bizarre stunts and "stupid whitewater tricks," which replaced the paddle twirling and simple surfing of the '70s. Rodeo, too, initially became a tool for individuality in the '80s. Like squirt, it became the domain of a small number of paddlers with a desire to be apart from the rest.

The New Facilitators: The Industry (the Plastic Manufacturers)

Whitewater activity, including rafting, continued to grow into the early '80s. In 1979, 40,000 people paid for trips on the American in California. By 1983, the number had risen to 120,000, a three-fold increase. Both Eastern Professional Rafting Outfitters and Western River Guides Association saw an overall increase in the number of people using outfitters for whitewater rafting trips. In 1984, the Coast Guard estimated that more than ten million people paddled canoe or kayak for recreation. The Simmons Research Bureau estimated that 437,000 new and used canoes and kayaks were sold (with no differentiation between whitewater and flatwater usage).

Even in the early '80s, the growth of the sport brought laments from both ends of the paddling spectrum, racers and river runners alike. Some paddlers voiced concern for the sport's inability to grow sufficiently to support all that comes with sheer numbers, "fame and funding for such things as major expeditions, racing facilities, and expanded skills." [2] Others bemoaned the loss of the rivers to the few who were brave enough to tackle them in times past, giving way to the throngs of weekend paddlers. Bart Jackson, editor of *American Whitewater,* wrote in 1980:

> There lies a false premise here, assumed by both sides: the sheer number of paddlers *does not* determine the character, future direction, or enjoyment of whitewater boating. Rather, the nature of our sport springs from the character of its indi-

[1] Carlson, Gary. End Notes. "Adding an Extra 'P' to Yuppie." *American Whitewater* Volume XXXIII, Number 6 (November/December 1988): 42.

[2] Jackson, Bart. Editor's Soapbox. "Growing Pains." *American Whitewater* Vol. XXV No. 6 (November/December 1980): 4.

> vidual participants, blended with their experiences on the river. Frankly, only certain types of people are drawn to whitewater, and the rewards it offers are not truly sought by everybody.

Although Jackson acknowledged that increased numbers of participants brought more clout with conservation and environmental issues and that races drew more contestants, he argued the sport would not change.

> ... it is the character of the individual participants who mold this sport, and because that remains unchanged, I do not forsee any revolution in the whitewater experience due to the larger numbers sharing it. The whitewater boater has been traditionally, and still remains adventurous physically and spiritually, innovative, cheap, and snarlingly independent. The river draws a wide variety of people, but all its devotees hold these traits. For this reason, I see little danger, or hope, of us becoming an intensely commercialized, "big bucks" sport. Though more equipment is being purchased, one of the best selling boating books remains a guide on how to build your own boat. In AWA and most other paddlers' magazines and newsletters, the most read articles are the "how to" pieces. The majority of equipment manufacturers and retailers remain small, survival shops, with less than a handful making the mythical big money strictly out of their whitewater operations. Yes folks, we are, and will continue to remain a home made sport. Curse or cheer as you wish.[3]

Through the early '80s, many manufacturers continued to concentrate on the markets in their regional areas. For most boat manufacturers, shipping continued to be the biggest contributing factor to the market regionalism. In 1980, Old Town and Grumman were some of the few who shipped nationally to a nation-wide network of retailers. But shipping wasn't the only factor. The most obvious resources for nation-wide marketing strategies, national magazines, were also hindered and limited. The three national magazines, *American Whitewater, Canoe,* and *River Runner* had small readerships. *Canoe,* the magazine with the largest readership, averaged fewer than 45,000 through the first half of the '80s. The only tradeshows for paddlesport manufacturers to attend were associated with National Marine Manufacturers Association (NMMA) or Sporting Good Manufacturers Association (SGMA). Paddlesports were a very small part of these shows. Although some paddlesport manufacturers attended, their marketing met with limited success because many of the smaller specialty outdoor retailers, who often carried paddlesport equipment, often did not attend these large shows. Rep networks that targeted the small outdoor retailers proved to be the more effective. Rep associations for outdoor products formed in both the East and West in the '80s to assist manufacturers and reps.

By the mid-80s, marketing as a whole for the outdoor sports market had grown enough to warrant its own magazine and tradeshow. In 1981, *Outdoor Retailer,* a magazine targeted for retailers in the outdoor market, began pub-

[3] Jackson, Bart. Editor's Soapbox. "Growing Pains." *American Whitewater* Vol. XXV No. 6 (November/December 1980): 4.

lication. The following year in 1982, the publishers of *Outdoor Retailer* sponsored their first show for outdoor products in Las Vegas. Paddlesports were a small part of the show with less than about a half dozen manufacturers present.

In the Fall of 1985, *Canoe*, under the leadership of its publisher Judy Harrison, sponsored a seminar to help grow the paddlesport market. She presented the results of market research for paddlesports that *Canoe* had earlier contracted. In 1986, the seminar became known as the First Annual Canoe and Kayak Industry Seminar and was co-sponsored by *Canoe* and *Outdoor Retailer.* Attendees included manufacturers, dealers, and representatives from ACA and National Association of Canoe Liveries and Outfitters (NACLO). Seminar sessions included topics such as advertising and insurance, effective dealer marketing, industry economics, and sports promotion. One of the hottest topics was risk management and the cost and availability of liability insurance. In 1987, *Canoe* pulled in other sponsors including DuPont because of the large market for their product, Kevlar, among canoe manufacturers. Attendance at the annual seminars continued to grow. In 1988, the seminar moved in with *Outdoor Retailer*'s yearly show, which also provided a venue for the manufacturers to showcase their products to retailers and buyers. Within ten years, one-third of the booths at *Outdoor Retailer*'s Summer Market was associated with paddlesports.

Industry attendees at the 1986 seminar voted to organize a trade organization, this time though, one that included kayak manufacturers. In September 1987, North American Paddlesports Association (NAPSA) was formed representing all paddlesport manufacturers, whitewater and flatwater alike. In 1988, NAPSA designated *Outdoor Retailers*' Expo West show as the official trade show for paddlesports. [*Author's note:* NAPSA continued to represent the bulk of the paddlesport industry until 1999 when it merged with the Trade Association for Sea Kayaking (TASK). The new organization representing all paddlesport manufacturers is now the Trade Association for Paddlesports (TAPS).]

NAPSA's purpose was to provide information and resources to grow the industry by growing the number of participants. This meant providing assistance and promotion beyond the paddlesport industry through outdoor writers and ad agencies. NAPSA hired Jeff Blumenthal of Blumenthal Agency, an ad agency, who helped to expand the promotion of paddlesports with a media kit campaign. The media kits, which included product explanations, manufacturer and retailer lists, and photos, were sent to over 5,000 ad agencies, newspapers, and other media. As a result of the media kit campaign, images of paddlesports began to proliferate in all kinds of media. Whitewater caught everyone's attention. Whitewater kayaks appeared in Mountain Dew ads and canoes appeared in Chevy Blazer ads.

Blumenthal also suggested the use of brighter colors in paddlesport products (prior to his suggestion, red and green canoes dominated the market). His idea was to draw attention to the brightly colored boats on top of a vehicle. This use of color served both the boat owner's and the manufacturer's purposes. Many of the manufacturers took his advice and expanded their color selection to include brighter colors.

All of the marketing efforts to expand the paddlesport market and the industry began to pay off. In a survey taken by *Canoe,* paddlesports, not just whitewater grew 33 percent between 1983 and 1987.[4]

BART JACKSON, as many others, did not see it coming when he wrote in 1980: "I see little danger, or hope, of us becoming an intensely commercialized, 'big bucks' sport."[5] Many did not anticipate the changing role of the industry as facilitators of the sport. Some did, though. Perception did; Bill Masters did, and they led the way.

Perception

With its entrance and acceptance by paddlers in the '70s, plastics were ready to drive the market into the '80s. For whitewater, this was particularly true. For the whitewater industry entering the '80s, it was plastic kayaks.

Aside from the market's acceptance of plastics by whitewater paddlers, another factor that contributed to their acceptance was their profitability for the retailer. Fiberglass kayaks were historically sold at $100 over production cost (a costly labor-intensive process) in order to remain within a competitive price range of backyard builders and homemade boats. This left very little room for profitability for both the manufacturer and the dealer. In contrast, rotational molding was a less expensive process in labor and materials (although mold costs often ranged from $20,000 to $35,000 excluding the cost of the rotational molding equipment). The savings to dealers for rotomolded kayaks allowed them to realize profits as high as 40 percent which was in the range of accessories' gross profit of 40 to 45 percent.

One company, Perception, was poised to take control, to dominate and shape the industry's future. In 1980, Perception had a complete line of whitewater products: two rotomolded kayaks, the Quest and Mirage, Royalex canoes including the HD1, and paddling accessories. In order to see for himself what all the talk was about concerning rodeo, Bill Masters flew out for the Stanley Rodeo. While there, Masters met Ken Horwitz, a Boise retailer and Hollowform dealer. During their meeting, the two men discovered that they had the same entrepreneurial skills and ideas. Later that summer, Masters hired Horwitz for Perception's sales and marketing. Horwitz's goal for Perception "was to turn Perception into the North Face of the whitewater industry."[6]

Horwitz proceeded to establish a rep network hiring known whitewater boaters, an idea he borrowed from other sports industries. Having been a retailer, Horwitz also understood many of the problems encountered by small specialty store dealers. He established a pattern for successful distribution across the country based on honesty and loyalty with dealers. Horwitz also limited the number of dealers in a given area to protect a dealer's territory and market.

During the '80s, Masters developed a reputation for ruthlessness in protecting his market share with aggressive business tactics. After all, he had spent considerable effort to not only expand the market for himself, but for the sport. In 1982, Perception had an estimated 33 percent share of the kayak market, followed by 25 percent for Hollowform, and 15 percent for Phoenix.

[4] Walbridge, Charlie (Safety). "Study of Whitewater Fatalities Reveals Relative Safety of Sport." *American Whitewater* Vol. XXXV No. 3 (May/June 1990): 24.

[5] Jackson, Bart. Editor's Soapbox. "Growing Pains." *American Whitewater* Vol. XXV No. 6 (November/December 1980): 4.

[6] McCourtney, Dave. "AWA Interview with Ken Horwitz." *American Whitewater* Vol. XXX No. 4 (July/August 1985): 33–38.

The remaining was comprised of the rest of the kayak manufacturers, both whitewater and flatwater combined.[7] [*Author's note:* This indicated that up to two-thirds of the kayak market was whitewater.]

As long as Hollowform was a competitor, Perception targeted ads at Hollowform's weaknesses, often associated with interior pillar design that could lead to hull collapse as well as hull thickness variability (and therefore flexing and oil canning). In 1981, Perception's ads highlighted their own strengths:

> Special design: interior pillars lock under the seat.
>
> Engineeering design: special ridge around entire cockpit to reduce chance of hull disfiguration.
>
> Adjustable seat for safest positioning of boater.
>
> Ultrasonically tested hull thickness varies for maximum strength and wear points.
>
> Thigh braces designed to position and hold front pillars secure against lateral slippage.
>
> "They ain't what they used to be!"[8]

After Hollowform ceased production of River Chasers, Masters was concerned that Tom Johnson might help someone else get started in the plastic kayak market. By this time, Perception had exclusive domain on the market and wanted to keep it that way. Masters sent Horwitz to visit Tom and Virginia Johnson in California to hire Johnson on retainer for Perception. "They [Tom and Virginia] saw right through the offer for a 'retainer' which would have neutralized Tom on the market or at least guaranteed his designs would only come through Perception."[9]

[*Author's note:* Regarding the actual kayak market size in the early '80s, the manufacturers themselves were, and still are, mum about their actual numbers. Bob Woodward wrote in 1982,

> Let the manufacturers speak for themselves: "7 to 9,000," Bill Masters [Perception]. "Smaller than most people think it is," Tom Wilson [Phoenix]. Elmer Good [Hollowform], "3,000?" Joe Sedivec [Seda], "5 to 10,000."[10]]

As Specialty Markets Consulting Services, operated through Perception, Horwitz and Masters assisted dealers with their businesses and marketing by educating them in how to become and remain successful. In March of 1981, Perception began its own newsletter, *Eddy Line,* that not only provided the latest product news and information to their dealers but also provided a means to disseminate information from dealers to other dealers. The same year, Perception also began annual attendance at NSGA shows and later *Outdoor Retailer* market shows to show dealers the new products available for the coming season.

[7] Woodward, Bob. "Kayak Industry Review/Preview." *National Outdoor Outfitters News* (January/February 1982): 27–29.

[8] Perception Ad. *American Whitewater* Vol. XXVI No. 2 (March/April 1981): 12.

[9] McCourtney, Dave. "AWA Interview with Ken Horwitz." *American Whitewater* Vol. XXX No. 4 (July/August 1985): 33–38.

[10] Editor. "Annual Canoe, Kayak, and Inflatable Reports." *National Outdoor Outfitters News* (January/February 1982): 8.

Under the name Ken Meysan, Horwitz penned articles for *Outdoor Retailer* that provided information to all retailers, not just Perception dealers, regarding canoe, kayak, and raft selection and marketing.

Perception kayaks, with their distinctive flowing water tape lines, were readily recognizable in non-Perception ads for paddling gear and accessories including Bermuda drysuits, Patagonia paddling clothes, Extrasport PFDs, and European manufacturer Harishock PFDs. Perception's consumer marketing also expanded beyond paddlesport magazines, capitalizing on the growing interest of non-paddlers in articles in *Adventure Travel*, *Outside*, and *Women's Sports*. A Mountain Dew ad appeared on TV showing a paddler in a Perception kayak making an eddy turn at the bottom of a drop. The ad left the impression that the river was in the Southeast, which played on both the origin of mountain dew, the name of home-brewed whiskey in the mountains in the South, and the movie *Deliverance*.

Perception was the first manufacturer to acknowledge and market the growing female population of whitewater paddlers. A *Women's Sports* issue (June 1981) featured an article featuring women in whitewater titled "Whitewater Reflections" by Lee Green. The article contained a full-page photograph of Jamie Grant using a Perception kayak and gear with Perception logos prominently displayed. The issue also contained an ad with the often used photograph of Kathy Blau doing a pop-up at the Stanley Rodeo in 1980 followed with text customized, as quotes from instructors, for the magazine:

> The lower skeletal structure of a female gives distinct advantages to the student. She'll pick-up the rhythm of the river and grasp control of the boat faster than her male counterpart.
>
> The woman kayaker always learns faster that technique, rather than muscle, is the secret and beauty of the sport. [11]

[*Author's note:* In 1989, Perception introduced the first plastic kayak, the Dancer XS, designed specifically for smaller paddlers. The kayak was designed to perform for 80 to 120 pound paddlers and met the need for small women and young paddlers.]

Aside from direct marketing and sales, Horwitz encouraged participation in conservation causes that directly affected the sport. In 1980, Perception sponsored the annual Conservation Award presented each year in October to a group or individual who contributed greatly to the preservation of free flowing rivers. The first Conservation Award went to David Brown of the Ocoee River Council for his efforts to preserve access to the Ocoee. Prior to working for Perception, Horwitz was embroiled in the preservation issues involving the North Fork of the Payette. Horwitz was also active in supporting AWA's conservation efforts.

After Horwitz left Perception in 1982, Perception continued expanding its marketing and "good citizen" efforts under the direction of Joe Pulliam. [*Author's note*: Pulliam met Masters in 1973 while both were at Clemson, building composite boats.] Perception sponsored Citizen's Races (slalom races) at NOC to encourage participation and exposure to slalom for the average paddler.

[11] Perception Ad. *Women's Sports* (June 1981): 57.

The meeting of Masters and Horwitz and their subsequent work together launched Perception on a successful marketing path that set the standard for the whitewater industry and established Perception as the market's leader. However, sales and marketing alone were not the only reasons for Perception's success. Perception provided good quality products and designs that met the changing needs of the sport throughout the '80s.

Bill Masters and Allan Stancil recognized that boats being used by river runners were still based on 4-meter (13' 2") slalom designs. They kept that standard for the Quest and Mirage. In 1981, they decided to focus on river-running performance. Instead of keeping the 4-meter standard, they developed their third design, the Eclipse, at 12 feet in length (12' 1"). Unfortunately, the Eclipse did not perform as well as expected. Masters and Stancil had still not figured out finished-hull shrinkage based on aluminum and plastic shrinkage for rotational molding. The Eclipse's finished shape after molding was not proportioned well. However, the Eclipse helped to break the 4-meter barrier. In 1982, Masters and Stancil finally got it right with their fourth kayak design, the Dancer at 11' 6" in length.

In 1982, Masters bought a piece of Aquaterra, a manufacturer of paddling accessories. The next year, Masters discretely started TREK as a direct competitor of Hydra. TREK introduced the Blazer kayak, a medium-low volume whitewater playboat, at an introductory low price of $379.95. Within a year, TREK folded into Aquaterra who marketed the Blazer as a touring kayak. The Blazer was similar to Perception's first kayak, the Quest. Aquaterra also produced the Mystic, a high volume river-touring kayak designed by Tom Johnson, from molds Masters purchased from Hollowform's new owner when that company ceased kayak production.

Masters continued to pursue the non-whitewater paddling market through Aquaterra, which eventually grew into a large business on its own with touring, then seakayaking, then sit-on-tops. [*Author's note:* Because the touring market was unproven at the time, Masters chose to keep the two companies separate. In 1989, Masters purchased Aquaterra outright. In 1997, the Aquaterra name was dropped completely, folding Aquaterra's products into Perception's product lines.]

Masters had a larger build, more suitable for larger volume kayaks, than his friend and co-designer, Stancil. Until the Dancer, all their designs were geared to accommodate paddlers up to 200 pounds. Stancil wanted a smaller volume boat for paddlers in the 150 to 180 pound range. With the increasing popularity of short composite boats, a shorter plastic boat met this demand. The Dancer was a short boat with a lot of rocker starting amidships in contrast to the Mirage that incorporated very little rocker until the ends. Other paddlers laughed at the shortness of the first prototype in fiberglass. The first time Stancil paddled it, he found it caught eddies really well without trying, perhaps too well, and he thought they had made a mistake. However, as he continued paddling, Stancil, a solid Class III paddler, found that he started outdoing much better paddlers. He attributed this to the boat, which prompted Masters and Stancil to rethink what they were looking for. After eight prototypes, the Dancer was finally produced in plastic. The name Dancer came from the fact that it "danced" in comparison to other boats. It was certainly quicker for spinning because of the amount of rocker incorporated in the design.

In marketing the Dancer, Perception advertised it as:

> The ultimate precision kayak. Radically short. Low volume. Uniquely designed for both Eastern and Western whitewater... Perfect for catching eddies, playing holes, pop ups.[12]

The Dancer with its short, high performance hull became the future of the sport. It permanently established Perception's position in the market and helped to solidify the trend toward short playboats.

"Gaggle of Dancers" South Fork of the Payette (ID), 1984 —courtesy of Rob Lesser.

Perception continued introducing designs reflective of current trends in the sport. In 1983, Hollowform was out of business and another competitor, Hydra, had yet to establish itself. In 1984, Perception introduced the Gyramax, designed by Stancil with the assistance of Davey Hearn. It was a low volume C-1 in contrast to the Sage C-1 design.

The following year, the Sabre was introduced as the first radical hard-edged plastic boat. It borrowed heavily from squirtboating and was very reminiscent of Whittemore's long squirt designs. Although the ads for the Sabre clearly capitalized on squirtboating, no reference was made that it was designed as a squirtboat. Instead, the ads called it "**3-D**imensional Paddling Fun."

> Small, flat and fast, Sabre is the 3-Dimensional kayak advanced paddlers have been waiting for... When you're in your kayak, on the top of the water, you're in an 'X, Y' plane—left and

[12] Perception Ad. *American Whitewater* Vol. XXVIII No. 4 (July/August 1983): 34.

right, forward and backward. But at the end of a drop, or whenever your boat plunges underneath the water, you're in a 3-Dimensional world, 'X, Y, and Z'. The Sabre allows you to respond to those underlying currents with a symmetrical new Hydrofoil™ design. Hydrofoil makes use of the river currents through which it passes, the same way the wing of an aerobatic airplane makes use of air currents to lift and pivot. We call it Aquabatics™. [13]

The last boat Masters designed himself was the Corsica in the late '80s. After that, Masters relied on other boat designers to keep Perception in the forefront of the market.

THE NAME GYRAMAX came from a combination of Masters' patented and trademarked Gyraflow™ rotational molding process and the Max series of slalom C-1's design by Davey Hearn.

Author's note: At publication, Masters has twenty-one patents in his name related to kayaking or canoeing and associated accessories and gear. He also has four patents related to rotational molding. Masters also trademarked many terms, particularly related to squirtboating, although was often not the first to use the terms.

In addition to introducing and setting a precedent for marketing and business tactics in establishing the dominance of Perception in the whitewater market, Masters also filed for patents and trademarks to further reinforce and maintain Perception's position.

Ever conscious of safety and potential legal liabilities associated with whitewater, Perception learned from Hollowform's mistakes regarding quality of the design and rotomolded hull. Masters designed and patented interior tubular pillars used in the early model kayaks ("Supportive framework for a boat" Patent No. 4, 227, 272 October 14, 1980). He later patented the seat that locked the whole system in place ("Frame system for kayak" Patent No. 4, 407, 216 October 4, 1983) that alleviated many of the problems such as hull collapse associated with River Chasers.

Although weight was a problem compared to composite boats, Masters did not lighten the amount of plastic used in the hull with resultant loss of hull thickness for fear of deck-hull collapse. Instead, at the advice of Don Banducci, an instructor at Sundance, Perception offered foam pillars as a replacement to the rigid rotomolded plastic pillars. Mirage II models were the first to have foam pillars.

In 1986, to further provide insurance in case of any safety related lawsuits, Perception hired Les Bechdel as a safety advisor. Bechdel, co-author of *River Rescue*, conducted on-site river rescue workshops for outfitters, whitewater schools, and Perception dealers that benefitted the entire sport.

DURING THE '80S, Perception established itself as the market leader in whitewater. Under Masters' business leadership, Perception became the most successful and dominant whitewater paddlesport company in America. But the success was not limited to Perception alone, the success spread to the entire market. As Horwitz explained:

> Through the strength of Masters' business skills and Pete Jett's production skill, my marketing allowed us to teach store owners across the country that kayaks did belong next to their downhill skis and sleeping bags. Once this happened, customers saw kayaks six days a week, ten hours a day and began to get interested in learning. [14]

Perception became the first American paddlesport company to expand into Europe on any scale exporting American produced whitewater boats and products. Finally, American products were in demand in Europe instead of the

[13] Perception Ad. *Canoe* Vol. 13 No. 2 (April 1985): 15.

[14] McCourtney, Dave. "AWA Interview with Ken Horwitz." *American Whitewater* Vol. XXX No. 4 (July/August 1985): 33–38.

reverse. In 1981, Perception licensed Ace (A.C. Canoe Products, manufacturer of Ace helmets) in Britain to manufacture and distribute Perception products. This was replicated in the mid-'80s in New Zealand, and in Japan by the end of the '80s.

Aside from Masters' recognized success in the whitewater market, his efforts were recognized far beyond even the paddlesport industry. In 1984, Perception was chosen "Business of the Year" in South Carolina. Masters' efforts as a businessman were also recognized when he was named Chairman of the Federal Reserve Board in Charlotte.

Other Plastic Kayak Manufacturers

Although Perception dominated the plastic kayak market (and C-1 market, small though it was) through much of the '80s, other companies attempted to garner a share of the market with limited success. In 1982, Hollowform ceased production of the River Chaser, its only viable whitewater kayak model. Hollowform's position in the market was replaced by a very similar company, Plastics Industries (Hydra), also a plastics molder. By the mid-'80s, Prijon, a well-known European manufacturer and designer of composite boats, also entered the plastic kayak market with blow molded kayaks. Another company, Noah, entered the plastic kayak fray during the mid-'80s with short-lived, limited, and regional success.

In 1981, Whitewater Boats in Cedar City, Utah, introduced two kayaks, the low volume Lochsa and high volume model Salmon designs of Dick Held, with Royalex hulls and fiberglass decks designed "to reduce the danger of entrapment."[15] (Both designs were based on Duffek's design of the '60s.) Developed at the same time and announced in the same *Canoe* issue was Old Town's all-Royalex Oltonar kayak, a Lettmann Mark IV design. Neither company's Royalex kayaks caught on. This was in part due to their late entry into the market but also to the one-piece advantages of rotomolded kayaks over two-piece thermoformed kayaks.

Hydra

Plastic Industries of Athens, Tennessee, an injection molding company, wanted to enter the rotational molding market and saw potential in rotationally molded kayaks. They contacted Tom Johnson. In early 1981, Johnson already owned an aluminum mold to produce a new 13-foot design when Plastic Industries contacted him. With no one else to mold it for him, he jumped at the chance to work with Plastic Industries. His new 13-foot design became Plastic Industries' first rotomolded kayak model which they marketed as the Taurus. Their first ads appeared in late spring touting it as "the finest whitewater kayak in the world."[16] By the time the first ads appeared, Plastic Industries had hired Ken Horwitz, formerly of Perception, and started Hydra as a division of Plastic Industries. Ken Horwitz was responsible for choosing the name Hydra.

Horwitz began a concerted effort to expand Hydra's product line. Johnson contributed two additional designs, the Centaur C-1, lower volume than Perception's Sage C-1, and the Duet C-2. The Duet was the first and only plastic C-2. The cockpits were offset but were not as close to the ends as older end-hole C-2s. The Duet's cockpits were about 5 feet from the ends. In 1983,

[15] Whitewater Boats Ad. *Canoe* Vol. 9 No. 1 (February 1981): 10.

[16] Plastic Industries, Inc. Ad. *Canoe* Vol. 10 No. 3 (June 1982): 3.

Paddler in a Hydra Taurus on the South Fork of the Payette (ID), 1984 —courtesy of Rob Lesser.

Hydra molded Don McClaran's P-51 Mustang, a short kayak (12-foot) he co-designed with Paul Lemke in 1980. The P-51 Mustang had been previously produced as a composite boat by Class VI of Utah. For a time, Hydra's Mustang and Perception's Dancer went head to head in the market. The Dancer was introduced in March and the Mustang in June. However, in October 1984, Plastic Industries decided to get out of the rotational molding business and sold Hydra to Bob Grossman of Rotocast Plastic Products of Tennessee, a custom rotational molder. This put Hydra in the same business situation and disadvantage as Hollowform had been, a non-whitewater oriented rotational molding company producing products for the paddlesport market.

In addition to the whitewater market, Hydra under Horwitz's direction, entered the non-whitewater paddlesport market to compete with Masters' Aquaterra. In 1984, Hydra produced the Minnow designed by Ann Dwyer (who later owned Kiwi Kayaks) and a sit-on-top waveski designed by Danny Broadhurst. Hydra also later entered the sea kayak market. [*Author's note:* Hydra is still owned by Bob Grossman of Rotocast of Tennessee.]

Horwitz left Hydra when Grossman purchased it, although some of the gorilla marketing tactics he introduced to take on Perception were continued. Under Grossman, Hydra went headlong into competition with Perception, even entering trademark and patent disputes with Masters. Like Masters with Perception, Grossman also supported other paddlesport activities to further the Hydra name. In 1985, Grossman donated $25,000 in seed money to the Knoxville Canoe and Kayak Festival. Not so coincidentally, Hydra's new manufacturing facility was in Knoxville.

In 1985, at their new facility with a new rock-n-roll oven, Hydra switched to a linear and repairable polyethylene whose name they trademarked, Tuf-Lite™. At the time, Perception still molded with cross-link resins that were not repairable. Hydra also patented its own footbrace.

Just as early Perception ads targeted Hollowform's weaknesses, Hydra's ads targeted Perception's weaknesses:

Noah

In 1977, Vladimir Vanha, a Czech defector, started Noah. He advertised his company as a combination of Czech designs and American technology and materials. After relocating his company from New York to North Carolina near NOC, Noah developed a following for his composite boats, the latest slalom designs, among local boaters. In 1983, Vahna introduced the Jeti, based on Snyder's Slice design, a short composite playboat 10 feet in length. The following year, Noah introduced the Jeti in plastic (rotationally molded cross-link plastic) with a final molded length of 9' 10". It soon attracted a following of its own and was affectionately referred to as the "spud boat" (as in potato-shaped) by its supporters, particularly in the Southeast. Though dismissed as a fad by its detractors, the Jeti gained popularity among instructors as a teaching boat and among diehard paddlers as a good playboat or steep creekboat.

Slim Ray, co-author of *River Rescue,* wrote, and predicted, during the water test of the Jeti for *Canoe:* "Short boats, of which the Jeti is currently the ultimate example, are here to stay." [18]

Vahna did not mold his own plastic boats. Instead, he contracted the molding using molds that he owned. When arrangements with his local rotational molder fell through for molding the Jeti, he sought other arrangements. This included pursuing blow molding instead of rotational molding for his new design, the Aeroquatic. He was able to contract its production using a custom blow molder in Chicago. In 1986, Noah announced its use of a new plastic for the rotationally molded Jeti, a higher density linear polyethylene, and introduced a new design, the Aeroquatic which eventually became known simply as the AQ. Two things were unique about the Aeroquatic: the 11-foot Aeroquatic had a set of shallow grooves starting behind the seat, called Accelerators™, inspired by evolution in surfboard designs; and it was blow molded, the first (and only) blow molded kayak produced in America.

Vahna received un-outfitted molded hulls at his facility in North Carolina where he completed the hulls for sale. The first few years of production went well with his blow molder in Chicago. However, the company was sold and the new owner was not interested in molding kayaks for Vahna. About the same time, it was discovered that the molder had produced about 1,500 kayaks using resin with no UV stabilizers. The kayaks were defective. The molder did not back his product and Vahna was stuck with 1,500 bad boats. Although Vahna had already pre-sold many of the boats and collected money for them, he did not have the money to replace the defective boats or return the money already collected. In 1989, a fire wiped out Noah's entire uninsured facility and inventory.

VLADIMIR VAHNA originally contracted the molding of his Jeti to Perception. Perception also molded Ann Dwyer's Minnow kayak for a time. Both arrangements were eventually terminated requiring both Vahna and Dwyer to seek other arrangements.

TWO SMALL AMERICAN COMPANIES entered the market with plastic kayaks in the late '80s: Infinity of Idaho and Wave Sports of Colorado. Both initially contracted out the molding of their single kayak designs. Infinity had their Infinity model and Wave Sport had their Lazer model. However, their entrance into the market was initially barely noticed except in their small regional markets.

[18] Ray, Slim. "Water Test: Noah Jeti Grande." *Canoe* Vol. 13 No. 1 (February/March 1985): 70, 76.

FROM THE VIEWPOINT OF BOAT DESIGN IN THE '80S, the Dancer was **the** boat—the first for many paddlers. It was fun and easy to paddle. Once the Dancer caught on, there were no boats that competed on equal footing. The only alternative to the Dancer were designs from Hydra and Noah. However, with the exception of the Mustang and later the Dragonfly, Hydra's designs were behind the times and Hydra's marketing didn't match Perception's. Perception's marketing made sure the Mustang and Dragonfly couldn't compete against the Dancer. Hydra's Centaur C-1 and Duet C-2 were just very small pieces of the market. Noah's Jeti was good and NOC pushed it through their classes. But Vahna was a one-man show. He was clever but didn't have the business skills to compete on anything but a regional basis. Paddlers influenced by NOC paddled the Jeti while everyone else across the country paddled the Dancer. Prijon's designs, the T-Slalom, T-Canyon, and Invader, were not competitive with the Dancer but they were not designed to be so.

Until 1990, Perception had no real competition in the plastic whitewater kayak market. That changed when Dagger, a Canoe company, introduced the Response, their entry into the whitewater kayak market.

Plastic Short Canoe Manufacturers

Mad River in the Northeast and Blue Hole in the Southeast dominated the plastic whitewater canoe market going into the '80s. Although Mad River did not intentionally enter the short whitewater canoe design fray in the '80s, some of their canoes qualified. With the exception of the ME and Flashback (both John Berry designs based on European slalom C-1 and C-2 designs), Mad River did not specifically target whitewater paddlers, but two of their canoes designed by Jim Henry, the Explorer (16-foot) and the Courier (14' 10"), were often used by whitewater paddlers.

In general, Mad River's whitewater canoe designs tended toward open canoe racing, both slalom and downriver, owing to their location in the Northeast with its focus toward open canoe racing, and the Henrys' interest in racing and wilderness canoe tripping. However, beyond canoe designs, Mad River's marketing encouraged whitewater growth just as Perception's did. In the early '80s, Mad River sponsored instructional weekends with ACA instructors across the country including dealers in the Midwest (Wisconsin), West, (Colorado), Southeast (North Carolina), and Northeast (Massachusetts). In 1985, this evolved into demo days called "You Can Canoe! Days" held at many of their dealers across the country supported by Mad River experts that traveled the country in RVs pulling trailer loads of boats.

Blue Hole, on the other hand, intentionally designed for, and marketed to, whitewater paddlers. In 1983, Blue Hole started the trend of marketing short solo canoes specifically designed for whitewater that were not just takeoffs from slalom C-1 and C-2 designs. Blue Hole's Sunburst, a 14' 6" design from Steve Scarborough, was the first. But it was Nolan Whitesell's 14' 3" solo Piranha design that revolutionized the ideas behind successful short solo whitewater canoes. By the mid-'80s, short solo whitewater canoes were being designed specifically for river running, and specifically as solo canoes.

But it was more than just the designs that allowed solo open canoeing to become an important part of the open canoe market in the '80s. Advances in technique helped to push the limits and expand into the realm of closed boats with descents of Class IV and V rivers. Solo whitewater canoeing technique evolved with design. Robert Harrison, Nolan Whitesell, and other open boaters of the Southeast drove these new advances in technique based on traditional whitewater skills and strokes. For both Harrison and Whitesell, the advances included keeping the river out of the canoe and using the river to do so. For Whitesell, it meant designing canoes to take advantage of his particular style of paddling that continued to evolve in conjunction with his design. For Harrison, precision maneuvers were the key. "The harder the rapid, the smaller your margin of error, and the greater the emphasis on precision."

Bob Foote on the North Fork of the American (CA), 1982 —courtesy of Carl Trost.

Harrison explained his technique:

> Start by "dissecting" a questionable rapid while scouting it. Recognize and isolate its particular waves, holes, eddylines and cross-currents. Then decide which holes and waves will put water in the canoe. Devise a route to avoid them, utilizing the remaining features of the rapid to your best advantage. Use your paddle to make minor corrections in the position, angle and momentum of the canoe. Let the river do the rest. [19]

Harrison broke this down even further regarding whitewater difficulty in general in relation to open canoes.

> Generally a canoe takes on water while diving straight off a ledge or into a hole, cutting through standing waves or being hit by a breaking wave. It only follows then, to stay dry, don't dive off ledges or into holes, don't cut through standing waves and don't let any waves break over the canoe. [20]

Traditional tandem canoeing techniques also evolved. By the early '80s, the use of the eddy turn pry by the bow partner in C-2 and OC-2 had almost disappeared. Although McNair's *Basic River Canoeing* which advised use of the pry was still widely used, later versions of AMC's *Whitewater Handbook* discontinued its use and replaced it with the cross-draw. Although traditional OC-2 designs did not change to affect the use of the eddy turn pry, racing OC-2s adopted the same close-centered approach as found in the new offset, close-centered cockpit designs of C-2s.

In end-hole C-2s (or traditional OC-2s), the placement of the bow person at the end of the boat made kayak style spins difficult. However, when a end-hole C-2 entered an eddy, a bow pry was very effective and allowed the boat to pivot into the eddy away from the pry. On the other hand, in close-center configurations (and with flatter hulls and more rocker) the boat could spin like a kayak around its center. The bow pry in this situation actually stops the forward momentum of the boat, cutting down the effectiveness of the turn. The

Jim Shelander of California (formerly a Southeast paddler) ran the Grand Canyon in 1979 in a Mad River Explorer. Two years later his friend, Robert Harrison of South Carolina, repeated the feat in an ME. This was followed by Nolan Whitesell in the early '80s and later by Bob Foote in an ME with his friend Bill Behrendt, both California boaters (and exceptions to the dominance of Southeast open boaters). Since that time, numerous open boaters have made successful runs down big water runs like the Grand Canyon and small steep creek runs from the Southeast to California.

[19] Harrison, Robert. "Solo Whitewater Canoeing." *River Runner* Vol. 13 No. 2 (April 1985): 32–33, 36–38.

[20] Ibid.

ROLLING AN OPEN CANOE was not new, although it became more standard practice among boaters with the advent of better outfitting.

In the early '60s, canoeists experimented with rolling techniques for covered open canoes, although inadequate outfitting along with the use of wider and longer canoes hindered its practicality on rivers.

cross draw in the bow both turns the boat and keeps the forward momentum going. Although both paddles are on the same side, the effectiveness and use of controlled leans further reinforces the use of the cross draw stroke.

By the mid-80's, outfitting evolved to meet the demands of the new designs. New solo techniques included rolling open canoes, which further helped to push the limits of river-running. Outfitting was no longer an afterthought. It was more than just leaning against a thwart and styrafoam for flotation. Outfitting was customized for the boater. Mad River no longer installed thwarts in standard locations for whitewater canoes but left it up to the buyer to install them where needed. Perception's rotomolded saddle became popular as well as ethafoam saddles (pedestals). Kneeling height dropped following the style of the C-1 turned OC-1 paddlers like Kent Ford. Twelve inches was too high and was lowered to 9 or 10 inches, or whatever was comfortable before the legs went numb. However, with all the advances in whitewater open boat paddling, particularly OC-1, it remained a niche market in the Southeast, the home of many of the advances in the '80s.

Whitewater solo canoes were not the designs that took off in the '80s. Flatwater, wilderness tripping, and freestyle solo canoes proliferated from designers like Mike Galt, Jim Henry, Gene Jensen, Pat Moore, John Winters, and David Yost.

Blue Hole

By the early '80s, market pressure from Mad River's ME and Perception's HD1 hurt Blue Hole's sales of the OCA model, originally introduced in 1975 before shorter canoes hit the market. The pressure was on for Blue Hole to introduce a shorter and drier boat than the OCA. Steve Scarborough came forward and told Bob Lantz and Roy Guinn that he could design a short canoe for them. In 1983, Scarborough's design, Sunburst, at 14'6" in length, became the first whitewater solo canoe under 15 feet in length that was not based on a slalom C-1 design.

Two years later, Blue Hole introduced the Scarborough-designed stretched 16' 6" Starburst. Although it was a good design, it went the "wrong way."[21] The market trend was toward shorter canoes, not longer canoes. Both Whitesell and Mohawk already had short canoe designs that competed with the Sunburst. [*Author's note:* The Starburst was actually a better design than Blue Hole's own OCA. The OCA was poor on secondary stability. It had a breakpoint. The Starburst had great secondary stability with no breakpoint. The Starburst actually competed well against the OCA model.]

In spite of competition among canoe manufacturers, there was also cooperation among manufacturers. Blue Hole sold the original OCA hull, which used aluminum gunwales, with both plastic and wood, to meet market demand. For the model with vinyl gunwales (model OCV), Blue Hole obtained vinyl gunwales from Mohawk. Mohawk used black vinyl and Blue Hole used brown. Because of the quantities ordered by Mohawk, Blue Hole actually benefitted from a cost savings when Mohawk tacked on Blue Hole's gunwale order to their own. For the model with wood gunwales (model OCB), Blue Hole shipped unfinished hulls to Merrimack Canoe where they were outfitted with oiled wood.

[21] Lantz, Bob. Interview by author 11 May 1997.

In 1986, in order to remain competitive with a short solo canoe, the Sunburst II was introduced as an improved version of the original. With higher ends, a deeper center, and more rounded entry lines, the Sunburst II corrected some of the wetness problems of the original design. The additional freeboard also provided more capacity for heavier paddlers.

By this time, Blue Hole had hit $1 million in sales a couple of times. Lantz wanted to do more. After watching Perception's explosive entry into the whitewater kayak market, Lantz was convinced rotational molding was the way to go for canoes, too. He contacted Bob Grossman of Rotocast Plastics in Miami to contract molding of a rotationally molded canoe. [*Author's note:* This was before Grossman formed Rotocast Plastic Products of Tennessee or owned Hydra.] Grossman agreed and Lantz provided a mold based on the Starburst design. Two years later, Grossman was still unsuccessful in molding the canoe.

Unfortunately, in anticipation of having rotationally molded canoes to outfit, Lantz extended the business financially with the purchase of an adjacent building. Lantz even bought out Roy Guinn's share of Blue Hole. Ultimately, Blue Hole was unable to recover financially. In 1989, Blue Hole's assets were liquidated and sold as a unit, molds and all, to Michicraft canoes, an aluminum canoe manufacturer in Michigan. Blue Hole, the first company to design and market plastic whitewater canoes, was lost in the increasingly competitive and changing plastic whitewater canoe market.

Michicraft produced a few plastic canoes but soon sold off everything at auction to Bill Masters. Masters in turn sold it all a few years later to a buyer in Virginia who now produces the OCA, Starburst, and Sunburst II models.

Canoes by Whitesell

Nolan Whitesell began his whitewater paddling doing traditional whitewater on rivers. In 1983, a new window of whitewater opened for him when he purchased a Sunburst from Blue Hole. Whitesell outfitted the front and rear sections of the canoe with airbags leaving the center open which allowed him to paddle-scoop water out after swamping. Reasoning that the barrier to attempting more difficult whitewater was the difficulty in rescuing a swamped canoe, Whitesell developed and perfected a self-rescue technique. He also developed his own rolling techniques for an open canoe. Although he was able to do more than he had ever done before with the Sunburst and the techniques he developed, he wanted to do more. He wanted to improve on the design of the canoe itself.

The idea of designing a boat intrigued Whitesell although he never intended to go beyond designing for himself. Having grown up building and repairing sailboats with his father, Whitesell knew fiberglass, but he had no interest in building a new design for whitewater. Fortuitously, an opportunity presented itself that allowed him to design a canoe for a manufacturer already building with Royalex. Darrell Leidigh, owner of Mohawk, initially entered the plastic canoe market in the '70s with Warsaw Rocket hulls like many other canoe manufacturers at the time. He later expanded and molded his own canoes. Although some of his models were marketed for whitewater, Leidigh wanted to seriously enter the short whitewater canoe market. In 1984, Mohawk entered the market with the Whitesell designed Mohawk's Scamp, a more traditional design that was 14' 4" in length and 34 inches in width.

IN 1981, Lantz worked with Mike Galt to develop a river cruising canoe. The result was the MGA (Mike Galt A model), a 17' 6" canoe with a slight V and with a broad bow to throw water. Lantz thought this was the first canoe with the "funnel-type" bow. It didn't do well in the market. The canoe was too long and heavy and was later used as a sailing canoe. However, Lantz intended to produce a mini MGA which he later thought might have changed the market situation had that project not been continually deferred.

Mohawk also agreed to mold a second boat specifically for Whitesell and marketed by Whitesell that allowed him to design and build with his own non-traditional ideas.

Whitesell's personal design was the 14' 3" by 34" Piranha with a high volume funnel-shaped bow, a pivoting bulge on the sides amidships, and a rounded arch hull fading into a shallow arch at the ends. It was radically different than any other canoe design at the time in Royalex or composite. In 1984, Whitesell ran the Colorado at 25,000 cfs on a test trip with four other boaters trained in both the rolling and self-rescue techniques he had developed for paddling big water. The success of his techniques and design was apparent when all five boaters ran the main routes down all the drops, including Lava and Crystal. Although some flipped, all rolled back up and remained in control. In 1987, Whitesell introduced an improved version that was available with outfitting as either a solo or tandem canoe.

The concept behind Whitesell's designs was that the traditional view of canoe design involved shapes that dealt with the current. His approach involved canoe shapes that dealt with the surface shapes of water. This allowed the funnel-shaped bow to stay on the surface instead of cutting through and made the design drier than many others. The pivoting bulge amidships was designed to provide combined maneuverability and final stability. Whitesell maintained his designs utilized water. "They go up and around rather than through waves. They take on any wave or curler and put the boat on top or use it to slide around."[22] The mid-ship bulge provided even greater rocker to the hull when paddled on its side.

As is often the case with new concepts, the first reviews of his boats (both the Piranha and Scamp) were mixed from both *River Runner* and *Canoe.* Tom Sebring described the Scamp for *Canoe* as a "large dumpling." Sebring continued, saying,

> Paddling the Scamp proved an interesting experience. The volume and stability of this canoe make it quite capable in heavy water. Unlike a true short-class slalom boat [compared to an ME or HD1] that demands constant attention lest it unthrone you, the Scamp is forgiving and stable, mostly due to the ample waterline width and soft bilges. In minutes we were side-surfing rollers, running drops sideways and backwards, and in general hamming it up real fine. It's just so easy to run big whitewater in this little boat.
>
> Surfing in particular was a blast. The giant bow provided enough buoyancy to keep the nose up and dry while permitting the bow to be brought back up into the current easily. One could sit in a three-foot wave and ferry back and forth on its surface.
>
> What you lose relative to a true slalom boat is the following: The Scamp is not as fast as narrower, racing-type boats. Waterline width and blunt entries make the boat less efficient paddling upstream to play... Eddy turns and peelouts were less precise and slower than with a sharp-bilged boat that carves these maneuvers.

[22] Koll, Chris. "Building an Open Boat to Perform." *American Whitewater* Vol. XXXIII No. 4 (July/August 1988): 32–25.

> In all fairness, though, this canoe is not intended as a technical slalom craft, but rather as a fun boat for bigger water.[23]

Whitesell proved his design, concepts, and technique in the whitewater he ran. Often described as a daredevil and risk taker, Whitesell preferred to say he paddled knowing and evaluating the risks being taken. In the fall of 1987, Whitesell successfully ran the Niagara Gorge in his Piranha during the brief three-week window that runs were sanctioned. He made many first descents in an open canoe on rivers in both the East and West including the Payette in Idaho. As Walbridge recalled:

> One of the finest moments in open canoeing has got to be when Whitesell made his daring Class VI run over the 12-foot 'Big Splat' ledge on the Big Sandy River [West Virginia]. Whitesell made this drop without swamping, mind you.[24]

In 1987, Whitesell provided another design for Mohawk, the Rogue (14' 2"). The Rogue was similar to the Piranha but with less rocker and no mid-ship bulge. Within two years, Mohawk introduced another short canoe from Whitesell that was initially advertised as the Rogue XL-13. In 1989, the canoe became known simply as the XL-13, the first in a series of "XL" canoes of different lengths. All of them included the same key elements of Whitesell's original Rogue design.

Advertising for the XL-13 further reinforced Whitesell's impact on whitewater open canoeing with his key design innovations.

> The XL-13's unique high-volume flared ends above the waterline create a boat that is extremely dry. The sleek entry at and below the waterline results in a boat that is easy to paddle and quick to accelerate. The short length (13' 3") and round bilges blend in to flared sides forward and aft resulting in a boat than can turn on a dime, is stable side-surfing and easy to roll.[25]

By the late '80s, some of Whitesell's design elements were being copied by other designers. The previous negative criticism and comparisons to traditional slalom-type hull designs were fading. The fact that "the Piranha's deep, full, and blunt-nosed hull is seen on water previously thought beyond the level of most open boaters"[26] was proof enough. The practicality of Whitesell's design elements provided him with recognition for his innovations for whitewater open canoes. In 1989, Pat O'Herren's description of the Piranha praised Whitesell's design elements:

THE THREE-WEEK WINDOW of opportunity, during the Fall of 1987 to run the Niagara Gorge was possible because of a suit brought by four paddlers against the Niagara Frontier Parks and Recreation Department. The suit was designed to compel the Parks and Recreation Department to grant permission to run the river. This suit was the result of the prior granting of permission for the 1981 ABC filming of Chris Spelius, Carrie Aston, Ken Lagergren, and Don Weedon's first legal descent of the Niagara Gorge. Legal maneuvering from the suit finally resulted in permits granted to three different parties during a three-week window after the peak of tourist season.

Author's note: For some of the paddlers, it was the first time they had legal permission to run the Gorge. In 1982, Pete Skinner made an illegal solo run. In 1985, Skinner was joined for another illegal run by Risa Shimoda-Callaway and Bob Baker.

[23] Sebring, Tom. "Water Test: Mohawk Scamp." *Canoe Vol.* 13 No. 1 (February/March 1985): 74–75.

[24] Walbridge, Charlie. "The Outer Limits of Open Canoeing." *River Runner* Vol. 5 No. 6 (Fall 1985): 7–9, 35, 40.

[25] Mohawk Ad. *River Runner* Vol. 8 No. 7 (December 1988): 14.

[26] O'Herren, Pat. "Canoes: Thirteen Great Solo and Tandem Open Canoes." *River Runner* Vol. 9 No. 7 (December 1989): 28–34.

> With its "pivoting bulge," the boat rolls at least as easily as our other two rolling leaders, the smaller Encore and Flashback II. But such an advantage is not often needed– unanimous top marks were garnered in eddy grabbing, side-surfing, and stability by all size paddlers. Peel-outs even provided whiplash potential, while the wider bow and lipped decks shed water very well.[27]

Whitesell revolutionized whitewater open canoe design. However, it was others who continued what he started with designing shorter and shorter canoes. Perhaps like some designers including Lantz with his OCA design, it was difficult for Whitesell to improve on what he felt was already perfect. As many people found out in the past, though, just when there didn't seem to be room for any real innovations, and that designs or technique had reached the ultimate, someone takes it up to the next level and the whole process begins again.

Dagger

For a brief time after leaving Perception in August of 1987, Joe Pulliam worked for Blue Hole. Pulliam was hired to assist with marketing even though he recognized that Blue Hole was a company with financial and image problems. But Pulliam soon realized that some of Blue Hole's problems were too much to overcome. He offered to buy Blue Hole from Bob Lantz but Lantz rejected his offer. Interested in starting his own paddlesport company, but realizing the kayak market required more capital than he had, Pulliam teamed with Roy Guinn, Peter Jett, and Steve Scarborough to form a new canoe company. In 1988, as Blue Hole went under, Dagger Canoe Company was formed by the four partners, using the Dagger name Scarborough used for manufacturing paddles.

Dagger's first canoe models were all Scarborough designs, the 14' 4" Caper, 16-foot Dimension, and 16-foot Legend. Only the Caper and Dimension were designed as whitewater open canoes. The following year, Dagger entered the market of short canoes when they introduced the 13' 2" Encore as the new solo playboat.

Scarborough's designs were similar to others introduced around the same time. However, it was not Dagger's canoes that gained attention in the whitewater market. In 1990, Dagger entered into the plastic whitewater kayak market with their introduction of the Response, designed by Scarborough. With the rotational molding experience of Peter Jett who had previously worked for Perception and Hydra, the thermoforming experience of Roy Guinn who was a partner with Lantz in Blue Hole, Steve Scarborough as canoe designer, and Pulliam who previously marketed for Perception, Dagger had a powerful team entering the paddlesport market in the '90s. They were poised to take on Perception.

[27] O'Herren, Pat. "Canoes: Thirteen Great Solo and Tandem Open Canoes." *River Runner* Vol. 9 No. 7 (December 1989): 28–34.

Squirtboating

Slalom racing's legacy was felt in the birth of a new sport—squirt—a sub-sport within whitewater paddling. Squirt was truly an American invention. It ultimately had far reaching contributions to whitewater and the future of the sport.

> Squirtech had its beginnings in the slalom-racing corner of the sport. Fierce competition finally gave racers the nerve to lean their boats the "wrong" way in a turn. The success of the move is now history, but it was hard to accept at the time. [28]

In the '80s, the term squirt evolved from Phil Coleman's original description of what happened to him. Coming out of an eddy above Tear Drop in the Cheat Canyon he "was propelled into the rapid at pumpkin seed speed." Squirt became defined as the "sinking [of] all or portions of a boat using currents and strokes in order to accomplish hot-dog maneuvers." [29] It described a whole new aspect of whitewater paddling.

Before squirt, boat hulls were designed as surface boats to use the currents and features on the surface of the water. Paddling was two-dimensional, moving the boat left and right on the river. Squirt added the third dimension using the sub-currents and features below the surface. Squirtboat hulls were designed to use the entire boat, hull and deck. The interplay of its volume not for maximal buoyancy as the previous surface boats had used to remain on the surface, but for minimal buoyancy was critical. As Snyder explained, "Maximum access boats have a 51 percent probability of floating." [30] That is, boats designed for squirt, for accessing the sub-currents, optimally barely float at the surface. Unlike surface boats where good and bad designs merely helped or hurt the effectiveness of their usage on rivers, squirtboat design was an integral and critical part in their usage. A boat that wasn't designed for squirt, for capitalizing on sub-currents, wouldn't work.

Jesse Whittemore backblasting in a Millennium Falcon on the Ocoee (TN), 1985 —courtesy of Rob Lesser.

In 1987, *The Squirt Book* written by Jim Snyder, was the first and only definitive manual on the squirt kayak technique. The book, illustrated by William Nealy, not only provided the fundamentals of squirtboating and river hydrology but provided an insight into the perspective and philosophy of squirtboaters. Snyder wrote:

> Squirtists should reflect on the spirit revealed in the history of our subsport. It is indomitable and inimitable, a rock in time, a stroke for all. It is the one point central to all squirt development.

[28] Snyder, James E. *The Squirt Book*. Birmingham, Alabama: Menasha Ridge Press, 1987.

[29] Ibid.

[30] Ibid.

Although the beginnings of squirt were tied to slalom racing, squirt evolved at the hands of ex-racers, sometime racers, raft guides, and boat and paddle builders on the Appalachian rivers. It was here that commercial rafting provided a livelihood, and the time, for early squirt paddlers to develop and explore this new aspect of whitewater. Many early squirt pioneers and innovators lived in the region. Area residents Phil Coleman, Jim and his brother Jeff Snyder, and Jesse Whittemore, along with others like Jim Stuart from the D.C. area, were all a part of this time and place that inspired innovations that led to squirt. But Jesse Whittemore and Jim and Jeff Snyder became the leaders. From their early experiments in design and squirt technique (squirtech), two divergent philosophies evolved. The most noticeable difference between the two was attributed to boat length. Whittemore's boats were long and built for speed, moving from eddy to eddy with grace and speed. Jim Snyder's boats were short and built for tricks in the eddy lines. Both could do bow and stern pivots, blasts and splats, but it was Snyder's Arc that radically changed the direction of squirt designs. The subsequent Jet and ProJet designs defined squirtboats in the '80s. These designs had floating hulls in the 10-foot to 11-foot range, concave decks, radiused edges, a lot of hard rocker, and cut so that the edge was at or below the waterline. Cut meant that the boat's volume was customized for the paddler's weight to obtain neutral buoyancy displacement at the surface, or approximately 51 percent buoyancy. It was achieved by removing an appropriate amount of hull from its edge prior to joining at the deck. Snyder's boats ultimately became the image conjured with the term squirtboat.

Like Wolf Bauer and others who coined new terms for whitewater in the '50s, squirtboating required new terms to describe not only the sub-currents and features, but the moves using these new-found features. While Bauer and others borrowed terminology from rock-climbing and skiing, squirtboaters related to the jargon of the '80s. In particular, they coined terms that were reminiscent of quantum physics which related to the discovery of new sub-atomic particles and their descriptive behavior. Squirt terminology included:

Blast Surfing a slide-type or pourover hole straight on, like a wave.

Boof To impact with the hull. A technique for flat landings from vertical drops.

Cartwheels To flip a kayak end-for-end continuously. Double enders followed by smashes.

Charc Charging arc. The angle of attack of a boat's long axis as it encounters local currents/features. Directly related to strategy or lack thereof in river running. A broad charc is perpendicular to the current; a steep charc is toward parallel. Also used in reference to people's attitudes, i.e., bad charc.

Meltdown To sink deeply below the foam pile of a hole during a downstream run.

Mush Move Dropping completely underwater on an eddy line, parallel to the grain, on a downstream run.

Mystery Move A bow and stern squirt done in close succession so that both ends of the boat sink completely underwater almost simultaneously. This is an entry technique for whirlpool rides. The reemergence from a complete submersion is called a black attack.

Screw Up A past vertical stern squirt done as a pirouette backender. A super screw up is a 270-degree spin with a full twist, which feeds you directly back into the eddy. A full-twist 360-degree spin of the bow is a mega screw up.

Shoulders The side structures of a wave. They support the peak.

Smash After the stern sinks, this move flips the boat end for end so that the bow is under. The tough half of a cartwheel.

Squeeze An underwater feature of an eddy line. The area where eddy currents are pitted most directly against downstream currents.

Sweet Spot Deadish area in the heart of a foam pile of a hole.

Swipe A bow squirt followed by a double ender done passing very near a rock. A bow-screw swipe is a bow-screw lead into a swipe exit done passing a swipestone.

Swipestone A stone with good characteristics for accomplishing successful swipes, i.e., rounded corners and a strong consistent pillow.

Third Point The position of the center of the mass/shape of the boat/rider.

Third-Point Charc The direction of travel of the third point. An imaginary line.[31]

[31] Snyder, James E. *The Squirt Book.* Birmingham, Alabama: Menasha Ridge Press, 1987.

"The Master," Jesse Whittemore, 1985 —courtesy of Rob Lesser.

Whittemore

Jesse Whittemore was one of the local guides and paddle builders working enough to have food, but more importantly, working enough to paddle. He guided for Cheat River Outfitters and lived at the guidehouse in Albright, West Virginia. Throughout the winter of 1981–1982, he paddled on the Cheat and on the Upper Yough, often with Jim and Jeff Synder. Whittemore discovered that paddling hard, keeping the boat moving like in slalom racing, provided opportunities to use the river currents. His skill skyrocketed. Using a Sonnet (a Sanna with a flattened deck designed by Phil Coleman), a chopped race boat, Whittemore did the first controlled squirt at Decision on the Cheat using a 30-degree Duffek stroke. Although Phil Coleman had squirted a few years before, squirts were still not a controlled and intentional move by paddlers. While the Snyders perfected their backsurfing and paddle throwing tricks, Whittemore perfected his squirts. Jim Snyder credits Jesse Whittemore with being a "catalytic character" of the time and influencing both he and his brother. As Jim Snyder recalled,

> His [Whittemore's] timely influence on the sport cannot be overestimated. He has spoon-fed the sport from its infant days to the present... The three of us [Jim, Jeff, and Jesse] made a habit of paddling almost every day that winter [1981]. Jeff and I were there to perfect our backsurfing and paddle throwing, while Jesse was in it just for the kicks. The chopped race boat he paddled was dangerously small for his large-framed body. It seemed that he could only keep one end of it afloat at any one time. Over and over, Jesse would break out of an eddy and sink his upstream hip and then his stern. He became quite skilled at head-high squirts. We watched spellbound as his squirts attained higher and higher limits. In a couple of short cold months, he was performing perfect backenders on eddy lines. It really looked like fun. Before long, it seemed we were going boating to watch Jesse. We knew that we had to get into the act before we fossilized.[32]

The following summer, after the guiding season for the Cheat was done, Whittemore was offered a job working for River Sport on the Yough. While there, he met Jon Lugbill and Norbert Sattler, World Champion slalom racers, who worked as instructors for River Sport. River Sport, located on the Middle Yough in Pennsylvania, is a paddling school, outfitter, and store, owned by Bob Ruppel. Although Whittemore never raced slalom, he admired their skill and spent time boating with Lugbill. He learned from the master of the stern pivot move.

Lugbill and Whittemore later wrote of their meeting in the summer of 1982 on the Yough:

> ...Jesse Whittemore looked upstream and noticed someone paddling a C-1 with great ability. He had heard Jon Lugbill was going to be around, and realized that it must be him. When Lugbill paddled down, Whittemore introduced him-

In 1975, Whittemore started boating with Explorer Post 757, led by Carl and Beth Flynn. The Post not only exposed him to building boats and women paddlers (the Post was about 50/50 men to women) but also the guides, the local boater folk heroes of the Yough.

While paddling on the New River, Whittemore saw a boater using an asymmetrically shaped paddle blade called the Slasher. He was infatuated with the design but he didn't know anything about it until he moved to Albright where he found out that the Slasher blade was a Jim Snyder design. Whittemore met Snyder, a resident of Albright, and inquired about the paddle. "Oh, you want that old model? Go to Keith Backlund. He's just down the road."[33] This was the beginning of Whittemore's longstanding friendship with Backlund and Snyder that fueled the development of squirt.

[32] Snyder, James E. *The Squirt Book.* Birmingham, Alabama: Menasha Ridge Press, 1987.

[33] Whittemore, Jesse. Interview by author 17 January 1998.

self. After seeing Whittemore zip in and out of eddies squirting and blasting, Lugbill figured out that this guy was actually the hot kayaker he had been hearing about. The two of them took off together, each showing the other their trick moves. That day, a racer and a river runner melded ideas to improve techniques beneficial to all canoesport. They learned from each other, and in analyzing the mechanics of squirting (pirouetting on the end of the boat), discovered some interesting offshoots.[34]

While paddling with Lugbill, Whittemore discovered front blasting. Lugbill imitated the move in his C-1. Lugbill, with the smaller and flatter bow of his C-1, discovered stern blasting. Whittemore imitated the move in his kayak. Convinced that what was needed for squirting was flat surfaces while maintaining hull speed, that is long kayaks, Whittemore designed the Millennium Falcon during the summer. It was based on the Equipe, the hottest slalom design at the time.

Whittemore paddled his Millennium Falcon the rest of the summer and during Gauley season. He still didn't have a bow squirt (bow pivot) down and while at the Gauley, a C-1 boater told him only C-1's would be able to bow pivot. Whittemore took up the challenge. He worked at it during the following winter until he could "yank it [the bow] down" with his stomach muscles.[35] However, even before he perfected the bow squirt, Whittemore pulled off the first pillow move that same Gauley season on Pillow Rock. (Whittemore's pillow move was witnessed by Greg Green and John Regan. Regan was inspired by it and got into squirtboating. Regan made the same pillow move on Pillow the next year.)

Whittemore sensed he was on the verge of something. He knew that it was too big, too fun, too cool for boaters ***not*** to be interested. He knew squirtboating would grow. In 1983, Joe Pulliam, then at Perception, came north to West Virginia. He paddled with Jim Snyder and Whittemore on the Big Sandy (at 7½ feet). Whittemore felt it was his day to shine. He yanked off as many squirt turns as he could and ran Big Splat, its first run, and got munched in the process.

Although there were no on-going conversations between Whittemore and Pulliam regarding squirtboating, Whittemore kept in contact with Pulliam at Perception. In the meantime, Whittemore continued to improve on his Millennium Falcon. His theories and philosophies about hull design solidified as his squirt skills and firsts continued. Whittemore concluded that a locking hull, the trend in slalom racing that began in the '80s, was required for the squirt moves he desired. Since squirtboating took boating away from merely surface moves by lowering hull volume, definitions for how the hull behaved had to evolve. A paddler in a floating hull had the ability to change direction merely by shifting weight. The boat hull typically had soft rails. A locking hull was the opposite. The locking hull provided the ability to lock into the current for a ferry and maintain it instead of getting washed out. The locking hull, in essence, provided and presented a controllable amount of volume and, therefore, resistance to the current. The floating hull could not do that. Whittemore also concluded that the critical locking part of the hull was just forward of the paddler's body extending toward the knees. This locking position was

Jesse Whittemore working on his first squirtboat, the Millennium Falcon, circa 1983 —courtesy of Kevin O'Brien.

PADDLES ALSO EVOLVED during squirt's evolution. Blade shapes and offsets changed to facilitate the new squirt moves. Offsets reduced from 90 to 60 to 45 degrees. Paddle shapes changed from the traditional rectangular slalom racing shape to the reduced area squirt tear-drop shape. Squirtboaters also preferred wood sticks whose construction was also amenable to shape and offset evolution.

THE BEGINNING OF THE FLOATING HULL versus locking hull controversy started with the difference between Prijon and Lettmann hulls in the '70s. Locking hulls proved to be the future for slalom racing. Richard Fox, a British K-1 slalom racer, designed locking hull characteristics during the '80s. His designs and the technique were the basis for his three World Championships wins.

[34] Whittemore, Jesse, and Jon and Jill Lugbill. "Squirt Boating: A New Dimension in Kayak Acrobatics." *Canoe* Vol. 14 No. 3 (June 1986): 58.

[35] Whittemore, Jesse. Interview by author 17 January 1998.

THE DEATH STAR was actually Jesse Whittemore's second design after the Millennium Falcon (note the *Star Wars* theme). It was a total flop, but Whittemore learned a lot; he made too many changes at one time in a single design.

The Cyborg was the sixth design after the Surge series. Although designed for the masses like the Sylon, it followed Snyder's lead in short squirtboat design with a gouged out (concave) bow and stern.

critical but position-sensitive to the paddler's weight. The designs most successful in initiating the turn placed the mass of the locking hull, a defined side wall, just forward of the paddler's weight.

Whittemore continued with long hull designs that were close to the traditional four-meter slalom length. Following the Millennium Falcon, he introduced the Sylon, Blaster, and Surge. These designs retained the hard rails with defined chines to create the locking hull and direction control in fast water, just like slalom designs. Although the hulls were fast allowing rapids to be attained (paddled back upstream), the lack of rocker reduced their turning ability and required stern leans to keep the bow from diving in steep drops. Whittemore's designs developed a niche of their own as cruising squirtboats.

The Sylon, similar to a Prijon '82, was designed for the masses. Although the flat chine wall was too far forward, it was a great surf boat. It allowed the paddler to actually climb up into a wave. The Blaster's cockpit was moved forward like that found in newer slalom kayaks designed by Fox during the same time. The Surge was small but had massive flat surfaces and was eventually abandoned even by Whittemore when he was chewed up on the Gauley during a competitive stunt rodeo.

Whittemore's contact with Pulliam, and the success of Whittemore's designs, resulted in "Blasting in the Third Dimension," a Perception sponsored tour of the South. Whittemore used Perception's new design, the Sabre, which was strikingly similar to Whittemore's cruising squirtboat designs for the tour. In March 1985, Whittemore was sponsored by Go With the Flow, an Atlanta-based retailer, and Perception at the Ocoee Festival where Whittemore provided a squirtboating exhibition using a Sabre and his own design, the Aramis Charger. Throughout the South, Whittemore taught clinics with Perception footing the bill. Perception also sent him to the Payette Rodeo in Idaho where he competed in the slalom race. He won paddling his Blaster kayak. The tours went well for Whittemore and Perception's Sabre. Perception also sent him to Europe for the '85 World Championships where he repaired the team's boats and paddled rivers with some of the best European boaters.

In addition to designing boats, Whittemore also developed his skills and techniques in composite boat building, Whittemore Laminates. Squirtboating was hard on boats and stronger materials, layups, selective reinforcements, and better seams were needed. Whittemore experimented with hand layups and vacuum bagging developing techniques for both. Not only were his designs in demand but so were boats built by him.

Whittemore built Jon Lubgill a 10½ pound race boat that was a masterpiece of technology. It was built of S-glass and Kevlar with a honeycomb core using higher than normal vacuum to lower the resin/fiber ratio as much as possible.

By this time, however, Snyder's short boat designs had emerged. Although Whittemore's designs overcame the dreadfully slow hull speeds of the shorter Snyder-style boats, his designs were more difficult to paddle and required more serious expert boaters, like himself, to successfully make the squirt moves. The shorter squirtboats were easier to paddle and became very popular, soon replacing Whittemore's designs in the squirt arena.

WHITTEMORE was successful because he was able to shake off the old concepts of paddling. Like Ford, Hearn, Lugbill, and Robison a few years before in C-1 boating, Whittemore forced himself to do uncomfortable things that went against the grain of paddling technique, like leaning upstream. Just as the efforts of their C-1 paddling paved the way to a revolution in C-1 boating, Whittemore's efforts paved the way for squirtboating.

Jim Snyder

Jim Snyder, an ex-racer, guide, boat and paddle builder, thought short boats were cool. The Snyders were not into long squirtboats like Whittemore's designs. Instead, they wanted to be able to do cartwheels and decided short was best. Jim Snyder also realized that low volume was the way to go but he was initially concerned about going too low in volume. In 1981, Snyder designed the Slice, a 10' 4" kayak, on a piece of paper. Following the Augsburg (Prijon) hull design theory, he incorporated soft chines and a short stern that kicked out behind the bow in turns. With the help of Bill Friend, Snyder stripped out the design for the plug to mold the boat.

During the winter of 1981–82, Snyder witnessed Whittemore's first vertical backender in his 13-foot (4-meter) modified race boat at Decision on the Cheat. Snyder later performed the same move in his 10-foot Slice. This confirmed for Snyder that he was on the right track and the divergence in design theory for squirt occurred. The next spring, Snyder chopped his Slice design to make the Trice, the first in a blitz series of designs "to combine high performance with passable comfort." The Trice culminated in the Baby Arc, a design resembling "a hollowed-out surfboard." [36]

Jim and Jeff Snyder (front to back) on the Cheat (WV), circa 1983 —courtesy of Kevin O'Brien.

Jeff and Jim Snyder (front to back) squirting on the Cheat (WV), circa 1983 —courtesy of Kevin O'Brien.

JIM AND JEFF SNYDER began paddling with the Mad Hatters Canoe Club (east of Cleveland, Ohio) before becoming raft guides. In 1969, Jim began guiding on the Yough to support his paddling habit which included slalom racing in the late '60s and early '70s as a junior competitor. Both Jim and Jeff were a part of the West Virginia boating, guide-ex-racer-boat builder, community beginning in the early '70s.

[36] Snyder, James E. *The Squirt Book.* Birmingham, Alabama: Menasha Ridge Press, 1987.

[37] Ibid.

JIM SNYDER wasn't interested in producing large numbers of the Slice himself. He approached Vladia Vahna of Noah in North Carolina about producing the Slice for him. Vahna didn't mold it for Snyder because he felt it needed softer lines before it would sell. Six months later, Vahna came out with the Jeti, one of the first short playboats that became very popular in the Southeast. The Jeti was actually a modified Slice of Jim Snyder's design.

The Baby Arc, born in January 1983, at a mere 24 gallons of volume, was "the most radical squirt design ever."[37] Jim Snyder wrote of its testing,

> The spring '83 floods were the format for the proving of the "dense-boat theory." In very big water, the small Arcs proved able to deliver a steady and superior ride. Punching eight-foot holes became quite fun with a boat that penetrated through as level as it entered. We also accomplished the first *screw ups* and *cartwheels* in these boats that spring.[38]

The Arc was the first squirtboat paddled on the Grand Canyon.

> In November [1983], John Regan, Greg Green, Jeff [Snyder] and I ran the Grand Canyon at 27,000 cfs in our squirt boats. We rode whirlpools that were 30 feet around with two-foot cores. All you could see was the top one foot of the rider's bow as he would swirl in the core with a cone of air reaching his lungs. This provided an unusual toilet's-eye-view of the world. In his baby Arc, Jeff would sometimes be completely swallowed by diagonal folds in the currents. His tiny boat also provided the most stable ride through the huge holes he punched. We had fantastic rides, including one in which I had a long talk with the Reaper, deep in a whirlpool at the bottom right of Lava Falls. He said any time I wanted to talk to God, I just had to drop in.[39]

THE PLUG for the Baby Arc was actually made from 2-inch thick boards nailed and glued together to make a 10 foot by 2 foot board. The board was then chain-sawed and ground down to the final plug form.

Following the Baby Arc, Snyder designed a progression of Arcs, with full bows, volume in the bow, that culminated with the commercial production of the Arc 6 design by Phoenix for the 1984 season.

In 1985, the series culminated in the Jet with toe tunnels. The Jet was pivotal in squirtboating for two reasons: it was the first successful design for the masses with more than one hundred sold the first year, commercially produced by New Wave Kayaks, and because of working with New Wave, Snyder bumped into John Lawson, a designer-engineer from Boston. Their ensuing conversations proved pivotal in assisting Snyder with the next major evolution in squirtboats, the concept using the wing design in the hull-deck shape and the reduction of bow volume.

The wing concept led to round leading edges like an airplane wing, with tight custom adjustments for weight displacement to maintain a 51 percent positive buoyancy. In order to do this, the design required foot bumps or toe tunnels. The follow-on design, the Pro Magnum, incorporated bumps on the stern deck called "Lawsons" in Lawson's honor because of his contribution to the design. The wing concept expanded in the Maestro, Shred, and Big Foot, all three derivations on the same concept. The Shred introduced the pointy bow.

New design terminology with better descriptors evolved because of the radical changes in design. The term rail and its descriptors augmented the use of the word chine to better qualify the hull shape. The rail was defined as the line or transition where the flat bottom curved upward toward the deck. A sharp rail described the use of an abrupt upward angle while the soft rail

[38] Snyder, James E. *The Squirt Book*. Birmingham, Alabama: Menasha Ridge Press, 1987.

[39] Ibid.

described a gradual curve. The term edge, where the hull met the deck, also required clarification for squirtboats. A sharp or hard edge described a flat deck joining a flat hull while a radiused edge indicated some rounding of the hull where the hull meets the flat deck.

Technique also evolved with these concepts. The advantages of the barely floating hull (51 percent buoyancy) which allowed boat response to subtle weight shifts was ideally suited for surfing the face of a wave but also made the boat extremely tippy and hard to control in pushy water. The extreme cut, while intended for subsurface moves, required that the boat was paddled on its edge to prevent the bow from nosediving. Of course, the shortness combined with the extreme rocker made the boats extremely slow.

But the success of these design concepts, which became the hallmark of squirtboating, was firmly entrenched in the evolution of squirtboating. Many other squirtboat designers incorporated the same concepts. Jim Snyder and squirtboating became synonymous.

CHANGES IN TECHNOLOGY, including modifications in rotational molding practices, have allowed intricate shapes, like squirtboats of the '80s and rodeos boats of the '90s, to be successfully rotationally molded. One of the first kayaks to take advantage of the changes in technology was the Engima, the first plastic squirtboat. The Engima, first produced in 1992, was manufactured by Outdoor Leisure Products of Britain, owned by Trevor Snook who later was a partner in Euro Kayaks.

A Niche Market

Squirtboating blossomed during the mid-to-late '80s and though it was not for everyone, it spread from East to West. Its niche was small because "almost every one went through the embarrassing stage of being an expert-turned beginner." [40]

West Virginia, the home of squirtboating, was far removed from California's Sierras in more ways than one. In the Sierra's, the cutting edge of the sport manifested in first descents in the '60s and '70s, particularly after plastic kayaks made the scene. At first, low volume composite boats with moves linked to slalom racing had no audience in the Sierras. This, along with the lack of squirtboating equipment and local expertise slowed the acceptance and progress of squirtboating in the Sierras in the '80s. However, squirtboating slowly picked up momentum, particularly after experts demonstrating skills and arrived on the scene. In 1988, Risa Shimoda-Callaway and Forrest Callaway demonstrated squirtboating at clinics at Sierra Kayak School. As in the East, squirt class divisions were added to rodeos in the West including the South Fork of the American in California and the Wenatchee in Washington.

Squirtboaters in the West, circa 1988 —courtesy of Wilderness Systems.

Squirtboating provided a way for those few boaters who took it up to stand out in the crowd, to distinguish themselves from everyone else who paddled the same standard plastic models with the same standard colors, and the same standard gear: Perception boats, Harmony paddles, Extrasport PFDs, and Pro-tec helmets, all in the standard four or five basic colors. Neither squirtboating hull shapes, particularly the short squirtboats, nor the size of the squirtboat market was conducive to plastic construction. Squirtboats were of composite construction with very different hull shapes and colors. The paddles

[40] Snyder, James E. *The Squirt Book*. Birmingham, Alabama: Menasha Ridge Press, 1987.

were often wood, not composite, with non-standard offsets of less than 80 or 90-degrees with non-standard blade shapes. Squirtboaters wore non-standard gear. They even paddled rivers differently, often choosing and exploring non-standard and non-traditional lines down drops. Squirtboating became a counter culture to plastic.

By the late '80s, animosity between squirt and surface boaters in plastic had emerged. Peter Cogan, a surface boater turned squirtboater, observed what happened when the counter culture of squirt met the traditional boating culture on a river in New England. In an article titled "Boat Wars" or "Rivalries Surface As Squirt Boats Submerge" he wrote:

> [For the squirt boater] the first wave is a beauty and we surf it for hours. I was on it... when a red, plastic "spud" boat dropped onto the wave from above, the paddler ignoring the five or so others waiting in line in each eddy on the sides of the wave. I paddled into the eddy, unwilling to be "spudded," wondering if this wasn't another case of plastic vs. glass, surface vs. squirt, roto-molded vs. radical. Regardless of his intentions, it was typical of a New England (and national?) problem: the peaceful coexistence of plastic and glass boats. While certainly not on par with the emergence of Eastern Europe as a global issue, it affects a core group of serious river runners, and demands attention.
>
> ...Essentially, it's as if new crafts[squirt boats] suddenly invaded the waters, taking over surfing waves and holes... and speaking a new language. Truly, these boats were being paddled by aliens.
>
> ...Plastic boats take work to move. They are limited in their range; they paddle on the surface only... They come in sedate blues and reds, banana yellow, simple black and whites. Perfect for the Puritan Paddler. Squirt boats, on the other hand, are radical. A squirt boating Puritan is a contradiction in terms. 'Splatter' graphics, for example, upset the entire surface boat reality... What God-fearing New Englander, for example, would ever be seen in a Screamin' Meanie? That's the devil's work, man. What staid New Englander would be caught doing a mystery move? It sounds illegal... Squirt boats are anathema to the New England work ethic. Because of their design and weight, you don't need to work as hard. Surfing a wave is the clearest example; you can use the tail and your body weight to move the boat, rather than pushing on the paddler [paddle]. In other words, you work less, and play more.[41]

Squirtboating gave composite manufacturing a short-term boost, particularly in the East. Snyder and Whittemore licensed their successful designs to other small manufacturers. As squirt grew, other designs were produced by designers including John Lawson (the popular Vulcan design) and John Schreiner (the popular Demon series), owner of New Wave Kayaks in Pennsylvania.

[41] Cogan, Peter. "Boat Wars." *American Whitewater* Vol. XXXV No. 5 (September/October 1990): 56–59.

Two composite companies that grew significantly as a result of squirtboating were New Wave Kayaks and Wilderness Systems in North Carolina. Although they produced race boats and wave skis, New Wave benefitted from their production of Snyder's Jet design. In 1986, New Wave sold more than 400 squirtboats. New Wave further enhanced squirt's popularity, as a counter to plastic, by offering both custom graphics and custom cuts determined by the owner's shoe size and weight, something that plastic manufacturers could not offer.

New Wave's market, initially in the East, expanded with squirtboating's popularity in the West. Squirtboating frenzy was delayed by a couple of years in the West, primarily owing to the geographic separation between the two areas. It finally began to be noticed when New Wave sponsored Jeff Snyder to compete in rodeos across the country. New Wave's custom-cut squirtboats and graphics were in such demand that they were producing nineteen boats per week and had a four to six month waiting list for orders. In the late '80s, New Wave sponsored Jim Snyder and others including Risa Shimoda-Callaway to demonstrate squirtboating in Japan.

A THIRD MANUFACTURER OF SQUIRTBOATS that helped to pick up the overflow need was Watauga Laminates in North Carolina owned by Chase Ambler.

JOHN SCHREINER purchased molds for race boats and wave skis in the '70s from Danny Broadhurst, a designer of wave skis and other boats as the starting basis of New Wave Kayaks.

In October of 1986, Andy Zimmerman and John Sheppard started Wilderness Systems within the first year of becoming squirtboaters themselves. Their first squirtboat was the Ferrier, their own design. They added others including cruising designs. They built Tom McEwan's White Bear, Wick Walker's Blackwater C-1, Richard Fox's Foxfire, and other squirt designs including Whittemore's Surge and Snyder's Prize. Wilderness Systems also provided custom graphics as well as aerodynamic, funky shaped squirt helmets that were a take-off from the once distinctive fireman's helmet used by a few early squirtboaters. The helmets, with custom graphics, were very popular with new squirtboaters. In 1990, Wilderness Systems built between 450 and 500 composite boats of all kinds including, squirt, race, and creekboats. Like other manufacturers, they had a six-month backlog of orders.

Neither Sheppard nor Zimmerman had any experience building composite boats. Zimmerman concentrated on marketing and Sheppard on boat building. Sheppard learned everything he could about materials and processes, including vacuum bagging, from John Abbenhouse of NorthWest Kayaks in Seattle. Wilderness Systems went from wet bagging with epoxy to dry bagging with vinylester. Wilderness Systems was one of the first paddlesport manufacturers to use Dow's Derakane 8084 vinylester resins.

Through Zimmerman's efforts, Wilderness Systems established a network of over sixty dealers, concentrating in the Southeast and Northeast. D.C. was their biggest area.

Squirtboating grew so fast in popularity that none of the manufacturers of squirtboats could keep up with demand, a fact that hurt its growth. The growing number of boaters also hurt squirt's growth. In the beginning, squirtboating was a way to stand out from the crowd in plastic, to look different. But when the fireman's helmet was made into a mold, everyone had one and everyone looked the same. Squirtboating's growth diminished its uniqueness. One of its basic appeals, individuality, was lost.

By the mid-'80s, with the popularity of Snyder's Jet designs, boaters who began whitewater just a few years before in plastic boats were able to buy squirtboats. Because they had no experience building their own composite

IN 1985, Perception's Sabre was their entry into the squirt market, though neither Perception, nor paddlers, identified it as a squirtboat. It was not like the Snyders' short designs that instantly conjured the vision of squirtboating. The Sabre's success was limited due to the fact that it was not a short design, and that squirt was not a sport for the masses. Low volume sterns with edges were not common except among race designs. The Sabre required more skill to handle than the average boat. But by the late '80s, low volume sterns with their accompanying stern moves, influenced by squirtboating, were more acceptable and handleable by the average boater.

boats and no experience repairing their own, they were not familiar with the weekly process of boat repairs that were a part of life for boaters before plastics. This, too, affected squirtboating. Squirt's growth was further hindered because it was not a beginner's sport and it was not a sport for the masses. At the same time, the availability of plastic playboat designs with some squirt characteristics, particularly lower stern volume, in the mid-to-later '80s appealed to more of the beginner and intermediate boater masses.

The continued growth of whitewater in general affected the growth of squirtboating. With the congestion of many of the popular rivers with plastic play boaters and composite squirtboaters, boaters began seeking less popular, less congested runs. Creekboating developed its own niche. Jim Snyder's Screamin' Meanie and Phil Coleman's New Vision were custom composite creek designs. In 1989, Perception came out with the Corsica, a plastic boat intended for creekboating. Creekboating, also not for beginners, took away from squirtboating.

IN THE EARLY '90S, many factors began contributing to the decline in popularity of squirtboating, including the rise of rodeo. But squirtboating forever left its mark on the sport and its future. It introduced new radical design innovations, radical technique innovations, and new concepts in river hydrodynamics for boaters. Squirtboating bucked the often conservative approaches taken in the past. It brought with it a sense of exploration and experimentation or "gee, why not try it and see what happens." At times, it also contributed to an attitude of, "What's the worst that can happen? Death?

The less than conservative attitudes that developed from squirtboating were a part of its sub-culture. Although often frowned upon by non-squirtboaters, these non-conservative attitudes provided the flavor of what it was all about for squirtboaters, a sense of fun and free spirit. In 1988, Alex Cooptavenus wrote of a friend, Tim Kelly, and his trick at Glen Park Falls on the Black River in New York that typified this.

> We were loitering in the eddy above the 15-foot Glen Park Falls... when Tim Kelly scratched his brush-cut head and announced, "I think I'm going to try a melt-down. I read about it last night in (Jim) Snyder's book. When you run the falls, instead of trying to stay flat when you launch off the lip so you can boof the bottom hole, you attain the green water on top then lean forward. You try to stay with the green water as it goes under the hole. Then your boat comes rocketing up on the other side of the boil." From the pool below the falls, we watched Tim make his run. His brightly colored Jet appeared at the brink of the falls and, sure enough, Tim leaned forward. The kayak plunged straight down into the maw of the hydraulic and after a moment, endered straight back up... still in the grip of the hole. For 10 heart-stopping seconds, Kelly vertically surfed the falls. I wish I could report that as a group, we jumped into action, initiating a rescue. The situation had the possibility of disaster. But instead, we simply sat back and laughed: "Look, he's back-blasting the falls. Tim, you didn't attain the green water... Twirl your paddle... [42]

[42] Cooptavenus, Alex. "Stupid Whitewater Tricks: Having 'Fun' Is the Only Rule." *American Whitewater* Vol. XXXIII No. 6 (November/December 1988): 28–31.

Many core squirtboaters who participated in squirt competitions migrated toward and helped—transform rodeo from its beginnings of showing off everyday river-running skills to playboating and hole-riding skills. Squirt's skills and technique influenced rodeo as did some of squirt's design concepts, including short boats. Jim Snyder acknowledged that squirt contributed to its "mutated pal," the rodeo of the '90s.

The Rest of the Industry

The rest of the industry benefitted from the growth and changes in marketing that plastics and Perception brought. Although plastic canoes and kayaks dominated the market, the sport's growth in the '80s was enough to support a few small composite manufacturers, particularly those that provided boats for squirt and racing, slalom, and wildwater competition. Other goods, including new accessories and gear, and services like paddling and rescue schools also expanded to meet the growth and popularity.

Coincidental with whitewater's growth was growth in other sports like climbing, hang gliding, and sail boarding. Outdoor accessories and clothing across all sports became more specialized. Everything from clothing to cartop racks developed for paddling. Clothing using new materials for warmth was developed for both on-water and off-water. Clothing and gear were also sized to fit women. Dry suits entered the market. Even footwear was developed beyond the standard wet suit diving bootie.

The dry suit was perhaps the clothing innovation with the most impact on the sport. Although available as early as the '60s, new materials made dry suits more cost effective and suitable for paddling. Dry suits first appeared in the mid-'80s. Dry suit usage among paddlers initially suffered from the wet suit versus dry suit safety controversy as well as their cost relative to wet suits. Critics of dry suits were concerned that a tear would allow the one-piece style suit to fill with water endangering the paddler. However, dry suits caught on and by the end of the '80s, paddlers had a selection of dry suits to chose from in style, materials, and manufacturer. Dry suits expanded the paddling season, particularly in the colder areas of the country. Many whitewater paddlers during the '80s paddled year round.

The entire retailer network benefitted and grew. With the increased number of paddling consumers, the number of whitewater retailers including mail order retailers increased, too. Some destination stores were able to remain open year round because of round paddling. By the end of the '80s, whitewater also began to enter the mainstream outdoor market with big name retailers like REI and EMS carrying whitewater boats and equipment.

Composite Manufacturers

Fewer composite boat manufacturers started up and survived in the late '70s and early'80s with the domination of plastic canoes and kayaks in the whitewater market. Those that did survive found their own niches and they were often associated with squirt and racing boats. They did not try to compete directly with plastics.

In the East, the niche for New Wave, Wilderness Systems, Watauga Laminates, and Whittemore Laminates was racing and squirt, although for a time squirtboats dominated their manufacturing. Small composite manufacturers with racing niches were often owned by racers or ex-racers like Valley Mill Boats in Maryland, owned by wildwater racer Andy Bridge. Millbrook Boats, owned by John Berry, and Nittany Valley Boats, owned by John Sweet, continued producing small quantities of boats into the '80s.

In the West, the niches for small composite builders were a little different, focusing on river running, a little racing, and playboating for rodeo. Squirt and racing were primarily sports of the East and manufacturing was left almost exclusively to Eastern composite builders. Class VI's niche in Utah was river-running and playboats. Whitewater Boats' owned by Dick Held, also in Utah, was primarily the same. Jaycox Boats, owned by John Jaycox, built a mix of river running, playboats, and racing boats for the Colorado boating community. Ultrasports' niche in California provided the small racing population with advanced lightweight composite race boats. By the '80s, the interest in whitewater racing in California had shrunk considerably from what it had been in the '60s and '70s, replaced by a new form of competition—rodeo.

CLASS VI, co-owned by Don McLaran, built the P-51 Mustang, as a shortened modification of a Lettmann Mark V. It was extremely popular in the West as a playboat. Because of its 26 inch width, it was marketed and sold as both a K-1 and a C-1. Class VI also built Bill Clark's Mistle design which was a modified Lettmann Mark IV. Both designs were popular for western river running and playboating.

While most composite manufacturers chose not to compete directly with plastics, one composite manufacturer, a survivor from the early '70s, did: Phoenix. Before plastic dominated the market, Phoenix sold more composite boats than anyone else. But plastics changed everything. In order to survive, Phoenix's owner Tom Wilson eliminated his dealer network and sold direct to keep retail prices low and competitive with plastic.

Phoenix clearly sought to market its products' strengths over what Wilson saw as the weaknesses of plastics. In the summer of 1982, Phoenix introduced Fiberlastic as its own trademarked composite brand. Two-page magazine ads highlighted many of the arguments against rotationally molded kayaks. The ads read:

> ... for today's kayaker it [Fiberlastic] means enhanced safety, lower weight, and a maintenance-free product. The new Fiberlastic™ WILDFIRE [the model] is not a soft rotomold or brittle fiberglass kayak. It is the product of years of research and experimentation in material science to create a product without the drawkback of these and other materials [compared to "rotomold," Phoenix fiberglass with nylon, and straight fiberglass]. The plastic fiber lamination of the WILDFIRE, which is immersed in a liquid tri-polymer resin and subjected to heat and pressure for added strength, survived two years of brutal prototype testing at the Nantahala Outdoor Center, a leading kayak school and rafting operation. At 37 lbs. of finished weight, the virtually indestructible

> WILDFIRE is the lightest and strongest plastic kayak on the market. And, its Break-A-Way™ cockpit area and foot length, non-obstructive support walls provide the extra margin of safety not available with rotomolds.[43]

By the mid-80s, Phoenix had three large sellers of its own, the Wildfire, the Spitfire series, and the Slipper series, which was first introduced as the Slipper kayak in 1975. In 1984, Phoenix also began to produce Snyder's Arc squirtboat. In order to be competitive with the custom cut versions of squirtboats that New Wave, Wilderness Systems, and Watauga Laminates offered, Phoenix offered the Spitfire, an 11-foot boat introduced in 1985, with five size options. However, in the end, like all the other composite boat manufacturers, Phoenix was unable to compete with plastics in the whitewater market and had to settle for a niche within paddlesports in general.

Paddling Schools

Within ten years of MKC's (Madawaska) and NOC's founding, paddling schools were founded across the country including Saco Bound in New Hampshire, Riversport School of Paddling and Whitewater Challengers, both in Pennsylvania, Appalachian Wildwaters in West Virginia, Whitewater Specialty in Wisconsin, World Of Whitewater and Otter Bar Lodge in California, and Sundance Expeditions in Oregon. Some schools specialized in courses for beginners. Others were geared more for intermediate and advanced paddlers. Some schools taught courses exclusively for kayak, particularly in the West, while others offered instruction in all boats. A few advertised their use of ACA certified instructors while others touted their use of expert-professional instructors, although not of slalom or wildwater like MKC, but rather rodeo and playboating.

MKC continued its long tradition of using the best-of-the-best from around the world. In 1982, MKC's instructors included World and European champions Kurt Presslmayer, Norbert Sattler, Gisela Grothaus, Gerhardt Peinhaupt, and Ulrike Deppe as well as the younger generation American champions Linda Harrison, Cathy Hearn, Davey Hearn, Eric Evans, Jon and Ron Lugbill, and Bob Robison, many of whom at one time were MKC students themselves. American racers were finally held in best-of-the-best esteem.

Both Otter Bar Lodge in California and Sundance Expeditions in Oregon used instructors with rodeo and playboating credentials. In the '80s, Otter Bar's instructors included Don Banducci, Arlene Burns, Rick Fernald, Cameron O'Connor, Chris Spelius, and John Wasson. Sundance's instructors included both Banducci and Fernald along with "Bat Man" Montgomery, the Glatte Brothers, Richard Ray, and Nancy Wiley.

One of the benefits that the schools brought to education and training was the development of better instructional techniques along with a better understanding of the evolving paddling techniques. Although unintentional, paddling schools were particularly helpful with regard to assisting with the dissemination of the latest techniques by hiring instructors from different areas of the country, and who taught at various schools. The cross-pollination of

[43] Phoenix Ad. *Canoe* Vol. 10 No. 4 (July/August 1982): 38–39.

information benefitted everyone. In the '80s, NOC continued to stand out among the rest, primarily for its staff's contributions to paddling instruction techniques and river rescue.

The kayak roll was one technique that benefitted from the cross-pollination. The sweep roll had traditionally been taught in the West. In the East, the C-to-C roll evolved from the screw roll through NOC. Chris Spelius named the new roll the C-to-C, but Ken Karsten led the teaching progression that evolved it.

Spelius maintained that the kayak roll evolved for two reasons in the '70s and '80s:

> Over the years kayakers have figured out how to sneak their way upright using body English; they have stopped forcing their way up with the paddle. This has led to easier, more reliable rolls with less stress and strain on the joints. Secondly, because of the large numbers of students being taught, instructors have devised effective systems for teaching the new techniques. [44]

Spelius was an instructor who taught at schools across the country. Eventually, he learned to teach what he described as the slash roll, a technique that evolved at Sundance Expeditions kayak school in Oregon. He called it the slash roll "because the paddle slashes cleanly through the water with no resistance" [45] while the long-used sweep roll uses downward resistance of the paddle on the water to support the kayaker's use of hips to snap the boat upright. The Slash roll's series of steps were the Tuck, Initiation, Sitting Up Diagonally, Cocking the Wrist, and Twisting the Torso. Spelius first taught this at Otter Bar. It soon caught on with other instructors.

NOC: Instruction

Author's note: NOC has the highest number of instruction days of any paddling school. This certainly contributed to NOC's abilities to try new techniques to see what worked and what didn't work.

From the beginning, NOC provided racers with a livelihood through both instructional and guiding jobs while at the same time providing a place to train practically year round. This helped NOC play a significant role in instructional advancements. In the mid-'70s, Gale Coward from ACA held an instructor clinic for NOC. This was followed by the appointment of Don Jarrell, Chairman of ACA's Training Committee from 1977 to 1980, as head of NOC's instructor program which was the beginning of NOC's and ACA's long-standing relationship regarding paddling instruction and education.

When NOC began, instruction was based on the American Red Cross's (ARC) latest manuals for instruction. However, over time NOC's instructors realized that they were not really teaching ARC's instruction, but were rather adapting it. At the same time, the instructional technique was largely "watch me and emulate me." That too, was slowly adapted. In the early '80s, instruction moved toward an emphasis on understanding what was really happening with the paddler's body, boat, and paddle. About the same time in the early '80s, Bunny Johns of NOC became Chairman of ACA's Training Committee. With NOC's classroom for instructors, instructional techniques, and paddling techniques, NOC influenced ACA's training and instructional programs.

[44] Spelius, Chris. Interview by author 14 November 1998.

[45] Spelius, Chris. "The Slash Roll." *Canoe* Vol. 17 No. 2 (May 1989): 50–55, 62.

The atmosphere at NOC was somewhat unique and lent itself to innovations in instruction. Among its staff was a high concentration of past and present slalom and wildwater racers. Although teaching slalom racing skills and technique was not an integral part of NOC's courses, the instructors sought to leverage as much as possible from their racing backgrounds to supplement traditional canoe and kayak instruction. In doing so, they found out what worked and didn't work in instruction.

Another contributor to NOC's success was its class size and ratio. At MKC and other schools, class size was 1 to 5, instructor to students. At NOC, it was 2 to 10. Although NOC's class size was larger while maintaining the same ratio, the additional instructor provided for peer review and peer growth for the instructors. This proved invaluable for innovations and advances in instruction. Dinner-time conversations were a sharing time with much brainstorming among the instructors. Shoptalk among the racers-instructors outside of dinner also led to innovations.

Multimedia

In the '80s, the publication of guidebooks and instructional books continued. Although the magazine *Down River* discontinued publication, it was replaced by *River Runner*, a quarterly publication, which premiered with its Fall 1981 issue and continued throughout the '80s. *River Runner* focused on whitewater river-running in rafts as well as canoes and kayaks, competing directly with *American Whitewater*. It was an excellent magazine with articles written by authors who knew whitewater. During the '80s, *Canoe* continued with its original format covering paddlesports in general. In early the '80s, with its new owners, *Canoe* shifted away from ACA, no longer serving as its official magazine but was rather endorsed by ACA. A subscription was no longer included with an ACA membership.

American Whitewater, dependent on articles contributed by its members from across the country, suffered through much of the '80s with thin issues, partially attributed to AWA's low membership numbers, but also from competition with *Canoe* and *River Runner*. But as the '80s wore on, fewer and fewer articles about boating in the West were included, indicative of a change in AWA's membership. In addition, more articles focused on the extremes of paddling, which was also indicative of the trend in its membership. In 1987, under new volunteer editor, Chris Koll, *American Whitewater* moved from their 6-inch by 9-inch format to an 8-inch by 11-inch format, the same size as *Canoe* and *River Runner*. Over the next few years, the quality of *American Whitewater* improved and though still a member magazine, was sold to the general public through a small number of paddlesport retailers.

The '80s also brought entertainment and multimedia to the sport. No longer were there just instructional books and guidebooks written for whitewater. Books were also written for entertainment. Some of the first books produced for their entertainment value were written by William Nealy. In the mid-to-late '70's, Nealy, a paddler with a talent for cartooning (actually a cartoonist with a penchant for paddling), produced river maps unlike any seen before with what became known as his trademark caricatures. In 1981, fourteen of his maps were included in Volume I of the *Whitewater Home Companion*, interspersed with cartoons with his characteristic biting, satiric commentary about the eccentricities of whitewater paddlers (which could only have been written by one of our own). Within a couple of years, maps were no longer the basis for his work and Nealy produced *Kayaks to Hell* and *Whitewater Tales of Terror.* In 1985, reviewers from *River Runner* wrote of Nealy's books,

> ...he left the river maps behind and concentrated on lampooning the thrill-seeking, crash-and-burn mentality of the tribe *Kayaker* (admittedly drawing from the ethos prevalent in the magazine of mercenaries, *Soldier of Fortune),* shuttle bunnies to feminists, equipment suppliers to preppies.[46]

Paddlers either loved his work or hated it. But regardless, it offered some of the first true tongue-in-cheek humor about whitewater paddling, a subject that had previously been treated very seriously.

In 1979, through a fortuitous chance meeting, Nealy met author and extreme boater Bob Sehlinger. A conversation with Nealy, Sehlinger, and Holly Wallace, Nealy's significant other (and now wife), eventually resulted in the formation of Menasha Ridge Press in Tennessee, known for its publication of whitewater oriented books.

The fast advances in whitewater open canoeing technique and equipment in the '80s was evident with publication of books that were obsolete soon after publication. Bill Riviere's book, *The Open Canoe,* published in 1985, was one such book. Riviere provided up-to-date information on construction materials and a brief history of open canoeing. He insisted that open canoes were not appropriate for Class IV and above because of the need to be covered and the need to be able to roll. The advances in design and technique, most notably present in boating circles in the Southeast, was not known widely beyond the Southeast.

Film and the new format, videos, also moved away from serious instructional and documentary-type subjects towards entertainment although safety and instructional videos continued to be produced. Rocky Rossi who started Gravity Sports Films around 1980 took advantage of the new and growing video technology. Rossi was one of the first to make videos of playboating that were shown and seen across the country. In 1981, Rossi started the Utah Gravity Sports Film Festival. Two years later in 1983, the Paddling Film Festival (now the National Whitewater Film Festival) in Lexington, Kentucky, premiered. It was sponsored by the BlueGrass Wildwater Association and Menasha Ridge Press.

Other videos followed, both amateur and professional. Videos, particularly of extreme boating, were popping up everywhere, just as the guidebooks had in the '70s about every conceivable run in the country. Not only were these videos made for entertainment but they documented the sport with its growing trend toward extreme boating.

SEVEN YEARS LATER IN 1992, Slim Ray's *The Canoe Handbook: Techniques for Mastering the Sport of Canoeing* finally provided an updated look at the subject. Ray wrote in his introduction:

> Solo canoeing is definitely one of the new trends. Ten years ago there were few purely solo boats... If you wanted to go for bigger water, you took up kayaking. Today there is a whole range of solo boats suitable for almost any purpose, and solo whitewater boats now run just about anything that can be kayaked... The style of paddling has changed also. Not for us the relaxed, ukelele-strumming cruises of the cautious backferrying of yesteryear. Today (apologies to the shade of Bill Mason) it goes toward aggressive playing and eddy hoping... What I have chosen to emphasize in this book is the sport of paddling as it developed (and continues to develop) at the Nantahala Outdoor Center in the seventies, the eighties, and into the nineties. NOC has been variously described as the Oxford (*Esquire*) and the Julliard (*Outside*) of the paddling world.[47]

[46] Combs, Rick and Steve Gillen. "William Nealy: In Full Candor." *River Runner* Vol. 5 No. 2 (March/April 1985): 15–18.

[47] Ray, Slim. *The Canoe Handbook: Techniques for Mastering the Sport of Canoeing.* Harrisburg, Pennsylvania: Stackpole Books, 1992.

The Changing Roles of the Old Facilitators: AWA and ACA

During the '80s, just as there were changes in the role of the sport's newest facilitator, the industry, there were changes in the roles of the old facilitators, AWA and ACA. Some of the changes were not apparent. They were subtle changes with regard to amateurism, both professional competitors, and professional staffs. In 1980, Bart Jackson, editor of *American Whitewater,* wrote:

> Another aspect unlikely to wane with growth is our amateur aura on all levels of the sport. The true energy of boating comes from the clubs plus a couple of national organizations, which are almost entirely volunteer run... More paddlers may mean more races and perhaps limited entry, but the nature of competition won't change. And frankly, the advent of the professional racer, or even the suspect semi-pro lies beyond the farthest horizon and poses little immediate worry, or hope... it is the local club or volunteer boaters who publish the newsletters, teach the skills of the sport, instruct and publicize safety and rescue techniques, and it is even these club members who promote most of the river-saving efforts made in this country.[48]

By the late '80s, changes in both amateurism of competitors and organization's staffs occurred. Rule changes governing amateur status allowed slalom and wildwater racers to become more than amateurs. Although maintaining their amateur status, they became paid competitors within their amateur status. Outside of slalom and wildwater competition, a professional circuit developed for the new form of competition: rodeo. Both ACA and AWA progressed toward paid professional staffs and with that, river-saving efforts were driven by the national organizations and supported by the grass roots efforts of clubs. Although clubs continued to be the mainstay of instruction, the growth of paddling schools, ACA certification for instruction (which could provide a livelihood), videos, and other clinics for rodeo skills also brought the paid, professional aspect of instruction and education.

AWA

In the mid-'70s, AWA's imperatives were divided into five areas: providing increased coverage and information included in the journal, an intensified effort to preserve whitewater streams, lobby against unwise legislation on equipment and use restrictions, national trips to learn about whitewater in other regions, and developments in other areas like guidebooks, standards, films, and books. These efforts continued into the '80s and in 1980, AWA had 127 affiliates including businesses, manufacturers, universities, and other clubs that supported these imperatives.

[48] Jackson, Bart. Editor's Soapbox. "Growing Pains." *American Whitewater* Vol. XXV No. 6 (November/December 1980): 4.

In the early '80s, one of the hot topics for debate was the river rating system. The debate resulted when previous paddling limits were pushed because of plastic and more paddlers began traveling cross-country to paddle rivers. Although AWA was not the originator of the International Scale, AWA inherited it in the United States (somewhat by default) because of its inclusion in AWA's Safety Code. AWA, therefore, inherited the debate.

In 1982, a flurry of discussions regarding overhauling the river rating system was prompted by an article published in *American Whitewater.* The article was written by Andy Embick, an Alaskan paddler with only two years of whitewater experience. Embick boldly proposed complete abandonment of the present river classification system replacing it with a system using "the vast knowledge of its experienced boaters to construct a list of standard runs for each region in the whole U.S."[49] He dismissed the use of six categories as ineffective. Embick felt that the rating categories failed for many reasons. Rating by danger failed because it was a function of the boater, his skill, equipment and judgement. Rating by describing problems failed due to terminology disparities. Rating by gradient or speed failed because it ignored obstructions and drop/pool situations. Rating by required skill level also failed because skill level was changing and a rating requiring specific skills, such as the need to roll, also failed. Embick proposed that each region designate standard runs that exemplified different classes or difficulty of water. Upon arriving at a consensus among local boaters, these designated runs would be expanded upon with experience from boaters with other regional and national experience. Consensus would be reached through guidance from both big water (West) and technical (East) experts. The ratings would also need to take into account all of the factors such as speed, gradient, obstructions, maneuvering required, continuous character, temperature, undercuts, and other river features.

Embick's proposal was met with considerable discussion. Coincidentally, during the summer of 1982, Charlie Walbridge, Chairman of ACA's Safety Committee and an eastern boater, paddled in Idaho and noted that the limits of whitewater boating had been extended since his previous trips west. Walbridge, too, felt the need to update the international scale, although focusing primarily on Class V criteria only. Walbridge also noted the difference in rating interpretation between western paddlers and eastern paddlers who were more consistent with European interpretations. Using *American Whitewater* as the forum, Walbridge initiated a discussion using between one hundred eastern and western paddlers by requesting comments from them regarding well-known runs.

Although recognizing that the "AWA Safety Code is less than perfect," O.K. Goodwin, AWA's Safety Chairman, disagreed with changes to the current system. Goodwin also stated that the "International Scale is probably most accurately applied by intermediate ability, open canoeists and low-intermediate kayakers."[50] This supported Walbridge's contention that only Class V needed better definition.

After collecting information from the one hundred eastern and western paddlers and pulling the information together into a chart, Walbridge sent the chart to a second group of paddlers who answered a request for help in *American Whitewater* and *Canoe.* Three concerns were apparent in the analysis of the information for compiling the chart. First, a clear distinction was made

[49] Embick, Andy. AWA Forum. "River Rating Overhaul." *American Whitewater* Vol. XXVII No. 3 (May/June 1982): 25–28.

[50] O.K. Goodwin. AWA Forum. "No Change." *American Whitewater* Vol. XXVII No. 5 (September/October 1982): 28–29.

between a Class IV rapid and a Class IV river. There was also a similar difference noted between drop-pool rivers and continuous rivers. The second concern involved regional differences among rivers such as drop-pool, continuous, rivers with boulder gardens, and rivers with tendencies for undercuts. (The chart did factor water level.) The third concern dealt with the over-rating and under-rating of rivers due to the region. In the Midwest and areas between the Appalachians and Rockies, rivers tended to be rated higher, often attributed to the lack of experience of local boaters and exposure to different kinds of rivers. The same was found in the East where many of the drops rated Class VI were simply not. However, in the West, many paddlers, with the introduction of plastic, had downgraded rivers over the previous five years with the result that most runs were one class lower when compared to eastern and European ratings.

In the end, Walbridge and others concluded, "The problem with river classification in this country is not the system, but the interpretation of it... We don't need new systems... we need consistency."[51] No real action was taken by AWA, or any other group, to attempt to resolve the issue.

However, by this time in the mid-'80s, AWA's membership was less than 800 and the number of affiliates was about half what it was in 1980. AWA as an organization struggled to survive let alone support any large initiatives. Conservation, river-saving fights, were often ineffective because AWA's efforts were diluted. AWA's focus was too broad for such a small volunteer organization. There were just too many efforts with too many complex issues for AWA to get its hands around. But then one person stepped up to the plate to bring focus to AWA's efforts. That person was Pete Skinner of New York.

Skinner was considered an extreme paddler. In the mid-80's, he became aware of the ramifications to rivers of the Public Utility Reform Program Act (PURPA) of 1978 which required public utilities to purchase all power generated by private hydro sites at "fair and reasonable rates" (which was generally construed to mean oil price equivalency). In essence, it gave independent power producers access to the grid and meant that many whitewater rivers were viewed as potential hydropower sites, a potential source of revenue. New York was one state that had a lot of potential hydropower sites. Skinner went from running whitewater rivers to realizing that he needed to protect them. He went "from self-grandizing to saving rivers."[52] His efforts began with writing an article a month to increase awareness, but then progressed to actually doing something. Instead of spending his weeknights repairing boats, Skinner spent his weeknights pursuing the issue.

Skinner soon learned that the standard phrase used by would-be hydropower developers, "renewable resources on existing site," was not as green as it appeared. Hydropower site development meant cutting trees, river level fluctuations, and a loss of habitat for fish and game. During the first couple of years, he learned the procedures the hard way for everything from gaining information to filing motions. He had no legal help and, of course, neither officials from state and federal agencies nor the hydropower developers offered any assistance. But within a few years, Skinner authored all AWA interventions in New York. These interventions became a template for all re-licensing interventions across the country. The Federal Energy Regulatory Commission (FERC) and the hydropower developers started taking Skinner seriously when he stumbled over procedural safeguards which he used to slow their projects.

PETE SKINNER began working for New York's Environmental Protection Bureau in the early '70s after graduating from college with a degree in civil engineering. Soon after he was introduced to whitewater kayaking, Skinner immersed himself in the sport. Beginning in 1974, he paddled in Idaho for seven straight summers. He also made other extreme runs including the Niagara Gorge.

[51] McCourtney, Dave. "AWA Interview with Charlie Walbridge." *American Whitewater* Vol. XXX No. 5 (September/October 1985): 19–27.

[52] Skinner, Pete. Interview by author 14 January 1997.

Some developers were even willing to negotiate at that point. In 1984, AWA made available prepared motions, based on Skinner's experience gained over the previous years, for intervention in hydropower projects before FERC.

During this time, cooperation between ACA and AWA regarding conservation issues also grew. Skinner, on behalf of both AWA and ACA, testified before a hearing of the Water Resources Council in support of reform of U.S. Army Corp of Engineers and other dam building federal agencies. [*Author's note*: During an interview, Skinner told me that he credits Mac Thornton with ACA with giving him the idea to pursue protecting New York's rivers. Skinner also credits Pope Barrow, AWA's conservation chairman, for all of his efforts and support during that time.]

Finally by 1986, the context of AWA's conservation efforts began to coalesce and became focused. AWA collaborated with other national organizations like American Rivers Conservation Council (ARCC), ACA, and Trout Unlimited. However, AWA's membership was down to fewer than 800 and AWA struggled to pay its bills to cover litigation and lobbying behind the river conservation efforts. AWA's directors decided to take on the Gauley Festival as a fund raiser for other conservation projects. In 1982, the Gauley Festival was held under the leadership of Dave Brown to help save the Gauley from the long tunnel project. The Festival continued as an annual event even after the long tunnel project was dead. Although AWA's first festival appeared to be a disaster as huge storm clouds rolled in, AWA actually netted about $2,000 and continued the festival's sponsorship. [*Author's note:* The annual festival now brings in about $30,000.]

YVON CHOUINARD, a climber with many first ascents, was also a whitewater paddler credited with first descents in the Sierras with other California paddlers including Reg Lake, also known for many first descents.

However, the Gauley Festival wasn't enough. Skinner, a past AWA director, looked for charitable donations to support AWA's conservation efforts. He traveled to California at his own expense to visit Yvon Chouinard, founder and owner of Patagonia, to ask for a donation. Chouinard asked Skinner how much was needed. Skinner told him $10,000. Chouinard responded "Done!"[53] In March, AWA received a letter that read: "Enclosed is a check for $10,000 to assist the American Whitewater Affiliation in their fight to stop the small hydro power ruination of our country's rivers. Let us know how you're doing from time to time."[54] That was the beginning of Chouinard's donations to AWA. The following year in 1988, Chouinard provided an additional $10,000 to assist AWA's nationwide hydroproject relicensing effort.

This was a major watershed event for AWA. It also coincided with other changes within the organization. AWA's Board of Directors was strong. They helped to transform passive, often older paddlers into boards that were involved and actively paddling, who were aware of the trends and needs of paddling in the '80s. Within months, AWA was again viable with renewed vigor.

Even the journal changed. After a six month absence through the beginning of 1987, *American Whitewater* was back in an 8½-inch by 11-inch format. (The name also changed from *American WHITEWATER* to *American Whitewater.)* Within a few short years, *American Whitewater* was published on a regular basis which drew back advertisers. Articles with extreme paddling and humor reflected the current genre of paddling. It was more in step with a younger generation of paddlers. *American Whitewater* went mainstream. In 1988, it was no longer a magazine just for AWA's members but was carried by whitewater retailers.

53 Skinner, Pete. Interview by author 14 January 1997.

54 Skinner, Pete. "AWA Fortunes Climb Thanks to Friendly Belay By Patagonia's Yvon Chouinard." *American Whitewater* Vol. XXXII No. 1 (January/June 1987): 21–22.

For all of his efforts, Skinner was named Perception's 1989 River Conservationist of the Year. Pope Barrow added praise to Skinner's recognition when he called him "River Rambo."

> Skinner is a one-man army. He's a Rambo, with 15 different kinds of weapons slung around his neck, except that in Pete's case, the weapons are motions, court pleadings, technical studies, financial analyses, site evaluations and press releases. Like Rambo, Skinner fires off a lot of ammo, easily several thousand rounds a year. No target is too big... And lately Pete's been hitting the bullseye with increasing frequency. [55]

During the '80s, a representative from FERC pointed out to Skinner one of AWA's weaknesses: AWA's staff was not very professional. If AWA wanted to make a difference, it must become professional even if that meant hiring professionals. In 1988, AWA's constitution and bylaws were amended. AWA's purpose was modified to reflect its changing role in the sport. The new constitution allowed for the appointment of a paid Executive Director to handle the administrative needs of the organization and serve as general manager of the business of the organization. Risa Shimoda-Callaway, a well-known extreme paddler and squirt paddler with a background in business, became the first Executive Director.

AWA's new purpose was to:

> Encourage the exploration, enjoyment, and preservation of American recreational waterways for man powered craft; Protect the wilderness character of waterways through conservation of water, forests, parks, wildlife, and related resources; Promote safety and proficiency in all aspects of white-water activities such as the navigation of moving water, teaching, teamwork leadership, and equipment design, by publishing and demonstrating developments in these and related fields; Promote appreciation for the recreational value of wilderness cruising and of white-water sports. [56]

Beginning in 1988, with a renewed sense of purpose, AWA took the lead in creating a nationwide inventory of whitewater rivers based on guidebooks and other knowledgeable experts. The intent of the inventory was to provide a database for many purposes, but mainly for the protection of whitewater rivers from any threats including hydropower, environmental pollution, access, and other conservation efforts. AWA's inventory was intended to be more complete than the Park Service's Nationwide Rivers Inventory.

AWA continued sponsorship of the Gauley Festival, proved successful for heightening river conservation awareness and support. Under Executive Director Shimoda-Callaway's leadership, AWA also embarked on a new role sponsoring rodeo competition with their support of the 1989 Ocoee Rodeo, cosponsored with Watauga Laminates.

RISA SHIMODA-CALLAWAY worked for Perception in marketing and new product development during the '80s and into the '90s.

Author's note: Curiously, AWA itself lost seven years of its own history for a while. Starting in 1989, *American Whitewater* provided a "who we are" ad which stated AWA was "organized in 1961 to protect and enhance the recreational enjoyment of whitewater sports in America." [57] It wasn't until the July/August 1993 issue that they partially corrected their mistake by writing, "AWA was incorporated under Missouri non-profit corporation laws in 1961." [58] Still no mention was made of the year of its original founding, 1954. Amazingly, with all the changes to the journals over the preceding thirty-plus years, the volume designation of the journals, although in roman numerals, remained correct, providing the correct dating back to 1954. However, this too changed. The November/December 1993 issue is Volume XXXVIII indicating AWA's correct age of thirty eight years. The January/February 1994 issue is Volume XXXIV, indicating a loss of four years.

[55] Koll, Chris. "Desktop Environmentalist." *American Whitewater* Vol. XXXIV No. 6 (November/December 1989): 26–29.

[56] Staff. AWA Constitution. *American Whitewater* Vol. XXXV No. 4 (July/August 1989): 40–42.

[57] Staff. "What is the American Whitewater Affiliation." *American Whitewater* Vol. XXXIV No. 2 (March/April 1989): 5.

[58] Staff. "The American Whitewater Affiliation." *American Whitewater* Vol. XXXVIII No. 4 (July/August 1993): 7.

In 1989, letters to AWA promoted the dropping of affiliation from its name saying that times had changed. AWA was no longer predominantly supported by affiliates but by individual memberships. Howls of indignation from ACA might have followed thirty years before. However, by this time very little was said.

Author's note: Many AWA members and directors were probably not aware of the earlier AWA and ACA controversies.

All of these events propelled AWA forward making it an organization with growing clout, particularly related to river conservation. By 1990, AWA, thirty-six years after its founding, remade itself to fit the changing needs of the times. This had been the intention of AWA's founders from the very beginning, to change and adapt as needed. With the changes in the '80s, AWA was well positioned for the changes and challenges of the '90s and its new role as a continuing facilitator of the sport.

ACA

In 1978, the Amateur Athletic Act was passed designating the U.S. Olympic Committee (USOC) as the ultimate governing body in the U.S. for amateur athletes. Because ACA was already a Group A member of USOC, and the officially recognized governing body by ICF for all canoeing and kayaking competition, ACA was automatically recognized as the governing body for all Olympic canoeing and kayaking events, both whitewater and flatwater. Group A designation were those groups that participated directly in Olympic sports. Ultimately, that meant that ACA's committees for competition, the National Slalom and Wildwater Committee (NSWC) representing whitewater, and the National Paddling Committee representing flatwater, could receive money to support their programs for Olympic competition from USOC.

Around the same time as the passage of Amateur Athletic Act, three changes were made within NSWC that affected American whitewater competitors. NSWC actively worked with all divisions to encourage more competitive paddlers. Through these efforts, NSWC finally became national across the country in all of ACA's divisions. ACA membership was strongly encouraged for anyone who wished to compete in ACA slalom and wildwater races. An additional $5.00 activity fee was added to a racer's membership. This activity fee was used to support a newsletter that disseminated information to registered racers across the country.

The increased numbers of competitors and a need to determine who could compete in the Nationals required a triage of sorts. This fact brought about the second change, a national ranking system. Past competitors Dave Kurtz and John Sweet established a framework for a national ranking system that allowed racers to determine their rank against one another even if they had not competed directly. Course difficulty was part of the equation and both races and racers were ranked in different classes: A/B being the more difficult that resulted in higher ranking and C/D the less difficult and lower ranking. A racer could determine his or her ranking through the National Whitewater Paddler Registration that was sent out to all ACA registered racers.

By the early '80s, the first signs of shifts away from the strict amateur rules required for competition occurred in all sports. It was apparent that ACA's current rules and definitions actually promoted elitism and were in Eric Evans own words, "an upper-class dilettante convention." It discriminated against all but the "wealthy kid whose parents foot the bill for equipment"[59] and who benefits from not having to work 40 hours a week to support himself. The third change was the implementation of a system that allowed racers to solicit financial support without losing their amateur status, therefore permitting more racers to seek national and international competition.

[59] Evans, Eric. Editor's Soapbox. "Amateurism on Trial." *American Whitewater* Vol. XXVIII No. 4 (July/August 1983): 4.

ACA established new guidelines that allowed amateur racers to sign waivers to compete for money as long as the money went directly to ACA's NSWC, and was earmarked for the racer. The racer then submitted legitimate receipts for training, racing, and travel to NSWC for up to 90 percent of his or her winnings, with NSWC retaining 10 percent.

These changes positioned ACA, and in particular NSWC, to benefit and support any potential future funding received from USOC. However, while all paddlers, racers or not, felt the changes to the amateur rules were beneficial, the other changes stirred controversy. This was particularly true in regard to fees imposed on the casual racer and the feeling that ACA only encouraged serious racers. Some of the controversy had to do with personal resentment towards what some paddlers considered ACA's heavy handed dealing with whitewater paddlers, vintages of old AWA and ACA rivalries. One AWA member wrote:

> In its latest attempt to extend control over the lives of the paddling public, the American Canoe Association has come up with a "National Whitewater Paddler Registration" which is supposed to establish a "direct personal communications chain" to reach everyone involved in slalom and wildwater racing. The links of this chain are forged by slapping a $12.50 annual fee on non-ACA-members wanting to participate in A/B class races ($5.00 if you're already rank-and-file ACA) and admonishing C/D race organizers to "encourage entrants to register so they too will be informed what is happening in the sport." An example of how this works is this summer's Esopus Slalom (ABCD) which cost $18.50 for a non-ACA-member ($12.50 plus $6 race fee for two classes). At those rates, the crowding of competitors during practice runs will quickly cease to be a problem.
>
> Consider the plight of Mr. Casual Racer. He's out there two or three times a year—for fun, friendly competition and to improve his river skills. He supports the U.S. Team, pays an entry fee for every race, and is still innocent enough to remember that a race can be more than just a date on an Olympian's training schedule. More to the point, he is shelling out bucks for club dues, subscriptions to canoeing magazines, newsletters, posters, T-shirts, and programs—and now someone wants to sell him a "direct personal communications chain" at $12.50 a shot (plus that much again for his daughter who's into racing as a junior paddler). Not just this season either—but the next and the next and the next after that. Is it surprising that Mr. Casual Racer is not thinking of trading in his paddle for a tennis racquet?[60]

What ACA thought was a positive step toward promoting the growth of the sport was perceived by some much differently and stirred controversy among some whitewater paddlers. In addition, ACA had to deal with controversy within its own organization pertaining to the allocation of funds from USOC.

[60] Varhola, John. "Letters from Readers." *American Whitewater* Vol. XXI No. 6 (November/December 1976): 185.

IN THE TWO YEARS AFTER THE 1984 WINDFALL, two organizations that promoted Olympic disciplines within multipurpose parent organizations successfully brought suit against their parent organizations. The U.S. Shooting Team split from the National Rifle Association and the U.S. Ski Team split from the United States Ski Association with all the money, leaving the parent organizations without Olympic connections and the prestige associated with it.

SOME PEOPLE WITHIN ACA felt its role in conservation was caught in the middle between two opposing forces: racers and recreationalists. Chic Dambach, past chairman of ACA's defunct NOCRC and then chairman of USCKT, was considered the man many people felt was responsible for America's first gold medals in flatwater sprint Olympics in 1988. (Greg Barton won the gold medal in K-1 1,000-meter sprint competition. Barton also teamed with Norman Bellingham to win the gold medal in K-2 1,000-meter competition.). Dambach expressed his conservation views during an interview with Dave Harrison of *Canoe*:

> 'I was always called upon as an ACA Council Member to vote for this or that river preservation motion, but secretly or half in jest I might suggest that a dam provided me with another ideal flatwater training site, plus a controlled water release for our slalom paddlers!' More seriously, Dambach said, 'The needs of racers and recreationalists are very different.'[61]

As one of the thirty-eight national governing bodies, ACA received $1.3 million, their piece of the more than $40 million profit from the 1984 Olympics in Los Angeles. ACA's National Congress voted to lock up the principal and spend only the interest generated on that amount, estimated at about $100,000 annually. This was considered an interim step until ACA set up a foundation to handle the funds. The initial distribution of the interest allowed 80 percent of the funds for the National Olympic Canoe Racing Committee (NOCRC), formerly the National Paddling Committee for flatwater, 15 percent to augment ACA's operating budget, and the remaining 5 percent returned to the principal. Two years later in 1986, the ACA foundation was finally established, but not without much internal squabbling. NOCRC's 80 percent allocation was not an absolute guarantee in future years. They threatened legal action against ACA to receive all the funds. After all, they were part of the only canoeing and kayaking events (flatwater sprint) participating in Olympic competition. After an absence of almost fifteen years, there was little indication that slalom would again be included in the Olympics.

After another two short years of relative calm within ACA regarding NOCRC and the foundation, two events occurred that again stirred up the controversy: two gold medal wins in 1988 for flatwater sprint and the announcement that slalom would be included in the 1992 Olympics in Barcelona. Now NSWC was entitled to a share of the funds, leaving NOCRC with less than their 80 percent share.

NOCRC forced a hearing before USOC that resulted in the establishment of the United States Canoe and Kayak Team (USCKT) in 1988. USCKT became the agent to receive and distribute funds for Olympic competition for flatwater sprint and slalom. NOCRC was satisfied with the formation of USCKT, although they were still not happy about sharing funds with whitewater paddlers. But the formation of USCKT left ACA in an upheaval with loss of purpose and staff as well as a 15 percent loss in operating funds. USCKT inherited the foundation fund, leaving ACA to make up the loss. At the same time, ACA was still responsible for maintaining the non-Olympic, grass roots, aspect of competition. (NSWC continued to handle everything not directly related to Olympic slalom competition though at times the boundaries were not completely clear.) In 1988, ACA incurred significant debt that resulted in an increase in dues and cut-backs in member benefits and services.

The formation of USCKT also took away a piece of ACA's original impetus for involvement in whitewater that began in the mid-'50s. The only undisputed areas left for ACA was conservation, safety, and education (and other vaguely defined services to all recreational paddlers). If ACA was to remain involved in whitewater outside of the remaining functions of NSWC, it was in safety, education, and conservation. Fortunately for ACA, the basis for safety and education was established in the late '70s under Commodore Chuck Tummonds' lead as "safety through education, not regulation." Safety and Education programs were well underway in the '80s.

[61] Harrison, Dave. "What's in a Canoesport?" *Canoe* Vol. 17 No. 2 (May 1989): 18–20.

In addition to continuing its direct role in safety through the efforts of its Safety Committee, ACA pursued public education through its training programs that included instructor certification. In the '80's, that role was further solidified through the efforts of ACA's Training Committee. [*Author's note:* Some thought Tummonds' forward thinking for ACA's role in safety and education was a stroke of genius. In the late '80s, it proved to be fortuitous for ACA.]

In the late '70s and early '80s, ACA solidified its cooperation with the American Red Cross (ARC), particularly through the efforts of Don Jarrell who worked for ARC but was also an active ACA member. ACA developed contracts with ARC for safety education and instruction. The U.S. Coast Guard also gave additional educational grants to both ACA and ARC. By the mid-'80s, ACA instructor training and certification workshops were well established across the country.

During the '80s, the instructor certification program was fueled not only by the need to develop better instructors for public safety and education, but also by the threat of litigation. At the time, liability insurance was difficult to obtain from most insurance providers. The use of certified instructors for training was thought to reduce legal liabilities should a lawsuit occur. ACA also provided a much-needed service to clubs by making available liability insurance for club activities including races and training. Clubs and paddling schools used, and advertised their use, of ACA certified instructors.

FOR DIFFERENT REASONS, but coincidentally about the same time, both AWA and ACA redefined their roles as facilitators in whitewater. AWA refocused its efforts towards active conservation and safety, and therefore inherently, education remained an integral part of AWA through the activities of the Safety Chairman and maintenance of the Safety Code. ACA strengthened its role in safety and education with its training and instructor certification programs. Like AWA's conservation efforts prior to the '80s, ACA's efforts were passive. As was appropriate for an organization that represented all paddlers, it was also related to general conservation instead of just whitewater.

Conservation

In the '80s, two conservation-related issues resulting from the sport's growth were access and its related issue, congestion. In the West, access was often associated with the desire to retain the wilderness experience of whitewater, with influence coming from the commercial aspect of river running. In 1980, the permit system on the Grand Canyon (the river experience that many non-paddlers associate with whitewater) went to an 80/20 commercial/non-commercial split, seriously impacting access of private paddlers. In 1984, 3,100 private boaters names (rafters and paddlers) were on the list for permits for the Grand Canyon, with only 220 summer launches granted each year. Private paddlers also had long waits to obtain permits to other popular wilderness rivers including the Middle Fork of the Salmon and Selway rivers in Idaho.

In 1982, Bruce Mason, a paddler from Oregon, wrote a letter to *American Whitewater* explaining his struggle to get permits for river running. In his letter, Mason wrote that in the early spring of 1982, river managers for the Grand Canyon informed him that he was number 1,345 on the waiting list. With an average of 220 non-commercial trips a year, that meant a potential wait of six years for a permit. For the Selway in Idaho, Mason was informed that he was number 45 on the permit for his first choice date, number 41 for his second choice, and 57 for his third choice, with only one launch per day allowed. For the Middle Fork of the Salmon in Idaho, Mason was number 11 on the waiting list for his requested launch date.[62]

Other access issues, not associated with obtaining permits, involved access to put-ins and take-outs across the country. These access issues were often associated with private ownership of land. Perhaps the most highly publicized extreme incident involved shootings by local land owners at the Sang Run put-in to the Upper Yough in Maryland. The shootings were actually pot shots taken at paddlers. In 1982, a court order stopped the shooting, but the Sang Run put-in was still an unfriendly area and paddlers were encouraged NOT to leave any shuttle vehicles in the area.

The unfriendliness toward paddlers could be attributed more to the incorrect association of what the locals perceived as paddler involvement in Maryland's designation of the Upper Yough as wild and scenic. Local resentment of the designation was often due to their misunderstanding of what the government could and could not tell them to do with their land.

While permit access issues were more often associated with rivers in the West, congestion issues were often associated with rivers in the East, though not exclusively. In both the East and West, the congestion was often associated with increased use by both commercial outfitters and private paddlers. In the West, the popularity of the Upper Sacramento grew in the mid-'80s. Eight commercial permits were issued in 1983, three more than in 1982. Popularity also increased on the Kings River (with its three authorized outfitters) as well as the Kern. However, unlike the Yough in the East, no restrictions were placed on private use to reduce congestion. In the East, ceilings on commercial use of many rivers also resulted from the increased popularity of whitewater rafting. In 1985, a ceiling for commercial use on the New was set ending the expanding commercial use of the river.

Congestion was particularly high during low water years with everyone scrambling to paddle the same dam-controlled rivers. The year 1987 was a low water year in the East that ended up putting the growing numbers of paddlers (private hardboaters) on the same rivers as the commercial outfitters. Paddlers had nowhere to paddle to escape the congestion. The New and Lower and Upper Yough were particularly crowded that summer. On the Upper Yough, with the two-hour release schedule, there were eleven outfitters trying to run trips with as many as sixty or more private boaters. This did not give a large margin of opportunity, or safety on this tight and technical river.

In the '80s, the Lower Yough was fully immersed in becoming the most regulated day river in the country, supporting over 100,000 rafters and paddlers each season. On the Lower Yough, where quotas were established at 192 private boaters a day, boaters were turned away for the first time on more than just holiday weekends during the summer of 1987. The inclusion of private

[62] Editor. Soapbox. "Five Letters." *American Whitewater* Vol. XXVII No. 3 (May/June 1982): 4–5.

rafts in the 192 quota number, at four per raft, was thought to unfairly discriminate against hardboaters, particularly since 960 commercial raft slots were allocated per day.

Access and congestion problems often paled in comparison to the loss of whole stretches of whitewater rivers. Though damming of rivers was not new in the '80s, the intensity of threats increased in the '80s as a result of PURPA fueling other hydro project developments and expansion. This hydromania, coupled with an increased awareness of access and congestion problems often on a personal level for paddlers, resulted in local grass-roots opposition to proposed projects that threatened whitewater rivers. People respond when it happens in their own backyard and that became the strength of the organizations supported by whitewater paddlers who wanted to preserve their way of life and their rivers. By the early '80s, individuals and organizations across the country organized against local projects (the same as Skinner and AWA) that threatened their rivers, such as the Ocoee in Tennessee, North Fork of the Payette in Idaho, Gauley in West Virginia, and Moose in New York.

California was ahead of other areas of the country with damming of rivers, projects (for hydro, flood control, and irrigation) that began in the early '60s. In 1981, the Stanislaus Initiative Campaign attempted to put a referendum on the 1982 California ballot to limit the base pool size for storage of the New Melones dam to below Parrott's Ferry, except in crucial flood years, which would protect the Stanislaus whitewater run for use. The New Melones dam project had already ended many of the whitewater runs on the Stanislaus. However, all attempts failed and the renowned Camp Nine 14-mile run from Camp Nine to Parrott's Ferry was inundated in late spring of 1982, about twenty years after the other whitewater runs were lost to the New Melones dam.

The Auburn Dam proposal, a Bureau of Land Management project from the '60s that was not yet built, reared its ugly head again in 1987 as a result of flooding the previous year in the Sacramento area. Proponents of the dam used flood control as the tactic to resurrect the project. However, an unlikely ally helped to bring the project to a halt. The Army Corp of Engineers reported the Auburn Dam was not needed. Proper operation of existing flood control and hydro facilities would have prevented the flooding.

One of the first successful fights to preserve a whitewater river was the battle for the Ocoee, a river that had only recently been discovered for whitewater. In 1913, the Eastern Tennessee Power Company erected a wooden diversion flume to generate power at Ocoee Powerhouse No. 2 (later acquired by TVA) and virtually eliminated all water in the section between Ocoee Powerhouse No. 3 and No. 2 on the Ocoee River. In 1976, an inspection of the wooden flume revealed severe deterioration that required its immediate cessation until repairs were made. After sixty three long years, the de-watered stretch of river now had the discharge from No. 3 running its course which revealed a 4½-mile stretch of Class III-IV whitewater. The river was discovered and paddlers flocked to it. Two years later in 1978, the National Wildwater Championships were held there. In 1979, six raft outfitters began operations. However, with the rehabilitation of the flume, TVA announced the flow would again stop unless there was guaranteed funding to offset losses due to lost power generation that recreational releases required.

Outfitters and paddlers realized their chances were slim against the TVA which was considered the most powerful power company in the country. Several paddling clubs and commercial outfitters united to form the Save the Ocoee River Council (later simply known as the Ocoee River Council, ORC) and hired David Brown, a full time paid professional. Brown's sole objective was to save the recreational resources of the river. He proved to be the right person. Brown formed a comprehensive plan, devised a means to generate funds to pay himself as well as the necessary cash to spread the word, and hired an attorney to defend ORC's interests.

In 1981, in order to draw attention to recreational water releases on the Ocoee and the threat to lose them, ORC sponsored the first Ocoee River Festival in August. The festival was a political-social event: part fund-raiser, part political action, and part whitewater rodeo event. Perception supported the fight to save the Ocoee with a drawing. For those individuals who contributed five dollars to ORC, they had a chance to win a new kayak or canoe of their choice. Perception also donated valuable time and effort to support the drawing across the country. The following year, the National Slalom Championships were held in conjunction with the festival.

Through ORC's strategies to increase awareness of the ramifications of the project, it was proven that the $5 million dollar loss over the thirty-year life of the project was far less than the loss of local tourism revenues in an area that was economically depressed. ORC's strategies resulted in a battle that pitted more than just the paddlers and outfitters against the TVA. The state of Tennessee, the federal EPA, and the Justice Department joined ORC in the fight once their awareness to the project was raised.

The combined efforts of the Ocoee festivals and other strategies developed by ORC worked. In the fall of 1983, Congress enacted legislation providing water for downstream recreational releases. The final outcome was a $7.4 million bill that established a recreation area on the Ocoee and provided for releases 117 days per year until 2019, although user fees were still imposed for rafting outfitters to offset power generation losses. Releases were scheduled from March through May for weekends, Thursday through Monday for summer, and weekends again in September. The first scheduled releases began in the spring of 1984.

With the success of the Ocoee, special task forces were formed for other save-the-river efforts. One such group was formed when two popular sections of the Moose River in New York were threatened by a small hydro power project with a proposed dam at Ager's Falls. The project would have de-watered the Bottom Moose (Class IV-V), considered one of the foremost expert runs in the Northeast, and the Lower Moose (upstream of the Bottom) with its Class II-IV run. Although the dam was eventually built, an agreement was reached in 1984 between the Moose River Corporation (a subsidiary of Long Lake Energy) and a coalition of paddlers and environmentalists led by AWA. The agreement included whitewater recreational releases for twenty days a year: ten scheduled ahead of time and the other ten on a request basis with at least five days warning. This was considered a victory and set a precedent in dealing with small hydro developers. The releases were scheduled for eight consecutive Sundays starting the third week of April and the first two Sundays of October. In the '90s, AWA developed the Moose River Festival around the annual releases.

In contrast to the Ocoee and the Moose, preservation of the North Fork of the Payette in Idaho was a long-fought conservation war that lasted much of the '80s and into the '90s. Idaho Power's North Fork Project threatened the Class V-V+ run (from Smiths Ferry to Banks) on the North Fork. The legend of the North Fork, the Mount Everest of Kayaking, was barely known outside of Idaho in the early '80s. Even then, it was the domain of only the bravest or craziest. (In 1975, the last 2 ½ miles above Banks was first run by Idaho boaters Keith Taylor, Roger Hazelwood, and Tom Murphy.) When Idaho Power's North Fork Project was first announced in the early '80s, the Idaho Whitewater Association was formed to fight the dam as well as other river preservation projects. Although there were many well-intentioned individuals who tried to save the North Fork, they ultimately lost, or so **they** thought. Idaho Power had the financial resources to win merely by attrition, or so they thought. Idaho Power was armed with a full-time professional staff, a paid legal staff, and very qualified hydrology and engineering experts. The paddling community was armed with kayakers concerned about the preservation of their favorite stretch of river. They thought they had a grasp of the facts, but in the long run, they provided little if any credibility to their position. Their lack of knowledge of the system or credibility working within the system, and perhaps naiveté doomed their efforts. The final blow came when Idaho Power asked the paddlers how many days they wanted with releases. Idaho Power sidetracked them from the bigger issue of stopping the dam construction in the first place by offering them releases assuming the dam was going to be built. Instead of seeing the ploy for what it was, the paddlers "innocently accepted this offer and huddled to come up with a number. The boaters thought they had gained ground, but actually had hastened their own defeat. The assumption that the project was necessary had slipped by them."[63]

However, apparently the project was not necessary and Idaho Power eventually abandoned their North Fork project. For a time in the mid-to-late '80s, the North Fork appeared to be safe. Expert paddlers from across the country went to Idaho to run the North Fork. In 1988, however, the North Fork was again threatened by two separate privately financed proposals to divert the North Fork to produce power for sale to California. One of the private developers was an Idahoan, J. R. Simplot, a potato baron. The other was an out-of-state group from Connecticut, Consolidated Hydro of Connecticut, who obtained a preliminary permit for a pump storage project that would have de-watered the river for all but seventeen recreational release days.

This time, however, the Idaho paddling community was larger and smarter. Friends of the Payette formed for the single purpose of preserving the North Fork. Friends of the Payette was formed out of Idaho Whitewater Association. Idaho Rivers United formed from Friends of the Payette which focused on the preservation of the Payette alone, while Idaho Rivers United focused on all Idaho rivers. Idaho Rivers United also joined in the battle. What they thought would be a short battle lasted over three years. New financial backers in 1990 lengthened the war, but efforts to preserve the North Fork continued. Friends of the Payette and Idaho Rivers United concentrated their efforts at the state level. They enlisted support from landowners, business owners, paddlers, business organizations, and consumer groups in what was considered "one of the largest environmental lobbying efforts in Idaho history."[64] The campaign included rallies, TV ads, yard signs and delivery of

LIKE THE GAULEY, the North Fork has its own season. While Gauley season occurs during the annual September/October drawdowns of Summersville Lake, North Fork season occurs in August when the flood gates are lowered on Cascade Reservoir for irrigation in the lower Payette river basin.

NOT ALL CONSERVATION EFFORTS were well-organized, nor supported for a common purpose. Whitewater interests were sometimes at odds with fishing interests. In the '80s, local paddlers on the Androscoggin "spent months negotiating weekend flow releases" with a developer, leaving fishermen "with fishless waters under such an arrangement."[65] Another example was negotiations for new releases in the de-watered upper Ripogenus Gorge above Great Northern's proposed Big A dam (short for Ambejackmockamus Falls where the dam was to be built) by one commercial outfitting group. The negotiations were made to compensate for the expected loss of the West Branch of the Penobscot which in essence admitted defeat without a fight and subverted the efforts of others who had not given up. In spite of this, the West Branch of the Penobscot was eventually saved from the Big A dam.

63 Horwitz, Ken. "How to Win a River, Lose a River." *American Whitewater* Vol. XXVII No. 4 (July/August 1982): 23–26.

64 Ibid.

65 Vilbig, Pete. "Or Not to Dam." *Canoe* Vol.10 No. 1(February/March 1982): 43.

as many as 600 letters a day to Idaho lawmakers. It intensified when a state bill to ban future hydropower development on the Payette River system came up for a vote. Wendy Wilson, director for Idaho Rivers United, reported to AWA: "Some legislators were getting phone calls and answering letters about the Payette all day long, and then at night they couldn't go home without seeing yard signs along the road."[66] Finally in 1991, Idaho lawmakers passed the bill with the hope that FERC, at the federal level, would honor Idaho's intent and interests in the preservation of the Payette. However, the battle was not over. It continued to be fought into the '90s.

In the mid-'80s, subtle changes began to occur regarding the atmosphere for hydropower projects. The general public became aware of the ramifications of the projects that affected them personally as a result of many different conservation groups across the country. It also caught the attention of legislators.

Hydropower licenses are good for fifty years before the owner is required to re-license. In the '80s, many of the Depression Era projects that created work in the '30s and '40s required re-licensing. A total of 320 licenses were scheduled to expire between 1986 and 2000. As a result of the increased public awareness of hydropower projects, in 1986, Congress passed the Electric Power Consumers Protection Act to govern the re-licensing of the old projects. Organizations like AWA, Friends of the Earth, the Audubon Society, the Sierra Club, Trout Unlimited, and American Rivers lobbied hard to incorporate their own specific interests into the Act. The Act included a provision that required equal consideration to recreation opportunities. The same year, whitewater recreation gained new status with the Water Resources Development Act that required FERC to give equal consideration to fish, wildlife, energy conservation, and environmental values in the licensing of hydroelectric plants. Recreation interests were to be considered ***if they intervene,*** which were the key words. This pertained to both new licenses and the re-licensing of hydro projects. In 1988, FERC reversed its earlier drive that supported small hydro developments with their decision to invalidate the subsidies offered to new private hydropower developments.

BY THE LATE '80S, it was estimated that there were over 1,000 organizations and groups throughout the country involved in river conservation. Lessons learned in hard fought wins and losses during the '80s improved the odds in favor of winning the battles. It was learned that education of the public regarding the issues worked; that groups that focused exclusively on a single effort, small though they might be, could be more effective than large groups with scattered interests and divided efforts; that volunteers were invaluable, but that paid professional staffs were often critical; that sometimes the groups not thought to be the best allies were; that intense lobbying of state and federal legislators worked; and that paddlers could become just as knowledgeable as the experts.

The Gauley

Until the '80s, the legend and legacy of the Gauley was its whitewater. In the '80s, the chronicle of the Gauley expanded beyond its whitewater rapids. In the early '80s, hydromania caught up with the river and it was again threatened by an Army Corps of Engineers project with the $150 million Long Tunnel Diversion. The hydropower project proposed to divert water through

[66] Editors. Conservation. "Idaho bans future dams on Payette." *American Whitewater* Vol. XXXVI No.3 (May/June 1991): 10.

a long tunnel from the Summersville Dam downstream to near Pillow Rock rapid de-watering Initiation, Insignificant, and Iron Ring. Construction was slated for 1990.

By this time, the legend of the Gauley was known across the country. Paddlers from the East and West converged on the river during the Corps' annual fall drawdown of the reservoir and the term "Gauley season" was coined for this event. In 1982, as soon as word spread about the long tunnel project, Citizens for the Gauley was formed with the support of the West Virginia Wildwater Association, CCA, West Virginia Heritage Association, as well as commercial outfitters (raft companies), and individual paddlers.

With the financial support of the commercial outfitters who relied on Gauley releases for their livelihood, Citizens for the Gauley River hired David Brown who had previously demonstrated his successful strategies for the Ocoee. The strategy that developed for both state and federal level intervention included the designation of Wild and Scenic River status (from Summersville to Swiss), inclusion of the same section into West Virginia Streams Preservation Act, and the adoption of a non-structural alternative plan to replace the long tunnel plan. The strategy also included additional whitewater recreational releases as a stated purpose for the operation of Summersville Dam.

In 1982, following Save the Ocoee's example, Citizens for the Gauley River started the Gauley Festival during the annual fall drawdown. The effects of the publicity surrounding the festival and other strategies were so effective that the Corps attempted to deny a release for the 1983 festival. However, action from West Virginia's Governor resulted in a release. One week after the Festival, on September 30th, the Corps officially dropped their plans for the Long Tunnel Diversion. Their reasons were that the project could not be economically justified and they couldn't find a power company who wanted the power.

The Corps made a political miscalculation during the 1983 annual fall release by refusing requests for peak flows and instead provided releases only from Friday night to Sunday night. This resulted in a $1.5 million dollar loss in tourist dollars for a state already beset by economic woes. This rankled West Virginia Congressmen Bob Wise, who demanded that the Corps "pay more attention to the other resources of the area" [67] which included whitewater recreational boating. In 1984, the Summersville Dam was the first to include in its operation a plan for the enhancement of whitewater recreation. The plan called for a minimum of twenty scheduled days at 2,400 cfs each Fall with special peaking flows for a few hours each day during dry years to preserve the recreation season. This was a tremendous win and evidence of the growth and evolution of the sport.

The plan became official on October 17, 1986, when Congress passed the Water Resources Development Act, the result of bill H. R. 900. The Act made whitewater recreation an official project purpose of the Summersville Dam ensuring a minimum of twenty days of releases during the fall drawdown. Congressman Nick Rahall of West Virginia was credited with the language that guaranteed the Gauley releases. The Corps later announced that the 20-day release accounted for $16 million in direct and indirect economic benefit to the region. In 1986, an estimated 33,000 people took whitewater trips down the Gauley.

West Virginia Congressman Nick Rahall proved to be whitewater paddlers' biggest ally in Congress, not only in protecting whitewater resources in his own state, but beyond. In 1988, Rahall again provided support of whitewater recreation and sponsored legislation that amended the list of thirteen Corps dams that specified whitewater recreation in their operation stating that the dams must "protect and enhance recreation" including "downstream whitewater recreation." [68] The thirteen included dams in Pennsylvania (Yough Lake Dam on the Youghiogheny and Walter Dam on the Lehigh), in Maryland (the Savage River Dam on the Savage, Bloomington Dam on the North Branch of the Potomac), in West Virginia (Bluestone Dam on the New and Summersville Dam on the Gauley), and Virginia (Bailey Lake Dam above the Russell Fork, in Kentucky, and Sutton Dam on the Elk).

67 Staff. Fluvial News. "Gauley: Long Tunnel Dies." *American Whitewater* Vol. XXVIII No. 6 (November/December 1983): 10.

68 Staff. Conservation Comment. "'Project Purpose' Approved." *American Whitewater* Vol. XXXIV No. 2 (March/April 1989): 14.

In 1986, with their purpose to exist finished, Citizens for the Gauley River disbanded. They gave their remaining funds, about $11,000, to the West Virginia River Coalition to protect other threats, both hydro and environmental, to rivers in West Virginia. AWA took over sponsorship of the Gauley Festival as a fund-raiser to support AWA's conservation efforts. By 1987, the festival took on a new dimension and was more than just an AWA fund-raiser. The Gauley Festival developed into an annual whitewater convention where paddlers from across the country came to renew old acquaintances and catch up on the happenings in whitewater paddling. In 1988, the festival was the largest non-competitive whitewater event in North America and the largest gathering of whitewater recreational paddlers.

In 1988, the Gauley River canyon was made a National Recreation Area, although about 99 percent of the land remained in private hands. In 1990, Congressman Rahall once again fought to preserve the Gauley. He pushed for federal funding for land acquisition for the Gauley corridor. At the same time, the Trust for Public Lands took the lead in acquiring land in the corridor in an effort to preserve it prior to purchase by the federal government.

THE GAULEY was just one of many rivers that transformed an area by its popularity. Towns in close proximity to put-ins or take-outs of many popular rivers were affected during the '80s. Ohiopyle on the Yough was the first more than a decade earlier, facilitated by its residents and state park. Burns on the North Fork of the Payette and Lotus and Coloma on the South Fork of the American, though not nearly to the same extent, were others affected by the popularity of whitewater.

In the '80s, the legend and legacy of the Gauley evolved and expanded, setting precedents in many different ways, directly and indirectly. The fight to save the Gauley was so successful it transformed the local area. By the end of the '80s, Summersville was no longer a small town. The put-in was orchestrated to expedite putting on. The river take-outs were no longer a choice between a long day's paddle taking out at Swiss or a shorter two-day paddle taking out at Peter's Creek with a mile hike out the railroad tracks. Take-out parking was more than just pulling off the side of the road.

The Gauley Festival became the mountain man, fur trapper rendezvous of the East. The festival, as with the rendezvous, was the season's end gathering place replete with festivities, singing and dancing, buying and selling, socializing, and contests of skill and ability. There were squirt and rodeo contests, both official and not-so official as paddlers competed on the river showing off their skills.

Ron Burke summed up the Gauley when he wrote, "Call it an ironic paradox: the 1980s were a decade of change so that the river [the Gauley] can remain unchanged in the future."[69] Some bemoaned the loss of the "good old days," the loss of the Summersville small town feel, the loss of the festival's small event feel. But the Gauley, and everything that goes with it, was *and continues to be,* a reflection of the sport itself.

Safety and River Rescue

The philosophy of "safety through education, not regulation" began in the mid-to-late '70s with the threat of federal regulation. The compilation of accident information was the beginning of the development of river rescue courses which began in the late '70s and into the '80s. Until the causes of river accidents were determined, along with discussion regarding prevention, rescue techniques could not be developed. Although this might not have been a purposeful approach, this was, in effect, how river rescue developed.

[69] Burke, Ron. "End of a Decade of Change." *American Whitewater* Vol. XXXIV No. 5 (September/October 1989) 42–43.

In October 1977, the first River Safety Symposium was held in Pennsylvania, sponsored by ARC, ACA, AWA, and Pennsylvania Fish Commission. Papers were presented on topics including training, legislation, safety and rescue, and equipment. The presenters included Russ Nichols, the film-maker involved in some of the first river safety movies, Ramone Eaton, former senior VP of ARC, Charlie Walbridge, ACA Safety Committee Chairman, Ralph McCarty, owner of Mountain Streams & Trails, and others with similar credentials in river safety. The symposium was well attended by government officials, manufacturers, and expert paddlers. The second symposium was held in March of 1978 in North Carolina and was sponsored by ACA, AWA, ARC and Carolina Canoe Club. Again, it was well attended. River safety had the attention of the extended whitewater community and those people directly and indirectly associated with whitewater.

During the same time, there were still few formal water rescue courses. Examination of accidents and fatalities by the River Safety Task Force (and its newsletter) brought out the fact that few rescue courses were designed for rivers with swiftwater let alone whitewater. Except for the growing use of carrying stuff-bag throw bags, very little other preparation was made by whitewater paddlers for rescue. River guides of whitewater outfitters were the exception, although their preparation, too, was meager. However, two separate accidents that resulted in fatalities, one in Ohio in April 1978 and the other on the Chattooga in October 1979, prompted action regarding the development of river rescue techniques for professionals like fire, police, and rescue departments and non-professionals like whitewater paddlers.

The accident in Ohio involved two boys in a canoe who ran a low-head dam and three firemen who attempted to rescue them. Only one fireman escaped. (During the late '70s and early '80s, a third of the 8,000 annual drownings were would-be rescuers.) This accident prompted the Ohio Department of Natural Resources' Division of Watercraft to begin a comprehensive approach for safety education for all Ohioans. In 1978, recognizing that Ohio had experienced whitewater paddlers in its clubs, notably the Keel-Haulers Canoe Club of Cleveland, AYH of Columbus, and the Ohio-Penn Division of the ACA, the Division of Watercraft invited the whitewater community to participate in the development of its River Rescue Training Program for fire and rescue personnel. It was the first of its kind in the country.

In October 1980, Ohio's Division of Watercraft and Department of Education co-sponsored a River Rescue Conference with Charlie Walbridge as the keynote speaker. Although designed for fire and rescue personnel, a key aspect of the conference was integrating paddlers into a municipalities rescue program where possible. The following year, the Division of Watercraft published an instructional manual written by Pam Dillon, ODNR's Special Projects Coordinator, on river rescue for fire and rescue personnel.

While state sponsored programs developed river rescue techniques for fire and rescue personnel, AWA and ACA began to pull together information for whitewater boating and safety. In early 1979, AWA sponsored the AWARE report (the AWA Research Effort) in conjunction with the Coast Guard and Ohio University. AWARE was a safety enhancement project designed around the paddling behaviors and habits of whitewater paddlers. During the spring and summer of 1979, prior to the Chattooga fatality, Drs. Harry Kotes and Don

THE STATE OF CALIFORNIA, recognizing their own unique problems with river rescue (Ohio has swift water and low-head dams and California has swift water, diversion canals, and remote whitewater rivers) assembled their own conference, called Water Rescue 79, of professional and volunteer rescue personnel in April 1979. Rescue 80 International was sponsored the following year. The outcome of the conferences was a three-day course in Swiftwater Rescue to further disseminate the information to professional and volunteer rescue personnel.

In the mid-'80s, California based Rescue 3 began teaching swiftwater rescue courses designed for life-saving professionals such as fire and rescue personnel.

Gordon of the Psychology Dept at Ohio University, with the assistance of Ramone Eaton, John Burton, Bunny Johns, and Payson Kennedy (all associated with NOC), began their data collection at NOC.

Unfortunately, NOC's contribution to river rescue was not based on a gradual learning experience as with instruction, or through its participation in the AWARE report. Instead, NOC's contribution was based on an unfortunate accidental death of one of its own guides, Rich Bernard. Bernard, running kayak safety boat on a NOC commercial raft trip on the Chattooga, drowned when his kayak pinned on an undercut rock at Jawbone.

> The stern of Rick's home-made fiberglass kayak [a Lettmann Mark IV with a ¾ layup substituting two layers of nylon in the hull and one in the deck for glass] had been caught by a submerged log, the boat had folded about three feet from the stern, and the front ten feet of the boat had been swept through a nearly 180 [degree] arc to a position parallel with the current. The entrapment position was thus with the bow pointing downstream and the paddler nearly upright, in the "toe touch" position, forced onto the bow deck by the powerful push of the current over his back, jammed between the deck and the rock over his head and to his right. Rick was almost completely invisible...

Though valiant attempts were made to free Bernard, the efforts by experienced guides were unsuccessful.

> The guides tried to hammer a paddle shaft between the boat and the rock and fed a rope through it underneath the rock. They got the rope through, but it slipped off. They tried to get underneath the boat on the downstream side, but the current was too strong. Attempts to tie a rope to the boat in any way were unsuccessful.
>
> After five hours of such attempts, and of brainstorming other possible methods, a last ditch effort succeeded in securing a rope around the kayak. This was done by two men on either end, one on top of the rock and the other on the rock upstream of the upstream eddy.
>
> A long loop was passed under the overhang and under the boat, and pulled up to the bend in the stern. Six men pulling upstream and across the current from the South Carolina side were finally able to free the boat. Rick was still in it, pushed up against the front of the cockpit.[70]

[70] Walbridge, Charles (Editor) and Burton, John G. "Fatal Accident on Section IV of the Chattooga River." *The Best of The River Safety Task Force Newsletter: 1976–1982*. Lorton, Virginia: The American Canoe Association, Inc., 1983.

Subsequent analysis of the accident concluded that there were no fundamental causes that contributed to Bernard's death. He was in the wrong place at the wrong time. At this time, whitewater river safety and rescue for paddlers consisted mostly of the use of a lead, sweep, and rope. Unfortunately, the accidental drowning of Bernard showed how limited these river rescue techniques were.

Bernard's death rocked the staff at NOC. Les Bechdel, in charge of rafting operations, was deeply affected. During the winter after the accident, Bechdel, a climber, realized that rescue techniques for whitewater were not nearly as advanced as those developed for climbing. There was much to be leveraged from climbing using vertical rescue techniques in the horizontal. Over the next couple of years, Bechdel worked with NOC guides and, through a lot of trial and error, developed new rescue techniques for guides and staff. Bechdel modified climbing practices including the Z-Drag, teller lower, and Tyrolean traverse for river use. By 1982, whitewater paddlers in general were interested in these new techniques. Bechdel began traveling and teaching safety and rescue training to guides as well as clubs. Bechdel also continued to learn and borrow from whatever sources he could. The result was the publication of the book *River Rescue* in 1983, a collaboration with Slim Ray, senior NOC photographer, who also had considerable experience paddling and teaching.

Les Bechdel was in communication with Charlie Walbridge and Pam Dillon of the Ohio Department of Natural Resources who were also interested in collaborating on a river rescue book. Bechdel felt it was important to get the information out to the whitewater community in a timely fashion and felt their geographic separation (Walbridge in eastern Pennsylvania and Dillon in Ohio) would have delayed and extended the project. Instead, Bechdel and Slim Ray, both at NOC, collaborated on the book.

By the mid-to-late '80s, cooperation and exchange of information for river safety spread across the country and across the professional rescuer and whitewater paddler boundaries. Charlie Walbridge, as the ACA Safety Chairman, participated in the ICF Safety Symposiums held in Europe. In 1990, the first international whitewater river safety symposium was organized by Slim Ray and was hosted by NOC with funding support by Perception.

Because of Bernard's death and the efforts of NOC's staff in developing river rescue techniques, NOC became involved in developing river rescue courses. NOC offered some of the first courses for the general whitewater boating community developed around the abilities and equipment available on whitewater rivers to whitewater paddlers.

In the early '80s, while NOC and others incorporated safety education through actual river rescue programs, ACA and ARC took the "Education, Not Regulation" philosophy to heart. Their approach incorporated safety education into their instructional "how-to" programs, not as river rescue, but with the thought that an educated paddler was a safer paddler.

By the mid-'80s, ACA began to look at education and instruction, not for "Education, Not Regulation" but for the sake of instruction. A mini-industry evolved and flourished around ACA certification of instructors. Instead of education for safety, the instruction tended to reinforce learning technique and style and the memorization of the official list of endless names of stroke combinations, required by the certification. Although it may not have been

NONE OF THE THEN CURRENT DISCUSSIONS regarding safety hazards and concerns were proven with Bernard's death; that fiberglass kayaks are safer than plastic kayaks because they'll break apart in a pin or that break-away cockpits are the answer to entrapment. John Burton, Director of NOC and National Slalom Champion, concluded that,

> As with any durable river-running boat, the stern area had extra reinforcement, and it had both inside and outside seems [seams]. The boat cracked and ended up with several holes near the bend but did not break apart. I would venture to say that any boat capable of withstanding repeated runs on Class III-IV rivers would not have broken apart in this instance.
>
> A "break away" cockpit, lacking synthetic material, also would not have helped: the stress was not such that it would have broken out.[71]

[71] Walbridge, Charles (Editor) and Burton, John G. "Fatal Accident on Section IV of the Chattooga River." *The Best of The River Safety Task Force Newsletter: 1976–1982*. Lorton, Virginia: The American Canoe Association, Inc., 1983.

a conscious decision, the move toward education for its own sake, not for safety's sake, became the underlying result for ACA's programs during the late '80s and into the '90s.

Although the education programs were effective, deaths continued to occur. The programs could not completely eliminate lapses in judgment by both experienced and inexperienced paddlers, nor could it eliminate accidental deaths of experienced paddlers pushing the limits.

In July 1982, Chuck Rollins, a well-known paddler from New York, drowned on the South Fork of the Clearwater in Idaho. He joined an expert boating trip in Idaho although he apparently did not have the skills to handle the kind of water he attempted. Rollins had trouble with many of the easier runs on the trip, including the Middle Fork of the Salmon, even before attempting the more difficult South Fork of the Clearwater. After his death, there was much discussion regarding the social responsibility of fellow paddlers in trying to dissuade a paddler, and a friend, from attempting a run that was clearly beyond his or own ability, and perhaps the paddler's ability to accurately judge his or her own abilities or the river.

During Gauley season the same year, Bob O'Connor, an experienced boater from the Georgia Tech Outdoor Program, drowned when he was trapped in a sieve on river-right of Initiation Rapid. Analysis of the death showed that "the most competent and best equipped people can never assure rescue. Prevention is the only way to avoid fatalities."[72] The incident occurred where several pinnings had previously occurred, but never before with a fatality.

Over one March weekend in 1986, four experienced paddlers drowned: three in the East and one in the West. One man drowned on the North River in Virginia in an end-to-end pin in a T-Slalom that lacked walls and flotation. He was paddling with only one other boater who swam the same drop and was unable to assist in a rescue. Another death occurred on the Lower Gauley at 20,000 cfs above Pure Screaming Hell when a squirtboater disappeared. The boater was later found in a strainer with his PFD and sprayskirt still on. The third eastern boater to die was actually not the result of a drowning but of a massive heart attack on the Tohickon in Pennsylvania. The western boater died on a commercial trip on the Jatate in Mexico when he bailed in a Class V drop and was trapped under a boulder. He had apparently misrepresented his paddling skills. The following month Donna Berglund, a well-known experienced whitewater paddler, drowned while training alone on a river in Montana.

The drought of 1988 in the East resulted in fewer fatalities with none among experienced paddlers. But in the West, there were five fatalities among experienced and inexperienced paddlers. One death occurred at Eagle Falls on the Skykomish when an inexperienced boater, although experienced as a raft guide, missed his line going over the falls. Another occurred in Oregon on the Sandy River when a squirtboater pinned in a chute that contained a tree. Idaho rivers claimed two more. An expert OC-1 paddler drowned on the South Fork of the Clearwater, and an experienced kayaker drowned on the notorious Miracle Mile of the Secesh River, a tributary of the South Fork of the Salmon. The last fatality occurred on the Poudre in Colorado with the drowning of a 63 year old kayaker at the Mishawaka Rapid (Class IV+). Walbridge wrote of these deaths and other near misses the same year:

[72] Walbridge, Charlie. "Accidents: The Drowning of Bob O'Connor on the Gauley River." *American Whitewater* Vol. XXVIII No.4 (July/August 1983): 25–27.

I'm concerned with signs that our vigilance is dropping, and that we are taking unnecessary risks. Very difficult rivers which once were run by "teams of experts, taking all precautions" are being paddled "on the fly" by loosely organized groups... I am also concerned at what I see as appalling lapses of good judgement. Great Falls, a class VI drop outside Washington D.C., has changed from a discreet expert run to a "rite of passage" for every would-be hot-shot in the area.[73]

[*Author's note:* This would portend the first death of a boater at Great Falls, Scott Bristow, almost ten years later.]

The spring and summer of 1989 had some of the best boating in the East in almost a decade. Unfortunately, it also had a high number of fatalities that involved experienced and properly equipped boaters. The fatalities during Gauley Festival weekends in 1989 and 1990 prompted the Close Calls Survey. The results were somewhat surprising indicating that of the readership that responded, 8 percent had been involved in a serious mishap on the river. That corresponded to roughly one in twelve paddlers. Accidents occurred on rivers in twenty-nine states. West Virginia had the highest number of accidents reported. Accidents occurred on rapids rated Class II through VI, but the majority (39 percent) was on Class IV rapids. Like a bell curve, Class II had 26.8 percent and Class V had 23.7 percent. The age group with the highest number of accidents was 30–39 years of age (46 percent)) followed by the 20–29 age group (at 23 percent). Additionally, 79 percent of the accidents involved men.

Safety Concerns and the Industry

Safety education in the '80s brought with it an awareness of the dangers involved in whitewater. Unfortunately, the '70s and '80s also brought an awareness of consumer protection and product liability lawsuits. As long as the industry and the number of whitewater paddlers remained small, the likelihood of product liability lawsuits remained small. However, the growth of the sport in the '80s increased that likelihood. Product safety was a vulnerable area in regards to whitewater. Not that manufacturers were making unsafe products. On the contrary, whitewater manufacturers understood the risk involved with the sport. But the probability increased that an inexperienced paddler might alter a product beyond the manufacturer's specs, or push the limits of the product because of his or her inexperience. No product could be designed to protect the consumer for all possible scenarios that might occur in whitewater.

The first product safety issue resulting from an accident that came into the spotlight involved the same argument used by a few of the composite manufacturers against plastic kayak construction in the marketing war: deck collapse. However, instead of involving a plastic kayak as some thought would happen, it involved a composite kayak.

In September 1979, a paddler who admitted he could have prevented his own deck collapse problem in the manufactured kayak he paddled, decided he needed to protect other paddlers through governmental agency regulations.

[73] Walbridge, Charlie. Safety Lines. "The Year's Tragedies." *American Whitewater* Vol. XXXIV No. 1 (January/February 1989): 22–23.

AWA PROVIDED AN OPEN FORUM for discussion of the Reif-Old Town controversy by publishing the views of Arnold Reif, Peter Sonderegger (Old Town's General Manager), and Charlie Walbridge (as ACA Safety Chairman). The first views appeared in the July/August 1980 issue of *American Whitewater* under the title "Equipment Safety—Who's Responsible." AWA continued publishing correspondence involving the case, as well as opinions from other paddlers, throughout the next year.

Arnold Reif was surfing at the Cohasset tidal basin on the Class III wave when the deck of his new Old Town Prijon Special Slalom collapsed. He managed to extricate himself but then he that he should have reinforced the deck prior to using his new kayak but that he failed to do so. Reif wrote to Old Town suggesting that they reinforce the deck with a vertical deck-to-floor bracing (an internal pillar or wall). Old Town's reply was that they redesigned their construction, which was to take effect in their 1980 whitewater models. Reif was not satisfied with their response. He responded to Old Town suggesting that they warn all owners of 1979 whitewater kayaks of the deck collapse danger and provide a free kit to remedy the defect. The controversy heated up when Reif copied his letter to the Maine Consumer Protection Agency. The letter eventually made its rounds to the Consumer Product Safety Commission in Washington, D.C., to Captain Lohmann, Chief of the Boating Technical Division of the Coast Guard, to ACA, and finally to AWA.

Reif was not satisfied with Captain Lohmann's response because Lohman determined that there was no construction flaw. The kayak was not defective. Reif recalled that Lohman's reasons were,

> (a) that kayakers must be aware that kayaks are not unbreakable, (b) deck collapse does not necessarily result in a fatality (c) paddlers commonly install deck braces for Class III rapids and above, and (d) requiring a recall would mandate all similar kayaks be provided with deck braces.[74]

Reif continued pursuit of the issue through ACA. Subsequent letters and conversations were exchanged between Reif and various Coast Guard officials who again restated that no construction flaw was found and that mandating the recall of approximately 250 Old Town whitewater kayaks purchased in 1979 was not within their mandate by Congress. Regulatory action was required only when there was proof of "substantial danger to life." No proof existed of deaths of paddlers due to deck collapse.

Fortunately for the sport, this incident occurred after a working relationship had already been established between ACA and the Coast Guard, in particular, between Charlie Walbridge, the ACA Safety Chairman, and Captain Lohmann with regard to the leveling flotation discussions of the '70s. Walbridge's response to the whole matter expressed what he had come to know and understand about the limitations of mandating regulations:

> Knowledgeable paddlers have long agreed that only the individual can be responsible for his on-river safety... Law administrators, with a few notable exceptions, view paddlers as a small group of freaks, somewhere between motorboat racers and hang glider pilots. Changing this misconception is a time consuming, frustrating job. And convincing government of our ability to regulate ourselves while possible has become a more than full time task for organizations like ACA and AWA. Therefore, I have no desire to spawn new legislative Frankensteins whose effects will deeply restrict my boating time and freedom. Besides, experience has taught us all that

[74] Staff. AWA Forum. "Equipment Safety —Who's Responsible." *American Whitewater* Vol. XXV No. 4 (July/August 1980): 27–33.

the only way to improve boater safety is to make paddlers aware of the dangers. If a person is ignorant, no amount of rule-making will help him.[75]

Reif, upon learning of the earlier leveling flotation discussions, re-directed his interest from the deck collapse problem to questioning the decision by the Coast Guard regarding canoe flotation. His crusade then became that of protecting the unskilled and uneducated canoe users who constitute the majority in the sport. Reif also questioned the relationship between the Coast Guard and the industry manufacturers and ACA implying that the industry did not represent the consumer's well-being to the Coast Guard. Reif felt that Pete Sonderegger, Old Town's General Manger and past editor of *Canoe* Magazine, and Charlie Walbridge, ACA Safety Chairman and owner of Wildwater Designs, could not and should not represent the consumer to the Coast Guard.

The deck collapse controversy elicited comments from paddlers across the country including Carl Trost who had studied whitewater boating fatalities in California during the '70s. Until Trost read of the deck collapse controversy, he was unaware that eastern kayakers took foam walls for granted in fiberglass kayaks. Trost's experience in California was the opposite and was more prevalent among western boaters: that it is better to not rely on pillars which might interfere with escape in the case of entrapment. Instead, light-weight decks were reinforced with ribs and the layups themselves were designed to break before the boat collapsed. In his twenty years of paddling, he had never seen pillars or walls in fiberglass boats on western rivers. Trost, however, supported and praised Charlie Walbridge and the Coast Guard while chastising Old Town for their less-than-magnanimous reply that added insult to injury.

The deck collapse controversy also elicited different solutions for composite kayaks other than the installation of interior walls for support, as used in plastic kayaks. In the early '80s, Phoenix developed and marketed its breakaway cockpit system. Using nylon in its whitewater layups for durability, the nylon lay-up around the cockpit in the deck was uninterrupted which allowed the cockpit itself to break out should the boat pin and fold. The folding action put the fiberglass-only areas under tensile stress and since glass is significantly weaker in tension than compression, it breaks or cracks apart.

In the mid-'80s, Rick Curtis and Tom Kreutz of Outdoor Safety Systems in Princeton, New Jersey, designed the Safety Deck System that allowed a section of the deck in front of the cockpit to be released in the case of entrapment, providing additional room to escape. The Safety Deck System was a removable foredeck section that included the knee braces and forward part of the cockpit rim. The foredeck section was released by pushing it forward in an emergency situation. After designing and building it, Curtis and Kreutz hired a patent attorney and applied for a patent. Unfortunately, Bill Masters of Perception had filed for a similar concept. In 1985, Masters received the patent (Patent No. 4,520,747). They also approached kayak manufacturers with the concept but were unable to win much support. New Wave Kayaks, Ultrasports, and Whittemore Laminates offered it as an option for their composite boats. However, few were sold. Even paddlers didn't feel the need for it. Curtis and Kreutz also realized their system was too labor intensive in production and decided not to pursue it any further.

SINCE THE LEVELING FLOTATION DISCUSSIONS of the '70s, ACA spent much time working with and educating the Coast Guard regarding the sport of whitewater. The Coast Guard, in turn, educated ACA and others regarding regulation by federal mandates and self-regulation of the sport. The Coast Guard admitted they were controlled by laws that did not allow flexibility once regulations were established, however good or bad those regulations were. The industry and the sport benefitted from an understanding of the complexity of the system in which the Coast Guard operated.

IN THE EARLY '80S, Teckna Survival Knives became popular among whitewater paddlers. Paddlers carried them on the PFD's should the need arise to cut a way out of a collapsed or pinned boat, or assist with other river rescue situations.

[75] Staff. AWA Forum. "Equipment Safety —Who's Responsible." *American Whitewater* Vol. XXV No. 4 (July/August 1980): 27–33.

Although the deck collapse accident involved a composite kayak, plastic kayaks were not completely immune from the same threat even though manufacturers such as Perception relied on the design and strength of its interior pillar supports to prevent deck collapse. However, accidents inspired two other potential improvements for plastic kayaks. Les Bechdel, realizing the difficulty of freeing a pinned kayak, came up with the idea of a broach loop adjacent to the cockpit. He approached Perception. The very name itself implied danger in the sport and Perception did not immediately pursue the idea. Instead, Perception later incorporated a security loop in the same location to prevent boat theft, although the security loop was strong enough to serve a dual purpose: a security loop and broach loop.

The other potential improvement was first noticed in kayaks imported from Europe, notably Prijon kayaks, that used a larger keyhole-style cockpit. Demonstration of the effectiveness of the larger cockpit during pin situations eventually helped to gain acceptance of their use in American designed kayaks in the early '90s.

THE SPORT AND INDUSTRY were sensitized to the potential for product liability lawsuits by the deck collapse controversy. On the whole, since the manufacturers of whitewater boats and products were often paddlers themselves, they took precautions in their designs and construction based on their paddling experience to ameliorate the risks as best they could. However, regardless of the amount of safety education or safety features built into whitewater boats, as Walbridge wrote: "only the individual can be responsible for his on-river safety.[76]

The '80s in Competition: Slalom

Although slalom racing had not been included in an Olympics since 1972, it experienced a resurgence in interest during the '80s. Slalom still held the promise and the potential of Olympic competition. However, interest in wildwater neither significantly grew nor declined.

Slalom courses, both formal and informal, sprang up across the country. Programs emulating the C-CATS developed encouraging young paddlers and hoping to repeat its success. A subtle shift in the home states of competitors occurred from the East toward the Midwest. ACA's Midwest Division contributed an increasing number of racers, particularly C-paddlers, in both slalom and wildwater, which was perhaps due to the Midwest's dominance in open canoe marathon racing.

In the '80s, a shift occurred in competition in the kind of corporate support it garnered. ACA encouraged both paddlesport and non-paddlesport sponsors. Aided by the popularity of whitewater rafting, non-paddlesport corporate sponsors began to participate. Television coverage of daring whitewater runs also helped. In the spring of 1982, four regional events and national finals were held at Six Flags theme parks. Billed as a Grand Prix (slalom racing for timing with no gate penalties), K-1, K-1W, C-1, C-2 and C-2M races were held on the man-made river rapids at various parks. The events were endorsed

[76] Staff. AWA Forum. "Equipment Safety—Who's Responsible." *American Whitewater* Vol. XXV No. 4 (July/August 1980): 27–33.

by ACA with prizes, including cash for national finals. Paddlers retained their amateur status as allowed by ACA's new rules governing amateurism. Six Flags continued to sponsor the events throughout the mid-'80s.

The popularity and success of festivals also encouraged corporate support. In 1986, Knoxville hosted the Knoxville Canoe and Kayak Festival, which was planned around canoeing and kayaking events, both whitewater and flatwater. The festival began May 31 with the North American Whitewater Rodeo on the Ocoee. It continued with the National Slalom and Wildwater Championships, the Pan American Cup Regatta on Melton Hill Lake for flatwater sprint competition, and U.S. Team Trials for Marathon Canoe racing. Other events included an outdoor recreational equipment exposition, family and corporate challenge canoe races, and canoe and kayak instruction clinics. Open boat surfing and a squirt contest were also held on the Ocoee.

Perhaps the single achievement that drove the popularity and awareness of slalom racing among racers and non-racers alike was the continued and remarkable performance of America's C-1 team throughout the '80s, the Decade of America's C-1 Domination.

America's Decade of C-1 Domination in Slalom

American wins at the '79 World Championships in Jonquierre were not, at first, considered spectacular to the world paddling community. The absence of the East German team and the less-than-stellar performance of the once strong Czech, Polish, and Yugoslavian teams threw a wet-blanket on the American wins. Everyone waited for the '81 World Championships in Bala, Wales.

American C-1 paddlers showed up with an all-new design, the Cudamax, a cut-down Ultramax with even lower volume for the low volume course. American domination of C-1 was reaffirmed. All C-classes, both in slalom and wildwater, were dominated by American paddlers. In C-1 slalom, Jon Lugbill again took gold and Davey Hearn took silver. In C-2M slalom, the American team swept all the medals. Liz (Boo) Hayman and Fritz Haller won the gold, Barb McKee and John Sweet won silver, and Karen Marte and Brent Sorenson won bronze. In C-2 slalom, Mike and Steve Garvis, the Garvii, won gold, and Paul Grabow and Jeffry Huey won bronze. It was the last year for wildwater C-2M competition in the World Championships. In wildwater, the C-2M team of Mike Hipsher and Bunny Johns won gold and John Butler won bronze in C-1.

In K-1W slalom, the American women continued to gain ground with Cathy Hearn's silver win, the best finish ever. However, in K-1 slalom, the American team continued to fall short in international competition. Their best finish was 13th.

In 1983, at the World Championships in Merano, Italy, American C-1 paddlers showed up with the Batmax, their latest C-1 design, which had wings that added 5 cm to a 65 cm hull width, but still meeting 70 cm minimum width requirement. The Batmax was much faster in forward speed than the previous designs. Once again, as in the '79 and '81 World Championships, the U.S. team in C-competition dominated the championships. Jon Lugbill became the World Champion for a third time. He also became the first man ever to win six gold medals in C-1 slalom (combined individual and team medals from the '79, '81, and '83 World Championships). Davey Hearn

LINDA HRRISON'S DECADE was the '70s. She was expected to win the gold so her bonze medal finish at Bala was a heartbreaking loss. Her run was clean until the last gate. Russ Nichols' film *Fast and Clean* documents her loss. The '81 World Championships were her last shot. Younger women were poised to take over. Cathy Hearn won a silver. In just two short years, Harrison's bronze at Jonquierre, the previous best, was beaten. However, Harrison's contribution to K-1W and her support and inspiration helped make it all possible. The style and aggressiveness she displayed ratcheted-up K-1W competition in America a few notches.

THE WIDTH CHANGE for the Batmax would have been too radical in the '70s. When the minimum width requirement changed from 80 to 70 cm in 1971, many of the first C-1 designs didn't immediately go to 70 cm, but stayed a little wider because of concern for instability. Ten years later, stability concerns were replaced by the desire for speed. Narrow widths provided that.

earned his third silver. In C-2 slalom, brothers Fritz and Lecky Haller won the gold with an incredibly fast and clean second run. Two other American brothers, the Garvi, took bronze. However, in kayak competition, the best K-1W finish was Cathy Hearn's 7th in both slalom and wildwater K-1W. A medal finish in K-1 continued to elude the American team. The best American K-1 finish was 33rd.

At the '85 World Championships in Augsburg, Lugbill and Hearn switched places. Hearn won the gold and Lugbill won the silver. Again, they won in a C-1 of their own design, the Super Batmax, the last in the Max series of designs.

In 1985, Lugbill was one of six winners chosen out of a field of 1,000 athletes in the "Search for Champions II" sponsored by Wheaties. His image was used on boxes of "the breakfast of champions."

The incredible domination of American C-1 paddlers continued in the '87 World Championships on the Isere at Bourg St. Maurice, France. Lugbill and Hearn again swapped finishes and American C-1 men swept the medals in their latest design, the Extra Bat. The Extra Bat reversed the trend in the C-1 Max designs; volume was added for the relatively big water of the Isere. Lugbill won gold, Hearn won silver, and newcomer Bruce Lessels won bronze. Lecky Haller and Jamie McEwan teamed in C-2 to win silver.

The next year, 1988, was an exciting year for Americans in slalom. International competition was brought to North America with the inauguration of a slalom World Cup and the Pre-Worlds that were held on the Savage prior to the World Championships. The Pre-Worlds were held on the Savage just as they had been ten years earlier in Jonquierre to make sure everything went off without a hitch to prepare for the World Championships. The World Championships were anticipated to be the biggest whitewater race ever held in North America. Because the Savage is located in a narrow canyon with a one-lane road on river left, traffic and logistics were carefully planned, including buses and a train that brought spectators to the site. Facilities were built for the races including spectator stands, judging stations, bridges, and walkways.

IOC also announced that slalom again would be an Olympic event at the '92 Olympics in Barcelona. Now, an American audience, not just racers, could watch Americans dominate in international C-paddling. Americans also had a strong chance to win a gold in the Olympics.

The inaugural World Cup in 1988, based on a series of seven races, was another success of American C-paddlers, as well as in K-1W. ICF designated the World Cup a demonstration sport to ensure it continued a quality event prior to official ICF sanctioning. Four of the seven races were held in North America on the Savage and Gull, both natural river sites, at Wausau with its man-enhanced rapids, and South Bend with its artificial course. The three European sites were Nottingham and Augsburg, both artificial courses, and Dublin which was described as current with one drop. Americans won three of the four cups. Dana Chladek won K-1W, Lugbill won C-1 followed by Davey Hearn and Jed Prentice with an American sweep of C-1 medals. Lecky Haller and Jamie McEwan won in C-2.

By 1988, in addition to the premier bi-annual World Championships, there were other major races including the Europa Cup, the Pan Am Cup, and the Mid-America Cup. But the World Championships, the longest continuous race, were considered the premier international championship event.

By the '80s, the growing number of artifi cial courses for slalom racing, particularly related to their concrete walls and narrowness, began to affect both slalom canoe and kayak designs. One of the changes effects that Hearn and Lugbill incorporated in the Super Batmax was a re-distribution of length between the bow and stern. For the Super Batmax, the bow (from cockpit to bow end) was shortened by 2 inches and added to the stern. This in essence shortened the length of boat for maneuvering the tighter courses, and also reduced bow damage caused by hitting the concrete walls. Because mandatory reverse gates were eliminated for the '85 World Championships, the extra length in the stern was inconsequential.

The idea for the World Cups had been bantered about for a while, but didn't happen until Richard Fox of Britain and Rade Koracevic of Yugoslavia joined forces and proposed the World Cup series. The World Cup Promotional Committee, headed by U.S. Team coach Bill Endicott, worked to obtain ICF sanctioning.

The Slalom World Cup was modeled after the World Cup series of races for skiing with 25 points for first place, 20 for second, 15 for third, down to one point for 10th through 15th. The final race in the series was weighted heavier with double the standard points.

The '89 World Championships were held in North America for the second time, and for the first time in the United States on the Savage River in Maryland. Jon Lugbill again reigned supreme capturing his fifth individual gold medal with Davey Hearn capturing his fifth silver behind Lubgill. They paddled the Fanatic, one of the last C-1s they designed together. The Fantatic was a more forgiving design, with softer chines, than the Extra Bat. In 1991, Hearn designed the Stealth, which proved to be a dog for racing. It had more rocker in the stern but became too low in volume with the rocker modifications. Lugbill, having come out of his first retirement to compete in 1991, tried the Stealth but switched back to the Fanatic.

In K1-W, Dana Chladek and Cathy Hearn captured silver and bronze, another incredible win, behind Myriam Jerusalmi of France. American C-2 and K-1 teams took no medals in slalom or in any of the wildwater events.

American wins on home turf on the Savage were an incredible culmination to an incredible decade. Lugbill's gold winning performance proved his mastery of his craft and had knowledgeable spectators entranced. The excitement and celebration was incredible but soon, all attention turned to the next prize, Olympic medals at the'92 Olympics in Barcelona.

The success of the American slalom teams which began in the late '70s and carried into and through the '80s was attributed to the flexibility of the American system of training and the selection process. Though unintentional, the system's evolution as the result of the lack of both governmental and limited national support and infrastructure, proved to be an advantage with the sport's changes and advances that occurred during that time. "This flexibility has given the Americans the opportunity to take advantage of the frequent rule changes and improved equipment of the seventies while the larger organizations of the Europeans are unable to adapt as quickly."[77]

The flexibility and variation in training methods also seemed to spark innovation in many areas. The continued Hearn-Lugbill designs from the original Max II and Ultramax C-1s turned the tide whereas the Europeans were watching the boats the Americans designed and copied them for the next year's races. The Americans, not the Europeans, were the innovators in canoeing designs both for C-1s and C-2s. American techniques, the result of their inter-relationship with design, were also copied by the Europeans.

Although the limitations of the national system made it difficult for new racers to become involved, the selection process seemed to ameliorate this deficiency. The team size remained larger to allow younger or less-experienced paddlers to experience competition and the final team selection process remained a winner-take-all, one-weekend event for selecting the top four in

Just as Jon Lugbill dominated international competition in the '80s in C-1, Richard Fox of Great Britain, dominated in K-1. Fox took a bronze at Jonquierre in 1979 but took the gold at Bala in 1981. Fox went on to become a three-time World Champion in the '80s. Fox also won on the Savage in 1989.

In 1981, Fox, like Lugbill and Hearn, designed his own boats for his style of paddling. Fox followed the design trend first begun by Prijon in the early '70s and continued with designs from Pyrahna and Nomad, two British companies. In the late '70s, Fox used the Equipe and followed with the Extreme, a Graham Mackereth design. Fox, working with Mackereth at Pyrahna, designed his first boat, the Extra, with a distinctive U-shaped chine forward of kayak's center that allowed Fox to carve his turns. Fox set up his moves in advance instead of relying on abrupt gate turns that many others used, including the Americans. Fox said that his technique evolved, partially from studying Lugbill and Hearn. Fox's Quattro and Foxfire designs followed the Extra later in the '80s.

[77] Ford, Kent. AWA Briefs. "Flexible Training Techniques Contributes to US Slalom Success." *American Whitewater* Vol. XXXIV No.1 (January/February 1989): 10–11, 46.

each class event. Other countries kept their team size small, only for the select few, and used various other processes for team selection including percentages, point systems, and coach selection.

By 1989, the rule changes for slalom racing that began in the early '70s had finally changed the sport from testing river-running ability to testing hand-eye coordination at high speed. Even U.S. Team Coach Bill Endicott felt that the later year changes seemed to promote a sport with better spectator appeal, including TV viewability. The continuing changes also raised concerns that it might even eliminate the premium on whitewater technique.

However, regardless of changes in designs, the changes in technique, the C-1 medal sweeps, and all the other medals won by American racers, the singlemost phenomenon that stood out in the '80s was Jon Lugbill. In 1984, just halfway through Lugbill's career, Eric Evans wrote:

> ...Advancements in sport spring from four basic factors:
>
> An iconoclastic psyche... The scaling of entrenched barriers through sheer force of will or the courage to plunge unfettered into the unknown has always been seminal to progress...
>
> Superior equipment... Technology judiciously applied has often been the catalyst to launch a sport onto the next plateau...
>
> Revolutionary training or techniques... Radically different approaches to basic problems and principles often yield frustration but every so often the results are dramatically effective...
> Sheer physical talent... blessed with physical gifts, gifts that came to redefine their disciplines...
>
> Until recently, however, no sportsman has promulgated change within his realm through leadership in all four areas.[78]

...that is, until Jon Lugbill. Lugbill, was head and shoulders above the rest in bringing all four factors to slalom canoeing. He redefined the barriers for C-1 slalom that remained practically his alone until the '90s. He accomplished what no one before had ever done in whitewater, totally dominating the competition through five World Championships.

Because of Lugbill's skill and speed, C-1 slalom scores were reduced to less than ten percentage points of K-1 winning scores– something few people previously would have guessed was possible. [*Author's note*: That is, until you watched him. Then you just might think it was possible for him to beat the K-1s.]

In whitewater competition, the bellwether for the sport was long considered to be the K-1 class. Even former C-1 and C-2 racer Tom Southworth once said "a country has not arrived in international competition until it wins in K-1."[79] However, that was before anyone ever dreamed that C-1 could be transformed into a class and a craft that could almost compete head-on with K-1. American C-paddlers in the '80s made it happen.

[78] Evans, Eric. "The Old Ways Will Not Do: Lugbill." *Canoe* Vol. 12 No. 2 (April 1984): 32–38, 40–41, 92–93.

[79] Editors. "Our Time Has Come." *Canoe* Vol. 7 No. 3 (May/June 1979): 38–41.

The New Competition: American Style

Rodeo, squirt, and extreme racing were three American-style sub-sports within whitewater that evolved in the '80s. The root of whitewater rodeos in the West and squirt and extreme racing in the East was competition. Friendly, unofficial, unregulated, and unstructured competition among paddlers, where the limits of the paddler, boat, and water were pushed, and where little or no structure provided for the endless potential for change.

Rodeo was playboating in a public forum. Squirt was, at first, personal competitions with the river and unofficial competitions among squirtboaters. It eventually morphed into rodeo. Extreme took wildwater racing to the next level. It was truly a ***wildwater*** race with an increased risk of injury, even death, and was meant for the most highly skilled. Extreme races were for the demonstration of the extreme upper-end of paddling skills.

Rodeo and Squirt

Two events occurred within rodeo that changed the sport and steered its course in whitewater. The first occurred at the 1979 Stanley Rodeo where the first cash prizes were awarded. The prizes were provided by Harrah's Corporation, owner of gambling casinos in Nevada, and also the owner of land on the Middle Fork of the Salmon. Prizes brought the eventual need to regulate and structure rodeo competitions to equitably distribute the winnings. The other

Boating crowd at Salmon River Days (ID), 1982
—courtesy of Rob Lesser.

Contestant at the North Idaho Whitewater Festival, 1986 —courtesy of Rob Lesser.

THE NORTH AMERICAN WHITEWATER RODEO was referred to and advertised as the Nationals although there was no national organization or consensus among event holders, who were primarily found in the West, that it be designated as such. This was the same situation that occurred with slalom and wildwater competition in the '50s between race organizers in the East and West. It also occurred in 1940 with AMC's designation of their race as the National White Water Championship.

event occurred the following year when Bill Masters showed up at the Stanley Rodeo to see what all the hoopla was about. From Masters' perspective, rodeo events were a marketing mother lode that could be used to draw more paddlers to the sport which meant a larger market. He could see it and was going to capitalize on it.

A paradigm shift gradually occurred that affected the entire sport of whitewater. Competitors went from professional amateurs, professional because they took winnings, to amateur professionals because they were new at being paid professionals. The sport now had quasi-professional paddlers, paddlers who were sponsored to compete in rodeos.

By 1985, almost a dozen rodeos were organized across the West; from the Sawtooths in Idaho, rodeo's birthplace, to the Cascades in Washington and Oregon, and south to the Sierras in California and the Rockies of Colorado. The list included the Animas River Races, Arkansas River Hotdog Contest, Blackfoot Whitewater Roundup, Chili Bar Rodeo, Clackamas Whitewater Rodeo, Colorado Whitewater Festival, Gallatin Get Together, Nugget Whitewater Roundup, Payette Whitewater Roundup, Salmon River Days, Stanley Whitewater Rodeo, Trinity Whitewater Races, and the Wenatchee Whitewater Rodeo.

The East had a couple of its own. In 1981, the first rodeo contest was held at the Ocoee River Festival and was included annually thereafter. In 1985, the Eastern Freestyle debuted on the Black River in New York. It was the first time that separate hot dog competitions were held for playboats and squirtboats.

Not only did the number of rodeos grow by the mid-'80s, but the size of the rodeos grew, not just in attendance, but in festivities. By this time, the classic rodeo was a weekend of festivities around three competitive kayaking: slalom, wildwater/downriver, and a hot-dog contest consisting of hole-riding. In 1986, the Upper Clackamas Whitewater Festival with its rodeo at Bob's Hole was in its fourth year. It had grown from a single day event with 45 entrants and 200 spectators to a weekend of free-style kayaking, bluegrass entertainment, and the largest inflatable slalom in the country with over 200 entrants and 2,000 spectators.

In 1986, the Nationals for rodeo competition were held in the East at the North American Whitewater Rodeo on the Ocoee. Because of its location in the East near a large squirtboater population, the rodeo included separate playboat and squirt competitions. Jeff Snyder, sponsored by New Wave, competed and won in a Jim Snyder-designed Jet manufactured by New Wave. This was the start of competitive squirtboating as incorporated into rodeo events. Two years later in 1988, the first squirt competition in the West was held at the Wenatchee Whitewater Rodeo.

In the '80s, the rodeos and festivities grew bigger and bigger. They became more than a hot dog contest and a party. Permits and insurance were needed which meant financial support was needed. Raffles were used to raise the funds necessary to break even. Manufacturers stepped in to lend their support. Perception led the way pouring time, money, and boats for raffles and prizes. For Perception, it was another dimension of marketing. However, all involved benefitted since left over money, which happened as the contests grew bigger, often went to support river conservation. Hydra also understood the value of supporting rodeos and offered prize money to the winners in rodeo competition at the Wenatchee and Ocoee rodeos: $1,000 for first place ($2,000 if won in one of their boats). The Dragonfly, introduced in 1988, was marketed as a low volume whitewater playboat for rodeo. Doug Wellman, won $2,000, the larger prize money, in a Dragonfly at the Ocoee rodeo. Rodeo now became involved in competition between manufacturers for the new market.

While squirt in the East evolved beyond its precursor, that of paddle twirling and tricks, rodeo in the West evolved toward paddle twirling and tricks. As hole-riding skills improved, rodeo technique evolved into an "eclectic wedding of technical virtuosity and pizzazz." [80] Judging vacillated between the entertainment value, the pizzazz with its crowd-pleasing moves and technical skill. By the mid-'80s, judging moved from using novice paddlers as judges to ex-rodeo champs. This helped the situation but also at times brought in favoritism, a problem later remedied by more organized rules.

Different geographic regions developed their own hotdog styles. Californians had their paddle spinning, Idahoans had their aggressive hole-playing. By the mid-'80s, rodeo technique appeared to stagnate in the West.

> Some time has passed since anyone demonstrated new tricks of skill in a hot dog contest. What's more, rodeo holes are often too small to fully challenge kayakers' abilities. At last year's [1985] low water Payette rodeo, eventual winner Bob MacDougal almost didn't compete because he felt his repertoire was too routine. [81]

At the same time, paddlers in the East, in their low-volume squirtboats, applied their tricks to rodeo. Instead of hole-riding in standard river running playboats with volume that kept the boats in the surface currents as used in the West, hole-riding in low-volume squirtboats offered a new realm in subsurface currents. Squirt also offered a solution to holes that were too small or were too low in volume.

As East went West to compete, squirtboaters provided the spark needed to ignite new innovations in rodeo techniques and provided a new generation of hole-riding moves. Retendos and other moves were the result, moves that used sub-surface currents to link a series of enders, pirouettes, and squirts in a "dynamic amalgamation of vertical air." [82]

It also sparked some East-West friction for a time. From 1985 through 1988, New Wave sent Jeff Snyder, Forrest Callaway, and Risa Shimoda-Callaway to rodeos in the West to compete. Shimoda-Callaway later recalled going to the Payette rodeo and the reactions of locals who were beaten by outsiders from the East. The same happened in 1989, when Chris Spelius toured western rodeos for Dagger using their new kayak, the Response. Not only was this "East meets West" in rodeo competition, but a manufacturer's paid-professional meets a professional amateur.

By the late '80s, rodeo with its unorganized rodeo circuit showed tremendous potential for the sport as a whole as well as for the industry. However, by the late '80s, rodeo struggled and stumbled mostly because it required a tremendous amount of volunteer effort. For some rodeos, particularly the longest running ones in the West, ten years meant volunteer burnout. [*Author's note:* The same thing happened with slalom races in the '60s and '70s that also required a tremendous amount of volunteer support.]

BY 1984, rodeos had four-digit-figures for prize money. For the Chili Bar Rodeo on the American in California, over forty manufacturers provided products and money for prizes worth over $7,000.

RISA SHIMODA-CALLAWAY, a squirtboater who went west, described the classic retendo move:

> The move is to do a forward ender and land back in the hole. This requires you to plan the upcoming move before you land. To execute the new, more difficult moves, paddlers use seams and current differentials, sometimes beneath the surface of the water, to initiate their next move. [83]

THE REPONSE was not designed as a rodeo boat. However, any boat that won rodeo events was considered a winning design. Spelius' wins in rodeos with the Response helped catapult Dagger into the kayak market. The same thing happened the following year with Spelius' rodeo wins across the country using Dagger's next design, the Crossfire.

80 Armstrong, John. "More Than You Ever Knew About Whitewater Rodeos." *River Runner* Vol. 6 No. 3 (June 1986): 36–39.

81 Ibid.

82 Singleton, Mark. " 'Fringe Sport' Makes the Big Time." *Nantahala Outdoor Center Outfitters Catalog* (1995): 60–61.

83 Ibid.

Mother nature also took her toll on some popular rodeos. Some holes changed or disappeared altogether after large floods that affected the quality of the hole for rodeo competition. The Clackamus Rodeo using Bob's Hole was one example where a flood degraded the character of the hole used for competition.

In 1989, the formation of the National Organization for Whitewater Rodeo (NOWR) was an attempt to give struggling rodeos a hand. Risa Shimoda-Callaway, Executive Director for AWA, was the force behind its formation. Prior to organizing NOWR, Shimoda-Callaway had organized the Ocoee rodeo for a couple of years. She realized that two of the biggest challenges for organizers across the country were the difficulty in obtaining insurance and in arranging sponsors. NOWR was created as a group of volunteers across the country that worked to enhance and promote all fourteen whitewater rodeos and festivals. With so many rodeos and festivals, scheduling problems arose. That, too, was resolved by the formation of NOWR. Entering into the '90s, NOWR was in position to facilitate an even greater role in rodeo's development as a major sub-sport of whitewater.

Extreme Races

The same stimuli and inspiration that spawned squirtboating spawned extreme racing by the same paddlers in the same location with the same livelihoods. They were ex-racers, sometime racers, raft guides, and boat and paddle builders on the waters of the Yough and Cheat.

A predecessor to extreme racing was called attaining, an activity that began in the '70s as informal races by raft guides on the Lower Yough. Attaining, negotiating and running rapids going upstream, was actually born of a necessity for the professional raft guides and safety boaters. This necessity became a sport in and of itself and was almost an art. More than brute strength, attaining required the ability to read and know all the nuances of the river and current in order to take advantage of it to paddle back upstream. Around 1980, attaining evolved into an annual event, the Annual Ohiopyle Upstream Race, with mostly word-of-mouth advertising, on Entrance Rapid on the Lower Yough.

The Annual Ohiopyle Upstream race is a mass start at the top of the rapid where the contestants paddle down and then back up finishing at the start. It is a 10-minute sprint with only one requirement that the contestant never gets out of his or her boat. This means that the contestant can do a hand-shoulder roll upstream across a rock if that proves to be the fastest way. John Weld wrote of the race:

> ...the happening members of Backlund usin', non Coast Guard approved PFD wearin' and T'Canyon ownin' 'in crowd' call this new sport 'attaining.'[84]

The first extreme race occurred around the same time, in 1981 on the Upper Yough. It was the brainchild of Jesse Whittemore. The Upper Yough Race, a sprint from start to finish, was aimed at the skill required to negotiate the famed Class IV-V drops of the Upper Yough. The race became an annual event although it was always intended to remain small for the skilled few. Its

[84] Weld, John. "Up, Up and Away." *American Whitewater* Vol. XXXV No. 2 (March/April 1995): 49–55.

publicity was intended to remain primarily within the whitewater community. The Upper Yough's location and relative inaccessibility along its course kept it that way.

Whittemore, along with his race-day competitor Roger Zbel, was acknowledged as one of the most knowledgeable about the Upper Yough. In addition to the Upper Yough race, Whittemore sponsored other races on the Upper Yough. "Slots-a-Luck" was designed as a natural slalom but with mandatory eddies, slots, and moves that had some big consequences like the possibility of dangerous pinning situations. Another was the "Attaining Wars" (a video was made with that name) which was an Upper Yough attainment race. It also had some serious moves with the same big consequences.

In contrast to the Upper Yough Race's low visibility, the next comer to extreme racing, the Great Falls Rapid Race in 1988 occurred in a National Park with TV and press coverage. Organized by National Wildwater Champion Andy Bridge and National Slalom Team Coach Bill Endicott, the race was by invitation only. Half of the racers were from the National Whitewater slalom and wildwater teams. The race was held in accordance with National Park Service regulations which allowed falls running only early in the morning from the Maryland side. The race started at 7:00 am and finished by 8:30 am.

Both the Upper Yough Race and the Great Falls Rapid Race set the stage for the profusion of extreme races that followed in the '90s.

At the first Great Falls Rapid Race, Dan Schnurrenberger, K-1 member of the 1988 National Wildwater team, took first followed by Jon Lugbill and Tom McEwan, both in C-1s. (Tom McEwan was one of the first to run Great Falls in 1976.)

Women and the Sub-sports

In the '80s, more women than ever began paddling whitewater. Changes in attitudes toward women that encouraged and supported them occurred and women paddlers, predominantly in kayaks, found their own niches in the

Nancy Wiley on the South Fork of the Payette (ID), 1984 —courtesy of Rob Lesser.

Kathy Blau (Shelby) at Houndstooth on the North Fork of the Payette (ID), 1981—courtesy of Rob Lesser.

sub-sports. This was further supported by the trend toward smaller volume boats along with the availability of accessories and clothing designed for smaller paddlers (although the increasing number of women helped spur the availability of smaller accessories).

In the West, women like Kathy Blau, Cameron O'Connor, and Nancy Wiley, already with established reputations as heavy-water paddlers, entered the rodeo scene. In the East, women like Risa Shimoda-Callaway, Debbie Pepper, and Susan Gentry-Wilson, gravitated toward squirt. In 1987, a women's class was introduced at the Upper Yough Race for the first time with five entrants.

Barb McKee recalled watching Shimoda-Callaway compete in one of the Six Flags races in the early '80s: "She was being window-shaded in a hole but she was laughing and enjoying it."[86]

Nolan Whitesell described Shimoda-Callaway's run of Niagara Gorge in her "¾ cut" Jet:

> I watched as Risa, just 15 feet from me, got completely swallowed by a whirlpool along the eddy line. The pool closed over her, and I saw no sign of her under the smooth surface until she blasted up seconds later, laughing and loving every minute of it.[87]

Although it was a long time coming, women in whitewater (outside of slalom and wildwater competition) were finally coming into their own and at a level equal to their male counterparts. In 1984, *American Whitewater* recognized that women were not covered in the sport and published a series of bios of women paddlers. Unfortunately, the bios drew criticism because of what some considered sexist remarks.

IN THE MID-'80S, 90 percent of *Canoe*'s readership was male but 25 percent of ACA individual members were women and an equal percentage had become certified instructors. Women participants in paddlesport races of all kinds increased 20 percent from the early to mid-'80s. Paddling club rosters began to reflect more of a 50/50 ratio. Although 25 percent of women were attracted to quiet water trips (flatwater and whitewater through Class II), 10–15 percent were paddling Class III and above and the percentage was growing.[85]

[85] Miller, Pam. "Women on Water." *Canoe* Vol. 12. No. 5 (September/October 1984): 22–29.

[86] McKee, Barb. Interview by author 23 and 24 January 1999.

[87] Whitesell, Nolan. "Niagara: The Easy Part." *River Runner* Vol. 8 No. 1 (February 1988): 11.

View from the Bridge

THE ROLES OF THE NEW AND OLD FACILITATORS gelled during the '80s. Plastics and playboating led the way spawning changes that shaped the sport. Plastics, as a material and a mass-production process, established total dominance in whitewater. Playboating became a facilitator. Through rodeo and squirt, the sport began to take on a new dimension, both figuratively and literally, and a new American-style competition emerged for whitewater beyond amateurism.

The industry took the lead. ACA and AWA found and settled into new roles that were mutually beneficial to themselves, to one another, and to the sport as a whole.

The market changed. The sport changed. Boater demographics changed. Based on a 1983 AWA survey, Bart Jackson wrote:

> One of the greatest surprises of the entire survey was in the income area. We had clung to the romantic visage of our readers being rag-clad boating bums who can scarcely scrounge the cash for their next roll of duct tape. Whether a view of the past or never-was, we found our respondents were considerably more well heeled.
>
> ... Both the time and the variety of ways spent in pursuing the perfect river are great, with many paddlers frequently trying several types of paddling craft. Certainly, they do not mind parting with their cash to get not only good boating equipment, but proper safety equipment. [88]

The boating experience itself changed. Rivers for first descents were harder to find. Access and congestion issues surfaced compounded by droughts. Creek-boating emerged to escape the crowds. Playboating, not just river-running, were a part of the experience of novices and experts alike. Squirtboating emerged and hole-riding set the stage for destination paddling in the '90s.

The rivers boated changed. As the experience and skill of boaters increased, a result of better designs, equipment, instruction and skills learned from playboating, boaters' repertoire changed. Some of the rivers "lost their mystique to familiarity." [89] In the East, the "Ten Best Hair Rivers" shifted from the New, Cheat, Gauley, Tygart, Chattooga, and the Black of the '70s to the Moose, Big Sandy, Watauga, Linville, Overflow, and Little Rivers of the '80s. Only the Upper Yough, Russell Fork, Blackwater, and Lower Meadow carried over into the late '80s. Tragically, within a year of AWA's "Top 10" listing in 1988, three deaths occurred on the listed rivers, one each on the Blackwater, the Upper Yough, and the Meadow, all three carry-overs from the '70s. In 1989, two kayakers within 10 days of one another drowned on the Meadow.

[88] Jackson, Bart. "AWA Readership Survey Results." *American Whitewater* Vol. XXVIII No. 2 (March/April 1983): 30–34.

[89] Gedekoh, Bob. "Appalachian Top 10." *American Whitewater* Vol. XXXIII No. 5 (September/October 1988): 42–49.

In 1985, the Cheat crested at an estimated 250,000 cfs at Albright at the start of the Gorge compared to its mean annual discharge of 2,207 cfs. According to USGS, the flood was "off the chart" and could not be classified with any reliability as to its probability of occurrence. It certainly exceeded the frequency of a 500-year flood.

Even the shuttle experience changed. Paid shuttles emerged, both non-optional, like the Lower Yough (dictated by the state park), and optional, like Glen Miller's pre-arranged truck shuttle for the Cheat and Big Sandy out the east road from Jenkinsburg. [*Author's note:* You load your boat, gear, and yourself in the back of a 2-ton 4WD pickup truck where a cooler of beer awaits your ride out.]

In some instances, rivers themselves changed. The Clackamas changed. Bob's Hole used for the Clackamas Whitewater Rodeo changed, shifted due to floods. Others changed subtlety, some not so subtlety. The "Great Flood of 1985," the result of Hurricane Juan that dumped up to 20 inches of rain in just two days (November 4 and 5) in western Virginia and West Virginia, spawned floods that forever changed the rivers in the area. The Upper Cheat watershed was devastated. Some of the rapids of the Gorge, Big Nasty, and Coliseum, changed forever.

The sport as a whole during the '80s experienced alterations similar to the Cheat Gorge after the 1985 flood. The effects were subtle in some areas and not so subtle in others. So, too, were the changes that the '80s brought to the sport. However, the final outcome was that the flood changed the Gorge forever, just as the changes initiated in the '80s changed the sport forever.

Shuttle vehicle, 1985—courtesy of Rob Lesser.

The course of the River at the end of the '70s, a braided river with two channels, was more firmly set in the '80s and the River itself grew and broadened. The character of the competition channel expanded with the additions of the sub-sports; whitewater rodeo, squirt, and extreme racing. The character of the river-running, cruising channel also continued to change with playboating brought on by its offspring. The currents, the designs and techniques, associated with each channel were fed by cloudbursts associated with playboating, squirtboating, and rodeo. The currents affected one another, changing and intertwining within each channel.

Whitewater, The Next Generation: the '90s

ALTHOUGH, BY THE MID-TO-LATE '80S, the first of the next generation—Generation-X—was lured toward whitewater, they were small in number and carried little clout. The sport still belonged to the Baby Boomers. They owned the companies and designed the boats. They were the World Champions. But that began to change in the early '90s.

The '90s brought our sport into the mainstream and to a level of maturity, for good or bad, that was recognized in other outdoor sports. The appearance of the homespun, low-key atmosphere of the past disappeared. The simple, uncomplicated, unartificial, and sometimes understated and undervalued aspects of our sport were gone, replaced with new boats, new concepts, new attitudes, and a fully-grown industry that controlled and directed the sport and its future. However, all of this came about because it was time. The roles of the new facilitators, the industry, and the old facilitators, ACA and AWA, were well defined and comfortable. It was finally time to transition from the second to the third generation of whitewater paddlers. It was also the time of Generation X, the internet age and the internet generation and by the late '90s, Generation Y.

Rodeo, merely a sub-sport in the '70s and '80s, evolved beyond its sub-sport status. From its humble beginnings of showing off river-running skills, rodeo with its freestyle moves took playboating to a new level and transitioned the sport, both directly and indirectly, toward the future. Although the '92 Olympics in Barcelona were the first time in twenty years that slalom was includs effect on whitewater in general was pretty small. The same was true of slalom racing in the '96 Olympics in Atlanta and the '00 Olympics in Sydney. TV coverage and publicity brought public awareness of slalom to a new generation, but it wasn't something that many people watching TV aspired to. Slalom racing was too controlled, perhaps too contrived, for a sport that was supposed to instill excitement. It didn't fit with the extreme sports of Gen-X, the X-Games. But rodeo and freestyle moves and boat acrobatics and playboating did. Marketing to, and the involvement of, Gen-X and Y propelled whitewater into the mainstream.

Rodeo playboating's moves and purpose paralleled and borrowed from other sports of the late '80s and '90s: skateboarding, snowboarding, BMX, and rollerblading. Boat Acrobatics and playboating moves and technique came from the twists, turns, and flips of body and boat gymnastics associated with kids sports. They were meant for younger, more agile athletic bodies and minds. Rodeo playboat marketing also paralleled and borrowed from the other sports. Manufacturers sponsored athletes and a whole new class of paid professional paddlers emerged. Whitewater truly evolved to include and support

1990

'92 Olympics, first in twenty years. Joe Jacobi and Scott Strasbaugh win gold in C-2. Dana Chladek wins bronze in K-1W

First World Whitewater Rodeo held on the Ocoee with rodeo-specific boats

Necky introduces the Rip, the first planing hull kayak

1995

Corran Addison of RP Savage Designs introduces the Fury, a radical planing hull kayak that fueled a new breed of playboats

'96 Olympics on Ocoee. Dana Chladek wins silver in K-1W

Paddlesport manufacturers merge

2000

professionals paid to train and compete for cash prizes, all for the purpose of selling merchandise. The sport's growth, particularly in the latter half of the '90s, was also affected by the country's economic prosperity. We had money to spend on everything from the latest boat design (which came out practically every six months) to new gear and equipment. We also invested heavily in time spent paddling, both nationally and internationally.

Rodeo playboating moved away from its original purpose of demonstrating river-running skills. River running was no longer necessary. An accessible hole or green wave was the only requirement, and its byproduct, destination paddling, took root. Park and play. That, too, paralleled other kids sports. A sign of the changing times was a shift in listing the top **river** destinations from the early '90s to listing the top **playspot** destinations in the late '90s.

Rodeo playboating moves and boats were not intended solely for Gen-X and Y paddlers, nor were the kids the only ones excited by rodeo/freestyle. The short boat trend furthered by rodeo designs influenced new designs for river running and creekboating and opened up opportunities for everyone, even older paddlers not specifically interested in competition. The short boats and new designs also opened up more opportunities for fun on more rivers. As one long-time boater said, "They up the fun meter." It's kind of like the difference between driving a winding mountain road in a Ford minivan or driving the same road in a Jaguar sportscar.

The '90s saw an accelerated learning curve, though it was not solely the result of new rodeo and river running designs. Better boats, gear, and instruction advanced our skills faster than ever before. We ran more rivers and paddled more days per year. We not only had dry suits that extended our paddling seasons, but we traveled more to access more water. A year in the life of a paddler in the '90s might have been comparable to three years in the '70s just in the number of days spent paddling. Add to this the ballsiness of Gen- X and Y with their slogan "No fear" and an increased understanding of river hydrology (in river runner/playboater terms advanced by squirtboating of the '80s), and these new paddlers pushed the limits of the sport; they upped the ante. Extreme paddling continued to reach new heights, literally, with new waterfall records and growing numbers of deaths among expert paddlers.

All of this contributed to continued growth in the '90s that attracted mainstream attention. Aside from sports coverage by an increasing number of cable channels and networks including ESPN and OLN (Outdoor Life Network), whitewater, particularly extreme events, caught media attention outside of sports, just as Blackadar caught public attention in the '70s. However, the impact was far greater in the '90s. Images of whitewater paddling were found everywhere from TV commercials to magazine advertising. The movie *River Wild* in 1995, like *Deliverance* in the '70s, spurred growth in whitewater, particularly rafting. Rafting use of the Ocoee grew 20 percent between 1994 and 1995, 16 percent on the New and Gauley, and 28 percent in Maine. [1]

The growth also brought congestion, and often for the first time in many areas, conflict between commercial rafters and paddlers. Congestion meant that we had to plan our trips to avoid prime put-on times. Congestion also meant crowded eddies at good playspots. Tempers flared. We became less polite with one another—river etiquette was ignored. Many long-time boaters lamented the changes to the whitewater experience which was the same

[1] Brown, David. "Guided Whitewater Rafting in Hot Demand." *Canoe & Kayak Industry News* Spring 1996: 1, 19.

reaction that previous boaters had in the '50s, '60s, and '70s with earlier growth in the sport. But this time, the congestion appeared more noticeable, the diminished whitewater experience more obvious.

Some of us also lamented that rodeo appeared to ruin the sport. It was valued too highly, gained too much attention, and moved away from whitewater's river running root. But we forgot or didn't realize that it was not rodeo alone that changed the sport. It was the next generation of paddlers testing the limits, making their impact just as many of us from the second generation of paddlers did in the '60s and '70s. By the end of the '90s, rodeo playboating and Gen-X and Y were well entrenched and intertwined with the sport and the industry. New and very different generations were well on their way to molding the shape and future of whitewater. A paradigm shift had occurred and there was no turning back the clock to an earlier time.

The Industry (Kayak Manufacturers) and Rodeo Playboats

The state of the industry and the sport in the '90s were molded by the second generation of whitewater paddlers, Baby Boomers (born after World War II through 1965), the same generation as the industry's kayak designers and business owners. By the late '80s, many people felt that the whitewater kayak market had evolved "from whiteknuckle paddling and expeditions to a fitness activity with more emphasis on enjoying the experience."[2] The whitewater kayak market was not the booming recreational activity it had been in the past. Instead, it was characterized with slow but steady growth coming from a more diverse group of people including women and older men looking for the experience of whitewater. The market, the audience with money, was getting older and was not as interested in the thrill seeking of their younger days.

The aging of the audience was not only reflected in marketing, but also in the new kayak designs. Designs from Perception and Hydra during the latter part of the '80s were traditional displacement-type hulls with no new radical concepts. Some squirt innovations were incorporated but those, too, were softened for the market audience. Perception, who for all practical purposes ***was*** the industry for whitewater kayaks, marketed primarily to the only market it knew, the Baby Boomer generation, of which it was a part. This one-manufacturer industry for whitewater also contributed, in part, to the slow growth. During much of the '80s, Perception's marketing director, Joe Pulliam, recognized that he never had to think of the market because Perception *was the market.*

Bill Masters acknowledged that during the mid-to-late '80s, Perception was marketing whitewater kayaks to existing customers, "designing boats for ourselves,"[3] the aging Baby Boomers.

In 1989, Dagger entered the plastic whitewater kayak market. Dagger was soon followed by New Wave and Wave Sport. Prijon of Germany, and a few years later Pyrahna of Great Britain, also seriously entered the American market in pursuit of a share of its whitewater paddlers. This brought much needed market competition that contributed to new ideas and innovations.

THE TREMENDOUS GROWTH in seakayaking during the '80s and '90s was also reflective of the same trends observed in whitewater: fitness, experience, and less thrill.

[2] Montgomery, Pam. "Kayaks '87." *Outdoor Retailer* Vol. 6 No. 7 (September 1986): 32–34, 36–39.

[3] Masters, Bill. Interview by author 14 December 1996.

The growth of the rodeo circuit and the development of the National Organization for Whitewater Rodeo (NOWR) in 1989, also spurred competition within the industry. Manufacturers scrambled to capitalize on the marketing potential of rodeo/playboating. The effects of the first two events were felt almost immediately. However, the third event, the generational transition from Baby Boomer to Generation X (born between 1965 and 1977), was more gradual and associated with more than a difference in age. It was associated with a difference in their respective eras that contributed to their different views and ways of thinking.

With a shift in generational focus, a new rodeo emerged, one that was different from its rodeo roots in the '70s. Until this new rodeo emerged, playboating remained a part of the river running experience and was marketed as a thrill experience that delivered all of those things that river running traditionally offered. Kayaks used for rodeo and playboating were river-running designs with some squirt characteristics for better hole and wave riding.

The new rodeo emerged from the festivals and the fun times associated with friendly competition. It also became a venue for competition for the market by the manufacturers. The new rodeo and playboating added more excitement to river running and provided a new challenge for the paddlers and manufacturers alike.

Rodeo truly developed as a sub-sport just as squirt did in the '80s. But rodeo went further than squirtboating. Where squirtboating started sponsoring athletes in the '80s for competition and demonstration, rodeo took it the next step with the introduction of whole teams of full-time professionals. In 1986, many people agreed that "the market needs new designs and new designers, but this won't happen until we manufacturers start seeing increased demand for new products."[4] Rodeo provided that demand and the industry and rodeo intertwined.

The Next Generation in California, 2000—courtesy of Brandon Knapp.

[4] Montgomery, Pam. "Kayaks '87." *Outdoor Retailer* Vol. 6 No. 7 (September 1986): 32–34, 36–39.

Market and sporting competition spurred innovation. Flat hulls, "planing hulls," were discovered and started a whole new revolution and evolution in kayak designs for surface moves. This was the opposite of squirt with its subsurface moves and designs. River running displacement-type hulls no longer worked for rodeo. Rodeo moves evolved to become as design dependent as squirt was and just as sensitive to profile and volume distribution as squirtboats were.

The innovations were further fueled by the growing interest by Gen-X in whitewater. Perhaps initially drawn to an extreme sport, rodeo also caught the attention of Gen-X paddlers for its gymnastic appeal with twists, turns, and flips from other Gen-X-type sports. With Gen-X paddlers came new attitudes towards competition and risk taking that were different than those of aging Boomers. One writer observed that they liked to compete because it "makes me [a young competitor] perform better" and that "the recent surge in extreme sports– from bungee jumping to sky surfing—is not an accident. The hip slogan of [the] Gen-X T shirt? No Fear." [5]

IN 1998, an estimated 14.8 million people participated in whitewater rafting and kayaking.

Just as the non-competitive side of the sport had in the past benefitted from competition and racing innovations, the non-competitive side benefited from rodeo, too. However, the non-competitive side was traditionally associated with river running and rodeo/playboating had moved away from river running. Rodeo was now the basis for playboating. Unlike squirtboating that used all river characteristics as a part of expanding the entire river running experience, new playboating skills and designs were developed for hole riding and wave surfing, only part of the river experience. Destination paddling evolved and hours were spent on one playspot on a river. For some paddlers, the rest of the river was almost inconsequential and even overlooked if the playspot was readily accessible. Rodeo, with all of its ramifications, changed the sport.

Playboating on the Ocoee (TN), 2000
—courtesy of Brandon Knapp.

Towards Flat Hulls and Short Boats

In 1989, three new companies, Infinity, Wave Sport, and Dagger, started production of plastic whitewater kayaks for river running and creekboating. Infinity, based in Idaho, misread the market and didn't survive. Wave Sport, based in Colorado, was small and was only able to develop a niche market in the West. However, Dagger was immediately competitive with Perception in Perception's own backyard in the Southeast.

Infinity Kayaks was started by three river runners, Judson Zenzic, Andy Laidlaw, and Les Bechdel. Zenzic, a marine designer, and Laidlaw, an architect, brought Bechdel on board for his experience in fiberglass and manufacturing (from his days working for Phoenix in the '70s). They started with the Infinity and initially contracted its molding before setting up their own rotational molding facility. Within a few years, Bechdel sold out. Ed Roper

[5] Hornblower, Margot. "Great Xpectations." *Time* June 9, 1997: 58–68.

was brought in as manager. A few years later, Infinity with its two kayaks, the Infinity and the Quantum, and a molded cat rig called the Infinicat, sold out to New Wave who purchased their molds and rotational molding machine to begin their own production of plastic whitewater kayaks.

Chan Zwanzig, owner of Wave Sports, began importing kayaks and accessories from ACE in Great Britain in 1987. Zwanzig worked with ACE to design a kayak that became known as the Lazer in the American market. By 1989, Zwanzig went into rotational molding himself and began production of the Lazer. Two years later, Wave Sport introduced a second kayak, the Excel, a larger version of the Lazer followed by the Micro, a shortened version of the Lazer, and the Extreme, a shortened version of the Excel.

However, unlike Wave Sport, Dagger was recognized in the market from its inception. With owners Roy Guinn, Pete Jett, Joe Pulliam, and Steve Scarborough's knowledge of and history in the whitewater market, Dagger successfully entered into thermoformed canoes in 1988. They produced their first kayak, the Response, in 1989. The Response was an immediate success. Their single mold ran 24 hours a day to meet market demands. Described as a shrunken Aeroquatic, it was predictable and forgiving with a flattened stern with rounded edges. Two years later in 1991, the Crossfire was introduced. It was slightly shorter in length with an increased bow rocker and sharper edges in the stern. The Crossfire was followed by the Vortex, a big-boy version of the Crossfire. In 1993, Dagger re-introduced Vahna's popular Aeroquatic design, the AQ II.

THE CROSSFIRE was one of the first kayaks designed using CAD software. No prototype was built or paddled before it was introduced to the market. Its predecessor, the Response, was built in wood-strip-prototype form for paddling and testing prior to production.

Chris Spelius in a Crossfire, 1991—courtesy of Robert Harrison.

Though Perception, and to a lesser extent Prijon, now had market competition with Dagger and Wave Sport, there was little impetus to drive any real changes in whitewater designs which were essentially all river-running designs with some rodeo playboating characteristics. Essentially, they produced variations on the same themes. In 1989, Perception introduced the Corsica, marketing it as a play and expedition boat (later called a creekboat), and the Reflex, a slalom-style training boat. A year later, the Corsica S, a smaller version of its namesake, followed and in 1993, the Sabre was introduced. The same year, Prijon, distributed by Wildwasser Sport USA in Colorado (Landis Arnold was the owner), introduced the Invader, another river-running design similar to the T-Slalom and T-Canyon.

By the first half of the '90s, all of paddlesports, not just whitewater, had grown significantly enough to warrant recognition by many people in the larger sporting goods industry. Attendance by paddlesport manufacturers at the yearly summer trade show sponsored by *Outdoor Retailer* grew considerably, taking up to close to a third of the show. By 1996, paddlesports, which included canoeing, kayaking, rafting, and all accessories, was an estimated $200.1 million market. Canoe and kayak sales alone were $99.1 million. That corresponds to approximately 165,000 boats per year at an average price of $600 per boat.

Beyond paddlesports' financial growth, the infrastructure was also well established. A veritable alphabet soup of organizations represented trades associated with paddlesports: AO (America Outdoors representing commercial rafting operations), NACLO (National Association of Canoe Livery Outfitters), TASK (Trade Association for Sea Kayaking), NAPSA (North American Paddlesports Association), along with ACA and AWA representing the paddling public. In 1994, a meeting was held in Atlanta bringing in the executive directors from all paddlesport organizations to consider how the organizations could work together more efficiently for the greater good of the sport. An outcome of the meeting were partnerships between ACA and NACLO, (which later became PPA, Professional Paddlesports Association) and TASK and NAPSA which later merged to become TAPS.

Rodeo competition continued to grow and expand. In 1990, NOWR was initially only supported by AWA and New Wave Kayak Products, although manufacturers and retailers continued to support individual events. However, the lack of attendance and scheduling conflicts began to hurt some of the events. The American River Festival-Chili Bar Rodeo suffered from poor attendance due to low water (the fourth year in a row) and schedule conflicts with Bob's Hole Rodeo on the Clackamas. Other events, such as the Wenatchee Rodeo, were not held at all due to lack of an organizer.

By the next year, NOWR, under the leadership of Risa Shimoda Callaway, took the lead in organizing a national whitewater rodeo circuit with a schedule of thirteen rodeos across the country. Soon, different sponsorship levels based on contributing amounts (premier sponsors, major sponsors, and contributing sponsors) were instituted to encourage increased sponsor participation.

NOWR's support expanded beyond the original two sponsors (AWA and New Wave) to include Dagger, Kokatat, Menasha Ridge Press, Patagonia, PD Designs, Lochsa Connection, *Canoe,* Crazy Creek, Bob Foote Products, ICS Books, Four Corners Riversports, Northwest River Supplies, *Paddler,* Rivers and Mountains, Sandpiper Publishing, Tightskirts, Northwest Design Works, Adventure Medical Kits, and Wildwater Designs.

NOWR assisted event organizers with planning, insurance, and publicity. In order to encourage increased participation, new events were added that combined downriver races with rodeo events. Open boat competition with shorter boats was becoming more popular. More women also entered all events in both rodeo and squirt competition.

With growing publicity and support of rodeos across the country, Dagger jumped into the rodeo market and competition employing Chris Spelius as their sponsored paid professional athlete. Spelius' rodeo successes in the Response and Crossfire gained recognition for both Dagger and their kayaks across the country. It pitted him against Rob Lesser, Perception's long-time western sales rep, in relatively friendly competition. However, Spelius' success in rodeo competition and its pay-off in Dagger's increased marketshare at Perception's expense, helped to bring an end to the laid-back competition that were rodeo's roots. In 1991, Perception countered Dagger by hiring Bob McDonough as a full-time competitor and designer.

In 1991, the Ocoee Rodeo at Hell Hole was by far the largest rodeo ever held with over one hundred competitors in squirt and surface classes including open and closed canoes. Bob McDonough won the K-1 Expert class and Kathy Bolyn won K-1W Expert class, two of the best rodeo paddlers in

THE STANDARD LENGTH for river running kayaks ranged from 10'4" for small volume kayaks like the Corsica S and Extreme to almost 11'4" for large volume kayaks like the Excel and Response.

the country. The level of skill in all classes was well demonstrated and was reflected in the increased levels of competition. Classes for Women's Intermediate Surface and Squirt and for Open Canoe were held for the first time due to the number and skill of competitors. The rodeo even drew a European competitor, German paddler Jan Kellner, sponsored by Pyrahna promoting their new boat, the Stunt Bat.

Likewise, three American competitors participated with twenty others from around the world in the first international competition in England at an event called the 1991 World Stunt Boat Championships. Though informally run in tidal conditions (which created its own challenges), the event was a start for international competition. After the event, competitors agreed to have a World Championship event every other year. A Pre-World event held in the off years would help event organizers prepare for the Worlds (the same strategy instituted in the '80s for slalom competition). The American competitors successfully campaigned to bring the first World event to North America in 1993.

IN 1992, DICK WOLD, a well-known ocean surf kayaker, showed up at the Payette Rodeo with a 6-foot surf ski. Although he won, its significance was neither seen nor immediately appreciated by the right audience. About the same time both Corran Addison and Bob McDonough tried surf shoes at a few rodeos but were unable to handle the designs on the waves. McDonough, working for Perception, designed the popular Pirouette series of whitewater kayaks for river running and playboating—all displacement hulls—before incorporating planing hulls in his designs.

Although NOWR had begun to establish the basics needed for such an event, the challenge was still great. Instead of relying solely on paddling clubs with legions of volunteers as slalom and wildwater racing had always done, NOWR and rodeo organizers worked to supplement support and sponsorship through the paddlesport industry. In 1992, a local group in the Southeast began to develop plans to host the event on the Ocoee. Led by Chris Spelius of Dagger and Bob McDonough of Perception, the group drafted a document that outlined the philosophy of rodeo and proposed guidelines for supporting it as an internationally recognized event. The document illustrated some of the similarities between rodeo and figure skating, gymnastics, aerobatics, and diving. NOWR began to standardize scoring guidelines for the various events based on those similarities.

In 1993, NOWR, now supported by AWA, joined forces with ACA to gain ICF recognition and sanctioning in order to gain access to the international paddlesport community to pave the way for rodeo's eventual inclusion as an Olympic event. As a result, the World Whitewater Rodeo Steering Committee was developed, made up of representatives within the United States. Many of the representatives were long time supporters and competitors of rodeo and squirtboating including Risa Shimoda Callaway (rodeo organizer and competitor), Jim Daly (rodeo organizer), Susan Wilson Gentry (competitor), Steve Scherrer (rodeo organizer), John Schreiner (manufacturer), Chris Spelius (competitor), Mark White (competitor and organizer), and Nancy Wiley (competitor and organizer).

Everyone's efforts paid off and the first World Whitewater Rodeo was held on the Ocoee in 1993. More than 100 competitors participated from Austria, Canada, Germany, Great Britain, Italy, Japan, New Zealand, Slovenia, Spain, Switzerland, and the United States. Events were held in K-1 and K-1W surface, OC-1 and C-1 surface, and K-1 squirt classes. C-1 squirt and K-1W squirt were exhibition events because the classes did not require participation from at least five countries (ICF requirements for international competition). In addition to "Hole Riding" which was typical of American rodeos, "Freestyle Through a Rapid" (a European-style event) was also a part of each class.

Competitors' sponsors included canoe and kayak manufacturers such as Dagger, Fanatic Designs, Mohawk, New Wave, Perception, Prijon (Wildwasser Sport USA), and Pyranha (Impex International), all hoping their boats would win. However, it was the new kayaks sponsored by Dagger, Perception, and Prijon following the lead of Pyrahna (who developed the Stunt Bat for rodeo competition) that were the real winners in the first steps toward new innovations in kayak design.

Until the early '90s, rodeo evolved faster in the West than the East, with Bob's Hole on the Clackamas as the focal point. That focal point shifted to Hell Hole on the Ocoee in the East. Many circumstances led to this change including the Ocoee's proximity to large population centers in the East and Southeast and Hell Hole's predictability due to dam releases. However, perhaps more importantly, Hell Hole's choice for the '93 World Whitewater Rodeo Championships and its proximity to Dagger and Perception, practically in their backyard where their teams could train and test prototypes, helped to cement this shift.

As the weeks drew nearer for the '93 Worlds, Dagger still didn't have what Spelius felt was a good design. Soon after Prijon's Hurricane came out for the 1993 season, Spelius paddled one and felt that it was the "new operating system. We can't go back."[6] Steve Scarborough and Spelius tried modifying the Vortex into the Mutex, which was a terrible boat. A new design, which became known as the Transition, was finally produced just a few weeks before the rodeo. During the week before the Worlds, the Dagger team paddled it all day, everyday in Hell Hole, along side many other competitors who were also preparing for the rodeo.

The Transition was Dagger's entry for the '93. Spelius said of the design:

> We knew the Ocoee hole didn't want to retain you, and for big thugs like [Mark] Lyle and myself, who were working hard on this project along with Steve Scarborough, we knew we had to maximize things. Cause we're big thugs, we wash out—little people, they're in there... The reason it was called the Transition was because I was showing it to Joe [Pulliam, president] of Dagger, and no boat has the transition from that sliciness [in the bow] to this giant puffiness in the knee area. The increased knee volume makes the boat more comfortable. And in the back, that makes the boat able to shred waves too. Our boat was made to do verticals and cartwheels, and when we're playing, that's the position we want to be in.[7]

Author's note: Some felt that Dagger copied the Hurricane in their transition design. Pulliam acknowledged to me that the profiles just made sense and that both were the result of the same evolutionary concepts.

[6] Spelius, Chris. Interview by author 14 November 1998.

[7] Singleton, Mark. "Hot Dogs Go High-Tech as Boat Designs Evolve." *Nantahala Outdoor Center Outfitters Catalog* (1995): 63.

Perception's entry was the Pirouette Super Sport, the last in the Pirouette series of designs by Bob McDonough of Team Perception. McDonough said of his design:

> The Super Sport originated as an idea I had for an advanced freestyle boat to compete with in the 1993 World Whitewater Rodeo. There were certain design criteria I wanted this boat to meet: it should surf waves easily, it should hole-ride with the best of them, and it should be pure fun to paddle downriver. Surfing waves with the ability to make quick cuts with the fine edge on the stern leading the carving action. The bow rocker is enough to surf well without too much of a detrimental effect on speed. When executing a turn on a wave with a lean, the edge on bow will lead turns. If the bow starts to purl, a simple lean will allow the bow's edge to carve back to the surface. The small stern volume enhances control on waves by reducing the lift on the rear of a boat that more volume can cause. [8]

In ads for the Transition, Dagger stated it won because of the Retendo Theory:

> ...it [the Transition] was designed to go to new levels: The low volume bow catches quickly to initiate "retendo" moves and slices freely to avoid pearling during a wild surf. The low volume stern carves out the turns and performs smooth vertical moves. The midsection enhances sidesurfing and the higher volume helps you in the hole. [9]

At the rodeo's conclusion, American men dominated the K-1 events. Jackson won edging out Shipley (both '92 Olympians in slalom) in K-1 Surface. Both paddled Transitions. McDougal in his Super Sport was edged out of the medals by a British paddler. Lyle, also paddling a Transition, gave an inspired performance in the prelims that electrified the crowds.

Both Perception's Super Sport and Dagger's Transition were available to paddlers in plastic for the 1994 paddling season. Dagger, thinking the Transition was too hot for the average whitewater paddler, detuned the design for plastic production from its original composite design. The plastic version was a little longer with a more rounded hull. The composite version was flatter and had edges. The length of all three kayaks, the Hurricane, Super Sport, and Transition, were in the 10-foot range, the standard for river running kayaks at the time.

Although Corran Addison, paddling for Prijon, didn't win in a Hurricane, many acknowledged that the Hurricane was the kayak that changed thinking regarding rodeo. The design was noticeably asymmetrical with the widest point aft of its center. It had a wide low volume stern. In contrast to other designs, the hull was also very flat for much of its length, particularly from under the seat to the stern which allowed for spinning and surfing. (The Hurricane, a blow molded kayak, retained its intended flatness in the hull because of the more rigid plastic used in its production.) However, the Hurricane, as well as the Transition and Super Sport, still retained their river-running characteristics with roots in their slalom heritage.

The '95 World Rodeo Championships were held in Augsburg, Germany, on the Eiskanal, the site for the '92 Munich Olympics. European paddlers were very prepared to compete on their home turf. In OC-1, the traditional North American event, two Germans beat out American Jeff Richards who won only a bronze in the event. Likewise in squirt, the best American finish was Bob McDonough's bronze. However, in K-1W and C-1 events, Americans Karen Mann and Allen Braswell won gold. Corran Addison finished with silver in K-1.

Although the Hurricane's hull was considered flat at the time, innovations that indirectly grew from its ability to spin and surf, a result of its flatness, would take rodeo designs beyond their river running roots towards combining kayak characteristics for hole-riding with those of a surfboard.

[8] Singleton, Mark. "Hot Dogs Go High-Tech as Boat Designs Evolve." *Nantahala Outdoor Center Outfitters Catalog* (1995): 63.

[9] Advertisement. *American Whitewater* Vol. XXXV No. 2 (March/April 1995): 29.

Flat Hulls and Short Boats

While many people felt that the Hurricane was on the verge of a new operating system for whitewater, no one knew exactly what that meant. The future and the vision were still pretty murky. With their newly released successful designs, Dagger, Perception, and Prijon continued with the new status quo. With the exception of moving toward shorter lengths, down toward nine feet, their new rodeo-playboat designs were variations on the same theme for the next couple of years. While Perception introduced nothing new for rodeo-playboats until 1997, Dagger introduced the Outburst, Animas, and the nine-foot RPM (Radical Play Machine), and Prijon, the 9' 4" Rockit and 8' 10" Fly.

In the meantime, Spike Gladwin and Corran Addison, two non-American designers, discovered the next crux to the new operating system, *very flat* planing hulls with *very hard* chines.

Their design concepts, introduced through North American manufacturers, spawned the next evolution in whitewater kayak designs. Although Gladwin and Addison came to the same basic conclusion regarding planing hulls, their inspirations were different.

For Spike Gladwin, a British slalom paddler, ocean surfing in kayak was the inspiration for his first surf kayak design, the Rip International. In 1993, Gladwin, an employee of Necky Kayaks in British Columbia, designed the Rip International with Mike Neckar, fellow ocean-surfer, former Canadian whitewater champion, and owner of Necky Kayaks. Like other surf kayaks and surf shoes dating back to the '70s, the hull was flat like a surfboard with bow and stern rocker. The design proved a success for ocean kayak surfing. Gladwin placed second at the World Surf Kayak Championships in Costa Rica. With the playboating trends of wave and hole surfing, Gladwin and Neckar tried it for river running and found that it also worked well as a river running playboat. In 1994, Necky introduced the Rip, a 9' 2" whitewater composite version. Within a year, it was produced in plastic at 8' 10" with a planing hull for river running.

Corran Addison competed in a Hurricane for Prijon when it was first introduced in 1993 and realized that although he used primarily surface currents for cartwheels, he also used the sub-surface currents of a hole. Addison used these sub-surface currents to change direction or boat orientation to link moves, "sticking" some part of the boat down into the sub-surface currents. Addison realized that since he needed to remain on the surface a majority of the time, he needed a hull that kept him there. A flat hull, like the Hurricane's, worked. However, Addison, bored with doing cartwheels for rodeos, also realized that a flat hull, like that found on a surf kayak, would allow spins on a green wave. A *very flat* hull, a planing hull, was the answer.

Addison was not new to designing radical kayaks. Believing he could design a better kayak for Perception than the Dancer he paddled (while believing the Dancer was one of the best designs available), Addsion bought a ticket and traveled from his home in South Africa to visit Bill Masters. Addison was 17 years old. He showed up with his prototype kayak at Master's doorstep. Addison's brashness impressed Masters who allowed him to stay and work at Perception.

THE TERM PLANING HULL IN BOATS, prior to its use in describing a flat hull used for rodeo kayaks, applies to motorized water craft. In naval architecture, a planing hull is defined as:

> A hull form with straight buttock lines [the lines of intersection of the surface of the hull with its longitudinal vertical planes], designed to develop positive hydrodynamic pressures on its bottom so that its draft decreases with increasing speed, enabling it to rise higher on the wave that it is generating.[10]

The term planing hull used to differentiate the new flat hull configurations from the older displacement hulls is actually a misnomer. All hulls are really displacement hulls because displacement of water is what makes a boat float. Playboat planing hulls, with their flat bottom surfaces, plane because of the size of the kayak and the weight of the paddler, that is, the kayak's displacement, combined with its use on moving water. Moving water replaces moving or powering the boat on water in the more traditional view of planing hulls.

It is the current, or moving water, whether it is on a river wave or ocean wave, which provides the power or rather, the speed, relative to the kayak. A flat hull offers little resistance or drag. It is therefore far easier to develop the positive hydrodynamic pressures that define a planing condition. Even the older displacement hulls, without the flat planing areas, could plane under certain conditions, just not as well or as controlled.

But, regardless of technical correctness, the two terms offer an adequate distinction between the new concepts and old concepts in kayak design and hydrodynamics.

[10] Parker, Sybil P. (editor). *Dictionary of Scientific and Technical Terms.* New York: McGraw-Hill Book Company, 1989.

Addison remained with Perception over the next couple of years and learned about design from Masters and Stancil, designers of the Dancer. Modifications of his design resulted in the Corsica. At the time, his designs were a little too radical; they were ahead of their time. In 1989, he developed a variety of designs: Lite Sabre, a cross between a Hurricane (Prijon) and an RPM (Dagger); the Blackout, a squirt design that was a cross between an Enigma (Euro-Kayaks) and a Blast (Dagger); and the Osprey with a flat hull, hard edges, and tubes that ran through the deck so that air traveling down to the water surface would "act like ball bearings." [11] In 1991, Addison left Perception to train for the '92 Olympics. He later paddled and competed in Europe where he met Prijon.

In 1994, Addison, with actress Selene Thoms, co-founded RP Savage Designs in North Carolina. A year later, Addison introduced the Scorpion, a very radically designed rodeo kayak. The Scorpion with its shallow arch hull was ultimately an evolutionary dead-end, but the following year in 1996, Addison incorporated some of the Scorpion's radical design features with a planing hull in his Fury and Gravity designs. Unlike Necky's Rip, the Fury at 8' 6" was designed for rodeo playboating with a planing hull, hard chines, and golf-ball sized divots (indentations) in the hull that were designed in to contribute to surfing and spinning dynamics. It was by far the most radical design but it was the beginning of a progression of rodeo playboats incorporating planing hull innovations. The Fury fueled the new breed of rodeo kayaks that followed.

Author's note: Around 1976, I recall watching Denny Cilensek, a member of the Keel-Hauler Canoe Club, paddle a very short (relative to the 13- foot standard at the time) surf shoe on the Lower Yough. Denny was ripping and shredding every possible surfing wave and surface on the river.

Although Gladwin and Addison were influenced by the same desire to surf in a kayak, Gladwin designed his first planing kayak for ocean surfing and found that it worked well for river running. Addison, on the other hand, designed his first planing kayak based on surfboards and ocean surfing for river surfing, rodeos, and river running. While both are credited with the introduction of the planing hull, Addison with his radical bad boy image, was able to market and push the concept by pushing the envelope and kick-starting the trend that brought the innovations to all paddlers, not just professional rodeo paddlers.

Others before Addison and Gladwin paddled surf kayaks on rivers. However, neither the purpose nor the timing was right. Rodeo playboating in the mid-'90s was the right combination.

While Savage and Necky pursued the planing hull concept in their Fury and Rip designs, others like Pyrahna and Wave Sport looked for their own new innovations. Unfortunately, these innovations resulted in a few one season winners. Still, other paddlers and designers did not immediately recognize, nor accept, that the planing hull was the next step toward a new breed of rodeo playboat. Nor did they understand that the average whitewater paddler was ready to take that step.

In the early '80s, Pyrahna of Britain, owned by Graham Mackereth, began production of rotationally molded kayaks for the European market that were distributed by Josef Sedavic using the Seda name for the American market. After Mackereth attended the '93 World Whitewater Rodeo on the Ocoee, he realized the potential of rodeo in the American market, geared up for production of new designs, and changed distributors. In 1994, Johann Forsberg

[11] Addison, Corran. Interview by author 30 December 1997.

began distribution of Pyrahna products through Impex International. Within two years, Impex imported eight different whitewater kayaks including river running, creekboat, and rodeo playboat designs.

After Pyrahna's earlier success with the Stunt Bat design, Mackereth introduced the Acrobat 300 and 270, and another in the Stunt Series, the Stunt 300, to the American market. All three boats were well received for about a season, particularly the Acrobat 270. The hulls of the Acrobats and Stunt 300 were anything but planing hulls. The Acrobats' hulls incorporated two concave areas on either side of the center while the Stunt 300 incorporated convex areas. When it was first introduced, the Acrobat 270 was one of the shortest rodeo playboats on the market at 8' 7".

Chan Zwanzig at Wave Sport spent considerable time and effort building five prototypes over almost two years to produce the Frankenstein. It, too, proved to be an evolutionary dead-end. The Stubby, at a very short 7' 5" was another. However, its use continued as a squashed Topolino, a forgiving introductory rodeo playboat and steep creekboat.

During 1996 and 1997, eight manufacturers introduced at least one new hot kayak for the river running, rodeo-playboat market (excluding creekboats) comprising both planing hulls and displacement hulls. The Whip-it and the Whiplash, both designed by Bob McDonough, were Perception's entry into the new planing hull design trend for rodeo playboats and was actually introduced mid-season. Wave Sport's Kinetic, designed by the team of Dan Brabec, Eric Jackson, and Chan Zwanzig, was Wave Sport's first real entry into the planing hull rodeo playboat market. At the same time Dagger and Eskimo (a German manufacturer) continued to design displacement hulls. Dagger's RPM, designed by Steve Scarborough, was the everyman boat. It gave paddlers a taste of some of the more radical rodeo ideas without being too radical. Eskimo's Kendo, designed by Jan Keller, a rodeo World Champion, was in the same category as the RPM. Many of the kayaks introduced during this time were in the 8 ½ to 9-foot range.

In 1996, Addison left Savage to start Riot, a new company in Quebec. Addison introduced three designs: the Antagonist, the Rage, and the Hammer. The Hammer, introduced in 1997, was the next generation of Addison's radical rodeo playboat designs. The name of Savage Designs changed to Savage V after Addison left to start Riot with Jeff Rivest, Savage's Canadian distributor. In 2000, Savage V folded.

Over the next few years, planing hull designs continued to evolve. It was, after all, a very new design concept for whitewater kayaks. Except for the concepts and understanding of squirtboating and squirt designs, there was very little past knowledge to rely on. Almost everything about the new hulls was new. In spite of the mumbo-jumbo science and physics that designers used for why their boats performed a certain way, they still relied on their intuitive senses and paddling their prototypes to test their latest theories and innovations. The size and shape of the "spin disk," the planing surface area, getting "release" for the spin disk, and the amount of rocker were all problems that each manufacturer encountered and solved. The release problem, perhaps the most significant, was resolved within a few years. Designers realized that an abrupt transition between the flat spin disk and hard wall vertical chine was

ESKIMO, a long time German paddlesport manufacturer initially worked with Prijon to produce blow molded whitewater kayak. For a time, Wildwasser Sport USA distributed Eskimo kayaks alongside Prijon until 1998 when Eskimo USA began distribution for Eskimo of Germany.

THE CAD PROGRAMS that practically all manufacturers now use for designing kayaks and canoes incorporate basic hydrostatic calculations which include displacement and waterline information.

THE PROLIFERATION of rodeo playboats continued into 1998 and 1999. All were designs with flat-spinning planning hulls around 8 feet in length including Dagger's Vertigo, Medieval, Vengeance, Centrifuge, and Ultrafuge; Eskimo's Zwo; Necky's Jive and Gliss; Perception's Mr. Clean; Prijon's Samurai; Pyrahna's Inazone 220, 230, and 240; Riot's Glide and 007; Savage V's Maniac; and Wave Sport's Z and XXX (Triple X).

part of the problem and incorporated a bevel or intermediary step, a "release chine," to free surface tension between the surfaces of the flat hull and the water.

By the 1998 and 1999 seasons, practically all whitewater kayak manufacturers had their own hot designs with flat-spinning planing hulls. Some designs were very rodeo specific while others were all-terrain playboats incorporating the hottest or latest rodeo innovations into a kayak intended for river running. Manufacturers also produced different sized rodeo playboats with the same new innovations to accommodate different weights of paddlers. They recognized the critical connection between planing hull performance characteristics and paddler weight. The desire for the hull to remain on the surface was now very dependent upon the paddler's weight and the boat's total volume or buoyancy, its *displacement.* Obtaining the correct volume or displacement was the reason that squirtboats were custom-cut for the paddler's weight. Instead of remaining *on the surface* for rodeo, squirtboats were designed for minimal buoyancy, with a 51 percent probability of floating. However, the spin disk did not act alone for the performance of a rodeo playboat. Changing direction or boat orientation required that the paddler stick some part of the boat down into the sub-surface currents. In 1998, Perception introduced the 3-d, designed by Shane Benedict, with deck characteristics reminiscent of squirtboats. It had foot bumps and scooping of the bow and stern, the squirt "wing concept."

However, the planing hull was more than just a design innovation. It was the beginning of the next transition in the sport. The new planing hull rodeo playboats not only brought design concepts from surfing but playboating technique, co-developed with the design concepts, brought gymnastic concepts from rollerblading, skateboarding, and snow boarding, all sports of Gen-X and the real audience for planing hulls. Planing hulls and everything associated with them embodied the future of the sport with the next generation of paddlers, the generation of "park and play" paddlers comprised of both Gen-X and Y.

In early 1998, Bozo Cardozo wrote of the proliferation of designs:

> Boats that looked radical five years ago are now trumpeted as "all-around" boats, and site-specific boats for creekin', surfin', and rodeo are popping out of molds like crazy. The rodeo and surf boats have given rise to a whole new game called "park and play." [12]

While many manufacturers jumped into the planing hull design fray early on, only a few initially understood who the planing hulls were really for, what it really meant to whitewater paddling, and that the sport was ready to transition. While Gladwin's Rip design was one of the first planing hulls, Necky failed to understand the full extent of what the planing hull was about and failed to grab its market. Addison on the other hand, was a visionary. He recognized the full embodiment of the planing hull and the paradigm shift it meant for the sport. Addison saw the transition coming because as a Gen-Xer, he was part of it himself. He recognized what it would take to bring whitewater to his generation and the next. Planing hulls fit the market of the now

[12] Cardozo, Bozo. "Goofy and Goofier." *Canoe & Kayak* Vol. 26 No. 1 (March 1998): 120–125.

generation. Addison was not bound by aging Boomer concepts and thinking. His designs were bold and brash, as was his paddling reputation with extreme paddling and falls running.

Chan Zwanzig (Wave Sport) also recognized the impact of the planing hull. Although an aging Boomer himself, Zwanzig was one of the first traditional owners and designers who understood the generational transition. In 1996, Zwanzig introduced the Kinetic and Godzilla, both with planing hulls. Based on kayak sales compared by model, he saw two different demographics emerge among paddlers, what he described as the "classic" and the "aggro." The classic was 30 years old and up (the aging Boomer), was into river running with some playing, and bought a new boat about every three and a half years. The aggro was 14 to 28, Gen-X and Y, was into instant gratification, shredding, and cartwheeling, though not necessarily extreme or difficult paddling. They wore noseplugs for their park and play style and bought a new boat about every year and a half. Zwanzig recognized what was happening, that Gen-X and Y were the next whitewater paddlers. His marketing and designs responded to the changing market.

Zwanzig saw the transition occur with his own sales. In 1996, his sales were 85 percent classic to 15 percent aggro based on model, traditional river-running displacement hull versus flat planing hull. In 1997, his sales ration was 75 percent to 25 percent, although he found that some of the aggro sales were also classic paddlers who had converted, not wanting to be left out.

Zwanzig immersed himself in the play of Gen-X and became a part of it himself. For a time in 1997, Zwanzig sported a pink and purple Mohawk haircut. Zwanzig hung with "the boys and girls, ripping, playing, and shredding."[13] In 1996, Zwanzig went out on a limb and supported a team of young paddlers. He gave them $10 a day and a credit card for expenses and told them to paddle and compete, which they did. Team Wave Sport developed and attracted hot competitors, young men and women alike.

Dagger and Perception, the two largest American manufacturers, like many of the other whitewater manufacturers were owned by aging Boomers and did not initially enter the planing hull design fray. For a few years, the audience for their designs continued to be their own generation and the new designs they produced were conservative based on playboating for traditional river running hulls. However, within a couple of years, Dagger and Perception hired their own Gen-X advisors, designers, and team members, and began designing for, and marketing to, Gen-X and Y paddlers.

It all happened fast: the changes in design, the changes in the market, and the changes in marketing. Within ten short years, the American market went from a single manufacturer that controlled the market to a market large enough to support more than seven. By 1998, just three years after the introduction of the planing hull, the proliferation of new models was on the verge of hurting the industry more than helping it. No one knew where it would stop and many looked to what had happened to high growth sports like sailboarding in the late '70s and '80s. The proliferation of specialized designs actually hurt the sports growth. The unprecedented growth of the whitewater market was further fueled by the growth of the American economy and the prosperity that it brought.

[13] Zwanzig, Chan. Interview by author 10 June 1997.

While the changes in design and the market continued, brought on by the transition from one generation to the next, the industry itself was ready for change, for a transition of its own. Mergers and acquisitions, a reflection of the overall economic growth of the late '90s, were part of that change. On June 26, 1998, a private group of Atlanta investors announced the purchase of Dagger Canoe and Perception. Although still operated as separate companies, Watermark brought the two industry leaders, and rivals, under a single company umbrella. Joe Pulliam as president, and Steve Scarborough as vice president of Engineering, continued in their roles in Dagger management while Bill Masters, although remaining as chairman of Perception, essentially retired.

The benefits to economic and market consolidation of all paddlesport products, not just whitewater, compelled other mergers. About the same time in July 1998, another announcement was made of a strategic sales alliance between Wilderness Systems and Mad River Canoe. This was a precursor to their merger in October under the Confluence name. Like WaterMark, both Wilderness Systems and Mad River maintained their independent company names and entities. Wilderness Systems' co-founder Andy Zimmerman was named CEO and John Sheppard, executive vice president of Manufacturing, for Confluence. Kay Henry, co-founder of Mad River Canoe with Jim Henry, remained on the board of directors but essentially retired from daily company operations.

Consolidation continued the next year. In January 1999, Old Town's parent company, Johnson Worldwide Associates (JWA), acquired Necky. In June, Confluence purchased Wave Sports adding whitewater kayak manufacturing to their holdings. Riot's founders, Corran Addison and Jeff Rivest, acknowledged that paddlesports was more than just the whitewater market. In the fall of 2000, they formed a parent company, Voodoo, that encompassed recreational paddling and seakayaking under the Azul and Sun product lines. By 2000, no independent plastic manufacturers remained in the whitewater kayak market.

Consolidation occurred in the overall paddlesport industry during the '90s. All three major entities, JWA, Confluence, and WaterMark, now contained within their holdings fairly complete paddlesport product lines that included whitewater.

JWA purchased Old Town from the Gray family in 1974 and by 2000, owned six other paddlesport companies including Carlisle Paddles, Extrasport, Necky, and Ocean Kayak.

Confluence, initially comprised of Mad River Canoe with its Voyageur accessory line and Wilderness Systems with its Trinity Bay and WindRider brands, added Sidewinder Whitewater paddles along with Wave Sport to bring whitewater kayaks into its holdings.

For WaterMark, both Dagger and Perception already had a complete line of paddlesport products for whitewater, seakayaking, and general recreational including Dagger Accessories, formerly Headwaters, and Harmony Paddles and Accessories.

Two other acquisitions occurred around the same time with roots tracing back to the early days of rotational molding and whitewater kayaking. Old Town purchased LPA Plastics, owned by Pierre Arcouette, a long-time contractor to Old Town for their rotationally molded recreational kayaks.

LPA Plastics is the single longest continuous manufacturer of rotationally molded plastic kayaks. The other was the purchase of Hydra's parent company, Rotocast Plastic Products of Tennessee, by Rotonics Manufacturing, the fourth owner in the series of kayak companies tracing its roots to the first whitewater kayak designed by Tom Johnson for Hollowform.

Coincidental with the industry's consolidation, a consolidation of design concepts also took shape. Bob Woodward, a long-time industry observer, wrote in 1999:

> A semblance of design standards has actually emerged as a result of the playboat wars of the past two years. Today's playboats are more symmetrical, with bows and sterns nearly equal in volume. The majority of the volume is centered around the cockpit, accounting for the "raised" cockpit look on many boats... Hard chines help in carving the boat move-to-move. Contemporary playboat ends are flatter, more "slicey." Boats have more rocker, so that the ends don't dive, particularly during spin moves. The most noticeable differences in design from boat to boat occur in hulls. Scoops in the nose and tail help create lift and make the hull "free." Channels, essentially borrowed from wakeboard design, aid tracking and separation from the water. A flat planing hull or raised spin disk makes the boat surf and spin with ease.[14]

The new designs seemed to bear a resemblance to older squirt designs from the early '80s, incorporating many of the same concepts for the same reasons. Their bows and sterns approached those of squirtboats for using sub-surface currents while the surfboard-like planing hull incorporated various features like scoops, channels, and beveled release edges to break surface tension, to free-up the hull from the water when needed. The chine wall with high volume mid-section not only provided a chine to catch and carve the water, but also another planing surface when paddled on that side. The mid-section volume provided the proper amount of volume or displacement for the paddler's weight for the boat to remain on the surface.

The rapid decrease in rodeo playboat length observed in the latter '90s ended settling around 8 feet with designs for smaller paddlers a few inches less, and for larger paddlers, a few inches more. Some of the later designs seemed to even decrease the length for larger paddlers to under eight feet in length. In general, river-running playboat and creekboat designs remained a little longer.

In 2000, Corran Addison obtained patents on two separate inventions associated with the performance of planing hulls: Patent 6,035,801 for the spin groove and 6,119,620 for a kayak with release louvers.

Because planing hulls present very little surface area to the water, there is little translational stability, "there is very little 'hull in the water' to provide a 'bite' to keep the craft on course." In order to increase translational stability, hull designs have incorporated features such as longitudinal grooves and bevels "that run parallel with the longitudinal axis of the kayak."[15] However, those

[14] Woodward, Bob. "Hot Stuff for Whitewater." *Canoe & Kayak* Vol. 27 No. 2 (July 1999):98–100, 102–104.

[15] United States Patent 6,035,801. Inventor: Corran Addison. March 14, 2000.

same features inhibit flat spins. Addison's purpose for the spin groove invention was to improve performance for flat spins. As described in the patent's abstract:

> The hull section [of the kayak] has a bottom surface circumscribed with a contour edge. At least an endless groove is formed in the bottom surface and spaced inwardly of the contour edge, whereby the endless groove traps water and provides a thrust bearing-like action enhancing translational stability during planing conditions and performance in a flat spin of a kayak. [16]

Another area that Addison sought to improve was hull speed. The short lengths and rocker of current designs reduced hull speed dramatically over older designs. In order to reduce drag, Addison invented the release louvers feature to reduce "adhesion of water molecules to the hull of a kayak at its trailing end" [17] thereby increasing hull speed. As described in the abstract the hull contains:

> one or more louvers provided in said hull at least in a stern section thereof to force water to separate from said hull whereby forming voids which are replaced with air from the water surface or water from the sides as said kayaks is displaced thereon. This reduces drag and the kayak benefits from a speed improvement. [18]

FOR 2000, the rodeo playboat designs included Dagger's Centrifuge and Ultrafuge; Eskimo's Quadro (Zwo's big brother—from 1999); Necky's Zip (with a concaved hull) and Bliss (Gliss's big brother—from 1999); Perception's Ultraclean, Amp, and Shock; Prijon's Alien; Pyrahna's Prozone series (225, 230, and 235): Riot's Disco, Trickster, and Prankster; and Wave Sports' Forplay.

However, in spite of the semblance of design standards, designing fever did not level off and the proliferation of designs continued. In the next season, 2000, a dozen new rodeo playboats hit the market and at least that many were anticipated for 2001.

The proliferation in rodeo playboat and kayak designs also affected open canoe designs for rodeo. Although open canoes had a class of their own for rodeo competition, few rodeos actually had enough competitors to make a class. At the '95 Rodeo Worlds in Augsburg, Massive Outdoor Products, a small Canadian manufacturer of composite boats, introduced their new canoe design, the 9' 1" Departure. Designed and paddled by Massive Outdoor Products owners Ian Thomson and Paul Danks, Departure was certainly a departure from traditional canoe designs. Their next design, the Air, took advantage of new rodeo standards for open canoes and turned many heads to the possibilities of competitive open canoes in rodeo. Thomson contended "that the canoe market has been fading in part because the boat designs haven't kept up with the growing interest in rodeo moves and what some are calling 'destination boating.'" Thomson's reasons for pushing OC-s and C-1s in rodeo was "because your center of gravity and freer range of body movements give you an incredible rotational torque and hip control that a kayaker doesn't have." [19]

In 1998, a few years after Thomson and Danks showed off their composite rodeo open canoes, Savage V introduced the Skeeter, designed by Frankie Hubbard. (In the '80s and '90s, Frankie Hubbard designed open canoes, many based on slalom C-1s of the late '70s and early '80s, for Dagger and Mohawk.) The Skeeter was a rotationally molded OC-1 only 9' 4" in length.

16 United States Patent 6,035,801. Inventor: Corran Addison. March 14, 2000.

17 United States Patent 6,119,620. Inventor: Corran Addison. September 19, 2000.

18 Ibid.

19 Editors. "Redefining the Sport." *Canoe & Kayak* Vol. 26 No. 1 (March 1998): 16.

Dagger followed within a couple of years with their rotomolded Quake at 8' 10" (27½ inches in width), and later the Aftershock at 8'4" and 26½ inches in width, practically the same width dimensions of C-1s.

Because of the Skeeter's size and cockpit design, the canoe could be rotomolded to eliminate oil canning, a deterrent from molding longer canoes. The Skeeter was short enough that there were no long flat areas that would result in excessive oil canning. The elongated cockpit design, reminiscent of decked canoes and closed canoes of the early '60s, also provided additional structural support eliminating the need for gunwales, while at the same time eliminating molding waste, that is, the area cut-out after molding to open the cockpit was small. Later, rotationally molded canoes such as Dagger's Aftershock introduced in 2000 were sold with uncut cockpit areas to allow the buyer to custom fit the cockpit.

JUST AS SLALOM COMPETITION drove design changes that affected river-running designs, so, too, did rodeo playboat designs affect the rest of the sport. However, the effects were greater than previously seen from slalom and went beyond the designs.

River Running Boats

Until the advent of flat planing hulls (essentially before 1996), river-running designs and rodeo boats were virtually one and the same as would be expected of rodeo's origin. Even the newer, hotter designs like the Crossfire, Hurricane, and Pirouette in the early '90s were soon adopted by the average paddler for river running. This followed the example set by slalom in the'60s to mid-'70s as paddlers' skills increased to match new design capabilities; the hot slalom boat for one year was the hot river-running boat the next.

In the early '90s, aside from the trend toward lower volume and shorter river running kayaks (and shorter canoes), and what was considered as newer playboat characteristics with flatter sterns with edges, very little really changed from the late '80s. Plastic kayaks dominated and because of the costs associated with introducing a new kayak design into the market, many manufacturers were reluctant to introduce any new radical innovations in design that might not pay back their design and mold costs. Design changes or innovations were, therefore, made in small steps.

In 1994, New Wave Kayak Products, one of the last manufacturers of squirtboats, entered the plastic whitewater kayak when they purchased the assets of Infinity Kayaks. During the next five years, New Wave produced the Cruise Control (designed by Jim Snyder), Sleek (designed by Jim Snyder and John Schreiner), Mongoose (Ken Sanders and Schreiner), and Buzz, a whitewater sit-on-top (designed by Snyder and Attila Szilagyi) before going out of the paddlesport business.

Dagger was the first plastic kayak manufacturer to introduce multicolored kayaks. This was achieved using different colored resins (powdered plastic) in the mold and allowing the colored resins to mix naturally during the molding process. A few years later, "molded-in graphics" were available to rotational molders and were adopted by many of the kayak manufacturers. New Wave, in particular, because of their long-standing tradition of producing highly graphiced composite squirtboats, adopted the use of molded-in-graphics and adapted the concepts to produce similarly graphiced custom plastic kayaks.

In 1995, kayaks used by paddlers for river running, now called whitewater playboats, included Dagger's Transition, Prijon's Hurricane, Perception's Overflow and Super Sport, New Wave's Sleek and Cruise Control, Wave Sport's Fusion, and Pyranha's Mountain 300, although Perception's Dancer and Corsica, Dagger's Response and Crossfire, and Prijon's T-Canyon and T-Slalom were still popular. Many of the newer kayaks were in the 10-foot range, plus or minus 6 inches, down about a foot from the '80s. The Mountain 300 at 9'7" and Sleek at 9'5" were two of the shorter designs.

South Fork of the Yuba (CA), 2000—courtesy of Brandon Knapp.

Grasping for the next innovation in whitewater, Dagger, Perception, and New Wave designed rotomolded sit-on tops for whitewater, reflecting the popular trend for such boats outside of whitewater. In 1995 and 1996, whitewater sit-on-tops debuted but the market proved to be limited and short-lived.

Creekboating, a variation of river running, became popular with the congestion brought on by the growth of whitewater and the desire to paddle yet unexplored sections of rivers. Creekboats were generally designed with blunter ends to reduce pinning possibilities for running tighter and steeper rivers. Perception's Corsica, introduced in 1989, was considered a good creekboat. Dagger's Freefall was the first American design to include a European keyhole-style cockpit and cut-away front pillar with a bulkhead footbrace. Other creekboats in the early to mid-'90s included Perception's Overflow, Pyrahna's Creek 280, and Wave Sports Descente, all in the 9½ to 10-foot range.

The hulls of creekboats designed at the end of the '80s, Jim Snyder's Screamin' Meanie and Phil Coleman's New Vision, tended toward the 11-foot to 12-foot range with fuller bows for buoyancy but with squirtable sterns and locking hulls. Noah's Jeti and AQ, were used as creekboats in the Southeast although they were designed with fuller sterns and without normal squirt characteristics. These features became the standard for creekboats in the early '90s.

Within a few short years of the introduction of flat planing hulls in rodeo playboats, designs for river-running boats began to adopt the planing hull. As planing hull design standards for rodeo playboats coalesced around 1998, so did standards for river running. While some designers like Zwanzig initially maintained that rodeo playboats were ideal for river running and creekboating, others de-tuned their hot rodeo designs for river running and lengthened the designs by about a foot. By 1998, kayaks designed and marketed for river running were in general about a foot longer than rodeo playboats, around 9 feet instead of 8 feet.

In 1998, Perception introduced the Arc (All River Craft) and Sparc (Small Persons All River Craft) designed for river running, joining Prijon's Fly, Riot's Hammer, Savage's Beast, and Wave Sport's X, among others, as whitewater playboats. Soon after, Dagger introduced the Redline and Infrared designs as planing hull river-running kayaks.

With the exception of Wave Sport's Y, creekboat designs retained their displacement hull origins although decreasing in length as was the trend for all other kayaks, now in the eight to nine foot range. However, one benefit from the design proliferation of planing hulls and the desire to provide a complete line of kayaks was that more, and newer, creekboat designs were available for paddlers.

In 2000, new creekboat designs included Dagger's Gradient, Perception's Phat and Axess, Prijon's Rockit, Pyrahna's Migo 230, Savage's Skreem, and Wave Sport's Y with new designs anticipated in 2001 from Riot, the Sick and Big Gun, and from Necky, the Blunt.

By 2001, every manufacturer of whitewater kayaks also produced a kayak for creekboating.

Still another benefit of market competition for the growing number of paddlers was the introduction of designs for different sized paddlers. With the impact of displacement (kayak volume and therefore size) on planing hulls came the recognition that paddler weight affected hull performance and that paddlers were looking for optimum performance characteristics. This, combined with the growing number of younger paddlers, contributed to designs for every sized paddler. This was a tremendous benefit and impetus for the entry of more women and younger kids into whitewater. In the mid-to-late '90s, a new generation of young and fearless Gen-X and Y women entered whitewater and was drawn to every aspect including rodeo and extreme paddling.

The mid-'90s were more than twenty years, a full generation, after Title IX in 1972. Gen-X and Y women were the result of the societal changes that occurred since that time which have allowed women to be viewed as equals, particularly among their peers of Gen-X and Y men.

In 1999, Christie Dobson wrote about women in paddling:

> Women have hit the mainstream in whitewater kayaking... They are competing in rodeos, exploring new rivers and creeks, and working at top positions in the industry... Just as they have done in countless other sports, women have surpassed the gender barrier in kayaking. No longer are they looked upon as lessers; they are running the same, if not harder, drops as men and are competing at a near-equal level... innovations in equipment have enabled them to climb the ladder faster and higher—especially in the world of freestyle and hairboating.[20]

[20] Dobson, Christie. "She'll Be Comin' Down the River." *Paddler* Vol. 19 No. 1 (January/February 1999): 80–89.

Woman kayaker on the South Fork of the Yuba (CA), 2000—courtesy of Brandon Knapp.

A benefit to all paddlers was the technique that developed from the new designs. This allowed the new paddler or an average paddler to become successful in a fairly short time. Rodeo and the new designs and techniques associated with it brought a proactive approach to dropping in a hole that was not common except by the gutsiest of paddlers.

Towards the end of the '90s, river running kayaks were called all-around, all-terrain, or even river playboats to differentiate them from rodeo playboats that were called freestyle or park-and-playboats. But the differentiation was more than just the subtle descriptions of the design. The two boat types, both within river running, also illustrated a divergence of paddlers. Just as specialized designs for slalom competition were part of the divergence between racers and cruisers (river runners) in the late '60s, specialized designs for rodeo competition seemed to move toward another divergence within river running in the '90s. This time a divergence seemed to occur between river runners, with their extreme boater contingent, and playboaters, with their park-and-play or rodeo boater contingent.

Gen-X and later Gen-Y began to gravitate toward extreme sports and, therefore, to whitewater. In the late '80s and early '90s, the social aspect of rodeo, combined with its acrobatic aspect, was similar to other Gen-X sports like skateboarding where everyone hung around the pipe at skate parks to watch others and to perfect their own moves and tricks. Hence, park-and-playboating or destination paddling was introduced to whitewater through the entry of the next generation into the sport. Although park-and-playboating was not without risks, it was far less risky than river running, especially extreme boating, the extreme end of river running. For some paddlers, the park-and-play environment and rodeo was more appealing.

In the mid-'90s, the apparent trend toward divergence between river runners and playboaters began with the increased popularity of rodeo. Rodeo, with all its hype in the market, became a sore point for river runners. Congestion was a result of rodeo's popularity. In 1994, Matt McCloud, a river runner, wrote a letter to *American Whitewater* expressing his concerns about the new park-and-playboaters. He wrote:

> The popularity and the potential of professionalism in rodeo is growing yet many good boaters are alienated admirers. The hole hawging numbers and manners of those that dedicate hours and hours of practice manage to piss off their fellow paddlers with the same dedication. Natural talent and sweet holes are scarce, aspirations do not seem to be.[21]

CLIMBING had experiences similar to whitewater during the '90s. Sport climbing with natural settings competed with wall climbing on man-made walls. In the case of wall climbers and park-and-playboaters (and rodeo boaters), watching videos, practicing, and hanging out watching others was all a part of gaining skill and experience while maintaining the social aspects of the sport.

[21] McCloud, Matt. "Change for the Worse." *American Whitewater* Vol. XXXIV No. 4 (July/August 1994): 10–11.

By the end of the '90s, the disparity between the two groups was more pronounced, based on many inherent differences in the basic appeal of both types of paddling. In early 2000, *Paddler* published two opposing opinions, one for river running and the other for park-and-play. Scott Lindgren, owner of Driftwood Productions, wrote:

> ... this Saturday & Sunday, the National Organization of Whitewater Rodeos is coming to a town near you. Brought to you by Kamel, Butt Light, Pimpto Bismol, Microsofty, and Phillipstick Morris. We have killer whitewater hole, the sickest downriver race, and all the rockstar rodeo'ers from around the world. And if that's not enough, we're gonna throw the biggest, most rippin' party ever at the Honkey Tonkin' Ho Pumpin' Bar. Naked chicks and more! And Loaded Gun Productions will be there, making their newewst, sickest kayak porn flick yet... Is this what kayaking is all about? Glam? Not! Rock Stars? Not! Winning a rodeo or competition? Not! It's all crap. Why? Because if that's why you kayak, you're kayaking for the wrong reasons... It's not about kayaking for the money or for the sake of being recognized, it's simply about wanting to paddle more than anything else. That is the core. This is competition amongst nature and I'll let the river be the judge of my ability—not some rodeo judge who tries to count how many ends I throw in a weak, overcrowded play spot.[22]

Erik Voake, owner of Loaded Gun Productions, expressed the opposite view and wrote:

> I've always tried to focus on freestyle kayaking in my life because that's the future of the sport—that's what generation X and Y are interested in today. While there is a need to keep the extreme/expedition aspect alive, it's not where kayaking needs to go... Playboating is simply more realistic for most people... I'd rather see people having fun on play runs than see them out on some remote creek– hurt, pinned and broken... Playboating is a lifestyle, bringing a fresh new image with it... We are drawing more interest from bigger magazines and television. Heroes are being created and kids are buying into it. Life is great... Playboating rules. You can only run so high a waterfall before it'll kill you—but I've never heard of anyone playing themselves to death.[23]

[22] Lindgren, Scott. "Rodeo, Schmodeo-Exploration is Where It's At." *Paddler* Vol. 20, No. 2 (March/April 2000): 36–37.

[23] Voake, Eric. "Playboating Rules Supreme." *Paddler* Vol. 20, No. 2 (March/April 2000): 36–37.

Although rodeo did not immediately affect canoeing, the continuing trend toward shorter boats did. Solo whitewater canoeing was firmly entrenched. As the traditional rules regarding the lengths of kayaks was broken, so too, were the rules regarding lengths of canoes. In 1990, Walbridge predicted, "Short canoes are going to open whitewater canoeing to large numbers of people who can't handle the bigger boats in use today. I expect canoes to continue to get shorter while retaining the blunt ends and the width needed to shed water in big rapids. Smaller, lighter boats translate to more fun on white water."[24] Just as shorter kayaks upped the "funmeter," shorter canoes did the same.

At the end of the '80s and into the early '90s, solo open canoes in the 13-foot to 14-foot range dominated the market including designs from Dagger, Mad River, Mohawk and Old Town. In 1990, Mohawk broke the 13-foot barrier with the XL 12 (12' 3") followed by the XL 11 (11' 4") the following year. In 1991, Dagger introduced the Impulse at 12' 8" — barely under 13 feet. In 1993, both Mohawk and Dagger continued the short canoe trend with the introduction of Mohawk's Viper series, the Viper 12 and Viper 11, and Dagger's Prophet.

In 1990, Old Town introduced the H2 Pro, designed by Scott Phillips. It was their last venture into solo whitewater canoes. While the H2 Pro, at 13' 8" did well in the market for a couple of years, Old Town did not introduce any shorter designs and therefore, did not keep up with the rest of the market dominated by Dagger, Mad River, and Mohawk.

Except for special Royalex classes, composite canoes dominated open canoe slalom and wildwater racing for their lightness. New and younger designers like Mark Clark and John Kazimierszyk replaced long-time designers and builders John Berry (Millbrook Boats) and Jim Henry (Mad River). Berry sold Millbrook Boats to Kazimierszyk to carry on his legacy of building and designing composite boats for racing, particularly open canoes.

A few composite designs by Clark and Kazimierszyk were produced in Royalex by Mad River. Kazimierszyk's Howler was one of the more radical produced by Mad River. It came out in 1991. The 15-foot canoe, paddled solo or tandem, featured an unusual-shaped prow bow with extreme flare like an aircraft carrier designed to shed water. The hull was a shallow arch, and more rocker was incorporated into the stern than the bow which put the pivot point just aft of center for better surfing.

Short solo canoes found popularity in rodeo competition and increasing numbers of open solo paddlers entered rodeo competition. The popularity of short solo canoes also found a niche in open canoe slalom which helped to establish classes specifically for short plastic canoes. By 1997, the three major manufacturers of solo open whitewater canoes, Dagger, Mad River, and Mohawk, had designs that covered the 11-foot to 14-foot range. Whitesell and the new Blue Hole also introduced their own short designs, Whitesell's Whirlwind at 12' 1" and Blue Hole's Sequel at 11 feet, both designed by David Sherrill.

In 1997, newer solo whitewater canoe designs in the 11-foot to 12-foot range included Dagger's Ocoee, Ovation, and Rival; Mad River's Outrage; Mohawk's Rodeo, the shortest at 10' 6", and shorter canoes in the Probe series.

Although the whitewater canoe market did not expand in numbers like whitewater kayaking, the market did expand beyond its usual members and geographic boundaries, beyond the Southeast. Short canoes opened up the market to more paddlers. Mohawk's XL 11 was one of the first to open up solo whitewater canoeing to smaller women. Its short size was conducive to smaller paddlers. Short canoes, along with the pioneering efforts of the expert

[24] Walbridge, Charlie. "Whitewater Hotshots: A Review of Three 13-foot Solo Canoes." *Canoe* Vol. 18 No. 2 (May 1990): 50–55.

few, also opened up more rivers to whitewater canoeing. The popularity that short canoes brought also helped to continue to push the upper limits of open canoeing.

Open whitewater canoeing even expanded in California, an area not known for open canoeing. In 1991, Larry Wade wrote:

> Open canoeing is now undergoing the transition kayaking did in the 1970's. This is the out rime (outcome) of first descents and new play moves. Boats that are explicitly designed for recreational paddling and which roll well have opened up a lot of runs in the past few years. Rivers that California guidebooks describe as "Totally Inappropriate" or "No Way" for canoes are now regularly paddled. These are runs that, until recently, only animals like Nolan Whitesell or Bob Constantini would even consider. All that was needed was a bad attitude among the general open boat population.[25]

Wade's article in *American Whitewater* also revealed a schism of sorts between open boaters with strong preferences toward either Mad River's ME or Whitesell's Pirahna, two very different designs, design philosophies, and accompanying paddling philosophies.

Woman canoeist on Section III of the Chattooga (GA/SC), 1999—courtesy of Julie Keller.

In the mid-'90s, whitewater canoeing was about five percent of the open boat community, based on Dagger's numbers for flatwater versus whitewater sales for open canoes. While most canoes were still used for Class II–III rivers, the number of canoes used for Class III–IV increased. However, the percentage used for Class V was still small. In 1995, roughly 50 percent of Dagger's market was whitewater. Of that, 80 percent was for whitewater kayaks, with the remainder for whitewater canoes.

[25] Wade, Larry. "Totally Inappropriate." *American Whitewater* Vol. XXXVI No. 1 (March/April 1991): 42–46.

With the introduction of rotomolded open canoes for rodeo such as Dagger's Quake and Aftershock, the length for solo canoes dropped to under 9 feet. Like rodeo kayak designs, these short rotomolded rodeo canoes were used for river running. Coincidentally, following the introduction of the very short rotomolded rodeo OC-1s, Dagger introduced the Phantom at 9' 10", the shortest thermoformed canoe produced.

In the meantime, in the early to mid-'90s, the market for plastic C-1s remained small. In 1991, Perception introduced the 12-foot Slasher C-1 and for most of the '90s, with the exception of kayak conversions, particularly the Hurricane because of its 26 inch width, only composite C-1s were available. In 1998, Dagger introduced the Atom C-1, the first truly short plastic C-1 (at 9' 8") produced for river running. It had a flat hull and hard chines.

About the same time the Atom was produced, C-1 conversions of rodeo playboats began to increase, not only for rodeo, but for river running. Allen Braswell, sponsored by Perception, converted a 3-d and began to push the limits of rodeo C-1 paddling. Braswell also became an advocate for C-1 paddling in the rodeo spotlight.

The new rodeo of the '90s brought much needed competition to the whitewater industry but the effects on the sport went beyond just rodeo. New manufacturers emerged and old manufacturers transformed. Instead of a lopsided domination by one or two, the market was shared by up to eight. All eight competed for the market of rodeo, playboats, and the next generation which was fueled by the new paradigm and the new operating system for design and technique brought about by flat planing hulls.

New designs evolved practically over night, driven by new discoveries and new innovations. Competition for the next new design or the next innovation drove the design machine. New designs came from eight manufacturers instead of just one or two. The bottom line in this industry became design, design, design. It expanded beyond just rodeo playboat to encompass all of whitewater. During the late '90s, each kayak manufacturer almost yearly introduced one or two designs for each category of whitewater, rodeo playboat, river running playboat, and creekboat. New radical designs appeared for whitewater canoeing, too.

Manufacturers no longer waited to introduce one or two new designs at the yearly *Outdoor Retailer* Summer Market tradeshow for the following season. Market competition led to mid-season launches. Now, new designs were shown and released for the Summer Market where in the past those same designs would not have been ready for production until the following winter. The Summer Market releases were often followed by other new designs in the spring. Almost three times the number of plastic whitewater kayaks designs were introduced from 1995 through 2000 than all the previous years combined since plastic kayaks were first introduced in 1973.

For the average whitewater paddler, the plethora of boats to chose from was astounding. Now boats were designed for a very specific purpose: small steep creeks, large volume rivers, all-around, park-and-play, and rodeo. Many paddlers owned more than one boat and chose among their stable like a golfer choosing the appropriate golf club. One paddler summed it up when he wrote: "There are no bad boats, only mismatches between boats and paddlers, and boats and rivers."[26]

[26] Cardozo, Bozo. "Goofy and Goofier." *Canoe & Kayak* Vol. 26 No. 1 (March 1998): 120–125.

Designing in the '90s was a long way from the tweaking of slalom racing boats in the '70s and '80s. Instead of one or two paddlers designing and building prototypes to paddle for themselves, now there were design teams and factory teams to test paddle the prototypes. Designs became nameless. Characteristic designer signatures were no longer obvious. The cost of introducing a new design changed. By the mid-'90s, a new design for rotational molding cost $60,000 to $70,000, more than double the cost of the mold itself which was far different than before. The launch of a single design was at significant cost, let alone the launch of six or seven in a single season.

The cost of doing business changed the industry. There was no longer room for small manufacturers to compete. Some manufacturers like Savage V went out of business. Canoes by Whitesell ended when Whitesell chose to retire. Consolidation of companies and resources and expansion within the larger paddlesport market became a solution for continued growth. WaterMark, Confluence, and Voodoo were formed for those reasons.

For paddlers, the increased cost of doing business meant escalating boat costs. In 1991, the average cost for a plastic kayak was $725. In 1995, it increased to $800. In 2000, it was $950. This is an increase of about 30 per cent since 1991 with two-thirds of the increase coming during the second half of the '90s. Unlike during the '70s and '80s, prices for kayaks in the '90s from a manufacturer often had a range with older models priced lower than the latest models (and kayaks designed for youth were even lower still). Although the price of solo Royalex canoes increased roughly the same from 1991 to 2000, in contrast to kayaks, two-thirds of the increase occurred during the first half of the '90s.

In addition to the cost benefits of consolidation, some manufacturers began attempts to slow the rising costs of new design launches. They also tried to assist their retailers in handling problems associated with too-soon-outdated stock with the elimination of mid-season launches. Confluence announced the end of their mid-season launches in 2000. Other manufacturers attempted to lower the price of older models to even lower than the norm, to benefit paddlers directly. In 1999, Riot offered their older models a full $300 less than the newest designs which was far lower than any other manufacturer.

The effects of the new rodeo on rodeo competition were unlike anything previously seen in whitewater (although analogies to sports outside of paddlesports could be found, particularly the newer sports of the '70s and '80s). Manufacturers worked hand in hand with organizations that supported rodeo competition. Their support wasn't offered as a necessary good will service to the support rodeo competition. They realized it was critical for both rodeo and the industry. In 1998, a meeting was held at the *Outdoor Retailer* Summer Market show with rodeo manufacturers and organizations in attendance. Professional athletes from the whitewater manufacturers worked with NOWR and American Whitewater to take rodeo to the next level of sanctioned international competition with the formation of the U.S. Freestyle Kayak Committee (USFKC) to govern the sport of freestyle kayaking as a sub-committee of NOWR. The first committee was made up of professional athletes representing Dagger, Necky, Perception, Pyrahna, Savage, and Riot along with two seats representing women athletes, two representing junior athletes, two at-large seats, and one advisory member with no voting status.

IN 2001, Riot entered the snowboard market thinking it was a natural crossover for their target audience. Kayaking in summer and snowboarding in winter are both activities of Gen-X and Y.

The relationship between skiers and paddlers is a long-standing traditional relationship. Many early paddling clubs were also associated with skiing and/or climbing like AMC, Buck Ridge Ski Club, and the Sierra Club. Many notable past paddlers were also skiers like Wolf Bauer and Roger Paris.

ALTHOUGH MOHAWK began selling direct to paddlers in 1993 at dealer cost with a savings of 30 per cent to the paddler, no other manufacturers followed their lead.

The effects of the new rodeo and the growth of whitewater also helped draw the attention of the mainstream to whitewater, particularly for advertising targeting Gen-X and Y audiences. Magazine ads and TV commercials with images of whitewater appeared for many products, particularly new trucks and SUVs. Nissan, Volvo, and Toyota, all included images of whitewater kayaking in their advertising. Perhaps the advertising that best evoked the lure of whitewater for professional Gen-X audiences was a TV commercial for the new 1998 Toyota 4Runner. The commercial depicted a young businessman waiting in big-city downtown traffic. Seeing a 4Runner waiting to enter traffic with a mountain bike and a kayak on top, the young businessman begins to daydream, thinking how neat biking and kayaking would be. Then he realizes that it is a Tuesday and the 4Runner owner is driving away, leaving work behind. He becomes envious of the 4Runner owner's life of adventure and freedom from everyday, workday drudgery.

Some advertising even evoked the lure of whitewater out of context from the sport itself. An ad for ID-Alert used a photo of a kayaker going over a waterfall with the caption:

> But what really scares him is running out of chocolate... Raging 30-foot waterfalls. Deadly Class 5 rapids. That's what he lives for. Being a diabetic is what could kill him. [27]

By the end of the '90s, estimates for the number of whitewater kayakers came in at over 700,000. Outdoor retailers thought the whitewater kayak market was the second hottest market in paddlesports behind recreational kayaks but in front of seakayaking and touring. Manufacturers thought it was third behind seakayaking and touring. Rodeo and playboating and marketing to the next generation were by far the biggest drivers for the growth. Erik Voake, owner of Loaded Gun Productions, expressed his view of the future and benefits of playboating on the sport and the industry when he wrote:

> In recent years we've suffered a lot of deaths within the sport—the majority of these occurring on Class V waters, often in remote areas. This has been a kiss of death to the sport. Anytime a newcomer hears of someone dying while paddling, it's an instant turn-off. Nobody wants to buy death... Besides, playboating is better for the industry. This is where media coverage is and I want to see the sport grow. Sure, the rodeo scene might get some people upset but it's just the beginning—give the circuit a couple of years and it'll be the best thing going. The sport is truly in its infancy... Paddling needs a facelift and it begins with playboating... Look at the surfing or ski industry. It used to be filled with stuffy old guys who had no idea what was going on or what the people really wanted—much like the kayak industry. Then the youth took over and they could do nothing about it because one day, all of a sudden, the kids owned it. Playboating rules. [28]

[27] ID Alert. Advertisement. *Time* Vol. 153 No. 8 (March 1, 1999): 70.

[28] Voake, Eric. "Playboating Rules Supreme." *Paddler* Vol. 20, No. 2 (March/April 2000): 36–37.

The '90s were the time for the generational transition, from aging Boomers to Gen-X and Y. However, even though playboating and rodeo marketing targeted the next generation of paddlers, aging Boomers were still a part of the market. The transition was going to take more than a couple of years. Aging Boomers were still paddling rivers and because of that, were contributors (though not solely) to a divergence that seemed to emerge within river runners, a divergence between more traditional river runners and steep creekboaters (even extreme boaters), and park-and-play-boaters. The character of the River was changing.

A sign of the change was that by in the in late '90s, listings were compiled of top playspots, holes and waves, instead of top rivers. A listing of the top playspots in the February 1998 issue of *Paddler* included Hell Hole on the Ocoee and Great Falls on the Caney Fork River in Tennessee; Hungry Mother on the Gauley and Upper Railroad on the New in West Virginia; Santa Rita on the Animas and Burns Hole on Derby Creek in Colorado; Bob's Hole on the Clackamas and Trestle Hole on the Deschutes in Oregon; Inflatable Hole on the Main Payette and Cedar Hole on the Lochsa in Idaho; The Wheel on Canyon Creek in Washington; McCoy's Rapids on the Ottawa in Ontario; and Super Hole on the Kootenai River in Montana.

Shuttle (CA), 2000—courtesy of Brandon Knapp.

DURING THE '90s, the sport witnessed many transitions. The industry moved from a small few to a great many. Rodeo evolved toward competition that was fully intertwined and dependent upon the industry. Designs changed from displacement hulls to planing hulls and technique changed with it. The market audience grew from aging Boomers to a mix of Boomers and Gen-X and Y paddlers. The rivers of northern West Virginia and western Maryland, the "cradle of whitewater innovation" since the '70s, and its innovators of the Boomer generation faded from the picture and were replaced by playspots like Hell Hole and Bob's Hole and teams of innovators with computer aided design (CAD) prototype kayaks. Destination rivers became destination playspots. A paradigm shift had truly occurred.

The Rest of the Industry

While planing hulls and Gen-X contributed to the paradigm shift for whitewater, the '90s and the beginning of the digital and e-commerce age also affected the industry. Manufacturers and retailers expanded on-line with their own websites. Traditional large retailers such as REI went on-line and new e-retailers formed such as PlanetOutdoors.com and Outdoorplay.com, which focused on the paddlesport market. In 1997, Outdoorplay.com developed by John "Tree" Trujillo, an Oregon extreme and rodeo boater, went on-line. It was designed to be more than just an e-retailer. They partnered with *Canoe & Kayak* magazine, ACA, AWA, NOWR and others to offer stories, interviews, product reviews, and links. By 1998, outdoor retailing in general was on-line.

For paddlesport manufacturers, support for the new e-retailers was not without controversy. Manufacturer to retailer loyalty was important and was considered essential in the development of the sport. E-retailing was too much akin to factory direct sales, a practice thought by many manufacturers and retailers to be self-defeating, even for the consumer, and they chose not to participate. Since the '70s, paddlesport manufacturers had supported their retailer base, a base that was particularly important for customer service both in consumer education and delivery. This strong connection between manufacturers and retailers developed because of inherent problems associated with shipping canoes and kayaks by commercial truck. Many manufacturers had solved these problems by establishing shipping networks and even setting up their own transportation with their own drivers. In some instances, retailers themselves did their own shipping.

While manufacturers had their *Outdoor Retailer* Summer Market to sell to retailers, consortiums of paddling groups as well as some of the larger retailers established their own consumer shows, some beginning in the '80s and continuing into the '90s. Though not exclusively whitewater oriented, a few of the shows attracted large numbers of paddling consumers. Canoecopia sponsored by Rutabaga in Wisconsin and Paddlesport sponsored by Jersey Paddler in New Jersey were two of the larger spring shows sponsored by retailers, attracting a diverse crowd including whitewater paddlers. The Great Minnesota Canoe Event in Minnesota and Canoe Expo in Ontario were two shows sponsored by a consortium of clubs and organizations.

Composite Manufacturers

With the exception of composite manufacturers who supplied slalom and wildwater race boats, composite whitewater manufacturers were a dying breed. The demand for composite boats for river running and squirt, where introduction of radical innovations was more practical, dropped dramatically in the early '90s as interest in squirt waned. In the late '80s, Wilderness Systems ceased production of whitewater boats. Phoenix settled on a very small niche in non-whitewater paddlesports. Watauga Laminants and Whittemore Laminates also ceased production. Even New Wave Kayak Products, a long-time composite manufacturer and the last of the larger composite companies, slowly began phasing out composite production when they entered the plastic kayak market and began producing their own plastic kayak designs.

Because composite construction allows small production runs (one and two boats) of specialized designs and lightweight layups, composite boats will undoubtedly always have a small niche in the whitewater market, even outside of building slalom and wildwater race boats. Small one- and two-man shops like PS Composites owned by Paul Schreiner in Pennsylvania will continue to support a small segment of the whitewater population, particularly aging Boomers, that prefers custom boats and designs. Composite construction also continues to provide the best medium for independent boat designers.

Paddling Schools

Although local schools came and went, the biggest schools across the country continued to be NOC, MKC (Madawaska), Otter Bar, and Sundance. In the '90s, clubs continued their part in providing instruction. Many felt that the quality of club instruction improved through the efforts of ACA's instructor certification program which helped to ensure better quality instructors and instruction. River safety courses also improved within club instructional programs with the availability of river rescue courses from ACA as well as other organizations and professionals.

Although many schools catered to adult paddlers during the '80s and '90s, many also developed programs for young paddlers following the example set by Camp Mondamin and Camp Merrie-Woode. Camp Mondamin continued to develop young whitewater paddlers, particularly carrying on their reputation for developing C-1 paddlers. Valley Mill Camp in Maryland also continued their whitewater programs exclusively for young paddlers.

Youth programs associated with slalom racing programs developed around USCKT's Centers of Excellence that supported youth racing programs. St. Alban's School's Voyager Program in D.C., under the leadership of Mark Moore, was one youth program that benefitted from their proximity to the Bethesda Center of Excellence. Others established their own schools with a slalom racing orientation. Bob Ruppel's Riversport in Pennsylvania developed a reputation for involving kids in slalom racing, prompted by his daughters' involvement in slalom racing. The same was true for Tom Long's Cascade Canoe and Kayak School in Idaho with his sons' involvement in racing. Long was also associated with the Payette Whitewater and Racing Kids of Idaho and in 1997, established a traveling slalom camp.

In 1997, Cascade Adventure Center in Hood River, Oregon, began the first program of its kind where kayak instruction was included as part of the local public junior high and high school physical education program using school pool facilities. Instruction and equipment were provided free of charge by Cascade Adventure Center owner John Trujillo (also owner of OutdoorPlay.com). In 1999, another unusual first was the establishment of Wolf River Paddling Club, Inc., a non-profit corporation developed to promote kids and paddling. The brainchild of the husband and wife team of Bob Obst and Colleen Hayes, it sponsored the ACA and USCKT sanctioned 1999 Wolf River Youth Paddling Camp.

While for-profit and not-for-profit paddling schools continued to evolve for kids, a few manufacturers recognized the need for supporting and promoting kids programs. In 1994, Perception began sponsoring youth instruction symposiums bringing in speakers experienced with kids' paddling programs. In 1994, the first Symposium on Youth Instruction was held at NOC where well known instructors and coaches shared strategies about working with kids. Speakers included Tom Long of Cascade Kayak School and Gordon Grant, former head of instruction at NOC. The following year, the symposium was sponsored at two different sites, at NOC and at Manor Camp on the Potomac in Maryland. Speakers included Tom Long, Gordon Black (head instructor at NOC), Peter Kennedy, and Mark Moore, an instructor at St. Alban's School Voyager Program in D.C. Symposium workshops were held again in 1995 and 1996 expanding across the country to include Portland (OR), Charlottesville (VA), Camden (ME), and Woodland Park (CO).

By the mid-'90s, rodeo began to develop its own following among Gen-Y paddlers, emulating the interest by their preceding generation in whitewater rodeo. Chan Zwanzig of Wave Sport recognized this and in 1995, announced an expansion of their support for youth kayaking by donating kayaks through the National Organization of Whitewater Rodeos. The overall K-1 expert winner of each freestyle event was given a kayak to donate to the youth program of his or her choice. Within a couple of years, Zwanzig also began sponsoring junior paddlers to Team Wave Sport.

In 1989, Peter Kennedy's Adventure Quest in Vermont was another school started exclusively for young boys that helped to develop young competitors. Adventure Quest program developed a whole new generation of competitors, both in slalom and rodeo. In 1994, calling themselves the "Extreme Squad" (later called Team Adventure Quest), young competitors participated in the Open Canoe Nationals, the Junior Worlds, the U.S. Team Trials, and several rodeos while touring the country. The success of Adventure Quest's program has been demonstrated with numerous medals won in national and international championships in slalom and rodeo.

In addition to developing their skills in slalom and rodeo competition, the Extreme Squad also developed their skills in extreme boating. In 1994, led by Chan Zwanzig and Dan Gavere, Extreme Squad members paddled the North Fork of the Payette at 2,000 cfs. The following year they ran the Green Narrows, led by Woody (Forrest) Callaway and the Kern brothers, Chuck, Willie, and John. While many people were impressed by the paddling abilities of the young Extreme Squad members, others were not impressed, questioning Kennedy's judgement for allowing 14 and 15 year olds to do the extreme runs.

In 1996, Adventure Quest began a tutorial program that allowed the kids to paddle and study abroad. The program expanded, becoming the Academy at Adventure Quest, a fully accredited independent private school.

Multimedia

Traditional printed media, long a resource for information, continued from the '80s into the '90s. *River Runner,* considered the leading whitewater magazine covering rafting, kayaking, and canoeing, abruptly ceased publication with its February 1991 issue and was replaced by *Paddler,* a combination of *River Runner* and two other magazines, *Canoe Sport Journal* and *Canadian Paddler.* Unfortunately, *Paddler* soon evolved into what some people considered a regurgitated *Canoe,* not the whitewater magazine that *River Runner* had been. Beginning in 1992, a free subscription of *Paddler* was included with an ACA membership benefit, the same way that a *Canoe* subscription had been included in the '70s and early '80s. In 1997, *Paddler* was sold to ACA's Paddlesport Publishing Inc., a commercial subsidiary of ACA.

Canoe, the oldest commercial paddlesport magazine, underwent a few transitions of its own during the '90s. In 1994, it even included a name change to *Canoe & Kayak.* In January 1998, Dave and Judy Harrison, the longest publishers of *Canoe* (14 years) sold the magazine to Cowles Enthusiast Media who in turn turned it over in a relatively short time to PRIMEDIA. The same year, *Canoe & Kayak Magazine* sponsored and developed a magazine for TV that appeared on cable on the Outdoor Life Network (OLN). During its first year in 1998, forty-two half-hour episodes aired. Although it covered all of paddlesports, many episodes capitalized on mainstream interest in whitewater, both rodeo and extreme boating.

Entertainment and multimedia continued into the '90s with the added flavor of Gen-X and Y tastes. Whitewater videos for entertainment with two prominent themes, rodeo and extreme boating, became as prolific as whitewa-

ENTERTAINMENT VIDEOS varied from hardcore whitewater porn with extreme paddling like *Aphrodisia* with its huge falls and drops to *Dashboard Burrito* and *Loss of Altitude* with their hardcore playboating and steepcreeking. *Falling Down* was about extreme kayaking with falls, and *Paddlemania* displayed an excessive enthusiasm for paddling. *Adventures of Johnny Utah* portrayed the mystical side of paddling (although filmed on the Narrows of the Green in North Carolina), and *Tales of the Paddlesnake* showed open canoe carnage incurred while looking for the mythical paddlesnake.

ter boats. Titles such as *Aphrodisia, Dashboard Burrito, Falling Down, Loss of Altitude,* and *Paddlemania* occupied whitewater paddlers on cold winter nights and during dry seasons.

Even instructional videos evolved more toward entertainment instead of just dry, basic, how-to videos. Advanced instructional videos for river running, playboating, and rodeo were produced such as *Searching for the "Gee Spot"* with Corran Addison and *Play Daze* with Ken Whiting.

The '90s were the real start of the internet age and whitewater paddlers, long known for being techies, gravitated toward giving and receiving their information on-line. Websites for water levels and weather were some of the first used by whitewater paddlers. Public information available from government websites such as real-time (almost) river gauge readings courtesy of USGS became standard bookmarks for many paddlers. Weather sites also provided up-to-date forecasts for determining where to go and what rivers might come up. In the spring of 1995, *American Whitewater* developed their own website to disseminate information, with links to all the important river gauge sites.

Clubs and individual paddlers also developed their own websites. A newsgroup, rec.boats.paddle, was developed for all paddlers to share information. Its users became affectionately known as "rbp'ers." A whole new club system and sense of community began to evolve without the confines of geography and distance.

COMPETITION in the American whitewater market and sporting competition in rodeo spawned and drove innovations just as slalom competition and competition for the perceived paddling market drove innovations in the '60s and '70s. However, as time proved, the slalom market was small and limited by the lack of interest by the larger American paddling public and by plastics. River running and plastics were interdependently linked and helped to cement the divergence between sporting competition and river running. Once the divergence occurred, specialization in slalom designs further cemented the separation although, as demonstrated with slalom C-1 design and technique contributions to squirtboating development, competition still influenced river running.

History seemed to repeat itself with rodeo. Rodeo competition diverged from river running. However, unlike slalom racing, rodeo competition appealed to the larger American paddling public. After all, rodeo was invented here and was an offspring of the younger American free spirit of the '70s. Slalom was a European invention with ties to more traditional (and sometimes) restricted European thinking with all kinds of rules and regulations. Rodeo and freestyle was a marketable commodity while slalom was not. Rodeo was also different than slalom in that non-competitive slalom had no lure, while non-competitive freestyle paddling did. Because of that, along with rodeo's loss of its river running roots, non-competitive playboating began to diverge from river running and a schism in interests ensued.

The course of the River set in the '70s, a braided river with two channels, river running and competition, broadened even more with events of the '80s, cloud bursts from the sub-sports of rodeo, squirt, and extreme racing. Coming into the '90s, both channels were strengthened by the three climatic-type events of the '90s: market competition, rodeo competition, and generation transition. However, a third channel, playboating, while not really a part of either the river running or competition channels, formed between the other two. It's currents, design and technique, were fed and influenced by rodeo competition.

Competition

The '90s ushered in the reinstatement of slalom competition as an Olympic event with three consecutive Olympics beginning in 1992. For American paddlers, the spotlight for slalom racing came with hosting the '96 Olympics in Atlanta. The '90s also saw a rise in rodeo and extreme, gaining recognition among whitewater paddlers on a level to that of slalom competition, particularly among Gen-X and Y paddlers. Rodeo and extreme racing began to get respect. Even a few slalom racers joined the ranks of professionals for rodeo competition and extreme races.

Slalom

As occurred in the rest of the sport, the late '80s and early '90s ushered in many changes that affected slalom competition. These changes took the form of a changing of the guard from both an organizational sense as well as within the competitors' ranks, a generational transition from aging Boomer and the oldest Gen-X paddlers to younger Gen-X and Y paddlers.

NGB STATUS carried with it the responsibility of owning and coordinating all aspects of competition including international competition that might be Olympic events in the future, including rodeo.

In 1988, organizational change began when USCKT was formed. Throughout the '90s, USCKT shared responsibilities with ACA, the long-standing ICF recognized NGB (National Governing Body) and owner of American slalom competition in coordinating U.S. participation in internationally recognized sporting events. Ten years later in 1998, the U. S. Olympic Committee (USOC) designated USCKT as the NGB for Olympic sprint and slalom beginning after the '00 Olympics. In 1999, USCKT changed their name to USA Canoe/Kayak.

Beginning with USCKT's inception, new marketing or promotional strategies were brought to slalom competition to promote its growth toward the goal of Olympic medals, particularly with the announcement of inclusion of slalom in the '92 Olympics in Barcelona. These strategies included promotion and support of athletes as well as slalom competition as a whole among the larger paddling public and in the mainstream. Official Centers of Excellence were established across the country for slalom (and sprint) to support and provide coaches and training facilities for athletes, building on already long-established informal training sites. By 1992, six Centers were established in Atlanta (GA), Betheseda (MD), Durango (CO), New England (CT), Nantahala (NC), and Wausau (WI).

While ACA continued garnering support at the local club and community level, USCKT expanded towards gaining larger corporate support outside of the paddlesport industry. Corporate support helped pay for events as well as provided cash support to athletes within the expanded rules of amateurism. In 1990, USCKT produced the Champion International Whitewater Series sponsored by Champion International, a paper and wood products company based in Stamford, Connecticut, and sanctioned by ACA and ICF. It was the first sanctioned whitewater slalom series to offer prize money, a total of $75,000. The series included four races: Durango, Wausau, Duluth, and South Bend. Cash prizes were distributed through 10th place finishes for each race. Individual athletes could win as much as $7,000 for winning all four races in his or her class. C-2 teams split the winnings.

Champion's sponsorship of the Series continued through 1995, although not without controversy. Champion's business practices regarding air and water pollution and the operation and management of its plant on the Pigeon River in North Carolina, long considered one of the worst polluters in the Southeast, were questioned. Many whitewater paddlers considered Champion's sponsorship a betrayal, a sell-out for the sake of money--and tainted money at that. Later corporate sponsors were less controversial and included Texaco and Anheuser-Busch.

USCKT EMPLOYED other strategies for earning money to support athletes. In 1995, USCKT sponsored the Whitewater Shootout. The race pitted recreational paddlers against Olympic paddlers Cathy Hearn, Davey Hearn, and Scott Shipley for a chance to win $1,000 if they were able to beat the Olympians in their respective races.

Coincidentally, with USCKT's gold medal strategies and corporate sponsors, professionalism (sponsored athletes) was brought to slalom racing for the first time. While some athletes welcomed the change as an indication of the sport finally developing toward a level found in other Olympic competition, other athletes were wary and concerned about where it might take slalom competition. As early as 1990, Jamie McEwan expressed his concern about professionalism and money creeping into slalom and what might come with it.

> The way it is now, if you forget your equipment the day before a World Cup race, in no time your German or French competitors come up with a helmet or life jacket so that you won't miss a minute of practice... The 14 year-year-old daughter of a friend of mine is successful in the highly competitive world of figure skating. After watching the Savage Worlds she wanted to change sports. "I'd never seen people competing who could still be nice," she said. It sounds contradictory, but the cooperation is greater exactly because the people are so independent—a bunch of loners rather than closely knit teams... No it isn't the influx in money that I fear most—it's the increase in bureaucracy. But as long as the racers don't lose their slightly crazed whitewater roots, as long as they remain true jungle boaters down to their rancid polypro underwear, then the sport will retain its unique, sometimes maddening, but always refreshing spirit.[29]

Surprisingly, even after two Olympics, McEwan's fears were not realized. The sense of cooperation and community among independent paddlers remained, even internationally. At the '96 Olympics, American K-1 paddler Scott Shipley provided his own boat to a Bosnian paddler, Samir Karabasic, after his boat was damaged beyond repair during the trials. For his action, Shipley was awarded the Jack Kelly Fair Play Award by USOC. After the Olympics, Shipley arranged a shipment of $40,000 worth of paddling equipment to Bosnia for young athletes.

29 McEwan, Jamie. "Flood of Change." *River Runner* Vol. 10 No. 1 (February 1990): 6,8.

Toward Olympic Gold

By the time the announcement of Olympic competition for slalom racing in the '92 Olympics in Barcelona was made, after a twenty year hiatus, many felt the American slalom program was up to the task. After all, American C-1 paddlers dominated international World Championship, and the newer World Cup competition throughout the '80s. American men in C-1 and women in K-1W medaled in slalom at the '89 World Championships on the Savage. Although old by some standards (five of the 20 members of the '89 team were on the '79 team, and three of the four medals in '89 came from those five), the anticipated '92 Olympic team was expected to garner Olympic medals.

However, the '91 World Championships at Tacen, Yugoslavia, brought a sobering reality to U.S. Olympic medal chances. The American team took only two silvers in individual competition, and a gold and bronze in team competition. Jon Lugbill and Davey Hearn finished out of the individual medals (Lugbill 4th and Hearn 17th) although the C-1 team of Adam Clawson, Jon Lugbill, and Jed Prentice won gold in team competition. Dana Chladek took silver in K-1W, and the K-1W team of Chladek, Kirsten Brown-Fleshman, and Kara Ruppel won bronze in team competition. The surprise finish was 18-year-old Adam Clawson's silver in individual C-1.

Although the team's poor showing was attributed to the course itself on the Sava River, the obvious could not be ignored. The team was made up of many paddlers who held team positions for over a decade, some even much longer like Lugbill and Hearn in C-1, Jamie McEwan and Lecky Haller in C-2, and Cathy Hearn in K-1W. Younger or newer paddlers were also on the team such as Scott Strasbaugh and Joe Jacobi in C-2, Kirsten Brown-Fleshman and Kara Ruppel in K-1W, Jed Prentice and Adam Clawson in C-1, and Scott Shipley in K-1. But their lack of experience in international competition showed.

The '92 Olympics came at a bad time for the U.S. team experience and age-wise. Toward the end of the '80s, many competitors felt that the years of fine-tuning technique of older racers was still an advantage over the quick reactions and recovery of younger racers. But the sport itself was changing, particularly in C-1 competition. The rest of the world caught up to the Americans. New and younger European C-1 paddlers raised the bar. Technique's advantage had diminished. The playing field was more level. More competitors than ever before were full-time athletes. By the '96 Olympics, there were ten international C-1 competitors who were capable of winning the Worlds.

Even the courses themselves began to favor speed. Slalom courses were shortened and the number of gates dropped from thirty to twenty-five to facilitate TV coverage. Clean runs without speed did not win. (At the '92 Olympics, the best C-1 finish was 110 seconds, by far the fastest international C-1 competition ever held.)

After the disappointing '91 World Championship finishes, two D.C. area paddlers, John Anderson and Scott Wilkinson, began a project to build a course for the Bethesda Center of Excellence that would replicate the features of the La Seu d'Urgell, the slalom venue for the '92 Olympics.

The project was officially developed by the Bethesda Center of Excellence and the slalom division of the CCA. However, it was the efforts of Anderson and Wilkinson that got the project off the ground. They convinced Potomac

Edison Power Company (PEPCO) Vice President Bill Sim of the feasibility of building a whitewater training site on the warm-water discharge canal at Dickerson on the Potomac.

Anderson and Wilkinson also convinced officials of the David Taylor Model Basin, where slalom racers had trained during the winter since the '70s, to allow them to use the facilities to build a scale model for testing. U.S. Olympic Coach Bill Endicott along with national team members Davey Hearn and Jon Lugbill provided their assistance in ensuring the course would resemble the course at Seu d'Urgell, Spain.

The entire effort escalated with a press conference, articles, and coverage by local TV stations. Efforts by Bill Sim resulted in cooperation and assistance by many corporations. With the help of the U.S. Navy, PEPCO, corporate sponsors, corporate and private volunteers, the artificial slalom course was built on the outflow discharge from the Dickerson Generating Station.

The result was a Class IV course that was 900 feet long and 60 feet wide with a vertical drop of 110 feet per mile (compared with 24 feet at Seu d'Urgell), with between 450 and 650 cfs (compared with about 325 cfs at Seu d'Urgell). Boulders were movable to change the course for training but also in the event PEPCO needed to have them removed. The estimated cost of the entire project was $250,000. In December 1991, the project, the Dickerson Whitewater Course, was completed providing year-round training.

Unfortunately, although the Dickerson course was modeled after the Seu d'Urgell course, the Olympic course was not what most paddlers had trained for. The twenty-five gates were placed in the top two-thirds of the 1,115-foot long course (340 meters) with only six upstream gates. The finish was a sprint over the lower third of the course. It was great for a TV audience, but technically easy for the competitors who trained for a more demanding course.

For the '92 Olympics, U.S. Team Coach Bill Endicott brought the best team possible, made up of many experienced athletes. He felt the team could win a medal in every event. In C-1, there were the favorites Lugbill and Hearn; in C-2 Jamie McEwan and Lecky Haller; in K-1W Dana Chladek and Cathy Hearn; and in K-1 up-and-coming Eric Jackson, Scott Shipley, and Rich Weiss. Unfortunately, Lugbill finished just out of medals with 4th and Hearn finished 11th. McEwan and Haller also finished out of the medals in 4th and no medals were won in K-1—with the best finish 13th. However, Chladek won bronze in a very competitive K-1W class and Joe Jacobi and Scott Strausbaugh won gold in C-2, a pleasant surprise for the American team.

While McEwan and Haller were disappointed in their 4th place finish out of the medals, Lugbill's 4th place seemed "a travesty that the man who redefined his sport during the 1980s not have an Olympic medal to add to his accolades." [30] McEwan said it was heartbreaking to watch as Lugbill was "relegated to fourth place by a feather-light touch of a gate, while Lukas Pollert, who had left gate 12 swinging wildly but was inexplicably given no penalty, got the gold." [31]

Endicott retired after the '92 Olympics. His resignation coincided with NSWC's restructuring of the whitewater coaching program, which placed a head coach with assistant coaches at the four Centers of Excellence: Atlanta, Bethesda, Durango, and Wausau. With the prospect of Olympic competition again in the '96 Olympics, this time on home turf, the slalom competition program kicked into high gear.

In 1992, McEwan returned to Olympic competition, twenty years after his bronze finish in C-1 at the '72 Olympics. In 1986, McEwan, realizing he would not be able to touch Hearn or Lugbill in C-1, began to compete in C-2 with Lecky Haller. In 1986, Haller and McEwan beat the favored team of Harris and Harris (brothers). At the '87 World Championships, they won silver.

Endicott's coaching career ended with one gold and one bronze in slalom at the '92 Olympics. His career spanned 21 years with national teams, 16 years as head coach, during which 52 international medals were won, 25 of them gold, most attributed to the C-1 reign of Lugbill and Hearn during the '80s.

[30] Gardner, Todd. "Bittersweet Dreams." *Canoe & Kayak* Vol. 20 No. 6 (December 1992): 7–8.

[31] McEwan, Jamie. "Five Ring Fever." *Canoe & Kayak* Vol. 24 No. 1 (March 1996): 110–111.

Aside from international competition, efforts to increase grass roots competition to support and encourage young competitors also benefitted from USCKT's and ACA's shared interest in building the next generation of gold medal contenders. In New England, the old traditional center of competition dating back many decades, a series of races was developed to encourage race participation and provide events for new and young paddlers. In 1994, the New England Cup Race Series, sponsored by NSWC, was established for both slalom and wildwater racing. An individual's best results in four out of the six slalom races or three out of the four wildwater races determined his or her final ranking for the series. This Cup series was added to the already popular New England Slalom Series which was sponsored by Mad River and designed for open canoe and unranked C/D decked boaters.

In the Northwest, grass roots competition took a slightly different approach than that found elsewhere in the country. Because NSWC and USCKT concentrated their efforts in the East, the Northwest region lacked the same level of support and coordination found in the Northeast. In the early '90s, a group of paddlers banded together to form the League of Northwest Whitewater Racers. The League's purpose was to coordinate and support grass root efforts for slalom racing covering Washington, Oregon, Idaho, northern California, and British Columbia. Within a few years, their efforts expanded beyond slalom to include wildwater racing and training sites. In 1995, the League began sponsorship of the Northwest Cup Series. By the late '90s, the League's success with increasing interest in competition was reminiscent of that found in the '60s, where paddlers trained and participated in races to develop their river running skills.

While Scott Shipley and Rich Weiss did not place as well as expected at the '92 Olympics, they made up for it the following year. The self-coached Weiss won silver in the '93 World Championships at Mezzana, the best and first K-1 medal finish ever by an American in World Championship competition. The same year, Shipley became the first American K-1 to win gold in the Whitewater Slalom World Cup. The following year, defending champion Shipley won bronze in the '94 Whitewater Slalom World Cup but recaptured the gold again in the '95 Whitewater Slalom World Cup as well as a silver in the '95 World Championships at Nottingham. American K-1 men were finally in a position to capture Olympic gold.

While Lugbill dropped out of serious training and competition after the '92 Olympics, Hearn continued competing. In 1993, Hearn won silver in the Whitewater Slalom World Cup, behind '92 Olympic gold medal winner Lukas Pollert. Hearn went on to win at the '95 World Championships, ten years after his first World Championship individual gold.

Preparation for a slalom venue for the '96 Olympics meant preparation of an all-new slalom race site in close proximity to Atlanta. Modeling the preparation for the first World Championships after the Savage in Maryland in 1989, federal, state, and local agencies along with local organizations worked together to develop the race site on the Ocoee in Tennessee. The U.S. Forest Service paid an estimated $14 million to develop the site, $1.8 million for the course. A section upstream from the popular whitewater run below Powerhouse No. 3 was chosen for the site. The river was narrowed into a channel and natural features and ledges were augmented to create the slalom course.

Controversy surrounded the modification of the Ocoee for use as a slalom site. The heart of the debate was the philosophy regarding river modification, economic development, and the future of whitewater paddling. At stake was the anticipated $60 million "transfusion" from construction and tourism into an economically depressed and environmentally ravaged area. AWA wrote:

> For some the creation of a permanent slalom racing site for the '96 Olympics is a chance to restore a river bed that is dewatered for most of the year, a chance to promote economic development in a depressed county in east Tennessee. For others, it is another insult in a long list of manmade intrusions in the area.[32]

The issue of streambed modification is complex and can range from dam building to changing a rapid to make it safer to changing a stream bed for economic reasons. Although the Ocoee streambed modifications were largely to ensure that the river and course remained stable in the event of a flood, AWA with its record against stream bed modifications, did not take a formal position and was not involved in any of the planning and development discussions regarding the site. Although they did not support it, they also chose not to take an official position. Instead *American Whitewater,* as in the past, was used as a forum for the controversy.

[32] AWA Staff. "Ocoee River." *American Whitewater* Vol. XXXV No. 2 (May/June 1995): 11.

For AWA with their stance against "human modifications to river systems (including dams) that are economically and environmentally unsound,"[33] stream bed modifications for economic and safety considerations were awkward, particularly concerning the Ocoee site.

The "old" river was to remain virtually indistinguishable from the "new." The modifications included bonding rocks to each other as well as the bedrock, installation of shear walls in the river banks where "abrupt jutouts are called to focus water on mid-stream hydraulics, or to cr[e]ate pull-out eddies or self-rescue pools."[34]

John Anderson, a former U.S. team member and architect for whitewater courses, wrote of his support. "The 1996 Olympic Games offered the impetus to re-water this neglected resource for competitive boating- and recreational traffic."[35]

However, Bill Hay, Editor of *Real Sport* (a quarterly publication that focused on outdoor sports in the Southeast) wrote an opposing view: "The Ocoee became the great American River Dream, a money making machine for everyone... Like any slum (in reference to the years of ecological and economic damage to the area), the Ocoee can be rescued, not to its former self, but to become a monument to some new greed and folly."[36]

The '96 Ocoee course was a rousing success. After the first two Olympics on man-made courses, at Augsburg in 1972 and Seu d'Urgell in 1992, the Ocoee was a pleasant return to using a natural river, albeit modified.

> Urban courses have brought the sport to the people. Over the years, rules have been simplified, resulting in faster races. This arguably has made the slalom more exciting and easier to understand, as well as marketable. Yet the nature of the sport was compromised: what originally pitted paddlers against whitewater has become more a test of speed, particularly on easier courses.[37]

Although only 14,000 tickets were supposed to be available each day for the slalom competition, over 15,000 spectators watched the competition, the largest crowd ever assembled for slalom competition. Slalom competition on a natural streambed captured the attention of the mainstream, at least during the competition itself. Unfortunately, American medal wins did not meet expectations.

The Olympic team was reduced in size from previous Olympic teams due to rule changes imposed by the IOC. Each country had to earn spots in the Olympics based on the previous standings in the World Championships. The team was made up of Rich Weiss and Scott Shipley in K-1, Cathy Hearn and Dana Chladek in K-1W, Davey Hearn and Adam Clawson in C-1 and the C-2 team of Horace Holden and Wayne Dickert. Again, as with the Seu d'Urgell course in 1992, the Ocoee course was fast and wide open which was not technically demanding but was great for TV coverage. Shipley, who was expected to medal, trained hard for a tight demanding course. Only Chladek medaled, a silver, besting her bronze in K-1W at the '92 Olympics.

[33] AWA staff (Conserve). "Ocoee River." *American Whitewater* Vol. XXXV No. 3 (May/June 1995): 11.

[34] Wright, Paul (Project Director, USDA Forest Service, Cherokee National Forest). 'Some Thoughts on Misconceptions about the Ocoee River Project.' *American Whitewater* Vol. XXXV No. 3 (May/June 1995): 16.

[35] Anderson, John. "The Ocoee River Project." *American Whitewater* Vol. XXXV No. 2 (May/June 1995): 13–14.

[36] Hay, Bill. "The Weeping Wall." *American Whitewater* Vol. XXXV No. 2 (May/June 1995): 14–15.

[37] Turner, Elizabeth (Boo). "Olympic Slalom." *Canoe & Kayak* (May 1996): 42–47, 50–51.

Dana Chladek won the silver medal at the '96 Olympics. (Although she tied for the gold on her second run, the tiebreaker was based on first run scores. Chladek had flipped and missed a gate that resulted in a 50-second penalty on her first run.) Her paddling career, which ended with her retirement after the '96 Olympics, included two Olympic medals (bronze in '92 and silver in '96) as well as two silver medals in the '89 and '91 World Championships. While other athletes often garnered more attention and fame, Chladek was the only American paddler to win two Olympic medals.

By the end of the '90s, the Ocoee slalom site appeared to become a "monument to some new greed and folly," a monument of limited use. Like the Savage site, which was built for the '89 World Championships and then virtually abandoned except for occasional team selection races, water releases for public use of the Ocoee site were few and far between after the Olympics.

In spite of the popularity of slalom racing at the '92 and '96 Olympics, slalom still did not have permanent Olympic status. Inclusion was left to the decision of the host country, and for the '00 Olympics in Sydney, there was considerable discussion between the international slalom community and Australia's Olympic Committee.

While inclusion of slalom in the '00 Olympics in Sydney was not guaranteed, ICF incorporated changes in slalom in 1997 that supported televised event coverage. Practice runs were no longer mandatory, gate touches were reduced from 5 to 2 seconds (missing a gate was still 50 seconds), and the final score was the total of both runs instead of the faster of the two. Because of the additional coverage time involved, television networks were not a proponent of the best of two runs. With the final score a combination of both runs, only the final run needed to be televised. This change, combined with more open course designs, now made slalom televised-coverage friendly.

The changes, while supporting televised coverage, brought what some saw as fundamental changes in slalom strategy, particularly for experienced international caliber competitors. Davey Hearn anticipated that "by not having practice runs and adding the two race runs together, we are going to see much more conservative and consistent paddling."[38] But for younger athletes not yet ready for international competition, the changes brought other problems. Tom Long, a long time advocate and supporter of young athletes, felt the loss of practice runs and the combined total for final score were detrimental to the development of young athletes.

> In the past, practice runs enabled us to tell the kids that they could miss the harder gates. Then on the first race run, we could tell them to clean it up a little. And by the second race run, they would feel comfortable enough to go for a clean run. Now this progression will not be possible, and kids will have a harder time getting two consistent runs. It might add some frustration.[39]

Following the '96 Olympics, Shipley returned to winning form for the '97 Championships in Tres Coroas and the '99 World Championships in Seu d'Urgell winning a silver at both. The only other American medal finish in World Championship competition was Cathy Hearn's bronze at the '97 World Championships. Shipley also won silver in the '98 and '99 World Cups, the only American to medal.

Following the '96 Olympics, Shipley returned to winning form for the '97 Championships in Tres Coroas and the '99 World Championships in Seu d'Urgell, winning a silver at both. He also won silver in the '98 and '99 World Cups, the only American to medal. The only other American medal finish in World Championship competition was Cathy Hearn's bronze at the '97 World Championships.

[38] Harkness, Geof (editor). "ICF Revises Slalom Rules." *Canoe & Kayak* Vol. 25 No. 3 (July 1997): 28.

[39] Ibid.

With the exception of Shipley, no other American team member finished well in either World Championship or World Cup competition after the '96 Olympics. Many competitors failed to even make the finals in World Champion competition with cutoffs at twenty for K-1 and fifteen for K-1W, C-1, and C-2 classes. Only Davey Hearn consistently made the finals.

The trend toward smaller teams, particularly in Olympic competition, reached its peak for the '00 Olympics in Sydney. The '99 World Championships were the basis for earning spots for the twenty country limit for '00 Olympics. For the U.S. team, only one spot was earned for each class, C-1, K-1, and K-1W. The American C-2 team was the first on the waiting list for countries that had not earned spots and was able to compete only after another country withdrew from C-2 competition. It was the last Olympics for many of the oldest athletes. Davey Hearn made the Olympic team but finished out of the medals in 12th place. Cathy Hearn was edged out for the team by Rebecca Bennett-Giddens who finished 7th. Scott Shipley had the best finish of any U.S. Team member, but again finished out of the medals in 5th place. (Although Shipley finished out of the medals in the '00 Olympics, he won silver in the Slalom World Cup competition the same year.) In C-2, Lecky Haller, another long time athlete, and his young partner Matt Taylor finished 12th. The U.S. team failed to win any medals, the first time that had happened in Olympic competition.

In 2000, the Whitewater Slalom and Wildwater Nationals were held on the Kern, the first time on the West Coast in more than twenty years. This absence illustrated the shift in domination of slalom racing, even for kayakers, to the East after the West's strong showing in the '60s and '70s.

In spite of ongoing efforts to educate the mainstream about the differences between canoeing and kayaking, the distinction seemed to fall on deaf ears. Nokia's ad in the Olympic spread for Time (September 11, 2000) erroneously referred to Joe Jacobi as "one of the world's best kayakers. ... Joe's kayak team ... competes in kayaking events around the world..."

By the '96 Olympics, many of the top American slalom athletes who made the Olympic team were over 30 years old, making the U.S. team one of the oldest in the world. Unfortunately, there was also an absence of an equally skilled pool of athletes ready to take their place. Some of this was attributed to the difference in slalom's popularity between the European and American paddling community. Slalom athletes, particularly from European countries with a long history of slalom competition, were encouraged and supported by highly organized club and national infrastructures, that were deficient in the American system, particularly for junior athletes. While the lack of a strong national infrastructure and bureaucracy proved beneficial during the late '70s and early '80s for American C-paddlers in regard to getting a head start on design innovations, it was not as effective for contributing to the continuous, on-going development of young athletes in the '90s.

Another impediment for the small pool of young athletes was attributed to dynasties. Athletes competed for many years, therefore, eliminating the chances of younger athletes coming up in the ranks to compete in World and Olympic competition. Long-standing dynasties have been common in slalom, particularly for national competition. The longest reign for any individual had been approximately ten years. Davey Hearn was C-1 National Champion eighteen times from 1976 through 2000. His longest continuous streak was seven years. While Hearn was National Champion, Jon Lugbill was five-time C-1 World Champion throughout the '80s, the longest reigning international champion.

Long-standing dynasties were not limited to the C-1 class. Eric Evans was nine-time K-1 National Champion through much of the '70s. During the '90s, Scott Shipley dominated K-1 national competition. Shipley was the continuous (nine-time) National Champion from 1991 to 2000. Linda

Harrison was a seven-time K-1W National Champion from the mid-'70s through the mid-'80s. Cathy Hearn's eight-time reign for K-1W spanned from the mid-'80s into the '90s.

While a single dynasty in a class can affect the development of young competitors, two parallel dynasties in a class can seriously affect development. This was the case in the C-1 class with the parallel dynasties of Lugbill and Hearn in C-1, two exceptionally talented competitors that brought C-1 paddling to a par equal to that of K-1 in international recognition. In 1979, Lugbill was just 18 years old and Hearn was 20 when their dynasties began.

The long-standing dynasty of Lugbill and Hearn was certainly a contributing factor in the development of young C-1 paddlers in the '80s and '90s. Although both men were great mentors, their domination left little room for younger athletes to gain the international experience necessary for World Cup, World Championship, and Olympic competition. Many young, very talented paddlers came and went during their dynasties such as Jed Prentice and Adam Clawson. Some pursued C-2 careers like Wayne Dickert, Lecky Haller, and Joe Jacobi. Unfortunately, the C-2 class has gone the way of the C-2M class in being fairly non-competitive with difficulty obtaining athletes from five countries to make it a class in international races.

Slalom takes a considerable amount of time to develop the necessary skills and technique. The rising level of competition required year round training which also required considerable commitment both financially and personally on the part of slalom athletes. Unfortunately, the combination of dynasties, the sheer amount of time needed to develop the skills and technique, and the weakness of the American system worked against developing a pool of young American athletes ready to replace the retiring stars during the '90s.

However, another factor was the rise in popularity of rodeo. For young athletes with an inclination toward competition, particularly for young Gen-Y paddlers, rodeo competition fit their interests more than slalom. The grueling workouts for slalom were not as much fun as rodeo workouts and could not offer the potential of the professional career that rodeo could. There were just too few incentives for young athletes to compete in slalom. But that didn't keep all young athletes away. Fortunately, changes in rules governing amateurism allowed athletes to compete in both rodeo and slalom. Some experienced slalom athletes capitalized on their training and successfully competed in rodeo and extreme competition as did Jason Beakes, Eric Jackson, Scott Shipley, and Rich Weiss. Their example helped to promote the training of young athletes for slalom competition. By the end of the '90s, young athletes including Aleta Miller, Rusty Sage, and Eric Southwick competed in both junior rodeo and slalom competition. Sage and Southwick later left slalom to turn pro in rodeo/freestyle competition.

Rodeo to Freestyle

As different as speed skating is from figure skating, so, too, was slalom and wildwater racing different from rodeo. In slalom, a competitor's score was based on speed and accuracy, judged by a clock. In rodeo, a competitor's score was based on moves and style, a choreographed routine, judged not by a clock, but by a group of judges. The events surrounding the first World Whitewater Rodeo in 1993 set the course for the evolution of the new rodeo competition, a course as different from either slalom or wildwater racing as were the inherent differences in their venues and objectives of competition. Rodeo's course evolved around and intertwined with professionalism, the industry, and a market for the next generation in a time and place far different than the course set for either slalom or wildwater in the '40s and '50s.

Rodeos, with NOWR's involvement, evolved towards more "show and glow" and away from its roots. Even its name changed from rodeo to freestyle which was reflective of changes that took it away from merely showing off river running skills. Event organizers such as those of the Payette Rodeo, opted to drop out of the NOWR circuit because they wanted to return to rodeo's roots. Other organizers were concerned that with professionalism, rodeos would go the way of slalom racing where races were put on for a select few. In rodeo, that meant a select few professionals that sometimes acted like prima donnas. The new rodeo was far removed from rodeo's beginnings in the '70s. The new rodeo's professionalism also went beyond merely winning prize money.

Like squirt ten years before, a whole genre of terminology developed for rodeo moves, particularly with the introduction of planing hulls that enabled moves far different than displacement hulls. Older moves based on displacement hulls included:

Rodeo on the Ocoee (TN), 2000 —courtesy of Brandon Knapp.

McTwist an elevated spin in which a paddler's boat is dynamically lifted and spun by the upstream water at the corner of the hole. The center of the boat stays in the same "sweet spot" of the backwash.

Pirouette a move following an ender in which the boat executes a 180 degree or more vertical spin and lands upright.

Whippet a retentive maneuver in which a paddler's boat travels vertically through an arc and lands back in the hole. The boat's end is pulled through the arc by the force of the downstream water under the backwash and the boat's midsection is held in the hole by the upstream push of the backwash.[40]

[40] Singleton, Mark. "Rodeo 101: A Primer of Hot Moves." *Nantahala Outdoor Center Outfitters Catalog* (1995): 70–71.

THE 1997 RULES governing rodeo included no boat measurement requirements for either kayak or C-1. However, boat measurement requirements were imposed for the OC-1 class in order to eliminate designs that might blend open and closed (C-1) canoes that would jeopardize the future of an OC-1 class.

Although no length restriction was imposed, other boat dimensions were required including a 14 inch minimum depth in the middle 2 feet of the boat's length; a maximum gunwale line drop of 3 inches from the middle section to either end; and a maximum tumblehome of 3 inches including gunwales and foam outfitting. Other specifications required removable flotation, attached only with a cord, and no solid bulkheads.

But the newer planing hulls allowed even more complex moves including 360-degree flat spins, split wheels, and Clean 360s. In 1998, Trophy Moves included the Airwheel Cartwheel, Loop, Olie, and Retentive Pirouette:

Airwheel A cartwheel where the paddler's weight is only supported by the first end of the cartwheel. Second end can be in the water but not supporting the paddler's weight.

Loop Front or back 360-degree vertical somersault in the hole without edging the boat and with no rotation or directional change.

Retentive Pirouette (360-degree) A 360-degree-or-better pirouette that lands back in the hole without the paddler washing out of the hole.[41]

By 2000, the list of freestyle moves had grown to seventeen and included variations on moves that limited paddle strokes or hand touches:

Clean 360 360 degreee spin on a smooth wave with only one stroke per 360-degress, no paddle or hand touch.

Super clean spin 360 spin on a smooth wave with no paddle stroke or hand touch per 360-degrees.

Clean cartwheel (aka washout) A cartwheel with two clean linked ends, no paddle or hand touch, per two ends.

Super clean cartwheel A cartwheel with two clean linked ends, no paddle or hand touch.[42]

In 1997, NOWR released the Whitewater Freestyle Event Format and Judging Criteria for all upper tier events, the first complete guidelines for rodeo events and judging. The standardized judging criteria required three components: technical moves, style, and quality of the ride. In addition to a standard event format, an optional event format was Freestyle Through a Rapid, an event with five gates modeled after European freestyle competition. For the next couple of years, changes were made in the judging criteria, although for the most part, the changes affected only the top tier rodeos and expert events.

Changes in 1998 included the addition of the Variety Moves Rule that applied to expert. Now, significant penalties (deductions) were required for not performing at least four of the ten for men, and three for women on the Variety Moves List. Trophy Moves added to a Variety Move could result in even higher scores.

In 1999, the three areas judged were redefined as technical, style, and variety. Technical scores were based on the difficulty of the moves. The style score reflected boat control, timing, rhythm, artistic expression, and choreography. Variety multipliers increased the technical/style score and were added for every

[41] AWA staff. "National Organization of Whitewater Rodeos (NOWR) 1998 Judging." *American Whitewater* Vol. XXXVIII No. 3 (May/June 1998): 30–31.

[42] National Organization for Whitewater Rodeo. "Freestyle Moves Defined." www.nowr.org 16 May 2001.

different move performed in a list of variety moves. High scores could only be obtained by the incorporation of a variety of different moves and ensured the highest level of technical skill among competitors.

Other changes were made for the 2000 rodeo season in developing a new standardized competitor classification system. The basis for the new system stemmed from research of similar competitive sports such as mountain biking, snowboarding, gymnastics, and skating. It was also created to facilitate "a foundation of amateur/local events and competitors,"[43] that is, a grass roots foundation for the development of competitors.

The new classification system developed three classes based on age: Junior, Senior, and Master. Four categories were based on ability and rodeo paddling proficiency: Beginner, Sport, Expert, and Pro. Judging for the two lowest levels was based on technique and style only. Judging for the highest two levels incorporated variety. Event organizers could choose to offer four mixes of categories ranging from the lowest amateur levels, Beginner and Sport, to the highest professional level, Pro only.

The classification system also required that all competitors register with NOWR (effective 2001 season) in order to compete in an NOWR sanctioned event. The cost of registration was $25, which included a membership with American Whitewater.

The new system was the same basic concept as the A/B and C/D ranking system instituted for slalom racing by ACA's National Slalom and Wildwater Committee (NSWC) during the late '70s. With its accompanying registration costs, this was the same concept that rankled many AWA members at the time ACA imposed their system.

By 1997, many if not all boat manufacturers sponsored either individual athletes or whole teams. These athletes were certainly professionals, training and competing full-time. In 1997, NOWR instituted a new race series specifically for Expert/Pro paddlers. The Point Series Championship was modeled after a multi-race cup series bringing the total number of rodeos in the NOWR circuit to twenty-one with three more added the following year.

Rodeo gained so much attention that traditional slalom venues added rodeo to their events. In 1998, the Wausau Canoe and Kayak Corporation, a slalom race sponsor on a slalom course in Wausau, Wisconsin, modified a hole for rodeo. The event was very unique from most rodeos with an urban downtown location, bleachers, and controlled water, something that rodeo organizers realized was as important to rodeo as it was for slalom. The event was a success.

The importance of controlled releases for rodeo events was demonstrated time and time again with last minute changes or cancellations in rodeo schedules. In 1996, Bob's Hole on the Clackamus washed out from February floods. Animas River Days didn't have the expected runoff which affected team trials that were anticipated to occur at either event. Fortunately, Bob's Hole returned later the same year after flooding in December. In 1998, low water forced last minute changes for a rodeo scheduled for the Canyon Creek Rodeo, part of the five-event Oregon Cup. Fortunately, the outcome provided a new venue for rodeo. The last minute change provided for a freestyle acrobatic waterfall

RODEO COMPETITION in Europe developed its own European Freestyle Kayaking Circuit. Rodeos were included in festivals, although not emulating the American festival practice. Instead, rodeo was included with town festivals, just as slalom and wildwater races were included dating back into the '50s. In Europe, festivals often attracted thousands of spectators for slalom races. European rodeos are different than American rodeos in that the score is based on one ride only with no practice.

[43] Abbot, Jayne H. NOWR NEWS Vol. XXXIX No. 6 (November/December 1999): 41.

contest, a vertical rodeo, at 15-foot Sunset Falls on the East Fork of the Lewis River in southeast Washington. A total of thirty-six competitors, including five women, participated. It was the first waterfall rodeo sanctioned by NOWR.

The same year, NOWR spearheaded the effort to modify Smiley's hole on the Ocoee Olympic slalom site to make it bigger and more suitable for rodeo. Just as Wausau Canoe and Kayak Corporation had done, NOWR took advantage of a first class slalom site for a rodeo contest. TVA and volunteer engineers and architects helped re-design and modify the hole, but their resulting efforts were less than satisfactory. It wasn't sticky enough and the hole was returned to its initial state. However, because of the trend toward smaller boats after 1998, Smiley's Hole was found suitable. It was the site of the 2000 Ocoee Rodeo.

Recommendations from the U.S. Freestyle Kayak Committee (USFKC), a sub-committee of NOWR, at the 1998 *Outdoor Retailer* Show included the establishment of the North America Cup and national championships along with team trials to determine the national champion and Freestyle Team, with East Coast and West Coast team trials. The North American Cup was based on cumulative points from three top rodeos. In its first year in 1999, the cup series included the Ocoee Rodeo, Animas River Days, and Wausau Whitewater Rodeo.

The North America Cup was a natural progression for rodeo. In the '90s, both American and Canadian manufacturers, competitors, and organizers contributed to the development of rodeo. AWA has a long history of Canadians in its membership and operated with little regard to the international boundary between the two countries. Even in the early years of slalom competition, Americans and Canadians, particularly in the Northeast and Northwest, co-participated in many slalom races, including the Eastern National Championships (although American finishes were adjusted to reflect American winners for the official championship titles).

In 2000, another series was incorporated into the twenty one-event NOWR rodeo circuit, the five-event Freestyle Championship Series sponsored by OutdoorPlay.com. This new event had a purse of over $150,000 offering $5,000 for Men's K-1, Women's K-1 and C-1 Pro divisions with an additional $7,500 split for overall category champions.

While the popularity and participation of paddlers, both athletes and spectators, continued to increase for NOWR's rodeo circuit, international competition also continued to draw larger numbers. In 1997, the World Freestyle Championships, formerly called the World Rodeo Championships, returned to North America, this time held on the Ottawa. A total of 235 competitors from nineteen countries, including Japan, Zimbabwe, and Finland, competed in eight categories in front of over 850 spectators. Both TSN (The Sports Network) and OLN (Outdoor Life Network) networks covered the championships.

Although four classes, mostly associated with women's events, didn't have enough contestants for competition, the remaining events were very competitive. With the exception of Open Canoe, swept by Canadian paddlers, and Men's Squirt, swept by American paddlers, the international community was represented in the event medal winners.

American and Canadian athletes did well in all events. Ken Whiting (Canada) won and Eric Jackson (USA) was second in Men's K-1. In Women's K-1, Nicole Zaharko (Canada) won the event followed by Jamie Simon (USA) in second. In C-1, Allan Braswell was 2nd and Adam Boyd was 3rd (both USA). In OC-1 Canadians swept the event. Mark Scriver won the event followed by Ian Holmes in 2nd and Lyle Dickieson in 3rd. In Men's Squirt, Americans swept the event. Clay Wright was 1st, Andy Whiting was 2nd , and Eric Zitzow was 3rd.

By the mid-'90s, rodeo competition was exported around the world, and not just in the traditional countries of slalom competition. In 1998, the Himalayan Whitewater Rodeo was in its third year. It was started in 1996 by Equator Expeditions of Katmandu.

The 1999 World Freestyle Championships were held in New Zealand. Although the championships were a success and well attended, the event was marred by the death of Nimh Tomlins, a member of the Irish team, who drowned when she jumped in the river to cool off.

Team USA had a strong showing and won the overall gold in the team competition in all seven classes. Individual World Champions were Eric Southwick in Men's K-1, Andy Beddingfield in Men's Squirt, and Eli Helbert in OC-1.

Like the '97 World Freestyle Championships, American and Canadian team members did well in many of the events. In addition to an American World Champion in OC-1, American Brian Miller placed 3rdin the event. In Women's K-1, Julie Dion (Canada) was 2nd and Brooke Winger (USA) was 3rd. In Men's Squirt, Clay Wright (USA) was 2nd and Brendan Mark (Canada) was 3rd. However, in C-1 the best finish for the American and Canadian teams was Allen Braswell's (USA) 4th place, beaten by British and French paddlers for the medals.

In less than five short years, rodeo competition evolved and developed at the same fast pace as the boat designs themselves. Just as the designs reached a consolidation of concepts for rodeo hulls, and the industry moved toward consolidation, the competition side of rodeo reached consolidation of its foundation. With the development of an organizational owner or caretaker in NOWR beyond strictly a volunteer basis, rodeo was on its way to developing the infrastructure and systems necessary for a competitive sport. While some similarities existed between slalom competition and what rodeo required, rodeo differed with its requirements related to professionalism and the intertwining and interdependence between its competition and the industry that supported it.

Rodeo both helped and hurt slalom, but in some instances the two actually developed a synergistic relationship. Rodeo, the American-style sport with free-spirited boat acrobatics, initially attracted young Gen-Y athletes and provided an arena to compete in. Slalom, the European-style sport with very different competition requirements, was not as attractive. Chris Spelius said, "Rodeo fits the United States character more than slalom racing. Bravado, macho, go-into-the-hole-as-if-it-meant-something! It's the way we are."[44] However, because it was demonstrated that slalom training benefitted

[44] Singleton, Mark. "'Fringe Sport' Makes the Big Time." *Nantahala Outdoor Center Outfitters Catalog* (1995): 60–61.

rodeo, many young athletes also competed in slalom. While rodeo took some young athletes away from slalom, it also brought a number of young athletes to slalom who were looking for a second sport in which to compete.

But slalom also helped rodeo. Controlled sites and controlled releases were found to be just as important for rodeo as they were for slalom. But developed slalom courses benefitted rodeo in more ways than just controlled releases. The courses also often provided better site conditions for spectators that drew larger crowds. Slalom courses and whitewater parks like the Wausau Whitewater Park, initially established for slalom, benefitted both sports. And because this brought a broader use, about a dozen similar whitewater parks sprang up across the country with still others proposed in the late '90s and the years beyond.

Extreme Races

The Upper Yough Race and Great Falls Race, both begun in the '80s, were two types of extreme races that were duplicated in the '90s. The Upper Yough Race was a Class V wildwater race down the famous Upper Yough from Sang Run to Friendsville. Paddlers were drawn to the race just to pit themselves against the local expert-extreme legends and favorites: Roger Zbel (the winningest competitor), Jim and Jeff Snyder, and racer/organizer Jesse Whittemore.

Other Upper Yough-type Class V wildwater races followed such as Gore Canyon in Colorado, the Watauga in North Carolina, North Fork of the Payette in Idaho, Upper Gauley in West Virginia, Russell Fork in Kentucky, Bottom Moose and Black River in New York, and Canyon Creek in Washington. Some of the races came and went in a few years. Others, like the Black River and Bottom Moose races, were started as a part of river festivals. Still others, like the Great Falls Race, were the start of a festival surrounding the race itself. In 1998, many of the extreme races were incorporated into a new series, the American Whitewater Cascade Series, sponsored by NOWR.

In 1990, Chan Zwanzig organized the first Gore Canyon race with support from Sun Valley Beer. Local favorite and legend John Jaycox won the 4-mile race in a little over 20 minutes. Although the racecourse was short, its difficulty was demonstrated when two safety boaters pinned on the course, one losing her Dancer to the river.

The Great Falls Invitational Race was a Class V+ sprint over waterfalls. Due to its extreme nature, the race was by invitation only. The race was run on the Virginia side of Great Falls with a total drop of more than 55 feet broken into roughly three drops. (There are four runs over Great Falls: the Virginia side, the Maryland side, the gorge through the island, and the "fish ladder.") The race started with U Hole followed by S Turn, both complex Class V drops. The last drop was the Spout, an almost sheer 22 foot falls. (In 1995, the route was changed to avoid hazardous water conditions down the usual run.)

Eric Jackson's first run time at the '93 Great Falls Invitational Race was so fast that he was considered the winner on that run alone. On his second run, he ran the course without a paddle, with two hand rolls, to show off for the crowds. Although this seemed to downplay the danger of extreme racing, another racer, Mike Januska, on the same day shattered his right ankle when he pitoned after losing his line on the falls. Januksa had broken the same ankle earlier in the year running the North Fork of the Blackwater in West Virginia.

In 1995, the first Russell Fork race was held and won by Jeff Snyder. The difficulty and danger of the race was illustrated with the requirement that each competitor fill out the "Acknowledgment and Assumption of Risk," which was more than just a standard risk release form. The form notified the competitor that in order to compete, he or she was required to have paddled the Russell Fork on at least three previous occasions. It also notified the competitor of previous deaths on the river, that the race was not an organized event with no prizes of any kind or entry fees, and that no safety was provided for the race. Initials of the competitor were required after each item on the form. The competitor's final signature relinquished anyone and everyone of all liability and acknowledged the foolhardiness of the event.

In 1996, the first Great Falls-type Class V+ sprint over waterfalls was included in the Gorge Games. Sponsored by the World Kayak Federation, the Gorge Games Extreme Race was by invitation only or pre-qualification. The race was held on the White Salmon River in Washington on a Class V section that included several Class V drops including 30-foot Big Brother Falls. A total of thirteen racers competed for a $1,500 total cash purse plus a free Wavesport boat that went to the winner. Eric Jackson, Olympian in slalom and World Rodeo Champion, won the race followed by Bryan Tooley, National Wildwater Champion, and Sam Drevo.

Although the Gorge Games were cancelled in 1999 due to lack of a sponsor, expanded Gorge Games that included a rodeo and extreme race were back again in 2000 with Subaru of America as the sponsor. The 2000 Gorge Games included windsurfing, mountain biking, climbing, and outrigger canoeing in addition to freestyle rodeo, a four-boat-at-a-time head to head race over Class IV Husum Falls on the White Salmon River, and the extreme race that included Big Brother Falls. The Games were televised on NBC.

In 1997, the section of the White Salmon used for the Gorge Games Extreme Race claimed Olympian Rich Weiss.

Initially, many of the extreme wildwater races, competitions held between local expert-extreme boaters, were non-ACA sanctioned events. However, some of the events qualified as ACA sanctioned events and were, therefore, eligible for insurance through ACA. These events were included in the race circuit for wildwater racers. In such instances, local extreme boater winners were often replaced by wildwater racers who trained for such events in their downriver canoes and kayaks.

For inclusion of a race into ACA's wildwater rankings, there were two basic requirements. One was that the race times, regardless of course length, were recorded for each competitor to allow the calculation of percentages from the winner. Another was that the race had to include at lease one composite or plastic downriver boat in the results.

Interest in wildwater competition began to decline in the '90s, overshadowed by slalom competition in the '92 and '96 Olympics and growing rodeo competition with international competition. The last time an American medaled in world competition was at the '85 World Championships. No American women even participated in the '96 and '98 World Championships. Beginning in 1996, the World Championships for wildwater were held every other even year, corrresponding to off years for the World Championships for slalom.

AWA and ACA

For both ACA and AWA, the '90s brought more refinement to their whitewater roles that had begun to coalesce in the latter half of the '80s. During the '90s, ACA began to remake itself into a truly national organization representing the interests of the general paddling public. ACA refocused its attention on safety, education, and instruction and entered into an active role in conservation. Whitewater, as a niche, was only a part of these areas. For ACA, one of its biggest and earliest whitewater roles was through competition as the long-standing NGB for Olympic competition and ICF representative. Although ACA's imminent loss of NGB status relegated its interest in slalom racing to a grass roots effort, ACA retained its national interest in whitewater through wildwater and open canoe competition

During the '80s, AWA remade itself to fit its changing needs and that of its membership. Conservation was one of its key focus points. AWA established a foundation for further changes in the '90s to meet the challenges for the next generation of whitewater paddlers: to transition from AWA, the American Whitewater Affiliation, of the past to American Whitewater for the future. The transition involved a change that included competition. In the past, AWA's long standing interest in representing whitewater paddlers excluded slalom and wildwater competition because of ACA's involvement. However, in the '90s, AWA entered into the competition arena through rodeo and not just for the sake of competition. AWA's involvement in rodeo competition was used to support and fund their river conservation efforts that had become one of their core functions in the latter half of the '80s.

ACA and AWA truly became organizations of the '90s. Both organizations concentrated on growing their memberships and transitioned from small staffs (or primarily volunteer staffs for AWA) to paid professional staffs. Both organizations also benefitted from locations in the greater D.C. area to further their involvement with governmental agencies regarding safety, education, and conservation issues.

AWA to American Whitewater

From its early years in the '50s, committees representing Conservation, Safety, and Education, through the Editorial and Guidebook Committees and *American Whitewater* publication, focused on the purpose for AWA's existence: to support the growth of whitewater in America. In the '90s, conservation and events became important focal points for AWA. In 1990, event sponsorship in support of conservation was added as another purpose for AWA with the sponsorship of the Gauley and the Ocoee Festivals. In 1993, access was added as an important part of preserving enjoyment of whitewater rivers for the future, just as conservation was important to preserving rivers.

The organization was re-invigorated with successes in conservation efforts and new leadership, along with membership growth from younger Gen-X members. By the end of 1990, AWA had 2,000 members, up from as few as 800 in the mid-80s. In 1991, *American Whitewater* was found in over 125 retail outlets.

[45] AWA Staff. Briefs. "Risa Shimoda Callaway Resigns as AWA Head." *American Whitewater* Vol. XXXV No. 3 (May/June 1990): 14.

[46] Alesch, Ric and Pope Barrow. "Summary of the AWA Five-Year Strategic Plan." *American Whitewater* Vol. XXXV No. 5 (September/October 1995): 93–94.

American Whitewater's turnaround was attributed to Risa Shimoda-Callaway and Phyllis Horowitz, Executive Directors in the late '80s and early '90s. Shimoda-Callaway was a driving force behind American Whitewater regaining its position as the "nation's leading whitewater organization."[45] Among other things, Shimoda-Callaway was responsible for establishing the whitewater marketplace at both the Gauley Festival and the Ocoee Rodeo, the retail distribution of *American Whitewater* and American Whitewater's product lines. In 1990, she resigned as Executive Director and was replaced by Phyllis Horowitz whose long time involvement with *American Whitewater* as Advertising Director helped to increase American Whitewater's revenues for conservation battles.

AWA's membership and influence continued to grow, and in 1995, it developed a strategic five-year plan. Its Mission Statement was "To conserve and restore America's whitewater resources and to enhance opportunities to enjoy them safely."[46] The plan was designed to address goals and strategies for whitewater river conservation, access, safety, and to promote whitewater through special events such as NOWR affiliated festivals and other events. The plan also proposed that AWA become the focal point for whitewater information on the "information superhighway" just as AWA had always been through *American Whitewater.* In the Spring of 1995, AWA's website began perpetuating one of their original purposes of education through dissemination of information.

AWA's website became an important medium for assisting paddlers with everything from information and links regarding river levels (U.S.G.S. stream flow data and phone gauge phone numbers) to updates on access, conservation, and festivals, to hosting Affiliate home pages.

The website was just the beginning of changes resulting from the strategic plan. By 1995, membership reached almost 4,600 paddlers and affiliates. The increased revenue derived from membership and events was sufficient to support more than two paid staff positions, Executive Director and Conservation Program Director. In 1996, Rich Bowers, Conservation Program Director since 1992, replaced Phyllis Horowitz as Executive Director. In 1997, AWA dropped the term "Affiliation" from its name. AWA became American Whitewater, reflecting the changes that occurred in the organization. A new Conservation and Hydro-Power Program Director was hired and an Events Coordinator was added to handle festivals and rodeos. In 1998, an Access Director was added to the staff. A Development Director was hired the following year. By 1999, American Whitewater's membership was over 8,000.

In the '90s, American Whitewater's promotion of safety in the sport continued as an integral program through its role as the caretaker of the river ranking system and the Whitewater Safety Code. Compilation, analysis, and publication of whitewater accidents also continued and were expanded to include a database of accident reports by year and state available over American Whitewater's website.

The debate that began in the '80s about overhauling the river rating system continued into the '90s. The general consensus among whitewater paddlers was that the problem associated with the river rating system originally involved the Class V classification alone. Classification of rivers was largely satisfactory for Class IV and below. Few felt that the de-rating of Class V to IV or IV to III was necessary because ratings were primarily intended for beginners or people running a river for the first time. But much discussion evolved around Class V and many felt that the classification needed a more open-ended rating system as reflected in the increased ability to run once unrunnable drops due to advances in equipment and technique. In the 1996 January/February issue of *American Whitewater,* AWA requested help from readers. American Whitewater's plan was to maintain the current classification definitions, adding a plus or minus to Class II through IV, and expand Class V (redesignated Class 5) to an open-ended decimal system, 5.x, like that used for climbing. American Whitewater requested that paddlers across the country create and submit their own river list according to the definitions for consolidation into one master list of rivers.

Based on the input, American Whitewater incorporated examples of updated and new classifications in the 1998 revision of the Safety Code that provided a benchmark for rivers and rapids across the country. The benchmarks were incorporated into the new Standard Rated Rapids by class which included examples based on river section and water level for four different geographic areas: North East, South East, Rocky Mountains, and West Coast. Plus and minus designations were added to classes beginning with Class II (no Class II minus, though) through Class IV. Class V rivers were split into two designations: the Roman numeric Class V (the lower of the two) and the open-ended decimal numeric class beginning with Class 5.1. In the 1998 Standard Rated Rapids, the highest listed rapids were Class 5.3 which was reserved for the most extreme drops runnable. This included S Turn on Lime Creek, Upper Narrow on the Narrows section of the Cache La Poudre, Rigormortis on Clear Creek Canyon, all in Colorado, and Jacob's Ladder and Nutcracker on the North Fork of the Payette in Idaho.

In the '90s, American Whitewater took on a higher level of involvement in conservation efforts across the country. By this time, American Whitewater was finally being taken seriously by many governmental agencies. Some of the fruits of American Whitewater's labors that started as early as 1984 regarding hydro regulation issues resulted in whitewater recreation issues being taken seriously in FERC and other federal agencies' decision-making processes. In 1991, American Whitewater's Nationwide Whitewater Inventory, begun in 1988, was adopted for use by the Bureau of Land Management, the National Park Service, and the U.S. Forest Service as well as other state agencies and conservation groups across the country.

In 1992, American Whitewater hired Rich Bowers as Conservation Program Director coordinating efforts of the network of almost thirty regional coordinators, the eyes and ears of American Whitewater. With input from the regional coordinators, established in 1990 to help American Whitewater focus on local issues of concern, yearly Top 40 issues were identified and ranged from a focus on specific river issues to broader access, conservation, hydropower relicensing, and safety issues. As learned from the late '80s in fighting hydropower development, American Whitewater took battles to court when necessary. Funding for legal help was provided by the Whitewater Defense Project which was supported by individual and club donations as well as from companies, foundations, and trusts. Initially begun by Pope Barrow in 1986, the Whitewater Defense Project was turned over to American Whitewater in 1988 to provide greater organizational support for its further development. Under the auspices of American Whitewater, the Whitewater Defense Project continued to grow providing financial support for many of the legal battles taken on by American Whitewater in the '90s.

American Whitewater's conservation and preservation philosophy was put to the test the protection of rivers in their natural state versus modification for the sake of safety or recreational releases. American Whitewater sometimes found itself at odds with other organizations that were often allies under other circumstances. On the Snoqualamie in Washington, American Whitewater did not support the removal of rocks while the area supporters of Wild and Scenic preservation did. American Whitewater was against the addition of the Hays Dam on the Russell Fork in Kentucky for flood control although it might provide better releases (the same argument PG&E used in California in the '70s to justify dams). American Whitewater chose to remain out of discussions regarding the '96 Olympic slalom site on the Ocoee, but was involved in the modification of Smiley's hole for the Ocoee rodeo.

By 1993, river access was recognized as an important issue involving the enjoyment of whitewater rivers. In the late '90s, access efforts expanded to actually acquiring land, permission, or leases for put-ins and take-outs to ensure access. Among other land purchases and leases, American Whitewater, with the help of the West Virginia Rivers Coalition and Friends of the Cheat, purchased land at the confluence of the Dry Fork and Blackwater in West Virginia with funds from American Whitewater's River Access Program first established in 1994 with a grant of $40,000 from the Conservation Alliance. Working with the U.S. Forest Service, BLM, state of Colorado, and CWWA, American Whitewater also helped to obtain land for the put-in to the Numbers section of the Arkansas. Land was also obtained for the take out for the Wautauga in North Carolina.

The most recent function added to American Whitewater, event sponsorship, developed throughout the '90s. In 1990, American Whitewater sponsored two events, the Gauley Festival and the Ocoee Rodeo. Ten years later in 2000, American Whitewater sponsored and co-sponsored four different categories of events: American Whitewater Festivals totaling eleven separate festivals, RiversLiv Series totaling twenty rodeos in American Whitewater's NOWR schedule, American Whitewater Cascade Series totaling seven extreme/downriver races, and OutdoorPlay.com Freestyle Championship Series co-sponsored with OutdoorPlay.com with five professional rodeos. In spite of the competitive nature of events associated with rodeo and extreme racing, all four categories of events were designed to support river conservation efforts.

American Whitewater's participation and sponsorship revolved around the original purposes for the first Ocoee and Gauley Festivals: to highlight and fund specific river preservation issues. While some festivals like the Gauley Festival were no longer required because protection and preservation were won, the festivals continued as celebrations of their success as well as sources for continued funding for other conservation efforts.

In 1994, American Whitewater added two additional festivals, one on the Kennebec on July 4th weekend and the other on the Deerfield in August to assist with access and release issues involving both rivers. Both festivals were set up to allow vendors to display their products, the same as the Gauley Festival Marketplace. American Whitewater also teamed up with

CWWA (Colorado White Water Association) for the First Annual American Whitewater/CWWA River Festival (Arkfest) in Salida in July after the Salida races. Arkfest, modeled after the Gauley Festival, was successful in raising money for river conservation projects in the state of Colorado. The festival coincided with the annual CWWA and Rocky Mountain Canoe Club's Arkansas weekends and the Colorado Cup races on the Numbers section of the Arkansas.

In 1995, the calendar of events expanded beyond the Gauley, Deerfield, and Kennebec Festivals with new events that included the Potomac Whitewater Festival and Rodeo, the Moose Festival and Whitewater Race, and the Russell Fork Rendezvous which was a joint effort with the Bluegrass Wildwater Association and ACA.

As the '90s rolled on, new festivals were added while some festivals (and rodeos) were discontinued or shifted away from American Whitewater's sponsorship. However, the model and success of American Whitewater's sponsorship of the Ocoee and Gauley Festivals was duplicated by other festival organizers across the country, like the Kern Fest in California, the Lochsa Festival in Idaho, and the Cheat River Festival and Race in West Virginia.

In 1995, NOWR became a part of American Whitewater to better sponsor and organize rodeo and related festival events. In 1998, American Whitewater event sponsorship grew to nine festivals with twenty-four rodeos in the NOWR circuit, and the addition of a new series, the American Whitewater Cascade Series that incorporated a total of eight extreme races. The NOWR rodeo circuit spanned North America including Canada.

The changes and organization that American Whitewater brought to NOWR contributed to the growth and uniqueness of the sport of rodeo. No other professional sport, or even amateur sport, was developed to support conservation efforts that benefitted the greater whitewater paddling community. In 1998, the Ocoee Rodeo was the largest festival, earning over $16,000 for American Whitewater's conservation efforts.

IN 1994, the Kennebec Festival release was 9,000 cfs due to higher than normal rainfall. The release was larger than the usual 4,800 cfs on weekends and still more than the sometimes 6,000 cfs on hot weekdays when Boston needs power. Water actually spilled over the 150-foot sluice normally reserved in case of flood. In 1995, the reverse was true when the festival was cancelled due to no water.

IN 1997, American Whitewater entered into a partnership with the World Kayak Federation (WKF), which was formed to support the professionalisation of rodeo competition as well as promote conservation and instructional programs. The partnership provided that American Whitewater advertise and promote professional events sponsored by WKF and in turn, WKF shared revenues to help fund conservation and access programs. Within a year, the partnership fizzled, as did WKF.

ACA

Changes that began with the formation of USKCT in 1988 continued into the '90s, particularly for ACA's role in whitewater. ACA struggled as an organization to find a new identity separate from international and Olympic competition. ACA was one of the few surviving multi-purpose organizations representing a pyramid with a base of recreational paddlers and a top with competitive paddlers (USCKT). However, a few people within ACA began to recognize that ACA was not successful as a national organization in affecting issues associated with recreational paddling. Its roots were still based in an ineffective club-like mentality. Other organizations such as the Sierra Club, National Audubon Society, and Appalachian Mountain Club (AMC) were far more effective in both representing and providing services to their members. An estimated 24.8 million people participated annually in canoeing, kayaking, and rafting activities in the mid-'90s, yet ACA's membership represented fewer than 0.05 per cent of that number.

Although recreation, conservation, safety, and training were long-standing committees within ACA's organization, ACA established new councils and activity committees in the '90s. The councils included Recreation, Conservation, Competition, and Safety, Education and Instruction (SEIC), the latter a combination of the previous safety and training committees rolled into one. While the purpose of the Safety, Education, and Instruction Council was well developed, certified educational courses in the pursuit of overall paddlesport safety and Recreation and Conservation were not. Active efforts were made to develop both conservation and the promotion of general paddling recreation. Membership development was also recognized as a key ingredient for success and ACA began to emulate other national non-profit organizations in their membership efforts.

In order to fully implement the changes, ACA also hired a professional staff who supported departments that were linked to the Councils, particularly the Conservation Council with the development of the Conservation and Public Policy Department with a paid director. Like American Whitewater, ACA expanded into event sponsorship and assistance. In 1998, a Programs and Special Events Department was established with its own program coordinator to provide event insurance/risk management, technical assistance, and event sponsorship to support ACA's Event Sanctioning and Support Program.

In addition to emulating other outdoor non-profit organizations with regard to membership campaigns, ACA also sought corporate sponsors, as did other successful outdoor/sports oriented organizations. ACA's first entry into corporate sponsorship, outside of Champion International's sponsorship of the USCKT whitewater slalom series, was Finlandia Vodka (Finnish National Distillers). Finlandia Vodka was looking for a good image, pretty outdoor pictures and a tie to the growing popularity of good environmental stewardship, with which to associate its name. ACA finally realized selling vodka was not in their best interest and their association with Finlandia Vodka was not continued.

ACA's next sponsor was Subaru who was interested in expanding their image from competitive skiing (Subaru was a sponsor of the U.S. Ski Team for almost twenty years) to family-oriented activities and green recreation. Recreational paddling and ACA fit the bill.

ACA EXPANDED into the representation of professionals and industry associated with paddling recreation, outfitters and liveries, with the establishment of a sister trade association, Professional Paddlesport Association (PPA), in the mid-'90s.

ACA also expanded to establish Paddlesport Publishing Inc. (PPI), a commercial subsidiary and in 1997, purchased *Paddler.*

The forerunner of SEIC's programs began in the latter half of the '70s with the earliest ACA instructor courses and emphasis on "safety through education, not regulation." During the '80s, paddling courses and safety programs expanded with the ultimate goal of increasing public safety, preventing injury, and saving lives. Tied in with it all was instructor certification, and the rationale that certified instructors implied better instructors, which meant increased safety for the paddling public and reduced liability. ACA viewed certification as another card in the deck in case of a lawsuit.

ACA's programs were not without controversy, both within and outside of ACA. The basic canoeing and kayaking courses separated paddling strokes into a myriad of combinations. Over thirty different named strokes were counted for open canoeing alone. Bruce Lessels, a professional instructor and founder of Zoar Outdoor in Massachusetts wrote,

> The greatest disservice done to paddling is breaking the sport into understandable parts for the sake of teaching, because students too often believe these divisions are inherent in the sport. While most paddlers think of strokes, leans and maneuvers as independent concepts, in real river situations no single component ever stands alone. [47]

Instructor certification became embroiled in controversy, often split along ACA and American Whitewater party lines. The controversy boiled down to an overemphasis of credentialed paddlers and their paddling abilities based on those credentials. ACA's national certification program was not deemed credible enough by many truly expert paddlers to warrant their involvement in the process. Without that name recognition and support of acknowledged expert paddlers, ACA's credentials were just plain lacking for many whitewater paddlers.

In defending their certification process, ACA's Executive Director Jeffrey Yeager argued for support of ACA's national certification process based on the position that credible national certification safeguarded public safety. He also argued that "certification as an ACA instructor is widely accepted as a credible indication of a person's paddling and teaching skills." [48]

Bob Gedekoh, Editor of *American Whitewater,* responded with a description of the prototypical ACA instructor named "Jack," the festooned badge carrying certified paddling and rescue instructor, who would have difficulty saving himself in a Class IV drop, let alone rescuing someone else. Gedekoh wrote: "There are too many ACA instructors out there like Jack, who sat through the requisite course... held on class three water... but who can not competently paddle class four whitewater and are totally incapable of negotiating class five." [49]

Gedekoh further wrote:

> Now I really wouldn't have paid much attention to all of this, except for the fact that Mr. Yeager announced, in the same editorial, that the ACA has received a $63,000 grant from the Coast Guard to expand their instructional program. They plan to use part of the money to hire a full time director of instruction and safety. Since that's my tax money, I hope they choose wisely. Because there are a lot of "experts" out there with excellent "credentials." Folks like Jack. [50]

While some took exception to Gedekoh's intimation that only Class IV and V paddlers should be credentialed, others agreed that the reasons behind credentials for some paddlers was to demonstrate on paper their abilities without having to demonstrate them on water. Still others, including a few ACA certified instructors, supported many of Gedekoh's opinions. One professional

[47] Lessels, Bruce. "Wholistic Paddling." *Canoe & Kayak* (December 1994): 17.

[48] Gedekoh, Bob. Forum. "The River Decides." *American Whitewater* Vol. XXXIV No. 1 (January/February 1994): 4–5.

[49] Ibid.

[50] Ibid.

instructor, John Weld, voiced his beliefs that "the ACA Certification Program has problems not only as a concept, but also in application."[51] He explained that for the professional instructor, the real measure was how well the he could teach the class, not just demonstrate the strokes and that no amount of certification can adequately replace "the social skill" with the "quantitative science" of paddling. Jess Gonzales, another long-time paddler (and paddle maker, owner of Gonzo Paddles) wrote:

> The over emphasis on credentals and qualifications is perpetuated by the unknowing of the ones who want the status of putting the years of hard and honest work that it takes to achieve mastering of any subject. Qualifications are not bestowed, they are earned after a very long period of honest and varied achievement.[52]

Controversy aside, ACA's instructional program grew tremendously in the '90s to over 300 instructor trainers and 3,000 instructors nationally. In 1999, ACA responded to the explosion of the number of paddlers tackling difficult whitewater with a new advanced whitewater certification in kayak and canoe. The Advanced Whitewater Certification course was designed by ACA with major input from Gordon Black, Director of Instruction at NOC. It first began in 1999 with a series of instructor trainer courses with regular courses offered on rivers of at least Class III in difficulty. A Basic Whitewater Safety course was also rolled out in 2000. All whitewater instructors were urged to seek endorsement for teaching it, too, "because safety really is our first priority."[53]

In 2000, ACA also began working with Garrett Community College's Adventure Sports Program in McHenry, Maryland, to develop a prototype program that was intended to lead to the development of a nationwide network of centers at colleges and universities. Officially designated an ACA National Center for Paddlesport Instruction, Garrett Community College would offer a full range of ACA courses taught by ACA certified faculty members.

Aside from ACA's involvement in instructional courses and certification for the purpose of increasing public safety, ACA was also involved in the development of the National Livery Safety System (NLSS) in partnership with ODNR Division of Watercraft and Professional Paddlesports Association. NLSS focused on canoe liveries and outfitters and included whitewater rafting and other whitewater activities. Videos served as the backbone for the System provided by a contract between ACA and Performance Video and Instruction, Inc., owned by Kent Ford. The System was later able to expand through a grant from the National Nonprofit Public Service Organization Boating Safety Grant Program administered by the U.S. Coast Guard. ACA's new efforts in the late '90s also targeted whitewater rafting, non-guided whitewater paddling, and coastal kayaking.

IN 1999, Mad River Canoe's "You Can Canoe! Days" became "You Can Paddle! Days" under joint sponsorship with Wilderness Systems. They also signed an agreement with ACA that encouraged ACA certified instructors to participate in the program across the country.

Although ACA had a Conservation Committee for many years, it wasn't until the '90s that their efforts came into focus and concentrated on recreation based conservation and protection of waterways for future generations. While American Whitewater focused on many different tools for preservation and access for whitewater resources, ACA focused on ensuring clean water for

[51] Weld, John. Letters. *American Whitewater* Vol. XXXIV No. 3 (May/June 1994): 9–10.

[52] Gonzalez, Jess. Letters. *American Whitewater* Vol. XXXIV No. 3 (May/June 1994): 13.

[53] ACA staff. "Basic Whitewater Safety- New ACA Course Rollout." *American Canoeist* (Spring 2000): 3.

waterway protection. In the early '90s, ACA's efforts got a big boost from their corporate sponsor, Finlandia Vodka, with the establishment of the Finlandia Clean Water fund. ACA convinced Finlandia Vodka that recreational use was important to the American people and paddlers. Through Finlandia's funding, ACA created a paid conservation position that helped kick-off the efforts in enforcement of the Clean Water Act. (The Clean Water Act is a 1977 amendment to the Federal Water Pollution Control Act of 1972. The amendment focused on toxic pollutants.) In the late '90s, ACA added a Director of Environmental Enforcement to its growing list of paid staff positions. Like American Whitewater's conservation efforts, ACA's clean water efforts relied heavily on support from local clubs and paddlers including working with them as joint plaintiffs in taking violators to court.

ACA's Event Sanctioning and Support Program provided a variety of services including liability insurance, promotional assistance, event sponsorship contacts, and event funding (loans and grants), services similar to American Whitewater's NOWR event support. In 1998, aside from competitive sanctioned events, ACA got into other sanctioned events such as consumer shows, festivals, and symposia for everything from flatwater, to seakayaking, to whitewater, sponsoring nine different events in its first year.

In 1998, ACA added the Rafting Activity Committee.

In 1998, the U.S. Olympic Committee designated USCKT as the National Governing Body for Olympic sprint and slalom starting after the 2000 Olympics. This meant that USCKT would take responsibility for all aspects of competition including international competition that might be Olympic events in the future. While ACA maintained their own national activity committees dealing with non-ICF disciplines, for whitewater that meant whitewater open canoe and rafting, ACA's role for slalom and wildwater competition involved grass roots efforts only following the 2000 Olympics.

In order to strengthen and encourage more grass roots conservation support, ACA's Bylaws were changed in 2000 to convert Conservation and Recreation Council seats to at-large seats. This change allowed more equitable representation of ACA's membership on the Council.

With these final changes to ACA's role in international and Olympic competition, ACA adopted a five-year strategic plan for 1999 through 2004 that encompassed ACA's future vision for itself.

> To become the nation's leading source of the most comprehensive and accurate information regarding all aspects of paddlesport... To become the leading national organization involved in enforcing the Clean Water Act in regard to pollution of recreational waterways... To establish a national waterway access land trust program with local management and oversight, to ensure waterway access and serve as local centers for ACA programs and activities... To dramatically expand the scope and availability of ACA's national instructional programs... To provide increased support and programming in the area of amateur athletics, particularly at the grass-roots level... To increase the Association's membership to 100,000 individuals.[54]

In less than ten years, ACA underwent fairly dramatic changes from its earlier club-based operation to a more truly national organization attempting to represent the interests of the general paddling public as a whole. In 1999, ACA's programs included Waterway Conservation/Access,

[54] Yeager, Jeffrey. "New Strategic Plan Sets Vision for Future." *Paddler* Vol. 19 No. 2 (March/April 1999): 16.

Safety, Education/Instruction, Recreation/Public Information, and Athletic Competition/Special Events. In 2000, ACA's website, first established in 1994, was revamped to become a resource of paddling information. By 2000, ACA's membership totaled more than 45,000.

Safety and River Rescue

River rescue courses continued to evolve from their beginnings in the late '70s and early '80s into the '90s teaching techniques to deal with entrapment, effective use of throw lines and belaying skills. Courses in the '90s began to emphasize more basic and practical solutions to solve river rescue situations including team wading to create a downstream eddy to assist with rescue and safe-wading skills to prevent foot entrapment, all passive techniques on the part of the victim. Courses also began to emphasize the need for active participation on the part of the victim, or potential victim. Self-rescue and aggressive swimming techniques were encouraged that would assist the swimmer using currents to ferry surf to reach an eddy to get to safety.

Rescue rodeos evolved playing off the original impetus behind cowboy rodeos: demonstrations of day-to-day skills and techniques. In 1991, the First Annual Nolichucky Rescue Rodeo was held, supported by American Whitewater and Western Carolina Paddlers. The rodeo was arranged around six events that included a rope throw for speed, accuracy, and technique; a self rescue incorporating a roll and a swim in Class II water; a team rescue in Class II; an equipment round-up in which teams scrambled to recover equipment dropped into the river from upstream; a rescue scenario in which the team encountered a victim of a common river accident playing a scripted role; and a first aid scenario in which the team demonstrated their mastery of skills similar to those taught in American Red Cross CPR and Advanced First Aid classes.

While river rescue in America developed as a result of accidents and fatalities in the late '70s and early '80s, European river-rescue developed independently with their own experience with accidents and fatalities. During the '80s, the European paddling community experienced an increasing numbers of accidents and fatalities as European paddlers pushed the limits of Class V-VI rivers, including fatalities among their expert paddlers. The European paddling community was rocked when eight kayaking fatalities occurred on Corsican rivers in a single two-week period. The result was an evaluation and the development of effective rescue techniques and gear by the leading European paddling club, the Alpine Kayak Club, which, in the process, transformed itself into a leader in boating safety without backing off on the difficulty of water paddled. In 1990, American paddlers involved in safety and river rescue saw for themselves European rescue techniques and gear in action at a river rescue symposium organized by Slim Ray and hosted by NOC with funding support by Perception. The symposium was well represented by river rescue experts from Australia, Austria, Britain, New Zealand, Russia, Norway, Germany, Switzerland, Japan, Canada, and France.

THE KEYHOLE COCKPIT DESIGN was the result of greater numbers of vertical pins on the steep vertical descents of the European rivers being explored during the '80s. The cockpit was designed to allow the paddler, while remaining seated, to remove his knees from the thigh supports and step out of the hull using the rim. Combined with a stern painter, this system allowed a paddler to extricate himself from a vertical pin.

IN 1992, the first American-made rescue PFD, the Max PFD System by Stohlquist, was introduced to the market. It was considered one of the biggest breakthroughs in years. The Max PFD System borrowed from European PFDs with additional improvements. It was a basic PFD with a quick-release belt harness, a retractable tow tether, and a self-storing throw bag. The latter two items, the tow line and small carabiner rated at 400 pounds, were designed to break should the paddler get into trouble during a rescue. (Jim Stohlquist, founder of CKS, Colorado Kayak Supply, developed paddling clothing in the mid-'80s under the Stohlquist company name.)

Rescue techniques used in Britain, Germany, and Austria were displayed. These techniques were well developed, borrowed heavily from climbing techniques, and were far more sophisticated than those currently used in American river rescue courses. Also presented were European boats and equipment that incorporated many of the newly developed ideas to increase the safety of the equipment and assist in river rescue itself. Safety equipment included face shields for helmets and PFDs designed as rescue life jackets with quick-release harnesses. The benefits of the keyhole cockpit, widely used in European kayaks, were also demonstrated.

However, because of differences between European and American approaches towards liability, American manufacturers did not immediately adopt many of the safety features of equipment already available from European manufacturers. This was particularly true regarding keyhole cockpits and bulkhead footbraces. Perception, the leading American manufacturer, came out with a compromise for their kayaks: a bulkhead footbrace kit to give the best of both systems. However, even though the kit provided a compromise, it still did not completely fix what some considered the problem with American rotationally molded kayaks, the need for walls to provide rigid structural support. The keyhole cockpit design with its bulkhead footbrace allowed a platform with an unrestricted area within the cockpit to allow a pinned paddler to step out onto the rim. The cockpit area of American rotationally molded kayaks was still restricted because of its reliance on internal wall support.

The European view toward liability was that of individual responsibility. The risk taker took full responsibility for his or her actions and was prepared to pay the consequences. In contrast, the American view toward liability often placed the responsibility back on the equipment manufacturer. In response to this view, a draft of the Paddle Safety Warning Label was introduced to paddlesport manufacturers at the 1991 *Outdoor Retailer* Show. The warning label, written with the assistance of John D'Orazio, an Atlanta attorney and friend of Bill Masters, was an attempt to limit charges of negligence and "Failure to Inform" which was the basis of most lawsuits in the country (outside of paddlesports). In 1992, Perception/Aquaterra began installing them on all their boats, including whitewater. This created a great deal of discussion among other boat manufacturers regarding the implications of a manufacturer not installing it when it was already in use by the leading manufacturer. In other words, it was worse not install it than to install it. As a result, the warning label became widely used by paddlesport boat manufacturers.

Accidents

There were fewer fatalities in 1991 than the previous year. However, fatalities in 1992 increased with the deaths of fifteen novice and expert paddlers. The high toll was attributed to a wet spring in the Southeast, late and heavy spring and summer rains in the Northeast, and record rains in Texas. At the same time, a drought in the West curtailed fatalities and accidents. The increase in deaths due to high water supported an accident study made the previous year. Walbridge wrote:

> Until the 80's one reported death per year was the norm; some years there were none. By the mid-eighties I began to expect several fatal accidents each year; as we enter the 90's we're creeping into double figures... The increasing number of paddlers can account for some, but not all, of this increase. With growth has come more river knowledge, better equipment, and improved paddling skills. The increased difficulty of the rivers being attempted probably plays some role; places which were once the exclusive playground of elite experts are now being visited by boaters of average ability... But the biggest change in the past ten to fifteen years has to do with the casual approach that many of us take to river running. This is especially true of high-water runs... Few people had run the tougher rivers more than once or twice before, so each run was like an exploratory. Eddy scouting was a new and radical concept then, we exchanged leads constantly, moving from eddy to eddy and side to side, probing the river. Regular slalom racing taught us a lot about paddling precisely; we learned to read the water and to run no drop blind. Major drops were scouted and treated with respect; people frequently carried. We were pioneers of a sort, and pioneers learn to be very careful. Times change... Freewheeling modern paddlers, armed with precise knowledge of rapids and water levels, often lose some of the respect which characterized our runs. This more casual attitude can result in a let-down in the wrong place, permitting those small mistakes that lead to serious trouble. The rapids aren't any easier than what I encountered in the 70's, and although gear and knowledge has improved, the consequences of error remain. And while we thought we were going to die when we messed up, nowadays the chance of serious injury or death in rapids considered extreme or dangerous is much higher... And no matter how much fun you're having, never ever forget what you are dealing with.[55]

Slim Ray, co-author of *River Rescue* and a leader in river rescue, was the victim of an accident on Sunshine Falls on the Green River Narrows in North Carolina that left him without the use of his legs. Fortunately, heroic efforts on the part of his fellow paddlers, all with considerable river-rescue experience and expertise, prevented the accident from becoming a fatality.

In 1993, American Whitewater studied fatalities over the previous decade and found that the top three killers of experienced whitewater paddlers were Pins (25 percent), Long Swims (25 percent), and Swimming into Entrapments (15 percent). Fatalities over the last decade showed California with the greatest number of paddling fatalities at thirteen, followed by West Virginia at twelve, Colorado at ten, and British Columbia, Idaho and New York, all with nine. The next closest was Pennsylvania with six. The rest of the twenty states had one and two fatalities each. By river, the Arkansas in Colorado had five, as

ONE FATALITY that defied common logic was that of Jessie Sharp. In 1990, Sharp paddled over Niagara Falls in his C-1 convinced he could run the falls successfully. He wore no helmet or PFD and was so sure of his attempt, that he left his car downstream and had dinner reservations for the evening. His run was witnessed by a few of his friends (?) and hundreds of tourists. "He twirled his paddle confidently as he went over the lip, but below there his 'run' fell apart. The drop was so huge that he could not hope to launch himself clear of the falling water as is done on smaller falls. His bow caught the water below, causing him to pitchpole end for end until he hit the bottom. His paddle appeared fifteen minutes later; his boat took an hour to surface."[56] His body was never found.

Because of his bizarre behavior, Sharp became a legend and a myth evolved around him for a few years after his death. "Jesse Lives" was found painted on outhouses, bridges, and rocks at rivers around the country. Tails of his appearance at different rivers followed the same folklore as Elvis sightings. The term "Jesse" also became known as "valiant, albeit misguided attempts to paddle the impossible."[57]

[55] Walbridge, Charlie. "Changes in Attitudes." *American Whitewater* Vol. XXXVIII No. 2 (March/April 1993): 36–39.

[56] Walbridge, Charlie (Safety). "New York Suffers Four Whitewater Deaths." *American Whitewater* Vol. XXXV No. 4 (July/August 1990): 27.

[57] Garrison, Carla. End Notes. "Carla's Glossary." *American Whitewater* Vol. XXXVIII No. 4 (July/August 1993): 42.

did the Chilco in British Columbia. The Gauley in West Virginia had four, and the Chattooga Section IV in Georgia, Squamish in British Columbia, and North Fork of American in California all had three each.

American Whitewater was always a medium to disseminate information to paddlers and to share river experiences, and it's dependence upon volunteer writers to submit articles for publication often reflected trends in the whitewater community. In the '90s, *American Whitewater* reflected a growing laxness in safety and judgement in the articles submitted for publication. Even Bob Gedekoh, Editor, noted the increased laxness:

> As for the failure of our authors to address safety issues, I think this reflects a problematic attitude in the paddling community at large. In many circles it seems that expressing concern regarding safety has become decidedly "uncool." There is not just a disregard for river safety among these people, there is an open disdain for it. This seems to be particularly the case with the younger generation of 'would be' hair boaters and creekers.[58]

Fatalities continued to increase every year through 1996. Although some attributed the increase to a laxness in safety and judgement, analysis of the fatalities showed that "most of the kayaking fatalities involved skilled paddler(s) in difficult water. Often there was no clear mistake made; the 'objective,' or random danger of whitewater was responsible."[59]

However, 1997 proved to be the worst in history, claiming nineteen lives, including those of acknowledged expert paddlers. Dugald Bremner, photographer and expert paddler, died on the Silver Fork of the American in California. Three other companions portaged the Class V drop he chose to run. Bremner's kayak was pulled stern first into an unseen crack at the top of a 15-foot waterfall and was wedged with just 18 inches of the bow showing. Chuck Kern, Perception's western technical rep and member of the U.S. Rodeo Team, drowned on the Black Canyon of the Gunnison on a drop that many portage. Kern bow-pinned under a slab of rock. Rich Weiss, an Olympic slalom racer and U.S. Team member, died on Class V water on the White Salmon River in Washington at Big Brother, a 30-foot waterfall rapid (2-foot lead-in drop followed by 27-foot vertical falls), while preparing for the Gorge extreme race. Joel Hawthorn, another expert paddler, died during the first descent of Warren Creek in Idaho. Scott Hassan, a longtime Class V kayaker, drowned in a drain-type sieve on the Meadow in West Virginia, a river he had run more than thirty times before. Todd Smith, another well-known Eastern paddler, died on Possum Creek in West Virginia.

Some might point to the use of inappropriate boats and equipment as a cause for the increasing fatalities, but that was not often the case. Weiss was in a Whiplash and Bremner in a Freefall, while still others used creek-type boats for the Class V runs. The argument that boats have advanced beyond the skill level of the paddler was also not valid since many of the victims were truly experts with a lot of Class V+ notches on their belts.

Coincidentally during the same time, other extreme-dangerous sports also experienced fatalities among their experts. In 1995, expert/pro surfer Donnie Solomon drowned while surfing followed in 1997 by surfer Todd Chesser.

[58] Gedekoh, Bob. Forum. *American Whitewater* Vol. XXXVI No. 4 (July/August 1996): 5.

[59] Walbridge, Charlie. "1996 River Accident Report." *American Whitewater* Vol. XXXVI No. 5 (September/October 1996): 29, 31, 33–34.

Fatalities also occurred in mountain climbing. In 1995, Rob Slater and female climber Alison Hargreaves were killed while climbing. In 1996, Rob Hall and Scott Fischer died followed by Allan Bard in 1997.

Walbridge wrote of the 1997 whitewater accidents,

> During the past few years an unsettling number of expert paddlers have been killed attempting difficult rapids. The only "cause" of these deaths is the demanding nature of difficult Class V drops, which are brutally intolerant of errors in water reading, boat handling, and judgement... Like the European experts who pursued the sport with similar intensity decades before we did, they sometimes die... Both the least experienced and the most skilled and daring paddlers are at risk, creating a "reverse bell curve" that has serious implications for high-level paddlers. [60]

While 1997 was the worst for fatalities in the history of American whitewater, 1998 proved to be even worse with twenty-five fatalities including six outside North America, two during expeditions. Five fatalities involved well-known expert paddlers on Class V water. Pablo Perez, a steep creekboater and rodeo competitor on Dagger's Team D, died on the Rocky Broad River in North Carolina. Doug Gordon, an accomplished paddler and former member of the U.S. Whitewater Team, died on an expedition sponsored by National Geographic and Malden Mills on the first descent of the gorge of the Tsangpo River in Tibet.

Tim Gavin, another extreme boater, died on the Upper Blackwater in West Virginia. American Whitewater's report of Gavin's death expressed what many felt about the deaths of so many expert paddlers:

> While many who knew Gavin were not surprised that he perished in a kayaking accident, the circumstances surrounding his death have left his friends puzzled and shaken... While Gavin was known to be a daring risk taker, no one could have foretold that he would die paddling a river that he knew well, at a low to moderate level, on a warm, sunny spring day in the company of a close friend—who is also an accomplished steep creeker. [61]

Nathan Vernon, a competitor at the Third Annual Dowd Chute Shootout on the Eagle River in Colorado (and sponsored by Jeep as part of the Jeep Whitewater Festival) drowned during the competition. The tag line for the event "Winners will be rewarded; losers will be resuscitated" proved all too ominous.

In 1998, the first kayaking fatality for Great Falls on the Potomac occurred (although twenty-nine people, all non-paddlers, had died at the falls since 1975). Scott Bristow, a well-known contributor to rec.boats.paddle, died running Great Falls on a fall Saturday afternoon with many spectators looking on. Although Great Falls had been successfully run by a few expert paddlers since the '70s, increasing numbers of paddlers running the falls prompted guidelines to ensure continued access to the falls. In 1986, the U.S. Park Service set up voluntary guidelines for running the falls that limited group size (for safety so that follow-the-leader was more controlled) and imposed time of day/week day restrictions (for lower public profile). In September 1989, NPS posted an announcement banning access to the falls across park land. The ban was rescinded after CCA protested NPS's legal and jurisdictional grounds for the

[60] Walbridge, Charlie. "Difficult Rivers Claim Expert Paddlers." *American Whitewater* Vol. XXXVII No. 5 (September/October 1997): 82–83.

[61] AWA staff. "Extreme Paddler Dies on Upper Blackwater." *American Whitewater* Vol. XXXVIII No. 3 (May/June 1998): 75–76.

ban. Bristow's death prompted welcomed and renewed dialogue between paddlers and local officials regarding issues surrounding the use of the area for paddling.

Summary of the U.S. Park Services' new voluntary guidelines in 1999:

> Boaters should avoid running Great Falls when visitation in the park is high. Morning runs are best. If you must go later in the day, go in a group no larger than four (4) and finish quickly. Never go in a large group, spend excessive time scouting, or carry back up for repeat runs when the park is crowded. Know the hazards of this Class V+ rapid before deciding to run it. Be aware that some of the dangers are not evident, even after careful scouting. And please do your part to protect access to this tremendous resource.[62]

Although only eighteen deaths (one fewer than in 1997) occurred in 1999, the fatality trend continued to include deaths of expert and skilled paddlers in kayaks while canoeing and rafting deaths were often associated with less experienced paddlers. In 1999, American Whitewater added River Safety as one of its Top 40 issues, a departure from the river conservation issues that were the basis for the Top 40. While data indicated that the sport was safer than ever for more conservative river runs despite the growing numbers of paddlers, it was the sport's experts that continued to die.

Cheslatta River (BC, Canada), 2000—courtesy of Dustin Knapp.

As reports of deaths and obituaries mounted in *American Whitewater* and rec.boats.paddle, the paddling community responded. Articles and editorials were written and published in *Canoe & Kayak* and *American Whitewater* and on various websites. Cautions, almost pleadings, were written by concerned paddlers as "Letters to the Editor" or posted on rec.boats.paddle and rec.boats.paddle.whitewater.

[62] AWA staff. "Boater Etiquette: Great Falls of the Potomac." *American Whitewater* Vol. XXXIX No. 3 (May/June 1999): 28–30.

Jonathon Katz, a regular contributor of humor to *American Whitewater* wrote:

> Never forget: whitewater boating is an open-ended sport, like rock climbing. There are always steeper, trashier rivers. 200 feet per mile isn't extreme anymore; the only limit is what you can get down and live to tell about. To get credit for a first descent you only have to be alive at the bottom... There's a difference between mountaineering and kayaking. If I set out tomorrow to climb Everest, the labor of the trek and the ever-increasing altitude would chew me up and spit me out. I'd fail and go home before I ever saw base camp. But I have some cash and a good car, and if I set out tomorrow there is absolutely nothing that would stop me from putting in at the top of the Narrows of the Green. Nothing except the quality of what's between my ears... The point? The only limits to our ability to put on at the top of rivers are those we impose on ourselves. And it just might be that at the top end of this sport, people are taking too many risks. Perhaps there are some hard rivers that should be paddled a little less. And perhaps there there are some that shouldn't be paddled at all. Maybe, just maybe, its time for the paddling community to back off just a little. Our parents call it discipline, and maybe we need some.[63]

Rich Kulawiec wrote:

> Let me start by saying that I really don't want to tell anybody what to run and what not to run. I can only make the decision for myself... But please, please, please folks: think carefully about your motivations and think about the consequences of your decisions. I'm not asking you to stay home: I'm asking you to THINK first... I'm growing tired of mourning my friends and heroes, including the ones that I never had a chance to meet. Yes, I recognize that some of that is part of the sport; always has been, always will be. But over the last few years– for whatever reason—it seems to me that we have lost a certain measure of respect for the river. We are now ALL paying the price for that. It's just not necessary.[64]

In 2000, the total number of fatalities for canoeing, kayaking, and rafting remained high at forty-nine for the year. Seventeen were kayak deaths with the greatest risk for inexperienced and very experienced paddlers in Class V water. Two well known Class V stretches, the Green in North Carolina and Gore Canyon in Colorado, claimed their first fatalities. Gore Canyon claimed two paddlers in two days.

[63] Katz, Jonathan. Letters. *American Whitewater* Vol. XXXVIII No. 4 (July/August 1998): 12–13.

[64] Kulawiec, Rich. Letters. *American Whitewater* Vol. XXXIX No. 2 (March/April 1999): 11.

ONLY TIME WILL TELL whether the pleadings to "don't do hard runs because everyone else is doing them," "don't paddle hard runs on an off day," "don't assume that just because you managed to get through something in one piece that you've mastered it can move on and up," and "please take into account the fact that your paddling companions (and other people on the river who don't even know you) will try to come after you if you screw up, putting themselves at risk on your behalf"[65] will affect paddler's decisions and reduce the mounting death toll, or whether new regulations and restrictions will be imposed in an effort to do so.

STRATEGIES using the Wild and Scenic Rivers Act of 1968 for river conservation battles evolved from its inception. Successes and failures of the different strategies during the '80s helped to hone American Whitewater's use of the Act in the '90s. In 1991, Pope Barrow, past ACA and American Whitewater Conservation Chairman, wrote of the Act:

> The Wild and Scenic Rivers Act is the Snow White of river conservation. It can be a beautiful thing. It has probably stopped the construction of more unwise dams and saved more rivers than anything else. The Federal Wild and Scenic Rivers Act is so essential to river conservation that most river protection organizations consider the care and feeding ot the wild and scenic rivers system to be ther Number 1 mission in life.

But he went on to say that it was not enough; it was not the only solution,

> There are currently at least 7 other river conservation techniques currently in use- or being tried. At first blush, these "7 dwarfs" seem a lot less attractive to river conservation buffs than Snow White, but sometimes they can do the job that the Wild and Scenic Rivers Act cannot do. The 7 dwarfs of river conservation are (1) rear guard litigation, (2) State designation, (3) State-managed Federal designation, (4) national recreation area status, (5) permanent wild and scenic studies, (6) bullet bills, and (7) Clean Water Act bans.[66]

[65] Kulawiec, Rich. Letters. *American Whitewater* Vol. XXXIX No. 2 (March/April 1999): 11.

[66] Barrow, Pope. "Wild and Scenic is not the *Only* Solution." *American Whitewater* Vol. XXXVI No. 1 (January/February 1991): 8–11.

Conservation

With successes in the '80s regarding river access and preservation from hydroprojects, American Whitewater, along with other national conservation organizations and local grass-root organizations, further joined forces in various river-preservation projects. ACA also entered into the fray in the '90s with their own conservation efforts and strategies that were very different from those of American Whitewater. ACA's conservation efforts targeted all recreational waters, not just whitewater, using the Clean Water Act as its focus and common denominator for all the recreational paddling activities.

In 1993, ACA created a position, Coordinator for Conservation and Public Policy, for their new conservation initiative. Their entry into conservation joined efforts with organizations such as American Whitewater, American Rivers, and the River Network, and began with two initiatives. ACA's Paddle Free Program was designed to provide a coordinated support network to respond to local threats across the country. Their Finlandia Clean Water Fund provided grants to local groups in support of river and waterway conservation efforts.

ACA worked with Champion International to clean up the Pigeon River in North Carolina and Tennessee, polluted by Champion's Canton, North Carolina, mill which was the object of controversy regarding their sponsorship of the slalom race series. In December 1997, a landmark agreement was reached regarding pollution of the Pigeon. ACA, Tennessee Environmental Council (TEC), the Clean Water Fund of North Carolina, the Dead Pigeon River Council, and a number of other partners fought the re-permit of Champion's Canton paper mill for pollution discharge, which had expired in 1994. The new agreement imposed tougher new standards. Shortly after the agreement was reached, Champion announced its plans to sell the facility. Any buyer was bound to the new and tighter requirements and standards.

The Pigeon River success supported ACA's strategy which furthered their efforts on other waterways, including taking on Westvaco, another pulp and paper company, with a facility on the Upper Potomac downstream from the confluence of North Branch and Savage. Where necessary, ACA entered legal battles in taking companies to court to enforce compliance with the Clean Water Act.

American Whitewater continued to remain the sole proponent focusing on issues affecting whitewater exclusively. In 1993, American Whitewater refined their conservation program into three project areas: River Defense,

River Conservation, and River Access. With other environmental and conservation groups recognizing the problems associated with hydropower development, American Whitewater was able to shift some of their attention to access issues. River Defense, which focused on hydropower development and which was the predominant piece in the '80s, was surpassed by River Access.

During the '90s successes of organized efforts by coalitions of similarly interested groups for whitewater access and releases included the Tallulah Gorge in Georgia, La Grande Canyon on the Nisqually in Washington, and Deerfield watershed in New England.

In 1913, water running through the Tallulah Gorge was rerouted for power generation for Atlanta. In 1991, Georgia Power filed for a new license, which affected the de-watered Tallulah Gorge. American Rivers, Georgia Canoeing Association, Atlanta Whitewater Club, America Outdoors, and American Whitewater joined forces to intervene in the future of the Gorge. The Gorge is unusual in that it drops 650 feet in the first half mile and has waterfalls such as Tempesta at 76 feet, Hurricane at 96 feet, Oceana at 50 feet, and Bridal Veil at 17 feet, most of which are runnable. American Whitewater requested whitewater studies of the Gorge. For two days in late May 1993, water was returned to the Gorge for a run by ten boaters representing all of the interested parties. Although a short run, the 1.8 mile run proved that it was a fantastic continuous Class IV run which included a Class V run of Oceana Falls, a 50-foot-long sloping falls about 150 to 200 feet in length with an optimal level of about 750 cfs. The results of the study also showed that the stretch was for more than just an expert-only run, which was the widely held opinion of non-paddlers. A five-year effort resulted in the first recreational releases in November 1997 based on a Memorandum of Understanding worked out between all the interested parties. Due to the fragile nature of the area, access was limited to 120 boaters per day; hikers and climbers were limited to 100 per day.

In 1994, efforts to gain access to LaGrande Canyon on the Nisqually River in Washington by American Whitewater resulted in access to the canyon to study it as a recreational site. Eleven boaters ran the canyon at two different release levels, 800 cfs and 1,000 cfs, and found it a premier whitewater run "with its magnificent canyon walls and exquisite scenery."[67] The first recreational releases took place in November and December 1998.

Around the same time that efforts were made to access the Tallulah and Nisqually Rivers for recreational releases, a settlement was reached with New England Power Company (NEPCO) regarding the protection of the Deerfield River watershed. The Settlement Agreement, reached in October 1994, was the culmination of a five-year effort of local, state, and regional federal agencies, NEPCO, and the conservation efforts of the Appalachian Mountain Club, American Whitewater, Conservation Law Foundation, Friends for the Liberation of Whitewater (FLOW), and Trout Unlimited. The Settlement Agreement included recreational whitewater releases, free access to all non-developed river resources and non-developed project lands, minimum flows for aquatic life and other fish passage, and wildlife enhancements to both the river and its surrounding lands. Recreational releases were provided on the

American Whitewater expanded their efforts beyond domestic conservation issues. The Bio Bio in Chile was one of the first rivers to gain attention by American paddlers. In 1991, American Whitewater joined forces with other groups to form River Conservation International (RCI) to save rivers world wide. In 1994, RCI merged with International Rivers Network (IRN) to provide more assistance to other organizations around the world fighting river development battles.

In 1994, the rejuvenated River Council of Washington (formerly the Northwest Rivers Council) established itself like other statewide groups in New York, Idaho, and West Virginia, "to create a mutually supportive network of 62 watershed communities that invests the social and political will of local people in a sustainable relationship with their natural ecosystem."[68]

67 Deckert, Mike. "Boof and Boogie." *American Whitewater* (September/October 1994): 21.

68 AWA staff. Access. "New Watershed Program Underway in Washington State." *American Whitewater* Vol. XXXIV No. 2 (March/April 1994): 28.

IN 1990, Eastern Professional River Outfitters and the Western River Guides Association merged to create American Outdoors, representing over 150 river outfitters and 35 manufacturers and suppliers to the outfitting industry. As a national organization of professional river outfitters, AO also became involved in conservation issues, particularly water flow and river access. However, because of the commercial nature of its members, it was sometimes at odds with other conservation organizations.

once de-watered Monroe Bridge section (Class III-IV) thirty-two weekends a year, and on the Fife Brook Section (Class II-III) one hundred and seven days a year.

Coalitions were also formed to provide funding for conservation efforts. In the early '90s, industry support expanded beyond individual corporate funding to specific organizations to the establishment of funding organizations that provided grants to various efforts. The Outdoor Industry Conservation Alliance, which included REI, Northface, Patagonia, and Kelty as its early members, committed funding to the alliance. Eventually, almost twenty-five outdoor companies donated $10,000 each to the alliance which was re-distributed as one-time grants to support grass roots efforts across the country. In the mid-'90s, ACA joined forces with the Bluegrass Wildwater Association and American Whitewater to co-sponsor the annual National Paddling Film Festival, the proceeds of which were used for conservation efforts.

In the '90s hydro project development battles continued, particularly for those projects that were involved in on-going licensing and re-licensing, and particularly in California. In spite of lessons learned from the New Melones Dam on the Stanislaus during the '80s and '90s regarding whitewater and the economic benefits to the local economy, the battle continued for the multi-purpose Auburn Dam. However, those same lessons, including public awareness and the influence of the paddling public as on the Tallulah and Nisqually Rivers were heeded to. But not without effort, especially in the re-licensing of two dams, the Rock Creek-Cresta project, on the North Fork of the Feather licensed by Pacific Gas & Electric (PG&E). Sections of the North Fork of the Feather again saw water in de-watered stretches (since the mid-'60s) in a controlled flow study in June of 1999. The sections on the North Fork of the Feather included the Class III / IV Rogers Flat section, the Class V Tobin section, and the Class IV Cresta section. The results of the study were the foundation for negotiating a schedule of annual releases in the new FERC license.

The war against the New Melones Dam on the Stanislaus was waged for most of fourteen years before the Camp Nine Section of the Stanislaus was lost in 1982 to rising water. Although tourism benefits of the reservoir the dam created were touted, neither the power boaters nor tourists flocked to it. Economic benefits were further lost when the dam proved more expensive to build than anticipated. This made its water overpriced and not much was sold for agricultural use.

However, the Camp Nine Section resurfaced, so to speak, because of drought in 1990. The local economy got a bigger boost during that summer than had been seen with the filled reservoir. Local paddlers as well as raft outfitters quickly took advantage of the re-surfaced river.

Unfortunately, in spite of lessons learned from the New Melones Dam, the multi-purpose Auburn Dam designed for the American River just wouldn't go away although it had the same potential economic problems. The dam threatened the North Fork and Middle Fork directly, and the South Fork indirectly. In 1992, 130,000 boated the South Fork and generated $30 million in local business. Estimates of up to 30 percent of that business would be affected by the loss of the North and Middle Fork runs. Coincidentally, the Auburn Dam was set to become the most expensive dam in history, likely to exceed $2 billion.

In 1996, Congress (again) defeated funding for the dam and instead approved money to improve levees downstream on the Sacramento and American for flood protection. This was still not the end. Congressman Doolittle, a Republican representative from California, vowed to continue to fight every single year for appropriations for the dam. Another Republican congressman from Wisconsin, Thomas Petri, drafted the shortest and most direct bill to come before congress titled "A bill to protect US taxpayers by preventing construction of a dam on the American River at Auburn, California." The bill had two provisions: "to ensure no funds given to Crop or Bureau of Reclamation for the project and that in the event that increased levels of flood protection were necessary, more efficient and cost effective projects would be proposed as preferred alternatives."[69] Supporters got behind both Petri and Doolittle in their opposing stands and so the battle waged on.

A few hydropower projects were also ultimately defeated, including the projects that threatened the North Fork of the Payette in Idaho. In 1990, the state of Idaho recognized the recreational and scenic value of protecting the river and finally banned future hydropower dams on the Payette River system, hoping the state's ban would be honored by FERC. Unfortunately, for a time, this did not seem to be the case. In 1993, the Gem Irrigation District with the permit holder, Western Power Inc., tried to take advantage of the fact that FERC still retained control of federal hydropower licensing and proposed a new project that would have destroyed the North Fork of the Payette for many recreational purposes. The project never received the federal permit to construct a dam and in the fall of 1999, the GEM project was officially declared dead when GEM withdrew their water rights application. The application had been grandfathered in with the Idaho Comprehensive State Water Plan in 1991 that would have protected the river, had the water rights application not been filed previously. With the withdrawal of the application, the North Fork of the Payette was saved from future projects.

FERC itself complicated the battles for a time when in 1991 it attempted to get around requiring recreational consideration for licenses by redefining some rivers, previously considered navigable, as unnavigable therefore releasing the rivers from federal licensing. This decision and interpretation was handed down concerning the Upper Yough in Maryland, long used for commercial rafting. The Upper Yough was deemed too rough and did not fit the strictest interpretation of being a water highway used in interstate commerce.

However, while FERC sent mixed messages, another player in dam construction projects, the Bureau of Land Management (BLM), changed its position. In November 1993, a conference sponsored by American Rivers, Inc., and co-sponsored by seven federal agencies was held to review national river policy and shape future direction for river protection. The time was appropriate to celebrate the 25th anniversary of the National Wild and Scenic Rivers Act. The conference was supported and attended by American Rivers Management Society, ACA, River Watch Network, REI, and National Audubon Society among others. At the conference, Dan Glaser of BLM in Denver indicated a fundamental change when he said that BLM

THE SEVEN FEDERAL AGENCIES sponsoring the conservation conference in 1993 were the National Park Service Rivers, Trails and Conservation Assistance Program, U.S. Forest Service, Bureau of Land Management, U.S. EPA, Bureau of Reclamation, and U.S. Fish and Wildlife Service.

[69] AWA editors. "Auburn Dam." *American Whitewater* Vol. XXXVI No. 2 (March/April 1996): 12.

was "out of the dam building business and into restoration. We will now use our engineering skills to manage the resources... breaching is now a consideration."[70]

In 1993, FERC also joined the dialogue and viewed decommissioning as an alternative to re-licensing to restore ecosystems and fisheries. Talks began in earnest regarding the Elwha Dam in Washington and the Edwards Dam on the Kennebec in Maine to restore salmon runs. In 1999, the Edwards Dam was removed. PacifiCorp signed a voluntary removal agreement the same year for the removal of the Condit Dam on the White Salmon River in southeast Washington for recreational and fishery benefits. The agreement was the outcome of over two years of talks between PacifiCorp and state and federal agencies including American Whitewater and thirteen other environmental groups.

While river preservation and conservation strategies focused on dam prevention and removal successes, another twist began to develop in the '90s: stream bed modification for safety and economic considerations. While not new, particularly in the West (Rapids on the Rogue River were dynamited many years ago to allow safer passage for tourism, fishing), the twist posed serious dilemmas for some organizations, sometimes positioning often-time allies against one another. During the '90s, both regulated and un-regulated, without agency approval, stream bed modifications occurred.

The most prominent regulated stream bed modification for economic reasons was the Ocoee site for the '96 Olympic slalom venue. In 1991, the state of Tennessee determined that the estimated $10 to 15 million needed to host the event and build the facilities would generate over $60 million in revenue over five years. Studies of the project also determined minimal impact to the area's natural resources.

In contrast, the most prominent unregulated stream bed modification for safety reasons occurred in 1993, the dynamiting of Quartzite Falls on Arizona's Salt River. The man behind it was William "Ken" Stoner who said he did it because it was a safety hazard, people had been killed there. Others thought he did it to eliminate congestion problems associated with the mandatory portage of the falls. Regardless of the motivation, Stoner and his accomplices were jailed for this un-regulated modification. However, the river was un-naturally changed forever.

Other stream bed modifications were proposed for public safety. The family of a paddler who drowned in Left Crack on Section IV of the Chattooga requested either modifications to Left Crack or the imposition of a mandatory portage which would create problems of its own. Because of the Chattooga's Wild and Scenic designation, no modifications were made. A similar situation occurred in 2000 when a young woman, part of a private party in rented duckies, drowned at Dimple Rock on the Lower Yough, the victim of entrapment in a cavern at the base of Dimple. The resolution has yet to be determined.

Access issues continued to grow, particularly with increasing numbers of whitewater paddlers. While permit requirements were common in the West, other access issues also arose in the East. In the early '90s, paddlers were arrested in Texas, Colorado, New York, and Washington in defiant trespass

[70] Stuhaug, Dennis. "America's Rivers: Promise of a More Protected Future." *Canoe & Kayak* Vol. 22 No. 1 (March 1994): 11.

for crossing private property to access rivers. In 1993, with increasing issues around access, American Whitewater recognized it as the "number one river issue" and added it to its purposes along with safety, conservation, and events. American Whitewater immediately targeted access issues involving the Lower Yough, the Kennebec, the Genessee River through Letchworth State Park in New York, and a number of small creeks in Georgia.

In 1993, American Whitewater issued their general policy statement regarding Critical Access Issues that fell into two categories: Governmental Limits on River Access and Private Limits on River Access. Altogether, there were seven separate issues:

1. Fees for Access to Rivers
2. Limits to Control Carrying Capacity and Allocate Use Among Different Groups
3. Limits to Access for Safety or to Avoid Liability
4. Access to Whitewater Affected by Water Projects
5. Bans on River Access for Environmental Protection
6. Access Points on Private Land
7. The Right to Boat on Streams Through Private Lands. [71]

Access issues were found across the country. By the mid-'90s, at least fifty rivers required permits for private boaters, mostly in the West. In 1993, a fee system was proposed for the South Fork of the American by the county's Parks and Recreation Division, under the direction of the County Board of Supervisors. The reasons were that private boaters should share in the expenses to maintain the county's services and improvements for paddlers as well as attempting to control the number of illegal "pirate" raft trips that didn't pay as the commercial trips must. In 1995, Central Maine Power, who began collecting a head fee in 1983 for rafters on the Kennebec, also started collecting a $1 fee from private boaters. CMP owned the dam at the entrance and the land at the put-in and collected the fee for maintaining facilities used by paddlers. For rafters, the fee was up to $6 per head which was included in the cost to run the river by commercial outfitters. An estimated 30,000 rafters were taken down the river annually.

Perhaps the most blatant access issue in the East, and the only one in the East that required permits for paddlers, was associated with the Lower Yough in Pennsylvania. In 1990, Ohiopyle State Park instituted a telephone reservation system for launch permits for hardboaters. Allocations remained at just 192 boaters or 10 percent of the total number of users. Two years later, Pennsylvania's Bureau of State Parks instituted a use fee of $2.50 for all private boaters, paddlers and private rafters, in addition to the $1.50 fee already required to purchase a ride on the mandatory takeout shuttle. [*Author's note:* Unless you want to walk up the half mile hill to the parking lot at the take out, you ride the shuttle]. The fee system was originally intended for use on the Yough, Lehigh, and Slippery Rock, although the State Park at the Yough was the only one to implement it. The fee was ostensibly used for the new reservation system and other services. The problem was that many of the other services were free to non-boaters. The park then claimed it was strictly for the reservation system, although boaters who did not get an advance reservation, but merely showed up to paddle, were also charged the same reservation fee. Of course, boaters objected.

[71] AWA staff. "Public Access to Rivers and Streams for Recreational Rivers." *American Whitewater* Vol. XXXVIII No. 2 (March/April 1993): 43–59.

Charging boaters and no-one else who used park services was a dangerous precedent, one that many boaters feared might spread across the country as other states looked for a way to fund maintenance of park services such as rest rooms, picnic areas, and hiking trails. Boaters were clearly singled out. On Saturday May 23, a protest was staged by paddling clubs from Pennsylvania and surrounding states that regularly paddled the Lower Yough for club trips.

On the day of the protest, picketers carrying signs appeared in town. The plan included a demonstration to continue until 3:00 p.m. at which time the picketers staged a mass put-in to circumvent the fees. However, park rangers invented new rules that day and at 3:00, the time after which a reservation was not required, when boaters approached the put-in, they were required to sign-in (new rule number one), and then were restricted to only fifteen boaters per half hour (new rule number two). Unfortunately, there were also other unnecessary instances of ranger official abuse of power, reminiscent of the protests of the '60s (before some of the boaters and rangers were even born).

In the meantime, a coalition representing paddlers calling themselves "Friends of the Yough" (American Whitewater, Three Rivers Paddling Club, Keystone River Runners and other Pennsylvania paddlers) worked within the system to review the fees. In 1994, an interim agreement was finally reached after numerous meetings between American Whitewater, ACA, Friends of the Yough, and other commercial interests with officials from the State of Pennsylvania. The agreement allowed boaters an option of using the reservation system or a free, space-available basis on non-holiday weekends. Over the next couple of years, other kinks were worked out in the reservation/fee system.

While access issues continued to increase in the East, the permit systems in the West were crumbling under their own weight. By 2000, the waiting list for Grand Canyon permits was up to about 6,500 names, more than double the number just fifteen years before. At the current allocation levels, the wait for access amounted to at least twenty-four years. The National Park Service did little to alleviate the situation for private boater access although many organizations, including American Whitewater attempted to work with the Grand Canyon National Park since the late '70s to resolve ever increasing long-developing conflicts over the Private Boater Waiting List. The Colorado River Management Plan (CRMP) instituted in 1980 increased the number of private launches to 240 to reduce the then six year wait for private boaters. The plan was ineffective. Over the next twenty years, updates to the CRMP were mandated including additions that included a Wilderness Management Plan to maintain the wilderness experience in the use of the Colorado River and adjacent lands. Unfortunately, the decision by the Grand Canyon National Park Superintendent to curtail the planning process of the CRMP and the Wilderness Management Plan in early 2000 left interested parties with few alternatives but to file suits against the National Park Service. In July 2000, a suit was brought against the Secretary of the Interior, the National Park Service Director, and the Grand Canyon National Park Superintendent by the Grand Canyon Private Boaters Association, American Whitewater, and the National Parks Conservation Association along with individual plaintiffs. It was anticipated that the suit would take at least two years to settle. In the meantime, the waiting list to run the Colorado River through Grand Canyon continues to grow.

While river preservation, keeping rivers flowing free from dams or with water releases, was the main issue for river conservation beginning in the '50s through the '70s, the '80s and '90s brought access and congestion issues from the growth of the sport itself. By the late '90s, some paddlers actually welcomed a permit system on some rivers to reduce increasing congestion problems. Congestion was so bad on rivers like the Yough and Ocoee in the East and the Deschutes in the West with commercial and non-commercial raft trips that boaters had to wait to run drops. Rafts and paddlers often vied for the same routes and playspots. Tempers flared. Any thought of playing at certain spots was often considered almost suicidal.

Dave P. posted on rec.boats.paddle on May 17, 2000 about the Deschutes:

> The horrors I have seen. For example the "cowboy" themed paddle raft descending a Class IV drop sideways while engaged in a spirited bucket fight with the drunken "Pirate" themed oarboat. Usually a crowd gathers on the rocks near Oak Springs to cheer when people go overboard... I've never seen hardboat paddlers even trying to play the holes on the Deschutes in the Summer. As far as ettiquette goes—hoo boy. Ya know how an oarboat will generally row upstream while preparing for a big drop to get the line right? This is apparently the cue for paddle rafts behind to ram the slowpoke... But the amazing thing about all of this carnage is that hardly anyone seems to be getting hurt... It's too bad when it starts to make sense to think about limiting access to public resources like the Deschutes.[72]

The whitewater river experience was in serious jeopardy. In 1994, Matt McCloud wrote:

> The river experience, as it has been known, is in jeopardy when one is elbow to elbow with stressed and hostile boaters, dodging erratically controlled rafts guided by indifferent summer workers. Even further up the watershed where commerical organizations can only dream of predictable flows, many times the experience is tarnished by full eddies and paddles clashing both up and down stream. No longer can a boat be left unguarded on shuttle car racks or equipment in the bushes while hitching a ride for risk of ending up in a flea market. As every motorcyclist once acknowledged one another with raised hand, boaters passing on the highway increasingly view other boaters with the same decreasing affections as groups polarize. The popularity and the potential for professionalism in rodeo is growing, yet many good boaters are alienated admirers. The hole hawging numbers and manners of those that dedicate hours and hours of practice manage to piss off fellow paddlers with the same dedication... The early romance of boating seems to be surfing an exploding wave. Soiled, like many other treasures, by those that loved and would love it.[73]

[72] P., Dave. "Ocoee = East Coast's Deschutes?" *rec.boats.paddle* May 17, 2000: 2:58 pm.

[73] McCloud, Matt. "Change for the Worse." *American Whitewater* Vol. XXXIV No. 4 (July/August 1994): 10–11.

The Gauley

In the '90s, the Gauley continued to be a reflection of the changes in the Sport. The Gauley Festival continued to grow, replete with all the commercialism brought by rodeo gatherings. In 1993, the Gauley Festival Marketplace had more than one hundred exhibitors representing manufacturers across the country as well as retailers, video, and book publishers. Gauley season was imitated on other rivers during annual releases. The Gauley Festival was called the Mecca of the sport and paddlers from across the country flocked to Summersville.

Mike McCormick, Olympian slalom paddler, wrote:

> Whitewater has only one pilgrimage to speak of. It occurs every fall when thousands descend on a sheer-walled valley in West Virginia. Paddlers go for two things: a bracing run of the Gauley River and a folksy bash known as the Gauley River Festival... [It is] playboating with a vengeance. Their daring one-upmanship leaves folks gasping in disbelief. They being the whitewater "professionals" who travel to the Gauley from across the country... By the end of the weekend, most everyone who has run the Gauley has been changed to some extent. Many are more relaxed. Some are more confident. A few are more crazed. All are relieved. They are the same people as when they arrived, but their perspective on life has, for a short time at least, been pushed off center. Now that's a pilgrimage.[74]

THE SUMMERSVILLE DAM is the second largest dam east of the Mississippi with releases of 44 billion gallons of water each fall during normal seasons. By the end of the '90s, an estimated 65,000 hardboaters and rafters, were running the river annually, most during the annual fall releases.

However, some longed to hold onto a piece of the old Gauley days. In 1988, vandals hacksawed and stole the iron ring for which Iron Ring rapid was named. Its loss symbolized another piece missing of the old Gauley days.

Iron Ring for many years was considered a Class VI rapid. The traditional river right route had a dangerous under-cut rock in the middle-left at the bottom with a semi-terminal hole below it. Any paddler missing their line was pushed towards or into the hole. By the mid-80's, a route starting river left and pushing right toward the middle missing two shallow holes and continuing cross-cutting the main current to the bottom proved the rapid to be runnable by all and it was no longer considered a Class VI mandatory carry. But, the aura of Iron Ring continued and the loss of the ring itself cut into the soul of many long-time paddlers.

In 1992, a somewhat unlikely local group joined forces to find the iron ring. No one knew what had happened to it, but a lead came in that suggested that a local, having had his fishing disturbed by boaters, had sawed it off and thrown it into the river. Dave Arnold, co-owner of Class VI River Runners, arranged for divers, including the former sheriff, to search for it in the river. On a warm summer day with the river at 400 cfs, Arnold and the divers headed down to Iron Ring with a high railer (a pick-up truck that can run on tracks) borrowed from Conrail. Unfortunately, the ring was not found. The reward offered by Arnold was raised from $100 to $500. However, no leads led to the iron ring. Discussions began with the Park Service to fashion a replica to replace the missing iron ring.

74 McCormick, Mike. "The Mecca of Our Sport." *Canoe & Kayak* Vol. 22 No. 1 (March 1994): 9–10.

Even the thundering experience at the put-in of the Gauley was about to change. While many thought the Gauley was finally safe in the '90s from hydro development, a new hydro project was proposed in spite of efforts by many during the '80s to preserve the river and adjacent land from development. In 1996, a new hydro project was proposed for Summersville on the Gauley. Neither construction nor completion of the project was expected to affect the federally guaranteed releases of twenty-two days for Gauley season. The hydro plant was licensed as "Run of the River" and the license still guaranteed Corp control of the flow. As the Army Corp of Engineers resource manager explained of the major change,

> If flows are of sufficient volume on a given day for turning the turbines, then water will be routed through the hydro plant... The water will then circulate through the plant's generating units and bubble out from a tailrace area in the old launching pool.[75]

"Bubble out" are the key words. The effect will be that the "awesome put-in for the Upper Gauley will be lost forever."[76] The roar and thunder of the Gauley, the shaking ground from water flowing outward through the tubes, a part of every Gauley paddlers' experience, will be replaced by a diminished Kennebec-like experience.

The existing Corp of Engineer tubes would still handle certain volumes outside the range designed for the hydro power plant, in the 800 to 4,000 cfs range. This meant that outside the range, a little bit of the old Gauley experience could be felt.

The Gauley, like the rest of whitewater, was headed for changes and an experience different than that of the past.

[75] Hamilton, C.J. "Hydropower at Summersville: Looking Toward the Future." *American Whitewater* Vol. XL No. 5 (September/October 2000: 82–83.

[76] AWA editors. "Hydro to Be Added To Summersville Dam." *American Whitewater* Vol. XXXVI No. 3 (May/June 1996): 14–15.

Epilogue

To say *The River Chasers* has been a labor of love for the past five years would not be entirely correct. It has been a passion spawned by a fascination with what I have discovered and uncovered about the sport that has been a part of my life for over twenty-five years. Scientist that I am, I approached the research of the subject as objectively and thoroughly as possible, gathering and collecting data from across the country, all the while attempting to keep to my original premise of writing about the significant people, places, and events that brought the sport to where it is today. As a scientist, I attempted to follow a structured methodology not only for the kind of information I was looking for and during the interviews I conducted, but in the outline and organization of each chapter. But as a writer, I found that I needed to allow my book, and each chapter, to evolve and flow with the evolution of the sport from decade to decade just as a river flows, routed, directed, and influenced by the geomorphological features it encounters.

As a scientist, I wanted to report all the data I collected. It was all so interesting and relevant to me, each piece a part of the larger database. But as a writer, I realized I wanted to convey the story of our sport and that meant distilling the data to an appropriate amount of detail. Using my river metaphor for the sport's history, my editor told me a few times that I needed to stay in my canoe, on the river, and to avoid those side trips where I would get out of my canoe and hike up the mountain. Those side trips were interesting but not necessarily relevant to running the river and were not relevant for this book.

But as a scientist, I understood and realized the influence and importance of materials on the evolution of the sport and that boat design and paddling technique were closely linked with materials. Their intertwining influences are certainly reflected in my perspective and understanding of whitewater and are included in this history.

Whitewater is more than just the materials, design, and technique. It is also the people drawn to it, the human aspect of the sport. As a paddler, I have long recognized that we all share many of the same personality or characteristic attributes. We are all thrill seekers in our own ways, whether it be solely based on the adrenaline rush of the excitement that whitewater can bring, the thrill of making the perfect move or the perfect combination of strokes, or even the thrill of seeing and being in an area that few people can get to.

In the early years, in particular, the non-human and human elements were closely intertwined. Many of the key paddlers were scientists and engineers, both degreed and non-degreed. Perhaps the draw to whitewater was the risk that could be calculated, situations that could be studied and analyzed, yet one that could also provide unseen variables that needed to be quickly ascertained and recalculated. Perhaps it offered a weekend escape as far removed from the regimented and structured work life that scientific and engineering professions required. Regardless of the psychological profiles and reasons, scientists and engineers were a sizable part of the people drawn to whitewater. They were the people who were so integral to the development of whitewater as a sport, providing structure and organization, from understanding how to run rivers and build boats to the development of a national organization. They were the kind of people who founded American Whitewater. In researching American Whitewater's history, I developed an appreciation and deep respect for its founders. Those engineers and scientists (professors and early conservationists, too) who brought organization where necessary but didn't over engineer it and didn't over structure it. Somehow they knew that what the sport needed was a loose structure that could be shaped and molded, that could evolve as the sport evolved. Whitewater paddlers then as now didn't like being told what they could paddle and when they could paddle, but the engineers and scientist paddlers also knew that some structure was necessary and that preservation of whitewater, the experience as well as the rivers, depended on it. My personal feelings for American Whitewater as an organization evolved and changed because of this.

I also learned that like minds solve similar problems in similar ways, the collective unconscious of paddlers. Quite often I discovered that while one person claimed to be the first to discover or make something for whitewater, the same was coincidentally occurring in another area of the country. This is appropriately illustrated in the first boat built using Kevlar. At least four different paddlers/boat builders I interviewed thought they were the first.

Although I tried to remain as objective as possible, my perspective of whitewater's history is, nevertheless, influenced by my experiences as a paddler. Over the years there have been many people I have paddled with and talked with who have had a significant effect on me. The significant places have been the rivers, the campgrounds, and the restaurants, places were we congregate to share our experience and experience the camaraderie of whitewater. The significant events have often focused around those people and places and my experiences paddling on the rivers, particularly on what I consider my home rivers in and surrounding West Virginia.

As a paddler, the writing of whitewater's history in *The River Chasers* has been a significant event. A history is a chronological record of significant events with or without an explanation of their causes. A history puts things in perspective and helps people find their place in time (and space), their place in perspective to the history. As a paddler, *The River Chasers* has done that for me. I hope it will do the same for others.

Now that I've run the river once, I want to run it a second time, this time exploring the side trips and getting off the river to hike up the mountains. I want to explore materials and boat design in more detail, explore the rivers we paddle from a different perspective, and explore the people in greater depth. As a paddler, I want to learn more. As a writer, I want to share it with others. *The River Chasers* is just the beginning.

Appendix A: National Champions

Information to complete this listing was taken from various sources including race results and souvenir whitewater racing programs published by ACA from 1969 to 1987. Information after 1987 was more difficult to obtain. Jennifer and Davey Hearn were extremely helpful in verifying and providing race results after 1987. Unfortunately, a few gaps remain associated with wildwater champions which is indicative of the loss of interest and status of wildwater competition in America.

1956

K-1 Slalom	Larry Zuk
K-1 Wildwater	none
K-1W Slalom	Carol Kane
C-1 Slalom	none
C-1 Wildwater	none
C-2 Slalom	*Paula Zuk & Larry Zuk
C-2 Wildwater	none
C-2M Slalom	*Paula Zuk & Larry Zuk
C-2M Wildwater	none

*C-2 and C-2M classes were combined.

1957

K-1 Slalom	Dick Stratton
K-1 Wildwater	none
K-1W Slalom	Carol Kane
C-1 Slalom	none
C-1 Wildwater	none
C-2 Slalom	Roy Kerswill & Larry Zuk
C-2 Wildwater	none
C-2M Slalom	none
C-2M Wildwater	none

1958

K-1 Slalom	Eliot Dubois
K-1 Wildwater	none
K-1W Slalom	none
C-1 Slalom	Bob Harrigan
C-1 Wildwater	none
C-2 Slalom	Charles Sauer & Donald Wescott
C-2 Wildwater	none
C-2M Slalom	Edith McNair & Bob McNair
C-2M Wildwater	none

1959

K-1 Slalom	Erich Siedel
K-1 Wildwater	Walter Kirschbaum
K-1W Slalom	none
C-1 Slalom	none
C-1 Wildwater	none
C-2 Slalom	John Berry & Bob Harrigan
C-2 Wildwater	John Berry & Bob Harrigan
C-2M Slalom	none
C-2M Wildwater	none

1960

K-1 Slalom	(F-1) Erich Seidel (R-1) Allen Schell
K-1 Wildwater	Ted Young
K-1W Slalom	none
C-1 Slalom	John Berry
C-1 Wildwater	none
C-2 Slalom	John Berry & Bob Harrigan
C-2 Wildwater	none
C-2M Slalom	Edith McNair & Bob McNair
C-2M Wildwater	none

1961

K-1 Slalom	(F-1) Eric Frazee (R-1) Dave Morrissey
K-1 Wildwater	Dan Makris
K-1W Slalom	Barb Wright
C-1 Slalom	Bill Bickham
C-1 Wildwater	none
C-2 Slalom	Bill Bickham & Dick Bridge
C-2 Wildwater	Bill Bickham & Phil Hugill
C-2M Slalom	Barb Wright & Phil Hugill
C-2M Wildwater	none

1962

K-1 Slalom	Claud Burk
K-1 Wildwater	Dan Makris
K-1W Slalom	Barb Wright
C-1 Slalom	Bill Bickham
C-1 Wildwater	none
C-2 Slalom	Bill Bickham & Bill Heinzerling
C-2 Wildwater	none
C-2M Slalom	Marilyn Trimble & Bill Bickham
C-2M Wildwater	none

1963

K-1 Slalom	(F-1) Dan Makris
	(R-1) Ron Bohlender
K-1 Wildwater	(F-1) Dan Makris
	(R-1) Ron Bohlender
K-1W Slalom	Barb Wright
C-1 Slalom	Bill Bickham
C-1 Wildwater	none
C-2 Slalom	Bill Bickham & Bill Heinzerling
C-2 Wildwater	none
C-2M Slalom	Barb Wright & Bill Bickham
C-2M Wildwater	none

1964

K-1 Slalom	Roger Paris
K-1 Wildwater	Ted Makris
K-1W Slalom	Barb Wright
C-1 Slalom	Tom Southworth
C-1 Wildwater	none
C-2 Slalom	Dave Guss & Tom Southworth
C-2 Wildwater	Glen Roberts & Jim Zacharias
C-2M Slalom	Barb Wright & Bill Bickham
C-2M Wildwater	none

1965

K-1 Slalom	Walter Harvest
K-1 Wildwater	Ted Makris
K-1W Slalom	Barb Wright
C-1 Slalom	Bill Bickham
C-1 Wildwater	John Berry
C-2 Slalom	Mark Fawcett & Dick Shipley
C-2 Wildwater	Bill Heinzerling & Rowan Osborne
C-2M Slalom	Barb Wright & Bill Bickham
C-2M Wildwater	Kathy Berry & Bob Harrigan

1966

K-1 Slalom	Roger Paris
K-1 Wildwater	Dan Makris
K-1W Slalom	Kay Harvest
C-1 Slalom	Tom Southworth
C-1 Wildwater	Bill Bickham
C-2 Slalom	Les Bechdel & Dave Kurtz
C-2 Wildwater	John Connet & Jim Raleigh
C-2M Slalom	Nancy Abrams & Tom Southworth
C-2M Wildwater	Gay Gruss & Mark Fawcett

1967

K-1 Slalom	Les Bechdel
K-1 Wildwater	Tom Johnson
K-1W Slalom	Barb Wright
K-1W Wildwater	Tammy McCollom
C-1 Slalom	Tom Southworth
C-1 Wildwater	Bill Bickham
C-2 Slalom	Les Bechdel & Dave Kurtz
C-2 Wildwater	Bill Heinzerling & Rowan Osborne
C-2M Slalom	Nancy (Abrams) Southworth &
	Tom Southworth
C-2M Wildwater	Gay Gruss & Mark Fawcett

1968

K-1 Slalom	Roger Paris
K-1 Wildwater	David Nutt
K-1W Slalom	Gail Minnick
K-1W Wildwater	Tamara DeBord
C-1 Slalom	Wick Walker
C-1 Wildwater	John Sweet
C-2 Slalom	Les Bechdel & Dave Kurtz
C-2 Wildwater	John Bryson & John Hummel
C-2M Slalom	Nancy Southworth & John Bridge
C-2M Wildwater	Gay Gruss & Mark Fawcett

1969

K-1 Slalom	Eric Evans
K-1 Wildwater	Art Vitarelli
K-1W Slalom	Jan Binger
C-1 Slalom	Don Joffray
C-1 Wildwater	Al Chase
C-2 Slalom	Ed Bliss & Dick Church
C-2 Wildwater	Brad Hager & Norm Holcombe
C-2M Slalom	Gay (Gruss) Fawcett & Mark Fawcett
C-2M Wildwater	Louise Wright & Paul Liebman

1970

K-1 Slalom	David Nutt
K-1 Wildwater	David Nutt
K-1W Slalom	Peggy Nutt
K-1W Wildwater	Peggy Nutt
C-1 Slalom	John Sweet
C-1 Wildwater	John Sweet
C-2 Slalom	John Burton & Tim Schell
C-2 Wildwater	Bill Endicott & Brad Hager
C-2M Slalom	Nancy Southworth & Tom Southworth
C-2M Wildwater	Barb Holcome & Norm Holcombe

1971

K-1 Slalom	Eric Evans
K-1 Wildwater	Dick Sunderland
K-1W Slalom	Cindi Goodwin
K-1W Wildwater	Peggy Nutt
C-1 Slalom	John Burton
C-1 Wildwater	John Sweet
C-2 Slalom	Steve Draper & Frank Schultz
C-2 Wildwater	Brent Lewis & Kevin Lewis
C-2M Slalom	Barb Holcombe & Norm Holcombe
C-2M Wildwater	Barb Holcombe & Norm Holcombe

1972

K-1 Slalom	Eric Evans
K-1 Wildwater	Eric Evans
K-1W Slalom	Carrie Lyn Ashton
K-1W Wildwater	Carol Fisher
C-1 Slalom	Jamie McEwan
C-1 Wildwater	John Sweet
C-2 Slalom	John Evans & Russ Nichols
C-2 Wildwater	Stin Lenkerd & Steve Piccolo
C-2M Slalom	Carol Knight & Dave Knight
C-2M Wildwater	Carol Knight & Dave Knight

1973

K-1 Slalom	Eric Evans
K-1 Wildwater	Tom McEwan
K-1W Slalom	Linda Hibbard
K-1W Wildwater	Carol Fisher
C-1 Slalom	Tom Irwin
C-1 Wildwater	Russ Nichols
C-2 Slalom	John Evans & Russ Nichols
C-2 Wildwater	Steve Chamberlin & Joe Stahl
C-2M Slalom	Lyn Ashton & Russ Nichols
C-2M Wildwater	Carol Knight & Dave Knight

1974

K-1 Slalom	Eric Evans
K-1 Wildwater	David Nutt
K-1W Slalom	Candi Clark
K-1W Wildwater	Carol Fisher
C-1 Slalom	Angus (Sandy) Morrison
C-1 Wildwater	Al Button
C-2 Slalom	Al Harris & Dave Knight
C-2 Wildwater	Steve Chamberlin & Joe Stahl
C-2M Slalom	Leena Mela & Paul Liebman
C-2M Wildwater	Rasa D'Entremont & George Lhota

1975

K-1 Slalom	Eric Evans
K-1 Wildwater	Bill Nutt
K-1W Slalom	Linda Harrison
K-1W Wildwater	Carol Fisher
C-1 Slalom	Jamie McEwan
C-1 Wildwater	Al Button
C-2 Slalom	John Evans & Carl Toeppner
C-2 Wildwater	Ben Cass & Wallace Dyer
C-2M Slalom	Marietta Gilman & Chuck Lyda
C-2M Wildwater	Louise Wright & Jim McConeghy

1976

K-1 Slalom	Eric Evans
K-1 Wildwater	Tom Ruwitch
K-1W Slalom	Linda Harrison
K-1W Wildwater	Carol Fisher
C-1 Slalom	David Hearn
C-1 Wildwater	Al Button
C-2 Slalom	Steve Chamberlin & Joe Stahl
C-2 Wildwater	Chuck Lyda & Andy Toro
C-2M Slalom	Susan Chamberlin & Steve Chamberlin
C-2M Wildwater	Margaret Clark & Mike Chamberlin

1977

K-1 Slalom	Eric Evans
K-1 Wildwater	Bill Nutt
K-1W Slalom	Jean Campbell
K-1W Wildwater	Leslie Klein
C-1 Slalom	Kent Ford
C-1 Wildwater	Angus Morrison
C-2 Slalom	David Hearn & Ron Lugbill
C-2 Wildwater	Jon Lugbill & Bob Robison
C-2M Slalom	Linda Aponte & John Kennedy
C-2M Wildwater	Louise Wright & Jim McConeghy

1978

K-1 Slalom	Eric Evans
K-1 Wildwater	Bill Nutt
K-1W Slalom	Linda Harrison
K-1W Wildwater	Leslie Klein
C-1 Slalom	Angus Morrison
C-1 Wildwater	Angus Morrison
C-2 Slalom	David Hearn & Ron Lugbill
C-2 Wildwater	David Hearn & Ron Lugbill
C-2M Slalom	Linda Aponte & John Kennedy
C-2M Wildwater	Margaret Osborne & Bern Collins

1979

K-1 Slalom	Dan Isbister
K-1 Wildwater	Dan Schnurrenberger
K-1W Slalom	Linda Harrison
K-1W Wildwater	Cathy Hearn
C-1 Slalom	David Hearn
C-1 Wildwater	Chuck Lyda
C-2 Slalom	David Hearn & Ron Lugbill
C-2 Wildwater	Ben Cass & Joe Stahl
C-2M Slalom	Barb McKee & John Sweet
C-2M Wildwater	Bunny Johns & Mike Hipsher

1980

K-1 Slalom	Chuck Stanley
K-1 Wildwater	Dan Schnurrenberger
K-1W Slalom	Linda Harrison
K-1W Wildwater	Cathy Hearn
C-1 Slalom	David Hearn
C-1 Wildwater	David Hearn
C-2 Slalom	Paul Grabow & Jef Huey
C-2 Wildwater	Paul Grabow & Jef Huey
C-2M Slalom	Barb McKee & John Sweet
C-2M Wildwater	none

1981

K-1 Slalom	Tom McGowan
K-1 Wildwater	Dan Schnurrenberger
K-1W Slalom	Linda Harrison
K-1W Wildwater	Carol Fisher
C-1 Slalom	David Hearn
C-1 Wildwater	Chuck Lyda
C-2 Slalom	Paul Grabow & David Hearn
C-2 Wildwater	Bern Collins & Stan Janas
C-2M Slalom	Linda Harrison & Paul Grabow
C-2M Wildwater	Bunny Johns & Mike Hipsher

1982

K-1 Slalom	Chris McCormick
K-1 Wildwater	Jon Fishburn
K-1W Slalom	Sue Norman
K-1W Wildwater	Carol Fisher
C-1 Slalom	David Hearn
C-1 Wildwater	Jim Underwood
C-2 Slalom	Mike Garvis & Steve Garvis
C-2 Wildwater	Mike Hipsher & Dave Jones
C-2M Slalom	Karen Marte & Brett Sorenson
C-2M Wildwater	none

1983

K-1 Slalom	Bruce Swomley
K-1 Wildwater	Jon Fishburn
K-1W Slalom	Linda Harrison
K-1W Wildwater	Carol Fisher
C-1 Slalom	David Hearn
C-1 Wildwater	Angus Morrison
C-2 Slalom	Alan Blanchard & David Hearn
C-2 Wildwater	Bob Bofinger & Howard Foer
C-2M Slalom	Elizabeth Hayman & Fritz Haller
C-2M Wildwater	none

1984

K-1 Slalom	Mike McCormick
K-1 Wildwater	Jon Fishburn
K-1W Slalom	Wendy Stone
K-1W Wildwater	Carol Fisher
C-1 Slalom	David Hearn
C-1 Wildwater	John Butler
C-2 Slalom	Fritz Haller & Lecky Haller
C-2 Wildwater	David Mason & Scott Overdorf
C-2M Slalom	Hanna Nekvasil-Coraor & John Coraor
C-2M Wildwater	none

1985

K-1 Slalom	Chris Doughty
K-1 Wildwater	Jon Fishburn
K-1W Slalom	Cathy Hearn
K-1W Wildwater	Cathy Hearn
C-1 Slalom	David Hearn
C-1 Wildwater	Angus Morrison
C-2 Slalom	Paul Grabow & David Hearn
C-2 Wildwater	David Jones & Brent Turner
C-2M Slalom	Dana Chaldek & David Paton
C-2M Wildwater	Mary Hayes & Mike Hipsher

1986

K-1 Slalom	Chris Doughty
K-1 Wildwater	Jon Fishburn
K-1W Slalom	Cathy Hearn
K-1W Wildwater	Cathy Hearn
C-1 Slalom	Jon Lugbill
C-1 Wildwater	Andy Bridge
C-2 Slalom	Paul Grabow & David Hearn
C-2 Wildwater	Mike Hipsher & David Jones
C-2M Slalom	Pat Kingman & John Anderson
C-2M Wildwater	none

1987

K-1 Slalom	Rich Weiss
K-1 Wildwater	Brent Reitz
K-1W Slalom	Dana Chladek
K-1W Wildwater	Cathy Hearn
C-1 Slalom	David Hearn
C-1 Wildwater	Andy Bridge
C-2 Slalom	Adam Clawson & Kent Ford
C-2 Wildwater	Mike Hipsher & David Jones
C-2M Slalom	Julie Albrecht & Ray McLain
C-2M Wildwater	none

1988

K-1 Slalom	Rich Weiss
K-1 Wildwater	Brent Reitz
K-1W Slalom	Kara Ruppel
K-1W Wildwater	Kathy Bolyn
C-1 Slalom	Jed Prentice
C-1 Wildwater	Andy Bridge
C-2 Slalom	Joe Jacobi & Scott Strausbaugh
C-2 Wildwater	Mike Hipsher & David Jones
C-2M Slalom	Julie Albrecht & Ray McLain
C-2M Wildwater	none

1989

K-1 Slalom	Rich Weiss
K-1 Wildwater	Jon Fishburn
K-1W Slalom	Cathy Hearn
K-1W Wildwater	Mary Hipsher
C-1 Slalom	David Hearn
C-1 Wildwater	Andy Bridge
C-2 Slalom	Joe Jacobi & Scott Strausbaugh
C-2 Wildwater	Mike Hipsher & David Jones
C-2M Slalom	Kara Ruppel & Joe Jacobi
C-2M Wildwater	none

1990

K-1 Slalom	Eric Jackson
K-1 Wildwater	Andy Corra
K-1W Slalom	Dana Chladek
K-1W Wildwater	Jill Runnion
C-1 Slalom	David Hearn
C-1 Wildwater	Andy Bridge
C-2 Slalom	Joe Jacobi & Scott Strausbaugh
C-2 Wildwater	Mike Hipsher & David Jones
C-2M Slalom	Becky Kassouf & Max Wellhouse
C-2M Wildwater	none

1991

K-1 Slalom	Rich Weiss
K-1 Wildwater	Brent Reitz
K-1W Slalom	Cathy Hearn
K-1W Wildwater	Mary Hipsher
C-1 Slalom	David Hearn
C-1 Wildwater	Andy Bridge
C-2 Slalom	Joe Jacobi & Scott Strausbaugh
C-2 Wildwater	Chuck Lyda & Dan Schnurrenberger
C-2M Slalom	Kara Ruppel & Joe Jacobi
C-2M Wildwater	none

1992

K-1 Slalom	Scott Shipley
K-1 Wildwater	Bryan Tooley
K-1W Slalom	Cathy Hearn
K-1W Wildwater	Heidi Becker
C-1 Slalom	Jon Lugbill
C-1 Wildwater	Andy Bridge
C-2 Slalom	Joe Jacobi & Scott Strausbaugh
C-2 Wildwater	none
C-2M Slalom	Cathy Hearn & Lecky Haller
C-2M Wildwater	none

1993

K-1 Slalom	Scott Shipley
K-1 Wildwater	Dan Johnson
K-1W Slalom	Dana Chladek
K-1W Wildwater	Renata Buddeusova-Altman
C-1 Slalom	Lecky Haller
C-1 Wildwater	Andy Bridge
C-2 Slalom	Marty McCormick & Eliot Weintrob
C-2 Wildwater	Martin Bay & John Pinyerd
C-2M Slalom	Abby Kingman & Bill Kelly
C-2M Wildwater	none

1994

K-1 Slalom	Scott Shipley
K-1 Wildwater	Nelson Oldham
K-1W Slalom	Cathy Hearn
K-1W Wildwater	?
C-1 Slalom	David Hearn
C-1 Wildwater	Andy Bridge
C-2 Slalom	Fritz Haller & Lecky Haller
C-2 Wildwater	?
C-2M Slalom	none
C-2M Wildwater	none

1995

K-1 Slalom	Scott Shipley
K-1 Wildwater	?
K-1W Slalom	Kara Ruppel
K-1W Wildwater	?
C-1 Slalom	Jon Lugbill
C-1 Wildwater	?
C-2 Slalom	Fritz Haller & Lecky Haller
C-2 Wildwater	?
C-2M Slalom	Cathy Hearn & Lecky Haller
C-2M Wildwater	none

1996

K-1 Slalom	Scott Shipley
K-1 Wildwater	Franklin Lewis
K-1W Slalom	Cathy Hearn
K-1W Wildwater	Carolyn Potter
C-1 Slalom	David Hearn
C-1 Wildwater	Andy Bridge
C-2 Slalom	Fritz Haller & Lecky Haller
C-2 Wildwater	Martin Bay & John Pinyerd
C-2M Slalom	Cathy Hearn & Lecky Haller
C-2M Wildwater	none

1997

K-1 Slalom	Scott Shipley
K-1 Wildwater	Franklin Lewis
K-1W Slalom	Kara (Ruppel) Weld
K-1W Wildwater	Carolyn Porter
C-1 Slalom	David Hearn
C-1 Wildwater	Michael Beavers
C-2 Slalom	Lecky Haller & Matt Taylor
C-2 Wildwater	Michael Beavers & John Pinyerd
C-2M Slalom	Cathy Hearn & Lecky Haller
C-2M Wildwater	none

1998

K-1 Slalom	Scott Shipley
K-1 Wildwater	Nelson Oldham
K-1W Slalom	Cathy Hearn
K-1W Wildwater	Carolyn Porter
C-1 Slalom	David Hearn
C-1 Wildwater	Tim Sampsel
C-2 Slalom	Lecky Haller & Matt Taylor
C-2 Wildwater	Scott Overdorf & Michael Vorwerk
C-2M Slalom	Mary Koeppe & John Koeppe
C-2M Wildwater	none

1999

K-1 Slalom	Scott Shipley
K-1 Wildwater	Nelson Oldham
K-1W Slalom	Rebecca Bennett
K-1W Wildwater	Lane Errickson
C-1 Slalom	David Hearn
C-1 Wildwater	Tim Sampsel
C-2 Slalom	Lecky Haller & Matt Taylor
C-2 Wildwater	none
C-2M Slalom	Mary Koeppe & John Koeppe
C-2M Wildwater	none

2000

K-1 Slalom	Scott Shipley
K-1 Wildwater	Andrew McEwan
K-1W Slalom	Rebecca (Bennett) Giddens
K-1W Wildwater	Jennie Goldberg
C-1 Slalom	David Hearn
C-1 Wildwater	Tom Wier
C-2 Slalom	Lecky Haller & Matt Taylor
C-2 Wildwater	Charles Albright & Norwood Scott
C-2M Slalom	Carolyn Peterson & Max Poindexter
C-2M Wildwater	none

Appendix B: American Individual Medalists for World and Olympic Slalom

1972 Olympics in Munich (Augsburg), Germany

C-1 Slalom	Bronze	Jamie McEwan

1973 World Championships in Muotathal, Switzerland

C-2M Slalom	Gold	Carol Knight & David Knight
	Silver	Barb Holcombe & Norm Holcombe

1975 World Championships in Skopje, Yugoslavia

C-2M Slalom	Gold	Marietta Gilman & Chuck Lyda
	Silver	Rasa D'Entremont & George Lhota
	Bronze	Micki Piras & Steve Draper

1977 World Championships in Spittal, Austria

K-1W Slalom	Bronze	Linda Harrison
C-2M Slalom	Gold	Marietta Gilman & Chuck Lyda
	Silver	Linda Aponte & John Kennedy

1979 World Championships in Jonquierre, Quebec

K-1W Slalom	Gold	Cathy Hearn
	Bronze	Linda Harrison
C-1 Slalom	Gold	Jon Lugbill
	Silver	David Hearn
	Bronze	Bob Robison

1981 World Championships in Bala, Wales

K-1W Slalom	Silver	Cathy Hearn
C-1 Slalom	Gold	Jon Lugbill
	Silver	David Hearn
C-2 Slalom	Gold	Mike Garvis & Steve Garvis
	Bronze	Paul Grabow & Jef Huey
C-2M Slalom	Gold	Elizabeth Hayman & Fritz Haller
	Silver	Barb McKee & John Sweet
	Bronze	Karen Marte & Brett Sorenson

1983 World Championships in Merano, Italy

C-1 Slalom	Gold	Jon Lugbill
	Silver	David Hearn
C-2 Slalom	Gold	Fritz Haller & Lecky Haller
	Bronze	Mike Garvis & Steve Garvis

1985 World Championships in Augsburg, Germany

C-1 Slalom	Gold	David Hearn
	Silver	Jon Lugbill

1987 World Championships in Bourg St. Maurice, France

C-1 Slalom	Gold	Jon Lugbill
	Silver	David Hearn
	Bronze	Bruce Lessels
C-2 Slalom	Silver	Lecky Haller & Jamie McEwan

1988 Whitewater Slalom World Cup

K-1W Slalom	Gold	Dana Chladek
C-1 Slalom	Gold	Jon Lugbill
	Silver	David Hearn
	Bronze	Jed Prentice
C-2 Slalom	Gold	Lecky Haller & Jamie McEwan

1989 Whitewater Slalom World Cup

K-1W Slalom	Bronze	Cathy Hearn
C-1 Slalom	Gold	Jon Lugbill
	Silver	David Hearn
	Bronze	Jed Prentice
C-2 Slalom	Silver	Lecky Haller & Jamie McEwan
	Bronze	Joe Jacobi & Scott Strausbaugh

1989 World Championships at the Savage River, Maryland

K-1W Slalom	Silver	Dana Chladek
	Bronze	Cathy Hearn
C-1 Slalom	Gold	Jon Lugbill
	Silver	David Hearn

1990 Whitewater Slalom World Cup

C-1 Slalom	Gold	Jon Lugbill
	Bronze	David Hearn

1991 Whitewater Slalom World Cup

C-1 Slalom	Silver	Jon Lugbill

1991 World Championships in Tacen, Yugoslavia

K-1W Slalom	Silver	Dana Chladek
C-1 Slalom	Silver	Adam Clawson

1992 Whitewater Slalom World Cup

none

1992 Olympics in Barcelona (La Seu d'Urgell), Spain

K-1W Slalom	Bronze	Dana Chladek
C-2 Slalom	Gold	Joe Jacobi & Scott Strausbaugh

1993 World Championships in Mezzana, Italy

K-1 Slalom	Silver	Rich Weiss

1993 Whitewater Slalom World Cup

K-1 Slalom	Gold	Scott Shipley
C-1 Slalom	Silver	David Hearn

1994 Whitewater Slalom World Cup

K-1 Slalom	Bronze	Scott Shipley
C-2 Slalom	Bronze	Fritz Haller & Lecky Haller

1995 World Championships in Nottingham, England

K-1 Slalom	Silver	Scott Shipley
C-1 Slalom	Gold	David Hearn

1995 Whitewater Slalom World Cup

K-1 Slalom	Gold	Scott Shipley
C-2 Slalom	Silver	Fritz Haller & Lecky Haller

1996 Whitewater Slalom World Cup

none

1996 Olympics in Atlanta, Georgia at the Ocoee River in Tennessee

K-1W Slalom	Silver	Dana Chladek

1997 World Championships in Tres Coroas, Brazil

K-1 Slalom	Silver	Scott Shipley
K-1W Slalom	Bronze	Cathy Hearn

1997 Whitewater Slalom World Cup

K-1 Slalom	Gold	Scott Shipley
K-1W Slalom	Bronze	Cathy Hearn
C-1 Slalom	Silver	David Hearn

1998 Whitewater Slalom World Cup

K-1 Slalom	Silver	Scott Shipley

1999 World Championships in La Seu d'Urgell, Spain

K-1 Slalom	Silver	Scott Shipley

1999 Whitewater Slalom World Cup

K-1 Slalom	Silver	Scott Shipley

2000 Olympics in Sydney (Penrith Valley), Australia

none

2000 Whitewater Slalom World Cup

K-1 Slalom	Silver	Scott Shipley

Appendix C: American Individual Medalists for World Wildwater

American paddlers won individual medals in only three world wildwater championships.

1975 Yugoslavia

K-1	Bronze	Al Button

1981 Wales

C-1	Bronze	John Butler
C-2M	Gold	Bunny Johns & Mike Hipsher

1985 Germany

K-1	Bronze	Jon Fishburn

References

Interviews by Author

Acton, Ted. 12 February 1999.

Addison, Corran. 30 December 1997.

Anderson, Fletcher. 23 November 1998.

Annable, Hank. 5 January 1997.

Arcouette, Pierre. 5 September 2000.

Arnold, Landis. 9 June 1997.

Ashton, Carrie (Lyn). 6 May 1997.

Backlund, Keith. 26 October 1996.

Bauer, Wolf. 26 June 1997.

Bechdel, Les. 29 November 1996.

Bell, Frank Jr. 11 May 1997.

Benner, Bob. 8 May 1997.

Berry, John. 15 and 16 January 1997.

Boser, Lee (Uniroyal). 4 November 1998.

Bowers, Rich. 12 March 1997.

Bradley, Steve. 7 October 1998.

Bridge, Andy. 8 May 1997.

Bridge, Dick. 10 March 1997.

Brown, Barb (Snyder). 6 January 1997.

Brown, David. 6 May 1997.

Burrell, Bob. 20 November 1998.

Burton, John. 13 May 1997.

Calloway, Risa (Shimoda). 13 December 1996.

Chamberlin, Steve. 14 September 2000.

Chamberlin, Susan. 12 September 2000.

Clark, Bill. 7 January 1998.

Cline, Marge. 20 October 1998.

Coffin, Stewart. 16 January 1996.

Cooper, Tom and Jane. 1 October 1998.

Corbett, Roger. 13 December 1998.

Demarre, Dan. 31 August 2000.

Demaree, Dave. 15 February 1997.

Demaree, Mimi (Hayman). 15 February 1997.

Derrer, Tom. 24 June 1997.

Draper, Steve. 11 March 1997.

Endicott, Bill. 27 January 1997.

Erdman, Cully. 25 March 1999.

Evans, Eric. 23 January 1997.

Evans, Jay. 3 January 1998.

Fawcett, Mark. 6 March 1997.

Fentress, Mike. 13 June 1997.

Ford, Kent. 6 June 1997.

Foote, Bob. 8 November 1998.

Furrer, Werner Sr. 14 November 1996

Galpin, Ginny. 18 January 1997.

Galpin, Sam. 18 January 1997.

Gardiner, Dee. 16 April 2001.

Gertler, Ed. 31 January 1997.

Gilman, Lew. 21 January 1997.

Good, Elmer. 8 September 2000.

Goodwin, OK. 4 February 1997.

Grant, Gordon. 13 May 1997.

Harrigan, Bob. 28 January 1997.

Harrison, Judy. 19 November 1996.

Harrison, Robert. 17 October 2000.

Harvest, Walter. 14 June 1997.

Hauthaway, Bart. 22 January 1997.

Hays, Hank. 19 June 1997.

Hearn, Davey. 25 May 1999.

—— 18 March 2000.

Heidemann, John. 29 January 1997.

Held, Dick. 24 May 2001.

Henry, Jim and Kay. 20 January 1997.

Holbek, Lars. 12 June 1997.

Holland, John. 18 March 2000.

Horwitz, Ken. 26 June 1997.

Hurka, Joe. 23 and 24 October 1996.

Irwin, Tom. 17 October 1998.

Johns, Bunny. 12 May 1997.

Johnson, Tom. 21 and 22 November 1996.

Kazimierczyk, John. 17 January 1996.

Kennedy, Payson. 11 December 1996.

Krautkremer, Steve. 21 January 1997.

Kurtz, Dave. 4 March 1997.

Lantz, Bob. 11 May 1997.

LeClaire, Keech. 26 March 1999.

Lesser, Rob. 1 July 1997.

Liebman, Paul. 7 February 1999.

Martin, Charles. 14 February 1999.

Masters, Bill. 14 December 1996.

McEwan, Jamie. 14 January 1997.

McEwan, Tom. 12 March 1997.

McDonnell, Marty. 10 April 2001.

McDonough, Bob. 13 December 1996.

McKee, Barb. 23 and 24 January 1999.

McLaren, Don. 2 July 1997.

Mitchell, Peggy (Nutt). 10 January 1997.

Morrison, Angus (Sandy). 15 November 1998.

Moyer, Lee. 25 June 1997.

Nichols, Gary. 29 September 1998.

Paris, Roger. 8 November 1998.

Parks, Bill. 2 July 1997.

Phillips, Scott. 21 January 1997.

Pulliam, Joe. 12 December 1996.

Rodman, Sayre. 5 November 1998.

Ruuska, Dan. 25 June 1997.

Samsel, Tim. 25 March 1999.

Schreiner, John. 24 January 1997.

Sharp, Turner. 6 January 1998.

Sindelar, Jim. 18 January 1997.

Skinner, Pete. 14 January 1997.

Snyder, Jim. 15 February 1997.

Southworth, Tom and Nancy (Abrahms). 2 January 1998.

Spelius, Chris. 14 November 1998.

Stancil, Allen. 13 December 1996.

Stiller, Dieter. 7 March 1999.

—— 26 June 2000.

Stuart, James. 16 January 2000.

Sturgis, Peter. 15 June 1997.

Sullivan, Dan. 10 March 1997.

Sweet, John. 19 December 1996.

Thomson, John Seabury. 5 February 1997.

Toeppner, Carl. 16 March 1999.

Trost, Carl. 17 June 1997.

Van Wijk, Claudia (Kerckhoff). 13 July 1999.

Walbridge, Charlie. 5 March 1997.

Walker, Wick. 1 February 1998.

Watters, Ron. 6 July 1997.

Whitesell, Nolan. 12 December 1996.

Whitmore, Bryce. 18 May 2001.

Whittemore, Jesse. 17 January 1998.

Wiley, Nancy. 6 June 1997.

Wing, Bill. 15 June 1997.

Woodward, Doug. 11 December 1996.

Wright, Barb. 6 July 1997.

Wright, Jackson. 6 October 1998.

Wuerfmannsdobler, Xaver. 15 March 1999.

Zimmerman, Andy. 16 December 1996.

Zuk, Larry. 13 and 14 February 1999.

Zwanzig, Chan. 10 June 1997

—— 12 August 2000.

Books

50 Years of the International Canoe Federation (English edition). Hans Egon Vesper and John W. Dudderidge. Florence, Italy: International Canoe Federation, 1974.

A Guide to the Middle Fork of the Salmon River and the Sheepeater War. Johnny Carrey and Cort Conley. Riggins, ID: Backeddy Books, 1977.

A Paddler's Guide to the Obed/Emory. Monte Smith. Birmingham, AL: Menasha Ridge Press, 1990.

A River Runner's Guide to the History of the Grand Canyon. Kim Crumbo. Boulder, CO: Johnson Books, 1981.

A View of the River. Luna B. Leopold. Cambridge, MA: Harvard University Press, 1994.

Advanced River Rafting. Cecil Kuhne. Mountain View, CA: Anderson World, Inc. 1980.

Adventure Travel. Pat Dickerman (editor). New York, NY: Adventure Guides, Inc. 1983.

The All-Purpose Guide to Paddling (Canoe, Raft, Kayak). Dean Norman. Matteson, IL: Greatlakes Living Press, 1976.

AMC River Guide, Volume 1. Maine Appalachian Mountain Club. Boston, MA: AMC, 1980.

AMC White Water Handbook for Canoe and Kayak (first edition). John T. Urban. Boston, MA: Appalachian Mountain Club, 1973.

AMC Whitewater Handbook, Third Edition. Bruce Lessels. Boston, MA: Appalachian Mountain Club Books, 1994.

America by Rivers. Tim Palmer. Washington, DC: Island Press, 1996.

Annals of the Former World. John McPhee. New York, NY: Farrar, Strauss and Giroux, 1998.

An Innocent on the Middle Fork: A Whitewater Adventure in Idaho's Wilderness. Eliot Dubois. Cambridge, ID: Backeddy Books, 1997.

Appalachian Waters 1: The Delaware and its Tributaries. Walter Burmeister. Oakton, VA: Appalachian Books, 1974.

Appalachian Waters 2: The Hudson River and its Tributaries. Walter Burmeister. Oakton, VA: Appalachian Books, 1974.

Appalachian Waters 3: The Susquehanna River and its Tributaries. Walter Burmeister. Oakton, VA: Appalachian Books, 1975.

Appalachian Waters 4: The Southeastern Rivers. Walter Burmeister. Oakton, VA: Appalachian Books, 1976.

Appalachian Waters 5: The Upper Ohio and its Tributaries. Walter Burmeister. Oakton, VA: Appalachian Books, 1978.

Appalachian Whitewater, Volume I: The Southern Mountains. Bob Sehlinger, Don Otey, Bob Benner, William Nealy, Bob Lantz, and Nicole Jones. Birmingham, AL: Menasha Ridge Press, 1986.

Appalachian Whitewater, Volume I: The Southern Mountains. Bob Sehlinger, Don Otey, Bob Benner, William Nealy, Bob Lantz, and Nicole Jones. Birmingham, AL: Menasha Ridge Press, 1994.

Appalachian Whitewater, Volume II: The Central Mountains. Bob Grove, Bill Kirby, Charles Walbridge, Ward Eister, Paul Davidson, and Dirk Davidson. Birmingham, AL: Menasha Ridge Press, 1987.

Appalachian Whitewater, Volume III: The Northern Mountains. John Connelly and John Porterfield. Birmingham, AL: Menasha Ridge Press, 1987.

Appalachian Whitewater: The Southern States. Bob Sehlinger, Don Otey, Bob Benner, William Nealy, Ed Grove, Charlie Walbridge, and Bob Lantz. Birmingham, AL: Menasha Ridge Press, 1998.

Assembling California. John McPhee. New York, NY: Farrar, Strauss and Giroux, 1993.

The Bark Canoes and Skin Boats of North America, Edwin Tappan Adney and Howard I. Chapelle. Washington DC: Smithsonian Institution Press, 1964 and 1983.

Bark, Skin and Cedar: Exploring the Canoe in Canadian Experience. James Raffan. Toronto: HarperCollins Publishers, 1999.

Basic Canoeing. American National Red Cross, 1965.

Basic River Canoeing (third edition). Robert E. McNair. Martinsville, IN: American Camping Association, Inc., 1968.

Basic River Canoeing. Robert E. McNair, Matty L. McNair, and Paul A. Landry. Martinsville, IN: American Camping Association, 1985.

The Basic Essentials of Kayaking Whitewater. Bill Kallner and Donna Jackson. Merrillville, IN: ICS Books, Inc., 1990.

Basin and Range. John McPhee. New York, NY: Farrar, Strauss and Giroux, 1980.

The Best of the River Safety Task Force Newsletter 1976-1982. Charles Walbridge (editor). Lorton, VA: The American Canoe Association, 1983.

The Best Whitewater in California. Lars Holbek and Chuck Stanley. Coloma, CA: Watershed Books, 1998.

The Big Drops: Tales from Bo Rockerville. Monte Smith. Boise, ID: Pahsimeroi Press, 1996.

Blue Ridge Voyages, Volume I (fourth edition). H. Roger Corbett, Jr. and Louis J. Matacia. Oakton, VA: Blue Ridge Voyageurs, 1973.

Blue Ridge Voyages, Volume III (fourth edition). H. Roger Corbett, Jr. and Louis J. Matacia. Oakton, VA: Blue Ridge Voyageurs, 1973.

Boat Builder's Manual: How to Build Fiberglass Canoes and Kayaks for Whitewater (second edition). Charles Walbridge. Penllyn, PA: Wildwater Designs, 1973.

Boat Builder's Manual: How to Build Fiberglass Canoes and Kayaks for Whitewater Using Contact Molding and Vaccum-Bagging Techniques (third edition). Charles Walbridge, Steve Rock, and Gary E. Myers. Penllyn, PA: Wildwater Design Kits, 1978.

Boat Builder's Manual: How to Build Fiberglass Canoes and Kayaks for Whitewater Using Contact Molding and Vaccum-Bagging Techniques (fourth edition). Charles Walbridge, Steve Rock, Gary E. Myers, and Chip Queitzsch. Penllyn, PA: Wildwater Design Ltd., 1979.

California White Water: A Guide to the Rivers. Jim Cassady and Fryar Calhoun. Cassady and Calhoun, 1984.

Call of the Colorado. Roy Webb. Moscow, ID: University of Idaho Press, 1994.

Canoe Building in Glass Reinforced Plastic. Alan Byde. London: Adam and Charles Black, 1974.

The Canoe Handbook: Techniques for Mastering the Sport of Canoeing. Slim Ray. Harrisburg, PA: Stackpole Books, 1992.

The Canoe in Canadian Cultures. John Jennings, Bruce W. Hodgins, and Doreen Small (editors). Toronto: Natural Heritage Books, 1999.

Canoeing. Laurie Gullion. Champaign, IL: Human Kinetics Publishers, 1994.

Canoeing. Joseph L Hasenfus. Washington, DC: American National Red Cross, 1956.

Canoeing: A Practical Introduction to Canoeing and Kayaking. Ray Rowe. Lincolnwood, IL: NTC Publishing Group, 1993.

Canoeing and Kayaking. Wolf Ruck. Toronto: McGraw-Hill Ryerson Limited, 1974.

Canoeing and Kayaking for Persons with Physical Disabilities. Anne Wortham Webra. Newington, VA: American Canoe Assocation, 1990.

Canoeing and Kayaking: Instruction Manual. Laurie Gullion. Newington, VA: American Canoe Association, 1987.

Canoeing and Kayaking Instruction Manual. Laurie Gullion. Birmingham, AL: Menasha Ridge Press, 1987.

Canoeing Guide to Western Pennsylvania and Northern West Virginia (eighth edition). Roy R. Weil and Mary M. Shaw (editors). Pittsburgh, PA: Pittsburgh Council American Youth Hostels, 1991.

Canoeing, Kayaking, and Rafting. Gary Paulsen and John Morris. New York, NY: Massner, 1979.

Canoeing Made Easy. I. Herbert Gordon. Old Saybrook, CT: The Globe Pequot Press, 1992.

Canoeing North Into the Unknown: A Record of River Travel: 1874 to 1974. Bruce W. Hodgins and Gwyneth Hoyle. Toronto: Natural Heritage/Natural History, 1994.

Canoeing Western Waterways: California, Oregon, Washington, and Hawaii. Ann Schafer. New York, NY: Harper & Row, 1978.

Canoeing White Water River Guide. Randy Carter. Oakton, VA: Appalachian Books, 1967.

Canoes and Kayaks for the Backyard Builder. Skip Snaith. Camden, ME: International Marine Publishing Company, 1989.

Carolina Whitewater: A Canoeist's Guide to the Western Carolinas (fourth edition). Bob Benner. Hillsborough, NC: Menasha Ridge Press, 1981.

Classic Northeastern Whitewater Guide (third edition). Bruce Lessels. Boston, MA: Appalachian Mountain Club Books, 1998.

Class Virginia Rivers. Ed Grove. Arlington, VA: Eddy Out Press, 1992.

The Complete Book of Canoeing and Kayaking. Paul Fillingham. New York, NY: Drake Publishers, 1974.

The Complete Guide to Kayaking. Raymond Bridge. New York, NY: Scribner, 1978.

Danger! Whitewater. Otto Penzler. Mahwah, NJ: Troll Associates, 1976.

Der Hadernkahn: Geschichte des Faltbootes. Ursula and Christian Altenhofer. Rotdornstrabe, Oberschleibheim: Pollner Vertag, 1989.

Dictionary of Scientific and Technical Terms. Sybil P. Parker (editor). New York, NY: McGraw-Hill Book Company, 1989.

Fabulous Folbot Holidays. Jack Kissner. Charleston, SC: Creative Holiday Guides, no date.

Fabulous Foldboat Holidays. Jack Kissner. New York, NY, no date.

Fast & Cold: A Guide to Alaska Whitewater. Andrew Embrick. Valdez, AK: Valdez Alpine Books, 1994.

First Descents. Cameron O'Connor and John Laszenby (editors). Birmingham, AL: Menasha Ridge Press, 1989.

The Floater's Guide to Colorado. Doug Wheat. Billings, MT: Falcon Press Publishing Company, Inc., 1983.

Fluvial Processes in Geomorphology. Luna B. Leopold, Gordon M. Wolman, and John P. Miller. New York, NY: Dover Publications, 1992.

Glacial and Quaternary Geology. Richard Foster Flint. New York, NY: John Wiley & Sons, 1971.

The Grandiose Rio Grande. Walter F. Burmeister. Charleston, SC: Creative Holiday Guides, 1978.

Handbook of Chemistry and Physics (51st edition). Robert C. Weast (editor). Cleveland, OH: The Chemical Rubber Company, 1970.

Idaho Whitewater: The Complete River Guide. Greg Moore and Don McClaran. McCall, ID: Class IV, 1989.

If We Had a Boat. Roy Webb. Salt Lake City, UT: University of Utah Press, 1986.

Kayaking. Alan Fox. Minneapolis, MN: Lerner Publications Company, 1992.

Kayak & Canoe Trips in Washington. Werner Furrer. Lynwood, WA, 1971.

The Kayaking Book. Eric Evans and Jay Evans. Lexington, MA: Stephen Greene Press; New York, NY: Viking Penguin, 1988.

Kayaking Made Easy: A Manual for Beginners with Tips for the Experienced. Dennis O. Stuhaug. Old Saybrook, CT: Globe Pequot Press, 1995.

Kayaking: The Animated Manual of Intermediate and Advanced Whitewater Technique. William Nealy. Birmingham, AL: Menasha Ridge Press, 1999.

Kayaking: The New Whitewater Sport for Everybody. Jay Evans and Robert R. Anderson. Battleboro, VT: Stephen Greene Press, 1975.

Kayaking with Eric Jackson: Whitewater Paddling Strokes and Concepts. Eric Jackson. Mechanicsburg, PA: Stackpole Books, 1999.

Kayaking: Whitewater and Sea. Kent Ford. Champaign, IL: Human Kinetics Publishers, 1985.

Kayaking: Whitewater and Touring Basics. Steven M. Krauzer. New York, NY: W.W. Norton, 1995.

Landprints. Walter Sullivan. New York, NY: Time Books, 1984.

The Ledyard Canoe Club of Dartmouth: A History. Thomas Falcon. Hanover, NH: Dartmouth, 1967.

Merriam-WebsterDictionary (Home and Office Edition). Springfield, MA: Merriam-Webster, Inc., 1995.

Modern Plastics Handbook. Modern Plastics and Charles A. Harper (editor). New York, NY: McGraw-Hill, 2000.

The Nealy Way of Knowledge: Twenty Years of Extreme Cartoons. William Nealy. Birmingham, AL: Menasha Ridge Press, 2000.

Never Turn Back. Ron Watters. Pocatello, ID: Great Rift Press, 1994.

Open Boat Canoeing. Bob Wirth. West Nycek, NY: Parker Publishing Company, 1985.

The Open Canoe. Bill Riviere. Boston, MA: Little, Brown & Company, 1985.

Oregon River Tours. John Garren. Portland, OR: Garren Publishing, 1991.

Paddle to Perfection. Mark B. Solomon. Boston, MA: Aquatics Unlimited, 1994.

Path of the Paddle. Bill Mason. Toronto: Key Portes Books, 1984.

Performance Kayaking. Stephen B. U'Ren. Harrisburg, PA: Stackpole Books, 1990.

Performance Kayaking Plus Play Paddling. Stephen B. U'Ren, Bob McDougall. Harrisburg, PA: Stackpole Books, 1990.

Pole, Paddle and Portage. Bill Riviere. New York, NY: Van Nostrand Reinhold Company, 1969.

Potomac White Water: A Guide to Safe Canoeing Above Washington. John Seabury Thomson. Oakton, VA: Appalachian Books, 1974.

Rising from the Plains. John McPhee. New York, NY: Farrar, Strauss and Giroux, 1986.

The River Masters: A History of the World Championships of Whitewater Canoeing. William T. Endicott. Washington, DC: William T. Endicott, 1979.

River of No Return. Johnny Carrey and Cort Conley. Cambridge, ID: Backeddy Books, 1978.

River Rescue. Les Bechdel, Slim Ray. Boston, MA: Appalachian Mountain Club Books; New York, NY: The Talman Company, 1989.

River Runner's Guide to Utah and Adjacent Areas. Gary C. Nichols. Salt Lake City, UT: University of Utah Press, 1986.

River Running. Verne Huser. Chicago, IL: Henry Regnery Company, 1975.

River Safety Report 1986-1988. Charles Walbridge (editor). Newington, VA: American Canoe Association, 1989.

River Safety Report 1989-1991. Charles Walbridge, (editor). Springfield, VA: American Canoe Association, 1992.

River Safety Report 1992-1995. Charles Walbridge (editor). Birmingham, AL: Menasha Ridge Press, 1996.

River Safety Report 1996-1999. Charles Walbridge (editor). Birmingham, AL: Menasha Ridge Press, 2000.

River Safety: A Floater's Guide. Stan Bradshaw. Helena, MT: Greycliff Publishing Company, 2000.

Rivers at Risk. John D. Echeverria, Pope Barrow, and Richard Roos-Collins. Washington, DC: Island Press, 1989.

River's End: A Collection of Bedtime Stories for Paddlers. Bill Sedivy (editor). Newbury, OH: Big Dog Publications, 1995.

Rivers of the Southwest: A Boaters Guide to the Rivers of Colorado, New Mexico, Utah, and Arizona. Fletcher Anderson and Ann Hopkinson. Boulder, CO: Pruett Publishing, 1982.

River Thrill Sports. Andrew David. Minneapolis, MN: Lerner Publications Company, 1983.

Running the Rivers of North America. Peter Wood. Barre, MA: Crown Publishers, Inc., 1978.

Sierra Whitewater. Charles Martin. Wayland, MA: Charles Fontaine Martin, 1974.

Soggy Sneakers. Willamette Kayak and Canoe Club, Inc. Seattle, WA: The Mountaineers, 1994.

Sports Illustrated Canoeing. Dave Harrison. New York, NY: Harper & Row, 1981.

Sports Illustrated Canoeing: Skills for the Serious Paddler. David Harrison. New York: Sports Illustrated/Winner's Circle Books, 1988.

The Squirt Book, Jim Snyder. Birmingham, AL: Menasha Ridge Press, 1987.

Virginia White Water. H. Roger Corbett. Springfield, VA: The Seneca Press, 1977.

Washington Whitewater (volume one). Douglas A. Norton. Seattle, WA: The Mountaineers, 1986.

Washington Whitewater (volume two). Douglas A. Norton. Seattle, WA: The Mountaineers, 1987.

The Water Encyclopedia (second edition). Frits van der Leeden, Fred L. Troise, and David Keith Todd. Chelsea, MI: Lewis Publishers, Inc., 1990.

Water Trails of Washington (revised). Werner Furrer. Edmonds, WA: Signpost Books, 1979.

West Coast River Touring: Rogue River Canyon and South. Dick Schwind. Beaverton, OR: The Touchstone Press, 1974.

Western Whitewater: From the Rockies to the Pacific (A Guide for Raft, Kayak, and Canoe). Jim Cassady, Bill Cross, Fryar Calhoun. Berkley, CA: North Fork Press. 1994.

Whale Rock: The New and the Gauley. Bob Downing. Akron, OH: Bob Downing, 1983.

Whitewater! Norman Strung, Sam Curtis, and Earl Perry. New York, NY: Macmillan Publishing Company, 1976.

Whitewater Canoeing. William O. Sandreuter. New York, NY: Winchester Press, 1976.

Whitewater Home Companion: Southeastern Rivers, Volume I. William Nealy. Birmingham, AL: Menasha Ridge Press, 1997.

Whitewater Kayaking. Jeremy Evans. New York, NY: Crestwood House, 1992.

White Water Kayaking. Ray Rowe. Harrisburg, PA: Stackpole Books, 1988.

Whitewater Rafting in Eastern America. Lloyd D. Armstead. Charlotte, NC: Fast and McMillan Publishing, Inc., 1982.

Whitewater Rescue Manual. Charles Walbridge and Wayne A. Sundmacher, Sr. Camden, ME: Ragged Mountain Press, 1995.

The Whitewater River Book: A Guide to Techniques, Equipment, Camping, and Safety. Ron Watters. Seattle, WA: Pacific Search Press, 1982.

White Water: Running the Wild Rivers of North America. Bart Jackson. New York, NY: Walker and Company, 1979.

The Whitewater Sourcebook (third edition). Richard Penny. Birmingham, AL: Menasha Ridge Press, 1991.

White-Water Sport: Running Rapids in Kayak and Canoe. Peter Dwight Whitney. New York, NY: The Ronald Press Company, 1960.

Wildwater: The Sierra Club Guide to Kayaking and Whitewater Boating. Lito Tejada-Flores. San Francisco, CA: Sierra Club Books, 1978.

Wildwater Touring. Scott Arighi and Margaret S. Arighi. New York, NY: Macmillan Publishing Company; London, England: Collier Macmillan Publishing, 1974.

Wildwater West Virginia. Bob Burrell and Paul Davidson. Parson, WV: McClain Printing Company, 1975.

Wildwater West Virginia: Streams and Creeks of the Mountain State (fourth edition). Paul Davidson, Ward Eister, Dirk Davidson, Charlie Walbridge. Birmingham, AL: Menasha Ridge Press, 1985.

Wood and Canvas Kayak Building. George Putz. Camden, ME: International Marine Publishing Company, 1990.

Youghiogheny, Appalachian River. Tim Palmer. Pittsburgh, PA: University of Pittsburgh Press, 1984.

You, Too, Can Canoe. John Foshee. Huntsville, AL: The Strode Publishers, 1977.

Magazines

American Whitewater. Journal of the American White Water Affiliation: Vol. 1 No. 1 (May 1955) to Vol. XLI No. 2 (March/April 2001).

Appalachia. June 1929; December 1931; June 1937.

Canoe/Canoe and Kayak. Volume 1, Issue 1, April 1973 through Volume 29, Issue 1, March 2001.

Down River. Volume Three, Number Nine, October 1976.

Down River. Volume Four, Number Three, April 1977.

Paddler. Volume 16, No. 5, October 1996 through Volume 21, No. 2, March/April 2001.

River Runner. Volume 1, No. 1, Fall 1981 through Volume 11, No. 1, February 1991.

River World. Volume 6, No. 1, April 1979; Volume 6, No. 3, June 1979.

Time. June 9, 1997; March 1, 1999.

Newsletters and Other Periodicals

ACA Yearbook. 1946 through 1969.

American Canoeist. Published by ACA, 1962 through 1972; 1980 through 2001.

CKI News (Canoe and Kayak Industry Newsletter). Published by Canoe America Associates. June 1987 through Fall 1997.

The Eddy Line (Georgia Canoeing Association). Vol. 30 No. 3 March 1995; Vol. 30. No. 4 April 1995; Vol. 30 No. 6 June 1995; Vol. 30 No. 7 July 1995; Vol. 30 No. 8, 9, 10, 11 August through November 1995; Vol. 31 No. 12 December 1996; Vol. 32 No. 1 January 1997.

ICF Bulletin. International Canoe Federation No. 3 1962 (July 1962).

National Outdoor Outfitters News. January /February 1982.

NOWR News. Vol. XXXIX No. 6 (November/December 1999).

Outdoor Retailer. Vol. 6 No. 7 (September 1986).

Paddlesport Business (formerly CKI News). Winter 1998 through Spring 2001.

River Safety Task Force Newsletter. Charles Walbridge (editor) Vol. 1 No. 1 (1977); Vol. 1 No. 2 (1978); Vol. 2 No. 1 (1978); Vol. 3 No. 1 (1979); Vol. 4 No. 2 (1980); Vol. 5 No. 2 (1982).

The Spray. 1954/55.

Whitewater '79 (Souvenir Program). Barbara S. McKee (editor): The United States International Slalom Canoe Association.

Whitewater Racing 1971 (Souvenir Program). Tom Wilson (editor).

Women's CaNews. Barbara S. McKee (editor). Vol. 1 No. 1 (December 1980) through Vol. 1 No. 6 (May 1981); Vol. 1 No. 7 (Summer 1981); Vol. 1 No. 8 (September-October 1981); Vol. 1 No. 1 (December 1981); Vol. 2 No. 2 (Spring 1982); Vol. 2 No. 3 (Summer 1982); Vol. 2 No. 4 (Spring 1983).

Movies and Videos

Fast & Clean (video). The 1979 World Championship Races at Jonquierre.

Give Us a River. Bob Betton 1960-61.

River Runners of the Grand Canyon (video). Don Briggs. Sausalito, California: Don Briggs Productions.

Salida slalom and downriver races (16mm movie). Larry Zuk. 1954.

Yampa and Green River trip with Hatch Expeditions (16mm movie). Larry Zuk. 1959.

Miscellaneous Documents

"A Member Looks Back," notes prepared for commemorative address for KCCNY 25th anniversary dinner. Ed Alexander. 1984.

American Canoe Association 100th Anniversary Yearbook. Lawrence E. Zuk (editor). Concord, MA: Minuteman Printing Corporation, 1980.

Colorado Kayaks. Advertisement. *American Whitewater* Vol. 4 No. 1 (Spring 1957).

Cruise Committee Report No. 1. Larry Zuk. Colorado White Water Association. 1955.

"Early Days of Kayaking on Puget Sound," lecture notes. Werner Furrer, Sr. February 1996.

Folbot catalog. 1935-1936.

"The French Slalom Canoe" (unpublished article). Larry Zuk. 4 July 1955.

"General Foldboating Terminology." Washington Foldboat Club courtesy of Larry Zuk. Circa 1955.

"Hints on Reading Fast Water" (unpublished article). Bob McNair courtesy of Larry Zuk. June 1953.

"How Many Rivers? Golden Memories of a Whitewater Explorer Scout Post" (unpublished article). Doug Woodward. 9 September 1996.

Interview of Cal Giddings by Roy Webb. 3 July 1984.

Nantahala Outdoor Center Outfitters Catalog. 1995.

National Organization for Whitewater Rodeo. www.nowr.org. 19 May 2001.

National Survey on Recreation and the Environment (NSRE), USDA Forest Service and the University of Georgia, Athens, GA. 1994-95.

Perception. Advertisement. *Women's Sports.* June 1981.

"Stewart Gardiner—River Pioneer" (unpublished article). Dee Gardiner. April 1993.

"Quick-Water and Smooth" (draft article). Coffin, Stewart. *Canoe Magazine,* 1985.

United States Patent 6,035,801. Corran Addison. March 14, 2000.

United States Patent 6,119,620. Corran Addison. September 19, 2000.

Washington Foldboat Club River Classification Chart courtesy of Larry Zuk. Circa 1950.

Waterways Unlimited. Advertisement. *American Whitewater* Vol. 4 No. 1 (Spring 1958).

"White Water Canoeing 1957-1970." Article by Gardner Moulton courtesy of Stewart Coffin. Connecticut Chapter of AMC. Date unknown.

Correspondence

Baldwin, Henry I. to Stewart Coffin, courtesy of Stewart Coffin. 19 January 1986.

Cabot, Thomas to Steward Coffin, courtesy of Stewart Coffin. 27 February 1985.

P. Dave, "Ocoee = East Coast's Deschutes?" *rec.boats.paddle* newsgroup. 17 May 2000: 2:58 p.m.

DuBois, Eliot to Fred Sawyer, courtesy of Stewart Coffin. 6 April 1955.

Evans, Jay to author, 10 January 1996.

Gardiner, Dee. E-mail to author, 17 April 2001.

Hatch, Don to "Fellow River Rats" courtesy of Larry Zuk 23 January 1957.

Holland, Alfred E. E-mail to author, 13 March 1999.

Hughes, Jerry to Al Holland, courtesy of Al Holland, 17 December 1998. (Original correspondence 20 April 1998.

McKee, Barb. Email to author, 4 September 2000.

McNair, Bob (Buck Ridge Ski Club). Correspondence to White Water Canoeists, 9 March 1954, courtesy of Larry Zuk.

McNair, Robert E., American White Water Affiliation Secretary, to Affiliates and Prospective Affiliates, Courtesy of Larry Zuk, 8 June 1956.

Moulton, Gardner to Stewart Coffin, 13 March 1985.

Perry, Earl. Email to author, 22 December 1998.

Rockwell, Dwight Jr. (of Rockwell and Newell, Inc., New York, a marketing firm hired by Grumman), to Harry Roberts at Wilderness Canoe, courtesy of Marathon Canoe. Date unknown.

Sawyer, Fred, AMC Chairman White Water Canoeing Committee to Ledyard Canoe Club, courtesy of Stewart Coffin. 20 April 20 1955.

Stuart, James. Email to author, 29 January 2000.

Stuart, James. Email to author, 31 May and 1 June 2000.

Stuart, James. Email to John Sweet, 4 May 1998.

Sweet, John. Email to author, 31 August 2000.

Yeamans, David. E-mail, 1 January 1999.

Yeamans, David. E-mail, 24 February 1999.

Zuk, Larry address listing, 13 April 1954.

Zuk, Larry to "Fellow River Rat(s)," 14 April 1954.